MW01484396

CAN EUROPE SURVIVE?

'A rare blend of intellectual honesty, institutional memory and insider access. Drawing on decades of engagement with European and global monetary affairs, David Marsh unpacks the challenges facing the euro and the EU – and the structural contradictions Europe has deferred for too long.' Udaibir Das, Visiting Professor, National Council of Applied Economic Research, New Delhi

'Europe is created through conflicts and common challenges but also a growing understanding that only together can we master our future. Marsh excels in presenting this discourse across time and space, with focus on monetary, financial and fiscal policy.' Robert Holzmann, Governor, Österreichische Nationalbank

'David Marsh's synthesis of the views and thoughts of policy-makers – including through an unmatched range of interviews – is both lively and perceptive.' Patrick Honohan, former Governor, Central Bank of Ireland

'A great achievement. Europe can be understood only in holistic fashion, combining historical, political and economic analysis. The inimitable David Marsh has yet again accomplished this objective.' Otmar Issing, former Board Member for Economics, European Central Bank

'A comprehensive, up-to-date analysis of the complicated challenges Europe confronts. Marsh's clear-eyed assessments provide a sober look at the choices ahead combined with cautious encouragement.' Jackson Janes, Senior Fellow, German Marshall Fund of the United States

'A fascinating read. The passages which dealt with events I experienced first hand, for example on German re-unification and the fall of the Soviet Union, were spot on.' Sir Paul Lever, former British Ambassador to Germany

'Europe has been the leading light in world affairs for most of the past 500 years. Yet it is now clearly lost. What went wrong? Marsh clearly explains how Europe drifted down.' Kishore Mahbubani, author of *Living the Asian Century*

'A bold revelation of the history and events that have brought Europe to its current state.' Sheila M'Mbijjewe, former Deputy Governor, Central Bank of Kenya

'An insightful, stimulating, provocative and sometimes anguished narrative of everything that is wrong with Europe. Marsh's strength is in interlinking the spheres of economic, monetary, fiscal, geopolitical and social issues contributing to Europe's predicament.' Rakesh Mohan, former Deputy Governor, Reserve Bank of India

'Most timely. This is a pivotal moment for Europe . . . As Marsh suggests, forging a new symbiotic relationship with China – and Asia – may well be one of the decisive moves that Europe could make for its future.' Ravi Menon, Singapore's Ambassador for Climate Action

'It is a pleasure to read this broad and fact-based account. The interviews and many telling quotations are extremely stimulating.' Ewald Nowotny, former Governor, Österreichische Nationalbank

'A really big hit that will attract a lot of attention. The book has the potential to become a standard work for understanding postwar politics, especially in the US–Europe–Russia triangle.' Bernd Pfaffenbach, former adviser to Angela Merkel and Gerhard Schröder

'A great work, tackling the key issues and bringing a wealth of historical information and interesting interviews with key players.' Sir John Redwood, former MP for Wokingham and adviser to Margaret Thatcher

'Europe, including the UK, faces a world where both hostile powers and erstwhile security guarantors treat it with barely disguised contempt. David Marsh's superb book examines how we arrived here, just over a generation after a unified West had seemed to end the Cold War as the unqualified victor.' Sir Ivan Rogers, author of *9 Lessons in Brexit*

'A historical-biographical European thriller, written with a light touch and a British taste for the whimsical. This is a real page-turner.' Janine von Wolfersdorff, Founder and Managing Director, Life Bridge Ukraine

'An impressively well-documented history of the two major challenges for Europe over the past fifty years: managing security in relation to the Soviet Union, later Russia, and advancing economic integration.' Niels Thygesen, Professor Emeritus of International Economics, University of Copenhagen

'A pleasure to read. By explaining so clearly Europe's present predicament in the context of the events and decisions that created it, Marsh illuminates the forces and factors likely to determine its future.' Lord Christopher Tugendhat, former Vice President, European Commission

'Immensely enjoyable. Marsh masterfully weaves the European story into the broader fabric of global developments.' William White, Senior Fellow, C.D. Howe Institute

'David Marsh, drawing on his deep knowledge from journalism and business, has compiled a masterly account of the political and economic development of today's Europe. Historians will undoubtedly draw on this book's considerable original material.' Lord Norman Lamont, former British Chancellor of the Exchequer

'Combining a journalist's wit and a historian's care, David Marsh sizes up both past and present with a rare balance of understanding between the people, the politics and the economics.' Philip Zelikow, author of *The Road Less Traveled*

'Europe faces an unprecedented challenge with the global breakdown of postwar certainties. David Marsh is the ideal author to point us to the dangers confronting Europe, and the way forward.' Lord Meghnad Desai, author of *The Poverty of Political Economy*

'A major contribution to the understanding of Europe's history: a fascinating, detailed account of the economic and (geo)political forces that have shaped this continent over the past fifty years.' Nout Wellink, former President, De Nederlandsche Bank

'A bleak, minutely researched and persuasive analysis of the "tide of adversity" that has brought Europe to its present pass. Stimulating and essential reading for anyone who wants to know how that happened.' Philip Short, author of *Putin: His Life and Times*

'A masterpiece – full of precious insights. In the present turmoil affecting Europe's status and credibility, David Marsh's extremely well-documented book will arouse enormous interest.' Jacques de Larosière, former Managing Director, IMF, and former Governor, Banque de France

'A magisterial account of Europe's variable geometry: the shifting currents of politics, culture and economics that investors must navigate in turbulent times in the global competition for capital.' Anne Simpson, Global Head of Sustainability, Franklin Templeton

'A magnificent book. It taught me a lot, especially on the intricacies of the relationships between Germany and Russia.' Charles Goodhart, co-author of *The Great Demographic Reversal*

'This characteristically stimulating book gives a vivid picture of the policy dilemmas facing Europe in the past, the present and the future. Marsh is persistently iconoclastic and interesting.' Harold James, author of *Seven Crashes*

'From the fall of the Berlin Wall to the invasion of Ukraine and tariff wars, Europe has been subject to revolutionary changes. Based on intensive research, there is no better guide to these events, and their implications for our future.' Lord Mervyn King, former Governor, Bank of England

'A bracing, clear-eyed account of a continent at a crossroads. Drawing on decades of experience and a reporter's eye for detail, David Marsh reveals how Europe is struggling to navigate an unpredictable America, a rising China and a revanchist Russia.' Edward Fishman, author of *Chokepoints*

'A privilege to read. David Marsh's meticulous research brought together over many years provides great insight into both challenges and opportunities for Europe, and deserves the widest possible circulation.' Gordon Brown, former Prime Minister of the United Kingdom

CAN EUROPE SURVIVE?

THE STORY OF A CONTINENT
IN A FRACTURED WORLD

DAVID MARSH

YALE UNIVERSITY PRESS
NEW HAVEN AND LONDON

For information about this and other Yale University Press publications, please contact:
U.S. Office: sales.press@yale.edu yalebooks.com
Europe Office: sales@yaleup.co.uk yalebooks.co.uk

Set in Adobe Garamond Pro by IDSUK (DataConnection) Ltd

Printed and bound in the UK using 100% renewable electricity at CPI Group (UK) Ltd

Library of Congress Control Number: 2025940613
A catalogue record for this book is available from the British Library.
Authorized Representative in the EU: Easy Access System Europe, Mustam‰oe tee 50, 10621
Tallinn, Estonia, gpsr.requests@easproject.com

ISBN 978-0-300-27300-7

10 9 8 7 6 5 4 3 2 1

In memory of
Meghnad Desai and John Kornblum
and in celebration of Elyssa

CONTENTS

ABBREVIATIONS

AAPD	Akten zur Aussenpolitik der Bundesrepublik Deutschland [Documents on the Foreign Policy of the Federal Republic of Germany] (German Foreign Ministry)
ABM	anti-ballistic missile
ADBI	Asian Development Bank Institute
ADST	Association for Diplomatic Studies and Training
AfD	Alternative für Deutschland [Alternative for Germany]
AFME	Association for Financial Markets in Europe
AIIB	Asian Infrastructure Investment Bank
BRICS	Brazil, Russia, India, China and South Africa (country grouping)
CBI	Confederation of British Industry
CDU	Christlich Demokratische Union [Christian Democratic Union, Germany]
CEPR	Centre for Economic and Policy Research
CER	Centre for European Reform
CFS	Center for Financial Studies
CIS	Commonwealth of Independent States
CPL	Clinton Presidential Library
CRM	critical raw materials
CSCE	Commission on Security and Cooperation in Europe
CSU	Christlich-Soziale Union [Christian Social Union, Germany]

DAX-40	Deutscher Aktien Index (40 top companies in German stock market index)
DBPO	Documents on British Policy Overseas
DE	Die Einheit [Unity] (East and West German foreign ministry documents)
DESE	Deutsche Einheit Sonderedition aus den Akten des Bundeskanzleramtes [German Unity, Special Edition of Federal Chancellery Documents] (West German Federal Chancellery)
DFDE	Diplomatie für die deutsche Einheit [Diplomacy for German Unity] (West German Foreign Ministry documents)
DM	Deutsche Mark
DS-OIPS	Department of State, Office of Information Program and Services (office releasing declassified documents under FOIA)
ECB	European Central Bank
ECJ	European Court of Justice
EFSF	European Financial Stability Mechanism
EIB	European Investment Bank
EMS	European Monetary System
EMU	Economic and Monetary Union
EO	Executive Order
EPP	European People's Party
ERM	Exchange Rate Mechanism
ESM	European Stability Mechanism
FCDO	Foreign, Commonwealth and Development Office (UK)
FCO	Foreign and Commonwealth Office (UK)
FOIA	Freedom of Information Act
FOMC	Federal Open Market Committee
FRBT	Federal Reserve Board transcripts
FSB	Financial Stability Board
GFTN	Global Finance and Technology Network
GWU-NSA	George Washington University, National Security Archive
HADB	Historisches Archiv der Deutschen Bundesbank [Historical Archive of German Bundesbank]

HWBPL	George H.W. Bush Presidential Library
IFMS	Institute for Monetary and Financial Stability
IISS	International Institute for Strategic Studies
IRA	Inflation Reduction Act
IWG	Interagency Working Group (US)
LNG	liquified natural gas
MAP	Membership Action Plan
NACC	North Atlantic Cooperation Council
NGEU	Next Generation European Union
NIC	National Intelligence Council (US)
NIS	Newly Independent States
NMD	National Missile Defence
NPT	Non-Proliferation Treaty
NRC	NATO–Russia Council
NSC	National Security Council (US)
OECD	Organisation for Economic Cooperation and Development
OMFIF	Official Monetary and Financial Institutions Forum
OMT	outright monetary transactions (ECB)
OSCE	Organisation for Security and Co-operation in Europe
PAAA	Politisches Archiv des Auswärtigen Amts [Political Archive, German Foreign Ministry]
PfP	Partnership for Peace
PPP	purchasing power parity
QE	quantitative easing
SALT-1	Strategic Arms Limitations Treaty
SMP	securities market programme (ECB)
SPD	Sozialdemokratische Partei Deutschlands [Social-Democratic Party, Germany]
START I / START II	Strategic Arms Reduction Treaty
SDI	Strategic Defense Initiative
TPI	transmission protection instrument (ECB)
UKNA	UK National Archives

DRAMATIS PERSONAE

ANDREW BAILEY (b. 1959) Bank of England governor from 2020, presided over massive Covid government bond purchases. Easy-going management style. Tried to eschew Brexit spats after Mark Carney's controversial tenure, survived attempted 2022 defenestration by Prime Minister Liz Truss and subsequent market turmoil.

JAMES BAKER (b. 1930) US politician and attorney, secretary of state and Treasury secretary under Ronald Reagan and George H.W. Bush. Skilled diplomatic craftsmanship over German unification. Helped secure Soviet compliance for united Germany in NATO, telling Gorbachev a neutral German state would be nuclear-armed.

BEN BERNANKE (b. 1953) American economist, chairman of Federal Reserve (2006–14) during global financial crises and European debt upsets. Pioneered quantitative easing government bond purchases, later followed with mixed results by Europeans. Adeptly analysed from sidelines the political psychology of European debt crisis.

JOE BIDEN (b. 1942) 46th US president (2021–5), vice president under Obama (2009–17). After initial missteps, maintained West's pro-Ukrainian coalition. Flawed, unduly late 2024 decision, forced by evident mental decline, to pass presidential candidature to Kamala Harris led to her heavy loss against Trump.

TONY BLAIR (b. 1953) British prime minister (1997–2007), succeeded in buttressing Labour Party image and promoting Europe-orientated economic modernisation. Failed to carry the country over misjudged unconditional support for US over Iraq war. Initially good relations with Putin and Schröder later soured with both.

GORDON BROWN (b. 1951) One of Britain's best postwar chancellors of the exchequer (1997–2010). Three-year prime minister-ship (2007–10) came adrift over financial crisis – despite his successful efforts to mitigate fallout through international economic cooperation. Scepticism about joining euro vindicated by later events.

GEORGE H.W. BUSH (1924–2018) 41st US president (1989–93). Second World War veteran and CIA director, vice president under Reagan. Presidency focused on foreign policy, playing steady diplomatic hand to end Cold War, showed exemplary understanding with Helmut Kohl, only to plunge afterwards into Gulf war.

GEORGE W. BUSH (b. 1946) 43rd US president (2001–9). Leadership defined by 9/11 attacks, 'war on terror' and international fallout from Iraq war. Forged initial bond with Putin but later Chirac–Schröder–Putin solidarity over Iraq greatly weakened western cohesion. Disagreed with Merkel over NATO extension.

DAVID CAMERON (b. 1966) British prime minister (2010–16), Conservative–Liberal Democrat coalition and later majority government. Sought to overcome internal party strife and heal rift with Europe with 2016 EU referendum, ended up exacerbating both. Resigned after losing vote. Brief return 2023–4 as foreign secretary.

MARK CARNEY (b. 1965) Canadian economist with Goldman Sachs experience. Governor of the Bank of Canada (2008–13) and Bank of England (2013–20). Switched to politics and became Canadian prime minister in 2025 on stoking Canadian anti-Trump sentiment. Helped stabilise sterling and UK economy after Brexit referendum.

JACQUES CHIRAC (1932–2019) President of France (1995–2007), prime minister (1974–6 and 1986–8) and mayor of Paris (1977–95). Stable two-year 'cohabitation' with Mitterrand. Relative success with 'centrist' economic policies strengthened French position in euro bloc.

BILL CLINTON (b. 1946) 42nd US president (1993–2001). Achieved economic prosperity, welfare reform, and trade agreements with Mexico and Canada. Presidency overshadowed by personal scandals leading to impeachment (though acquitted). Strong bond with UK's Blair. Fell out repeatedly with Yeltsin over NATO enlargement.

JACQUES DELORS (1927–2023) Whimsical, soft-spoken, effective European Commission president (1985–94), architect of 'single market', influential in EMU project and ECB independence (1989 Delors Report). As French finance minister, reversed early Mitterrand economic errors, forged essential bond with Kohl.

MARIO DRAGHI (b. 1947) Well-versed Italian politician, economist, academic, banker, civil servant. Governor of Banca d'Italia (2006–11), European Central Bank president (2011–19). Italy's prime minister (2021–2), failed to become Italian president (2022). Powerful role in 'saving euro'. Author of European competitiveness report (2024).

WIM DUISENBERG (1947–2005) Dutch politician and economist, former finance minister and president of Dutch central bank, first president of European Central Bank (1998–2003). Credited with establishing ECB council as a working body, renowned for straightforward and sometimes gaffe-strewn public interventions on euro.

TIM GEITHNER (b. 1959) President of Federal Reserve Bank of New York (2003–9), Treasury secretary (2009–13), played key role during financial crisis focused on economic recovery and financial reform. Helped secure euro in 2012 through intense financial diplomacy and behind-the-scenes exchanges with ECB president Draghi.

MIKHAIL GORBACHEV (1931–2022) Eighth, final president of Soviet Union, Communist Party general secretary (1985–1991). Personal chemistry with Kohl enabled German unification. 'Tragic hero': initiated glasnost and perestroika, ended Cold War, presided over Soviet dissolution leading to Yeltsin economic chaos and rise of Putin.

BORIS JOHNSON (b. 1964). British journalist and politician. Cross-party following as mayor of London (2008–16). Won Brexit referendum with Leave stance. Prime minister (2019–22), quit parliament over Covid deception. Pro-Ukraine stance helped stiffen European resolve.

JEAN-CLAUDE JUNCKER (b. 1954) Luxembourg finance minister (1989–2009), overlapping as prime minister (1995–2013). European Commission president (2014–19), winning job despite UK opposition. Reinforced Luxembourg position as arbiter of Franco-German relations, helped shore up EU stability to counter euro crisis fallout. Diplomatic sparring over Brexit with May and Johnson.

MERVYN KING (b. 1948) London School of Economics background, governor of Bank of England (2003–13), with crucial role during financial crisis. Fell out with Gordon Brown over stance on fiscal–monetary coordination. Sceptic on EMU, Brexit supporter with views emerging only after stepping down as governor.

KLAAS KNOT (b. 1970) President of Dutch central bank (2011–25). Maintained traditional Dutch alignment with Bundesbank but developed own voice on monetary policy and financial regulation. Clashed with Draghi over extended quantitative easing in 2019, assisted Lagarde in subsequent psychological truce. Potential ECB successor.

HELMUT KOHL (1930–2017) Chancellor of West Germany, then Germany (1982–98), pivotal role in German reunification and EU widening and deepening with forging of euro. Personal links with Bush and Gorbachev made unification possible. Underestimated in first half of sixteen-year rule, overestimated in second. Failure to restructure German economy gave successor Schröder leeway for economic reforms.

CHRISTINE LAGARDE (b. 1956) International law background. French finance minister (2007–11), IMF managing director (2011–19), ECB president from 2019. After Draghi squalls, succeeded in reinforcing ECB leadership and governing council crisis coordination. Mistaken late start (along with other central banks) in post-2021 anti-inflation monetary tightening.

JOHN MAJOR (b. 1943) Prime minister (1990–7), important role stabilising British economy and position in Europe (Maastricht treaty opt-out) after Thatcher upheavals, aided by understanding with Kohl. Undermined by EU controversies, 1992 currency turbulence. In 1997 bequeathed favourable economic backdrop to Blair.

THERESA MAY (b. 1956) British prime minister (2016–19), took over from Cameron in unsettled period following Brexit vote. Made heavy weather of Brexit negotiations, handicapped by sniping from pro-Johnson camp within and outside government. Demonstrated near-impossible task of uniting disparate Conservative policies on Europe.

GIORGIA MELONI (b. 1977) Leads right-wing Brothers of Italy party (neo-Fascist roots), Italian prime minister since 2022. As Opposition leader built good relations with Draghi, helping governmental continuity in economics and Ukraine support. Conservative nationalist policies, strong stance on immigration, link to Trump.

ANGELA MERKEL (b. 1954) German chancellor (2005–21), first former East German citizen in that office. Kohl protégée, succeeded in displacing Christian Democrat rivals. International reputation as stabiliser in Germany and Europe tarnished over Putin/Russia–Ukraine war and German problems with immigration, energy and economy.

FRIEDRICH MERZ (b. 1955) German chancellor since May 2025. Lost early 2000s power struggle with Merkel, international business career, 2022 comeback as CDU chairman. Former European Parliament member, wants to strengthen French ties. Qualifies US policies as 'America first, second and third'. Anti-Merkel stance may prove favourable with Trump.

FRANÇOIS MITTERRAND (1916–96) President of France (1981–95), first Socialist leader under Fifth Republic. Correcting early economic missteps, helped establish EMU to counter German unification impact and develop European independence. Despite setbacks over joint economic and military policies, emotional bond with Kohl symbolised Franco-German partnership.

JOACHIM NAGEL (b. 1966) Plain-speaking Bundesbank president since 2022 after earlier Bundesbank posts and spells at KfW development bank and Basel-based Bank for International Settlements. Strong 2022 push for overdue ECB tightening. Stability-minded market operator, pro-European risk-taker with diplomatic touch, strong personal link to Lagarde, potential ECB successor.

BARACK OBAMA (b. 1961) 44th US president (2009–17). Nobel Peace Prize laureate, first African American US president, strong role with Geithner in galvanising Europe over EMU crisis. Known for the Affordable Care Act and global diplomatic engagement. Left Hillary Clinton as disappointing Democrat candidate in 2016 election.

VLADIMIR PUTIN (b. 1952) Multiple terms as Russia's president and prime minister since 1999, shift to authoritarianism, centralised rule, intensified China partnership. Grievances over Soviet dissolution and NATO enlargement. Steady waning of initial US-European pro-Putin stance, West became adversary after 2022 full-scale invasion of Ukraine. Partial rehabilitation under Trump's second presidency, emphasising sidelining of Europe.

RONALD REAGAN (1911–2004) Hollywood actor, Republican governor of California and then 40th US president (1981–9). Crucial relationship with Britain's Thatcher. Bequeathed a booming economy, massively higher public debt thanks to tax cuts and miliary spending, and tough line on Soviet Union heralding end of Cold War.

WOLFGANG SCHÄUBLE (1942–2023) Long-time central figure in Germany's CDU, key role with Kohl over German unity, rivalry with Kohl and Merkel deprived him of chancellorship. Wheelchair-bound after surviving 1990 assassination attempt. Finance minister (2009–17), controversial stabilisation policies during euro financial crisis.

HELMUT SCHMIDT (1918–2015) West Germany's chancellor (1974–82), strategic thinker and economic manager, stumbled over Bundesbank policies. Strengthened NATO ties and prepared European monetary union on Franco-German foundations. After chancellorship, maintained influence as author and newspaper publisher.

OLAF SCHOLZ (b. 1958) Postwar Germany's fourth Social Democrat chancellor (2021–5). Maintained Schäuble's generally conservative policies as finance minister (2018–21) under Merkel. Supported Ukraine over Russian aggression but held back by poor communication skills. Lost 2025 election after his coalition collapsed.

GERHARD SCHRÖDER (b. 1944) Reform-minded Social Democrat chancellor of Germany (1998–2005), able to improve competitiveness through cutting deals with the left. Early sceptic on euro. Fell out with Blair and Bush over Iraq war. Repaired relationship with Chirac as a result of rupture with US. Maintained friendship with Putin after full-scale invasion of Ukraine – tarnishing image in West.

BRENT SCOWCROFT (1925–2020) US national security adviser under Presidents Gerald Ford and George H.W. Bush. Influential behind-the-scenes thinking on East–West relations helped end Cold War on American terms, solid partnership with Kohl's right-hand-man Teltschik pivotal in breakthroughs on German unity after Berlin wall fell.

KEIR STARMER (b. 1962) British Labour Party leader since 2020, lawyer-turned-politician. Prime Minister after landslide win in 2024 elections offering pragmatic alternative to troubled years of Conservative leadership. Rebuilding EU relationship, difficult economic balancing act. Held back by political management shortcomings. Cordial relationship with Trump, although US in driving seat over Ukraine.

RISHI SUNAK (b. 1980) UK prime minister (2022–4), chancellor of the exchequer (2020–2), first Asian-origin British PM, though seen as interim figure. Notwithstanding significant personal wealth, presented down-to-earth stance as antidote to Johnson and Truss turbulence, stabilised EU relations and helped calm political landscape.

HORST TELTSCHIK (b. 1940) Kohl's foreign-policy and security adviser until 1990. Crucial counterpart for US and Soviet Union over German unity. Ambitions to become defence minister thwarted by coalition rivalry. Became BMW car company board member. Directed Munich Security Conference for global dialogue including Russia.

MARGARET THATCHER (1925–2013) Britain's prime minister (1979–90), dubbed 'Iron Lady' enacting free-market reforms, maintaining strong US ties (Ronald Reagan), defence commitments. Helped Cold War thaw by 'discovering' Gorbachev, relations with Kohl soured badly over her resistance to German unity. Opposed EU monetary union deepening.

JEAN-CLAUDE TRICHET (b. 1942) Veteran French Treasury official, became Banque de France governor (1993–2003), European Central Bank president (2003–11). Presided over low inflation but build-up of euro area instability, early work on repairing subsequent euro financial crises. Long-term believer in European federation.

DONALD TRUMP (b. 1946) 45th (2017–21) and then 47th (from 2025) US president, controversial businessman and media figure. Exaggerated populist rhetoric and 'America-first' politics. Polarising international stance, harbours Putin-like grievances over allegedly losing out over past foreign and trade policies. Brought back Putin 'out of the cold' in 2025. His actions likely to strengthen China.

LIZ TRUSS (b. 1975) Shortest-tenured prime minister in British history, resigned in October 2022 after precipitating 'mini-budget' financial crisis in September 2022 for which she continues to deny culpability. Held Cabinet positions under PMs Cameron, May and Johnson.

FRANÇOIS VILLEROY DE GALHAU (b. 1959) Diplomatically adept governor of Banque de France since 2015, previously chief operating officer of BNP Paribas. Maastricht treaty veteran, adviser to finance minister (later prime minister) Pierre Bérégovoy. Franco-German family roots (Lorraine/ Saarland).

URSULA VON DER LEYEN (b. 1958) Tough-talking technocratic European Commission president since 2019, advocating stricter policies on Russia including sanctions and Ukraine military assistance. Unsuccessful spell as defence minister under Merkel.

JENS WEIDMANN (b. 1968) Economic adviser to Angela Merkel (2006–11), Bundesbank president (2011–21), embroiled in frequent ECB discord with Mario Draghi. Since 2023 chairman of Commerzbank, Germany's second biggest stock market-listed bank, object of politically fraught takeover attempt by Italy's Unicredit.

XI JINPING (b. 1953) China's leader since 2012, general secretary of Chinese Communist Party, president since 2013. Switch to authoritarianism, two-term presidential limit lifted in 2018. 'Xi Jinping thought on socialism with Chinese characteristics' now part of Chinese constitution.

BORIS YELTSIN (1931–2007) President of Russia (1991–9). Strong anti-communist position. Rivalry with Gorbachev brought down Soviet Union, economic upheavals paved way for Putin as prime minister in 1999, later president. Squabbling with Clinton over NATO enlargement. Yeltsin foretold an eventual Russian war over Ukraine.

ACKNOWLEDGEMENTS

This book started gestation in 2021 as a relatively modest update on the development of the European single currency. But thanks to the encouragement of Jo Godfrey, my indefatigable editor at Yale University Press, it quickly broadened and deepened. By the end of 2022 it had grown into a plan to review the multitudinous strategic developments that shaped Europe's present circumstances, starting from the upheavals of 1989. Over the thirty months of this gruelling undertaking, the accompanying rush of events – most of which, it has to be said, have been uniformly negative – has been all too evident. The volume of new and old material to process and the number of day-and-night hours this demands have both mushroomed. This is an ambitious project, accomplished at speed. And it would not have been possible without the help of many people whom I would like to thank here.

The long list of interview partners is recorded on separate pages. I set down my gratitude for their openness and patience as we waded through abstruse questions from past and present, sometimes during multiple sessions, including painstaking yet necessary checking and authorisation of statements. Singling out individuals is invidious, but the enlightenment – diverse, unexpected, even in parts entertaining – from three past presidents of the European Commission – José Manuel Barroso, Jean-Claude Juncker, Romano Prodi – represented, for me, a highlight. Horst and Gerhild Teltschik were hospitable and forthcoming when I travelled twice to stay at their home on the Tegernsee to improve my knowledge of the tumultuous times we experienced in 1989–90. John Kornblum was hugely constructive and motivating in many interactions in Berlin, especially in 2022. We spent many hours discussing preparations for this book. Meghnad Desai as always was a source of inspiration; wisely, he proposed, early on, thinning out some of the cast of multiple characters piling up into the script. The deaths of John in December 2023 and Meghnad in July 2025 robbed me and many others of cherished friends. I must record my special debt to four other interlocutors – Horst Köhler, Edzard Reuter, Wolfgang Schäuble, Helmut Schlesinger – each of whom I had got to know (like Kornblum and Desai) in the 1980s and 1990s. They gave me their time and thoughts (and approved their quotes) but sadly passed away while this book was being written.

Some early ideas were sketched out over dinner in Rome with Antonio Armellini and Edoardo Reviglio. John Nugée provided inimitable orientation. Many friends read through text, pointed out errors, suggested improvements. Andrew Adonis, Bill Keegan, Ivan Rogers and Tom Scholar reinforced my thinking. Philip Short gave untiring assistance not only in adding his own sagacious input from decades of studying Russia and China but also in proposing ideas for structural improvements, most of which I quickly implemented. Jin Liqun took an energetic and productive interest in the task. Support and illumination after reading earlier or later drafts came from Ashok Bhatia, Guy Chazan, Udaibir Das, Charles Goodhart, George Hoguet, Robert Holzmann, Otmar Issing, Mervyn King, Norman Lamont, Jacques de Larosière, Paul Lever, Pawel Kowalewski, Klaas Knot, John Neill, Ewald Nowotny, John Orchard, David Owen, Bernd Pfaffenbach, Jessica Pulay, Lars-Henrick Röller, Peter Sedgwick, Anne Simpson, Christopher Smart, Mark Sobel, Robert Stheeman, Niels Thygesen, Christopher Tugendhat, Jens Weidmann, Nout Wellink and Ernst Welteke. Wolfgang Proissl helped behind the scenes. Michael Best was a stalwart. Stefan Kornelius came up with a useful intervention. Markus Leitner and Wegger Christian Strømmen supplied crucial insights.

None of this came from nothing. Many partners in this enterprise comprise personalities and institutions I first became aware of during my work at Reuters, the *Financial Times* and Robert Fleming in the formative quarter-century up to 1999. Therefore I would like to set down my appreciation to all three organisations (the latter now subsumed into J.P. Morgan) and the colleagues who worked there for the latitude and learning they imparted. In the archives, I would like to thank Carmen Partes and her colleagues Mario Aulenbacher and Martin Reibe of the Historical Archive of the Deutsche Bundesbank. At the Political Archives of the German Foreign Office Birgit Kmezik, Uwe Schulz-Kopanski and Karolin Wendt provided valuable aid at crucial moments. Patrick Salmon and Richard Smith, historians at the British Foreign, Commonwealth and Development Office, were, as always, supremely helpful. I am thankful to Joachim Nagel and colleagues Marco Leppin, Ingrid Herden and Christian Erb for their backing. Along with guidance from Jo Godfrey I benefited from the careful editing of Rachael Lonsdale and Dave Watkins. Thanks to others on the Yale team: James Williams, Frazer Martin, Stuart Weir, David Campbell, Chloe Foster, Amanda Cordero and Ruth Killick. Among my colleagues at OMFIF I am grateful to Afroditi Argyropoulou, Caspian Davies, Simon Hadley, Sarah Maloney, Sofia Melis, Ben Rands, Avnish Patel, Rina Patel and Katie-Ann Wilson for their commitment and back-up. My board colleagues Phil Middleton, Maggie Mills, Mark Burgess and Jai Arya were always there when needed. My brother Peter provided useful encouragement.

For their forbearance while this enterprise snowballed, my heartfelt thanks go to Veronika, Saskia and Renaud, Sabrina and Chris, and Elyssa, born into the project, for reminding me of what is important.

Many generous people have aided my endeavours to avoid errors of fact, interpretation and judgement; flaws and errors that remain are mine alone, and, along with other insights, I look forward to receiving notice of them. As has often been said, historians write in retrospect, journalists with an eye on the future. Both try, as I do, to reconstruct on paper the political and economic building blocks of great and unsettling events.

David Marsh
Wimbledon, July 2025

The author and publishers would like to thank the following for permission to reproduce texts, statements and extracts from previous works and archival records:

Professor Giuliano Amato for an extract from a conversation with President François Mitterrand (1992), obtained via the Institut François Mitterrand; Dr Ben Bernanke for an extract from a statement to the Federal Open Market Committee (2011), obtained via the Federal Reserve archives; Emmanuel Moulin, secretary-general of the Elysée Palace, for an extract from President Emmanuel Macron's Sorbonne speech (2024); National Security Archive, George Washington University, for an extract from Anatoly Chernyaev's diary (1989); the Politisches Archiv of the German foreign office for extracts from transcripts of the following conversations: Charles de Gaulle and Willy Brandt (1966), Mao Zedong and Helmut Schmidt (1975), Leonid Brezhnev and Helmut Schmidt (1981), Helmut Kohl and Mikhail Gorbachev (1991); Random House for an extract from *The Russia Hand: A Memoir of Presidential Diplomacy* by Strobe Talbott (2002), recording a statement by Professor Fritz Stern (1996); Thames & Hudson for an extract from Professor Alan Bullock's essay in *The Twentieth Century* (1971); the UK National Archives for extracts from the following letters: Winston Churchill to Harry Truman (1945) and John Major to Helmut Kohl (1992), and for an extract from the transcript of a telephone call between Prime Minister Harold Macmillan and President John F. Kennedy (1963).

FOREWORD
Joachim Nagel

Europe is at a critical juncture in its history. Groundbreaking decisions are needed to ensure we are well-equipped for the future. Improving economic competitiveness, strengthening political unity, and securing as much strategic autonomy as possible in the shifting new global balance of power are just some of the current major geostrategic and European policy challenges that David Marsh addresses in his new book. This work marks a continuation of his decades of activity as a writer and commentator on European affairs that underpin his tremendous overview of historical and contemporary themes and actors.

As president of the Deutsche Bundesbank and a member of the ECB Governing Council, I am both one of the actors in this book and an addressee of its analyses and appeals. While I can concur with many of the evaluations and assessments, I find myself at odds with others. This mixture of agreement and disagreement shows me just how extremely thought-provoking this book is – not just for a specialist audience in the fields of finance, banking and central banking, but for all those interested in current political affairs. I find the recurring theme of political responsibility and accountability particularly stimulating. David Marsh places this question firmly in the foreground and, through his historical reflections, offers a perspective that helps us discuss our strategies for the future.

Chapter by chapter, Marsh guides us through the historical development of Europe, right up to today's geopolitical and economic landscape. He points to the fragility of social, political and – not least – monetary structures in a world increasingly characterised by populism, neonationalist movements, political adventurism and instability. The end of the East–West divide, the transformation of the Soviet sphere of influence, German reunification, the reshaping of Russian politics, the global financial crisis, the European sovereign debt crisis, Brexit – these and other events set the framework for Marsh's reflections. The project of European unity and integration has long been considered the key to peace, prosperity and security on a continent plagued by wars and crises. European monetary union was and remains a key part of this strategic process. But Marsh also highlights the difficulties of monetary union and its structural problems in an environment of competing national interests.

The introduction of the euro was intended to bring Europe closer together – not only monetarily and economically, but also politically. Conceived as a monetary union of sovereign states that lacked an existing political entity, monetary union was linked to the prospect that Europe could develop further in the direction of a federal state. Let us not forget that economic integration in the postwar period was above all a continental peace and security project in which economic integration was seen as the ideal strategic path. The focus at the time was on overcoming the Franco-German conflict that had destabilised continental Europe for decades, if not centuries. The East–West confrontation and postwar transatlantic cooperation merely formed the geostrategic backdrop to this peace project. It was in this environment that monetary union was established – in the historical period in which the collapse of the Soviet Union and the Warsaw Pact reshuffled priorities. The backdrop, which had been stable for decades, now became the dominant strategic field of action: the primary aim of European integration became to stabilise and transform the political landscape on the continent based on the model of liberal, capitalist, market-based nation-state democracies.

In the day-to-day business of monetary policy, the fundamental and overarching significance of our policy area is sometimes overlooked. David Marsh has succeeded over the decades in linking the issues of central banking with major strands of contemporary history. By opening horizons, his analyses serve as a guide. They show once again that, in a continent of 'many Europes', and multiple speeds, the further political integration of euro-area countries, which is necessary for the euro, has stagnated of late. The integration of the euro area remains incomplete.

It is a monetary union without a fiscal union. Progress is necessary on the capital markets union and the banking union. The ECB Governing Council has all too often had to act to overcome crises. With his book, Marsh puts his finger on the sore spot. At the same time, he provides encouragement to find pathways towards the completion of European monetary union.

David Marsh looks at Europe in general, and Germany in particular, from a British angle: for readers from continental Europe, a stimulating and enlightening viewpoint. Of particular interest are, first, the concept of the nation-state as a quasi-supreme actor; second, the ostensible goal of politics as a question of power and prestige; and third, the familiar observation that Europe is not the USA. Nineteenth-century thinking in national terms continues to live on in many political cultures today. In the chapter 'The Trouble with Britain', Marsh points to the persistence of British anguish at the loss of empire and to a British yearning for global recognition and exceptionalism that found concrete expression in Brexiters' fantasies about the role the United Kingdom could (re)assume in a world outside the EU. Marsh underlines how vibrant and potent nationalist methodology can still be in the historical-political debate. In his text, too, it is 'nations', 'powers' and 'institutions' that remain the main actors in history. Europe is at the centre; yet Europe is more than a few powerful countries.

I am grateful that reading David Marsh's stimulating book has refocused my attention on the topic of responsibility and accountability in Europe. Surely all those in positions of responsibility – including in Europe – should continually ask themselves where an excessive emphasis on the 'national' in political practice has led us in the past, and where it is currently leading us. As we see in present circumstances, an emphasis on the 'national' is gaining ground not only in theoretical terms. It is also being interpreted politically, in offensive fashion. We see this in Russia's expansionist ambitions, but also in the desire expressed by politicians to expand their national sphere of influence through economic or even military pressure.

David Marsh's splendid contemporary historical overview benefits from his enormous wealth of contacts in European institutions, particularly those involved in monetary, financial and economic policy. It offers a wealth of further topics, theories, events and actors that guide the reader to the following crucial questions: What is Europe? What can it be? What does it want to be? What role does Europe want to play – and what role should it play – in the future? What central values does it want to invoke? And what impact can Europe's path have on other parts of the world? Marsh shows us that European history, both in the short and long term, can be understood as a history of competition among political systems. In this sense, it has shown that Europe is strongest when it is built on shared values, cooperation, balance and collective security. And it is at its weakest when political division, nationalism and nationalistic competition gain the upper hand.

INTRODUCTION

EUROPE'S COMMON GOOD

Europe has a set of primary interests which to us have none; or a very remote relation . . . Why, by interweaving our destiny with that of any part of Europe, entangle our peace and prosperity in the toils of European ambition, rivalship, interest, humor or caprice?

George Washington, 1796[1]

We must be clear on the fact that our Europe, today, is mortal. It can die, and that depends entirely on our choices. But these choices must be made now.

Emmanuel Macron, 2024[2]

Trump, with his character, with his persistence, he will restore order [in Europe] quite quickly. And all of them, you will see — it will happen quickly, soon — they will all stand at the feet of the master and will wag their tails.

Vladimir Putin, 2025[3]

From Helmut Kohl's gargantuan frame, words generally tumble forth like a waterfall. But this time, in the evening of 9 November 1989 during a governmental visit to Warsaw, the West German chancellor was 'virtually speechless'.[4] Breaking off at 9 p.m. from a festive banquet with Polish prime minister Tadeusz Mazowiecki at the former Radziwill Palace, Kohl telephoned a key aide to get confirmation of news from Berlin that would change the course of Europe and the

1

world. 'Mr Chancellor, the Wall is falling,' he was told. 'Ackermann,' Kohl asked, 'are you sure?'[5]

The first telephone indications from Kohl's office in the West German capital of Bonn had surfaced at about 7.30 p.m., as Kohl's limousine convoy set off for the palace from the Parkowa government guest house.[6] As part of the journalistic entourage accompanying the chancellor, I was in a group that saw him that Thursday evening after he called in at the Marriott hotel after dinner.[7] Poland was emerging gingerly from forty years of Communism. A move towards reunification of its frequently troublesome western neighbour, responsible for partition, bloodshed and turmoil over much of the past two centuries, was a moment of tribulation as much as triumph. Poland feared it would be squeezed again between two historic enemies, Russia and Germany.

By 10 p.m., Kohl had been told that hundreds of East Berliners had crossed peacefully to the western part of the divided city. He appeared poleaxed by an event that would bring huge uncertainty for Poland as well as for much of the rest of Europe. 'The wheel of history is turning faster,' the chancellor proclaimed – but he added that no one could foretell the time when German unification might take place. Kohl conceded he was in 'an acutely difficult situation' with his Polish hosts. He was doing his best to avoid 'false signals' that could trigger 'dangerous emotions'.

Lech Wałęsa, the shipyard electrician who had become the ground-breaking leader of the Solidarity movement that brought Mazowiecki into office in August, had met Kohl for an hour before dinner. With Communism breaking down across eastern Europe and emigration pressure mounting daily in East Germany, he told the chancellor that the Wall would last only one or two weeks. 'Revolutionary chaos' would break out and Poland would once again become a 'victim of history'.[8] Kohl played down any prospect of radical transformation, countering that the East Germans had been demonstrating peacefully for reforms and wanted 'change, not revolution'.

Around 7 a.m. the next day, 10 November, Wałęsa told Horst Teltschik, Kohl's foreign-policy and national security adviser, present at all the big moments of the 1989–90 reunification drama, that his prediction the evening before had come true much more quickly than expected. 'The Wall has fallen and Poland will pay a price. Everyone will concentrate on East Germany.' National daily *Gazeta Wyborcza*, in its Friday issue, proclaimed in its front-page story, 'Europe without the Wall . . . No one knows what the consequences will be.'[9]

My 10 November despatch from Warsaw was published in the *Financial Times* on Saturday morning.

> Yesterday's wave of humanity washing through the Berlin wall marks the crumbling away, almost literally overnight, of the ugliest symbol of the post-war world – and the pushing into place of the building blocks of a new Europe. Rarely in history can an event desired by so many, deemed possible by so few, have happened with such remarkable speed. The build-up of protests over the past month in East Germany unleashes a torrent of questions over the future of central Europe to which neither East nor West has ready answers.[10]

After the passage of three and a half decades – four French presidents and German chancellors, five US presidents and nine British prime ministers later – the world has moved on. Europe has reacted at great speed to the startling February 2025 rapprochement over Ukraine between Donald Trump and Vladimir Putin.[11] Friedrich Merz, the new German leader, has announced 'Germany is back' with a gigantic debt-fuelled spending package on defence and infrastructure that appeared to overturn decades of German and European policy imperatives.[12] However, the move, enacted through a hurried amendment to the constitutionally enshrined 'debt brake' in force since 2009,[13] will require significant further Europe-level reforms to allow it to work effectively.[14] Merz has further widened his distance from long-term rival and former chancellor Angela Merkel, and shorn up a flagging partnership with France, by declaring support for French nuclear energy – a major change in German policy with wide-ranging security as well as economic implications.[15] The European Union is moving into a new phase of activism after Trump's attack on globalisation. All these developments – and many more that lie behind Europe's trials – can be traced back, one way or another, to that momentous November 1989 evening.

The purpose of this book is to make sense of these interlinkages in politics, economics, defence and security affairs – examining how, when and why they came about, and where they may be leading. Putin's

February 2022 full-scale invasion of Ukraine and subsequent barbarities flowed partly from Russia's insistence on depicting itself as a victim of the West, both after the end of the Cold War and in earlier periods of history, with special reference to Germany's 1941 invasion. Kremlin–White House entente, followed by a raft of highly protectionist Trump tariff announcements, seemed to demote the Europeans to bystanders, end eighty years of Euro-Atlanticism, and restore Putin to a global front-row seat. Under a balefully re-energised Trump, 'America First' apparently translates into 'Europe Last'.

Russia's 2022 action brought, for Putin, a set of consequences that can be described, mildly, as bitter-sweet. His strategic plan did not foresee the aftermath: an upsurge in Ukrainian nationalism, hundreds of thousands of Russian war deaths, fresh NATO enlargement through accession of two previously neutral states, Finland and Sweden, and further consolidation of American financial and military power. Yet, three years later, Trump's alignment with Putin over Ukraine reconfirmed the extraordinary psychological and political parallelism between the two men.[16] Russia's president appeared within reach of fulfilling a long-desired goal of a form of parity with America – a campaign sizeably boosted by Putin's red-carpet welcome on his August 2025 Alaska visit.

The outcome for Europe was less nuanced, and more bitter. The invasion destroyed the plans of Germany, Europe's strongest economy and banker of many European projects, to capitalise on Russia as a source of cheap energy and a buyer of industrial exports and technology. These circumstances laid the foundation for a US economic surge which – for a time, at least – reinforced America's international dominance. Domestically, the economic gains were perceived not only as unevenly distributed but also as a prime source of inflation – helping pave the way for Trump's November 2024 re-election. The president's grievances against alleged past economic mismanagement and other nations' exploitative trade practices[17] sit awkwardly with the reality that the US has been at the heart of the post-Second World War economic order.[18] Furthermore, over the past decade, the US economy has outperformed the rest of the industrialised world.[19]

Europe's vulnerability to American might in the four vital spheres of political economy – energy, defence, industry and money – rose dramatically. Furthermore, the invasion and its aftermath strengthened a Russia–China partnership that – despite Beijing's caution about US sanctions-induced disturbances to its international economic and financial position – could grow into a formal alliance, much to the West's discomfort and detriment. And it increased further the oft-stated, long-ignored need for the Europeans to care and pay far more for their own security, or otherwise risk a return to pre-1945 instability and tragedy.

All this took place at a dire time for the Old Continent, struggling with faltering economies, strained budgets, Atlantic alliance disruption, socially divisive immigration pressures, and the weakest political leadership since the 1930s. Europe's tasks are daunting – in summary, the 'six Ds': deglobalisation, demographics, decarbonisation, digitalisation, defence[20] and, ominously, debt, epitomised by the rising cost of Europe's welfare systems and the huge public borrowing necessary to finance them.

It is hard to avoid a neat, although austere, conclusion. Europe, together with the US, won most of the old arguments over the supremacy of capitalism and the failures of Communism. Since the fall of the Wall, it has lost many of the new arguments, lost its leadership, and lost its way. In the four decades up to 1989, Europe as a collective body got the big questions mainly right. In the equivalent period since then, it has got many of them wrong.

One set of facts on government finances illustrates the European malaise – and the difficulties of coping with increased spending demands, especially for defence and economic countermeasures after Trump's 2025 broadsides. In 1999, eleven countries led by Germany and France started economic and monetary union (EMU) and the euro. At the centre of the monetary and fiscal arrangements was a rule setting a 'reference value' limiting public sector debt to 60 per cent of gross domestic product (GDP), against around 70 per cent at the time.[21] Membership has since grown to twenty with the accession of nine mainly small countries. Successive efforts to comply with public finance targets have been dismal failures. The debt ratio rose to 90 per cent in 2024, with five EMU members (Belgium, France, Greece, Italy and Spain) exceeding 100 per cent.[22] But this has been a general world trend. Public debt in the UK and the US in 2024 stood at 103 per cent and 115 per cent of GDP respectively. For the thirty-four-member Organisation for Economic Co-operation and Development (OECD) group of industrial countries it was 115 per cent – against a 72 per cent average in the ten years before the 2007–8 financial crisis.

The central issue of public finance was just one of the questions which became more virulent during three years of research and writing. I have been aided by insights from 160 interviews with authoritative figures – most of whom are quoted 'on the record' – as well as from the uncovering of unpublished archives from the US, Britain and Germany. Many main themes were clear from the beginning, but developments since 2022 have sharpened the focus. Why did Germany, during the chancellorships of Gerhard Schröder and Angela Merkel, place its large gamble on the benignity of Russia? Why were so many warnings neglected about the explosive potential of the Russia–Ukraine stand-off? Can Germany under its new leader Merz recover economic fortune?

Why has western political leadership proven so vulnerable to populist opportunists? What mistakes could have been avoided over NATO's eastward expansion? Can Europe successfully combine the principles of promoting economic growth, paying adequately for its own defence, and countering climate change – or will it fail on all counts? Did Europe err in its one-sided commitment to monetary union before all the factors supporting it were in place? Why have France and Germany been getting on so badly – and can a combination of Emmanuel Macron (in the relatively short period he still has at the Élysée Palace) and Merz stop the slide?

How did Putin at the turn of the century hold so many European leaders in thrall? Will he at some stage be rehabilitated? Through his apparent upgrading by Trump, has he done so already? Why, exactly, did Britain leave the EU? After a bleak period of political mediocrity – the UK has run through more prime ministers than Italy since 2016 – can it prosper outside? Or even, as one of the possibly beneficial repercussions of Trump 2.0, return to the European fold?

Beyond all these questions lie deeper issues. Europe has been the leading light in world affairs for most of the past five hundred years. In a rough and dangerous environment, can it maintain the main components of what has become, since the Second World War, the prized 'European way of life' – multiculturalism, democracy, prosperity, education, industrial prowess and social protection? To what extent have these benefits reflected a form of post-1945 subsidy by the rest of the globe, encompassing a grandiose and, for most of that period, outward-looking US, and developing countries largely locked into economic subservience to Europe? Now that this favourable constellation is coming to an end, will Europe succumb – not for the first time in history – to external forces, in a world now moulting into antagonistic US and Chinese spheres of influence? The term 'superpower' is in some ways a misnomer because the US and China are wrestling with their own acute difficulties. But this makes them still less disposed to show clemency to a continent that seems to have lost its way.

There has been no shortage of analysis of the past, and planning for better times, by this bloc of old, proud, rich nations: collectively, the world's third biggest economic and trading area after the Americans and Chinese. But the European Union and surrounding non-member states – now including the UK – have shown deep-seated shortcomings in implementing a strategy for success in the twenty-first century. A long period of travail for Europe started at the time of the 1973 oil-price shock sparked by the Yom Kippur war. This ignited an inflationary surge which enshrined the power in and over Europe of Germany's independent Bundesbank, most importantly in imparting a net deflationary bias to the operation of monetary union when it started in 1999.

To help overcome Europe's manifest inability to establish anything even remotely resembling a genuine political union, I try to outline new meaning for the old idea of a politically and economically interwoven Europe of 'concentric circles'. All sides need to respect differences but build a framework that respects both solidarity and national interest. A parallel, wider concept – developed by Jacques Delors, European Commission president from 1985 to 1995, postwar Europe's most impressive and most disappointed leader – is 'variable geometry'.

This applies, too, to relations with the US and China. In dealing with individual European countries, the superpowers will inevitably practise a policy of 'divide and rule'. Maintaining an equilibrium within the EU and with partners outside is an enormously problematic balancing act. Britain will not rejoin the EU in the next ten to fifteen years; no one can afford the inevitable blood-letting that a renewed membership referendum would bring. Yet a reinvigorated partnership between Britain and continental Europe, in the four key areas of energy, defence, industry and money, linked by trade and technology, remains the best way forward for promoting European resilience.

However unrewarding this may appear with Trump in the White House, reinforcing or perhaps restoring Europe's relationship with the US has to remain an overall strategic goal. This can be achieved solely from a position of strength. And this, in turn, can come about only through greater European solidity and solidarity – including countries such as the United Kingdom which are not in the EU.

'Variable geometry' holds the key when the US is turning in on itself and China is gearing up to become a prime beneficiary of Trump's simplistic and self-harming economic policies. Europe would be well served by returning to the basic principles of the 1950s, as well as those exposed by Delors, to become a more constructive and cohesive economic whole. For all the reasons that Britain knew about in the 1960s, redis- covered in the 1980s and 1990s, appeared to forget in the 2010s, and can now reapply, trading with Europe makes considerable sense.

There are also great benefits to be realised by linking up with like- minded countries outside Europe, one of which is Canada, even though the 'gravity model' of economics dictates that trade ties attenuate with distance.[23] Opportunities for services trade can be widened further under the variable geometry model, including opening up sectors and regions that have concentrated on manufacturing. All this necessitates considerable efforts in enhancing productivity and investing in educa- tion, difficult yet not impossible at a time of public sector penury.

EUROPE'S PREDICAMENT

The background to these challenges is unpropitious. Five big factors behind Europe's predicament are summarised in Chapter 1. The deterio- ration in leadership authority and longevity since the 1980s tells its own story. Germany is undergoing a period of economic stagnation – although at a far higher level of wealth – not seen since the 1930s. France, since the Second World War a more traditional source of European instability, is navigating its own stretch in the doldrums. In many European countries, the rise and, in some cases, entry into government of far-right parties have produced a backlash against internationalism and a reduction in readiness for compromise on which modern democracies depend. The breakdown in Franco-German understanding, shortcomings in European financial firepower and Britain's Brexit perturbations have compounded the disarray.

There is a real fear (Chapter 2) that Europe will be squeezed by China and the US over trade, security and technology – becoming a 'playball' in Sino-American rivalry, to adapt words of former German president Richard von Weizsäcker. Less than three months after his second inauguration, Trump's enactment of aggressive tariff policies and willingness to force a peace deal in Ukraine if necessary over the heads of the Europeans sparked a fresh upsurge of European solidarity. This has been coupled with a new drive, powered by much more government borrowing, especially in Germany, to lower dependence on American military muscle. But it is still far too early to say whether Europe has the economic and industrial strength and political will to implement genuinely go-it-alone policies in a hostile world.

Chapter 3 deals with the long strands of history connecting Russia and Germany, encompassing the post-1945 reset under Willy Brandt's *Ostpolitik* and then the complex interactions leading to the breaching of the Berlin Wall. Putin, in November 1989 a sullen witness in Dresden to the hollowing out of Soviet power, embodies intriguing elements of continuity in long-running Russian thinking about the so-called 'European home'. The concept can serve ambivalently, as his persona shows, as a means both of providing pan-European stability and security and of buttressing a Russia-first mindset reminiscent of past imperialism.

Chapters 4 and 5 relate the eleven-month scramble to negotiate German unification after the Wall fell, and then the tortuous decade-long journey from the disintegration of the Soviet Union to Russia's break with the West – encapsulated above all else by Putin's landmark speech to the Munich Security Conference in February 2007. In the helter-skelter of events, three basic facts – of seminal importance for the drama of Ukraine and thus for the present and future course of Europe – stand out.

First, America was in control at nearly every step of the way. Chancellor Helmut Kohl was naturally an important actor in the reunification process. But the key influence stemmed from Washington. The most crucial role was performed by often underrated President George H.W. Bush – described, with cut-glass irony, by Strobe Talbott, one of America's arch-power players during the Soviet–Russian transition, as 'the perfect gentleman . . . a good sport, a gracious winner, skillful at assuring Gorbachev that he won't be sorry for what he has done, which is nothing less than presiding over the capitulation of the Soviet Union in the Cold War.'[24]

Second, the West failed – despite much professed benevolence – to give the Soviet Union, and then Russia, sufficient respect and recognition as a fallen, depleted and wary one-time superpower to prevent it lurching back in pursuit of the lost trappings of triumph. This was a fine, perhaps impossible-to-navigate dividing line. The western view was crystallised, in Russian eyes at least, by President Barack Obama's dismissive description of the country in 2014 as a 'regional power'.[25] During the 1990s, Russian interlocutors were given myriad assurances, at different times, from disparate people, and hedged with varying caveats, that NATO did not intend to enlarge its membership eastwards. That it did so, under pressure from formerly Soviet bloc countries, and under different conditions to those envisaged in 1990, does not excuse Russian aggression. But it does provide some explanation for Russia's perception, built on the legacy of history, that western 'betrayal' had heightened its vulnerability to outside forces.

Third, the danger of war if Russia's hand was forced over Ukraine was voiced freely, over the two decades before 2022, in many leadership conversations involving players as diverse as James Baker, Bill Clinton, Boris Yeltsin and Putin. Authoritative Americans, backed by much documentation on past statements and encounters, affirm that the US tried continuously to treat post-Cold War Russia as a friend and partner. Yet opposing truths can exist in parallel. A stream of top-placed European politicians – and some Americans – at the time regarded policies towards Russa as akin to the victors' treatment of defeated Germany after the First World War. There is plausible evidence that the US cynically regarded the risk of bitterness in Russia and, eventually, war in Ukraine as an acceptable price for American dominance in the region of central and eastern Europe.

The post-Cold War quid pro quo on the German side was to advance further with policies set by Chancellor Willy Brandt in the 1970s, with antecedents stretching back to the nineteenth century and beyond. These focused on trade and energy exchanges with Russia aiming to bolster stability in both East and West through massive imports of gas traded for western technology. The drawback for Germany – somewhat incongruous in a nation fabled for risk-aversion – was that it neglected to consider until it was far too late what might happen if things went wrong. The negative outcome of this failed gamble, with immense effects on the whole of Europe, was compounded by a supremely awkward juxtaposition.

Correlated German bets on continued stable relationships with China, America and France all turned sour at the same time.

Another interconnection is this: without the fall of the Berlin Wall and unification of Germany, Europe's 'single currency', the euro, would not have come about in the twentieth century – perhaps not at all. Here, in contrast to the risk-management shortcomings over Russian geopolitics, there were multiple German warnings during the 1980s and 1990s about the perils of starting EMU too early. The admonitions from the Bundesbank and others were prescient but, probably inevitably in view of the French-led calls for rapid post-German-unification change, went largely unheeded.

The initial lack of adequate safeguards for the single currency raised the need for Europe, from 2010 onwards, to enact far-reaching financial stabilising mechanisms. These had two seminal effects – both countering the euro's original Germanic 'stability-orientated' principles and also creating a new divide between Britain and the rest of Europe.

The avowed policy of 'bringing the D-Mark into Europe' and making the European Central Bank (ECB), more or less, a clone of the Bundesbank was the sole means available in the 1990s to persuade the Germans to abandon their currency. Yet, reflecting the sheer weight of EMU's non-Germanic-leaning members, the euro bloc's initial Bundesbank-like format was never likely to be durable. All constituents have now come to terms with this reality.

The euro system's innate instability and the evolution of the entity at its centre, the many-faceted European Central Bank, forms the centrepiece of Chapter 6. The story of the bank – and the plotting, politics and personalities behind it – is in many ways the story of Europe. One of the twists of monetary union, which I relate in detail, centring on the twinned personalities of Mario Draghi (the ECB's third president) and Tim Geithner (US Treasury secretary in the first term of President Barack Obama), highlights a principal, somewhat ironic message of this book. European action from 2010 onwards to shore up the single currency took place only after political intervention from the US, a country from which the Europeans were supposed to be making themselves monetarily independent. Moreover, the single largest European fiscal adjustment since German unification – Germany's relaxation of the 'debt brake' – occurred not because of combined European action but as a result of the pressure of events in the US.[26]

As Chapter 7 describes, the requirement for EMU, as it evolved, to embody a series of inbuilt self-stabilising mechanisms provided a fundamental reason for David Cameron's calling of the 2016 EU referendum and the schism that followed. The missteps of the four short-tenured Conservative prime ministers in the eight years after Cameron are now being at least partly corrected – by a Labour prime minister, Keir Starmer, facing far tougher economic conditions than when Tony Blair took over from John Major in 1997.

Starmer's instinctive propensity to put self-preservation ahead of ideology makes him innately cautions about a fundamental rebalancing towards the European Union. Trumpian polices are raising both Britain's relative attractiveness to European partners and its potential gains from a realignment. However, the UK's economic weaknesses heighten vulnerability to the forces of foreign capital, especially those orchestrated by a US real-estate developer-cum-president who owns Scottish golf courses and displays a fondness for the British royal family. So Starmer and his government will be highly susceptible to divide-and-rule blandishments from both Trump and Xi Jinping in coming years.

Under Trump, American political intervention in Europe has become blunter and still more transparently self-serving. Yet Trump will have to ensure that he does not overplay his hand.

Europe, it is true, has taken American protective power for granted for too long, enjoying freedom, amassing wealth and enlarging living standards behind the US military shield. But, in doing so, the Europeans themselves have reinforced built-in American geopolitical strength.

Through accepting the hegemony of the dollar, the Europeans have contributed to an increasingly close interweaving of US military capability with the country's reserve currency status.[27] That (for America) benevolent juxtaposition could be undermined or reversed if Trump overextends American muscle-play and takes ever greater economic and political risks with trade and budgetary policies and with the dollar's monetary role.[28] After years of uncertainty over the European currency, the risks for the US economy wrought by Trump's recklessness constitute an important prop for the international role of the euro.[29]

In Europe's attempts to stand up to America's new policies, the ECB may have to move further from a 'Bundesbank-pure' model and take on a more overtly political role. As the only EU institution with genuine international clout, the ECB has already developed considerably since its birth in 1998. However problematic this may be for the original protagonists behind EMU, a further transition may be necessary – for example, by purchasing government bonds helping to finance additional European defence spending. This would bring an important new aspect governing the ECB's statutory 'independence'.[30] It would amend an element of the bank's foundational purposes in the direction favoured by France's president from 1982 to 1996, François Mitterrand, as well as, latterly, by Emmanual Macron. Under the Merz-led government, it is vital that Germany and France find a common voice on this question. Yet another Franco-German split would be playing straight into the hands of Trump and Putin.

Looking beyond purely monetary matters, Trump and his administration have to be aware of a deeper threat. A protectionist, bellicose and unreliable America could further reinforce China's persistent desire to portray itself as a champion of globalisation and multilateralism.[31] This could end up driving a range of nations from the Global South – as well as, perhaps, Europe itself – into the Chinese fold. Such a development could badly erode America's global power – presumably, not one of the forty-seventh president's second-term aims.[32] Already, after the protectionist announcements of Trump's first half-year back in office, that move seems under way.

Where will it end? Chapter 8 outlines some possibilities. Like all the books I have written, this one tells of work in progress. Although tangible evidence of success thus far is threadbare, Europe can move towards an age of resilience. After a steep path towards (re)integration after the Second World War, European unravelling cannot be an option. Shakespeare's Macbeth (but not, I hope, his ending) comes to mind. 'For mine own good / All causes shall give way: I am in blood / Stepp'd in so far that, should I wade no more / Returning were as tedious as go o'er'.[33]

In Ukraine, much blood – and treasure too – has flowed. Stemming the needless waste of both, and rebuilding structures in both East and West, must be the way forward.

Europe, and that includes the United Kingdom, needs to come together and redefine what is its 'own good'. And then find the means, from all available resources – including, come what may, a strong bedrock of joint European–American interests – to accomplish it.

1

THE RECKONING

If one thing seemed certain at the close of the Second World War, it was the end of Europe.
          Alan Bullock, vice chancellor, University of Oxford, 1971[1]

We Europeans represent 8 to 9 per cent of the world's population, produce around 25 per cent of global gross domestic product and account for 50 per cent of global social spending. Without competitiveness we will not be able to maintain the prosperity of our country and Europe.
          Angela Merkel, German chancellor, 2012[2]

The magnitude of economic disaster stemming from economic and monetary union, relative to any reasonable forecast of Europe's strength as an economy, has been very large. Europe has not been successful in maintaining its relevance as a major global force.
          Larry Summers, former US Treasury secretary, 2023[3]

Across the frequently unsettled contours of Europe, ambition has given way to fracture. Russia's war in Ukraine together with upheavals triggered by climate change, Chinese–American rivalry, the Covid-19 pandemic, the globalisation of industry and finance, and, in 2025, the Trump renaissance confront the Old Continent with an uncomfortable panoply of challenges. Many of these difficulties rest on long-lasting legacies of the Second World War. Three epoch-changing events unfolded in unexpected manner: the fall of the Berlin Wall in

1989, the unification of Germany in 1990 and the break-up of the Soviet Union in 1991. Helmut Kohl, the 'Chancellor of German Unity', did not expect to see his nation reunited in his lifetime.[4] Yet all three developments, linked in a chain of Soviet collapse, took place in a span of just over two years. For western nations seemingly catapulted still further onto the victorious side of history, these events signified both triumph and tribulation.

The dismantling of the ugly edifice dividing the capital of the former German Reich made Europe 'whole and free',[5] but it brought a cathartic shock whose longer-term effects were not immediately perceived, and have become more pronounced over time. The shifts under way can most graphically be described by extending nomenclature developed by Louis Halle, a US State Department official under President Harry Truman.[6] The ending of the Cold War signalled by the events of 1989–91 ushered in the fifth great crisis in the European balance of power since the end of the eighteenth century – after the upsets wrought by Napoleon's France, Kaiser Wilhelm II and Adolf Hitler in Germany, and finally Josef Stalin with 1945-era Soviet expansionism.

The post-1989 tumult placed on trial a world order that was never fully settled, and is now giving way to a far more diffuse and unpredictable set of structures. Centres of political power and economic influence are gradually moving away from the West towards countries loosely known as the Global South, with China and India standing out in pole positions. Just as it faces these multiple external tests, Europe has been turning inwards. Its most important component, Germany, three and a half decades after reunifying, remains split culturally and politically between East and West. It has been stagnating economically since 2019 – the most intractable combination of political and economic circumstances since the Federal Republic's foundation in 1949.

France, the second biggest economy after Germany among the countries that share a single currency, the euro, has been weathering the most volatile period of political instability since the Fifth Republic was set up in 1958. The single most damning indicator of insidious Franco-German strains undermining the solidity of the euro concerns divergences over public debt in the two countries. The French have been profligate while Germany has practised its own form of fiscal orthodoxy. The two countries' debt-to-GDP ratios were virtually identical in

2007, just before the global financial crisis, but France's has nearly doubled since then while Germany's (after rising in subsequent years and then falling back) has remained unchanged.[7] According to the elder statesman of European finance, Niels Thygesen, the ninety-year-old Danish economics professor, for eight years chairman of the European Fiscal Board monitoring European public sector finances, 'France has replaced Italy as the major problem country within the euro area.'[8]

Britain, under a new prime minister, Keir Starmer, following the Labour Party's landslide victory in the July 2024 election, is still coping with the psychological drama of leaving the European Union in 2020. Emphasising the fraught nature of politics on both sides of the Atlantic, the start of Trump's second term coincided with a political vacuum in both France and Germany succeeding the collapse of both countries' governments. Furthermore, the threat of a trade war caused by an initial round of large-scale US tariffs could precipitate further inflation as well as a fall in output – the wrong medicine at the wrong time for an ailing Europe.[9] Under Trump's influence, Europe in 2025 embarked on a bid to correct its trajectory and steady its passage. Yet this is a race against time which Europe by no means is certain to win.

In the immediate post-Berlin Wall years, Germany appeared to benefit massively from the new structures following the crumbling of Communism in the East. Most notable was the introduction of the euro as the centrepiece of economic and monetary union, intended, among other objectives, to set up a harmonised market free of currency fluctuations that would aid national exporters (led by the Germans) throughout the continent. Now, partly as a result of the direct and indirect effects of the Ukraine war, but also reflecting China's industrial aggressiveness in targeting Germany as a market for its own increasingly sophisticated products, the accomplishments of the past three decades have been fading fast.

A politician with plenty of experience in dealing with Germany – and who lost more skirmishes than he won in political jousting with Chancellor Merkel – is David Cameron, Britain's Conservative prime minister during six disturbed years of European relations. His premiership ended with Britain's rejection of EU membership in a referendum he called in 2016 – the biggest failed gamble in modern UK political history. After a period in the political wilderness and then a brief spell in 2023–4 as foreign secretary in the last, doomed Tory government, Cameron now casts an acerbic eye on the latest German experience: 'EMU appeared to be working very strongly in favour of the German economy by effectively suppressing the price of exports, but now everything has turned against them: Putin, Ukraine, gas, China and Trump. That all combines to make the situation much more difficult.'[10]

PROLIFERATION OF PUZZLES

After its stellar recovery from the ruins of the Second World War, and the relatively brief post-unification interlude, Germany has unquestionably fallen upon harder and harsher times. The roll call of German success in the immediate postwar decades was conditioned by one eminent (probably inevitable) failure: the inability of the western powers which, together with the Soviet Union (after 1941), overcame Germany in 1939–45 to organise a peaceful and democratic system across the whole of Europe. Peace and democracy took hold in the western part. The East was left to the Soviets, and Germany was partitioned.

The set-up was unpleasant for many people living to the east of the Iron Curtain,[11] but division proved opportune. It enabled western Europe to establish a stable modus vivendi between Germany and France, neighbours which over the previous hundred years had become mortal enemies, generating havoc and bloodshed for themselves and the rest of Europe. The pre-1989 status quo permitted countries on both sides of the divide, living under different political systems and with different growth rates, to engineer the recovery – political, economic and moral – of a desecrated continent. It brought the US into partnership with western Europe to guarantee the peace, governed by a generally solid mutual understanding and division of responsibilities – always on American terms but with enough leeway for Europeans to have their say. And it allowed the West Europeans to advance economically with sufficient strength that they were ready for an all-important turning point.

When a more liberal-minded Communist regime in Moscow, predictably and dangerously, ran into trouble by trying to reform an unreformable system, western Europe and America, together, could supply support and salvation to countries emerging from the disintegrating Soviet imperium.

Since the West's victory over Communism, Europe's fortunes have turned downwards. Europe and America have been unable to find an acceptable common denominator in key strategic areas, particularly over defence. They have made numerous miscalculations in handling a renascent, frayed and psychologically unstable Russia. Understanding between Germany and France has unravelled. Europeans and Americans have been unsteady and irresolute in dealing with China, whose globalisation drive added to economic competition at just the time when eastern Europe emerged on to world markets as low-cost industrial players.[12] China has now started a new phase of forcible industrial expansion, combined with a Russia-leaning stance in the Ukraine war and in geopolitics more generally, that confronts the West with important threats to security as well as economic wellbeing.[13]

Europe has taken a series of wrong turnings over the flagship project of economic and monetary union, introduced in 1998–9 to reinforce trading and investment links between European nations, counterbalance America's monetary supremacy, and prevent a Franco-German rupture after reunification. Germany has displayed epic shortcomings over energy policies, especially the build-up of dependence on Russia – one of the reasons for the fall in German gross domestic product in 2023 and 2024 that has cast a pall over the continent. And all sides made mistakes that led, via contorted routes, to Cameron's promise in 2013 of an EU membership referendum, its enactment in 2016 and the UK's departure (a tortuous three and a half years after the vote) in 2020. Whatever the precise long-term effects on Britain, this break has deepened and accelerated the stream of bad news for Europe.

Caught in the force field between the two economic superpowers, Europe has to make sense of a proliferation of puzzles. American policies towards China are bedevilled by uncertainty and unpredictability. Can 'Trump the deal-maker' co-exist with 'Trump the competitor'?[14] Will he achieve a trade deal with China which can yield the US considerable benefits, or a trade war from which America might suffer a great reverse?[15]

However that conundrum is resolved, the unsavoury reality for Europe is that both the US and China are likely to resort to similar divide-and-rule tactics to separate individual European countries – including the UK – from the European mainstream.[16] A foretaste of conflicts was delivered shortly after Trump's 2024 election win. One of the president elect's advisers set down recommendations to Britain and its new Labour government: Britain should prioritise trade relations with the US and separate itself from a 'socialist Europe'.[17] Almost simultaneously, Pascal Lamy, a former director of the World Trade Organization and ally of Jacques Delors, gave the opposite advice. He said Britain should focus on the EU, as it did three times as much trade with Europe than with America.[18]

Chinese president Xi Jinping weighed in by telling Starmer that Britain and China 'should deepen political trust for mutual benefit'.[19] Trump will steer a zigzag course guaranteed to sow confusion and doubt. He will veer between supporting Europe's nebulous, oft-articulated desire for 'strategic autonomy'[20] – providing cover for weakening US ties[21] – and applying pressure for individual countries to enact trade and military deals that benefit America. Trump's election win, and actions thereafter, may galvanise Europe to make steps towards greater self-sufficiency and unity[22] – as happened with German's defence and infra-structure package. That would be a favourable outcome. Yet there remain still too many factors fostering furthering fissures rather than solidarity among the Europeans.[23] Larry Summers, former Treasury secretary and a strong critic of what he sees as the euro's deflationary effects, says:

> Trump's policy towards Europe has been very misguided, but there is a silver lining. It has caused some rethinking in Europe about the need to take more responsibility for national security, and has promoted a shift towards a less extreme fiscal view in Germany. I don't think the moment of major change in Europe has yet come. I have compared Europe to a museum and we are not yet at the point where I would withdraw that comparison. They've turned a corner, but they haven't turned the corner.[24]

Clues to the future can be deduced from past patterns. The overall message is that the EU has been an excellent club for the middle-income ex-Soviet bloc countries which joined twenty years ago, much less so for the higher-income pre-existing members, which have seen their relative prosperity diminished.[25] Subdividing European political and economic history into four roughly forty-year periods since the first unification of Germany in 1871 yields a compelling overview.

Economic output per head (equating with living standards) rose only scantily in the first two periods. The first was the forty years of industry-fuelled growth, rising populations and social upheaval up to the 1914 outbreak of the First World War. Then came, between 1914 and 1949, the period of conflict and disruption up to the start of the Cold War and the establishment of the East and West German states.

After 1949, following the years of devastation, the picture improved on both sides of the communist–capitalist divide.[26] With East and West in an ideological and military stand-off, but not at war, annual output per head in key countries rose two to four times as fast as during the conflict-strewn previous forty years. The Communist-led East did twice as well as in the previous period, but still grew at only half the pace of the West. In the latest four decades, since the heady days of 1989, prosperity has increased far more slowly in the larger countries of western Europe, while the eastern newcomers to the EU, fortunately for them, have been catching up fast.

The new laggards include Germany, France and Italy, the three most important EU members, founders of the European Economic Community under the Treaty of Rome in 1957, as well as the UK, which entered late, in 1973, and has now departed. A sharp, synchronised slowdown in economic growth among the four principal nations of western Europe, accompanied by rising public debt, both feeds off and feeds a political malaise that forms a baleful counterpoint to war and disturbance in the East.

Europe's monetary union has imparted a deflationary bias. The states which have done best out of the EU in the past twenty years are those that are not in the euro. Among the different European categories, Britain, the perpetual European latecomer, made the right decision by staying outside the euro bloc at the outset of the single currency.[27] By contrast, it quit the EU at a vulnerable time for the world and European economy, and has made heavy weather of its initial period outside. Whether Britain's relative fortunes improve depends on (presently rather bleak) prospects for European recovery, as well as on the performance of the Labour government that took office in 2024 promising rapprochement with the EU, but not re-entry.

All this forms a subset of the wider picture. For five hundred years Europe, despite many phases of penury and perturbation, has regarded itself as the cradle of world civilisation.[28] 'Europe' as a concept grew both eastwards (to Russia and Asia) and westward (America).[29] Those times of expansion and elevation are now over. Merkel, a former citizen of the collapsed Communist-run German Democratic Republic, who became chancellor of Germany seven years after Kohl left office and subsequently equalled his record of sixteen years in power, was unsurpassed in providing expert diagnosis of Europe's predicament. Her tragedy was that, despite unbeatable stamina, an uninterrupted outpouring of wise-sounding statements and a massive workload of international meetings, she was unable to do much about it. Indeed, her own mistakes – some due to external circumstances, others home-grown, some resulting from the inevitable constraints of her cloistered first thirty-five years in Sovietised East Germany – intensified Germany's predicament after she left office in December 2021.

According to Heather Conley, a long-time German specialist, president of the Washington-based German Marshall Fund think-tank in 2022–4 (and thereafter senior adviser), 'Merkel's great talent was being able to stay at the European Council working till 4 o'clock in the morning. By sheer stubbornness and the force of will to find consensus, she was able to work out seemingly impossible compromises. It was the psychology of "Stability über Alles". However, there is a fine line between stability and stagnation.'[30]

Merkel's East German upbringing limited her emotional appeal to many citizens in western Germany, but gave her sufficient distance from the European mainstream to put the continent's condition into sobering perspective. Already in 2012 she stated:

> We witnessed in the GDR and in the entire socialist system that an economy which was no longer competitive was denying people prosperity and ultimately leading to great instability. I find it worrying that many people in Europe simply assume that, alongside the US, Europe provides the only frame of reference for the world – that Europe is traditionally strong and that the world looks to us.[31]

Merkel's analysis of Europe's poor competitive position resembled the picture Kohl presented to his compatriots after reunification. Repeatedly warning that Germany was 'living beyond its means',[32] he urged: 'We must change our mentality, go down new paths, become more flexible. Otherwise we will fall behind in international competition.'[33]

But there was no follow-through. Like Merkel, Kohl failed to implement significant reforms in the second half of his chancellorship. The German economy was rescued by restructuring carried out under Kohl's successor, Gerhard Schröder, as well as by the later benefits of booming trade with China and temporally high-spending countries inside monetary union. According to French political and security analyst François Heisbourg, senior adviser at the International Institute for Strategic Studies, 'Schröder had already done Merkel's job for her by introducing reforms from which he suffered and she benefited.'[34]

Former diplomat Kishore Mahbubani, swashbuckling Singaporean best-selling author and professor, adopts a decidedly undiplomatic tone on Europe's predicament. He summarises the conundrum in blunt fashion: 'In 1980 the European Union's economy was roughly eight times as big as China's. Now it's roughly the same. In 2050, the EU will be half the size of China. So why is it still going around mouthing insults at China? There is too much arrogance among the Europeans. They have to find ways of being geopolitically astute.'[35]

Jin Liqun, chairman of the Asian Infrastructure Investment Bank (AIIB) since its establishment in 2016 and one of the best-known and most seasoned Chinese financial technocrats, imparts a less strident but equally sobering message. 'China has made remarkable progress in technology and manufacturing over the past 30 to 40 years. The competitiveness of Chinese manufacturing industry is such that it will be very hard for American and European competitors to deal with.'[36] Jin is a long-term finance ministry official and banker who previously chaired the supervisory board of the country's sovereign wealth fund, China Investment Corporation. He was one of the key initial forces behind setting up the AIIB – an ambitious undertaking spearheaded by China, now encompassing 110 shareholders (including all the leading European economies but not the US and Japan). He warns Europe and America against regarding China as a 'rival or even an enemy'.

The AIIB forms an important part of a three-decades-long Chinese effort to reduce the de facto supremacy of the US- and European-led Bretton Woods institutions set up in 1944, the International Monetary Fund and the World Bank. From this perspective, Jin's strictures show unwavering consistency with a long-term Chinese effort to reform the world's geopolitical and financial architecture. His message is that western efforts to 'contain' China will be counterproductive. There are vast ways, he says, for Europe and China to cooperate, but – despite current travails – China will be operating from a position of increasing strength.

> Delinking is unlikely to keep China trapped a couple of notches behind the West in science and technology. The Chinese have woken up to the risk of relying on technological transfer from the West. It is impossible to revert to the old days when both sides considered it attractive and viable for China to open its market in exchange for access to western knowhow. Now that the Chinese companies, in particular the private investors, have doubled down in investing massively in R&D in high-tech fields, nobody will be able to stop such an aspirational and highly motivated nation from catching up.

TESTS ON THREE FRONTS

The changed geopolitics emanating from China's rise forms the background to tests on three fronts that Europe must somehow try simultaneously to master.

First, for all the show of solidarity in its reaction to Russian aggression in 2022, Europe must confront centrifugal forces endangering prized projects of European unity. Increasing political fragmentation and polarisation, above all a strong rise in support for far-right parties, represent both cause and effect of the fraying electoral consensus on the European Union's aims and objectives. An important background factor reflects an international trend: proliferating use of social media, reflecting, amplifying and frequently distorting news and opinions on societal ills. Problems centre on immigration and integration of ethnic groups seeking a haven in Europe from conflict-torn parts of the world, as well the general impact of heightened global competition on previously robust economic sectors. Immigration can help allay the long-term economic consequences of Europe's poor demographic outlook generated by ageing societies and slacking productivity. But these potentially positive long-term effects are countermanded by the negative shorter-term consequences for public acceptance and social cohesion.

Further strains arise from mounting fiscal pressures on European governments, and the European Central Bank's manifest difficulties in setting an appropriate level of interest rates for a diverse euro membership held back by a lack of political unity. Britain's EU exit has left deep-lying tensions, not least over Europe's reduced budgetary resources and fragmented capital markets. Britain outside the Union may still have a strong role to play in Europe. But the initial phase as a non-member has been a fragile time for the UK and the rest of the continent. Another headache stems from a worthwhile but highly risky endeavour – the planned further enlargement to half a dozen former Soviet bloc countries (several states from the western Balkans, with an enlarged list including Ukraine and Georgia) in 2030 and beyond.[37] This could tax the EU beyond its strengths.

Second, Europe needs to come to terms with the incontestable dominance of the United States as the word's semi-reluctant super-power, torn domestically by political and economic divisiveness that looks likely to worsen under the second Trump presidency. Trump's return confirmed the break with a more comfortable age. In the four vital spheres of political economy – energy, defence, industry and money – Europe's relative weakness against and dependence on the US have increased significantly.

Trump and his 'America First' administration have shown themselves incapable of handling this position of supremacy with either sensitivity or sophistication. Despite the galvanising influence of Trump 2.0's initial waywardness, the prized goal of the European Commission – building 'strategic autonomy' – is unlikely to be achieved in any but the most limited sense.

The difficulties of cajoling the EU's multinational membership towards uniformity as a complement or a counterweight to America have been laid bare on multiple occasions.

Two painful examples before and after Trump's re-accession came from the EU's failure to find any significant responses to the post-October 2023 Gaza war between Israel and the Hamas military-terrorist organisation and to the June 2025 Iran–Israel flare-up – prompting Trump's withering put-down: 'Europe is not going to be able to help in this.'[38] Europe's eclipse as a bloc with international influence has been given additional emphasis by Trump's espousal of economic and political ties with the oil-rich nations of the Gulf[39] – underlining statements by Saudi Crown Prince Mohammed bin Salman that the Middle East can be 'the new Europe'.[40] For reasons of history and money, the only western state with any influence on Israel and its regional rivals is the US. Dealing with Trump brings huge practical and psychological problems. But, in view of America's geopolitical weight, the only practicable way forward for Europe is to relaunch transatlantic cooperation – if it can, from a position of economic strength. Generating this favourable position depends not on slogans but on policies to promote growth and investment in a way (easier said than done) that does not leave individuals and societies lagging behind.

Third, the continent must find a way of cooperating with yet also helping to constrain China, America's opaque, threatening Asian challenger. China's president Xi has not gone as far as Putin, who has scorned Europe for suffering economic losses by 'fencing itself off and creating a new Iron Curtain'.[41] Yet both leaders have shown disdain for Europe's flagging economic weight. China – still growing at a substantial pace despite an economic slowdown in 2023–4 – is not averse to using commercial ties with the Europeans as a lever to gain advantage in economic negotiations with Washington.

In relations with Beijing the Europeans must navigate a path that avoids the dual perils of quiescence or overconfidence. In a rare admission of semi-regret over past failures, Merkel has admitted her country adopted 'naive' policies in dealing with China earlier in the 2000s.[42] China's build-up of overcapacity in key industries – lowering world prices for high-quality technical goods necessary for Europe's 'green transformation' – exposes the Europeans to a serious dilemma. They have to choose between dependence on Chinese technology or protecting their own key industries. Either option will prove expensive.

Furthermore, Europe has to set up and manage systems for controlling flows of 'dual use' equipment and know-how to China that can be used for either civil or military purposes – especially useful for bolstering the Russian armed forces, estimated to have grown 15 per cent since the full-scale 2022 invasion of Ukraine.[43] And Europe will need to find a measured response in cases where industrial partners are involved in human rights abuses in regions such as Xinjiang. All this needs to take place at a time when the Trump administration is introducing large-scale tariffs against Chinese imports.

A slowdown in Chinese sales to America might trigger a fresh Chinese export surge towards Europe – which could in turn spark retaliatory European trade action. In commercial as well as political and military matters, Europe does not need systematically to side with the Americans in all fields of Chinese interaction. But adopting risk-mitigation policies would be facilitated if Europe can somehow strengthen its position vis-à-vis the US.

Balancing the twin exigencies of cooperation with and competition against China requires an effort of analysis and resolve at present well beyond Europe's means. With efficient exchanges of information among the Europeans, and a high degree of concertation with America, it may become possible. The chances of the latter condition being met are smaller with Trump in the White House than if the Democrats had continued in power. Yet the Europeans need to seize the opportunity of an alliance with Trump's America – while at the same time attempting to maintain a modicum of self-reliance and self-confidence. However modest may appear the chances of success, this is a balancing act that Europe has to try to accomplish.

Handling any one of these three gargantuan tasks would be a strain. Coping with all three at once will impose barely tolerable burdens on states and electorates that since the end of the Second World War have largely been rewarded by success – but now face the risk of a downward spiral.

In past periods of EU unrest, Germany, as the strongest economy, has normally been available to supply capital, credibility and staying power. Germany's agreement to increase government borrowing will have some positive effects on the European economy. But the military- and infrastructure-orientated spending will be centred on Germany and may end up exacerbating rather than overcoming fragmentation of European defence efforts.[44] In a more fraught age, the European escape route from peril that was once strewn with German largesse is looking more exacting.

Germany has now become a more fragile state. It is likely to remain so – a dark gift bequeathed from beyond the grave and beyond the Wall by Erich Honecker, the last significant East German leader. Polarisation between the country's eastern and western regions is epitomised by the surge in the eastern states of the radical right Alternative for Germany (AfD) party, as well as, more recently, the far-left Sahra Wagenknecht

Alliance (BSW) party, formed under the one-woman leadership of the titular ex-Communist Sahra Wagenknecht. Both prey on deep-lying dissatisfaction in the new regions of the Federal Republic over the longer-term effects of unification. Both parties sympathise with Russia, oppose more German military assistance for Ukraine, and rail against immigration and European integration.[45]

Heather Conley says, 'After 30-plus years of integration, the former East Germany is showing a nostalgia and neuralgia for Soviet systems and thinking.'[46] She likens the eastwards affinity to 'a Stockholm syndrome with Russia: a lingering feeling of [East German] inferiority with the West that can never be shaken'. French political specialist François Heisbourg sees it in similar psychological terms. 'The Russians gave the East Germans the supreme convenience of absolving them of responsibility for the Third Reich. They were not the perpetrators; they were the victims.'[47]

A EUROPE OF 'CONCENTRIC CIRCLES'

If the Europeans make the right choices, an age of resilience may still be in store. Europe could become the essential link between China and the US in a constructive constellation of global power. A Europe made up of 'concentric circles'[48] – representing different levels of political and economic integration, linked by a common sense of mutual purpose – would be in Europe's and the world's best interests. A parallel concept for driving the path forward is 'variable geometry'. The idea was revitalised by Jacques Delors, when he presided over the birth of the European single market in 1993 and gave strong impetus to the drive to the euro. At an earlier period of doubt over Europe's future, in 2004,[49] Delors stated that the sole way of preventing the EU from effective collapse was to allow smaller groups of countries to forge ahead with deeper integration and their own forms of cooperation.[50] The Delors spirit summarised by his biographer Charles Grant maintains that 'if the Europeans can pool their economic, diplomatic and military resources, they will hold their own among the superpowers and exert a benign influence on the world'.[51]

More likely, however, is a less edifying outcome where the Europeans are compressed by the US and China, losing sanctity, prosperity and security as well as their centuries-old sense of centrality. Europe's problems can no longer be resolved by a firm commitment to common goals by the two central states, Germany and France, because both are affected by a deep malaise.

To achieve a more benign result, the Europeans will have to take uncomfortable measures and accept unpalatable truths. One of them is that, in view of massive fiscal pressures now and in the future, Europe cannot do everything. It will need to set priorities and make painful choices to achieve a better balance between maintaining social cohesion with high-cost welfare, boosting international competitiveness with effective industrial polices, and living up to NATO requirements for spending 2 per cent of gross domestic product on defence.

During Trump's second term, this commitment has risen to a still more uncomfortable and difficult to achieve 3.5 per cent. The longer-term goal for overall widely defined defence outlays (including ancillary areas like civilian infrastructure, transport connections, cybersecurity and medical preparedness) has been set at 5 per cent[52] – accepted by Merz early in his tenure, and subsequently a European norm.[53] Undoubtedly, Europe will make a more effective contribution to the alliance than it has hitherto. Trump is not the first US president to state that the US has no wish to play an overt and overweening role as the world's policeman and protector. Still less does it wish to pay for the privilege, especially to shore up the defence of Europeans who appear incapable of either organising and financing their own efforts, or acknowledging their debt to America with anything but ill-disguised gracelessness.

Europeans' penchant for placing greater value on social and cultural aspects rather than pure monetary income is worth preserving. But that can happen only if the fundamentals of economic performance improve. Already, the benefits of the 'European way of life' – shorter working hours, longer holidays, better chances for family life, improved health care, maternity leave, higher life expectancy – are incontestably declining. They will disappear altogether unless Europe makes the right choices. Accepting a sizable degree of American leadership may turn out to be the least unpalatable of the difficult decisions ahead.

Any discussion of Europe's role in the world has to take place against the background of one escapable fact: Europe's relative international decline, put into stark relief by the Russia–Ukraine war. Marshalling indignation about NATO's eastern expansion and dream-like assertions of Russia's imperial mission, Putin has assembled an obsessional make-believe narrative to rationalise horrendous aggression. This brings a time of reckoning. The period when a German chancellor – in the form of Social Democrat (SPD) Helmut Schmidt, in office in West Germany from 1974 to 1982 – could take on a position as broker between the Soviet Union and China is long past. America's superiority in the key fields of defence, finance and technology has opened a widening gap. European countries must accept that they have lost their grip over essential levers of national and global power.

In past decades and centuries, Europe has united to confront a perceived external threat, whether religious (as in the case of the Crusades) or militaristic/ideological (Soviet Communism). The present European constellation seems inadequately suited to reproduce such a unifying spirit. The seminal western European agreement of the past fifty years – the Maastricht treaty which laid the groundwork for economic and monetary union – was drawn up in a fit of Euro-optimism. European leaders believed that the end of the Cold War trumped all the other outcomes of the twentieth century.

The aspiration was that Europe would soon recover its place as one of the world's great powers. That egoism was shattered less than five years later on the killing fields of Bosnia in the Yugoslav civil war. The American-led NATO air force intervention in the Balkans in 1999 exposed the misconception that Europe had the political dynamism and military clout to bring to a peaceful conclusion conflict in its own backyard. The illusion of European resurgence – summed up by an assertion from the Luxembourg foreign minister that 'the hour of Europe has arrived'[54] – survived that setback. It even withstood, for a time, the international economic unrest of 2007–8 and Europe's sovereign debt crisis initiated, improbably, by the financial woes of Greece, a small country with a proud and ancient history, making up just 0.25 per cent of the world's economy. The myth was finally demolished by Putin's attack.

European cohesion had already come under strain as a result of the post-2007 economic slowdown. Notwithstanding the West's impressive (and largely unexpected) solidarity over Ukraine, the overall objective has suffered further setbacks. Despite recalcitrance from Germany over additional military contributions – reflecting especially 1939–45 war trauma – the US and European allies united in stiffening Ukraine's defensive capabilities. The question is whether these efforts will suffice. The issue would be less stark if the US and NATO has made fewer mistakes in the run-up to the war. Arguably, if NATO – above all the US – had airlifted troops into Ukraine along the predicable and predicted Russian invasion routes in late 2021, Putin would not have attacked.

Putin's full-scale invasion shifted the balance in vital spheres of the political economy. Russia's large neighbour, which Moscow had long regarded as its domain, had dared embark on a dangerous liaison with the West. The wrenching experience of war on its eastern flank has, for the EU, produced at least some partially positive outcomes. The Europeans, led by Germany, took speedy decisions to lower dependence on Russian fossil fuels. The Europeans made some right choices to repair some of the cracks in the construction of the single currency. The UK departure – accompanied by many UK missteps in EU negotiations where the British were frequently outmanoeuvred – reinforced, at least initially, internal EU solidarity. But beyond all this lies a perception that the wheels of power in Europe and the US are frequently turning in different directions.

To master the machinery of US and European relations in an ever more complex world, both sides will need to draw on greater reserves of intelligence, sensitivity and statecraft than they have been able to deploy in the past two decades. The key to the future is a careful check of aspiration and achievement – calibrating policies and planning against the unforgiving background of cold-blooded calculation and hard facts. The destruction and subsequent division of Europe in the Second World War, and the enormous accomplishments since then, provide parameters for measuring the looming trials. Europe can look back with pride at postwar rapprochement between France and Germany, the overcoming of dictatorships in Greece, Portugal and Spain, the collapse of the Iron Curtain, and the extension of the European Union to twenty-eight states (now twenty-seven with Britain's departure). But past success provides no guarantee of continued advance.

On any hard-headed analysis, sooner or later, before or after Putin leaves office, Europe will need to find an accommodation with Russia –

a course which may produce fresh complexities for transatlantic relations. Hans-Friedrich von Ploetz, one of Germany's most crisis-hardened diplomats – a former ambassador to NATO, Britain and Russia – is equally forthright when commenting on the proposition by Annalena Baerbock, Germany's foreign minister from 2021 to 2025, that the post-invasion freeze on Russian–German business ties is permanent. 'Baerbock's idea of that we will never do business with the Russians again is idiotic. We will rebuild links. Russia will remain Russia.'[55]

CONTINUITY AND PARADOX

In all these issues there are abiding elements of continuity – and of paradox. The Germans have stuck to the belief, real or pretended, that unifying Europe is in the best interests of a peaceful international order. The French – faithful to the view that they are the world's most exquisitely civilised nation – favoured this goal because it would best serve France, and hence the rest of mankind. The UK, for reasons of history, geography and culture, has clung to the concept of being a nation apart. The UK's pretensions towards exceptionalism are in many ways more effusive, irritating and infantile than those of France. They have been exposed, temporarily at least, as fanciful. It is too early to make a full judgement of the long-term effects of Britain's withdrawal from the EU. But negligence and incompetence of successive Conservative governments since 2016 failed to turn the exit into even a modest initial success. All this has been happening at a time when France, under the internationally energetic yet domestically debilitated presidency of Emmanuel Macron, has witnessed a further weakening of the traditional strong bond with Germany.

Britain has had six prime ministers since 2016 – one more than Italy.[56] Five poorly functioning Conservative leaders between 2010 and 2024 – Cameron, Theresa May, Boris Johnson, Liz Truss and Rishi Sunak – have contributed to a dive in Britain's international reputation. Britain's world image has been shaped for two centuries by a concept of organisation and discipline. Yet the country managed to bring to its helm two leaders – Johnson and Truss, in charge successively in 2019–22 – who became international bywords for mismanagement. The perception of post-referendum shortcomings provided an all-pervading reason for the Conservatives' crushing defeat in July 2024 and the ascent of a Labour government, for the first time since 2010. Sunak, in office for twenty-one months after Truss, proved to be a technocratically adept prime minister but a hopeless politician. He achieved the rare accomplishment of uniting voters on both sides of the Brexit divide. The Tories were punished both by Brexiters who believed the government should have better handled the referendum outcome, and those who were already against the decision, and whose opposition had since hardened.[57] The 2024 election result graphically confirmed the sobering 1980s testimonial of John Major, Margaret Thatcher's successor as prime minister: 'Europe is a wolf coming up the path to devour the Conservative Party.'[58]

Developments surrounding Britain's departure from the EU have frequently, for better or (mostly) for worse, defied expectations. Elsewhere in Europe, too, results have turned out different to those intended. Germany has lavished financial and political capital on shoring up monetary union, designed (among other reasons) to secure German exports by preventing other currencies from devaluing. Yet successive Berlin governments have undercut the effectiveness of Germany's export efforts by heaping costs on industry.

One of the reasons for monetary union was to make Europe more self-sufficient by instilling monetary discipline into a group of like-minded trading partners, increasing their ability to promote prosperity and wellbeing with their own resources and without the disruption of competitive devaluations. In fact, twenty-five years after the introduction of the euro, Europe is as dependent on the rest of the world as it has ever been. This reflects the maintained supremacy of the US and the dollar, the greater importance of China and other members of the Global South, and Europe's reliance on energy and raw material imports from countries prone to disruption or instability.

Germany stands out for its wrong-headed energy strategy centred on build-up of undue dependence on Russian gas – accelerated by the exit from nuclear energy after the 2011 nuclear disaster in Fukushima.[59] This was a combination of policies for which Merkel, like Kohl from the Christian Democratic Union (CDU), and her predecessor Gerhard Schröder, from the SPD, bear a large measure of responsibility. Schröder in 2006 defined Putin's 'vision' as 'the reconstruction of Russia as a world power, which can negotiate, talk and act on the same level as the

US'.[60] Schröder still believed that the Russian leader wished to fulfil that objective through 'strategically ever closer ties to Europe' which would become 'irreversible' – and German support would be crucial.

Schröder's statement, at a time when Putin's drift away from mainstream Europe was becoming palpable, was self-serving. After he departed as chancellor in November 2005 and handed over to Merkel, Schröder promptly took up the chairmanship of the Swiss-based Russian–German Nord Stream company running gas pipelines from Russia to northern Germany through the Baltic Sea.[61] The SPD was in coalition with Merkel for twelve of her sixteen years as Germany's leader. In the periods since they left office, both leaders' flaws have been on public display. Schröder becamee persona non grata in his own party, and across most of the West, for refusing to break off ties to Putin after the Russian invasion – although at the end of 2024 there were signs of reconciliation with the SPD.[62]

Merkel was widely overestimated as a global figure during her time in office. Publication of her defensive and non-revelatory memoirs in November 2024 gave rise to more criticism than commendation in the German media.[63] Belying her image as a consummate European crisis-fighter,[64] in her book, she stubbornly refuses to acknowledge the negative European repercussions of many of the big decisions during her chancellorship – ranging from the guarantee for German bank deposits in 2008 to the nuclear exit in 2011 and the opening to refugees in 2015. Her claims in the book about an arm's-length relationship to Russian gas projects (including the Nord Stream 2 pipeline where Schröder was actively involved[65]) were cast into serious doubt by detailed German media revelations in May 2025 on her active role supporting Russian energy cooperation during her period as chancellor.[66]

Merkel sensibly (in contrast to Kohl in 1998) decided not to stand for a fifth term in the September 2021 election. After the SPD unexpectedly won a wafer-thin majority, she gave way to Olaf Scholz, her former finance minister, a poor communicator – unpopular even in his own party[67] – who projected all Germany's manifold uncertainties onto the world stage. Like Helmut Schmidt, Scholz is a former finance minister from Hamburg, but there the resemblance ends. Whereas Schmidt spoke with wit and mesmeric cadence, Scholz's messaging is mechanical, diffident and diffuse.

Immediately after Russia's invasion, Scholz's government took constructive decisions to fulfil some of the strategic expectations from Germany's allies. Yet the sheer weight of multiple objectives posed a heavy constraint. Scholz had a miserable time as chancellor at the helm of Germany's first fully fledged three-party federal coalition. When historians draw up their judgments, he may be ranked the least successful of Germany's post-1945 chancellors, falling below even Kurt Georg Kiesinger, the graceful but luckless chancellor of West Germany's first 'grand coalition' in 1966–9.[68] Fractiousness progressively gained the upper hand, leading to the collapse of the Scholz government in November 2024, a day after the US election. Following a German general election in February 2025, seven months ahead of the scheduled date, Scholz was replaced as chancellor by Merz, the combined candidate of the CDU and its Bavarian Christian Social Union (CSU) sister party.

COMEBACK FOR MERZ

Merz's victory came amid a surge of support for the far-right AfD, which doubled its score to become the second biggest group in the German federal parliament, the Bundestag.[69] The AfD became the strongest party in each of the five eastern German states (outside Berlin)[70] – and leading CDU figures from the region admit that the AfD could top the polls across the whole of Germany at the next election scheduled for 2029.[71] In spite of the AfD setback, the result capped a remarkable comeback, twenty years after Merkel sacked Merz as leader of the conservative parties' parliamentary grouping in the Bundestag. The outcome was welcomed by Britain, France and other NATO partners. This reflected both CDU/CSU plans to revitalise the economy as well as Merz's more energetic support for Ukraine than the diffident Scholz, still influenced by Russia-supporting sections of the SPD. A fluent English speaker with a business background (and therefore regarded with suspicion by many in Germany), the new chancellor is well at home in transatlantic circles. His long-term adversarial relationship with Merkel – with whom the president had frosty encounters during his first term – may represent a useful benefit during Trump's second term.[72]

Befitting Germany's status as by far Europe's biggest trading partner with China, both Scholz and Merz are aware of the often contradictory pattern of relations with Beijing. As Scholz wrote in 2017, 'China's rapid growth allowed the world economy to rise above the slowdown after the financial crisis. However, this led to rising imports from China into the western industrial nations, with negative effects on employment.'[73] He added that problems for 'ordinary workers' from 'low wage Asian competition' are no 'populist invention' but an economic fact which unsettles more and more people and puts globalisation in a critical light. Merz comments on Chinese realities far more stringently. 'China's rise within a few decades from one of the economically most backward states to one of the world's biggest economies is a unique success story . . . a win–win for both sides.'[74] But hopes of political reforms had been dashed. 'The Chinese Communist Party has maintained its original Leninist character . . . one-party rule, sweeping state propaganda internally and externally, severe censorship, powerful secret services, personality cult and rigorous persecution of political dissidents at home and abroad.'

The US and Europe recognise that, by bringing China into the world trading system in a bid to help push the Chinese regime towards a form of western-style democracy, they indulged in a form of self-harm. Although China's entry into the World Trade Organization in 2001 has benefited the world economy in many ways, not least in triggering a two-decade-long bout of downward pressure on inflation, the effects have been one-sided. China has taken advantage of the opportunities to expand manufacturing capabilities into many industrial and technological fields that were once the West's preserve. This has been one of the reasons – along with the march of factory automation and digitalisation – undermining the industrial base in numerous countries, including America. The resulting social dislocation has contributed to trends driving voters towards extremist parties that weaken the West's own democratic foundations.

Worse may be in store. Immigration triggered by a rise in globalisation and an opening of borders has driven the rise of the populist right. But if populism spurs a sharp fall in immigration, then the declining birthrate across much of the West will lower the number of active workers as a proportion of overall population – exacerbating labour shortages and stoking higher underlying inflation.[75]

In another field, the march to the European single currency has provided its own profusion of contradictions. One of the greatest ironies of monetary union is that European action from 2010 onwards to buttress the single currency took place only after political intervention from the US, a country from which the Europeans were supposed to be making themselves monetarily independent. Cross-border banking and financial activity across the euro area is still held back by a maze of internal regulations and standards, toughened following the 2007 financial crisis – a barrier to Europe's development.

Another juxtaposition goes some way towards explaining a Europe-wide stalemate over necessary reforms. Recognition has risen across Europe of some of the basic flaws in the euro's construction. But so too has political hostility to enacting changes generally agreed as vital for securing its long-term future. EMU's difficulties have increased both the need for and the resistance to greater integration. Monetary union was formed to make Europe more stable. However, when binding together disparate currencies results in instability, as has happened with EMU, efforts to recreate equilibrium become much more difficult and add a further source of instability. Systemic paralysis provides the basic reason why the EU's progression towards a unified 'federal state' – often predicted by Brexiters – will not take place. Kohl ruled out the 'United States of Europe' as long ago as 1993.[76] With populist parties all over Europe making common cause against centralising power in Brussels, that prognosis looks definitive.[77]

Resistance to greater European unity has not been difficult to discern. In 1992, Ulle Ellemann-Jensen, the pro-Maastricht Danish foreign minister, said, 'The whole idea of European co-operation has simply become too far removed from the daily lives of our people. The Danes showed they were sick and tired of reading in the newspapers or hearing on the radio every morning that new things had been decided over their heads.'[78] Twenty years later, the story continued. Jochim Gauck, Germany's president in 2012–17 – a former Lutheran pastor and anti-communist civil rights activist in East Germany before the Wall collapsed – summed up the mood with equal directness: 'The European Union leaves too many people feeling powerless and without a voice. There is more to this crisis than its economic dimension. It is also a crisis of confidence in Europe as a political project.'[79]

The EU took a significant step towards greater financial autonomy with its landmark decision in July 2020, under the impact of Covid-19, to start issuing bonds in its own name, for the Next Generation EU Fund, with the proceeds geared towards measures to reinforce Europe's economic structures and ability to resist future downturns. However, the historical importance should not be exaggerated. Even after three years of efforts by the European Commission, the bonds have not been awarded full sovereign status by global rating agencies, holding back their acceptability on world markets.[80] Scholz's forecast, as finance minister in 2020, that the decision on bond issuance was driving Europe towards a 'Hamiltonian moment' seems unlikely to be fulfilled.[81] In 1790, America's first Treasury secretary Alexander Hamilton initiated a move towards fiscal union of the nascent United States.[82] The European Union has a long way to go before it reaches that goal, even for a smaller group of members. For the wide (and widening) group of current members, the objective seems unobtainable.

Counterproductive effects have burst through in other fields. These include the quantitative easing (QE) policies of massive purchases of government bonds carried out by the US Federal Reserve, ECB, Bank of England and many other central banks over the past fifteen years. These measures were designed to help return economies to a stable footing after the international financial crisis of 2007–8 driven by banking failures resulting from disorderly financial markets and excessive risk-taking. However, because QE was extended too far, particularly after the 2020 Covid-19 outbreak, central banks' actions were a factor driving social polarisation – through distortions in the housing market, further disruptive financial market behaviour, and eventually (coinciding with the Ukraine invasion) a big rise in inflation. There is some empirical evidence that loose monetary policy, by lowering productivity gains and growth, can contribute to widening gaps in income and wealth – a catalyst for polarisation across Europe.[83] One of the most influential European politicians of the past fifty years, Wolfgang Schäuble, the long-serving German parliamentarian, said as finance minister in 2016 that 50 per cent of the AfD's voting rise was due to QE policies by the ECB's then president, Mario Draghi.[84]

Undesired negative effects extend to 'green transformation' measures raising costs on industry and households. These aim to provide citizens with greater long-term security in a world facing the huge drawbacks of climate change, but they impose shorter-term burdens particularly on lower-income individuals and families which can further stoke disillusionment and unrest. None of these measures is wrong in itself, but in a highly sensitive, interconnected social and economic environment, enactment needs to be handled with great care to ensure that countervailing forces do not gain the upper hand.

The equation of effects and counter-effects throws up many insuperable difficulties. In five areas, Europe has been struggling. European success depends on achieving clear improvements in all these crucial fields.

1. Shortcomings in European leadership have intensified

Short spans of government office have co-existed with greater polarisation, fragmentation of traditional party structures, and near-constant crisis management. When the Wall crumbled in 1989, the leaders of the six main West European economies, making up 90 per cent of the then twelve-member European Community's economy,[85] had held office for an average seven and a half years. Kohl, chancellor of West Germany, France's François Mitterrand, Margaret Thatcher in the UK, Giulio Andreotti of Italy, Spain's Felipe González and the Netherlands' Ruud Lubbers were politicians of distinction and experience.[86] Collectively they had helped steady Europe after a fraught 1970s marked by inflation and economic upheaval caused by two large Middle East oil-price rises.

At a time of Soviet and Russian instability, they supplied a stable West European leadership core, vital counterparties to Mikhail Gorbachev and, later, Boris Yeltsin – and, above all, for the US administration, which was always in the driving seat. The Europeans were frequently at odds. Mitterrand, Thatcher, Andreotti and Lubbers were all sceptical about German reunification. Thatcher – who was to lose her job to John Major just a year after the Wall fell – was the most overtly hostile; Mitterrand, the most thoughtful and constructive (in terms of securing what he believed to be France's best interests). Yet at crucial moments, their stature overshadowed personal weaknesses and enabled decisions, in alignment with the US, based on intelligent compromise.

A pivotal external European unifying force was President George H.W. Bush, who had taken office in Washington as Ronald Reagan's low-key successor in January 1989. Spurred on by a battery of highly effective advisers, largely operating behind the scenes, Bush immediately started to prepare Kohl for the possibility of unification. Defeated by Bill Clinton in 1992, Bush was a one-term president. But he earns his place in history as having played a central, often undervalued role in helping reshape Europe and producing what James Baker, his secretary of state, called 'a new Atlanticism for a new era'.[87] The historical record shows that, throughout the unification process and thereafter, US influence was pivotal. America supplied the essential concept; Kohl, aided eventually by Mitterrand, was instrumental in carrying it out.

Another key personality on the European side was Delors, a former French finance minister, as president of the European Commission. He took the Brussels job in 1985 with Kohl's crucial backing and provided an essential ingredient of power-broking acumen to strengthen the Franco-German partnership at a time of great strain.

At the end of 2024, the leaders of the six prime European countries – Germany having gained in size and population with reunification in 1990 – averaged a mere three years in office. Of the six – Scholz, Macron, Starmer, Giorgia Meloni (Italy), Pedro Sanchez (Spain) and Dirk Schoof (Netherlands) – the two newcomers, Starmer and Schoof, had both been in their jobs for just six months.[88] The senior in terms of years at the helm (seven and a half) was Macron, nearly three years into his second five-year term. But there were still signs that he had not fully overcome his well-paraded handicap when he moved into the Élysée in 2017: his previous lack of experience of holding any kind of elected office. Macron's finely honed intellect and flamboyant phraseology incite more hostility than affection.[89]

Philip Zelikow,[90] a US diplomat, lawyer and academic who was part of Bush's German unification team and has maintained influence in successive administrations – including, in 2023–4, over using in the war effort Russian assets seized in the West after the aggression against Ukraine – draws a contrast between the two periods: 'It's hard to see who is providing European leadership. It's never just one person. In the period leading up to and after German unification we had Kohl and Delors working together with Mitterrand. In issue after issue, Kohl and

Delors were at the core. They were able to drive through a coherent European strategy that appears to be missing today.'[91]

One of the drawbacks facing the men and women running European governments in the 2010s and 2020s is the much greater leverage of smaller parties to disrupt overall policies. The geopolitical and economic circumstances of the 2020s – bringing to the fore two issues that particularly inflame public opinion, inflation and immigration – have contributed to an upsurge in radical parties that have often splintered off from larger ones. For sitting governments, the resulting combination has been toxic. Elections in 2024 were the most unfavourable for incumbents since records started 120 years ago.[92] America's Democrats, Britain's Conservatives, Macron's Ensemble coalition, Japan's Liberal Democrats, Scholz's SPD, Austria's centre-right Austrian People's Party (ÖVP), even Indian prime minister Narendra Modi's previously dominant Bharatiya Janata Party (BJP), suffered unprecedented reverses.

The early months of 2025, in three key elections around the world, brought a break with this pattern. The global reverberations of Trump's January White House comeback helped to increase support for sitting governmental parties opposed to the policies and the polarisation of the returning president. The most startling – and perhaps reassuring – episode took place in Canada. Popular distaste for Trump's diatribes against America's large northern neighbour gave a decisive boost to a previously flagging Liberal party. Anti-Trump sentiment combined with his own adroit electioneering propelled Mark Carney, a former central banker (and Goldman Sachs partner) to leadership of a G7 country.[93] The former head of the Bank of Canada (2008–13) and Bank of England (2013–20) took over the Liberal party leadership and premiership from outgoing prime minister Justin Trudeau in March. He won a general election the following month,[94] profiting from his perceived economic prowess and forceful defence against Trump's stated ambition to reduce Canada to one of America's constituent states.[95] In May, in two other staunch allies of the US, Australia and Singapore, anti-Trump electoral sentiment helped bring victories for the existing governments – led respectively by Anthony Albanese (Labor Party)[96] and Lawrence Wong (People's Action Party).[97]

However, it is too early to say whether the tide has turned sustainably in favour of incumbents. Macron's domestic electoral setbacks followed a string of lacklustre French presidents since Mitterrand's fourteen-year rule – unpredictable Jacques Chirac, who held the post for twelve years, and two uninspiring single-term presidents, Nicolas Sarkozy (2007–12) and François Hollande (2012–17). Macron was re-elected in April 2022, but quickly lost his National Assembly majority in subsequent parliamentary elections. After his party fared badly in the June 2024 European elections,[98] with the French electorate polarised between radical right- and left-wing parties, Macron dissolved the National Assembly and called early elections in June–July 2024 – resulting in a hung parliament with no clear majority. This further constrained his capacity to carry out a reformist economic programme, making him a high-flying lame duck.

Macron's plight worsened with the ousting through a no-confidence vote of the centre-right government he engineered under the stewardship of Michel Barnier. The veteran Gaullist politician, as a European commissioner, had supervised four years of EU exit negotiations with Britain in 2016–20. Barnier's ejection in December 2024 after ninety days in office made him the shortest-tenured prime minister in France's Fifth Republic.[99] In view of her gradually expanding scores in elections in 2012, 2017, 2022 and 2024, Marine Le Pen, front-runner in the far-right National Rally, has been widely seen as a likely winner in France's presidential contest in 2027.[100] But her party has to overcome the setback of a court judgement in March 2025 which banned her from standing for office for five years after being found guilty of embezzling EU funds.[101]

A populist victory for the right in France would bring echoes of a similar upheaval in Italy. In October 2022, Draghi, an ice-cool technocrat from the Bank of Italy and European Central Bank, who had become a generally successful crisis-fighting prime minister in February 2021, gave way to Giorgia Meloni. The leader of the hard-right Brothers of Italy party became Italy's first woman prime minister after winning a strong popular mandate in the September 2022 general election. In the Netherlands, Geert Wilders, leader of the nationalist Party for Freedom (PVV) secured an unprecedented unforeseen victory in the Dutch elections in November 2023. In Germany, Scholz found himself at odds not only with his own fractious coalition and the mainstream CDU opposition but also with the restive anti-euro, anti-immigrant AfD, which has gained extensive ground since its formation in 2013.

Britain, too, is not immune from the continent-wide trend. The landslide win for Labour in July 2024 resulted from a combination of the UK's first-past-the-post electoral system, astute tactical voting in many key constituencies, and the ascent of the radical right, anti-EU Reform party, effectively neutralising the Conservatives in many parts of the country. A striking sign of the entrenchment of Reform in the UK came from municipal elections in mainly suburban and rural areas in May 2025. The radical party won around 40 per cent of seats contested. This was the first time the share of the Conservative and Labour vote had fallen below 50 per cent in a nationwide poll – showing the unravelling of a two-party system that mirrors developments around Europe.[102]

The reasons for the rise of the pan-European populist right have been broadly similar to those driving extremism in the US. There is widespread antipathy among a large section of the electorate towards a political establishment felt to have neglected ordinary voters, especially on emotive issues such as immigration. This coincides with a twenty-year period of intense global economic competition when many sectors have been disrupted by structural change. The 'dark side' (to use the phrase of Enrico Letta, a former Italian prime minister) of the EU's freedom of movement rules may also have had a negative effect on economic and political cohesion in some countries.[103]

There are some brighter spots. A pro-EU centrist coalition under Donald Tusk took power in Poland in December 2023 following Tusk's October election victory which ended the eight-year rule of the right-wing nationalist Law and Justice party (PiS). In Greece, Kyriakos Mitsotakis won a second term as conservative prime minister in June 2023, as the country rejected extremist parties and returned to a new growth path following a decade of unrest. Sanchez, Spain's socialist prime minister, beat off a challenge from the conservative opposition, including the far-right Vox party, and clung to power in the July 2023 election. But 2024 saw a further populist right surge in mid-year European parliament elections which produced a voting bonanza for populist parties. There followed in September 2024 large gains by the far-right AfD and left-wing BSW in landmark elections in eastern Germany, a forestate of Germany's general election result in February. Later in September, Austria's far-right Freedom party scored a historic victory in parliamentary elections, consolidating pro-Russian, anti-establishment forces in central Europe – although Herbert Kickl, the Freedom party leader, failed in his attempt to become Austria's first hard-right post-1945 chancellor.[104] In parallel, Belgium agreed a coalition government headed by Bart De Wever, leader of the right-wing New Flemish Alliance (N-VA), the country's first nationalist prime minister.[105] The pattern of light and shade continued in the first half of 2025. A centrist candidate, Nicuşor Dan, won an important presidential election in Romania against nationalist opposition, but the far right scored notable gains in a Portuguese general election which punctured the country's long-standing duopoly between right- and left-wing establishment parties.[106] In a blow to Tusk, on 1 June nationalist Karol Nawrocki beat his liberal rival Rafał Trzaskowski to win Poland's closely fought presidential election. This maintained a strong power base for the right-wing Law and Justice party, heralding further uneasy cohabitation with the Tusk administration – and, in particular, difficulties between Warsaw and other European capitals over EU policies.[107]

2. Germany's unsteady state has been undermining Europe

The German economy has stagnated in the eight years between 2018 and 2025 – by far, the longest phase of low growth since the country's post-Second World War rebirth, and unusual even against the volatile standards of the 1920s and 1930s.[108] Many years of efforts to make Russia a long-term partner in industry and energy have been wrecked by Putin's aggression and Germany's lack of strategic planning. The economic relationships have been unhinged between Germany as the world's fourth largest economy and the US and China, the first and second biggest.[109]

For all the Chinese leadership's diplomatic blandishments preaching harmony and multilateralism, Germany has had little choice but to join in the western campaign for 'de-risking' economic engagement with China. This may, over the longer term, put Germany on to a more stable geopolitical footing, but in the short term it will damage jobs, investment and growth. German exports to China have fallen significantly at the same time as the Chinese trade surplus has risen to a record high.[110] And the dependence of Germany and the rest of Europe on imports of raw materials from China vital for the transition towards clean energy and a decarbonised economy has been attracting rising concern.[111]

When Merkel stepped down after the 2021 election, she left behind a failed succession plan, a fractured CDU, and a stagnating economy. Among the factors behind the timing of the Russian invasion of Ukraine, Putin seems to have calculated that Germany would be weakened and unbalanced following Merkel's departure. Given the country's high share of manufacturing in total economic output, and heavy reliance on imports of energy and raw materials, Germany's political and industrial establishment had collectively gambled that Russia would continue to support the German economic model. That bet has now been comprehensively lost.[112] Merkel, who speaks Russian as a result of her East German schooling, overstated her ability, honed in scores of bilateral conversations, to exert a restraining influence on the Russian leader. Jean-Claude Juncker, European Commission president in 2014–19, previously Luxembourg's long-serving prime minister, ascribes his traditionally inclusive view of European developments to the Grand Duchy's position sandwiched between Germany and France – a seminal influence in times of both war and peace.[113] He says of the former chancellor, 'Merkel used to say to me that I was too soft on Russia. However, I think she practised a policy which was somewhat naive. She spoke much of the time to Putin in Russian. I feel she may have somewhat overestimated her influence on him.'[114]

Larry Summers, a former Treasury secretary under President Bill Clinton, and a strong critic of EMU's deflationary impact, does not mince his words about the former chancellor: 'Merkel's strategy of importing cheap energy from Russia to support manufactured exports to China has ended up a disaster. I cannot remember anybody who has registered as big a revision in how they were regarded, between when they were in office, and how they were seen after they left, two or three years later.'[115]

José Manuel Barroso, president of the European Commission between 2004 and 2014, with party affiliations (like Juncker) to the right-of-centre European People's Party parliamentary grouping, takes a similar view:

Merkel was leaning towards the SPD in her policies over Russia, rather than taking a traditional somewhat harder CDU line. We saw the SPD relationship with Schröder, who after he left office became effectively an employee of Putin.[116] The overall idea was that the Germans could help the Soviet Union become a more stable state, governed by the rule of law and market economics. This hope has turned out to be an illusion.[117]

Heather Conley of the German Marshall Fund adopts a still more uncompromising tone.

The Germans are very loath to change strategy unless they are absolutely forced to do so. Cheap Russian energy, dependence on Chinese markets for exports, and reliance on American defense represented an impossible trilemma in an era of strategic competition and an emergent two-bloc system. Don't forget it was not an act of German will which ended these dependences. It came through the actions of other countries.[118]

On the economic and budgetary front Germany has become a victim of its own contradictions. Germany habitually lectured other European countries for many years about their failings in macroeconomic orthodoxy. This was a prime reason for introducing the 'stability and growth pact' embedded in the Maastricht monetary union arrangements in the 1990s.[119] Yet the Germans have fallen foul of their own budgetary rules designed to prevent state excess. The Scholz coalition's three-pronged notion that the country could simultaneously maintain extreme budgetary rectitude, avoid tax increases, and fund high public expenditure (supporting Ukraine, fighting climate change, and keeping high social spending) was exposed at the end of 2023 as an elaborate fiction – one of the reasons behind the break-up, after months of internal wrangling, of the Scholz coalition twelve months later.

The celebrated 'debt brake' – a stipulation for a near-balanced annual budget – was embedded into the German constitution in 2009, marking the high point of the country's assumption of moral authority over the rest of the euro area. The constellation was always economically questionable and politically fragile. It unravelled as a result of a

German constitutional court ruling in November 2023 that the Scholz government had unlawfully used opt-outs from the debt brake in promulgating its 2021 budget. This formed part of the tortuous background for the eventual relaxation of the debt brake after the CDU/CSU won the February 2025 election.

Jean-Claude Juncker – despite his customary closeness to Germany and its leaders – confesses to quiet satisfaction over the German budgetary disarray: 'When I heard about the constitutional court judgement [in November 2023], my first reaction was to smile. The Germans have never properly fulfilled the criteria of the stability pact, even though this is something they invented.'

German budgetary missteps have had continent-wide repercussions. The much-improved economic track record in 2023–4 of peripheral EMU members such as Greece, Portugal and Spain that suffered in the European debt crisis has had helpful effects on European cohesion.[120] But Europe's overall position in the world has suffered. As Juncker puts it, 'The momentum has gone from German economic orthodoxy.' The setback exposed deep-seated incompatibility at the heart of Scholz's three-party coalition – and started the countdown to its demise a year later.[121] Furthermore, as a consequence of corrective measures removing some short-term support to German investment spending, the 2023 constitutional court decision further impeded the euro area's already anaemic economy.

In her sixteen-year reign Merkel coexisted with twelve US, French and German presidents and nineteen British, French and Italian prime ministers – as well as eleven party chairs from an often rudderless Social Democratic Party, her coalition partner for three-quarters of this time. Endurance does not always signify accomplishment. Thomas Matussek, a senior German diplomat who worked in the German chancellery under Schmidt, and became ambassador to Britain, India and the United Nations, cites five German chancellors who had 'the courage to push through necessary measures against the tide of public opinion'.[122] He lists Konrad Adenauer (over western integration and West Germany's rearmament within NATO), Willy Brandt (normalisation of relations with the Soviet Union and eastern Europe), Schmidt (nuclear rearmament), Kohl (common currency) and Schröder (labour reforms). Merkel does not figure on the list. One of her doughtiest conservative German critics, historian Michael Stürmer, a former adviser to Kohl, opines, 'Belying her widespread image as a politician who thinks before she acts, Merkel places great weight on short-term tactical scheming rather than implementing strategic ambition.'[123] One of her closest associates, Uwe Corsepius, her key adviser on European affairs during much of her sixteen-year chancellorship, comments on her character in more nuanced terms:

> Merkel is a physicist and a former environment minister. She knew that most Germans are against further development of nuclear power. After Fukushima, she realised that the risks involved were too large. A consensus on further use of nuclear power was out of reach. It was a form of pacification. It meant that she would deprive the opposition of an emotional topic and open her party for new coalitions. It's no point carrying out intellectually a very solid policy if you are not able to win the election.[124]

Merkel's short-term successes paved the way for longer-term erosion. Germany benefited from a growth boost in the second decade of the twenty-first century resulting from a combination of propitious circumstances – including cheap Russian gas. German economic specialist Friederike 'Fritzi' Köhler-Geib, for five years chief economist at the state financing agency KfW until she joined the Bundesbank board in November 2024, notes that in Germany's 'golden decade' up to 2020, GDP per capita grew faster than any other Group of Seven industrial nations apart from the US.[125]

But in the next decade 'international dependencies' made Germany extraordinarily vulnerable to 'challenges going well beyond the classic cases of business conditions', 'increased geopolitical conflicts and trade restrictions', 'Chinese concentration risk', 'high export dependence' and 'an unusually large share of manufacturing industry'. Köhler-Geib states, 'Challenges like decarbonisation are more difficult to master [in Germany] than in service-orientated economies, especially since the motor car industry is facing a deep technological transformation and the US as a major competitor is pushing through decarbonisation using subsidies, rather than higher CO_2 prices.'

She adds that President Biden's industry programme – principally the Inflation Reduction Act (IRA) of 2022, a misleadingly named set of legislative measures aimed at rebuilding America's industrial prowess, often with highly protectionist features – compounded America's subsidy-driven pressures on the German economy.

Lars-Hendrik Röller, the softly spoken Berlin professor who for ten years up to 2021 was one of Merkel's main confidants as her chief economic adviser, concedes that German reliance on Russian gas went too far[126] – and that the Merkel years left much unfinished business:

> The economy during Merkel's period was buoyed up by external factors: low interest rates, low energy costs due to cheap gas from Russia, exports to China, continued globalisation and an active role of the US defending Europe. As a result, we did not do many traditional reforms, such as lowering corporation taxes, or carry out any wide-ranging reforms to improve conditions for business.[127]

During the Scholz chancellorship, as Röller describes it, 'the external factors changed and the economy has been suffering. This created an opportunity for the government to implement wide reform measures because the population was ready to make some form of sacrifice.' But Scholz failed to take that opportunity. A diminishing minority of German voters believed he was up for the job – and his chancellorship came to a dismal end in 2025.

A withering judgment stems from a man who played a central part in German manufacturing in the 1980s and 1990s. Edzard Reuter, a member of the SPD since 1946, was chairman of motor and technology company Daimler-Benz from 1987 to 1995. His father, Ernst, was the legendary SPD mayor of divided West Berlin when the US organised an airlift of vital supplies to prevent the city from postwar paralysis from a Soviet blockade. Under Edzard Reuter's aegis, Daimler was briefly ranked the world's eighth biggest company by turnover.[128] A year before he died,[129] over afternoon coffee at his home in a rural Stuttgart suburb, the ninety-five-year-old industrialist delivered what amounted to Scholz's political epitaph: 'An aloof, uncharismatic Hamburger, he was never able to articulate what he wished to do as chancellor.'[130]

Taking over the chancellorship in May 2025 as Germany's tenth post-Second World War leader, Merz has considerable attributes to help him succeed where Scholz failed. He can list as positive factors intellect, business experience as an internationally active lawyer (including his time as German supervisory board head of US asset manager Blackrock), and a global policy approach honed though his decade-long chairmanship (to 2019) of the Atlantik-Brücke (Atlantic Bridge), a private non-profit association set up in 1952 to promote German-American understanding and friendship. Merz's associates have computed that he has been in the US 150 times.[131] Counting against him are lack of governmental experience – caused principally by a two-decades-long mutual antipathy with Merkel, which forced him into virtual exile during her sixteen-year rule – coupled with occasional high-handedness and lurches into ill-judged outbursts of temperament. What appears to be mutual antipathy between Merz and Germans in the eastern part of the country represents an important shortcoming, in view of the rise of the AfD and the region's sensitivities over a still palpable economic lag compared with western Germany.[132]

Merz's biggest and most perilous handicap, however, is his lack of a significant majority in parliament.[133] Stefan Kornelius is one of Germany's most talented and experienced journalists, combining both international and domestic policy insight with a sceptical opinion of Angela Merkel – whose memoirs he criticised for her refusal to acknowledge errors and to provide a judgement on the 'radicalisation' of Putin.[134] Kornelius expertly summed up victorious Merz's post-election predicament in a leading article in the *Süddeutsche Zeitung* a day after the poll.[135] Just over two months later, Kornelius took up a post in Berlin as Merz's chief government spokesman and head of the federal press office.[136] Kornelius pointed out how one-third of the electorate in the 23 February contest had voted for extreme parties, with political fragmentation greatly reducing the established parties' parliamentary strength and depriving the new chancellor of a comfortable working majority. He underlined how Merz during the campaign had repeatedly announced that he would spend the majority of his working time on foreign policy, on Europe and the US.

> That's a noble promise, but it hasn't been truly tested for its suitability – neither by voters, who may still believe they're in Angela Merkel's comfortable world, nor by the states of Europe, the objects of the future chancellor's foreign policy desires. In any case, the EU

partners' hopes of salvation don't stand up to the harsh reality of the election results.

The shift to the far left and far right, Kornelius wrote, 'confirms the fear of a Germany that is unstable on foreign policy issues'. Donald Trump's 'divorce announcement' had an effect in lowering commitment to NATO in Germany and the rest of the continent. Kornelius underlined European anxieties about Germany as 'a western European mini-hegemon that shifts its weight sometimes to the left, sometimes to the right, perhaps rediscovering its supposed kinship with a dictatorial Russia'.

A week before Merz (on 3 March) unveiled a widespread relaxation of Germany's 'debt brake' restraints on government spending, the government spokesman-to-be wrote that the new chancellor, even more than Scholz, would need the power of the budget to finance Germany's foreign leadership pretensions: 'A chancellor can travel through Europe, attend summits, and look determined. But the ability to assert oneself, as we know from Angela Merkel, always depends on the ability to pay.' Now, Kornelius opined, Merz faced a double burden: 'First, Germany is no longer the much-vaunted (economic) engine of Europe; the country must first earn this role again through tough reforms. And second, the country lacks the budgetary strength to finance the security spending of this new order.'

The message was certainly not lost on the politician who was to become Kornelius's new master. Whether or not Merz can live up to his spokesman's strictures is one of the larger questions of his chancellorship.

3. Franco-German weakness splits Europe and undermines euro

A breakdown in Franco-German understanding has been a primary factor behind Europe's geopolitical shortcomings – summarised magisterially in a combative report on competitiveness for the European Commission unveiled in September 2024 by Mario Draghi, the former Italian prime minister and ECB president.[137] Stronger cooperation between Berlin and Paris over the past twenty-five years, by promoting more cross-border mergers and exchanges in finance and industry, would not have resolved all of Europe's difficulties. But such steps would have alleviated some of the fragmentation in banking, finance and defence from which it now suffers.

Revealingly, J.P. Morgan, the premier US bank, has a stock-market value significantly larger than the combined total of the top dozen stock-market-quoted banks in the member countries of monetary union.[138] In the immediate aftermath of Trump's election victory, the surge in the New York stock market increased the gap still further.[139] Of the world's top fifty technology firms, only four are from Europe. In defence, the key to American supremacy is concentration of power. The US spends twice as much on defence as the European Union's entire membership.[140] But it produces just one basic type of battle tank – compared with twelve operated in Europe.[141]

Looking at the longer-term political landscape, veteran French political scientist Dominique Moïsi points to 'a greatly missed opportunity' over Macron's landmark speech promoting European integration at the Sorbonne in September 2017, just after Merkel won an inconclusive victory in her final general election.[142] All of this produced consequences for the quintessential European project spawned by Franco-German partnership – the euro. 'We have been unfortunate in recent years in that we have had a combination of strength and weakness in Berlin and Paris. A German chancellor has often been in a position of strength when the French presidency has been weak, and vice versa.'

Moïsi is pessimistic about prospects:

The strategic autonomy that Macron is talking about depends on Franco-German relations. The French remained obsessed with Germany. But the Germans don't even pretend to learn French any more. In Berlin's view, Warsaw is more interesting, more important and maybe more threatening than Paris. Possibly the emotion the Germans most feel about the French is indifference.

Moïsi was no fan of Merkel's successor. 'I found Scholz rather unimpressive and arrogant. He's been irritated by Macron – who is the most intelligent of the European politicians.'

Looking towards Paris, Gerhard Cromme, one of Germany's best-known industrialists, with fifty years in business on both sides of the Rhine, has a similar view. He started his career at French glassmaker Saint-Gobain before chairing German manufacturing giants ThyssenKrupp and Siemens. He says of the French president: 'Macron comes across as highly intellectual and somewhat arrogant. He expects everyone to follow his line both at home and abroad.' Cromme underlines the power of personality: 'Underpinning of important projects such as monetary union comes only if there is political rapprochement between France and Germany. This was very strong with Mitterrand and Kohl. It has slipped back since then.'

Scholz's inability to build a rapport with Macron stood in marked contrast to the close bond between Helmut Schmidt and Valéry Giscard d'Estaing in the 1970s – a partnership that paved the way to the European single currency. The malaise has consequences for the whole of Europe. According to Marek Belka, a former Polish prime minister and president of Narodowy Bank Polski, the country's central bank, a member of the European parliament for five years until 2024, and an ally of Donald Tusk, 'France and Germany are now weaker. This means Poland becomes a major part of the landscape of Europe. The Polish election [in 2023] changed Europe's dynamics. This makes Poland a more important European player.'[143]

At one stage in 2024, says Sylvie Kauffmann, editorial director of the French daily newspaper Le Monde, 'Diplomats joked that Warsaw could even help Berlin and Paris with some couples therapy.'[144] But even that idea quickly turned sour. Faced with a still-strong populist, anti-German opposition, Tusk has insisted on demands, notably about the legacy of the Second World War, that Germany has not been prepared to meet. As a result, Kauffmann believes 'the Polish–German relationship is now, in its own complex way, even worse than Germany's with France'.[145]

François Villeroy de Galhau, the urbane governor of the Banque de France, the French central bank, is aptly qualified to build bridges between the two countries. Born in Strasbourg, a fluent German speaker, the man who terms himself as one of EMU's arch pragmatists,[146] is part of the family that co-owns ceramic manufacturer Villeroy

& Boch, domiciled since the late eighteenth century in Saarland in western Germany.

Villeroy de Galhau has had convivial relations with successive Bundesbank presidents – formerly Jens Weidmann (who speaks French),[147] and since January 2022 Joachim Nagel. But cordiality has its limits. Villeroy has highlighted a sizable reason for the slippage in relations – divergence in energy policy. France has been voicing increasing irritation at German assertiveness over opposing nuclear power not just in Germany but throughout Europe – a policy that has contributed to increasing Europe's overall energy dependence on Russia. This deep-seated French antagonism contributed to the German nuclear change of heart enshrined in the May 2025 Macron–Merz energy announcement (although against the wishes of Merz's SPD coalition partner) on 'climate neutrality, competitiveness and sovereignty'.

> France and Germany share the same goal of a decarbonised, independent and competitive energy mix. But they disagree on the means of achieving this: France will not give up on nuclear power and will use renewable energy alongside this, while Germany has begun its exit from nuclear power. As we will not overcome these differences, we should accept them, instead of exporting them throughout the rest of Europe.[148]

Disagreements and miscommunication between Berlin and Paris have impeded efforts to resolve the inherent difficulties of running a single currency among nations without a fiscal union. Remarkably, no French speakers were invited to an official Berlin finance ministry conference in June 2024 commemorating the twenty-fifth anniversary of the euro.[149]

A range of panellists criticised French economic and budgetary policies, with the exception of Nagel, who praised his relationship with the Banque de France. Otmar Issing, a veteran European central banker, board member for economics at the Bundesbank from 1990 to 1998, who took the same job at the ECB when it was established that year, castigated Macron's proposal to change the legal objectives of the ECB, in a second Sorbonne speech in April 2024.[150] The idea of widening the ECB's mandate to include fiscal stability and the environment was an attack on the ECB's Bundesbank-like independence, Issing said. 'It would lead to chaos.'

Issing recalled President François Mitterrand's statement in 1992,[151] looking ahead to establishing the ECB: 'These technocrats [the ECB board and council] should not think that they will determine monetary policy', because that was 'a matter for politics'. Issing added that 'lack of respect for independence of the central bank is a French tradition'.

For good measure, Florian Toncar, the fervently free-market deputy German finance minister in 2021–4, highlighted the poor French fiscal position. He praised his ministry's success in reining back the softening of European deficit and borrowing rules proposed in 2022 by Macron in France and Draghi in Italy. Just a week after France's credit rating was lowered by the US rating agency Standard and Poor's, Toncar warned that French fiscal weakness could harm Europe's overall credit standing on world capital markets.[152] The top triple A rating on European Commission New Generation EU (NGEU) bonds depended on the triple A rating of five EU states, he said – Denmark, Germany, Luxembourg, Netherlands and Sweden.[153] 'One slip, and there is a danger that the NGEU bonds would be downgraded. If you take one card away from the pile, then the whole pile could move or slide.'

To overcome some of the single currency's basic deficiencies, enterprising European policy-makers have invented a range of devices – each bearing with its own set of mysterious-sounding acronyms – to prevent the edifice from collapsing. Measures to bolster heavily indebted southern euro members were coordinated with the International Monetary Fund (IMF) and ECB in a manner that kept the monetary union intact and allowed its later enlargement to twenty states from the initial eleven (twelve with the adhesion of Greece in 2001, a step which turned out to be disastrously premature).

The latest scheme – named the 'transmission protection instrument' (TPI) to denote a protective mechanism to prevent undue rises in capital market interest rates in vulnerable countries like Italy – was unveiled in July 2022.[154] Speculation gained ground in late 2024 that France might seek recourse to the mechanism in view of French political instability and growing budget deficits.

EMU enlargement needs to be placed in perspective. The larger, more solvent countries that chose not to join from the outset remain non-members – the UK, Sweden and Denmark. At Maastricht, Kohl was firmly convinced that, because of pressure from the City of London, the British government would choose to join in the anticipated first wave of membership in 1997. He also thought Switzerland, a neutral country outside the EU, would become a member.[155]

Poland and the Czech Republic, the largest and best performing of the ten mainly central and eastern European countries that joined the EU in the 2004 enlargement, have chosen to remain outside. The eight single-currency adherents since Greece have entered in two phases: before the 2007–8 financial upheavals, Cyprus, Malta, Slovakia and Slovenia; since then, Estonia, Croatia, Latvia and Lithuania. All eight are tiny countries: their combined economic weight is roughly the same as Austria's.[156] Bulgaria, due to join EMU in 2026, has the economic size of Latvia and Lithuania combined.

Using the methodology favoured by the ECB to make allowance for differences in purchasing power among different countries, the nine new joiners since 1999 (including Greece) have a combined economic weight equivalent to Argentina, Malaysia or the Philippines – and smaller than that of Thailand or Vietnam.

The euro is attractive for smaller countries seeking protection from economic storms. But it has been unable to bring in the larger non-euro member economies. This has not been helpful for Europe's overall equilibrium. Of the EU's fifteen largest economies, only ten are in the euro.[157] More widely, counting the UK, Switzerland and Norway – three relatively large economies outside the EU – the picture becomes even more diffuse. Only six of Europe's top ten economies, and nine out of the top sixteen, are in the single currency.[158]

The most important step in preventing the break-up of monetary union took place in summer–autumn 2012 through an unpublicised concordat between Merkel and Draghi, early in his spell as ECB president, which started in 2011. They tacitly agreed that she would not criticise unconventional ECB action (via quantitative easing) to protect the euro by buying government bonds of the over-indebted states.

This was the background to Draghi's celebrated 'whatever it takes' statement in London in July 2012, hailed as saving the euro from collapse.[159] The unspoken trade-off was that Merkel could keep the matter from passing through the Bundestag and thus sidestep critical public scrutiny. The Covid-19 outbreak which emerged in March 2020 provided the ECB with an important justification to intervene to buy bonds of more vulnerable euro members, resulting in a large volume of quantitative easing that has left a legacy of political as well as economic drawbacks. The rise in inflation in 2021–2 to the highest levels for half a century, partly prompted by the after-effects of Covid-19 as well as by the Russian–Ukrainian war, prompted an accelerated round of interest-rate tightening. In 2022–4, the ECB managed to avoid extra travails. But there could be no guarantee that these more stable circumstances would persist.

Ben Bernanke, chairman of the Federal Reserve board from 2006 to 2014, up to and beyond the financial crisis, played a major role in US efforts to steady European economies during sovereign debt turbulence. He sees EMU as having made impressive advances in the past fifteen years, although with unfinished business. 'The steps needed to cement its status are generally well understood but in many cases out of the ECB's control. Perhaps most important are measures to strengthen the fiscal positions of economically weaker members and to develop mechanisms to deal with situations in which a country is having difficulty meeting its debt obligations.'[160]

As part of a compromise solution by the ECB's multinational leadership on raising interest rates to deal with inflation, the central bank agreed in July 2022 the shadowy – and so-far untested –TPI to make further interventions in case of need. Implementing this could bring considerable political risks for the central bank, which is one of the reasons why the ECB wishes it to remain, for the time being, well out of the public eye.[161]

Tim Geithner, US Treasury secretary during the financial turbulence, was the senior partner to Bernanke in American and international crisis recovery measures. Geithner emerged as a fierce critic of what he saw as European (and especially German) hesitancy over protecting the continent from 'carnage' during the Greek debt crisis that erupted in 2010 and rapidly spread to other exposed euro members.[162] In three years of frequently ill-tempered exchanges with the Europeans, Geithner undertook marathon efforts to prevent a euro collapse that could have severely harmed the world economy and Barack Obama's re-election chances in the November presidential contest. In discreet phone calls to Merkel,

Sarkozy and other leaders, Obama backed up Treasury secretary's proposals for shoring up the euro with 'overwhelming force'.[163]

Geithner's well-publicised recommendations for using European taxpayers' money went further than governments, especially from the northern countries, were willing to accept.[164] He persuaded Draghi in July 2012 to ignore protests from the Bundesbank, telling the ECB president, 'You're going to have to leave them behind.'[165] A decade later, Geithner believes the euro will survive – but his verdict contains a warning. 'My sense is that they have done a lot to have in place a better framework and a better mix of tools to try to make sure the borrowing costs of member countries do not widen out terribly. It's not designed to give complete protection, but it's better.'[166]

That admonition gained sharpness after the Trump election victory. In the immediate aftermath, Nagel and Villeroy de Galhau in November 2024 launched a damage-limitation exercise with a call for 'joint French–German action' to revive Europe, saying that otherwise the continent would be 'condemned'.[167] The US election was a 'wake-up call . . . France and Germany should stand strong together'.[168]

For all its fervour, the statement drew attention to a point of weakness: in less disruptive times, such a declaration would come not from central bankers but from the French and German governments.

4. Europe's performance suffering from lack of financial firepower

Europe's underlying economic growth rate has fallen precipitously over the past thirty years. The continent's weight by comparison with the two economic superpowers has collapsed. In the 1980s, western Europe steamrollered towards the end of the Cold War on a wave of success. The five years before the Wall fell marked a high point of Europe's economic prowess. In 1988, France, Germany, Italy and the UK all had bigger individual economies than China's. A quarter of a century later, by 2022–3, China's economy was substantially larger than the six leading European economies combined.[169]

In 1985 to 1989, the six leading European economies achieved average annual growth of 3.6 per cent.[170] In the five years before the

Russian invasion of Ukraine, the Europe-Six's growth rates was lower by a factor of four. With performance hit by the Covid-19 outbreak in 2020, despite a rapid rebound in 2021, these six economies managed average expansion of a mere 0.8 per cent. The US economy showed a much more steady trajectory, with average growth over the two periods at 3.6 per cent in 1985–9 and 2.1 per cent in 2018–22. In other words, based on these growth numbers, Europe has been roughly one-third less dynamic than America in recent years.

Jacques de Larosière, doyen of European economic technocrats, believes faulty European monetary policies have contributed to widening the gap between the US and Europe since the financial crisis of 2007–8.[171] De Larosière – who has headed the French Treasury, the IMF, the Banque de France and European Bank for Reconstruction and Development – says the ECB's low (at times negative) interest rates have been responsible for much weaker European corporate investment and productivity. 'Zero interest rates have discouraged long-term investment and promoted short-term speculative placements and asset bubbles. Comparable GDP levels are now very unequal – which is a reason for the absence of European diplomacy in our American world.'[172] In a searing indictment of policies in his own country, de Larosière writes that France's 'dangerous decline' has been exacerbated by 'the lack of interest in economic and financial issues shown by all our presidents since François Mitterrand'.[173]

US crisis-fighting abilities have been strengthened by the international status of the dollar as the world's No. 1 reserve currency, whereas the euro's underlying problems have held back the Europeans in international competition. Biden's decision to deploy heavyweight fiscal resources to fight the Covid-19 virus in 2020–1 gave a strong boost to international inflation, from which Europe suffered more damage than the US. The Biden administration raised US resilience further with the quixotically named Inflation Reduction Act, providing a fillip to infrastructure and high-tech investment.

Tim Adams, a former US Treasury undersecretary for international affairs, who runs the Institute of International Finance, a Washington financial lobby group linking most of the world's leading banks, reported in summer 2023 'a constant flow of companies coming to Washington, showing interest on how to get a piece of the action [under the IRA] and negotiate deals'.[174] The IRA inspired the European Commission to signal a similar level of support for European companies. According to Adams, America's advantages lie in attracting companies from around the world: 'Availability of many suitable investment locations, abundant, cheap and secure energy, plus the desire by some European companies to establish a base in the US out of concern that they might otherwise be hit by US sanctions.'

Gordon Brown, UK chancellor of the exchequer for ten years under Tony Blair, followed Blair for three years as prime minister in 2007 – an experience which ended badly with the financial crisis and ejection in the 2010 election. He says lack of European progress in key financial and economic policy fields adds up to a severe handicap vis-à-vis the US.

> Europe has a structural problem with no fiscal union which prevents it from competing on subsidies to the same level as the US. It needs to come up with a better form of coordination between fiscal, industrial and monetary policy. But the structure and politics of Europe – no fiscal union, no capital markets union, no majority voting on foreign policy, the inflexibility of the growth and stability pact – make this very difficult.[175]

Brown's view is backed by a figure from another part of the policy spectrum. Jürgen Stark is a conservative former German finance ministry official, deputy president of the Bundesbank, and board member of the European Central Bank. He resigned from the ECB in summer 2011 primarily because of his uneasiness over the bank's negotiations over bond purchases with politicians such as Italian prime minister Silvio Berlusconi, which he saw as endangering its independence. Stark terms an 'uncomfortable irony' that, while Britain is outside EMU and now the EU, London is by far Europe's most important financial centre. 'This is one of the reasons why capital markets union has made no progress. There is no way that Europe can meet aspirations for the decarbonisation transformation without a full, efficient cross-border capital market.'[176]

Christian Sewing, chief executive of Deutsche Bank – Germany's largest, although a long way down the world's league tables compared with its heyday – says small and fragmented European capital markets lead to inefficient allocation of capital and reduce corporate financing possibilities. 'Time is running out because Europe's capital markets continue to fall behind.'[177]

Absence of integrated capital markets provides one reason why, in spite of many individual success stories, European industry cannot muster the technological and financial strength to confront challenges from faster-growing parts of the world.

Industrial policy set by the European Commission and key EU member states is unlikely to raise performance significantly at a time of strategic divergences between the main European economies. Past campaigns to improve Europe's competitiveness have fallen short – the 2000 'Lisbon strategy', aiming to make the EU by 2010 'the most competitive and dynamic knowledge-based economy in the world',[178] and the 'Europe 2020' plan for 'smart, sustainable, inclusive growth'.[179] Draghi's bleak EU competitiveness report put forward scores of recommendations – but, not surprisingly, did not allocate responsibility for what had gone wrong.[180]

One of the best-respected names in world finance, Ravi Menon, managing director of the Monetary Authority of Singapore for twelve years up to 2024, subsequently chairman of Singapore's Global Finance & Technology Network (GFTN), asks – somewhat heretically – a crucial question. Did Europe set wrong priorities by driving forward with monetary union at the expense of other policies?

> For Europe, having a vibrant and integrated capital market is likely to yield more benefits than monetary union. Notwithstanding its many advantages, monetary union has in some ways been a distraction, absorbing considerable policy bandwidth at the cost of efforts to integrate capital markets, consolidate the banking sector, build interoperable digital infrastructures, and co-ordinate green technology development.[181]

Underlining Europe's lag in driving innovation and funding for dynamic new companies, the EU accounts for just 5 per cent of global money in venture-capital funds, against 52 per cent in the US and 40 per cent in China.[182] Although many European companies have become leaders in niche areas, more than 60 per cent of the world's highest-valued companies are from the US.[183]

The gap in valuations has widened sharply over the past twenty years, mainly on account of the success of digitalisation in the US and the rapid growth of high-tech companies led by Apple, Microsoft, Nvidia, Alphabet and Amazon, each with stock market capitalisation of $2–3 trillion in 2024 – roughly equivalent to the combined size of Germany's top-forty stock-market-listed companies.[184]

Øystein Olsen, one of the inspirational figures behind Norges Bank Investment Management (NBIM), the world's biggest sovereign fund, can aptly survey Europe from outside the EU. For ten years governor of Norges Bank, the central bank of Norway, with overall responsibility for NBIM, Olsen points out that its $1.7 trillion of assets under management is less than the average size of the top-five US-listed companies. 'The EU economy lacks dynamism. This is one of the reasons why NBIM over the past 10 years has been trying to correct its previously overweight position in Europe and move more into Asia, China and the US.'[185]

Ana Botin, who chairs one of Europe's largest and most successful banks, Spain's Banco Santander, warned already in 2023: 'Europe has a range of options. When we are on the right side of that range, we are unbeatable – a combination of entrepreneurship and not leaving anyone behind. But if we're at the other end, we're going to be a museum. I don't like it when the Americans and others call us a museum. But that could be the outcome.'[186]

5. Britain's fragility on the EU sidelines has been negative for Europe

British and French European policies have been diametric opposites, but they have ended up with similar debilitating results. France has made a permanent habit of harnessing Germany to the mission of improving French economic prowess. By departing from the EU, Britain has tried to escape the thrall of its neighbours. The British decision rested on the exaggerated notion it could take full control of its destiny in an uncertain world. The result has been a weakening of UK foreign trade, investment and growth compared with what could have been expected from a continuation of membership.

Repercussions have rippled throughout the continent. In a sense, a split would have happened anyway, in view of the European Union's need from 2010 onwards to decide a much stronger set of collective measures to preserve the sanctity of the single currency – leading to a de facto division between members and non-members of the euro. The UK's departure has had some positive effects, aiding the solidarity that saw the collective Next Generation financial mechanism passed (after much wrangling) in 2020. Yet Britain's short-term weakness has cast a pall over the whole of Europe.

Cameron's six years as prime minister were punctuated by multiple misjudgements in Britain's EU relations, including a penchant for overestimating Germany's willingness to help Britain in European bargaining. But he realised, correctly, that, with the need to repair part of EMU's fundamental structures, the UK and the EU's core were heading down different paths.

A reminder of Brexit emotions comes from Christine Lagarde, a former French finance minister and IMF managing director, who took over from Draghi as president of the European Central Bank in 2019. She refers to the controversial nature of the Leave campaign (in which Boris Johnson was a leading figure[187]). Speaking in 2023, she went out of her way to defend the role of Mark Carney, governor of the Bank of England during the referendum period, and prime minister of Canada after March 2025.

> I feel sorry for Britain because the country is on its own and not shielded by the collective that is the European Union. Bodies like the IMF were dutiful in pointing out what might happen if the UK left the European Union, in terms of loss of GDP and loss of value. The IMF was criticised in some quarters but the forecasts turned out to be accurate. Some thought that people like Mark Carney should not speak out. But if they hadn't done that, then they could have been criticised for not giving appropriate warnings. The programme of the Leave campaign was essentially built on lies – such as the slogan that the EU was costing the UK £350 million a week.[188]

Johnson symbolised more than any other politician the propagandistic, at times jingoistic, nature of the referendum campaign – and the consequent damage to Britain's international reputation. Johnson's career as a member of parliament came to an end in 2023 when he resigned his seat, after having already been ousted as prime minister in 2022. His seemingly innate inability to tell the truth, a prime factor behind both departures, has gained him notoriety as well as affection from voters who prefer their facts served well embroidered.[189]

Dominic Grieve, a barrister who was a Conservative MP from 1997 to 2019, attorney general under Cameron in 2010–14, and chaired the House of Commons intelligence and security committee in 2015–19, was a leading figure trying to impose parliamentary standards of control over Brexit procedures in 2018–19. He says, 'Johnson is a pathological liar. He lies brazenly, openly and repeatedly. He reminds me of a type of client I sometimes defended in court as a young barrister – very engaging but not someone to whom one would entrust anything. He has the classic characteristics of a con man.'[190]

Pasquale Terracciano, Italy's ambassador to the UK during the referendum period, had multiple dealings with Johnson. 'By the time I finished as ambassador, I ended up resenting him. Johnson claimed that UK cyclists were dying because EU legislation was preventing changes in lorry cab design. I checked with Iveco [the Italian truck maker] on this. It would cost £2,000 more to build this into UK lorry cabs as a separate part of the UK vehicles legislation, whereas under single market legislation it would cost £200. Johnson got his facts wrong.'[191]

One of the best-respected British politicians of the past forty years, Kenneth Clarke, a former Conservative chancellor of the exchequer under John Major who built a considerable following in the UK and abroad for his pro-EU stance, has had ample experience of Johnson – and is not impressed.

> I have known all along that temperamentally he was not interested in running a government. He had various bees in his bonnet, where he could come into the office and ask people to carry out various tasks for him. But he doesn't put in the work, he doesn't read his briefs. The one thing he likes is being a celebrity. He has a few bright ideas and leaves others to get on with it. He doesn't understand that

his tendency for fibbing, telling untruths, on a large number of issues has led to a general lowering of standards in public life. He has intensified a level of contempt for the political class that I have not seen previously in my political career.[192]

Kim Darroch is one of Britain's most senior diplomats who, as the UK's permanent representative (ambassador) to the European Union in 2007 to 2011, encountered Johnson when he was a swashbuckling Eurosceptic *Daily Telegraph* correspondent in Brussels.

Darroch's diplomatic career ended in July 2019 when copies of some of his diplomatic despatches as British ambassador to the US, containing less than flattering accounts of Donald Trump's policies and performance, were leaked to the popular Conservative-supporting newspaper *Mail on Sunday*. Johnson, a year after standing down as foreign secretary, en route to becoming prime minister after the resignation of Theresa May, pointedly refused to back him.[193] Reflecting on Johnson's time in Brussels, Darroch recalls in 2023, 'He was writing legendary stories about the supposed new regulations on cucumbers and condoms. Even as a mere journalist he displayed charisma, he had humour, he was fun, he was entertaining. He was the pied piper of the Brussels journalists. A lot of his news stories were complete crap, but people were quite fond of him.'[194]

Later, as ambassador, Darroch re-engaged with Johnson on his Washington visits as foreign secretary in 2016 to 2018 – when Trump clearly preferred speaking to Johnson rather than to his boss, Theresa May. 'He wasn't allowed to see Trump. No. 10 were sensitive about the risk of his establishing warmer personal relations with the president.' According to Darroch, Johnson as foreign secretary 'had not changed one iota' from his Brussels days.

I could get half the White House staffers and officials to come to drinks and canapés with him. He would move around the room speaking to everyone, sprinkling stardust. We had annual receptions for the patrons of the Washington Shakespeare Theatre. One of these receptions coincided with a Johnson visit. I asked him whether he would speak. He readily agreed. He gave a brilliant speech composed entirely of Shakespearean quotations.

A more rounded view of Johnson's record comes from a political ally, Jacob Rees-Mogg, an arch-campaigner for leaving the EU, former Cabinet minister and leader of the House of Commons, who lost his House of Commons seat in the 2024 election. He says Britain's position outside the European Union reinforced the Ukraine defence effort at the start of the war against Russia. 'We would not have been able to deliver the weapons if Britain had been part of the EU. Other counties, such as Germany, would have been highly reluctant to supply necessary armaments at that stage.'[195] Rees-Mogg adds: 'Boris Johnson made this type of decision on instinct. Cameron might have made a similar decision. Theresa May would have spent time asking for papers on the subject and would have lost the opportunity for quick action.'

The lowest ebb in the tide of British prime ministers was reached with Liz Truss in September–October 2022 with a peculiar exercise in self-destruction: 'The most ambitious and disastrous budget in modern British history'.[196] Her resignation as the country's shortest-tenured prime minster was the prelude, less than two years later, to the Conservative Party's biggest ever election defeat. Her government's ill-judged budgetary announcement which precipitated, notoriously, one of the biggest financial-market sell-offs ever recorded illustrated how politics and economics set limits on 'go it alone' policies – a lesson that was not lost on other European countries.[197]

The UK's departure changed the broader signal that Europe sends to the world. Merkel's former adviser Uwe Corsepius says, 'When Britain left the European Union, there was regret that Germany had lost a partner for liberal market-oriented policies in Europe and with whom one could carry out a proper strategic dialogue. There's not many countries like that in Europe.'[198]

Otmar Issing, the ECB veteran, believes the UK outcome has upheld his gloomy pre-referendum forecast:[199] 'The British exit has led to an increase in protectionist tendencies. This has happened at the same time as there's been a tendency towards more state intervention in the world economy, exemplified by the rise of China and developments such as the American Inflation Reduction Act'.[200]

Even before Trump's re-election, Americans, too, espoused sobering views. According to Bob Zoellick, former World Bank president, deputy secretary of state under George W. Bush, an American of German descent (his forefathers came from Schwerin in eastern Germany), and author of a major book on 200 years of American diplomacy:

> Brexit is not good for either the British or the EU. We became accustomed to see the EU being driven forward partly by British policies, and now it's up to other countries to put themselves into this place. Unfortunately, in international affairs, Britain has been pushed more to the periphery.[201]

According to Bob Kimmitt – undersecretary at the State Department under George H.W. Bush, US ambassador to Germany just after unification, and deputy Treasury secretary for four years under George W. Bush – the US has witnessed a shift in its European centre of gravity from London to Berlin. He sees this as bringing drawbacks.

> The Germans will never carry so comfortably the responsibility of the special relationship that we have had with Britain, and still have, to a considerable degree, in the military and intelligence fields. There has been a deepening of economic and commercial ties between the US and Europe over the last 30 years. But the tenor of the overall economic relationship has declined since the end of the Cold War, especially post-Brexit.[202]

The warming of EU–UK ties since the British election in 2024 – a development that Trump's polarising return has helped to spur – represents, Kimmitt believes, welcome progress, from both a Republican and overall American perspective.

> In view of its importance in the economic and political-military fields including intelligence, Britain's twin relationships with America and Europe can be mutually supportive. The US will be very pleased to see a buildup of production and services in the European defence industry, but this will take time. If, in this more constructive post-EU phase, Britain can reinforce useful and attractive links with the Europeans, this will be useful and attractive for America as well.[203]

Into all these areas, America's forty-seventh president casts a considerable shadow. Speaking well before Trump's renaissance, Richard Clarida, a former vice chairman of the Federal Reserve, and (like Kimmitt) a Republican formerly at the Treasury under George W. Bush, sees longer-term risks from the build-up to protectionism. 'This will seem initially to be politically appealing with costs that are economically manageable. However, over three to five years such policies could add costs to individual countries. This could end up suddenly producing a lot of economic pain which could itself spill over into political unrest.'[204] Geopolitically, Clarida believes, Europe is in trouble. 'The geoeconomic model which served Germany, in particular, pretty well over 30 years is no longer functioning in the same way. It's possible Europe will end up being squeezed by China on trade and by the US on technology.'

The last few years have been difficult for Europe. Before it gets better, Europeans should brace themselves for worse.

2

BETWEEN THE SUPERPOWERS

This issue of a settlement with Russia before our strength has gone seems to me dwarf all others.

Winston Churchill to Harry Truman, May 1945[1]

If Europe in the next 10 years still remains incapable of uniting politically, economically and militarily, it will suffer. The Europeans must learn to rely on themselves.

Mao Zedong to Helmut Schmidt, 1975[2]

They have to open up to American products. Europe is very closed. We don't sell cars into Europe. We don't sell essentially agriculture of any great degree. They sell millions and millions of cars.

Donald Trump, shortly before announcing US–EU trade deal, 2025[3]

Given its comparable size as an economic and trading bloc,[4] Europe might have expected to play an important part in the political and ideological struggle between China and America. Hope has outstripped reality. The 2000 Lisbon Plan for 'new goods and services . . . a powerful engine for growth, competitiveness and jobs'[5] has proved as fruitless as the EU's 'global strategy' for foreign and security policy in 2016.[6] In 2019, Ursula von der Leyen started her first five years as European Commission president with the aim of establishing a 'geopolitical Commission'.[7]

Josep Borrell, the Spanish politician who served as the EU's singularly underwhelming chief representative for foreign affairs and security

policy between 2019 to 2024, set the stakes high. In 'geostrategic competition' between China, Russia and the US, he maintained, 'the EU has to
learn to use the language of power'.[8] Yet, outclassed on the world stage,
he became a metaphor for the EU's growing international irrelevance.
Borrell showed rueful honesty about the consequences of failure. The
EU faced the choice, he said, 'of becoming a player, a true geostrategic
actor – or being mostly the playground'.[9] This aptly summarised the
EU's losing position in the singularly one-sided trade deal forced
by President Trump in July 2025.[10] In similar vein, Richard von
Weizsäcker, Germany's ultra-eloquent president from 1984 to 1994,
warned in May 1989, six months before the fall of the Wall, against his
country – recovered from war and ruin, powerful, yet divided and
exposed – becoming a 'playball' in the centre of a shifting continent.[11]

Applied to the 2020s superpower balancing act, von Weizsäcker's
sobering phrase presents an apposite description of what Europe has
become. Mario Draghi's competitiveness report published in September
2024 summed up how Europe had failed to redeem its promises.
'Europe must profoundly refocus its collective efforts on closing the
innovation gap with the US and China, especially in advanced technologies. Europe is stuck in a static industrial structure. This lack of
dynamism is self-fulfilling.'[12]

Towards the end of her first five-year term, von der Leyen – a strong-
willed politician widely criticised as a failure during her five previous
years as German defence minister[13] – had scaled back some of her more
grandiose ideas, including a 'sovereignty fund' to reforge technological
strength.[14] At the beginning of her second term, in December 2024, the
landscape darkened – and the opportunity for European self-renewal
grew. As Borrell's successor at the end of 2024, the politician in charge
of enhancing the EU's foreign policy footprint is Kaja Kallas. The
combative former Estonian prime minister is on a Russian 'wanted' list
because of her strong support for western military action over Ukraine.[15]
She started her new job striving to rally support for a unified European
line on the Russian war, castigating German chancellor Scholz for
timidity over backing Ukraine[16] – and drawing some comfort from the
fall of Bashar al-Assad's Russian-backed regime in Syria at the end of
2024. 'Russia is weakened, and you cannot put your bets on Putin. He
does not support you when you need him.'[17]

Trump back in the White House has dramatically scaled down the US administration's view of Europe's global importance – and, through his policies on Ukraine and Russia, as well as his chaotic trade and fiscal policies, has strengthened China's hand in political and economic bargaining with the West.[18] He has simultaneously raised the stakes for Europe's attempts to restore diminished room for manoeuvre. But the starting-off point, for the Europeans, is far from propitious. For all the solemn pledges and affirmatory proclamations, Europe has descended to the grade of an also-ran. It will take enormous effort to re-establish rank and status. For different reasons, in ways that will reverberate unfavourably towards Europe, China and the US look set to extend their importance as repositories of economic and political power. Both countries, at vastly different stages of political and social maturity, face immense domestic trials – but they also have greater potential than a fractured Europe to emerge stronger from their manifold challenges.

The dramatic increase in the size of the Chinese economy over the past thirty years, confrontation with America that seems to be increasing in Trump's second term, and Chinese ascendancy from the supplicant of the 1970s to potential dominance over Russia have greatly weakened Europe's ability to take a constructive intermediary role. As von der Leyen's predecessor Jean-Claude Juncker waspishly explains, in dealing with Trump, the Commission president is handicapped by some fundamental factors. 'Trump doesn't make deals with nations, still less with the European Union, which he doesn't take seriously. He makes deals in personal conversations, with a handshake . . . Trump decides policies man to man. Which is difficult with Ursula von der Leyen, because she is not a man.'[19]

Moreover, Europe's technological and industrial lag with America has become increasingly evident. This has hoved into full view as a result of the US economic boom inherited by Trump in 2025, buoyed by extra stimulus from Biden's Inflation Reduction Act. With only a slim chance that Europe's re-energised growth initiatives in early 2025 will achieve a quick turnaround, the competitive gap between the US and Europe is likely to widen further.

One of the many imponderables is whether the dollar's strength – an initial feature of 'America First' trade policies – will tail off sustainably or be reinforced by Trump's tariffs and other actions. Trump's cavalier approach on further increasing US government debt by backing steep tax cuts without due regard to increasing revenues is a particular source of worry for world bond markets.[20] Many economists believe that the Trump administration's forecasts that tariffs will generate sufficient revenues to contribute sizeably to narrowing the budget deficit are hopelessly overblown.[21] However, in industrial strategy backed by aggressive tariffs, the US plainly has very strong policy instruments. 'When European countries confront the US on its industrial policy, they are confronting a bipartisan issue where the US competes for jobs and investments via industrial policy. This will have clear long-term implications for Europe, no matter who is president,' says Heather Conley of the German Marshall Fund.[22] Nathan Sheets, a former top US Treasury official, and chief economist for US bank Citi since 2021, sees America's dominance in fields such as artificial intelligence and advanced computing helping to increase the dollar's sway over the euro and other world currencies.[23]

Although the three economies are comparable in overall economic size, at times of crisis Europe looks much more vulnerable than America or China. As economist Richard Baldwin puts it, 'The US is the world's sole military superpower. It spends more on its military than the 10 next highest-spending countries combined. China is now the world's sole manufacturing superpower. Its production exceeds that of the nine next largest manufacturers combined.'[24] These two set of statistics, for the Europeans, throw into stark relief the scale of the tasks ahead.

NEW OLD PROBLEMS

Trump's trade measures unveiled in April 2025 confirmed and exceeded premonitions about the fragility of transatlantic ties. Extending well beyond that, his protectionist announcements effectively ended nearly a century of efforts to promote wealth-creating international economic exchanges[25] – 'the nail in the coffin of globalization'.[26] The across-the-board hikes brought US tariffs close to levels not seen since the Smoot–Hawley Tariff Act of 1930, which incited a global trade war and deepened the Great Depression.[27] Furthermore, in his plans to 'make America wealthy again'[28] Trump revealed hitherto unsurpassed ability to harm the constituency he was duty-bound to protect – the American people.

A historical lesson neglected by Trump and his advisers is the mixed legacy of the tariffs unleashed by one of his political heroes, William

McKinley, America's twenty-fifth president between 1897 and 1901.[29] The tariff policies (both before and during his presidency) of the so-called 'Napoleon of Protection'[30] led to enhanced prosperity but also higher prices, for which his Republican party was punished by the electorate.[31] Later in his career, McKinley softened his line on tariffs and moved heavily in the direction of free trade.[32] A day before he was shot by an assassin (he died a few days later), he gave an extraordinary speech in Buffalo. McKinley did not refer to classical economist David Ricardo and his law of comparative advantage. But he expounded the intellectual framework for waves of international tariff reductions which became the mainspring of global prosperity after the Second World War – before being jettisoned, 124 years after his death, by the forty-seventh president.

> What we produce beyond our domestic consumption must have a vent abroad. The excess must be relieved through a foreign outlet, and we should sell everywhere we can and buy wherever the buying will enlarge our sales and production, and thereby make a greater demand for home labor. The period of exclusiveness is past. The expansion of our trade and commerce is the pressing problem. Commercial wars are unprofitable. A policy of good will and friendly trade relations will prevent reprisals. Reciprocity treaties are in harmony with the spirit of the times; measures of retaliation are not.[33]

In his 'Liberation Day' presentation, Trump proclaimed 'better-paying American jobs [sic] making beautiful American-made cars, appliances, and other goods' in what would become 'a new golden age' for America.[34] But the announcement generated no fervour, rather fears about a recession at home and upheaval abroad. The US stock market fell 10 per cent – the biggest two-day fall since the 2020 Covid pandemic.[35] The Federal Reserve forecast slower growth and higher inflation.[36]

As Richard Haas, a foremost US foreign-policy expert, put it:

> What the tariffs will not do is trigger Trump's promised wholesale renaissance in American manufacturing. Many of this country's

manufacturing jobs have disappeared for a variety of reasons. Yes, in some cases because of the practices of other countries – above all China – unfairly subsidizing exports to this country. Targeted tariffs are justified in such cases. But jobs also disappeared because of new technologies that increased productivity and reduced the need for workers.[37]

Abroad, Haas foresaw significant setbacks to America's international structure of alliances that hitherto had 'provided the US an enormous advantage' in dealings with China and Russia. 'The tariffs will create new economic opportunities for China as countries look to reduce their exposure to US policy and unpredictability.'[38]

Concern about Europe's vulnerability to sometimes arbitrary American actions is hardly new. Neither is a US propensity – visibly a key component of Trump's playbook – to try to split Europe through country-by-country soundings and negotiations. But Trump has taken both sets of behaviour patterns to new levels. Contrary to popular belief, Henry Kissinger, Richard Nixon's secretary of state, never sought a centralised voice of power in Europe, but attempted always to gain advantage by speaking one by one with individual nations. Kissinger's alleged remark 'Who do I call if I want to speak to Europe?' is often advanced to symbolise Kissinger's wish for Europe to act in unity on the world stage – but he never uttered it, preferring instead to practise (like Trump) the tactics of divide and rule.[39]

There has been no shortage of American warnings – neglected or ignored over the years by many European states – about Europe's unwillingness or incapability to devote sufficient resources to its own defence. Yet US ambivalence about European military ambitions has been never far from the surface. As two European academics pointed out in 1998, 'The US calls for greater collective European action but insists on American approval before any joint European initiative, especially in security matters. American policy-makers decry the European culture of dependency on US leadership while insisting in the same breath that it continue.'[40]

Six decades ago, John F. Kennedy called upon the European NATO members to live up to their 'commitments'.[41] In the early weeks of the George H.W. Bush administration, six months before the Wall fell, US military chiefs were reminding each other of years of enjoinders by Congress for European governments to shoulder a greater share of the West's defence burden.[42] Robert Gates, George W. Bush's defence secretary, reflecting on Europe's lag in meeting the 2 per cent of GDP target after the 2007–8 financial crisis, summed it up ruefully in 2014, 'Telling the Europeans to increase their defense spending was about as useful as shouting down a well.'[43] In 2014–16 – after the Russian takeover of Crimea – Bush's successor Barack Obama said on three different occasions, politely yet firmly, that the Europeans had been 'complacent', the US 'can't do it alone' and the gap in outlays with America had become 'too large'.[44]

Travelling to the annual security conference in Munich in southern Germany represents a pilgrimage of choice for international foreign-policy specialists. In one of the many landmark Munich speeches over the years, Mike Pence, Trump's vice president in his first term, provided one more element in a long series of finger-wagging about European defence. Speaking in 2017, immediately after Trump's first inauguration, he urged European nations to do more to fulfil their 2014 NATO defence spending pledges – a 'minimum security commitment', set at 2 per cent of their gross domestic product. Only the US and four other NATO members met the target, Pence said – but this did not, he averred, affect America's commitment to the Atlantic alliance.[45] 'Today, tomorrow, and every day hence be confident that the US is now and will always be your greatest ally. President Trump and the American people are fully devoted to our transatlantic union.'

Eight years later, speaking at the same conference, J.D. Vance, Trump's vice president at the start of his second term, delivered the same basic message: 'It's important in the coming years for Europe to step up in a big way to provide for its own defense'.[46] But the speech was significantly less cordial than that of his 2017 predecessor. Berating the Europeans for allegedly infringing principles of free speech, particularly in social media, Vance coupled his exhortation with an extraordinary warning: 'The threat that I worry the most about vis-à-vis Europe is not Russia; it's not China; it's not any other external actor. And what I worry about is the threat from within: The retreat of Europe from some of its most fundamental values.'

For many, Vance's ill-placed diatribe represented the ultimate evidence of a breakdown in the transatlantic relationship. It was abrupt – but predictable.[47] A compilation of interviews of foreign-policy experts under the auspices of the German Marshall Fund published at the end of the first year of the Biden administration in January 2022 came up with bleak findings.[48] The report revealed widespread fears about 'decoupling' resulting from America's progressive 'pivot to Asia', the disastrous 2021 US pull-out from Afghanistan, and a perceived deterioration of American democracy.

Trump's arrival crystallised those worries in previously unsurpassed fashion – even against a historical background where, over the past century, Europe's dealings with America have frequently thrown up patterns of light and shade. In 1920 the US Senate refused to ratify the country's membership of the League of Nations established under President Woodrow Wilson.[49] In the late 1920s, the British and American navies formulated plans for a potential Anglo-American war.[50] Up to and during the German invasion of Poland in September 1939, a strong majority of Americans, according to opinion polls, opposed sending troops to Europe.[51] The influential 'America First Committee' campaigned against President Franklin Roosevelt in 1940–1 to keep America out of the conflict.[52] The movement was countered by the Roosevelt and Churchill Lend-Lease agreement in December 1940[53] and the signing the Atlantic Charter in August 1941[54] – but was overcome only after the US entered the war four days after Japan attacked Pearl Harbor in December 1941.

Roosevelt's successor Harry Truman inherited Roosevelt's policy of bringing US troops back from Europe within two years of the conclusion of hostilities.[55] Immediately after the end of the war in Europe, Churchill – disturbed by reports of imminent withdrawals of American troops to the Pacific – warned Truman in May 1945 of Russian power to maintain 'very large armies in the field for a long time'.[56] Describing (ten months before he introduced the phrase to a wider public) how 'an iron curtain is drawn down upon their front. We do not know what is going on behind,' he wrote. 'Anyone can see that in a very short space of time our armed power on the Continent will have vanished except for moderate forces to hold down Germany.'[57] Already in July 1944, the

British were warning that Germany might need to be 'converted to an ally to meet the Russian threat of 20 years hence'.[58]

With the surrender of Japan in August 1945, Truman promptly moved to his own version of 'America First', cancelling Lend-Lease aid to Britain, the Soviet Union and France, and announcing a comprehensive economic plan for the US. But by 1949, as Bob Zoellick has written, 'A small group of American statesmen . . . created a new sense of national involvement in – and even responsibility for – problems around the globe.'[59] The Truman Doctrine announced to Congress on March 1947,[60] and the plans for European reconstruction outlined three months later at Harvard by his secretary of state, George Marshall,[61] were reactions to a state of desperation and drift in Europe – and expectations of a creeping Soviet takeover.

Marshall warned at Harvard of 'revolution' in Europe from 'millions of people in the cities slowly starving'. According to Marshall's speech-writer, Charles 'Chip' Bohlen, a foremost Soviet expert and diplomat who later became US ambassador to Moscow, 'Stalin's seeming indifference to what was happening in Germany made a deep impression on Marshall. He came to the conclusion that Stalin, looking over Europe, saw the best way to advance Soviet interest was to let matters drift. This was the kind of crisis that Communism thrives on.'[62] Truman and Marshall were given staunch support by the substantial figure of Ernest Bevin, Britain's foreign secretary in the 1945–51 Labour government of Clement Attlee. 'Bevin got the full horrific measure of the brutal Soviet megalomaniac better than any other leader of his generation,' according to his biographer Andrew Adonis.[63] The Foreign Office's foreboding was of 'Communism on the Rhine'.[64] Victor Gollancz, the British publisher and humanitarian, of German-Jewish and Polish-Jewish descent, buttressed Bevin's campaign with a harrowing first-hand account in 1947 of starvation in the British zone of occupied Germany.[65]

Stalin's tactics transformed American plans. As Benn Steil, the historian of the Marshall Plan, has written, initial designs for the postwar international economic order did not take into account the threat of political instability and a growing ideological and military struggle with the Soviet Union – forcing a speedy switch in policy as the new reality emerged. 'Many of Truman's top advisers had by 1947 come to see western unity and recovery as the only viable alternative to a new

American military engagement in Europe.'[66] The greatest danger to the security of the United States', wrote the newly established Central Intelligence Agency in 1947, 'is the possibility of economic collapse in western Europe and the consequent accession to power of communist interests.'[67]

In the eight decades after the Marshall Plan, transatlantic vicissitudes were commonplace. But episodes such as the bungled attempted Anglo-French takeover of the Suez canal in 1956,[68] the 'Nixon shock' leading to the 1971–3 break-up of the Bretton Woods monetary system,[69] Ronald Reagan's 1980s strictures against German gas-pipes for the Soviet Union,[70] and the fall-out from the 2007–8 financial crisis[71] and the 2000–15 euro upsets[72] were all acted out against a differentiated but generally stable geopolitical backcloth. In 1957, President Dwight Eisenhower went as far as to say he hoped he would 'live long enough to see a United States of Europe coming into existence'.[73]

The Trump administration in 2025 brings new and disquieting features. On the one hand, in contrast to the uncertain pre-Marshall Plan period, Europe is now a continent of prosperity and technological strength with the ability to pay its way in the world. If the military alliance with the US is weakened or ended, the Old Continent, by drawing on its own resources, including heightened government financing capability in the manner that Germany has now decided, has a viable alternative to reliance on America. On the other hand, the threatened rupture comes at a time of immense home-grown difficulties, complicating further the challenges thrown up by the six Ds: deglobalisation, demographics, decarbonisation, digitalisation, defence and debt.

PESSIMISM AND PRESCIENCE

Europe's lacklustre institutional status is closely in line with the pessimistic but prescient prediction in 2008 by the US National Intelligence Council (NIC).[74] It correctly foresaw continuation of a 'perceived democracy gap dividing Brussels from European voters' and slow progress 'toward the vision of a cohesive, integrated, and influential global actor'.

Continued failure to convince skeptical publics of the benefits of deeper economic, political, and social integration and to grasp the nettle of a shrinking and aging population by enacting painful reforms could leave the EU a hobbled giant distracted by internal bickering and competing national agendas, and less able to translate its economic clout into global influence.[75]

In a similar vein, five years earlier Wiliam Hitchcock, a US academic specialising in the global history of the twentieth century, called on Europe to 'find a better way of mobilizing its people and generate the open, proud and sincere support that any truly united community requires'. In *The Struggle for Europe*, he suggested that the European Union might otherwise 'come unglued'. And he asked: 'Might Europe return to the old ways of rivalry, conflict and war?'[76]

The NIC report foresaw, with some accuracy, that Europe 'could pay a price' for its heavy dependence on Russian energy. The NIC did not predict war. But it did forecast how 'growing corruption and organised criminal involvement in the Eurasian energy sector 'might spill over to infect Western business interests' – an accurate enough depiction of Putin's efforts to 'weaponise' energy exports.

What the NIC was not able to discern is how a still more threatening external environment might correlate with and feed upon a set of internal pressures. These were inflated by the gradually growing negative effects of China's entry into the world trading community over the last twenty-five years, together with, most recently, the consequences of China's tacit partnership with Russia over Ukraine.[77] China has been sending ambivalent signals itself about Europe, terming the Europeans 'partners, not rivals',[78] but also criticising Europe's complicity with America in allegedly contributing to the war in Ukraine.[79]

Tensions caused by the war, American fears about China's rising economic and military power, and Beijing's aggressive promotion of exports to compensate for domestic economic weakness have combined to hit Europe harder than any other region.[80] On several fronts Europe is being squeezed in a Sino-American pincer. In economics, Europe faces high-productivity America and high-subsidy China, both homing in on industries the Europeans sought to energise and nurture for future prosperity.[81] On the eve of Trump's 2024 election victory, the IMF warned that Europe's economic weakness in comparison with America was due to widen further by the end of the 2020s.[82] In the strategic and military field, the continent has had to field accusations from the US over insufficient defence efforts, and simultaneous Chinese contentions that it is siding unduly with the Americans in a rerun of the Cold War. Institutionally, Europe has to balance a popular revolt in many member countries against EU centralisation and the 'Brussels knows best' mentality with the reality that combating US and Chinese dominance in technology, industry and finance requires a pooling of European forces.

The diversity and richness of its cultures and heritage represent one of Europe's prime strengths, much upheld and prized in a world progressively coming under the influence of the two economic leaders. Yet to regain control over its own destiny, Europe may need to pull back on diversity and resort to more centralised policies in some key spheres. This applies precisely to the fields where Europe has the greatest deficits – in defence procurement, monetary-fiscal coordination, energy planning and industry policies. This may be seen as diminishing some of the cherished European 'values' of devolved governance, democratic individuality and freedom of self-determination. But the setbacks will be still greater if Europe succumbs in the economic battle now under way, and falls comprehensively by the wayside.

As a post-US election analysis in November 2024 from the European think-tank Centre for European Reform put it: 'Many described Trump's first presidency as a wake-up call for Europe. But by and large, Europeans ignored that call. With Biden's election they tried to convince themselves that Trump's presidency had been an aberration. As a result, they now face the disruption of Trump's second term much less prepared than they could have been.'[83]

Yet in this interplay of forces, a further degradation of Europe's position will bring risks that are likely to reverberate within America. Some in the US may regard the burying of European hubris as a welcome culmination of Europe's long retreat from post-colonial superiority. But a further heightening of Europe's vulnerability to the economic and political consequences of American isolationism and, potentially, the formalisation of a Sino-Russian alliance would leave America itself badly weakened.[84]

Just as the US was constrained to come to the aid of an exposed and demoralised Europe in the aftermath of the Second World War, a further downward spiral in Europe's fortunes might require American remedial action to defend its own national and international interests.

Barry Eichengreen, the California-based economic historian, points out that, at a time when 'economic relations between the US and China have never been worse', the stand-off brings grave problems for the whole world.[85] Key global questions ranging from climate change and low income countries' debt burden to the handling of artificial intelligence and international drug trafficking can be resolved only through cooperation between the US and China. The Trump administration puts it in decidedly more forceful terms. According to Marco Rubio, Trump's secretary of state, 'We welcomed the Chinese Communist Party into the global order, and they took advantage of all of its benefits and they ignored all of its obligations and responsibilities. Instead, they have repressed and lied and cheated and hacked and stolen their way into global superpower status.'[86]

In view of weak, divided leadership and pressures on Europe's economic model, the array of multiple tensions sounds a special warning for the Old Continent. Whatever the travails facing the leaders of the US and China, and whatever the long-term outlook for the two economies, both countries have the critical mass to face up to coming tests. Europe does not have that backbone of resilience. Germany, in particular, faces unprecedented pressure on its export-orientated system. For the first time, it has to ward off direct competition with China in key industries that have been at the heart of Germany's post-Second World War revival. An extrapolation of Germany's poor performance of the past few years would suggest this is a tussle the Germans are highly unlikely to win. Failure of the German model would spell ruin for many larger European aspirations.

The missteps leading to Germany's disastrous build-up of energy dependence on Russia represent the single largest contribution to the factors undermining the continent's power relationships. How did Europe's biggest economy become so dangerously exposed? Angela Merkel's former advisers are more inclined to discuss this issue than the chancellor herself. Christoph Heusgen, Merkel's foreign policy and security adviser between 2005 and 2017, says:

We allowed deliveries of Russian gas to build up to a level which represented undue reliance on Russia. We assumed that the Russians would be reliable suppliers, as had had been the case in the Cold War. In retrospect this was somewhat naive. In addition, we allowed storage levels of gas in Germany to sink to levels that were too low. All these questions underline the need for Germany to bring together security and economic issues in a National Security Council. A decision on this is overdue.[87]

Controversy during Merkel's tenure over German support for Russian gas deliveries focused on two sets of pipes running through the Baltic Sea to the North German coast – Nord Stream 1 (agreed in 2005 just days before the German parliamentary election that brought her to power) and Nord Stream 2 (agreed in 2015).

In her memoirs, Merkel says her qualms over Nord Stream 2 (she had none over Nord Stream 1) reflected her worries that Ukraine would be deprived of transit fees – a problem that was resolved through a parallel accord with Russian state energy company, Gazprom, in 2019. Heusgen says: 'The idea of Nord Stream 2 came largely out of nowhere. There was never a big ministerial roundtable to talk about it. It was mainly supported by German industry and by the SPD, particularly by Sigmar Gabriel, the economics minister.'

Donald Trump's administration, in his first term, created the legal basis on security grounds for sanctions against firms involved in building Nord Stream 2. In her memoirs, Merkel dismisses this as special pleading. 'The US was chiefly interested in its own economic interests, as it wanted to export to Europe liquified natural gas obtained through fracking.'[88] Russian gas was cheap, abundant and heading for many other European countries beyond Germany. Merkel's successor Scholz initially went ahead with Nord Stream 2 but stopped the launch of the nearly completed project in February 2022.

Merkel writes: 'Finding political acceptance for this decision before the outbreak of war in 2022 would have been much harder, if at all possible, both in Germany among commercial and private users of gas and in many of the EU member states.'[89] One of Merkel's closest advisers at the time says, 'She was more aware of the risks than others in the government. There was always a note of distrust in her dealings with Putin.' But her powers were limited. The adviser adds: 'It was hardly likely that Merkel, when she came into office, would have been able to withstand what industry wanted. The industrialists would have said: "How can a politician stop this important exchange? She is relatively inexperienced, and from the East, she anyway doesn't understand anything about business."'

Industrialists, for their part, accuse Merkel of attempting to shift responsibility. Jürgen Hambrecht, chief executive between 2003 and 2011 of BASF, the world's biggest chemical company and a prime force behind the two Nord Stream programmes, points out the importance of gas as a feedstock for chemicals. 'We [German industry] have always seen the Russians as reliable partners . . . If the German state had been interested in reducing geopolitical dependence on Russia, it could have intervened on several occasions. Concerns about sovereignty are not the main priority for a company like BASF and its shareholders, that is an issue for governments.'[90]

He cites the deal between Gazprom and BASF's subsidiary Wintershall in 2015, giving BASF a stake in upstream activities, in exchange for Gazprom acquiring storage and distribution facilities in Germany. 'If the German government had thought that storage capacity was a relevant factor for national security, the state had every possibility of intervening, but decided not to do so.' A particularly vigorous denunciation of Germany's vulnerability over Russian gas comes from Robert Habeck, the Greens economy minister in the failed government of Olaf Scholz. 'We had to grapple with a fundamental, dramatic misreading of the geopolitical situation that we inherited from the grand coalition [under Merkel]. It was an epic, historic miscalculation to build our prosperity on the promise of eternal friendly relations with Vladimir Putin.'[91]

LONGER-TERM FRAGILITY

According to Haizhou Huang, a prominent Chinese economist and external member of the People's Bank of China monetary policy committee, German's energy conundrum illustrates a longer-term issue of now-emerging trade fragility.[92]

You have to go back to 1944–5 and the establishment of the Bretton Woods system. The D-Mark (and Japanese yen) was set at too low a rate when Germany joined the Bretton Woods System, and the undervaluation gave a trend boost to German manufacturing during the postwar period. After the Plaza Accord on weakening the dollar in 1985, Germany remained competitive as a result of the triple stimulus from unification, expansion of the European Union to central and eastern Europe, and establishment of economic and monetary union, which prevented other countries from devaluing. But this protection has eventually ran out.[93]

Europe at least has now woken up to the size of the coming trial. The Ukraine invasion has induced a new sense of fragility. Bob Zoellick said in 2023:

> The war in Ukraine ended Europe's holiday from history. There was a view particularly in Germany that the EU had moved to a post-modernist structure where economic issues were of paramount importance and Europe could avoid the complications arising from use of force by aggressive neighbours. There could have been lessons learnt from the Balkans in 1991, where it turned out that Europe had to be rescued from its predicament by American miliary intervention. The Europeans saw the Yugoslav war as a relic of the past, a legacy of the post-Cold War break-up, whereas we now know it was also a precursor to what could happen in the future.[94]

The industrial threat from China, meanwhile, has gradually permeated into the heartlands of Germany's manufacturing sector. According to Edzard Reuter, in the 1980s Germany's best-known industrialist, 'We have to face up to the unbroken rise of China.'

Reuter – a member of Germany's Social Democratic Party between 1946 and his death in 2024 at the age of ninety-six – regarded European vulnerability through a long lens of personal experience. 'In Europe we find ourselves caught in a world split between these two powerful nations. The danger for European countries is that we could become economically colonised by China.'[95] Ola Källenius, Reuter's 2024 successor as chief executive of Mercedes-Benz, has mounted a call for large-scale matching subsidies from Germany and Europe to counter China's prowess in electric vehicles.[96]

Ken Clarke, a pillar of the pro-European faction of Britain's Conservative Party, reflects caustically on the dual squeeze:

In the 1990s and 2000s, I was feeling relatively optimistic that Britain had learnt how to develop its economy in a globalised world. Britain was one of the three pivotal players in the European Union. And our close political and cultural links to the Americans gave us some additional clout in a world where China was challenging America's status and Russia was a fading but dangerous force. We've lost all that. Britain has become a satellite state of the United States.[97]

In the aftermath of the Second World War, private sector enterprise, a revulsion against corporatism and monopolies, and the collective force of societies seeking recovery from ruin provided the European Economic Community's ideological foundations. But in a world where statism has come to the fore, the overriding politics of Big Government is becoming the dominant force. National security concerns have entered the field of economic policy-making. China and the US are using their national balance sheets – through aggressive subsidies, export controls and tariff policies – to distort competition and win advantage in sectors ranging from electric vehicles and machine tools to quantum computers and artificial intelligence.[98]

The shift to 'state capitalism' brings into conflict two alternative models of how to run Europe. This is a rift that has been present since the first moves towards monetary union in the 1960s and 1970s, and now seems likely to deepen. Broadly speaking, a northern cluster of countries – headed by Germany, including the Benelux states, the Nordic group and most of the newer EU members from central and eastern Europe – back the concept of relatively restrained state intervention and a more market-orientated system to allow private enterprise to flourish. A southern group, with its strongest traditional adherents Italy and Spain (backed by the north–south straddling France) has advocated a greater role for the state and larger recourse to public finance to steer the overall direction of the economy. The relationship is complicated by one dominant factor: the first group presides over relatively solid state finances. The second group has traditionally been weaker in public finance (although, like Italy, it may have strong private industry and high savings among private households) – and thus, at moments of crisis in monetary union, may need to draw on the capital of more solvent countries highly unwilling to loosen their purse-strings.

The gap between the two categories widened, at one stage seemingly irredeemably, during Europe's 2010–15 sovereign debt crisis. North–south fault lines have significantly hampered Europe's ability to present a united front against the US and China. After the sovereign debt crisis erupted, ECB president Mario Draghi stated, in a moment of rare candour in May 2013, 'No one ever imagined that the monetary union could become a union divided between permanent creditors and permanent debtors, where the former would perpetually lend money and credibility to the latter.'[99] Ignazio Visco, who took over at the head of the Banca d'Italia when Draghi left to join the ECB, pointed out six years later the long-running nature of the split. 'The tide of the global financial crisis and the sovereign debt crisis has long fallen, but its poisonous legacy and geopolitical tensions are fuelling distrust, fears and even prejudices once thought long buried.'[100]

The report on the parlous state of European competitiveness vis-à-vis China and the US, unveiled in September 2024 by Draghi in his new role as Europe's most Delphic elder statesman, laid bare this split – without engendering significant optimism that it could be overcome. He called for a far more muscular European industrial and innovation policy and an annual extra €800 billion in investment, funded partly by pan-European borrowing, to counter an 'existential' threat.[101]

The report raised fresh controversy. The European Commission served immediate notice it would take up Draghi's proposals in seeking to extend borrowing for the Next Generation EU fund under plans laid down in 2020 at the start of the Covid pandemic.[102] But Draghi's advocacy of common borrowing was immediately rebuffed by Christian Lindner, Germany's finance minister in Scholz's lacklustre government, worried that burgeoning European debt would damage Germany's own credit rating.[103] One of the major challenges for Chancellor Merz will be to reconcile German distaste for more common European borrowing with the traditional need to support France and the newfound desire to revive and re-arm Germany.

According to Draghi, a combination of low growth, low productivity and difficult-to-fulfil requirements for high public spending on decarbonisation, digitalisation, defence and social welfare raised the threat that Europe 'will lose its reason for being'.[104] The near-dystopian mood was decisively more downbeat than the last major European report in which Draghi was involved, drawn up nine years previously by five presidents of major EU entities (when Draghi was head of the ECB).

The 2015 report, under the aegis of the then Commission president Juncker, set out an ambitious plan for completing economic and monetary union through adding financial, fiscal and political union.[105] None of these goals has been achieved. 'A deep and genuine EMU,' Juncker wrote in 2015, 'would provide a stable and prosperous place for all citizens of the EU member states that share the single currency, attractive for other EU member states to join.' In 2024, Draghi offered a far bleaker scenario. 'Never in the past has the scale of our countries appeared so small and inadequate relative to the size of the challenges . . . We have reached the point where, without action, we will have to either compromise our welfare, our environment or our freedom.'[106]

As the Draghi report highlights, lack of scale is a supreme source of European frailty against the economic superpowers. The continent has been unable to build on 1980s and 1990s progress under Commission president Jacques Delors to establish a genuine single market with economics of scale promoting successful worldwide firms.

Maintaining pockets of economic and industrial sovereignty and cultural individuality has suited the consensus-based European social model. It fulfils widespread popular desire to curb big business monopolies and maintain a degree of self-determination and control over families and individual lives. Antipathy for cross-border European mergers that cost jobs and disrupt communities is a prime example of this sentiment. But the fragmentation of the European marketplace may leave Europe with the worst of all worlds. Companies are often regarded as too large for the good of the societies they serve, but not large enough to be fully competitive globally – leading to consequent losses of jobs, investment and living standards that harm rather than uphold Europeans' values and social aspirations.

CHINA'S STRENGTH, EUROPE'S WEAKNESS

China's strength has become Europe's weakness. The Old Continent's relative competitive position has deteriorated over two decades, in line with greater Chinese self-assertiveness. The shift has accelerated further as a result of the Ukrainian conflict and the economic slowdown in China, which is making Chinese companies more active in turning to foreign markets to boost profitability and compensate for domestic economic difficulties.

Trump's rapprochement with Putin in the early weeks of his second term appeared to have further strengthened China's hand. A possible reason for Trump's behaviour may be the wish to concentrate on China as America's principal adversary by somehow engineering a communality of interest with Russia. Some have interpreted Trump's revived Russian overtures as a 'Reverse Nixon' strategy: driving a wedge between China and Russia in the same way as President Nixon's surprise visit to China in 1972 was designed to weaken the Sino-Soviet axis.[107] However, if there is a plan in this direction, it is highly unlikely to work.[108] 'Reverse Nixon' seems far more likely to separate Europe from America than Russia from China.[109] Well-regarded German financial analyst Norbert Tofall points out that the latter notion is based on a misreading of Russian and Chinese strategic interests. 'Russia does not want to be China's junior partner. But does this make Russia a partner of the United States? Or is it not more realistic in the true sense of the word that China and Russia will first try everything together to reorganize international relations and the global economy in their interests?'[110]

These factors worsen the dilemmas for European governments. Countries like Germany – which have businesses and sectors in areas where China is increasingly competitive – find themselves badly weakened by intensified Chinese efforts to gain market share abroad. These efforts will be increased further as China diverts exports to Europe in the wake of much higher US tariffs.[111] At the same time, Europe is highly dependent on imports from China for raw materials and technologies needed for 'greening' European industry.[112] China's predominance in metallic elements which are key ingredients for high-tech products and processes has been well known for years; over the past decade, China been increasingly exploiting this prowess to buffer its geopolitical position.[113]

Links with China were designed to make Europe more resilient, not more exposed to peril. The status quo stands in crass contrast to the aims entertained by politicians such as Charles de Gaulle – the trailblazer, with France's diplomatic recognition of China in January 1964 – or, a decade later, Helmut Schmidt. Europe expanded economic ties with China over the past sixty years to further its own prosperity, but with a side-effect that paralleled the reasons for developing the single currency: to build greater independence from the US as the leading global economy, but one that was also widely suspected, through economic ill-discipline, as potentially leading the world astray.

Europe hoped to profit in several ways from the rapid growth of a large Asian nation that would, over time, become (again) a major economic force and a source of better geopolitical balance. Playing the China card would provide a much-prized destination for European exports. A major incentive for de Gaulle was that it would mitigate the constraints of Europe's overarching economic and monetary relationship with the US.[114] Furthermore, over time, it was thought likely to introduce gradually greater democratisation into a state bound into an innately Chinese model of governance – an outcome that could benefit the West as a whole and Europe in particular. The strategy has, however, not gone according to plan. The bilateral economic relationship with China has been lopsided, with Beijing holding the upper hand. With regard to balance with the US, whatever the longer-term doubts about the 'hegemony of the dollar', the US retains a leadership role in industry and finance. And, perhaps most important of all, far from adapting to western styles of government and shifting strategically to the West, China has become more authoritarian.

Some elements of the early Sino-European relationship held important clues for the future. Schmidt's experience of federal office as defence minister and finance minister buttressed his role in foreign affairs. In his first visit to Beijing as chancellor, in 1975, he was confronted by a rambling and physically ageing Mao Zedong.[115] Obsessed with the military superiority of the Soviet Union, Mao was convinced that war between the Soviet Union and the West was only a matter of time. 'Peaceful co-existence is not possible. Europe is too soft and disunited and is terribly afraid of war.' When Schmidt argued back (in a projection of what was to happen under Gorbachev two decades later) that a future leader in Moscow might abandon Brezhnev's insistence on preserving the Soviet empire, and return to softer principles of Leninism, Mao energetically contradicted him, according to the German transcript, with a torrent of five 'No's'. On Schmidt's query on the reasons for Mao's adamance, the aged leader answered, 'Because they have so many nuclear weapons.'

Both before and after leaving office in 1982, Schmidt advocated building up a relationship with the Chinese that would put the two countries on a semi-equal footing. In 1999, he criticised Gerhard Schröder, shortly after he became chancellor, for supporting Russia's entry into the Group of Seven industrial nations – which then became the Group of Eight.[116] Characterising Russia as a 'sickly dwarf' by international economic standards, Schmidt asked why the West was allowing Moscow to join but leaving 'economically healthy' China on the outside. Schröder's explanation was that Russia was 'far too important' for Europe, especially Germany, not to engage in 'strategic partnership'.[117]

Chinese support for Russia is hardly selfless. It provides a means for Beijing to build up a strong hold over a country which, up to the end of the Cold War, had been by far its superior in the international rankings. The past decades' inversion of the Moscow–Beijing relationship is a source of new tensions that could cause great complications for Europe and the US. As Merkel has stated, 'By becoming a partner of China, Russia is effectively falling into the hands of its increasingly powerful neighbour.' In her memoirs, she notes this is the 'opposite phenomenon' to the weakening of the Moscow–Beijing axis promoted by Nixon in 1971–2.[118] Taking Merkel's argument a step further, if – for whatever reason – Putin's grip on Russia became looser, the Chinese connection could turn into an indirect mechanism for a shift towards further Russian authoritarianism. Whatever happens, Europe would be likely to be a bystander, preoccupied with and absorbed by its own travails.

The period when 1970s and 1980s European leaders could be effective intermediaries between the Soviet Union, China and the US is highly unlikely to return. One of the best American analysts of modern Russia, Bill Burns, ambassador in Moscow under George W. Bush, and director of the Central Intelligence Agency under Joe Biden, opines, 'Much as Russia chafed at the idea of being the junior partner to the US after the end of the Cold War, it's a safe prediction, over time, the Russians are going to chafe at being the junior partner to China too.'[119]

New sources of friction introduced by the second Trump administration are likely to add complexity to the equation. Europe is likely to observe, and seek to react to, such antagonisms from the sidelines.

The aftermath of the full-scale Russian invasion of Ukraine has made the Chinese more forceful in competition with Europe. This may be part of an overall Chinese stratagem aimed at weakening Europe in a conflict that has been in many ways a proxy war between the US and China.[120] In the worldwide geopolitical fissures generated by the war, the Chinese and Russians have appeared to be playing ever more openly on the same side. While avoiding direct full-scale military backing for Putin, Beijing has deployed its partnership with Russia as part of a long-term effort to dislodge the US from its pole position in the world order – a stance that has provoked a mixed response from Europe.[121]

Beijing has hardened its diplomatic line in high-profile areas[122] and has constantly declined involvement in attempted Ukrainian peace overtures where Russia has not been present.[123] Instead, in 2024, China pressed, together with Brazil, for its own 6-point peace plan that advocated freezing the conflict to allow Russia to maintain occupation of parts of eastern Ukraine. Beijing has refrained from direct delivery of lethal weapons. But it has supported the Russian economy by purchasing oil, selling dual-use goods that can be deployed in the military effort, and helped to circumvent western economic sanctions.[124] According to US estimates, in 2023 roughly 90 per cent of the imports that Russia needs to sustain its war came from China.[125]

Xi has used numerous opportunities to declare fellow-feeling with Putin, boasting repeatedly about driving forward changes in world political structures that 'we have not seen for a hundred years'.[126] In May 2025, comprehensively rebutting any notion of a 'Reverse Nixon' effect, the Chinese president showed that like both Trump and Putin, he can wield the instrument of exaggerated historical rhetoric. On the eve of a visit to Moscow to mark the eightieth anniversary of the end of the Second World War, Xi alleged a parallel between modern-day US 'hegemony' and the 'arrogant fascist forces' of 1945.[127] Beijing has ignored past requests by German chancellor Scholz and French president Macron to prohibit supplies of machine tools and components that that are no longer available from Europe or the US. China has been holding well-publicised joint military exercises and reinforced armed-forces ties with Russia and allies such as Iran and North Korea. Through sanctions, the US has slowed down the transit of some dual-use goods – which China organises partly via Hong Kong.[128]

After the Biden administration publicly suggested that it was considering sanctions on Chinese banks, Beijing announced that it was imposing export controls on dual-use drones.[129] According to US intelligence reports, Beijing has been directly aiding Moscow with technology for warfare. In return Russia has been alleged to hand over closely guarded know-how on submarines and missiles which could directly affect the US and its allies.[130] If these reports are true, they would indicate that China has gone through a period of experimenting with crossing American military-strategic 'red lines' in the economic interplay with Russia.

The economic and technical background is of crucial significance. Size matters. Although China's growth rate has slowed, in the period 2019–24 China's GDP in current dollar terms rose by $3.6 trillion, according to the IMF. This is equivalent to the total size of the UK economy in 2024.[131] China's startling development over the past three decades was initially complementary to Europe's, but, during the first twenty years of the twenty-first century, with a relentless Chinese drive into higher-value products, an important shift started to unfold – with significant repercussions especially for Germany. As Pierre-Olivier Gourinchas, chief economist of the International Monetary Fund, put it in 2023,

> Germany made two strategic mistakes. The first one was excessive reliance on Russia's cheap energy. The second was the auto sector's excessively slow adaptation to the shift towards electric vehicles. The sector is now waking up to the reality of massive Chinese competition in the EV sector, in Europe and in China. The two mistakes are not independent: in both cases they reflect a strategic failure to address excessive concentration risk for critical inputs. This is likely to generate a big conflict between industrial objectives and the aim of greening the economy.[132]

The Rhodium consultancy group pointed out in a major study in early 2024:

China [is] emerging as a formidable competitor to Germany in the industries it once dominated . . . German firms are likely to see their market shares in China erode, while coming under significant pressure from Chinese competitors at home and in third markets . . . Against the backdrop of a stagnating German economy and more volatile political environment, job losses in key German industries could trigger a backlash that has been largely absent until now, even as the government line on China has hardened.[133]

Another European research study, from the Forum for a New Economy, highlights how 'strategic dependencies on autocratic countries, like Russia and China, grew along the way, but were ignored'.[134] As a result, Germany finds itself 'dangerously exposed . . . In the span of three years, the perfect storm of a global pandemic, Russia's war against Ukraine, and an ensuing energy crisis, as well as growing Sino-American tensions, have laid bare the risks of this exposure being weaponised.'

In an important departure from their usual focus, economists from the European Central Bank in September 2024 intensified the debate over Chinese competition, pointing out the threat to the euro area manufacturing sector that employs over 20 million people and makes up 15 per cent of euro area GDP.[135] The share of sectors in which China is directly competing with euro area exporters is now close to 40 per cent, up from 25 per cent in 2002.

> Two decades ago, China competed mainly in low-value sectors, such as clothing, footwear, or plastic. That mostly affected southern euro area economies, which were exporting the same types of goods. As China's exports have moved up the value chain, they are challenging more and more European exporters, including those in high value-added industries like automotive and specialised machinery.

Adding to Europe's woes, Chinese competitiveness has been buoyed by a sizable decline in export prices. This reflects a combination of factors: a fall in the Chinese property market, lowering prices for construction products such as steel; government subsidies for advanced manufacturing sectors; and excess Chinese capacity that sharpens domestic competition, depresses profit margins, and drives Chinese firms to expand abroad.

According to the ECB economists, further bad news for Europe lies ahead:

> The competitive pressure from China is set to intensify significantly. Production plans for green energy technology such as battery electric vehicles entail a sharp rise in output, which is projected to significantly outpace growth of domestic demand, further compounding existing over-capacities in these sectors. China is also investing substantially in additional export shipping capacity. For instance, the scheduled delivery of additional shipping vessels is projected to significantly increase China's annual export capacity of cars multiple times over between 2023 and 2026.

Faced with similar pressures, Trump has resorted to large-scale tariffs against China.[136] Europe, while resorting to its own tariff machinery and considering 'buy European' measures in response to Trump's trade warfare, does not have recourse to the same muscle power.[137]

CHINA SHIFT FAILS TO MATERIALISE

Building over-capacity in key industries runs directly counter to many benevolent-sounding yet misleading Beijing indications over the last ten to fifteen years of a stark shift in the basic design of the Chinese economy – away from exports towards domestic consumption.[138] The reality has been different. The state of affairs underlines President Xi Jinping's shortcomings, especially setbacks during and after the Covid-19 outbreak, coinciding with the extension of Xi's term in office in 2022 to beyond the normal two terms, and the elimination of all apart from Xi loyalists in the country's highest echelons.

On numerous occasions, China said it wished to reduce dependence on heavy investment in globally important industries, lower its trade surplus, and boost domestic consumption. This would have spelled good news for western companies trying to sell into Chinese markets as well as for those western optimists who felt, naively, that developing a consumption-based middle-class society was the key to China attaining some characteristics of a western democracy.

Key Chinese think-tanks frequently tell western visitors that over-reliance on export-orientated growth cannot end successfully; they claim that the shift to export-led expansion is a temporary phase to bridge the country over a difficult post-Covid period when economic growth has bene running well below government targets.[139] Unquestionably, through its unbalanced industrial policies, China is storing up pain for its own economy. But because in many of these areas Europe is the target for aggressive Chinese trade practices, the greatest suffering is likely to be borne by the Europeans. As Charles Grant from the Centre for European Reform has pointed out, the heady ambitions surrounding China's membership of the World Trade Organization in 2001 have evaporated. 'Europeans have abandoned hope that China will play by the rules on trade and investment. They accuse it of stealing intellectual property, denying Europeans reciprocal market access, using excessive amounts of state aid to help its firms take over European ones or win contracts at the expense of European competitors, and much else.'[140]

Joerg Wuttke, a long-time executive from BASF, now working for an American advisory firm, lived in China for more than twenty-five years as the German chemical company's chief China representative, before moving to Washington in summer 2024. He points out how increased Chinese competition on foreign markets reflects domestic frailties.

> China cannot get the economy going. The country has become more unpredictable. There used to be a straight line between strong growth and strong leadership. Decision-making is now very slow because Xi controls everything. It was thought that the rise in Xi's authority and the appointment of his supporters in key positions would speed up decision-making. In fact, it is the opposite because the people lower down the hierarchy are fearful about what those higher up think about their actions.[141]

Wuttke underlines how Europe's exports to China have declined as the Chinese become more self-sufficient. 'The top 10 companies in Europe are maintaining their Chinese engagement but medium-sized firms are not getting involved. German exports to China are less than exports to Poland. The 27 countries of the EU export to China about as much as to Switzerland.' He adds: 'Europe is now becoming less important for China. The Chinese have successfully secured investment in China by the largest German companies. This reduces the relevance of imports. And China has acquired technology in many areas and no longer needs to import this from abroad.'

Indeed, imports from – rather than exports to – China represent the field where Beijing's policies, for the Europeans, are of crucial significance. Europe is keenly aware of its dependence on China for critical raw materials vital for the 'green transition'.[142] Europe is not alone here: Australia has been in the vanguard of countries trying to limit Chinese influence over its raw-material sector.[143] This raw-material dependence creates a separate race to safeguard international supply chains, where Europe is falling behind. Alongside its dominant position in processing and refining, China is actively investing in mining assets in Africa and Latin America and overseas refining via its Belt and Road initiative, where Chinese foreign investment in metals and mining rose to $10 billion in the first half of 2023 alone.[144] The US has deployed the IRA, the bipartisan Infrastructure Act and defence funding to build up domestic processing, refining and recycling capacity, as well as using its geopolitical clout to secure the global supply chain – but Europe has been slow at promoting similar initiatives.

Chinese officials are quick to underline the potentially counterproductive effect of western efforts to rein in China's industrial power. Jin Liqun, head of the Asian Infrastructure Investment Bank, says President Biden's ban on exports of high-performance semiconductors has strengthened China's indigenous industry.

> The embargo on exports of chips to China has caused American chip companies prohibitively high cost. There is now massive investment in China's high-tech industry. Probably in less than 10 years, China will produce chips of single digit nanos at incredibly low cost, exporting to many countries in the world. Even if Americans want to sell the chips to China, the answer will be 'We are sorry, but we don't need them anymore'.[145]

Rakesh Mohan, a veteran Indian government official and academic with a long track record in industry and technology, and a former deputy governor of the Reserve Bank of India, is one of the foremost Indian voices calling for greater trade cooperation between India and China. He says Biden's industry action over chips exports 'may be doing China a favour by forcing the Chinese to develop their own products and invest even more in scientific and technology development. They now have no longer any choice but to develop their own industry.'[146]

Jin's and Mohan's arguments received highly public support in May 2025 from an influential source – Jensen Huang, chief executive of Nvidia, the leading US chipmaker. He said the attempt to cut off the flow of advanced AI chips gave Chinese companies 'the spirit, the energy and the government support to accelerate their development. All in all, the export control was a failure.'[147]

Jürgen Hambrecht is a German industrialist well acquainted with long-term Chinese thinking. He built extensive activities in China as chief executive of chemicals giant BASF between 2003 and 2011. 'If you look to BASF's Nanjing petrochemical site, the investment has helped transform parts of the Chinese industrial system, in areas like management skills, employee participation, environmental standards and health and safety.'[148] He believes American technology constraints will bring no more than short-term relief. 'Longer term, the Chinese will be able to build up their own strengths in semiconductors, including the high-end. They don't just think in five-year dimensions, they think in 20-year terms.'

The Chinese will not, however, have it all their own way. There are many signs that Chinese companies are fulfilling an important part of Trump's policies by stepping up plans to build manufacturing capacity in the US to avoid tariffs.[149] US semiconductor experts highlight how China will run into cumulative obstacles as US restrictions gain momentum and the Chinese industry faces bureaucratic, organisational and financial hurdles in pursuing wide-ranging innovations. Paul Triolo, a Washington-based semiconductor analyst, points to a July 2023 speech by Hou Jianguo, president of the China Academy of Sciences, underlining the scale of the challenge and calling for 'acceleration of the seizure of a number of scientific and technological commanding heights in order to strongly protect national development and security'.

Hou's statement underlines Beijing's requirement to avoid 'economic dependency and encirclement'.[150] The official Beijing view, Triolo says, is that 'it is not sufficient for Chinese companies to catch up to their western counterparts in strategic technological areas; rather, they must achieve some level of dominance to evade technological choke points in the future.'

The US high-technology tussle with China will evolve further under Trump. Whatever happens, Europe's dependence on Asia as a whole, and especially Taiwan, for semiconductor supplies looks likely to enmesh the continent into a wider set of vulnerabilities.[151] China's ultimate stance, and America's reaction, in the latent conflict with Taiwan, will be of crucial importance for Europe in trying to frame its Asian strategies. Japan has remained a staunch US ally and has also launched a series of initiatives to increase its strategic and military influence in Asia and the Indo-Pacific. Yet the refusal to take sides over the Ukrainian war displayed by India, Indonesia and many other developing nations in Asia, Africa and Latin America raises questions about the western power base in southern and South East Asia.

These countries together with the so-called BRICS group – Brazil, Russian, India, China and South Africa, now supplemented by several further members – have thrown down the gauntlet to the US.[152] They are engaged, directly or indirectly, in an ambitious effort to weaken the primacy of the dollar and American financial markets, and, with that, erode global American economic leadership.[153]

These efforts have to be put into long-term historical perspective. America has long been wary of China-led efforts to dislodge the US from its pivotal position. The Obama administration in 2015 displayed considerable initial hostility to the Asian Infrastructure Investment Bank (AIIB) – and particularly the UK's role in joining as Europe's first major shareholder.[154]

The bank is firmly established as a form of smaller, less central but permanent counterweight to the so-called Bretton Woods institutions, set up in 1944 as war was still raging in Europe and Asia. China's attempts to challenge the post-Second World War order have sometimes been dubbed as a bid to set up a 'Beijing Woods' system. However, the AIIB has been careful to espouse the full gamut of western governance and operating standards. These include carrying out co-financing with both the World Bank and the Asian Development Bank, adhering rigorously to US-led financial sanctions against Russia and its allies, and maintaining a central role for the dollar in financing and lending.[155]

American antipathy to AIIB and its actions could intensify under Trump – which may influence the AIIB's expansionary plans. Sensitivities have increased since America-led sanctions efforts have resulted in a spate of countervailing moves to downgrade or circumvent the dollar's role in international trade and payments. A meeting of BRICS members in October 2024, in Kazan, capital of the semi-autonomous Russian republic of Tatarstan, was provocatively set to coincide with the annual gatherings of the IMF and World Bank in Washington. It was a diplomatic success for Putin. Yet it failed to take any concrete new steps towards de-dollarisation. As China expert Herbert Poenisch pointed out, BRICS was starting to look increasingly like a 'paper tiger'. The Kazan summit offered nothing new in economics and finance.

> A new cross-border payments system and even a common BRICS currency were on the table, with rumours of a petroyuan being established to replace the petrodollar. Russian government officials produced volumes of studies on many topics, ranging from agriculture, education, environment and energy to sports and counterterrorism. However, the lack of adoption of any responsibilities by the participating countries and the failure to establish new institutions to manage the transition to a new world order showed a lack of political will to turn these proposals into a reality.[156]

Despite this lack of decisive shorter-term action, the Kazan gathering was symptomatic of a wider movement. Many countries among the world's emerging market economies, increasingly reliant on Chinese largesse in lending, investment and trade, have resisted supporting the US and Europe in sanctions against Russia. Asia as a whole, having recovered more resolutely than Europe from the financial and economic upsets of the 2007–8 crisis, is in a much better state to choose its partners for growth and development – a lesson which the Europeans have no choice but to take seriously.

In the meantime, India's growth spurt and closure of the population gap with China has made the superpower race more complex. India will play a major role in the future world-power equation. India's veteran foreign minister Subrahmanyam Jaishankar lived in both the Soviet Union and the US as a Cold War diplomat. He says the world is now returning to a 'natural order' before colonialism where the countries that were the main losers of developments over the past two hundred years – above all China and India – are slowly regaining dominance. 'I am not an advocate of the theory of the decline of the West. Europe and the US will remain very strong and there will be many areas where they continue to be leaders. But they will have to make compromises – and work much more closely with others to develop an idea of what the future should look like.'[157]

Kishore Mahbubani, the outspoken former dean at the National University of Singapore, who believes that western economic 'incompetence' has now become structural, warns Europe not to neglect South East Asia. He points out that, from 2010 to 2020, the ASEAN bloc of South East Asian nations, with its $3 trillion gross domestic product, contributed more to global economic growth than the EU with its $17 trillion GDP.[158] From a similar vantage point Ravi Menon, former managing director of the Monetary Authority of Singapore, now chair of GFTN, describes Europe's future tasks:

Europe suffers from poor demographics which is holding back economic growth. Europe will need to integrate more with the Global South: China, India, Southeast Asia, and others. Despite the encouraging rhetoric, I have not seen a concerted and tangible European effort to connect more intensively with these countries and benefits from enhanced trade and investment links.[159]

For China, too, the future will not be unidirectional. Jude Blanchette, a China specialist at the Washington-based US Center for Strategic and International Studies, opines that the fractured relationship with Washington could set back the progress of globalisation on which China's economic prospects depend.[160] Blanchette points out how some Chinese experts, even those with deep knowledge of the country's foreign policy and security apparatus, have been taken aback by the effect of US sanctions over Ukraine. Among Chinese experts cited by Blanchette, international relations scholar Li Wei was alarmed by the West's 'unprecedentedly united' effort to sanction the Russian economy, which offered a 'vivid demonstration of the tools of economic power'. Hang Bei, an analyst at the People's Bank of China, predicted that US leverage over key payment and settlement mechanisms, including the Society for Worldwide Interbank Financial Telecommunication (SWIFT) system, would allow it to threaten Russia's 'national financial security'. Economist Wang Da likened the expulsion of Russia from SWIFT to a nuclear attack.[161]

In handling China, Lars-Hendrik Röller, Angela Merkel's economic adviser, with deep experience of dealing with China, says, 'The most important priority is to improve economic performance in Europe. We have to form a proper strategy for Europe as a whole.' Pointing to considerable evidence that 'the country is now paying the price for the inefficiencies and overheating that we have seen in parts of the Chinese economy over the past 15 years', Röller believes that Europe – despite everything – has a chance of adopting a China policy that does not need slavishly to copy the American line.

> There are a lot of problems in China, seen in the political crackdown against corruption, doubts about a fiscal stimulus, bankruptcies in real estate. The Chinese are returning to some basic questions: how to raise productivity, improve the education system, promote entrepreneurialism, counter demographic problems. Europe can follow policies that do not need to copy the Americans. In existential questions, Europe will side with America, but there is an opportunity for an independent path.[162]

THE COMPLEX OF AMERICAN POWER

In the complex of American power, the psychology of mutual trust – or lack of it – plays a large role. At a crucial stage in the run-up to Russia's full invasion of Ukraine, Biden sent emissaries to Berlin and other capitals in December 2021, shortly after Scholz moved into the chancellor's office in Berlin following formation of a three-party coalition in the wake of the September election.

The Americans delivered two key messages: a war between Ukraine and Russia was highly likely, and, once it came, Russia would attempt to use gas deliveries to Germany and Europe as an economic weapon. The message was taken seriously by Scholz's policy-making team, who had largely followed him to his new job from his previous post as Merkel's finance minister under the CDU–SPD 'grand coalition'. The result was a frantic effort to imbue Germany's gas dealings with Russia with an element of risk management that, during Merkel's sixteen-year chancellorship, had been singularly lacking. Jörg Kukies, Scholz's top economics official as state secretary in the chancellor's office (and subsequently finance minister after the collapse of Scholz's coalition in November 2024), recalls the circumstances on his arrival at his new post in December 2021.

> Scholz asked his advisers, 'What is our plan B if Putin cuts off energy supplies, especially gas?' There was no Plan B, neither in the Chancellery nor in the Economics Ministry. The Chancellor's response was clear: 'We need a Plan B of alternative suppliers – and fast, very fast.' The overall perception was that the Russians, going back to the Soviet Union and the most difficult periods of the Cold War, historically did not abuse their energy and food exports as weapons. But already there were intelligence reports indicating a military move against Ukraine.[163]

Daleep Singh, the key White House official who travelled to Europe (together with his colleague Amos Hochstein) relates sharing US intelligence about the build-up to war.

> This was much more than simply troop movements. We were talking about deploying field hospitals, blood banks, and so on, indicating that it would be fighting. Our German counterparts did not reveal any skepticism about our message. We told them they have a big problem since Russia was likely to use gas as a weapon. We told them they needed to reconfigure pipelines. They needed to buy liquefied natural gas from us and diversify supplies. This would need investment in the terminals on the Baltic Sea. We agreed a bargain under which we would open up oil reserves in a big way to bring down the price, flooding the market with oil.[164]

Singh gives credit to Kukies, who had worked with the chancellor in his previous job as finance minister. 'He saw this as a challenge and took to this as a banking deal, whereas his predecessors may have looked at the issue more as a mathematical equation. It helped matters that we both came from the same background at Goldman Sachs.' The episode underlined the closeness of the relationship between Biden and Scholz – both leaders whose long political careers ended badly at around the same time. Furthermore, it symbolised an enduring pattern of US involvement with Europe at moments of tension and crisis. Yet closer examination reveals that the ability of the largest European economies – Germany, France and the UK – to influence the superpower relationship has greatly fallen since German unification. This reflects not just the decline in Europe's relative economic size, but also the continent's diminishing geopolitical clout. Britain's withdrawal from the European Union, together with subsequent UK policy-making confusion and excessive prime-ministerial turnover in London, provides a significant further reason.

The paradoxical reality is that West Germany as a divided country before unification was a more substantive geopolitical player than united Germany thereafter. This reflects three factors: the change in the power balance with China, personality differences which intruded later into the German–American leadership equation and – above all – the leverage over East and West provided by the country's uncertain status. The built-in uncertainty over motives and intentions of West Germany, separated by the postwar East–West demarcation line and much played upon by Soviet strategists, gave the Bonn government significant leeway in handling America, especially as the Federal Republic's economic muscle grew in the 1960s and 1970s. West Germany could exert a hold over its western allies because of fears of the disruption that the divided country could provoke if it ever chose a 'go-it-alone' route promoting national unity at the cost of western integration.[165]

Hans-Georg Wieck, a 1980s head of the Bundesnachrichtendienst, the German foreign intelligence service, coined a somewhat scurrilous adage: 'We are strong because we are weak.' His elliptical reference meant that West Germany's exposed position on NATO's front line, together with the diminished sovereignty stemming from postwar division, gave it a disproportionate hold over its foreign partners.

Perceived unreliability made its neighbours highly receptive to the German point of view. Put brutally, Germany's strongest card in dealing with its western partners was to exploit the worry that it might be tempted to break loose from them.[166]

A prime example came with the first controversial overtures on *Ostpolitik* – the policy of rapprochement with the Soviet Union and eastern Europe espoused by Willy Brandt when he became chancellor in 1969. Brandt regarded rebuilding relations with the East as the key, at some far-off and completely undetermined date, to eventually winning back nationhood – a policy which eventually brought dividends under Helmut Kohl (and goes some way to explaining the close relationship between the two men). When Brandt's confidant and forward-thinker Egon Bahr outlined early notions on *Ostpolitik* to Kissinger in 1969, Nixon's security adviser at first believed that a new West German line on the East was incompatible with Germany's required solidarity within NATO. 'Too many memories might inhibit the requisite trust,' Kissinger recalled. 'And we were uneasy that Moscow might seek to manipulate the process.'[167] But Germany's disruptive potential was such that, rather than actively opposing the idea, Kissinger and Nixon overcame their scepticism. In a constructive compromise, they sought 'to pull the Soviet Union into negotiations on a wide range of East–West issues by integrating *Ostpolitik* into Nixon's new policy of building bridges to China'.

Division and wartime memories made West German policy-makers innately more cautious and risk-averse than post-unification Germany, especially with regard to building up undue reliance on the Soviet Union for energy supplies. The early stages of Brandt-inspired gas deals attracted suspicions from elsewhere in Europe about where intensified Soviet–German economic relations might lead: in 1969–70, discord among the western allies marred the start of a series of gas-for-pipes agreements between West Germany and the Soviet Union.

A top German foreign-ministry official – Axel Herbst, in charge of foreign trade relations – registered alarm about complaints from France that Germany was granting the Soviet Union loans for a February 1970 pipeline deal at unduly favourable interest rates. 'In view of the great economic and political interest in negotiating the delivery of Soviet gas to the Federal Republic, and German pipes to the Soviet Union,' Herbst called on the government to observe 'a minimum of rules for western countries' trade relations with the Soviet Union'.[168] The gas deals opened the way for further economic cooperation. Reporting on widespread interest in Soviet business from large German companies such as Mercedes-Benz, Siemens, Mannesmann and Thyssen, Herbst wrote: 'From a Soviet viewpoint there is a direct connection between large-scale gas deliveries and some big business transactions now under discussion.'

The West German government, coping with the challenges of the Cold War, understood that over-dependence on Russian gas could bring problems. In the run-up to the deal, in June 1969, Herbst wrote: 'The federal economic ministry believes 20 per cent is a reasonable maximum for the share of Soviet gas in total German consumption.'[169] Herbst's boss, Günther Hakort, state secretary at the foreign ministry, added a handwritten comment: in his view, the estimate appeared 'high'.

After unification – and especially when Merkel closed off other options by deciding to accelerate closure of nuclear power stations following Japan's 2011 Fukushima nuclear catastrophe – that caution was cast aside. At the time of the Russian invasion in February 2022, Germany's imports from Russia accounted for 55 per cent of its gas deliveries from abroad. Conley of the German Marshall Fund recalls, 'I was in Berlin the day after the Fukushima accident. I could see the emotion of the demonstration against nuclear energy. Without the flows of cheap gas from Russia and without nuclear energy, Germany will have higher energy costs, given the energy intensity of German industry – and this will add greatly to industrial costs and reduce global competitiveness. Gas imports will never be as cheap as they were before.'[170]

Another throwback comes with evidence of West Germany's one-time pivotal role in the global foreign-exchange upsets of the early 1970s. The break-up of the Bretton Woods currency system laid bare the weakening of the dollar's international role and the emergence of West Germany – despite Cold War division – as a major economic player.

A surprisingly upbeat assessment of Germany's authoritative place in the world came in 1974 from Fred Bergsten, who worked with Kissinger at the National Security Council, and went on to coordinate international economic policy at the US Treasury under President Jimmy Carter.[171]

> There are only two economic superpowers in the world today: the United States of America and the Federal Republic of Germany. Their active joint leadership is essential for the host of immediate problems which now plague the world economy: to avoid relapse on all continents into destructive nationalistic policies and to rebuild a stable international economic structure. Such leadership should be exercised through a series of concentric circles of decision-making, centered on their own bilateral relationship and radiating out through the other industrialized countries (primarily the rest of the EEC and Japan) into the existing global institutions.[172]

West Germany's role in foreign affairs was never greater than in the months before and immediately after the Wall fell. President George H.W. Bush pre-emptively reinforced his personal relationship with Kohl during what he and his advisers correctly believed would be a seminal time in East–West geopolitics. But in the years following Bush's optimistic May 1989 affirmation that the US and Germany would be 'partners in leadership',[173] the bonding with America has come under frequent strain. This applied notably to the disagreements over the Iraq war between Bush's son George W. Bush and Kohl's successor, Gerhard Schröder.

Tension also built during the era of Angela Merkel – over German obduracy on the European debt crisis, in going ahead with the Nord Stream 2 gas pipeline with Russia, and in refusing to join in military deliveries to Ukraine in the early stages of the war. A top Berlin security official explains how the Biden administration's faltering performance over the poorly handled Afghanistan military withdrawal in August 2021[174] contributed to Putin's decision to invade Ukraine six months later.

> It was not a coincidence that Putin chose this moment to strike. His diagnosis may have been that the west was disunited after the chaotic withdrawal from Afghanistan the previous summer and an apparent lack of leadership in Europe and the US. The build-up of Russia's

reserves of gold and foreign exchange gave him a kind of war chest. But, at the same time, you can also consider that Putin's hand was forced. He had to act then, because Ukraine was slipping away from him. It was becoming increasingly difficult to bind Ukraine into the Russian sphere.[175]

Martin Selmayr, a German civil servant who built up a high profile in Brussels, played a leading role in EU foreign affairs in 2014 to 2019 as chief of staff to European Commission president Juncker and then briefly secretary general of the Commission. (After a spell in Vienna as the EU's emissary to Austria, he moved to Rome in 2024 to become the bloc's ambassador to the Vatican. He arrived in time to appraise the political repercussion of the transition caused by the death of Pope Francis and the election of Leo XIV as the first American pontiff.) Like the Berlin official, Selmayr believes that, for Putin, the US withdrawal from Afghanistan indicated that 'America had reached the limits of its empire'.[176] An even more important factor may have been 'because Merkel was no longer there to exert any influence on him . . . The European Union, he thought, was a joke, and had been debilitated by Corona. He saw the EU and the West in general as decadent.' Selmayr notes Putin's miscalculations over issues such as the steely pro-Ukrainian policies of the Greens in Scholz's government, and over building Russia's foreign-exchange reserves, 'not realising that half could be frozen immediately'.

American officials and politicians with experience of Germany have a long track record of using psychological imagery to explain the frequently tortuous shape of relations. Richard Burt, US ambassador to Bonn in 1985–9, described handling the Germans as like dealing with a disturbed infant.[177] 'I'm like a psychiatrist who has to see a child from a broken home with complex problems. I take time with that child, and then I have to go back to Washington to explain it to the child's parents.'[178] Merkel used to say that the Americans treated the Europeans like children. She scolded her fellow leaders for not showing more discipline in their negotiations.[179]

Larry Summers, President Bill Clinton's Treasury secretary, an acerbic voice in the transatlantic relationship, describes a conversation with President Obama in 2010 during the sovereign debt crisis:

I told him the way to understand what was happening in Greece was to imagine a family, where Dad had been highly abusive many years ago and since reformed, Mom was flighty and nervous, and concerned above all to make sure that Dad didn't go back to his bad ways. And the children were in need of support from Dad, but were residually scared of Dad. The Dad being Germany; Mom, France; and the children, the Club Med.[180]

In reaction, Summers says, Obama showed 'amusement and interest'.

A similar psychological approach was displayed by John Kornblum, a veteran State Department official who played an important role at various stages of the Cold War, ending his diplomatic career as ambassador to Germany – and continuing as a resident of Berlin until the year of his death in 2023. The trauma of division, disorder and suspension between East and West, according to Kornblum, left a legacy that makes careful handling imperative.[181] 'The Germans are on our [the American] side, but they don't want to admit it. They're not going to sell out to the Communists, but they are not Atlanticists. They are worried about becoming a plaything between the superpowers. This goes back to an old fear.' Given the burdens of German history, Kornblum believes America had no choice but to apply psychology to Germany over the underlying factors behind reunification.

> Sensitivity to German feelings was one of the reasons why we [the US] thought it was appropriate to praise the East Germans as much as possible for the fall of the Wall. I was able to sell to Washington the idea of celebrating the East German popular revolution even though it didn't really take place. What was happening was that the Soviet Union was coming to an end – and this made reunification inevitable.

A depiction of Germany coping with growing pains and still not quite reaching adulthood has been advanced by Wolfgang Schmidt, Germany's chancellery minister in 2021–5, Scholz's closest government associate and coordinator of the country's intelligence agencies. Schmidt contributed significantly to Scholz's unexpected success in the 2021 general election – as well as to his subsequent fall from grace, reflecting widespread economic problems and the general malaise of his three-party coalition. Speaking in October 2022, Schmidt said Germany was still a 'teenager' in foreign and security policies. 'We are getting into a situation that Americans have known for decades: people want us to lead . . . We are in the teenager years in that role. We are not yet an adult when it comes to foreign security policy. In teenager years you have a lot of hormones, there's a lot of overshooting and shouting, you are not very sure of yourself and don't know where your place is.'[182]

The theme is taken up by Horst Köhler, Germany's federal president in 2004 to 2010, who resigned amid a barrage of criticism of a radio interview in which he defended Germany's intervention on the side of the US in the Afghan war as necessary to protect the country's economic interests.[183] Born in what was German-occupied Poland in the Second World War, Köhler spent most of his first fourteen years as a refugee. Köhler has been an extraordinary witness to Germany's innate historical upheavals. He was a top German finance ministry civil servant in the 1980s and 1990s. During the unification period, as a prime Kohl confidant, Köhler negotiated both monetary union between East and West Germany and the final withdrawal of Soviet troops from the eastern part of the country. He was chief negotiator for the Maastricht treaty that, in 1991, paved the way for the birth of the euro. Moreover, he played an important role in the currency crises of 1992–3. A unique career path saw him become president of the European Bank for Reconstruction and Development and managing director of the International Monetary Fund before, for six years, becoming Germany's head of state.

Asked in late 2023 – just over a year before he died in February 2025 – whether Germany had completed its journey towards being a fully grown-up country, Köhler replied, 'Not yet,' adding, presciently, that – after the shock of the Russian attack on Ukraine – the country needed a change of mindset and a redistribution of resources to reinforce defence capabilities. His words presented a chillingly accurate foretaste of the realities to which, with the new government in 2025, Germany and its leaders were becoming confronted.

Scholz has coined the phrase 'Zeitenwende' after the Russian invasion of Ukraine, meaning that Germany can no longer hide from its responsibilities brought by the size of its economy and population in the centre of Europe. But Germany was and still is not prepared for the security challenges we now face. People and political parties are still not aware that this new situation demands not least a substantial reshuffling of financial resources.[184]

Friedrich Merz is a politician who understands the dimensions and the difficulties of 2020s-style realpolitik. Whether he has the instruments and the staying power to surmount the challenges is still far from certain. Whatever happens, according to Bob Kimmitt, a Republican with experience of the top echelons of both Bush administrations, Merz's long association with the US will be of vital significance. 'The transatlantic partnership may go through the most turbulent time since the breakup of Bretton Woods system. It will be a bumpy ride and we will need to put on our seat belts, but we will pull through.'[185] Kimmitt believes closer commercial and financial ties with a 'business-friendly Trump administration' will be crucial.

> In addition to his private sector experience, Merz had over 10 years of working with Americans of both parties through his chairmanship of the Atlantik Brücke. He understands the American mindset. He can garner significant goodwill by focusing on Trump's interest in securing manufacturing jobs for the US. German companies in the US already employ 850,000 Americans. Merz can work with Trump on trying to double that figure.

A NEW APPROACH

In handling the complicated superpower conundrum, Europe requires a new approach that adopts the late Horst Köhler's prescribed elements of responsibility. In 2019, the EU approved a strategy document declaring that China was simultaneously partner, competitor and systemic rival.[186] The EU has maintained the triple description since then, but now places more emphasis on systemic rivalry.[187] China's handling of the Covid-19 virus did not help its relations with the EU. Beijing refused to accept international scrutiny, and would not accept any criticism that it may have been the source of the virus.[188] In December 2020, shortly before Biden took office, China and the EU agreed on the text of a 'Comprehensive Agreement on Investment', to facilitate investment between them.[189] Merkel pushed strongly for the treaty, which was opposed by the US and CDU party stalwarts such as Wolfgang Schäuble – 'I would have left it for a few months and discussed it with the Americans'[190] – and subsequently put on ice.

As Draghi's report makes clear, the EU's competitiveness is under pressure from several sides: from weaker foreign demand, especially from China, faltering domestic economies and a declining position in advanced technologies. Alongside combating these competitive pressures, Europe has to refine its approach on sanctions and tariff policies, partly in harmonisation, partly in competition with the US in areas like electric vehicles.[191] Far from attempting to carve out its own single-minded strategy, Europe has to find its place in a complex interweaving of positions among the allies and subordinates of the superpowers.

Washington's success in prevailing upon its partners to increase pressure on Beijing has led Xi to complain about 'containment, encirclement, and suppression'.[192] But if America's now ramped-up 'containment' succeeds, and China is forced into a position of greater self-reliance and autarky, Europe is likely to end up the loser in the balance of international power. The Old Continent is by no means alone in the world with its problems: pockets of technological backwardness, resistance to societal change, demographic pressures and populist politicians are a feature of many nations. But the combination of tasks and complexity of internal fault lines make finding solutions much more onerous.

Europe once harboured the ambition to hold the world in its hand. After the fall of the Berlin Wall, and especially in view of the twenty-first-century challenges stemming from the revival of Russia and China, Europe faced the strategic necessity of building up muscle in industrial, economic, defence and foreign policies. It has failed in that task. As some Europeans themselves predicted, the continent has become akin to a residual item in world politics.

Is Europe destined to bounce, from side to side (or sphere to sphere), as a 'playball'? The economic and political constraints drastically reduce the options. The clarion call of 'strategic autonomy', by itself, is not a valid option. Yet Europe must try to secure international viability on terms consistent with its culture and values. Nurturing a strong alliance with the US has become enormously more difficult under Trump 2.0.

But it cannot be given up as a goal, provided Europe can resist fracturing and recover a position on the world stage that exudes strength not weakness.

The need has been made more pressing, possibly existential, by the perils stemming from Europe's eastern neighbourhood – and, especially, from the man running Russia.

3

RUSSIA, GERMANY AND THE EUROPEAN HOME

In the French view, nothing can happen – especially on reunification – without a complete change in relations between the states of Europe, especially East and West . . . Russia will attack neither Germany nor France nor America. It must develop its own country and needs the help of the West.

Charles de Gaulle to Willy Brandt, West German
foreign minister, 1966[1]

Europe was, is, and shall remain – as a result of history and geography – the common home for the people of our two states as well for others in this part of the world.

Leonid Brezhnev to Helmut Schmidt, 1981[2]

I think Putin never expected the G7 to react as quickly and decisively to the invasion as was the case. Nor did he expect the degree of sanctions, including the freezing of roughly half of Russian central bank assets. The alliance was stronger across the EU 27 than he would have expected. He surely anticipated less solidarity and greater dispersion.

Jörg Kukies, state secretary, German
chancellor's office, 2023[3]

Vladimir Putin's story unfolds through Germany's Cold War relationship with Russia: forged in blood and treasure, financed by gas and technology, culminating in German unification and the tragic unfulfilled promise of an economic symbiosis between two unequal partners. This convoluted chronicle of hope and grief is of pivotal importance for untangling the story of modern-day Europe. Post-1945 German–Soviet rapprochement up to the 1989 opening of the Berlin Wall, an ensuing decade of chaos and decline, and Putin's quarter-century of consolidation after 1999 are studded with attempts to build constructive relations between these two pivotal European powers – often to the discomfiture of Germany's western allies and partners.

During an improbably lengthy period after he took over the leadership in 1999–2000, Putin maintained the enticing notion, attractive above all (but not only) to the Germans, that Russia was a seminal part of what Moscow's leaders traditionally called the 'common European home'. Alternating as prime minister and president since 1999, Putin has laconically declared, 'Somebody will come and replace me at some point,' adding (probably unnecessarily), 'I will make sure that such people will get support.'[4] In a national poll that was a long way from being fair and free, but whose outcome no doubt reflected the combined will of the Russian people, Putin was overwhelmingly re-elected president in March 2024, shortly after the death in a penal colony of his highest-profile opponent, Alexei Navalny.

Whatever his eventual succession, he has single-handedly done more than any other post-1945 leader to reshape Europe. Throughout centuries of upheavals, notwithstanding its near-continuous history of domestic tyranny and economic mediocrity, Russia has maintained a permanent sway over the European mindset. Putin has combined this historical appeal with his own multiple oscillating personalities. Alternately beguiling, bemoaning, berating, this 'deliberate political chameleon'[5], with 'killer's eyes, able to move from sensitive soul to hard nut in one blink',[6] has exerted a defining influence on the twenty-first-century world.

At the time of the Wall's opening, with the West Germans fearing an insurge of Soviet tanks, and peace and war hanging in the balance, Putin was an anonymous KGB operative in Dresden, enraged by Moscow's impotence at a time of 'paralysis of power'.[7] A decade later, a fading President Boris Yeltsin propelled this unheralded administrator and low-grade secret policeman from the shadows into the storm. With Russia 'balancing on the brink of preserving its territorial integrity and sovereignty', Putin declared himself the servant and builder of the 'Russian idea' – encompassing patriotism, solidarity and self-belief in Russia's greatness.[8]

Profoundly troubled by the Soviet Union's inability to maintain its pivotal European position hard-won in the Second World War, Putin reflected in 2000, the year he became president, 'We would have avoided a lot of problems if the Soviets had not made such a hasty exit from eastern Europe.' He drew a more general – and abiding – conclusion: the need for firm action against adversarial forces. 'Only one thing works in such circumstances – to go on the offensive. You must hit first, and hit so hard that your opponent will not rise to his feet.'[9]

Putin's notion of community with the western part of the continent, demonstrating continuity with decades of Soviet and Russian thinking, was targeted particularly on Germany – but engendered considerable sympathy across Europe. Mutual self-interest was the watchword. With Germany in the lead, the West expressed a fervent desire for political and economic cooperation to bring this huge, mineral-rich land and its wayward, archaic practices into line with the industrial nations. Bernd Pfaffenbach, a long-standing German economics official and adviser to Schröder and Merkel during their chancellorships, says,

> I was always convinced that co-operation between the two countries was the way forward . . . We believed in the concept of 'Wandel durch Handel' [transformation through trade]. It stretches back to Willy Brandt and Egon Bahr [Brandt's security adviser]. The aim of a common European economic area, including Russia, was put forward at the time of unification. It seemed like a proposition from which everyone would gain.[10]

Pfaffenbach was long-time co-chairman of the German–Russian Strategic Working Group, bringing together industry representatives from both countries:

> German industry had a strong reason to engage with Russia. We thought that this was enhancing, not reducing, political and economic security. It was helpful that Russia could build up its infrastructure and gain access to secure export markets for gas. This

led to a sharp increase in Germany's energy dependence on Russia. But we thought the risk was manageable.

Rolf Martin Schmitz, former chief executive of German energy company RWE (a major component of the country's electricity generating system), commenting shortly after Russia's full-scale invasion of Ukraine in February 2022, spoke for many: 'The energy dependency on Russia was rational, everyone profited. Just that the plan didn't foresee a despot like Putin. That wasn't part of the equation.'[11]

The traditional strength of Russian–German ties – symbolised by Otto von Bismarck's policy of 'never cutting the connection to St Petersburg'[12] – has found reflection in numerous seminal personal relationships. Kohl recovered from a disastrous start with Mikhail Gorbachev to build up a close bond with the Soviet leader, elected general secretary of the Communist party in 1985. The tight emotional connection made Kohl vulnerable to Moscow's frequent attempts to extort much-needed hard currency in return for Soviet favours.[13] Yet Kohl quickly came to terms, as Gorbachev's grip on power diminished, with his political demise. The chancellor built an almost equally strong rapport with Yeltsin. The two were united by strong shared characteristics: stamina, stubbornness and a proclivity never to forget personal favours and slights.[14]

Personal connections acted as an overlay to a web of intersecting interests stitched together in good times and (mostly) in bad. According to John Lough, a security specialist who was NATO's first representative in Moscow in 1995–8 during the turbulent years of Boris Yeltsin, Russian–German links reflect 'a complex mixture of cultural biases, instincts and sensitivities built up over centuries', including two large-scale twentieth-century wars and forty-five years of Cold War confrontation.'[15] In the German national psyche, 'a sense of guilt for Nazi crimes inflicted on the peoples of the USSR' had led to counterproductive results. 'In its stubborn quest for "strategic partnership", Germany inadvertently ended up supporting the emergence of a Russian regime hostile to its interests and values . . . It legitimised and reinforced a deeply corrupt and increasingly repressive and authoritarian Russian system, emboldening it to deploy force against its neighbours and to attack western institutions.'

In a similar vein, Christopher Mallaby, British ambassador to West Germany in 1988–92 (from October 1990, united Germany), wrote in 1989 that 'the appalling crimes of Nazism' led to Germany's 'lack of self-confidence and a tendency toward guilt' – factors behind 'uncritical enthusiasm for Gorbachev and willingness to believe that the Soviet threat has gone'.[16] Michael Stürmer, during his heyday Germany's globally best-known contemporary historian, a 1980s adviser to Helmut Kohl, believes the emotional detritus of Germany's historical misdemeanours played a critical role in shaping the close yet opaque relationship between Putin and Angela Merkel. 'She was the perfect person for Putin to work on, coming from East Germany, as a pastor's daughter, believing all the time in German guilt from the Second World War.'[17]

Putin became a central figure in a rapidly shifting geopolitical kaleidoscope. Broadly speaking, his love affair with the West extended up to his open revolt in Munich in 2007 against an American-led 'unipolar world' and thereafter moved in stages towards full-scale breakdown. But the process started a decade before his accession. The principal Russian actor was Gorbachev, presiding over the collapse of the Soviet Union in 1991 and simultaneously handing power to his rival Yeltsin. Gorbachev was distraught at the dismemberment. As described by his authorised biographer, William Taubman, Gorbachev was a 'tragic hero'[18] who venerated his role model, Vladimir Lenin, initiator of the Bolshevik dictatorship that succeeded the Tsarist empire, and architect of the Union of Soviet Socialist Republics.[19] A juxtaposition both piquant and tragic: Lenin brought down Russia; Gorbachev, the USSR.

As one of the most fastidious chroniclers of the Soviet downfall, Vladislav Zubok, has put it: 'Gorbachev certainly did not expect in 1985 to be remembered as the leader who destroyed the country that he tried to change.'[20] 'A fallen icon at home', in the words of biographer Gail Sheehy, yet 'the first Soviet leader to be a cult figure in the West'.[21] The ending of the Soviet Union – Lenin's heroic creation – was for Gorbachev 'the cross I shall bear till the end of my life'.[22] Putin famously called the collapse 'the greatest geopolitical catastrophe of the twentieth century'[23] – a phrase destined to act as psychological cover for much that would afterwards ensue.

'A COMBUSTIBLE COMBINATION OF GRIEVANCE, AMBITION AND INSECURITY'

A comparison between the Russian president and the most notorious figure in German and possibly world history may appear fanciful and even outrageous. But the parallel with Adolf Hitler has been drawn by no less a personality than Germany's longest-serving member of parliament, Wolfgang Schäuble – an internationally renowned minister with first-hand experience of the ending of the Cold War, who for thirty-three years until his death in 2023 was wheelchair-bound after an assassination attempt in 1990. At the time of the Russian takeover of Crimea in 2014, Schäuble generated controversy when he reflected on similarities between Russia's annexation and Hitler's seizure of the Sudetenland in Czechoslovakia in 1938, on the pretext that Nazi Germany wished to protect the 3-million-strong German-speaking population there.[24]

Holding the job of finance minister, but with an elder stateman's licence to speak on broad swaths of policy, Schäuble outlined in 2014 – with considerable prescience – what could happen next. 'The Russians could say: "There are fascists in the [Ukrainian] government, they are threatening our Russian population."' In 2023, Schäuble returned to his argument with an old man's relish: 'There is a parallel between Hitler and Putin. I made this point in 2014, and was criticised.' Schäuble spelled out his reasoning in a conversation in his spacious office in the Bundestag – of which he was president from 2017 to 2021 – in one of his last long interviews before his death at Christmas 2023. 'Hitler made clear in *Mein Kampf* that he wished to revise the Versailles treaty as one of the main results of the First World War. He carried that out, most evidently by occupying the Rhineland. In the case of Putin, we had all the warning signs, but we failed to heed them. We were blind to the signals.'[25]

Politicians frequently indulge in amateur psychoanalysis. Winston Churchill in 1935 depicted Hitler as 'a child of the rage and grief of a mighty empire and race which had suffered overwhelming defeat in war'[26]. There are parallels with Putin's own psychological background: 'a combustible combination of grievance, ambition and insecurity', in the words of Bill Burns, director of the Central Intelligence Agency during Joe Biden's presidency and a former US ambassador in Moscow.[27]

In a telegram in 2006 to Condoleezza Rice, George W. Bush's secretary of state, Burns wrote,

> Putin sees considerable room for maneuver in a world of multiple power centers, with the US bogged down with difficulties, China and India on the rise in ways which pose no immediate threat to Russia, and the EU consumed with internal concerns. After years of being the potted plant of Great Power diplomacy, Putin, and many in the Russian elite, find it very satisfying to play a distinct and assertive role.[28]

Burns has described Putin as 'pumped up by years of high oil prices and wounded pride'.[29] Robert Gates, George W. Bush's defence secretary, called him 'haunted by lost empire, lost glory, and lost power'.[30] Putin's assertiveness – medieval ferocity fuelled by modern weaponry and ancient quarrels – has been on murderous display against Ukraine, a most graphic demonstration of the traditional Russian view of the world. As Cold War US diplomat Louis Halle has put it, Russia's 'defensive expansion' over five centuries from the fifteenth century's Ivan the Great has been driven by 'the lack of defensive frontiers in a world of mortal danger on all sides'.[31] Putin appears to embody a strong element of Josef Stalin's thinking, seeing Russia 'encircled by sinister forces that purposed its destruction . . . so powerful that the greatest guile was necessary in dealing with them.'[32] Depending on how Putin adapts his behaviour patterns, there may be another parallel with the start of the Cold War. Another American historian of the era, Herbert Feis, a top official under Herbert Hoover and Franklin Roosevelt, wrote in 1957: 'The Russian people [in the immediate post-Second World War period] were entitled to the fullest equality and protection against another assault on them. But under Stalin they were trying not only to extend their boundaries and their control over neighboring states but also beginning to revert to their revolutionary effort throughout the world.'[33]

Former Kohl adviser Michael Stürmer takes a cold-blooded view of Putin's historical continuity. As head of an official German political and strategic research group and foreign affairs columnist for leading German newspapers, he became a frequent attendee at Russia's Valdai discussion group featuring grandiose Putin monologues delivered to multifarious groupings of Kremlin aficionados. Stürmer earned an unfavourable reputation among some US officials as being overly close to the Russian president. Yet, less than a year after the full-scale invasion, Stürmer offered an assessment closely matching western intelligence agencies' opinion of Putin's brutalist neo-imperialism.[34]

> Behind the Ukrainian war is the strategy of rebuilding Russia's claim to be a European and world power, even if the gross domestic product and the terrible state of Russia when you drive through the countryside do not live up to it. Crimea and Ukraine were nothing but a first step in a multistage process. Putin wishes to consolidate his dictatorship, set an alternative to the western model and restore Russia's place in Europe.'[35]

Stürmer sees Stalin as Putin's forerunner. 'When Stalin arrived in Potsdam for the peace conference in 1945, he was met by Averell Harriman, the American ambassador, who asked him if he was pleased to be in Potsdam. Stalin's reply was that Alexander had made it all the way to Paris.'[36]

In 1947, Stalin repeated his remark about the Red Army reaching Paris, underlining, in the view of John Lewis Gaddis, another leading Cold War historian, that Stalin's goal was not 'a balance of power in Europe, but rather to dominate the continent as thoroughly as Hitler had sought to do'.[37] Gaddis's conclusion is that Stalin's postwar goals were 'security for himself, his regime, his country and his ideology, in precisely that order'[38] – a set of priorities that could also apply, more than seventy years later, to Putin.

In a contemporary setting of jet-age diplomacy, Putin gave an insight into his obsessive personality at an extraordinary meeting in Brisbane, Australia, in November 2014 with Jean-Claude Juncker, the former Luxembourg prime minister, who just ten days earlier had started a new job as president of the European Commission. The session kicked off as a late-night bilateral meeting between Merkel and Putin following a formal leaders' dinner at the Group of Twenty summit, which Putin attended despite an international outcry over the annexation of Crimea nine months earlier.[39] Juncker joined the meeting shortly after midnight in Putin's spacious Brisbane hotel suite. The two men stayed talking until 4 a.m. after Merkel left at 2.15 a.m.

Martin Selmayr, Juncker's hyperactive chief of staff, who attended the later stages of the talks, reports that much of the conversation was taken up with Putin discussing the Minsk agreement reached two months earlier.[40] This was an initial failed attempt to bring a ceasefire between Ukraine and Russian separatists fighting across eastern Ukraine. Putin showed himself 'obsessed' with Crimea, making copious references to Kievan Rus', the medieval Slavic state spread across the territory of Ukraine, Belarus and part of Russia (with a name derived from the city that is now Ukraine's capital). The territory is claimed by all three modern states as their cultural and spiritual forerunner. At around 3 a.m., Putin went into a room in his suite, bringing out an old book in Cyrillic, full of his notes and annotations on Russian history, 'clearly something he had read and studied many times'. Putin declared: 'This book shows that the origins of Russia lie in Ukraine. This is a key part of Russian history – Ukraine is our territory.' The conversation, as related by Selmayr, then took a semi-comedic turn:

> Juncker said: 'The book is in Cyrillic, which I do not read. For me, it has the same value as a cookbook in my kitchen at home in Luxembourg. By the way, I have a book in Luxembourg which tells me that Prague was founded by the Grand Duke of Luxembourg. So when I get back home, should I tell the Luxembourg army to conquer Prague?' Putin initially was stony-faced, but then laughed. This was Juncker's way of telling Putin that his line of reasoning was foolish and at odds with the lessons from history.

The session delivered a further glimpse into the siege-mentality mindset of a man under constant pressure. Putin instructed Juncker, when he went to the bathroom, to use toilet paper on the cupboard from the left-hand side of the closet. This was the product he brought specially from the Kremlin to the summit, for fear of being poisoned. Juncker joked: 'This is a five-star hotel, and you think that you have better toilet paper in the Kremlin.'[41]

A vulnerable leader is susceptible to strategic mistakes. Taking on centralised power in a state accelerating towards totalitarianism, Putin has presided over a hollowing-out of Russia's technological capabilities, an unfavourable lurch towards a war economy, and primitive coarsening of its once sophisticated diplomatic machinery.[42] He has destroyed much of the basis of hopes that Russia could become a modern state.

While snuffing out resistance within Russia, he has greatly stiffened the political and military resolve of his adversaries in the West – and (through the accession of Finland and Sweden in 2023–4) accelerated the widening of NATO towards Russia's western borders.[43] To his east, he has made his homeland vulnerable to blackmail, coercion or subjugation – possibly all three – by a reinforced, resurgent and far from totally reliable China.[44]

As Philip Short, author of the most forensic biography to date, has noted, 'The longer Putin remains in office, the more deeply Russia will become mired in stagnation and economic decline and the sharper will be the social tensions festering below the surface.'[45] Yet none of these shortcomings makes the Russian president irrational or even unique. Putin's much embroidered 'historical script'[46] for the Ukraine invasion has been focused on countering a world led by America, 'the self-proclaimed winner of the Cold War'.[47] This is the playbook of a man both embittered and emboldened by misadventure. The broad lines of his trajectory were set many years in the past.[48]

LEAP FROM THE DARK

Putin's notoriety stems from a mixture of interwoven factors. His ascent was both spectacular and banal. He leapt from almost complete obscurity in the late 1990s to become very quickly a seminal European and global figure.[49] Rodric Braithwaite, Britain's well-regarded ambassador to the Soviet Union and then Russia in 1988–92, knew Putin from his St Petersburg years. In advancing to prime minister and then to president, 'He seemed inscrutable, a shadow from the secret world. When you looked more closely, there always seemed to be less to Putin than met the eye.'[50]

Barbara Hay, a British civil servant who was one of the first western diplomats to deal with him during his administrative years in St Petersburg in the early 1990s, speaks in a similar vein: 'I never saw anything in him at all. He had nothing much to say. He would never be one to start a conversation. He never smiled or showed signs of life. He looked like a bit of a bruiser, as he had been in his youth.' Asked whether he appeared to be 'grooming' western politicians and functionaries who could be useful for him in future, Hay says: 'He didn't appear quite clever enough to be cunning.'[51]

According to Pierre Morel, a diplomat who worked closely with President François Mitterrand in the 1980s and was French ambassador to Russa from 1992 to 1996, Putin never lost the indelible hallmark of the KGB, the Soviet intelligence service which he joined in 1975 – although he never became an exalted official.

> In my view he has always been a KGB man from top to toe. I first met him in St Petersburg in 1992 when he was working with [Mayor] Sobchak. When he gave you his cold-eyed look, you had the feeling that between his eyes and you was a file which he had read, and would shortly be adding to. He was silent, drab and some-what unpleasant. He was already a survivor of the broken former KGB system. Everything in Russia at that time reflected that rupture.[52]

In August 1999, when Yeltsin appointed Putin – the fifth time in seventeen months that Russia's president had replaced his prime minister[53] – the British foreign office greatly exaggerated Putin's foreign-intelligence experience. Tim Barrow, private secretary to Robin Cook, the British foreign secretary (who later became ambassador to Moscow and then UK national security adviser until late 2024), reported to the prime minister's office at 10 Downing Street: 'He [Putin] served for 15 years for the KGB in East Germany'[54] (overstating by a factor of three his time outside the Soviet Union).

With greater accuracy, the British civil servant described the desig-nated new prime minister as 'firm, cool-headed and businesslike', 'intel-ligent and thoughtful' with 'good organisational skills', but lacking social competence. (Yeltsin, somewhat bizarrely, described Putin as 'very sociable' in a phone call a month later with Bill Clinton.[55]) Barrow hinted at a darker side. 'We have had friendly contact with him on intel-ligence liaison matters, although this has produced little of substance,' Barrow wrote. 'The FSB [the KGB's successor] retains important influ-ence throughout Russia, and will have access to compromising material on a range of political figures.'

Immense fluctuations in Putin's standing form part of his aura. No other political personality has switched so comprehensively in only two decades from unknown status to a position of companion of and confidant for western leaders, and then back to a role as pariah and outcast, at least among the main industrialised countries.

Putin's partial rehabilitation in 2025 at the hands of Trump marked a further milestone.[56] Already in Trump's first term, a somewhat incongruous personality convergence with the US president was discernible. According to Fiona Hill, a British-born Russian specialist who served under Trump in the National Security Council in 2017–19, 'Trump came to more closely resemble Putin in political practice than he resembled any of his American predecessors.'[57]

Writing in 2021, Hill listed overlapping characteristics that provide strong background to the Putin–Trump manoeuvring of 2025: 'manipulation and exploitation of the domestic media, appeals to their own versions of their countries' "golden age," compilation of personal lists of "national heroes" – and their attendant compilation of personal lists of enemies.' Hill recounted pitilessly how Putin and Trump share the same enemies: 'cosmopolitan, liberal elites; the American financier, philanthropist, and open society promoter George Soros; and anyone trying to expand voting rights, improve electoral systems, or cast a harsh light on corruption in their countries' respective executive branches.' Believing that Putin was 'the richest man in the world' Trump told associates that he admired 'the way he ran Russia as if it were his own private company'. Trump freely admitted, according to Hill, that he wished to emulate Putin: 'He [Trump] saw the US as an extension of his other private enterprises: the Trump Organization, but with the world's largest military at its disposal.'[58]

A pattern of dependence based on economic interests was set by Gerhard Schröder, German chancellor in 1998–2005, who formed the closest relationship of any western counterpart. He overstepped normal (at least for most western European politicians) boundaries of decorum by quickly taking up top positions at Russian and Russo-German corporations after leaving office. A landmark event was Putin's journey to Berlin for the signing of the Nord Stream 1 pipeline project in September 2005, ten days before the general election which led to Schröder losing office. Putin's participation was arranged in a highly unusual phone call between Schröder and the Russian president a month earlier.[59]

A decidedly secular and unsentimental chancellor, Schröder claimed implausibly to be impressed by Putin's 'Christian beliefs' and 'mission for Russia as part of Europe'. Schröder hailed his 'numerous conversations' before and after Putin's landmark Bundestag speech in Berlin in September 2001,[60] shortly after the 9/11 terrorist attacks on the US, when the Russian president received a standing ovation after proclaiming, 'Stable peace on the continent is a paramount goal for our nation.'[61] Schröder's refusal to cut ties with Putin after the full-scale invasion of Ukraine brought him near-universal opprobrium in Germany and throughout the West.

Rice, secretary of state under George W. Bush (whose relations with Schröder plummeted into deep freeze over the latter's refusal to support the US over the Iraq war), says, 'We were all particularly appalled that Schröder stepped down as chancellor and then only three weeks later took up a job as part of Gazprom.'[62]

David Owen, a former UK foreign secretary who himself built a career in Russian business after leaving politics, takes an unemotional view of Schröder's Russian ties. 'Perhaps he never understood Germany's need for NATO and for an alliance with America. He could have become wealthy if he had stuck to building up German economic relations with the rest of the EU and the US, but it was a fateful option for him to choose to do it with Russia.'[63]

THE NEWCOMERS

In the early 2000s, Putin's and Schröder's newcomer status at international meetings drove the two men together, according to Hans von Ploetz, a veteran German diplomat, and ambassador to Russia in 2002–5.[64] Putin's KGB training – fostering capability to home in on targeted individuals[65] – put Schröder in his sights from early on. 'They were both outsiders,' von Ploetz says. 'Everyone else spoke English, and they didn't. They both spoke German. They both came from humble backgrounds, they were brought up in harsh circumstances after the Second World War: Putin in the backstreets of Leningrad; Schröder, impoverished, in a village without a father, his mother working as a cleaning lady.'[66]

A long way removed from the aggressive and assured figure of the 2020s, on his first meeting with Schröder in 2000, 'Putin was so nervous that his cheek muscles were trembling,' according to the German diplomat assigned as note-taker for the meeting. 'After the dinner he sank with relief into the Chancellor's arms.'[67] In a similar vein, a leading German journalist in Russia who interviewed Putin for the heavyweight weekly *Die Zeit* in 2000 described him as 'shy' and 'modest'.[68]

Roderic Lyne, in 1987–90 deputy mission chief under Braithwaite at Britain's Moscow embassy before returning as ambassador in 2000–4, highlights Putin's rough origins: 'He was a small kid from a poor area in Leningrad and was being beaten up by the bigger kids. He was not particularly talented and not amazingly bright. So he did two things to get back at the big kids: learn judo and join the KGB.'[69]

The roughness never wore off. Barack Obama described him as 'projecting an almost satirical image of masculine vigor (Putin riding a horse with his shirt off, Putin playing hockey), all the while practicing a casual chauvinism and homophobia.'[70] Putin reminded Obama of 'the sorts of men who had once run the Chicago machine or Tammany Hall – rough, street smart, unsentimental characters who knew what they knew, never moved outside their narrow experiences, and who viewed patronage, bribery, shakedowns, fraud, and occasional violence as legitimate tools of the trade.'

The behavioural psychology of international summitry facilitated Schröder and Putin bonding. José Manuel Barroso, who met Putin twenty-five times during his ten years as president of the European Commission in 2004–14, describes the atmosphere of the summits Putin attended. 'Obama was a cool guy, the celebrity. Everyone wanted to go up to him and be seen with him. Merkel was very approachable. She always went round to say Hello to everybody and also to the staff.' In a remark testifying to the notorious *froideur* of their relationship, Barroso claims that Putin was the one person with whom no one else was particularly interested in engaging. 'Partly because he doesn't speak English, also because he's not very sociable. And also because Russia was not perceived to be as important as others in the room.'[71]

For all this, Putin understood how to cast a spell. Religious belief was an apt instrument of influence. Before they met face to face, George W.

Bush regarded Putin as 'one cold dude'.[72] Shortly after meeting Putin in 2001 in Slovenia on the first of what would be more than forty encounters in eight years, he famously said: 'I looked the man in the eye. I found him to be very straightforward and trustworthy . . . I was able to get a sense of his soul.'[73] Later, he wrote, 'Putin would give me reasons to revise my opinion'.[74] The 2001 remark was not popular among Bush's own entourage. Rice wrote, 'I visibly stiffened,' on hearing her boss's comment. 'We were never able to escape the perception that the President had naively trusted Putin and then been betrayed.'[75] Other interlocutors' accounts of their first encounters with Putin have been less flattering.[76]

Bush was well known as a born-again Christian. At the Slovenian meeting, Putin showed the American president a baptismal cross given by his mother which, he claimed, had been sanctified during a visit to the Holy Sepulchre church in Jerusalem and rescued from the flames of a dacha fire. Rice termed the tale 'rather syrupy . . . I never really knew what to make of this story . . . It's hard for me to imagine Putin, the former servant of atheistic communism, as a religious man.'[77]

Over the years, the nature of Putin's religious beliefs have become no less enigmatic. Speaking in 2024, Rice said she was uncertain whether 'like Josef Stalin, [Putin] uses the Church to show the Russian heritage [in his policies]' or whether 'he is, in an almost messianic sense, a believer'. In the light of Putin's later development, she revised her previous view that he may have invented the tale of the cross. 'We see how he relies on somewhat Rasputin-like religious figures. Maybe there's something more there.'[78]

With Trump back in the White House, the ploy with Rice's boss was repeated in the changed circumstances of 2025. Reporting on Trump's visit to Moscow in March 2025, Steve Witkoff, Trump's real-estate associate turned special envoy, recounted how Putin had told him that he had prayed for 'his friend' Trump after he was targeted in an assassination attempt during a campaign stop in Pennsylvania in July 2024. The Russian leader had an artist paint a portrait of Trump and gave it to the American president as a gift. Putin said that after the attack 'he went to his local church and met with his priest and prayed for the president . . . not because . . . he could become the president of the United States, but because he had a friendship with him, and he was praying for his friend.'[79]

Juncker, who first met Putin in 2001 as Luxembourg prime minister before becoming European Commission president, relates another episode illustrating Putin's desire to show off his apparent piety. The Russian leader held up Juncker in Moscow in 2005 by insisting that he visit Putin's private chapel in the Kremlin.[80]

Putin attempted a parallel tactic with Juncker's predecessor Barroso. On his first meeting with the new Commission chief, shortly after the former Portuguese prime minister switched to his European post in 2004, Putin launched an overblown ploy to use religion as a political lever. The Russian leader had built up a close relationship with Romano Prodi, Barroso's Italian predecessor. Since Barroso also came from a Catholic country, surely, Putin enquired, the same principles would apply? Another reason, Barroso says, why 'Putin believed he could have some kind of complicity with me' was his belief that he could rely on cross-border Christian solidarity to support Russia's conflict against Islamic separatists in Chechnya. But the manoeuvre backfired.

Putin asked me how many of 'us' – and by that he meant Christians – there were in the world. He thought that was a way of getting on good terms with me. In fact it had the opposite result. I don't like to see people use religion for political purposes. This was a sign of his cynicism. I cannot believe he was speaking with sincerity. As a former agent of the KGB, he did not appear likely to be leading the life of a good Christian.[81]

PETER THE ADMIRED

Jacques Chirac first met Putin at a dinner at the Élysée Palace in September 2000. The French president from 1995 to 2007 had a rocky initial relationship because of the war in Chechnya. Eventually, the relatively youthful Kremlin politician came to regard his French counterpart as an experienced source of advice.

According to Claude Blanchemaison, French ambassador to Moscow in 2000–3, 'Jacques Chirac lent himself to the game with good grace. They forged a relationship of trust and esteem which was consolidated over time.'[82] In 2019, Putin termed Chirac the western politician who had impressed him most: 'a true intellectual, a real professor, a very level-headed man as well as very interesting'.[83] In the same conversation, Putin stated that his most admired leader was Peter the Great, the creator of Greater Russia. 'He will live as long as his cause is alive.'

When Putin appeared for the first time at an international summit, at the Okinawa Group of Eight session in Japan in July 2000, Lamberto Dini, Italy's foreign minister in 1996–2001 (and former prime minister), says, 'He appeared capable and knowledgeable. He was highly respected.'[84] Putin – who impressed Dini by his mastery of detail without need for briefing documents[85] – gained many continental Europeans' sympathy for his resistance to Ukraine's NATO membership. 'Bringing Georgia and Ukraine into NATO had been the US policy since the time of [Bill] Clinton,' Dini says. 'A solid NATO flank on Russia's western border, from the Baltics to the Caucasus republics. You can understand that this looks like encirclement.'

Michel Camdessus, the French monetary technocrat who led the International Monetary Fund in 1987–2000, showed similar approval for Putin's technocratic skills. He came across Putin on the second day of the G8 summit at Evian, France, in June 2003, where Camdessus had a mandate to represent Africa.[86] 'I went for a stroll in the large ornate garden next to the lake. I found myself passing the time with Putin. He came up to me, saying he recognised me as the head of the IMF. We spoke for 40 minutes. Putin showed himself unexpectedly expert in conversing on the politics and economics of world gas markets.'[87]

Tony Blair, British prime minister between 1997 and 2007, was immediately struck by Putin's stature as a 'Russian patriot'.[88] As late as 2010, Blair reflected, in somewhat maudlin fashion, on their first meeting, in St Petersburg in March 2000. 'We were the same age and seemed to share the same outlook . . . I never lost that initial feeling for him or the thought that had circumstances transpired or conspired differently, the relationship might have prospered.'[89]

Blair was renowned for his close relationship with the US; in July 2002 he wrote to George W. Bush (over Iraq policy), 'I will be with you, whatever.'[90] Yet Blair's declared empathy with Putin was based partly on their shared belief that, in world politics, America was overplaying its hand. 'Vladimir later came to believe that the Americans did not give him his due place. Worse, he saw them as circling Russia with western-supporting democracies who were going to be hostile to Russian interests. Blair realised that Russian resentment could end up reverberating against the West. 'I realised then how deep was his feeling that Russia had just been ignored by the US and his determination that they should see it eventually as a mistake. The difficulty was that I half agreed with him about the unilateralism.'[91]

Jonathan Powell, Blair's chief of staff, who returned to the international front line in 2024 when Starmer appointed him Britain's national defence adviser, underlines the scale of the Blair–Putin fluctuations:

> After the erratic figure of Yeltsin, Putin appeared a chance for a new start, a moderniser. The falling out started in 2003 when he threw in his lot with Schröder and Chirac over the Iraq war. It became obvious that power was going to his head. He became progressively more autocratic and corrupt. The final meeting was when Blair and I met Putin alone, apart from interpreters, at the Heiligendamm summit [northern Germany] in 2007. Blair told him exactly what he thought of him. This was the last time they met.[92]

UNWILLING CHARACTER WITNESS

Putin's personality mix of technocracy, tenacity and thuggery has been on near-constant display to Merkel. Germany's first female chancellor is the western leader with the longest continuous exposure to the Russian president – a total of twenty years, of which sixteen were during her time as leader.

When Merkel, then leader of the Opposition as head of the Christian Democratic Union, encountered Putin for their first meeting in the Kremlin, in 2002, Putin fixed her with a long steely gaze to test her resilience.[93] Her proficiency in Russian (which she learned to a high standard at school, but now tends to play down), Putin's knowledge of German, and the sheer length of their relationship make Merkel, potentially, a superior character witness. But she is also a supremely unwilling one.

Merkel's autobiography contains 120 references to Putin, more than Bush, Obama and Macron combined. She dutifully recounts meeting dates, mealtime arrangements[94] and aeroplane movements – but avoids imparting any but the most banal insights on the Russian president's psychological make-up or geopolitical objectives.[95]

Putin's frequent conversations with Merkel, by telephone and in person, would normally start in German, a language in which Putin combines the Saxon accent of his Dresden days with the soft tonality of the secret policeman.[96] He would switch to Russian for more complicated passages.[97] Merkel is able, when she wishes, to modify her sphinx-like approach to Putin, on condition that she does not give too much away. In line with this innate caution, Merkel has fashioned a well-honed and somewhat contrived story of how the Russian leader brought his pet labrador in an attempt to throw her off balance in front of media representatives. This was early in her chancellorship, on her trip in January 2007 to see him at the leadership's resort residence of Sochi on the Black Sea.[98]

Merkel's security adviser, Christoph Heusgen, in what would appear an unwise move for dealing with an ex-KGB officer, had earlier told Putin's foreign-policy adviser, Sergei Prikhodko, about Merkel's fear of dogs. Koni the labrador duly turned up in Sochi, arriving at the same time as Merkel as she waited for Putin before a group of journalists. 'I could tell from Putin's facial expression that he was enjoying the situation,' Merkel records. 'Did he just want to see how someone reacts under pressure? Was it a little demonstration of power?'[99] Merkel says she reflected phlegmatically (to herself): 'Never complain, never explain.' In fact, she complains rather a lot. In her book Merkel highlights Putin's 'canine power play' as a sign of his readiness to 'disrespect others'.[100] Her adviser Heusgen says Putin was practising 'KGB-style intimidation tactics' but he 'missed his objective', since Merkel 'showed no reaction and told the dog that he should devote his attention to the journalists'.[101]

Gavin Barwell was chief of staff to Britain's prime minister Theresa May, who developed a constructive relationship with Merkel during May's three-year tenure.[102] Barwell says, 'Merkel understood the nature of Putin. She liked to tell the story of how Putin knew that she didn't like dogs, and yet he famously brought his black labrador to one important meeting to unsettle her.'[103] The sheer regularity of Merkel's trademark labrador allusions may suggest that she has overplayed the story to divert attention from other more significant elements in her Putin relationship.

Horst Teltschik – a tousle-haired foreign-policy expert who became Helmut Kohl's all-purpose foreign-policy and security adviser, and later chaired the Munich Security Conference – is no big fan of the former chancellor. He emphasises: 'Merkel and Putin have had numerous conversations, but we know very little in any concrete way about what went on between them.' Teltschik came across Koni when meeting Putin in Sochi in February 2007, a month after the Merkel encounter, preparing for what would become a notorious Putin speech berating the US and the West at the Munich conference later that month. 'The dog was not threatening, it was well behaved. It wanted to be stroked.'[104] Of Putin, he says: 'He has changed greatly over the last 10 to 15 years. It's like the difference between day and night. In Sochi, I got to know him as a friendly person. He was laughing and joking. In the evening they produced a Russian band that played for us.'

Beyond canine manoeuvres and orchestrated bonhomie, Putin follows long-standing preoccupations in trying to draw in Europe to counter a world overly geared towards America. As late as June 2021, in a grandiloquent essay commemorating the eightieth anniversary of Germany's invasion of Russia in the Second World War, Putin praised Europeans' attempts to move on from the 'tragedies of the first half of the last century' by sealing economic accords aimed at 'constructive interdependence'.

He hailed German industrialists as 'pioneers' in the 1970 deal to supply pipes for importing Russian gas. He complained that the Europeans had 'forgotten' verbal assurances on not expanding NATO. And they had supported the US in the 'unconstitutional armed coup' in Ukraine in 2014 that ousted Viktor Yanukovich, the pro-Russian president. Just eight months before the invasion of Ukraine, Putin mapped out a plan for 'a comprehensive partnership with Europe . . . Our common and incontestable goal is the security of the continent without dividing lines, and a single area for equal cooperation and collective development.'[105]

The historical continuity was incontestable – and not only the parallels to the chaotic period thirty years previously. In April 1991, seventeen months after the Wall fell, Yuli Kvitsinsky, deputy minister for foreign affairs under Gorbachev and a former high-profile ambassador to West Germany, already well known for his role in Soviet–US arms negotiations,[106] addressed a conference in Prague on the future of

European security. Declaring opposition to a central tenet of western policies, Kvitsinsky questioned whether western European integration 'promotes or inhibits the emergence of a new common European home'.

In forthright tones, he laid down the Kremlin's thinking. The Cold War was thought to be over. But this Soviet diplomat, for one, believed a new one was about to begin. What he called 'a new European differentiation' would 'hamper the continent's political and creative potential . . . and in the long run, lead to a new division of this continent, to rivalry and confrontation between its parts'.[107]

Kvitsinsky extended the phraseology already developed by Gorbachev in a speech in the same city four years earlier. The Soviet leader outlined his support for a 'common European home' resisting 'accumulation of military arsenals in Europe, against everything that is the source of the threat of war'.[108]

Gorbachev's concept was framed with two linked objectives: to persuade the West Germans to turn away from full reliance on the American nuclear umbrella, and to show that the Soviet Union could act as a countervailing force to President Bush's vision of a 'Europe whole and free'.[109] Gorbachev's line followed a pattern set by Leonid Brezhnev, Soviet leader between 1964 and 1982 – a man whose legacy (along with his family's collection of privileges and honours) Gorbachev otherwise systematically dismantled.

Brezhnev's final visit in 1981 (a year before he died) to Helmut Schmidt in Bonn was a time of tension over US plans to station new medium-range nuclear missiles in Europe to counter an earlier Soviet missile build-up. In a pathos-ridden reference to the Russo-German past, Brezhnev told Schmidt: 'We were neighbours before America was discovered.' He added a doomsday touch, never far below the surface in German–Russian dialogue. Everything possible had to be done, the Soviet leader proclaimed, 'to save our common home – Europe – from new, still more fearsome tragedies'.[110]

Nearly half a century has passed between Brezhnev's final journey to Germany and the discourse of the Russo-Ukrainian war. Yet, word for word, the language of the Soviet general secretary in 1981 could well have been uttered by the Russian president in 2025.

ENERGY AND TECHNOLOGY TO THE FORE

More than a decade before Brezhnev's Bonn farewell, the path towards the Putin upheavals was laid down in the late 1960s as West Germany sought to overturn a legacy of blood and bitterness. If war and its aftermath have supplied the psychological backcloth, energy and technology have been the common denominators in modern Russia's most important western relationship.[111]

The breakthrough came with a political thaw. The key actor was Willy Brandt, who with good reason (despite the briefness of his five-year rule) can be regarded as Germany's second most consequential post-Second World War chancellor after Konrad Adenauer. Brandt provided the political and emotional cement that, a decade and a half after his chancellorship, helped bond together again, under Helmut Kohl, the two elements of war-sundered Germany.

Brandt supplied, a day after the Wall fell in November 1989, a phrase that has become an iconic slogan of German unity:[112] 'What belongs together grows together.'[113] The trail to that destination started in Moscow.

Following parliamentary elections in September 1969, Brandt, who had been foreign minister in the previous grand coalition between the CDU and SPD, became West Germany's first Social Democratic chancellor. The new leader's remarkable career was forged during his time as an émigré in Norway, a Second World War fugitive from Nazi Germany. He became mayor of Berlin during one of the most tense periods of the Cold War, coinciding with the building of the Wall dividing the city in 1961. In August 1970, Brandt visited Moscow to sign a treaty that would seal his name as the architect of *Ostpolitik* – normalising his country's relations with the Soviet Union and eastern Europe.

The treaty, for several years the focus of intense East–West diplomatic exchanges as well as fierce political disagreements in Bonn, attempted to draw Germany and the Soviet Union away from the oppressive history of Hitler's 1941 invasion. By forging rapprochement with the Soviet bloc, the treaty simultaneously enshrined West Germany's place in the western alliance and opened it to the East. This astute combination laid the foundations for the eventual unification of the two Germanys twenty years later. It also opened the way to deepened technology, trade and energy ties between Germany and Russia that became a major component in the rise and fall of the political relationship under Putin.

Ruhrgas, the giant German energy conglomerate, was designated as the Soviet Union's German gas partner. Egon Bahr, state secretary in the chancellery, Brandt's friend and master strategist on East–West relations, wrote in an internal memorandum that the Soviet Union believed Ruhrgas had an ideal position as a monopoly 'susceptible to external influence'. Bahr's phrase 'Wandel durch Annäherung' – 'change through rapprochement' – marked the opening stage on a long-term route to reunification by crafting agreements with East Germany that recognised the postwar status.[114]

America was watchful. Henry Kissinger, the US national security adviser – a German national born in Bavaria in 1923, who emigrated to the US in 1938 as a Jewish refugee fleeing Nazi persecution – was in a masterful position to analyse the double-edged repercussions of *Ostpolitik*. As he wrote to President Nixon in February 1970, 'Although Brandt has stressed that his Western policy has priority, German attention is heavily focused on the East.' Kissinger outlined American and allied qualms about German motives, noting 'suspicion or fear that eastern policy is acquiring its own momentum and will lead Brandt into dangerous concessions'.[115]

While even his critics credited Brandt with 'sincerity and wisdom', some of his advisers such as Bahr were 'deeply mistrusted', Kissinger wrote. The Germans might, in future, face 'agonizing choices' between East and West. Brandt and his key associates such as Schmidt, defence minister (and future chancellor), saw themselves as conducting a 'responsible policy of reconciliation and normalisation with the East'. But, according to Kissinger, they faced a twofold problem: 'to control a process, which, if it results in failure, could jeopardize their political lives, and if it succeeds could create a momentum that may shake Germany's domestic stability and unhinge its international position.'[116]

In the UK, the mood was more positive. Underpinned by fellow-feeling between Brandt and Edward Heath, Britain's Conservative prime minister, Britain – on the threshold of joining the European Economic Community in 1973 – accorded *Ostpolitik* full support. 'One short-term effect . . . should be to ensure that Herr Brandt remains strongly interested in Western European integration,' wrote Roger Jackling, British ambassador to West Germany, in a closely printed eight-page note in June 1970.[117] 'Herr Brandt has always emphasised that the Federal Republic can only safely seek an opening to the East if it keeps its feet firmly embedded in NATO and the European Communities.' A classic diplomatic quid pro quo was shaping up: German backing for the UK's EEC accession was of paramount importance. The upshot was, the ambassador wrote, that West Germany would remain fully interested in western Europe 'at a time when we [the British] most need their support'. Jackling believed the treaty could pave the way to eventual reunification.

> A united western Europe should not only be attractive enough to the West Germans to retain their full participation but should also be stable enough to absorb the accession of a second German state should that ever prove possible. A weak and divided western Europe would not only be less able to bring about such a change but would also be hard put to contain it once achieved.

France, on the other hand, made little secret of its qualms. 'The French are perplexed and uneasy about the treaty,' according to a despatch from the British embassy in Paris.[118] 'Distrust of rapprochement between Germany and Russia has deep historical roots in France.' Despite official approval for the treaties, the German embassy in Paris wrote of the French government's 'worries beneath the surface' over a weakening of French status as a Second World War victor power with joint responsibility for Germany and Berlin.[119] Less than a month before the treaty was signed, Maurice Schumann, the French foreign minister, made clear he was 'very worried' that the Soviet Union was using the leverage of the new treaty to gain concessions that would undermine the power of the four wartime allies over Berlin.[120]

Leverage was, for the Soviet Union, an instrument that could bring great advantage. Alexei Kosygin, the Soviet prime minister, emphasised the rewards to Brandt in Moscow in August 1970: 'Naturally we do not wish to separate you from your western allies. But we wish to put our relationship onto a new footing . . . Cooperation in science, economics and technology holds great perspectives . . . Our territory and our mineral deposits are so enormous that we will be able to satisfy the needs of the whole of Europe.'[121]

In his reply, Brandt underlined the familiar centrepiece of German state relations: Germany could gain advantage from an improved relationship with the Soviet Union only if it remained firmly anchored in the western alliance. This was a principle that he had inherited from Adenauer. Even if he had wished to do so (which is doubtful), he could not have given it up, in view of the West's misgivings about Germany's new eastwards shift.[122]

In the afternoon, after the treaty signing, Leonid Brezhnev, the Communist party chief, received Brandt for a four-hour audience. It was time to broach directly some longer-term Soviet goals. This was less a conversation, more an exchange of monologues[123] – and a transparent attempt to tempt Brandt away from the West. Citing de Gaulle's espousal of French independence from the US within NATO, Brezhnev urged the Germans to follow a similar approach. 'The more independence a state has in its foreign policy, particularly with regard to the Soviet Union, and the more it can represent its own interests in Europe and the world, the broader will be the possibilities for expanding cooperation between our states.'[124]

Brezhnev considered it 'completely abnormal' that the Federal Republic should be hampered in its ability to make 'fundamental decisions' on policies towards the East. 'The Federal Republic should take the place in the world that corresponds to its economic and technical position.'[125]

With supreme disingenuousness, Brezhnev denied having 'underhand plans' for the Germans 'to develop a relationship with us at the cost of its relations with other countries, particularly the US'. But the thrust of his arguments was clear. 'The alleged Communist danger from the East is a propagandistic concept, which serves certain interests, certainly not the interests of peace and cooperation above all between our two countries as the biggest and most important states in Europe.' Warming to his theme, Brezhnev complained – in terms that would be familiar to Putin-watchers fifty years later – about America's bid to 'immortalise its world influence'. The US had 'spread its tentacles' in Europe and Asia. 'I can imagine that your people and your party are seeking ways of freeing yourselves from this yoke.'

CHAOTIC AND MIGHTY RUSSIANS

The 1970 gas-for-pipes deals launched by Brandt in Moscow set down a marker for a long journey. At every stage, western leaders displayed contradictory emotions. Frequent dismay that Russia was slipping backwards, politically and economically, was combined with affirmations that, with a little more help from its friends and a modicum of goodwill and good management, the chaotic and mighty Russians might build prosperity and fraternity with their rich yet fearful western neighbours.

Towards the Russians, Europe and the US offered technology, credit and hope. In exchanges with each other, the western countries voiced a mix of apprehension that the Russians could, once again, slip back towards enmity, coupled with worries that one particular state in their own grouping – Germany – was trying just a little too hard to win Moscow's favour. With an intensity proportionate to the degree of suspicion they provoked, the Germans assured their allies that such suppositions were completely unfounded.

Conspiracy theories flourished. The accession in 1985 of a relatively youthful and reformist Mikhail Gorbachev to the Soviet leadership – after a hiatus caused by the successive deaths of three elderly party chiefs – Brezhnev, Yuri Andropov and Konstantin Chernenko – created opportunities as well as anxiety that Germany would succumb to blandishments from the East. At a summit meeting in Reykjavik in October 1986, Gorbachev and President Ronald Reagan came close to agreeing a ban on all nuclear weapons – a step that would have been generally popular in Germany but would have uprooted the prime tenets of European defence policy.

Shortly afterwards, Kohl gave a notable interview to the US magazine *Newsweek*. In a bid to show domestic and international opinion he was taking a hard-headed line on the new Soviet leader, he compared Gorbachev's aptitude for public relations with the policies espoused by Josef Goebbels, Hitler's propaganda chief.[126]

The explicit wording of the published interview was a first-order diplomatic gaffe. Friedhelm Ost, the chancellor's breezily lackadaisical official spokesman, unthinkingly cleared for publication a passage from Kohl's freewheeling conversation which was bound to cause the Russians serious offence. With equivalent absurdity, Yuli

Kvitsinsky, Soviet ambassador in Bonn, blamed what was evidently largely an act of German public relations incompetence on Machiavellian action by the Americans, who, he wrote later, were 'obviously not happy with the pace of developments in Soviet–German relations'.[127]

Only days previously, Hans-Dietrich Genscher, Kohl's relentlessly well-travelled foreign minister, had been in Moscow proclaiming the advantages of 'growing interdependence' between the two economies and offering German help in Soviet modernisation.[128] *Newsweek* tape-recorded Kohl's exchanges with its journalists in Bonn, so the published version was difficult to refute. Kohl admitted later he had been 'stupid' to mention Gorbachev and Goebbels in the same breath.[129] Kvitsinsky wanted to register a formal complaint in a personal meeting with Kohl, but had to be palmed off with Wolfgang Schäuble, Kohl's chancellery minister, to whom he handed a protest note.[130]

The ambassador demanded formal withdrawal of the assertions. Horst Teltschik, the foreign policy expert who had worked with Kohl for a decade before he became chancellor, was present at the meeting. Later Kohl's right-hand man during the frenetic period of German unification, Teltschik fulfilled a combination of roles: coordinator, political sounding board, and diplomatic go-between with foreign governments. The broad array of tasks and his personal closeness to the chancellor made Teltschik a perennial rival to Genscher, the foreign minister – and scuppered Teltschik's well-founded desire to become defence minister after the 1990 elections,[131] a job for which he was eminently well qualified.

In 1986, as Schäuble's deputy in the chancellor's office, Teltschik recorded for posterity the uncompromising Soviet message. Kohl had to formally distance himself from the interview. Otherwise, 'normal relations [with the Soviet Union] would be impossible'.[132]

Hermann von Richthofen, political director of the German foreign office, on an official visit to Moscow the next day, received the stiffest of reprimands from Anatoly Kovalev, first deputy Soviet foreign minister, who said trust had been 'severely damaged' and demanded that Kohl should apologise publicly. Explaining that the wounding remark had so far been kept out of Moscow's state-controlled media, Kovalev asked: 'Can you imagine how our people would react if we told them what the chancellor told *Newsweek*, what indignation that would provoke, and how that would affect bilateral relations?'[133]

Reporting back to Bonn, von Richthofen termed the Soviet démarche 'sharp' and 'provocative'.[134] The Russians were irritated that news about the interview had permeated into the Soviet Union through the German radio station Deutsche Welle as well as Voice of America. The German station had been criticised only weeks earlier for 'broadcasting lies and insults' and practising 'psychological warfare' against the Russians. 'The misdeeds of the Third Reich have not been forgotten, also by younger Soviet politicians,' von Richthofen told his ministry. 'We are skating on thin ice.'

Intensive diplomatic repair work by Genscher, Teltschik[135] and Richard von Weizsäcker, the German president, helped lower the temperature and heal the wounds. Kohl won the January 1987 elections. He told Mitterrand in March 1987 he regarded Gorbachev with 'sceptical sympathy'. Voicing sentiments from his *Newsweek* interview, Kohl added, 'Up to now we have words not actions. He doesn't want a democratic state, as many believe, but communism that works efficiently.'[136]

Nuclear arms matters were paramount. The French president – who earlier in the 1980s had supported deploying intermediate-range nuclear missiles in Germany to force the Soviet Union into disarmament – expounded his support for the so called 'zero option'. Both NATO and the Warsaw Pact should scrap intermediate-range weapons. Nuclear security in Europe, he told Kohl, should be based solely on strategic missiles aimed at the Soviet Union, not tactical weapons that would hit Germany and neighbouring states. This echoed a core belief of the disarmament movement on both sides of the East–West German divide: 'The shorter the range, the deader the Germans' became a slogan in both German states.[137]

In his conversation with the West German chancellor, Mitterrand dwelled on parallels with past wars that would feature in his language during the coming years of unification negotiations – and would return with a vengeance during the 2020s preoccupations with Russia and Ukraine. War in Europe would no longer resemble 1914, he told Kohl. In the event of a Soviet invasion of West Germany, 'French tactical nuclear missiles would not fly very far. They would land in Germany.

Should I, to save Germany, destroy Hamburg and then expect gratitude from the Germans?'[138]

Beyond these dystopian reflections lay cautious hopes of peaceful change. A German foreign-office analysis, prepared for a new round of East–West diplomacy, praised Gorbachev's 'common European home' as a 'significantly more subtle strategy than in the past', but warned that the Soviet Union had not changed its underlying objective: a European system of 'security and cooperation excluding the US and favouring a Soviet leadership role'.[139]

By the time that Kohl travelled to Moscow in October 1988 for his first official visit to the new Soviet leader, references to the Goebbels affair were no longer part of diplomatic discourse. But the frosty atmosphere of Gorbachev's initial reception – when his German visitor was made to walk the length of the reception hall to meet his Soviet host – left no doubt in onlookers' minds that the snub had not been forgotten.[140]

In a lengthy two-part pre-visit interview in Moscow with the German news magazine *Der Spiegel*, Gorbachev spelled out his rejection of a unified Germany in categorical terms. 'Any attempt to blur the boundaries between the two sovereign German states, let alone to indulge in power play, would be unacceptable if not catastrophic. In this question there must be full clarity.[141]

In a revealing exchange with the magazine's founder and publisher Rudolf Augstein, Gorbachev placed responsibility for the division of Germany with the western wartime allies rather than the Soviet Union, which favoured a single 'anti-fascist' state. In terms that were repeated almost word for word in Putin's anti-western Munich Security Conference diatribe of February 2007, he railed against a US-dominated international order. 'The times have passed when one country or a group of strong and powerful states can force their views on the rest of the world, sometimes in quite brutal fashion.'[142] He rejected as a sign of western condescension suggestions of a form of 'Marshall Plan' for the Soviet Union. This indicated, he said, a 'retreat into old arrogance in which the Soviet economic train needs the capitalist locomotive to get over the mountain'.[143]

At the Kremlin banquet at the end of the first day, Kohl praised Gorbachev's concept of 'a common European home . . . The house would need many doors and windows, and all residents had to be able to go in and out at will.'[144] But the common home manifestly did not encompass German unity – at least, not yet. Division was 'unnatural', Kohl said, but it could be healed 'only with the approval of the powers responsible for Germany as a whole'. Gorbachev rammed home the point, paraphrasing lines from Goethe: history had divided Germany – and any attempt to change the situation with 'unrealistic policies' would be 'unpredictable even dangerous'.[145]

Although nowhere near anyone's official agenda, overcoming German division was rapidly moving closer to the surface. Throughout 1988 and into 1989, a combination of Gorbachev's attempts to reform the Soviet system and East Germany's refusal to follow suit had provoked East German street demonstrations and further efforts by many ordinary citizens to leave for the West. The Soviet leader was anything but sure-footed.

Anatoly Chernyaev, one of his closest advisers, wrote in May 1989, 'Inside me, depression and alarm are growing, the sense of crisis of the Gorbachevian idea. He is prepared to go far. But what does it mean? His favourite catchword is "unpredictability". And most likely we will come to a collapse of the state and something like chaos.'[146]

There was, indeed, a sense of inevitability about the economic failings eroding the Soviet state. One of Britan's best-regarded and most versatile diplomats is John Kerr, who early in his career worked at the Moscow embassy in 1967–70 (where among other things he acted as interpreter for Prime Minister Harold Wilson).

After spells on nuclear planning[147] and secondment to the Treasury, Kerr ended up in quick succession as Britain's representative to the European Union, ambassador to the US, head of the Foreign Office and master negotiator of European treaties. Kerr recalls writing a 'rather pompous' missive from Moscow when he left in 1970, making three predictions. One turned out correct.

The centrally planned Soviet economy wasn't working. Most Gosplan [state planning commission] statistics were misleading. Cumulated at national level, the declared size of the Soviet economy, and the growth rates achieved, seemed implausible, though accepted by the IMF and OECD. The IMF at the time showed the East

German economy as larger than ours [the UK]. I thought it all a house of cards. I didn't think the Soviet economy could for ever be protected from market forces, and I predicted that, once exposed to them, it would collapse.[148]

Very few, though, could foretell the speed with which the cards would come tumbling down.

GERMAN UNITY: POSSIBILITY, OPPORTUNITY, REALITY

Internally, his state was fraying; externally, the Soviet leader was enjoying worldwide attention and acclaim.[149] A well-received visit to West Germany in June 1989 prompted a further outpouring of 'Gorbymania'. 'Nothing is permanent under the Moon,' the Soviet leader told a press conference at the end of his four-day stay. 'The Wall could disappear when the preconditions which brought it about cease to exist.'[150] An exodus of East Germans to the West (mainly via other East European countries) ushered in events that triggered the collapse of the Soviet Union and, a decade later, the arrival of Putin. Developments in the US, the Soviet Union and the two German states brought circumstances where German unification – desired by very few in the international community, and feared by many – became first possibility, then opportunity, then reality.

The East German economy was crumbling under the burden of 'spiralling western loans, interest rate costs and new credits' raised to pay off debt-service costs rather than to fund investment.[151] Compared with the Americans and Soviets, France and Britain – the other two wartime victor powers with formal legal responsibilities for Germany – were minor players: emotionally and politically ill-disposed towards a united Germany, with roles that flowed and (mostly) ebbed as the drama unfolded.

Having unleashed the Second World War, Germany had been extinguished in its aftermath. Dismantling the German state had brought Europe apparent stability yet at the same time prompted new tensions which, unless resolved, might unleash a third world war. The equation determining the fate of Europe's pivotal nation was governed by intertwined factors. Germany's fission in 1949 had been a product of worsening US–Soviet relations. So détente, when it came, was almost certain to weaken the forces of division.[152] And economics – expressed as the relative attractiveness and dynamism of the competing systems of East and West Germany – was likely to exert a supreme influence.

In a sentiment pithily expressed by Otto Reinhold, East Germany's chief ideologue, a retreat of Marxism–Leninism across the Soviet empire would generate greatly different consequences in different countries. It would leave Poland and Czechoslovakia under a different regime, but still as individual states. In East Germany, under a gerontocratic leadership whose principal ideology had become contemptuously dubbed 'Marxism–Senilism',[153] the ending of the state system would have far bigger consequences. It would redraw the map of Europe and resurrect a united Germany.[154]

The German equilibrium was fragile; there was scant enthusiasm to test what would happen if it ended. Ronald Reagan in 1987, on a West Berlin visit whose wisdom was strongly doubted by Kohl and his advisers, had stood in front of the Brandenburg Gate and publicly called on Gorbachev to 'tear down this Wall'. But this was stage management designed to lambast the 'evil empire', as Reagan labelled the Soviet Union, rather than to provoke operational change.[155] Reagan's deputy George H.W. Bush, who became his successor in January 1989, set down a policy that, although still fundamentally cautious about Gorbachev, took a more activist line.

Brent Scowcroft, Bush's national security adviser, a former associate of Kissinger, wrote to the president in March 1989, 'Today the top priority for American foreign policy in Europe should be the fate of the Federal Republic of Germany.'[156] Scowcroft recommended that the US goal in Europe should be to overcome division through acceptance of common democratic values. The concept of a 'commonwealth of free nations' was offered as an alternative to Gorbachev's 'common European home'. The internal discussions in Washington were played out against the background of forceful Soviet moves on reducing conventional armaments in Europe, crystallised at a ministerial meeting on European security in Vienna in March 1989.[157]

Returning from the gathering, Bush's secretary of state, Jim Baker, urged the president to 'get off the dime' and move ahead fast in conventional arms control to prevent Gorbachev gaining the upper hand over

European and German public opinion.[158] Baker's penchant for 'activism' itself led Bush to 'take the competition to Gorbachev's "end zone" in Eastern Europe'.[159] This led to a fateful letter from Bush to Kohl in May 1989 outlining a 'historic chance of transforming East–West relations'. The letter stated that the past forty years had been spent on a Soviet containment strategy; a new policy was now needed to bring about a deep-seated shift in Soviet institutions and armed forces.[160]

The tone in Bonn was, initially, much less forceful. But as East Germany's political and economic fragility became steadily more apparent, the strain of emigration pressures intensified. At first cautiously and then at speed, Kohl cast off the standard caution of Germany's *Ostpolitik* and moved to greater activism directly encouraging the fusion of the two German states. Internally and externally, East Germany was being undermined. A key factor strengthening Kohl's hand was the support, both overt and tacit, of the Bush administration. Yet German unification was not a popular concept, either in Germany or abroad. The word 'reunification' or *Wiedervereinigung* had semi-revanchist overtones. It implied unifying the state in the still formally legal borders of 1937, including large slices of Germany's historical eastern lands that had been granted to Poland in the 1945 settlement. Kohl's preferred phrase was 'Vollendung der staatlichen Einheit' – 'fulfilling state unity' – an expression that could be interpreted as a series of political steps rather than a territorial claim.[161]

Kohl was fully aware that warming Soviet–American relations would have consequences for Germany. Highlighting the relaxed mood at the Soviet leader's inaugural visit to Washington,[162] he pointed out during a two-hour interview in the chancellor's office in February 1989: 'When Mr Gorbachev is in the White House, and when they sing with President Reagan songs in the evening there together like "Moscow nights", people ask themselves whether the threat is the same.' But for a long period he was disinclined to show any enthusiasm for a rapid break with the status quo. He affirmed that unification could take place only over a lengthy period as part of a growing together of Europe. And he ruled out any question of an 'Anschluss' of the German Democratic Republic to West Germany.[163] Only twenty months later, through a mechanism that took place via Article 23 of the Federal Republic's Basic Law (constitution), that was exactly what happened.

Speculation and sensitivity about rapprochement between the two Germanys demanded many exercises of diplomatic contortion. Vernon 'Dick' Walters, a long-time soldier-diplomat and CIA veteran who had served in trouble spots all over the world, started broadcasting that German unification was imminent soon after he arrived in Bonn as US ambassador in April 1989. Teltschik, Kohl's national security adviser, was well aware that American thinking on unification 'was far ahead of the Germans at this time'.[164]

Both Teltschik and Walters earned the wrath of their respective bosses by pushing ahead on the issue with what appeared like unseemly emphasis. Baker and senior State Department officials believed Walters's claims were preposterous. 'Baker believed that the Bush administration, which had tied its Soviet policy to Gorbachev, needed to help its Soviet partner in his struggle with conservatives and the military high command that opposed German unification.'[165] Baker admonished Walters for his statements and cut him out of further diplomatic dealings.[166]

Teltschik generated a similar reaction when in July 1989 he told a Bonn newspaper that the 'German question' was moving back on to the agenda, implying that the Bonn government was far more active in preparing for reunification than was actually the case. This sparked irritation not only in the chancellery but also from Kohl's Free Democratic Party (FDP) coalition partners and the SPD Opposition.[167] His competitor Genscher, one of the FDP leaders, called upon the chancellor to sack his foreign-policy aide. Teltschik was forced to issue a statement to calm the controversy. Kohl's view was that patience would bring its own reward. 'Time is working for us.'[168]

On 4 October 1989, Gorbachev was invited to East Germany by its beleaguered leader, Erich Honecker, for celebrations to mark the state's fortieth anniversary. As soon as Gorbachev landed in East Berlin, he realised how quickly time was running out. On the eve of Gorbachev's departure, Britain's ambassador Braithwaite wrote from Moscow: 'Gorbachev's problem is now to control the forces he has unleashed. I do not think the Russians know how to do that.'

Gorbachev goes to the GDR without a coherent policy. His overriding need for stability there conflicts with forces he himself has generated. While he shuts his eyes and hopes that the German question will go away, events on the ground are overtaking him . . . Far, far down the road, the Russians see a solution, or rather an elision, in the golden age of a Common Europe Home: but it must not be built as a German Schloss. In its vague and unrealistic obscurity, this matches the Federal German hope that the German problem can somehow be made to go away through 'European Union'.[169]

Gorbachev wrote later: 'I sensed something was wrong when we were driving into Berlin from Schönefeld airport. Along almost the entire route to the residence there were solid rows of young people chanting "Gorbachev! Gorbachev!" – even though Honecker was sitting right next to me.'[170] In the evening he was feted by a march-past of youth activists, with Honecker standing glumly by.[171] Reacting to the cries of 'Gorbi! Gorbi!', Günter Mittag, the East German economics chief, known principally for industrial incompetence and a penchant for manipulating statistics, muttered, 'A scandal. They should have organised it better.'[172] Mieczyslaw Rakowski, a former Polish prime minister, among the East bloc dignitaries watching the torchlit parade, told the Soviet leader: 'Do you understand these slogans they are shouting? They're demanding, "Gorbachev, save us once more!" These are party activists! This is the end!'

Just before leaving East Berlin, Gorbachev set what effectively became an epitaph for the East German state with a withering remark to the country's leadership: 'Life publishes harshly those who are left behind.'[173] The weekend of commemorations deteriorated into widespread protests, leading to imprisonment of hundreds of demonstrators.

In mid-October, as a reaction to the fortieth-anniversary debacle, Egon Krenz, a former East German Communist youth leader, was appointed to replace the ageing and plainly incompetent Honecker. A shambling fifty-two-year-old of no evident proficiency, Krenz was an unlikely promoter of a fresh start. East Germans nicknamed him 'horse face' and 'the teeth'.[174] One of his first acts was necessary but not sufficient – promising that East Germany would stop shooting people trying to cross the border.

On 1 November, Krenz travelled to Moscow to unveil to Gorbachev the full extent of his country's economic malaise. According to the East

German note-taker, he described his predecessor in derisive tones: 'Comrade Erich Honecker obviously considered himself No. 1 in socialism, if not in the world. He no longer had any idea of what was happening.'[175] Krenz presented dire economic data; he may have deliberately exaggerated East Germany's plight as a means of attracting additional credits from both East and West.[176] If that was the case, the ploy misfired. Gorbachev weas shocked by Krenz's numbers for foreign borrowing ($26.5 billion) and deficits. 'The GDR needed new loans to pay off old debts.'

According to the transcript. 'Gorbachev asked whether these numbers were exact. He had not imagined the situation to be so precarious.' Gorbachev advised Krenz to tell the East Germans that 'they had lived beyond their means'. He cited the international unpopularity of German unification. But he failed to acknowledge the evident conclusion: domestic economic and political pressures driving the two Germanys together would substantially outweigh resistance from countries like the UK and France.

Gorbachev told Krenz of his latest talks with Thatcher, Mitterrand, Polish leader Wojciech Jaruzelski and Giulio Andreotti, the Italian prime minister. 'They all viewed the question of German unity as extremely explosive . . . Nor did they want the Warsaw Pact and NATO to dissolve . . . The balance of power in Europe should not be disturbed, since nobody knew what the repercussions would be.'[177]

With barely concealed desperation, Gorbachev on 6 November told Moscow's ambassador in East Germany, 'Our people will never forgive us if we lose the GDR.'[178] But that was exactly what was happening.

The Berlin Wall fell on 9 November. An edifice erected in infamy collapsed in ignominy.[179]

This was not an explosive demolition. The Wall was ground down by protest, decay and the realisation that the masters it served were no longer in charge. Indeed, they – and much else – were destined, sooner than anyone expected, to disappear.

4

TURNING POINTS

The Wall will remain still in 50 and 100 years, if the reasons for it are not removed.

Erich Honecker, January 1989[1]

The Berlin Wall has fallen. This is no longer a matter of socialism, but of a change in the world balance of power, the end of Yalta, the end of Stalin's legacy and the defeat of Nazi Germany. This is what Gorbachev has done!

Anatoly Chernyaev, November 1989[2]

The Americans were in a very triumphalist mood after the fall of the Wall. They were saying, 'Gorbachev would be left alone in the Kremlin with a dozen hussars.'

Norman Lamont, former UK chancellor of the exchequer, 2023[3]

In the years of global drama after the opening of the Wall, one key tussle took centre stage: the battle for the soul of the Soviet Union. The struggle was set to shape the future of Europe for decades, leading up to the war in Ukraine and beyond. Over that period, Russia was lost to the West. Who was to blame? According to Mark Sobel, a long-time US financial diplomat who headed the Treasury's Soviet office in the 1990s: 'US commentators asked: "Who lost Russia?" as if it were America's fault. It wasn't our fault. Russia lost Russia. The lack of economic stabilisation. The unholy orgy of privatisation, the oligarch culture and

148

the collapse of 1998. It is unlikely that any new democracy could have survived all that. Since then, Putin has emphasised dreams of an imperial past as a means of staying in power.'[4]

The full story is undoubtedly more complex. A decidedly pro-American British prime minister, Tony Blair, described US 'arrogance' towards Russia as 'counter-productive to our cause';[5] an Atlanticist Italian head of government, Romano Prodi, says America behaved towards the Soviet Union and Russia like a post-First World War victor power.[6] A crucial period, setting the pattern for all that happened later, was the interval between the crumbling of the edifice dividing Berlin and the reunification of Germany eleven months later. Dissolution and renewal ran together across Europe.

Central to the sense of post-Cold War grievance, prevalent in much Russian psychology, is the claim that Germany's unification coincided with betrayal: that the West's broke promises, made at the time of unification and repeated thereafter, not to expand NATO eastwards.[7] Behind this lies another cruel juxtaposition. Two pivotal countries underwent turning points, in diametrically opposite directions. Germany rose and the Soviet Union fell.

Putin grew up in a period when Germany had been eradicated from the map by the collapse of Hitler's regime and postwar territorial division.[8] The Soviet Union, by contrast, had risen from the backward factionalist agrarian state of the 1917 revolution to become, after America, the second superpower. Yet in 1990–1, within a little over a year, Germany re-emerged, while the Soviet Union was extinguished.

The radical change in fortunes brought its own anxieties: one important reason for the Soviet Union's hard-won 1990 acquiescence in German membership of NATO reflected Moscow's fear of an untethered and dangerous united Germany. At a key point, James Baker, Bush's secretary of state, a (normally) highly disciplined negotiator, unashamedly sought to exploit traditional Russian anxieties about invasion from the West. In a ploy to overcome the Soviet leader's antagonism to united Germany's membership of the alliance, Baker told Gorbachev in February 1990 that Germany had to be in NATO so that it would not 'again become a generator of instability in Europe'. Baker went further than was generally known (and certainly much further than he disclosed to the Germans) by affirming that a neutral unified German state could arm itself with nuclear weapons.[9]

US diplomats involved in the process were acutely sensitive to what the Soviet Union would regard as a painful loss – an injury that it might, by the Americans' own reckoning, wish one day to rectify or overturn.

Two officials with important roles in George H.W. Bush's German reunification team, Philip Zelikow and Condoleezza Rice, wrote in 1995 that the US goal of consolidating the democratic revolution in Europe and reducing Soviet military power in eastern Europe would cause Moscow 'a reversal of fortunes not unlike a catastrophic defeat in war'.[10] US officials were striving to persuade the Soviets to straddle two contradictory positions: 'to accept this result and believe that they retained an appropriate, albeit diminished, role in European affairs'. In past episodes such as at the Congress of Vienna (1814–15) and the Congress of Berlin (1878) – although not, crucially, at Versailles in 1919 (which the authors omit to mention in that part of the book) – 'accommodating the interests of a defeated power had been a familiar aspect of balance of power politics'.

Bearing this out, during the internal power struggle in Moscow immediately after the puncturing of the Wall, one of Gorbachev's closest aides, Andrei Grachyov, noted: 'Our European neighbours are eager not to aggravate the Germans, not to repeat the mistakes of the Versailles Pact. But they must be careful not to put the Soviet Union in the position of Weimar Germany – especially since we were not defeated in a war.'[11]

As Soviet power crumbled, the goal, Zelikow and Rice wrote, was to prevent 'a lasting bitterness [in Moscow] that would lead them some day to try to overthrow the European settlement'. As these officials' reflections show, America's top foreign-policy officials were fully aware that the US was playing with fire. Gorbachev, of Russian–Ukrainian descent, wished to make every effort to ensure his ancestral lands stayed together. At a meeting in the White House in November 1991, shortly before Ukraine voted overwhelmingly in a referendum to leave the Soviet Union, and six weeks before the Union broke up, Bush and Baker spoke to Alexander Yakovlev, Gorbachev's adviser, about the all-important issue of Soviet nuclear weapons on Ukrainian soil – and possible conflict between Russia and Ukraine if they were separated into two countries.[12] Pointing out the large number of Russians in Ukraine – 12 million, 'many in mixed marriages' – Yakovlev asked the secretary of state what kind of a war he envisaged. Baker replied, clinically, and (it turned out) accurately: 'A normal war.'

Whatever magnanimity may originally have lain behind US objectives towards the Soviet Union and Russia, the consensus among credible observers is that, across a span of years, America treated Russia as a vanquished adversary. The Soviets had to be handled carefully, but – however uncomfortable this was for Russian egos – one fact was incontrovertible: they had lost, and America had won.[13]

Romano Prodi, who in three different spells was Italian prime minister and president of the European Commission almost continuously from 1996 to 2008, had many exchanges with Russian leaders, which continued after he stepped down in 2008 from his second term as Italian premier. He says, 'The Americans treated the Russians a little like the western allies treated Germany after the First World War. There was a touch of Versailles about this.'[14] Norman Lamont, British chancellor of the exchequer in 1990–3, was in contact with Gorbachev and other Russian figures in the early 1990s, participating in extensive conversations on western aid for Russia. (He concluded – like many – that Gorbachev had little idea about economics).[15] Lamont attests: '[Nicholas] Brady [US Treasury secretary in 1988–93] said he thought it was in everyone's interest for the Soviet Union to disintegrate, and he was one of the few people to dare to say such a thing.'[16] Pierre Morel, French ambassador to Russia in the 1990s, says, 'My impression was that the Americans wanted to lay down the law to Russia. They saw themselves as victors of the Cold War.'[17]

Bringing to health what Morel called the 'mad, bad complex Soviet industrial system' would be immensely difficult. In addition, even if that aim had been feasible, America was not anxious to see a former adversary rise quickly to its feet. So there was huge distaste for pumping large volumes of western funds into the Soviet Union and Russia. A post-Second World War 'Marshall Fund'-type aid programme for Russia was never seriously considered. 'There was no handbook to deal with a superpower empire that has collapsed,' says Roderic Lyne, a British East European specialist who was No. 2 in the British embassy in Moscow when the Wall fell, and became Russian ambassador in the early 2000s.

> The Soviet Union faced several challenges simultaneously. The end of the empire, including the Warsaw Pact. The collapse of the Soviet Union, which took place by accident – neither Yeltsin nor Gorbachev wanted that. The attempt to develop democracy, where Russia had no experience, apart from some slender examples before the revolution. And transformation of a command economy into a market economy – setting free markets, liberalising prices – where in the past everything had been set by Gosplan. And all this in a huge country.[18]

Although Germany had a much more direct interest in economic stabilisation, a German foreign office document (from 1993) drew similar conclusions: 'History shows that reform policies in Russia are always difficult and often fail . . . While Tsarist Russia from Peter the Great to 1914 followed [reform] developments in the rest of Europe, at least in part or with a time lag, 70 years of isolation from the rest of the world have in many instances maintained pre-1914 structures and thought processes.'[19]

However, the series of upheavals was far from being pre-ordained. Brent Scowcroft, Bush's national security adviser, was the crucial American counterpart to Kohl's Horst Teltschik during the reunification saga. Reminiscing in 2009 on the twentieth anniversary of the fall of the Wall, Scowcroft reflected that history might have taken a different turn. Had he overcome a Hamlet-like inability to make up his mind, Scowcroft opined, Gorbachev could have stopped unification. Gorbachev was under constant pressure, from different factions in the Kremlin and elsewhere in the Soviet political and military spheres, to take a sterner line on Germany and NATO.[20] Yet the Soviet Union let East Germany slip out of its hands.

> Gorbachev was intelligent, very cerebral and I would say rather indecisive. And that stood in our stead. Helmut Kohl and George Bush were the only ones that wanted German reunification. The Russians didn't; the French didn't; the British didn't. Had Gorbachev been a different kind of a person he might have mobilized the British and French with him, and together they probably could have kept German unification from happening. He didn't do that.[21]

ROLLERCOASTERS AT VARYING SPEEDS

Reflecting their different vantage points, in the weeks after the fall of the Wall, the US, the Soviet Union, Britain and France were focused on disparate aspects of rapidly moving events. The outcome was on a knife edge. Unsurprisingly, the Second World War allies' conditions for ratifying German unification went through distortions and changes. A series of rollercoasters was moving at varying speeds and sometimes in different directions. The scene was set for a diplomatic re-enactment of the 1939–45 conflict: a new encounter – under reshaped conditions and alliances – between wartime victors and vanquished. The eight-month-long 'Two plus Four' negotiating process assembled the two defeated and dismembered German states and the four countries on the winning side in 1945. After a final late-night September 1990 scramble in the 'whited sepulchre' of the Oktyabrskaya Hotel in Moscow,[22] the legal text was laid down for reuniting the two Germanys. Wholly improbably, it contained agreement on an issue that the Soviet Union declared, at the start of the process (and at intervals while it was in train), would be impossible to achieve: united Germany would be a member of NATO. The eastwards shift in the alliance to cover the territory of East Germany was the prelude to further steady enlargement during the coming twenty years – a substantial factor behind Moscow's subsequent resentment over western strategies.

Soviet and Russian bitterness about NATO undoubtedly has some basis in fact. As an authoritative analysis from George Washington University recorded in 2017, 'Baker's famous "not one inch eastward" assurance . . . was part of a cascade of assurances about Soviet security given by western leaders to Gorbachev and other Soviet officials throughout the process of German unification in 1990 and into 1991.'[23] All this took place against a backdrop of Soviet fragmentation whose scale and speed took everyone aback. According to Scowcroft, 'I remember being surprised at the Russians acquiescing to NATO expansion. They complained, but they acquiesced. And I think I underestimated what it was really doing to Russia. I think we all did. We were humiliating Russia, not intentionally, but nevertheless that was the net result.'[24]

Like many, Helmut Kohl dramatically underestimated the pace of change. In October 1988, he said he did not expect to live to see unification.[25] In February 1989, he vehemently rejected any idea that West Germany would ever absorb East Germany through an Anschluss.[26] Two weeks after the fall of the Wall, he conjectured that reunification would take five to ten years.[27] In January 1990, he estimated it might happen in 1995.[28] With regard to the future of the Soviet Union, Kohl again failed to appreciate the underlying dynamic. He told François Mitterrand in April 1991 that it was 'impossible' that the Soviet Union would break up into individual states. But, just eight months later, it happened.[29]

Vladislav Zubok notes a scenario put forward by American diplomat and Soviet specialist George Kennan in 1946: 'internal dissension' that could 'weaken Soviet potential and lead to [a] situation similar to that of 1919–20'.[30] Zubok went on: 'Kennan did not think this option likely, yet it describes quite well what happened to the Soviet Union in 1991. Nobody, including the most sagacious observers, could predict that the Soviet Union, which had survived the epic assault of Hitler's armies, would be defeated from within, by its internal crises and conflict.'

James 'Jim' Collins, a US State Department Russian specialist who was chargé d'affaires in the US embassy in late 1990 (and became ambassador to Russia in 1997 until 2001), confirms the lack of fore-knowledge. 'When I went to Moscow in the fall of 1990, and I got my briefing from the [US] intelligence agencies, people were expecting that within five years one of the Soviet republics might have a significant degree of autonomy. No one expected the Soviet Union would disappear.' As Collins describes it, the Russians' own shortcomings in assessing what was going on would have wide-ranging consequences.

> The Russians thought they had assurances that, if the whole of Germany came into NATO, there would be no NATO expansion further east. For the Soviets, it was already a concession that NATO would remain in being when the Warsaw Pact disappeared. They assumed that, in the new Europe 'whole and free', the Soviet role would continue, alongside America; that the old superpower structure would not be dismantled.[31]

Gorbachev, Collins says, found himself trapped by a bitter, self-contradicting conundrum. Only an economically strong Soviet Union could stand up to America. 'Gorbachev realised that the Soviet Union would be an economic force only if it reformed. The problem was that the reforms led to such disruption that the Soviet system itself was destabilized.'

Reflecting this contorted background, diplomatic bargaining in the period straddling the fall of the Wall and the dismemberment of the Soviet Union only twenty-five months later was studded with fluctuating claims and pledges, often of dubious conviction – delivered frontally in conversations between leaders and through copious back-channels. Since the Soviet Union had the most to lose and could also do the most damage, many of the messages were directed to Moscow. Seeking compliance with an objective known to be antithetical to traditional Soviet interests, the West had strong self-interest in ruling out that NATO would expand beyond united Germany's eastern border towards Soviet/Russian territory.

A political struggle unfolded among the western allies – and within the West German government – over whether NATO's 'jurisdiction' would even extend to the territory of the German Democratic Republic. At a time when the Warsaw Pact was on the point of being dismantled, the West's many mollifying declarations over NATO enlargement, hedged with differing levels of conditionality, seemed plausible. Many of those who offered them believed these pledges were true. But these statements offered a very poor guide to what eventually happened. In the thirty years between 1990 and 2020, as a result of growing signs of instability in Russia, coupled with former Soviet bloc states' historically well-founded fears of a return to aggressive policies in Moscow, NATO enlarged its membership from sixteen to thirty countries.[32]

Well-orchestrated Russian statements alleging western betrayal are patently disingenuous. Factual analysis, and the testimony of interlocutors with plentiful experience of the Russian mindset, tell a fuller story.[33] Jean-Claude Juncker, well-versed in exchanges with leading Russians, explains: 'Putin maintains that the West lied to him over NATO's eastern extension. However, we did not decide to expand NATO. We simply did not say "No" to the eastern countries who wanted to join.'[34] Hans-Friedrich von Ploetz, Gerhard Schröder's choice as German ambassador to Russia, previously West German ambassador to NATO, built up a strong relationship with Putin (speaking solely in German) in the early 2000s and was well aware of Russian sensitivities. He says, 'We did not expand

NATO. They [the eastern bloc countries] broke down the doors to get in.'[35]

Teltschik, at Kohl's side during all the seminal moments of the unification saga, points out that the former Warsaw Pact states' wish to join NATO in the 1990s was because 'they wanted to improve their security not only against Russia, but also against Germany. This was especially the case for Poland.'[36] Braithwaite, British ambassador to the Soviet Union and subsequently Russia, who, with some sympathy, recorded myriad declarations to the Russians by western leaders ruling out NATO's future expansion,[37] says, 'The East Europeans were putting great pressure on us to join. Understandably, given their long experience of an overbearing Russia. The British in particular felt guilty about betraying Poland and Czechoslovakia to the Germans in 1939.'

An inability to understand developments in Russia remained a continual feature of the West's relationship. The roll call of missteps includes multiple miscalculations over Ukraine as well as the build-up of European and German energy dependence through successive deals on gas deliveries. The dashed promise of the Gorbachev and Yeltsin years gave way to a further period of initial optimism and then progressive disillusionment under Putin. Angela Merkel, the sole western politician who could speak both German and Russian, had the longest record of high-level engagement with Putin. Maintaining time-honoured German principles of seeking common accord with its sprawling eastern neighbour, she signally overestimated her capacity to influence the Russian leader. In her memoirs, she puts forward the unverifiable contention that, had she and other western interlocutors been able to speak to Putin during the Covid-19 lockdown period, the Ukrainian war could have been averted.[38] That assertion sits awkwardly with her oft-proclaimed belief that Putin, 'living in a reality of his own creation', could not be trusted.[39] But, whatever the West's mistakes, they provide no justification for Russia's war of aggression. Braithwaite provides an apt summary:

The West's policy towards Russia after the Soviet collapse was often arrogant, ignorant, and inept, like its policy towards Germany between the wars. But the claim that the West is to blame for provoking Russia's war against Ukraine is very wide of the mark.

Whatever their imagined provocations, Hitler was responsible for invading Poland and Putin was responsible for invading Ukraine. Georges Clemenceau was later asked who was responsible for the First World War. He said it was unclear. 'But I know for certain they will not say Belgium invaded Germany.'[40]

INTERLOCKING HOPES AND FEARS

In the immediate aftermath of 9 November, the West German government was at the epicentre of reverberating hopes and fears across many nations. The personal experiences and prejudices of each country's leader played an overwhelming role. West Germany had to reassure both western and eastern neighbours that united Germany – despite the huge challenges of integrating two highly unequal components – would be as constructive a future partner as it had been in the four decades of division.

Messages to interlocutors in different capitals had to be calibrated with extreme care. France posed a thorny problem. François Mitterrand showed ambivalence on military questions, reflecting France's withdrawal under Charles de Gaulle from the integrated command structure of NATO. The French president, like nearly all his predecessors, was obsessed by his country's economic and industrial inferiority against Germany. Consequentially, Mitterrand was determined to make progress in a vital area – to tie the D-Mark into a European economic system through accelerated implementation of previous proposals for economic and monetary union.

Mitterrand's desire that a new single currency should come under political control ran counter to German insistence on an independent central bank. One of Mitterrand's closest political allies, Pierre Bérégovoy, French finance minister during reunification and prime minister for a short time afterwards, never relented in his suspicion of an enlarged Germany.[41] A member of the Resistance in the Second World War, he urged the French people to vote for the Maastricht treaty in France's 1992 referendum so Germany would remain 'integrated into Europe' and unable 'to follow its own will'.[42] The clash of cultures was destined to persist as an enduring source of tension over European monetary arrangements in the 1990s and beyond.

For the two principal West German actors, Kohl and his foreign minister Genscher, dealing with the Soviet Union and the three often fractious western members of the Second World War coalition demanded a supremely delicate balancing act. As the edifice of the postwar construct started to buckle, a rich melange of subterfuge, bluff, counter-bluff, overstatement and miscalculation ran through the diplomatic manoeuvrings of the four 1945 victor powers. On the defence and military side, with its eye on Moscow's resentments and suspicions, West Germany had to play down any thought of strengthening NATO. Equally, the West Germans had to counter the view – heard in Washington and Paris but above all in Margaret Thatcher's Britain – that Bonn would seek somehow to free itself from its bonds with both East and West.

Kohl termed Thatcher's opposition to German unification 'near-hysterical', based on 'emotional enmity towards Germany'.[43] For Charles Moore, her biographer, 'as a child of the "home front" in the Second World war, she had a visceral dislike of German power.' Obsessed by British 'sacrifice' in both world wars, 'to her, the sins that had caused these tragedies had never been fully explained.'[44] For western policy-makers, the ultimate threat was that Bonn would opt for neutrality as the price of unity, a deal held out by Josef Stalin in 1952.[45] Thatcher, worried about 'a German state so large and dominant that it cannot be fitted into the new architecture of Europe',[46] wrongly believed she could rely on Mitterrand to slow German unification.

Mitterrand's capacity for disguising his intentions was aptly described by Britain's ambassador to France: 'The French would not stand against [the] tide, whatever they may say in private.'[47] Some influential figures in Moscow, on the other hand, believed America would block unity, avoiding the need for the Soviet Union to take action.[48] Echoing thoughts frequently voiced by both Mitterrand and Baker, as well as by Genscher (a man she distrusted), Thatcher argued that unification would destabilise Gorbachev and disrupt Soviet reform. The prediction turned out to be regrettably accurate. Hardly surprisingly, given the complexity, Gorbachev failed to master the torrent of events. He emerges from the narrative as a vainglorious and somewhat shallow politician, zigzagging his way through to an essentially tragic destiny.[49]

Contradictions and antagonisms that had lain semi-dormant for forty years burst to the surface. At a stormy dinner for European leaders at the Élysée Palace on 18 November, Kohl recalled the long-standing NATO commitment to a united Germany.[50] Thatcher replied that these promises dated from a time when no one believed reunification was possible. When Kohl told her, 'You will not stop the German people following their destiny,' Thatcher 'stamped her foot in rage' – an outburst that, Kohl observed, appeared to find Mitterrand's approval.[51]

For forty years Britain had espoused a policy aimed at unifying a democratic Germany within the transatlantic alliance. In 1989–90, the goal suddenly came into view. Yet, as David Manning, a long-serving British diplomat, ambassador to the US in the early 2000s and later Tony Blair's foreign policy adviser, points out, 'Thatcher was reluctant to embrace and capitalise on what was an enormous foreign policy success.'[52] Thatcher's cloudy judgement over Mitterrand's designs on Germany was similar to her erroneous belief in 1988–9 that Karl Otto Pöhl, the Bundesbank president, would block the path to monetary union in the European committee set up to plot the path to a single currency. And it set the tone for a long trail of British missteps in dealing with Germany that would continue into the Brexit era.

Thatcher's miscalculations on Germany coincided with the rapid erosion of her power base both internationally and at Westminster. Towards the end of her eleven years in office, the British prime minister's influence in Washington was running perilously thin. American and French diplomats were complaining behind the scenes to the British civil service about the prime minister's high-handedness. Mitterrand showed 'puzzlement' and 'irritation' in his dealings with her. Bush was 'uncomfortable' with her 'dismissive references to the Germans, and more particularly to Genscher, in their private conversations'.[53]

According to Charles Powell, Thatcher's ubiquitous foreign-policy adviser,

There was a feeling in Washington that President Reagan had been unduly influenced by Thatcher. The US was losing support from France and Germany. Hence the need to push back under George H.W. Bush, and [for America] to provide support for unification when the time came.[54]

A hint of another reason for the distance that opened up between Thatcher and other western leaders when Bush became president comes from John Kerr, the consummate British diplomat, later ambassador to the US and head of the Foreign Office, who led the Washington embassy's political section during Reagan's presidency. This was a period when Reagan's espousal of the Strategic Defense Initiative (colloquially known as 'Star Wars') for nuclear missile defence,[55] as well as the plan at the 1986 Reagan–Gorbachev Reykjavik summit for complete elimination of nuclear weapons,[56] sparked considerable anxiety from the British – who feared a lowering of American commitment to European defence.

> Mrs Thatcher treated George Bush like dirt. When she came to Washington to see Reagan, he used to come to the embassy, often to have a late dinner with her to prepare for meeting with the president the next day. George was an extremely gentlemanly character, supremely loyal to Reagan. He would hear her out, on issues such as Reykjavik or Star Wars, but never respond combatively: she found this irritating. And he would never even hint at any personal disagreement with Reagan's views, even on issues, like both Reykjavik and Star Wars, where I knew his were different, and closer to ours.[57]

MITTERRAND 'CAVES IN'

Thatcher's confidant Powell says she got on well with Mitterrand 'until he caved in on German reunification'. In her resistance to speedy unification, 'Mitterrand egged her on', Powell says. 'However, once Mitterrand reached an understanding that the Germans were willing to go ahead with monetary union, he became less fussed over reunification.'[58]

British efforts to instrumentalise Gorbachev in 1989–90 to slow down unification comprehensively backfired. Powell's younger brother, Jonathan, then a junior Foreign Office mandarin – later to become Tony Blair's chief of staff and, in 2024, Keir Starmer's national security adviser – provided one of the British government's pithiest pieces of unification analysis. Soon after the Wall was breached, the younger Powell travelled to Berlin, from where he wrote that the British ploy of exploiting Moscow's antipathy to block or brake unification was destined to fail. According to

German academics he consulted at a Berlin conference, 'The people of the GDR were not yet asking for reunification but in their hearts they all demand it.'[59] The key factor would be economic. 'People in the GDR wanted to live like the people of the FRG [Federal Republic of Germany], and not to be second class Germans.' The message blunted a crucial though unstated element of British policy on Germany: 'Unless the Russians speak up we will be unable to convince the Germans that it is they who are stopping reunification. They are convinced that Gorbachev has enough on his plate in the Soviet Union and will not interfere to prevent German reunification.'

The German position was made still more fragile by rivalry and dissonance within the Bonn coalition. Kohl and Genscher were simultaneously partners and rivals in the twin challenges of striking a bargain on Germany's future and navigating shoals of international and domestic opinion. The tide turned in dramatic fashion at the end of November when Kohl unveiled his '10 points' for German unity, outlining a plan for 'confederative structures' and eventually a 'federation' of the two German states.[60] The proposals were concocted in secret. The chancellor and his entourage pointedly kept Genscher and the western allies in the dark on the idea, on the grounds (as Kohl described later) that the proposals would have been 'talked to death'.[61]

Kohl and his advisers formulated the plan after a mysterious visit to Bonn on 21 November by Nikolai Portugalov, an influential adviser to Gorbachev, who 'electrified' key aide Teltschik with what appeared to be an emollient Soviet line on unification. Portugalov – a gregarious, will-o'-the-wisp envoy who spoke beguilingly accented German and was a frequent guest on German TV talk-shows – was, according to Teltschik, 'known as something of a hardliner, so I was surprised that he came with this idea of Soviet movement in the direction of German unity'.[62] Portugalov read out a seven-page handwritten note, which was subsequently handed to Teltschik and then to Kohl. The document stated that, over the medium term, the Soviet Union could give a green light to some form of German confederation – on condition that there should be no 'foreign nuclear presence on German soul'.[63]

The Portugalov visit led to a hectic weekend of action: formulation of the 10-point plan on a Saturday (25 November) and Kohl's announcement in the Bundestag the following Tuesday (28 November). In Bonn's hothouse atmosphere, secrecy was paramount. 'If we had talked about it with the allies, they would have asked for time to consider it,' Teltschik says. 'If we had mentioned it to our coalition partners, it would have become the subject of a newspaper interview by Genscher the next day.'[64] Genscher sanctimoniously claimed later that such deviousness 'would never have come to my mind'.[65] Recognising – and bolstering – his sound relationship with George Bush, Kohl intelligently made a symbolic exception for Washington, sending an untranslated version of the 10-point plan the night before the speech to the White House, knowing that the content would not be read and digested until some hours after he had made his intervention public.

The initiative surprised the British in particular. Christopher Mallaby, British ambassador in Bonn, was held in high esteem by Kohl and Teltschik for his intellectual prowess. But he had difficulty balancing straightforward reporting of the German disruption with what he knew to be Thatcher's emotional antipathy both to Kohl and to any prospect of unification. Particularly early on in the process, Mallaby – coveting as his next career move the top job in London as permanent undersecretary (a post he did not get)[66] – geared his reports to an undue extent to what Thatcher wished to hear.

On the eve of Kohl's Bundestag announcement of the 10-point plan, the British embassy in Bonn seemed oblivious to the febrile activity in Kohl's office. Mallaby wrote to the Foreign Office in London, with trademark superciliousness, 'There is a feeling in the air that the federal government, especially Kohl, is not rising to this historic moment and looking like the master of events.'[67] Kohl, for his part, was at pains to deal confidentially with Washington in preference to France and Britain. Kohl spoke to Bush for thirty minutes after the speech, telling him that unification was a 'long-term process'.[68] He did not wish to confront the issue of united Germany's alliance membership. 'They [East Germany] will remain in the Pact, and we [West Germany] in NATO.' Kohl told Bush he would be pressing ahead with economic and monetary union, using the dual opportunity to both criticise Thatcher's obduracy on money and stress Bonn's European mindedness. 'It is a great mistake on Maggie's part to think that this is a time for caution. It is an iron law that there will be no going alone in German policy.'[69]

An aggrieved Genscher, listening from the government's parliamentary benches to Kohl's statement on the previously unsighted 10-point plan, was obliged to swallow his displeasure. He responded with forced magnanimity by telling Kohl that he liked the speech. His annoyance intensified when Teltschik mischievously relayed Genscher's approval to German newspapers.[70]

The chancellor's office and the foreign ministry produced strikingly divergent summaries of the international reaction to the plan. Teltschik highlighted generally positive statements from Baker and Mitterrand and a neutral reaction from Thatcher.[71] Genscher's ministry broadcast a much more negative interpretation, reporting that western countries had generally reacted with 'surprise and scepticism. Critical undertones are unmistakable.'[72]

More trials awaited. Genscher withstood a frosty encounter with Thatcher in London. The British prime minister told him of a Moscow visit by Alan Greenspan, chairman of the Federal Reserve, who passed on news that the Soviet Union was suffering from massive inflation and was close to collapse.[73] Genscher informed Douglas Hurd, Thatcher's foreign secretary, that Germany was countering fears of an 'eastward drift' by pressing ahead with western European integration and called on the UK to join a future single currency[74] – not a message the fiercely non-integrationist British prime minister wished to receive. From London, Genscher crossed to Paris where an indignant Mitterrand told him Europe was in a comparative position to the eve of the First World War.[75]

COMPLEXITIES ON VIEW

The complexities were on full view as Gorbachev and Bush prepared for a shipboard summit in Malta in early December. En route, the Soviet leader stopped in Rome, where he announced his hope for a 'common European home' of sovereign and economically interdependent European states.[76] In a bleak memorandum preparing Bush for the Malta meeting, Scowcroft wrote that the Soviet Union had lost control of policy towards eastern Europe. Furthermore, it was opposed to German reunification, which Moscow thought would 'rip the heart out of the Soviet security system'. The Soviets' 'worst nightmare' was a reunified Germany allied with NATO. 'The Warsaw Pact, having lost its East German anchor, would quickly disintegrate and the Soviet line of defence would begin at the Ukrainian border. The gains of the Second World War, having been bought so dearly, would be gone.'[77]

During their discussions on 2 and 3 December, Bush and Gorbachev disagreed politely over whether history had decreed there should be two German states. But, otherwise, Gorbachev showed more flexibility than Scowcroft had feared – demonstrating swirling views in dealing with Germany that would be repeatedly displayed later in the unification saga. Gorbachev's 'relaxed demeanor' in Malta convinced Bush's advisers that the Soviet leader would be 'malleable' on the German question.[78] On the eve of a NATO summit, Bush briefed Kohl on the exchanges over dinner in Brussels: 'Gorbachev's problem is uncertainty . . . We need a formulation [on German unity] that doesn't scare him, but moves forward.'[79]

Genscher faced a further difficult encounter with Gorbachev in Moscow on 5 December. The Soviet leader vigorously attacked the 10-point plan. He accused Bonn of setting an 'ultimatum', 'throwing explosives on the fire' and acting like 'an elephant in a China shop'. Kohl's declaration contained 'dangerous elements . . . Every Soviet family sees this, as well as the most important partners in East and West.'[80] On 6 December, Gorbachev returned to the attack when he received Mitterrand in Kyiv. The French president told him that German unification would upset the European balance. Gorbachev repeated his complaint that Kohl was behaving like 'an elephant in a China shop . . . Help me to stop reunification. Otherwise I will be replaced by a general – and you will bear the responsibility for war.'[81] A fraught European leaders' session in Strasbourg on 8 December – for Kohl the most 'tense and unfriendly' he had ever attended[82] – featured overt hostility from Thatcher and Giulio Andreotti.[83] In two bilateral meetings with Thatcher, Mitterrand repeated the warning he had given Genscher a week earlier: Germany could face 'encirclement' from a redrawn pre-First World War triple alliance of Britain, France and Russia.[84]

The reunification bandwagon was, however, gaining unstoppable momentum. On 19 December, Kohl flew to Dresden where he was greeted at the airport by cheering East Germans; reunification, he told an accompanying aide, was now 'in the bag'.[85] As evening fell, he told crowds milling over the ruins of the Church of Our Lady, destroyed by Anglo-American bombs in February 1945, 'My goal remains – should the hour of history allow it – the unity of our nation.'[86] Kohl conceded that many of Germany's neighbours were watching 'with concern and some with fear': understandable, 'in view of the history of this century'.

Kohl's bargaining chip was European integration. 'The German house – our common house – has to be built under a European roof.' Yet constructing 'the German house' would demolish a principal Soviet prize of the Second World War. That devastating setback for Moscow was now well-nigh unavoidable, risking a Moscow backlash. A memorandum from West Germany's embassy in Washington on 12 January 1990 underlined what was at stake. 'Steps on the German question should not endanger the democratic upheaval in eastern Europe and the Soviet Union (Gorbachev).'[87] The Warsaw Pact, deprived of its East German bulwark, was nearing break-up, with the Hungarians and Czechoslovaks announcing plans for Soviet troop withdrawals.[88]

Later in January, Gorbachev summoned his advisers to the Kremlin to discuss the German question. Nikolai Ryzhov, chairman of the council of ministers, told the group that, with the Wall gone, the East German economy was crumbling and 'all the state institutions are falling apart too'. Gorbachev's key adviser Anatoly Chernyaev backed a six-state negotiating model – which later became Two plus Four – for an agreement on Germany. 'The German unification process cannot be stopped, but we need to make sure that it takes place with us present and not against it.'[89] Teltschik warned Kohl of Gorbachev's vulnerability. 'In view of the Soviet Union's weaker status as a major power in the world and in its former area of hegemony', the Soviet leader required 'stability and reassurance' and 'particularly urgently in the economic field, evidence of success'.[90]

On NATO membership, Genscher adopted a line designed to provide maximum comfort to the Soviet Union – a policy that Kohl and Teltschik, egged on by the US and Britain, succeeded eventually in modifying. The foreign minister declared in a newspaper interview in late January that bringing East Germany fully into NATO would 'close the door on a united Germany'.[91] In a much-cited speech in Tutzing, southern Germany, three days later, Genscher rejected the idea of a neutral Germany, but affirmed, 'There will not be an extension of the

NATO territory towards the East, that is, towards the borders of the Soviet Union.'[92] Scowcroft labelled as 'troubling' Genscher's 'obvious detour around a four-power role in reunification'.[93]

The German embassy in Moscow reported that the Soviet Union still seemed to be wavering on whether the new German state could be within or outside NATO.[94] Responding both to Gorbachev's statement on 30 January recognising that unification would take place, as well as Genscher's 31 January line on NATO, Thatcher termed the overall picture 'very worrying'.[95] Hans-Friedrich von Ploetz, Germany's assertively Genscherite ambassador to NATO, was determined to put a positive gloss on the matter. He outlined a position that was demonstrably true: alliance members generally agreed that West Germany's proposed continued NATO membership 'will improve the overall western position'.[96] Whatever deal was in the making with Moscow, the West looked likely to be the winner.

PERPETUATING THE NATO CONUNDRUM

In the diplomatic stand-off between Moscow, Washington and Bonn, deception and distrust were only superficially overlaid by copious flows of nervous energy. Genscher flew to Washington on 2 February to persuade Baker that NATO should be extended neither to East Germany nor to other states in eastern Europe; both alliances should become part of a new European security system.[97] Kohl and Genscher prepared to fly to Moscow for what would clearly be a crunch meeting. Briefing Mitterrand about the forthcoming visit, Kohl told the French president of Gorbachev's appeal that Bonn should help calm the 'catastrophic effects' of continued massive East German emigration.[98] On 6 February, Genscher told Douglas Hurd, the visiting British foreign secretary, that 'when he talked about not wanting to extend NATO, that applied to other states beside the GDR. The Russians must have some assurance that if, for example, the Polish government left the Warsaw Pact one day, they would not join NATO the next.'[99]

The same day, Kohl responded to Gorbachev's plea, in dramatic and hastily decided fashion: to help stop the flood of migrants crossing to the West, the government would unify the East and West German currencies. Wrong-footing the independent Bundesbank, the chancellor announced the West German government would introduce the D-Mark into East Germany.[100] Pöhl was aghast at the decision – communicated into the TV cameras in Bonn while he and Helmut Schlesinger, the Bundesbank deputy president, were in Berlin on a mission to speak to East German officials about ways to stabilise the eastern economy.

Kohl's decision helped calm the population outflows from East Germany and sealed the path to unification in October. But stabilising Germany destabilised Europe. The Bundesbank's manifest unhappiness at lack of consultation was one of the many reasons why Pöhl resigned the following year.[101] The eventual decision to fix the D-Mark exchange rate, against the Bundesbank's advice, at an overvalued level against the East Mark contributed to higher German inflation and the need for higher German interest rates, with widespread consequences. In the exchange rate crises of September 1992 and thereafter, Britain and Italy left the exchange rate mechanism (ERM) of the European Monetary System, the forerunner of monetary union. A series of other countries devalued their currencies or allowed them to float downwards after the ERM was de facto suspended in August 1993 – a state of affairs which left the D-Mark seriously overvalued on currency markets and brought Germany into recession in 1993.

Aware of the disruption that fusing the East and West German currencies would generate, as he emerged from a meeting with Horst Kaminsky, president of the East German State Bank, Pöhl was determined to scotch rumours of German monetary union. Responding to questions from journalists, he said he and Kaminsky agreed it was 'premature' even to consider 'such a far-reaching step' – shortly before Kohl announced his offer of an 'immediate' extension of the D-Mark to the East. An internal Bundesbank note records Pöhl's summary of the East Berlin position and his anger at being overridden by Bonn:

[Functionaries in East Berlin] don't want a new government, they want to come into the Federal Republic, 80 per cent of the population think like this. They want reunification. They've all had enough. The chancellor has decided [monetary union] by himself. I don't believe that on Monday [the day before the announcement] he knew that. Everything has been done by shooting from the hip, without any preparation. I have sharply criticised the procedure. What would happen if I said that in public? The question is: can the Bundesbank, although it has been unbelievably badly treated, go into confrontation with the government? That is not something one can do. I believe that we have no other choice, since we at the Bundesbank are obliged by law, than to behave loyally towards the government. All we can do is to give our advice and try in the negotiations to limit the damage, to enable something sensible to come out of it.[102]

The currency dispute between government and central bank formed a dramatic backcloth to the Kohl–Genscher trip to Moscow. Shortly before they were due to arrive, Baker flew to the Soviet capital.[103] On 9 February, he told, first, Soviet foreign minister Eduard Shevardnadze and then Gorbachev (in separate conversations) that the threat of European instability – and of Germany becoming a nuclear-armed state[104] – provided the reason why neither the US nor the West Germans favoured neutrality for the nascent unified state.[105] According to US archives, Baker appears to have given a still blunter warning to Shevardnadze than Gorbachev about united Germany's potential for acquiring nuclear weapons. Baker was undoubtedly playing on the Soviet foreign minister's well-articulated fears of German instability, including his worry about the 'neo-Nazis gaining power in Germany'. Shevardnadze voiced anxiety about the 'Republicans' party (at the time the main far-right force in West German politics) gaining 20 per cent of the popular vote.[106] The statement was prophetic. The populist right-wing Alternative for Germany party scored 20.8 per cent in the German parliamentary election in February 2025.

In his admonition to Gorbachev, Baker seemed, rather successfully, to be fanning the embers of Soviet distrust of Germany. 'If Germany is neutral, it does not mean it will not be militaristic. It could very well decide to create its own nuclear potential instead of relying on American nuclear deterrent forces.' Further, Baker raised the spectre of American military withdrawal from Europe adding to potential instability. If Europeans decided they no longer wished an American military presence, 'We will bring our troops home.'[107]

Resorting to a playbook of Genscher-like emollience, Baker coupled these warnings with abundant reassurance that NATO would be a supremely non-threatening force. In the coming decades, many Russian representatives, with Putin to the fore, would highlight this message of reassurance as prime evidence of western duplicity.[108] According to the fullest available account, from the Gorbachev Foundation, Baker told Gorbachev: 'We understand that not only for the Soviet Union, but for other European countries as well, it is important to have guarantees that, if the US keeps its presence in Germany within the framework of NATO, not an inch of NATO's present military jurisdiction will spread in an eastern direction.'

The narrative is backed up by the German archives, courtesy of a diplomatically worded letter (which appears to leave out important details) from Baker to Kohl on 10 February 1990. Later in the conversation, according to the Gorbachev Foundation account, came this key exchange:

> Baker: I want to ask you a question, and you need not answer it right now. Supposing unification takes place, what would you prefer: a united Germany outside of NATO, absolutely independent and without American troops; or a united Germany keeping its connections with NATO, but with the guarantee that NATO's jurisprudence or troops will not spread east of the present boundary?
> Gorbachev: We will think everything over. We intend to discuss all these questions in depth at the leadership level. It goes without saying that a broadening of the NATO zone is not acceptable.
> Baker: We agree with that.
> Gorbachev: It is quite possible that in the situation as it is forming right now, the presence of American troops can play a containing role. It is possible that we should think together, as you said, about the fact that a united Germany could look for ways to rearm and create a new Wehrmacht, as happened after Versailles. Indeed, if Germany is outside the European structures, history could repeat itself.[109]

SUITABLY SANITISED SUMMARY

As he departed from Moscow, Baker asked aides to assist the soon-to-arrive Kohl by preparing a (suitably sanitised) summary of his conversation with Gorbachev.[110] The Baker letter handed to the chancellor included the key rhetorical question of whether Gorbachev would prefer Germany as a neutral state or tied to NATO membership, 'with assurances that NATO's jurisdiction would not shift one inch eastward from its present position'. But Baker's message made no mention of his discussion with Gorbachev on united Germany acquiring nuclear weapons or rebuilding the Wehrmacht, or of the US withdrawing troops.

Adding to the contorted messaging, the White House, dissatisfied with news reaching Washington that Baker's reassurances to Moscow had gone too far, drew up a second letter, this time from Bush, again scheduled for Kohl to read when he arrived in Moscow. Bush's message reaffirmed that a united Germany would stay in NATO, eschewed any commitment about the alliance's enlargement, and endorsed an idea for 'a special miliary status for what is now the territory of the GDR'.[111]

This was the plan that was eventually agreed when unification took place eight months later. But when Kohl met Gorbachev for a two-and-a-half-hour session on 10 February, accompanied on the German side solely by Teltschik, the chancellor took the line of least resistance: he adopted as his leitmotif the Baker formulation ruling out NATO widening rather than the more stringent Bush formulation that the whole of Germany would remain in NATO.[112] Comforted by Kohl's assurance that 'naturally NATO cannot extend to the present area of the GDR', Gorbachev agreed that unification was a matter for the Germans to decide. This would be embedded into a European process including security questions to be decided in close cooperation with Washington, Paris and London.[113] Teltschik was jubilant. 'Gorbachev agrees reunification. A triumph for Helmut Kohl, who will go down in history as the Chancellor of German Unity.'[114]

Dissonance rumbled on in the Bonn government over NATO's extension to East Germany. Kohl was forced to broker a compromise between Genscher and Gerhard Stoltenberg, the Bonn defence minister, who, to American distaste, came down on Genscher's side.[115] Pressure was building on another front, over Kohl's refusal to commit Germany to recognising East Germany's border with Poland (the Oder–Neisse line) in a future unified German state.[116] The scene was set for Bush and Kohl to meet on 24 February at Camp David in the wooded Maryland hillside.[117] Bush's plan was 'to coordinate the path to reunification, keep Germany on the NATO reservation and get a declaration on the Oder–Neisse line'.[118] He succeeded in the first two aims but not on the third. In advance of the Kohl meeting, Bush had an hour-long telephone call with Thatcher, who voiced Gorbachev's fear 'that the border of the alliance has moved closer to him'. She again emphasised her qualms about Germany 'in the heart of a continent of countries, most of which she has attacked and occupied'[119] – and alarmed Bush and US diplomats with hints of an alliance with the Soviet Union against 'German dominance in Europe'.[120] In his Camp David exchanges with Kohl, Bush adopted a much more constructive line on Germany – and made clear that Washington, not Moscow, was now in the driving seat: 'The Soviets are not in a position to dictate Germany's membership of NATO. What worries me is talk that Germany must not stay in NATO! To hell with that. We prevailed and they didn't.'[121]

With consummate subtlety, Bush resorted to the key instrument of Second World War memories to play off Kohl against Thatcher. The president, whose secretary of state, only a fortnight earlier, had informed the Soviet president and foreign minister that a neutral Germany might acquire nuclear weapons, told the visiting German chancellor: 'We don't fear the ghosts of the past; Margaret does.'[122] In his Camp David conversation with the US president, Kohl was at pains to emphasise (twice) that Germany would not become a nuclear weapons power: according to the German account, he said, presumably without irony, this would be 'deadly' for relations with its neighbours.[123]

Bush speculated that convincing the Soviets about Germany's NATO membership could end up as a matter of cash. Kohl affirmed that Moscow might be 'quite glad if the Germans are in NATO' – but the Soviets wanted a price, which they might be more willing to name to the Americans than to Germany.[124] Jovially, Bush remarked: 'You've got deep pockets.' Baker told Kohl and Bush, 'Gorbachev and Shevardnadze believe US forces [in Europe] are a stabilizing presence.'[125] Four days later, at a meeting in London of foreign ministry political directors from the US, France, West Germany and the UK, the four western allies agreed on a formula for the whole of united Germany becoming part of NATO. There would be no expansion of the alliance's military presence to the GDR. But, as Britain's representative on the group, the pugnacious Foreign Office political director John Weston, adamantly insisted, NATO security guarantees would cover the whole of Germany.[126] In response, the Soviet Union pointed out to Bonn that

Germany's NATO membership 'would alter the balance of the post-war settlement and strengthen the West against the East'.[127] The message pithily summarised the new status quo. America and its allies, quite clearly, held the upper hand.

Camp David set the tone for a helter-skelter series of international meetings in spring and summer that cumulated in unification on 3 October. Kohl received a substantial boost from a convincing victory in the 18 March GDR elections for East Germany's pro-unity Alliance for Germany, leading to eastern CDU leader Lothar de Maizière becoming the country's first and last democratically elected prime minister. The Soviets continued to show strong qualms over NATO.[128] Gorbachev briefly sided with Moscow conservatives who wished to prevent at all costs the alliance crossing into East Germany.[129] The Soviet military retreat from eastern Europe, and the prospect of a united Germany within NATO, horrified Soviet army commanders. Sergey Akhromeyev, Gorbachev's military adviser, a Second World War hero, vented his outrage on the flight back from an official US visit in April: 'For 70 years the Americans have been trying to destroy our Union. Finally they have reached their goal.'[130] Less than a year later, despised by his children, with the Soviet Union in ruins, he committed suicide.[131]

Confirming a widespread perception of Soviet destitution, Kohl and Bush's Camp David surmise proved correct: German money would bring Gorbachev into line. On 13 May, Teltschik flew in a military plane on a secret mission to Moscow accompanied by Hilmar Kopper and Wolfgang Röller, the heads of the Deutsche and Dresdner Banks, who agreed to provide DM12 to DM17 billion in short- and long-term credits. Gorbachev acceded to Teltschik's suggestion that Gorbachev receive Kohl in his Caucasus homeland to prepare a long-term cooperation agreement and seal the accord on German unity.[132] Gorbachev termed the prospective bilateral treaty 'a pillar of the European home'.

'A COLOSSAL BRIBE FROM WEST GERMANY'

Charles Powell, Thatcher's adviser, who built a solid bond with Teltschik that continued well into the post-unity decades, saw it more prosaically. 'The Soviet Union had been greatly antagonistic to unification. The economy was collapsing. The cost of bringing back the Soviet troops from East Germany was daunting. The key factor was what amounted to a colossal bribe from West Germany to help defray these costs.'[133]

Powell's interpretation is confirmed by a letter from Kohl to Gorbachev on 22 May. The chancellor stated the Bonn government would guarantee a private bank credit for up to DM5 billion 'in the expectation that your government . . . will do everything necessary for required decisions bringing a constructive solution to current problems'.[134] The Germans were, however, more or less on their own. Kohl's letter came shortly after Bush told the West German chancellor in the White House the US could not join in financial help for Moscow because of popular American antagonism over the Soviet clampdown on protests in breakaway Lithuania[135] – just one of numerous occasions when the US refused financial assistance for the failing one-time superpower.

Kohl's 'deep pockets' were necessary but not quite adequate to seal the NATO deal. In a conversation with Mitterrand on 25 May, Gorbachev spelled out his suspicions about NATO's long-term goals. He asked: 'Are the Americans thinking to use NATO to create some sort of mechanism, an institution, a kind of directory for managing world affairs?'[136] He outlined that 'a united Germany could become a kind of space . . . covered by both organisations [Warsaw Pact and NATO]'. He related that he had told Baker how Moscow was aware of America's 'favourable attitude' towards East European countries withdrawing from the Warsaw Pact and joining NATO – and then floated the idea of the Soviet Union itself joining a (greatly modified) western alliance. Buffeted in different ways by influences at home and abroad, Gorbachev was still testing diverse scenarios.

Visiting Washington a week later, he showed further signs of equivocation. His warm welcome in the US represented a sharp and benevolent contrast to his increasingly strained position at home, where Yeltsin was rapidly consolidating power. By a narrow vote on 29 May, Yeltsin secured the presidency of the Russian parliament. A fortnight later, in a still more important step, he engineered a landmark affirmation of Russian sovereignty which effectively legalised Russia's separation and amounted to 'a declaration of political and economic war against the central state' – setting off a string of similar declarations in other Soviet republics, notably, and most consequentially, in Ukraine.[137]

Domestic pressures on Gorbachev were rapidly getting out of hand. The Soviet leader was seemingly oblivious when he made what the Americans termed a 'rambling' presentation in an afternoon session on 31 May at the White House.[138] Gorbachev started off by stating that united Germany could be a member of both alliances, or neither. He told Bush to be even-handed: 'You are extremely concerned about the health of united Germany, from which you calculate the health of NATO. You are so concerned about it that you forget about the health and interests of the Soviet Union.'[139]

There followed an American masterstroke. Bush mentioned that, according to the principles of the 1975 Helsinki Final Act, all nations had the right to choose their alliances. Should this right not apply to Germany? To the astonishment of the Americans, and the consternation of his own advisers, Gorbachev 'nodded and agreed matter of factly that this was true'.[140] Sergey Akhromeyev and Valentin Falin, head of the Foreign Ministry's international department, a key German specialist, 'squirmed in their seats'. Bush's officials were sufficiently startled that they asked the president to get Gorbachev to repeat the statement, which he did[141] – allowing Bush to broadcast agreement on 'the matter of alliance membership' at a harmonious closing press conference on 3 June.[142]

A still more decisive breakthrough came with Kohl's mid-July visit, brokered by Teltschik two months earlier, to Moscow, and then to Gorbachev's home region of the Caucasus, where the Soviet leader formally agreed that a united and fully sovereign Germany could stay in NATO.[143] However, to take account of Soviet sensitivities, and somewhat ominously in view of developments in later decades, NATO was not mentioned in the closing communiqué. Work started on a 20-point cooperation treaty that laid the groundwork for substantial German economic and technological assistance to the Soviet Union.[144]

Reflecting displeasure in Moscow that Gorbachev had been too generous to the Germans and Americans, the Russians fought hard to extract last-minute concessions from the West. A major distraction from Germany surfaced on 2 August when Iraq under dictator Sadam Hussein – an important client of the Soviet arms industry – invaded neighbouring Kuwait and occupied the country in two days. To the relief of Bush and Baker, this catalysed an unexpected US–Soviet rapprochement. Moscow's agreement to back US opposition to Iraq's annexation was announced on 3 August, in a statement by Eduard Shevardnadze, standing side by side with Baker in the lobby of Vnukovo II airport outside Moscow.[145]

Baker considered this marked 'the day the Cold War ended'.[146] But the scramble to complete German unity was set to move to a tortuous denouement.

A dramatic last-minute showdown took place at the Two plus Four foreign ministers' signing ceremony in Moscow's Hotel Oktyabrskaya, which Gorbachev was due to attend.[147] The US, Britain and France – with different degrees of vigour – wished to prevent Russia from setting conditions that could militarily constrain the unified Germans and their allies. Key issues were the status and stationing of foreign armed forces on GDR soil after unification, both before and after the four-year deadline for Soviet troops' withdrawal from East Germany. Would NATO forces be able to 'cross the line' of the East–West German border in the event of a crisis?[148]

Soviet foreign-ministry officials called on western participants in their hotel bedrooms in the early hours of the morning of 12 September, protesting that western stubbornness would delay the signing ceremony and could even scupper unification. But the West stayed firm. According to John Weston, the hawkish British foreign office political director, 'The Russians were running around the hotel in the middle of the night, trying to alarm us into making concessions. I said to myself: "Here we are, Gorbachev is coming to the hotel. We are preparing to sign tomorrow. Let us sit on our hands. They are going to give in. It is important to give the final say [over NATO troop movements] to united Germany."'

The legal statute upholding NATO's right to move troops east of the Elbe laid down an important marker for the years ahead. As Weston puts it: 'Giving NATO these powers for crossing the line was a necessary precaution. The protocol that we came up with had not been invented simply by me. It was observing the interests of the others at the table. There is a point beyond which you cannot budge.'

He adds: 'The idea was to stand firm on the basis that you never knew what to expect. Now we do know: it's called Ukraine.'

5

PATH TO BREAKDOWN

Anyone who thinks that the hour has now come to make the Soviet Union smaller, or rather to destroy the Soviet Union, is a donkey, because in the end there would only be ruins. It would be a fruitless destruction that did not serve peace.

Helmut Kohl to Mikhail Gorbachev, July 1991[1]

Why do not the Poles, Czechs and Hungarians deserve security and consideration every bit as much as Russia, especially since they have far more reason to worry about being attacked by Russia than the other way around?

Fritz Stern, November 1996[2]

Russia has only been great when it's been ruled by great men like Peter the Great and Alexander the Second.

Vladimir Putin to Condoleezza Rice, 2005[3]

The unification of Germany broke the mould of Europe. Many delicate, interconnected state-to-state relationships – some conflictual, some contradictory, some cooperative – had to be split apart, reconfigured and put together again. Once the pell-mell dash to unity was formally completed, on 3 October 1990, a broader, longer and still more fateful set of political, financial and diplomatic manoeuvres got under way. During the first chaotic decade encompassing the Soviet Union's dismemberment and Boris Yeltsin's rise and fall, the West could still – for all the travails – harbour hopes of partnership with Russia, though NATO's enlargement was a perpetual thorn in Moscow's side.

In the second decade, the turn-of-the-century accession of Putin – 'a fitter, healthier, and more sober version of Yeltsin'[4] (although seen initially by many as merely an interim figure) – brought new waves of confidence interspersed with fresh vicissitudes. The terrorist attack on the US on 11 September 2001 cemented a brief period of complicity between Putin and the Americans.

Over the five years following 2007–8 the mood again darkened. Putin lost patience with the West. And Russia attempted to bolster with increasingly desperate and brutal means its status and hold over the territories on its western boundaries – above all, Ukraine.

Along the path to breakdown, there were many staging posts. Force fields fluctuated with the passage of events. Tensions ebbed and flowed between centrifugal and centripetal forces within the Soviet Union and Russia; between the Americans and Europeans over their different historical backgrounds and economic perspectives; and between the East European states, their erstwhile Soviet masters and the West over relations with and within NATO. The largest area for friction was between the US and Russia, jostling within a new post-Cold War framework that seemed to have brought overwhelming advantage to the Americans.

Constant reminders of US supremacy provided a bitter counterpoint to the contest between the contrasting personalities of Gorbachev and Yeltsin. The Americans had a ringside view of the personal struggle at the helm of the failing superpower. According to Scowcroft's analysis in 2000, this bitter rivalry was a crucial factor behind the Soviet unravelling.

> The Soviet Union was disintegrating almost completely because it was the way Yeltsin could get rid of Gorbachev. He really pulled the Soviet Union out from under him. Here was the President of a political entity that no longer existed. I think if that had not been the case, if there had not been that enmity, I think there still could have been some kind of a Soviet Union today. Because Yeltsin, ipso facto, was not trying to destroy the Soviet Union.[5]

Gorbachev's faithful, fatalistic speechwriter Chernyaev believed his boss should have retired into private life immediately after he was awarded the Nobel peace prize on 15 October 1990 for his part in ending the Cold War.

Instead, Chernyaev lamented, Gorbachev wasted time in pointless pursuits such as examining critical domestic letters (delivered in large batches by the KGB) accusing him of sins such as winning 'the imperialist's prize for ruining the USSR, selling out eastern Europe, destroying the Red Army, handing over all our resources to the US and the mass media to the Zionists'.[6]

Chernyaev noted in his diary a month afterwards,

> The country is in ruins and panic. All the newspapers are predicting riots, civil war, and a coup . . . The era [Gorbachev] stirred up has truly gone beyond him. The things he wants to avoid with his carefulness, with his gradual steps, with compromises – all of it has already happened and in the worst form, with bloodshed on the peripheries and the danger of a serious famine.[7]

The war in the Middle East over the Iraqi invasion of Kuwait ended triumphantly for Bush; the collapse of a Moscow-brokered peace plan brought humiliation for Gorbachev. There was now no alternative, Chernyaev concluded, but to accept junior status in the relationship with Washington.[8]

Kohl was worried that Bush might be about to drop the Soviet president. He was grateful for Gorbachev's role in unification, but was concerned that the continued Soviet troop presence in eastern Germany (being dismantled gradually ahead of the planned complete withdrawal in 1994) maintained Moscow's grip over a future Germany. The chancellor telephoned Bush in February 1991 to ensure that the Americans 'continue to regard [Gorbachev] as an ally' despite his efforts to make peace with Saddam Hussein. Bush assured Kohl, 'He [Gorbachev] wants to consider his country as a great power with interests in the region, and he wants to be taken seriously. I have told him we feel the same way.'[9] Gorbachev's problems piled up. Yeltsin called for Gorbachev's resignation on Russian national television.[10] Richard Nixon, the former president, urged Bush to shift support to Yeltsin from Gorbachev.[11]

On the military-strategic front, signs had been multiplying since early 1990 that eastern European countries were bidding to join NATO.

Moscow issued a stream of complaints. Britain joined efforts to persuade Moscow officials that NATO development would not harm Soviet security. John Major, the British prime minster, who took over from Thatcher in November 1990, told Gorbachev and Dmitry Yazov, the Soviet defence minister, in consecutive separate meetings on 5 March 1991 in Moscow that Soviet fears of NATO expansion were based on 'a misunderstanding' and that 'nothing of the sort will happen'.[12] The political directors of France, the UK, the US and Germany, known as 'the Quad', meeting in Bonn the next day, approved a British paper setting out a consensus discounting NATO membership for central and eastern European states. The paper stated unambiguously, 'It would be important not to ostracise the Russians. We could not offer East Europeans membership or associate membership of NATO.' Jürgen Chrobog, political director at the German foreign office, stated that the prohibition of NATO membership to 'Poland and the others' followed directly from negotiations on German unification concluded five months earlier, which had made clear that NATO would not be extended eastward.[13]

The mollifying stance did not quell Moscow's unease. Less than a fortnight later, Gorbachev told Genscher that NATO was heading for 'confrontation'; he protested that 'old instruments against the Soviet Union' were gaining the upper hand over the wish for 'common European structures'.[14] Foreign minister Alexander Bessmertnykh warned that 'the borders of the Cold War should not be extended to the western border of the Soviet Union'. A NATO 'bridgehead' to the central and eastern European states would 'damage Soviet security'.[15] But there was discontent from the east Europeans, too; after President Vaclav Havel visited NATO headquarters on 21 March, German officials pointed out disappointment in the Czech press about the alliance's unwillingness to speed up new membership.[16]

A month afterwards, Dieter Kastrup, Genscher's state secretary, discussed with Manfred Wörner, NATO secretary-general, Soviet 'worries' that Poland and the Czech-Slovak federation were preparing NATO applications 'without delay'.[17] Wörner stated that the US had adopted Germany's cautious stance over eastern enlargement, 'but the relationship of these states with the alliance can develop'. He added that, in military-political circles, the Soviets saw NATO as an adversary, 'at least potentially'. Kastrup underlined the need to avoid alarming Moscow: 'It is desirable that foreign ministry communiqués say that the alliance does not wish to extend to the east.'

In fact, eastern states' desire to accede to NATO rose in direct proportion to growing signs of Soviet political downfall and anxiety about post-Soviet fragmentation unleashed by the simmering conflict in Yugoslavia. Chrobog, Genscher's fiercely loyal political director, later German ambassador to the US during a particularly fraught period for German–American relations under Chancellor Gerhard Schröder, told his British, French and US opposite numbers on 24 April the West should tone down speculation that Gorbachev would soon be dislodged.[18]

In a phone call with Kohl a week later, Gorbachev said he knew the Americans were leaning towards Yeltsin because his rival wished to free the Baltic states from the Union.[19]

Genscher suggested to Baker that eastern countries should join the European Union first, and then NATO – the opposite of what happened.[20] In response, Baker bleakly emphasised Soviet 'chaos' and said he could not rule out eventual membership by former East bloc states.[21] Klaus Blech, Germany's Moscow ambassador, accurately predicted that, unless Europe gave Moscow 'confidence' in its continental dealings, it would face the rise of a 'nationalistic Greater Russia within an unravelling Soviet Union'.[22] German officials emphasised the need for 'NATO liaison' with the former eastern bloc to show that the West respected the 'legitimate security interests' both of the Soviet Union and of eastern Europe.[23]

America's unwillingness to disburse large-scale financial assistance became blatantly evident. Nicolas Brady, the hardline US Treasury secretary, told Bush, with startling candour, that America should back reforms, on condition that they were not backed by adequate funding. Giving the Soviets 'any money to stay as they are' would be an 'absolute disaster'.

America's strategic priority had to be 'changing Soviet society so it can't afford a defense system'. Introducing 'a market system' would mean 'they can't afford a large defense establishment'. In a statement that confirms Russian fears (at the time, and in the years to come) that America was bidding effectively to cancel Russia's position as a world power, Brady proclaimed: 'A real reform program would turn them into a third-rate power, which is what we want.'[24]

'SINCE HE WAS SO DEVOUT, HE SHOULD SWEAR ON THE BIBLE'

Yeltsin won the Russian elections on 12 June. Bush gave him a warm welcome a week later in the White House, greeting him as the first democratically elected Russian leader in a thousand years: 'He was engaging and fascinating, and his infectious laugh made him easy to like.'[25] Bush was impressed, too, that, like Gorbachev, he arrived in a well-tailored suit. Yeltsin's inauguration plans were well under way – a prime occasion for him to show off. With withering irony, in early July, Gorbachev related to Kohl in a long conversation how Yeltsin planned to have himself 'crowned' as 'president of Holy Russia' in his formal investiture on 17 July.[26] 'I told him that since he was so devout, he should swear on the Bible.' He added that he had warned Yeltsin to behave moderately at the ceremony and 'stay sober'.

Gorbachev voiced his anxiety about the Americans: the Americans were backing Yeltsin because 'he spoke constantly about private capital'. Gorbachev was perturbed about 'civil war and anarchy' in the Soviet Union; separatist conflict in Yugoslavia was having a 'great impact' on the Soviet republics. In a sign of fraying German nerves about eastern Europe's increasingly overt NATO ambitions, Bonn officials took steps to water down a German public affairs information leaflet on the alliance's accomplishments, amending a passage stating that former eastern bloc states were seeking NATO membership, and reinforcing language stressing demilitarisation and peace frameworks across Europe.[27]

In an important symbolic gathering that in the end yielded far less than Gorbachev had earlier hoped, the Soviet leader attended the G7 summit in London in mid-July. He berated the western nations 'for spending $100 billion to conduct a regional war in the Persian Gulf', but not directing funding to help his country embark on a new economic system.[28] He told disparaging jokes about himself.

Two Russians were complaining as they stood waiting in line to buy vodka. One declared impatiently that the line was too long, and he was going to go and shoot Gorbachev. After disappearing for a couple of hours, the man returned to his friend, who asked, 'Well, did you shoot him?' The man shook his head. 'No, the line over there was longer than this one.'[29]

Behind the jocularity lay bitterness. Gorbachev hesitated to ask directly for large-scale western credits, partly out of pride, partly because he had been warned that the request would largely fall on deaf ears.

Aware that America had scored yet another victory by heading off requests for aid, Bush commented to Scowcroft that Gorbachev in his London performance appeared 'out of touch'.[30] With his sales patter starting to run dry, the once supreme purveyor of perestroika was 'facing bankruptcy'.[31] Gorbachev admitted he understood why the West was reluctant to dispense more funding. He told Baker later in Moscow,

> Things disappear around here. We got a lot of money for German unification, and when I called our people, I was told they didn't know where it was.[32]

Moscow's weakness, and a de facto hardening of American power in Europe, brought a particular headache for François Mitterrand. A week after the London summit, the French president met Kohl for a frank exchange in the Bavarian resort of Badessee – the village where many of Hitler's blood-thirstiest Nazi rivals had been arrested prior to their execution, in the infamous 1934 'Night of the Long Knives'. Mitterrand treated Kohl to a lengthy critique of American influence, saying that the US wished to create a 'foreign legion' in Europe for waging wars overseas:

> The Soviet Union is going downhill. At the same time the US presence in Europe is diminishing. Therefore, the Americans want compensation: to increase their power in Europe, with structures emphasising European dependence on the US . . . together with a new mission and role for Britain.[33]

In August 1991, Strobe Talbott, a long-time Soviet specialist and journalist (destined to play a strong role in US–Russian relations under Bill Clinton when the latter took over in the White House from Bush in 1993[34]) penned a brutal summary of American power and Russian weakness. 'The USSR has conceded so much and the US reciprocated so little for a simple reason: the Gorbachev revolution is history's greatest fire sale. In such transactions, prices are always very low.'[35]

Signs of Soviet instability intensified on 19 August, the start of the failed two-day coup against Gorbachev by Moscow hardliners, which set the path to the collapse of the Communist party and, just four months later, the Soviet Union itself. Anxieties about the repercussions of Soviet implosion, combined with Yeltsin's enhanced strength as leader of the resistance to the plotters, heightened the former eastern bloc states' desire to seek security within NATO, and simultaneously elevated German wishes to play down the prospect. Wörner joined with German and US officials in proposing 'an upgrade short of expansion' in the form of a NATO-affiliated organisation that would circumvent the difficult question of direct membership.[36] In September, speaking to Genscher in Moscow, Gorbachev claimed the Union's position was again strengthening; yet Ukraine and Kazakhstan's splitting off could unleash 'a great conflict'.[37]

On the same trip, Genscher met Yeltsin to discuss matters of greater practical significance – trade cooperation based on German energy and commodities purchases to allow Moscow access to foreign exchange.[38] Growing tension in Yugoslavia added to concerns. Mitterrand, in conversation with Kohl in Bonn, voiced fears that Germany's probable move to give diplomatic recognition to Croatia, coupled with France's traditional support for Serbia, could split Europe. Once again, Mitterrand said, he was reminded of 1914.[39]

Reality over the growing likelihood of NATO expansion was gradually breaking through in Bonn. A foreign ministry briefing paper for Genscher spelled out the alternatives of 'NATO association' as well as 'liaison', but underlined how Article 10 of the NATO treaty laid down that any European state capable of contributing to North Atlantic security could be invited to join.[40] Pointing out how Jan Krzysztof Bielecki, the Polish prime minister, had used a 10 September Washington visit to ask for speedy integration into the European Community as well as NATO, the document stated that enlargement was looming.[41] Amid worries in Bonn that the Soviet Union saw this as against its interests,[42] Genscher was forced to deny to Boris Pankin, Soviet foreign minister (who had taken over from Shevardnadze in December 1990), that eastern European states were working to join the alliance.[43] Recalled by Gorbachev to serve a brief final spell as the last Soviet foreign minister, Shevardnadze in late October voiced his fears to Genscher in Moscow:

'Soviet disintegration will mean instability for Europe. If the Soviet Union is destroyed, that will destroy what has been built up in the last few years.'[44] Shevardnadze added a bleak final warning: 'Yeltsin would probably not call for the return of Crimea to Russia. But it is conceivable that other, fascist leaders [in Moscow] will demand this.'

Steadily but inexorably, disintegration was under way. In the run-up to the Ukrainian independence referendum on 1 December, Bush and Baker met Gorbachev's adviser Yakovlev to discuss the potential for conflict over parts of the fragmenting Soviet imperium (when Baker predicted 'a normal war' in Ukraine).[45] In Washington, the Bush administration canvassed options internally for Ukraine to join the NATO liaison programme.[46] On his first foreign visit after his presidential inauguration, Yeltsin revealed to Kohl in Bonn his masterstroke for dislodging Gorbachev: to remove his Soviet power base by uniting Russia, Ukraine and Belarus in a confederation.[47] The plan, he told Kohl, had necessarily been kept secret from Gorbachev. Yeltsin already realised Ukraine would vote for independence, telling Kohl that the Ukrainians had placed orders for printing banknotes in Canada. Underlining that 6 million Russians lived in Ukraine (in a sign of lack of precision that went far beyond mere statistics, only half the figure reported to Baker and Bush by Yakovlev), Yeltsin forecast a possible referendum in Crimea that could lead to the territory's merger with Russia.

Coinciding with Bush's and Baker's discussion in Moscow of a possible war over Ukraine, Yeltsin gave Kohl in Bonn an identical warning of future storms. 'We are dealing here with a dangerous national development, an adventure, that one must fear will end in bloodshed.' But he also outlined hopes: the 'monster' of the KGB had been destroyed, and – one day – the Soviet Union would become 'an institution like the European Community'. When German ministers joined the German and Russian leaders for a wider meeting, Theo Waigel, the German finance minister, intervened with a blatant pitch for business. 'The Soviet Union has always been a good debtor. Medium and long term, it will be a rich country. Germany has been strongly engaged. If Russia is now making new investments, for example in natural resources, then it makes sense that countries that have been particularly engaged in the past should now receive favourable treatment.'[48] Yeltsin replied: 'There are enormous prospects for building ties between Germany and Russia.' He saw this as 'a barrier against possible unrest in Europe' and 'a bridge to Europe'. He added: 'I can say with great conviction that German companies will be treated as a priority.'

As predicted, the Ukrainian referendum resulted in a massive pro-independence vote. A fateful two-day negotiating session on 7–8 December in Belarus brought together Yeltsin with Ukraine's leader Leonid Kravchuk and Stanislas Shushkevich of Belarus: yet another turning point, of epic dimensions. With one momentous act,[49] Yeltsin sealed the end of the Soviet Union and of Gorbachev. Before informing his dethroned rival, the Russian leader telephoned Bush with news that the three Slavic Soviet core states had agreed to set up a 'Commonwealth of Independent States' (CIS) – which, he claimed, would be shortly signed too by Nursultan Nazabayev of Kazakstan.[50] The move would free Russians from 'the global centre that has issued commands for over 70 years'.[51] The CIS was enlarged to eleven states on 21 December at a summit in Alma-Ata. Yeltsin telephoned Bush on 23 December to tell him that Ukraine and Belarus would become non-nuclear states.[52] 'We will have no explosive processes.' The same day John Major told Gorbachev by telephone, with Majoresque understatement: 'We are aware that the coming months are going to be very difficult.'[53]

On Christmas Day, Gorbachev made his televised resignation speech. Shortly before, he telephoned Bush to tell him he was resigning as commander in chief and transferring nuclear weapons control to Yeltsin. 'The debate in our union on what kind of state to create took a different track to what I thought right.'[54] Demise was undignified. Handing over supreme command and the nuclear codes was a scrambled affair. Yeltsin, enraged by Gorbachev's TV address, refused to come to his office. Gorbachev portrayed his 'expulsion' from the Kremlin as one further step in a perpetual downward spiral.

> We were forced to move to different lodgings within 24 hours. I saw the results in the morning: heaps of clothes, books, dishes, folders, newspapers, letters, and God knows what lying strewn on the floor ... Developments in the country took an alarming term The so-called 'shock therapy' – a 'cavalry-attack' on our economy – brough enormous hardship for the people of Russia. Power was in the hands of irresponsible, incompetent people who were both ambitious and ruthless.[55]

A succinct epitaph on Gorbachev as 'a tragic figure'[56] came from Gorbachev's adviser Anatoly Chernyaev. 'History wanted something different from him than he wanted from it . . . The empire disappeared in a unique, original way.'[57]

ELEMENTS OF CATHARSIS

Gorbachev's unceremonious departure ushered in the Yeltsin years. They fused diverse elements of catharsis: a swirling battle for control over the sprawling post-Soviet landmass, the push and pull of western efforts at binding in Russia to post-Cold War security arrangements, concerted efforts to bring order into the ex-Soviet nuclear arsenals – all against the backcloth of a colossal, doomed economic experiment.

Shadowboxing over NATO expansion continued with a new set of actors after Bush lost the November 1992 presidential election to Bill Clinton. Speaking in 2023, Rodric Braithwaite, Britain's ambassador to Russia at the time, recalls fears in Moscow that Russia could follow a similar course to Germany after it lost the First World War: 'a failed attempt at democracy and the rise of an aggressive dictator. Millions of ethnic Russians had been left outside Russia when the Union disintegrated, and hundreds of thousands were returning to Russia as destitute refugees. It would be easy enough for a future dictator to exploit their plight as Hitler had exploited the position of the Sudeten Germans.'[58] Economic misery and chaos took hold.

> By the winter of 1991–2, the state was unable to pay its teachers, doctors and officials for months at a time. Military officers – men with guns – had no pay and nowhere to live: they did not take to arms, but many went into organised crime. Old ladies were having to sell their family treasures on the streets. Yeltsin did his best to cope. His economic advisers, young men in their twenties like [Yegor] Gaidar[59] and [Anatoly] Chubais,[60] were from the Soviet elite. The measures they took were botched and were much criticised in Russia and abroad. The critics – including the highly-paid Western consultants – failed to come up with convincing alternatives, perhaps unsurprisingly, since no-one had any experience of dismantling a state economy on a continental scale.

A sense of powerlessness to stop a remorseless decline was conveyed by a telegram sent to Washington in March 1994 by Wayne Merry, the US embassy's top Russian analyst, lamenting that 'shock therapy' tactics had led to disarray and destitution.[61] 'Sadly, very few of the multitudes of American "advisors" in Russia since the Bolshevik demise acquainted themselves with even the most basic facts of the country whose destiny they proposed to shape . . . Even the most progressive and sympathetic of Russian officials have lost patience with the endless procession of what they call "assistance tourists".'[62]

But reformers saw no alternative to radical change. Pierre Morel says of reformers like Gaidar and Chubais: 'The system was so rotten that they saw the danger of a Soviet comeback. The new leaders had to break the mould. They couldn't move step by step, they had to make the changes irreversible.'

Gaidar and others like him said they saw themselves as in a battle – the first wave out of the trenches, the first to be mown down in gunfire. There was a sense of drama and personal risk. Always the threat that it would end unhappily. I found it a bit terrifying. I called Chubais [in charge of privatisation] to say that what he was doing was confiscating the property of the nation. I told him this could come close to civil war – it was a kind of aggression against the nation. His answer was that, if this didn't happen, the red barons would be back tomorrow. This would mean the return of the Soviet Union. It was a battle for survival.[63]

Manoeuvrings over NATO contained similar explosive potential. The fundamental issue was the impossibility of combining four mutually exclusive imperatives. First, Russia wanted security from the West and to retain its place at the top table of world diplomacy. Second, ex-Soviet bloc states from central and eastern Europe were desperate to escape forcible return to a zone of Russian influence. Third, Clinton wished to win favour both from his defence establishment and ethnic east European voters in key electoral constituencies. Fourth, western Europe was anxious not to antagonise Russia.

Western concerns about enraging Yeltsin and Moscow hardliners diminished after the last Soviet-era troops (and accompanying nuclear weapons) left eastern Germany in 1994. Meanwhile, other former Soviet bloc countries' desire for insurance against Russian instability increased with displays of force by Yeltsin against opponents in Moscow and separatist movements in Chechnya and elsewhere.[64] As violence and instability in Russia mounted, and the civil war in disintegrating Yugoslavia reached a new crescendo with the American bombing of Russia's ally Serbia, suspicion and tension ratcheted upwards on all sides. The German foreign ministry was in no doubt that, in attempting to find a balance between Russia and Ukraine, the West was setting off a powder keg. Klaus Neubert, veteran head of the East European department, pointed out in January 1993: 'Without the enormous economic and military potential of Ukraine, which made up 40 per cent of the former Soviet armaments industry, the Soviet Union would never have become a world power.'[65] Ukraine's independence 'would place continual limits on a future Russian great power policy'. Neubert pointed to the 'psychological irreconcilability 'of competing Russian and Ukrainian claims on Kievan Rus' as their national bedrock.

In a sign of Ukraine's 'deep-seated complex' regarding the West, Neubert accurately pinpointed Ukrainian suspicions (that the Americans later admitted were justified): once problems such as the removal of Soviet nuclear weapons had been resolved, the West 'could lose all interest in the poor and economically run-down country'. International concerns surfaced at a NATO foreign-ministers meeting in Brussels in February 1993. Yeltsin's foreign minister, Andrei Kozyrev, underlined that Russia should not be excluded from NATO enlargement considerations. In an exchange over Ukraine, James Bartleman, Canada's ambassador to NATO, warned that a future conflict between Ukraine and Russia would make the Yugoslav war look like 'child's play'.[66] Bartleman's 1993 premonition about the linkage between nuclear arms removal (eventually sealed in a 1994 agreement[67]) and a Russo-Ukrainian war accurately foreshadowed a chilling remark by Putin to Bill Clinton two decades later.[68] The nuclear withdrawal set the pattern for a chain of events that made conflict well-nigh inevitable.

The West was aware that, not least because of the growing campaign for NATO enlargement, Yeltsin was facing severe resistance from anti-reform politicians in Russia. At an extraordinary meeting in Moscow in

March 1993, where Kohl stopped on the way back from a gruelling trip to Asia, the German chancellor offered the Russian president support for what Yeltsin hinted could be 'extreme measures' to counter 'reactionary' forces in the Russian parliament threatening a showdown with the president.[69] The former Communist party was reorganising, Yeltsin reported – 'a danger one should not understate'. Yeltsin explained he was considering emergency action similar to Charles de Gaulle's assumption of power through suspension of the French National Assembly in 1958. Pressed by Yeltsin to forecast reaction from other G7 states, Kohl said he thought they would back Yeltsin and further reforms.

In an attempt to bolster western cohesion, Kohl wrote immediately to Clinton, Mitterrand and Major informing them of his Moscow talks.[70] He recommended that the West support 'stabilisation' and warned his partners that Yeltsin might take 'extreme measures' in the stand-off with parliament – a prediction that came to a head in October when 187 people died after Yeltsin declared emergency rule and ordered tanks to fire on the White House parliament building to put down an insurrection. As the likelihood of escalation intensified, Clinton and Kohl stretched charm and plausibility to breaking point to attempt to keep Russia on side. Balancing these volatile parameters in a shifting equation of European and American power proved an unrealisable task.

A precisely argued paper on NATO enlargement from Germany's ambassador Hermann von Richthofen pointed this out in June. He advocated 'flexible and differentiated interim measures' to try to bridge the irreconcilable positions of Russia and the former Warsaw Pact states.[71]

Yeltsin himself set off discussion of NATO expansion through public remarks in Warsaw in August. In an echo of Gorbachev's fateful admission to Bush in May 1990, Yeltsin acknowledged the Helsinki Final Act right of countries to choose their alliances, and expressed 'understanding' for Poland's wish to join.[72] The evening before, during a private tête-à-tête, an inebriated Yeltsin had been coaxed by Lech Wałęsa, the Polish president, into a much further-reaching concession committing Russia to support Poland's intention to join NATO as soon as possible.[73] Following the public debate generated by his statement, Yeltsin wrote to Clinton on 15 September to express 'uneasiness' about 'the scenario of quantitative expansion of the alliance by adding east European countries'. To counter perceptions of Russia's 'neo-isolation' and avoid contravening 'the spirit' of the September 1990 German unification agreement, Yeltsin said he favoured 'a truly pan-European security system'.[74]

America made a concerted but ultimately fruitless effort to convince Yeltsin and his advisers that the Partnership for Peace (PfP) programme[75] – launched in September–October 1993 to upgrade the North Atlantic Cooperation Council[76] – was an alternative to NATO expansion, rather than a precursor.[77] The US and its allies mounted what amounted to a complex double game[78] – simultaneously pushing ahead with preparations for expansion later in the decade[79] and telling the Russians that a future European security system would include, not exclude, them.

On 22 October, Clinton's secretary of state, Warren Christopher, embarked on a mission of reassurance to the Russian president's hunting lodge at Zavidovo outside Moscow.[80] The Partnership for Peace, he told Yeltsin, was an attempt to defuse Russia's 'neuralgic' concerns that it would end up 'on the wrong side of a new division of Europe' as NATO expanded.[81] With what tuned out to be overdue haste, Yeltsin termed Christopher's proposal 'a brilliant idea – a stroke of genius', saying that it resolved Russian worries about relegation to 'second class status'.[82] According to the State Department account, Christopher added: 'We will in due course be looking at the question of [NATO] membership as a longer-term eventuality' – an aspect that Yeltsin appeared not to take seriously. Kozyrev, accompanying Christopher, believed that his American counterpart and his aides deliberately left 'unfinished business' rather than 'presenting the full scope of his president's policy'. Kozyrev's conclusion was that, on the basis of the emollient version of the truth, Yeltsin had 'solid ground' to assume that the topic of enlargement 'had been exhausted and that Clinton was intent on the Partnership for Peace instead of NATO enlargement as his new policy'.[83]

CONTRADICTIONS AND AMBIGUITIES

The internal and external contractions and ambiguities at the heart of PfP provided the reasons both for its superficial attractiveness, and for its eventual downfall. It furnished grounds for disquiet among both supporters and opponents of NATO expansion, since they each imagined that, through a flexible interpretation of the concept, their aims would be thwarted and their adversaries would gain the upper hand. A sobering State Department document in December 1993 underlined Moscow's fragile psychological condition. 'It sticks in their [the Russians'] craw that NATO appears poised to dictate the terms of the new order and Russia has no choice but to accept a late invitation to a table that has been pre-set by Washington for 45 years. At bottom, even our most enlightened colleagues in Russia have not fully adjusted to the loss of their status as a supposedly co-equal superpower.'[84]

A German foreign office paper earlier in the year came to a similar conclusion: Russian statements dwelling on 'pre-1914 thought categories' and weighing up miliary options showed 'how little Russia has come to terms with "loss of empire"'.[85] Nationalist anti-reform politicians gained ground in December 1993, the first parliamentary elections in post-Soviet Russia. Germany's assessment was that this shift would increase central and eastern European pressure to join the EU and NATO.[86] 'They [ex-Warsaw Pact states from central and eastern Europe] were disappointed by what we [the West] had to offer in Partnership for Peace.' Countering this, Kozyrev threatened that, if Poland and the other central European states joined NATO, the former Soviet countries 'could form a new Warsaw Pact-style bloc'.[87]

With relentlessness bordering on desperation, Clinton insisted on presenting PfP in a positive light. But the painful implausibility of his desired compromises was revealed in January 1994 when he stopped off in Prague on his way to see Yeltsin in Moscow. In talks with Czech president Vaclav Havel, Clinton attempted to reconcile the irreconcilable, making three at least partly contradictory points. First, that the PfP was 'a track that will lead to NATO membership'. Second, that it would not 'draw another line dividing Europe a few hundred miles to the east'.[88] Third, that another line might indeed arise in the future. 'Ukraine especially does not want to be pushed back onto Russia's orbit. Future events may force us to draw a line; nothing we are now doing prevents that.'

At lunch the next day, Clinton made clear to the leaders of the Czech Republic, Poland, Hungary and Slovakia that he would not acquiesce in any new Russian attempt to divide Europe into spheres of influence.[89] Wałęsa treated the lunch guests to a selective rendering of his feat the previous August in cajoling a drunken Yeltsin to sign a paper (which Wałęsa said he still had in his possession) approving Poland's NATO membership. 'Russia had signed many agreements, but its word was not always good: one hand held a pen; the other a grenade.' Immediately after the lunch, in a prepared press conference statement, Clinton put his seal on the issue. The question was 'no longer whether NATO will take on new members, but when and how'.[90]

In Moscow, Clinton told Yeltsin that PfP would provide the opportunity 'to do something that has never been done since the rise of the nation state itself – have a Europe that is truly integrated and not divided.'[91] But Clinton was aware that even his charismatic brand of political marketing might be inadequate to meet reality. He bluntly told Yeltsin of other world leaders' forebodings (which he insisted he did not share) that the Russian leader might be 'fighting a losing battle against the forces of history'.[92]

The sparring over NATO enlargement reinforced Vladimir Putin's simmering resentment. As an official in the St Petersburg administration working under the dominant figure of Anatoly Sobchak, the mayor, Putin had only a limited external profile.[93] But he used it to good effect.

When he spoke in a high-level St Petersburg dialogue with German and European officials and political scientists in August 1994, Putin delivered a strong hint of what was to happen in 2014 and 2022. He blamed Gorbachev for 'clumsy action' in causing the 'liquidation of the Soviet empire'. He touched on 'other territorial issues', pointing out that 'Russia voluntarily gave up vast territories to the former republics of the Soviet Union in the interests of general security and peace in Europe; including those territories that have historically always belonged to Russia,' highlighting Crimea, northern Kazakhstan and the 'Kaliningrad region' (presumably in a reference to Lithuania). 'There are now suddenly 25 million Russians living abroad, and Russia simply cannot afford – if only in the interests of security in Europe – for these people to be arbitrarily left to their fate.'[94]

A German historian participant reacted immediately – and with some prescience – to Putin's 'vision of a quintessentially Russian territorial designation' based on the 'Asian tradition' that 'territories impregnated in Russian or Slavic blood have the right to remain in Slavic possession forever'.[95]

Ahead of a visit to Poland and the Baltics, Clinton telephoned Yeltsin on 5 July – shortly before a later-scheduled meeting at the G7 summit in Naples – to allay the Russian president's anxieties about ex-Soviet bloc countries joining NATO. Clinton repeated the mantra on NATO expansion: 'no timetable and no requirements'.[96] Yeltsin responded that the Poles were undertaking 'a great propaganda campaign' to incite Belarus to unite with Poland. 'People say they want to join NATO to become stronger and stronger. They talk about threats. Russia is not a threat to anyone.'

When he addressed the Polish parliament two days later, Clinton fulsomely elaborated on PfP, but he said it was 'only the beginning', repeating the 'no longer whether, but when and how' phrase coined six months earlier.[97] Germany was becoming increasingly reconciled to Poland's NATO membership. Janusz Reiter, Poland's long-serving ambassador to Germany, discussed the issue with Chancellor Kohl when Andrzej Olechowski, the Polish foreign minister, visited Bonn in July 1994.[98] Kohl told the ambassador that he knew that an important background reason for the Poles' wish to join reflected worries about Germany's as well as Russia's policies towards its neighbours.

Two important PfP opponents – Richard Holbrooke, the outgoing US ambassador to Germany, and Volker Rühe, the German defence minister – used a ceremony for the departure of western troops from Berlin in September 1994 to call for swift NATO expansion.[99] Back in Washington, Holbrooke spurred aggressive behind-the-scenes action to accelerate exactly that development.[100]

Declassified briefing papers confirm that the Clinton administration recognised that Ukraine might be a casualty: 'Expansion will leave [Ukraine] wedged between an Alliance it can probably never enter, and Russia.'[101] With chilling cynicism, Washington officials resolved that no acknowledgement of this potentially fatal halfway-house position should be made until removing the territory's nuclear weapons was well under way, to avoid giving the Ukrainians the pretext for maintaining their atomic arsenal.

In his public diplomacy, Clinton stuck doggedly to reassuring Russia that its interests were not being undermined – even though in background conversations his officials were arguing the opposite. In September, Clinton repeated to Yeltsin at the White House: 'inclusion, not exclusion'. For Poland, Hungary and the Czech Republic, there was 'no timetable for NATO expansion . . . We're going to move forward on this. But I'd never spring this on you.'[102]

BEEFED-UP NATO COMMITMENT

The November mid-term elections in the US produced a fresh hardening of the American stance. The Republicans' feat in gaining control of both houses of Congress – for the first time since Eisenhower's presidency – reflected wins in key constituencies favouring the Republicans' pro-NATO expansion policy. Ahead of a planned Partnership for Peace signing ceremony in Brussels on 1 December, Anthony Lake, Clinton's hawkish national security adviser, brushed aside German concerns and engineered a beefed-up NATO communiqué affirming the alliance's 'welcome' for enlargement and working towards a timetable on it.[103] Yeltsin's foreign minister, Kozyrev, was under growing pressure to push back against the US from nationalist factions in Moscow, in particular Yevgeny Primakov, head of the foreign intelligence service and later foreign minister and prime minister.[104] Kozyrev arrived in Brussels the evening before the ceremony. But he refused to sign Russia's PfP document after the US pushed through changes in NATO accession agreements for Hungary, Poland and the Czech Republic.[105]

An enraged Yeltsin phoned Kozyrev at the Russian embassy to complain, interrupting his tennis game with the Russian ambassador. He 'screamed' (according to Kozyrev) that the Russians had been duped by Clinton and his secretary of state. 'What do you say of your beloved Americans? Where is your friend Christopher? He had promised to give you advance warning. What happened to Bill? How could he have done this to me again?'

Clinton and Yeltsin exchanged anxious letters.[106] On 5 December, when both men attended the Budapest summit of the Conference on Security and Cooperation in Europe, Yeltsin erupted with his strongest anti-NATO outburst, leaving Clinton 'stunned and angry'.[107] With strong undertones of statements Putin was due to make in the following decade, in his public speech Yeltsin accused the US of trying to run the world from Washington. He asked: 'Why are you sowing the seeds of mistrust? . . . Europe is in danger of plunging into a cold peace.'[108] Clinton – who had been wary about travelling to Budapest so soon after the disastrous mid-term elections – told his advisers afterwards he was 'pissed off' by Yeltsin's statements.[109] The debate on NATO was not only about Russia: it also concerned the prospect of a reawakened military role for Germany. In December, Henry Kissinger emphasised (just as Baker and Bush had reminded Gorbachev in 1990) how a 'vacuum between Germany and Russia' could unleash German aggression: 'If this request [for NATO widening] is rejected, and the states bordering Germany are refused protection, Germany will sooner or later seek to achieve its security by national efforts, encountering on the way a Russia pursuing the same policy from its own side.'[110] Kissinger's warning echoed a phrase in the influential pamphlet by two leading German Christian Democrat politicians, Wolfgang Schäuble and Karl Lammers. Three months previously – in a much-cited text regarded as a key pillar in the 'concentric circles' model of European integration – they had argued for a flexible system built round a 'hard core' of France and Germany. This, they wrote, would ward off the danger of a 'destabilising vacuum' in mid-Europe under which Germany 'might be called upon or, through its own security imperatives, be tempted to carry out the stabilisation of eastern Europe alone and in the traditional manner'.[111]

Departure of Soviet forces from eastern Germany, Ukraine's denuclearisation and progress on US–Russian weapons cuts, allied to concern about violence in Bosnia, prompted more moves on NATO expansion in 1995. In January, Clinton broke new ground by calling it 'inevitable'.[112] When Clinton visited Moscow in May to mark the fiftieth anniversary of Second World War victory, Yeltsin told him at the start of a rambling three-hour encounter, 'I see nothing but humiliation for Russia if you proceed.' NATO expansion would be 'a new form of encirclement', representing 'betrayal on my part of the Russian people'.[113] Suggesting that the issue be postponed until 2000, Yeltsin touched a raw nerve with Clinton, stating that, in forthcoming elections in both countries, 'extremists and hardliners are exploiting this issue for their own purposes'. Clinton responded by hinting that accord on a 'gradual' timetable for NATO would help Moscow integrate with the West through relaxed rules on technology exchanges and allowing full Russian participation in extended G7 summits.

Clinton pointed out how domestic electoral pressures were forcing his hand on NATO. 'The Republicans think they can take away those states [Wisconsin, Illinois and Ohio] by playing on the idea of NATO expansion.' The two leaders agreed a fragile compromise: postponing NATO enlargement until after both countries' 1996 elections (in June–July and November). An important landmark in Yeltsin's campaign against his Communist rival Genady Zyuganov was sealed in a telephone call between the two presidents in February 1996 – opening the way to a large, virtually condition-free loan from the International Monetary Fund.[114] Yeltsin could boast at election rallies: 'My pockets are full.'[115]

Further support for Yeltsin came from the Russian oligarchs.[116] Primakov, his wily new foreign minister who took over from Kozyrev in January, reinforced his backing for Yeltsin with a vigorous campaign against NATO enlargement, backed by a series of well-documented claims.[117] At the heart of the Primakov case was the contention (just as Yeltsin had suggested to Clinton in September 1993) that Germany's 1990 unification agreement limited or prohibited further NATO expansion. The State Department took the Primakov dossier sufficiently seriously that it assigned two hawkish top diplomats, John Kornblum and John Herbst, to assemble a detailed rebuttal of the Russian arguments.[118]

On a visit to Moscow in April 1996 to prepare for a nuclear safety summit of the 'Political Eight' (the G7 plus Russia), Talbott – now his old friend Clinton's deputy secretary of state – noticed a sign of Russia's 'wider options for the future'. Yeltsin's vast Kremlin office had been lavishly redecorated with statues of Peter the Great, Catherine the Great and Alexander II.[119] En route to Moscow, Clinton spent a day in St Petersburg. Putin as the key aide to Mayor Sobchak, in charge of security, was responsible for keeping the president from meeting local people.[120] Yeltsin enlivened the Moscow encounter by subjecting Clinton to a Primakov-inspired diatribe in front of the press over America's allegedly 'go-it-alone' Middle East policies.[121] Clinton once again mollified his host with talk of 'a cooperative, equal partnership', proclaiming, 'None of us has any intention of sidelining Russia.'

In a telephone call after Yeltsin's convincing second-round victory in July, the Russian leader urged 'massive' foreign investment 'now that it is clear that the people of the US do not see Russia as a threat or source of global instability or expansion'.[122] Yeltsin sounded 'listless' on the call: 'not the now-familiar thick-tongued quality we associated with drink [but] the sound of sickness'.[123] The political thaw after Yeltsin's win did not last long. When Talbott flew to Moscow shortly after the Russian election, Primakov again confronted him with evidence that Baker, Kohl, Major and Mitterrand had all given assurances to Gorbachev that former Warsaw Pact counties would not enter NATO.[124]

'A STRATEGIC BLUNDER OF POTENTIALLY EPIC PROPORTIONS'

The mood soured as the US presidential election neared in November 1996. In the week before the poll, George Kennan, the Cold War diplomat whose celebrated February 1946 memorandum on 'Soviet containment' had set the framework for post-1945 superpower relations, fired the first salvo, at a private dinner at Columbia University, in what was to become a public campaign against NATO enlargement. He termed it 'a strategic blunder of potentially epic proportions'.[125] Clinton's 5 November election victory came on the same day that Yeltsin was admitted to the Moscow Cardiological Centre for a seven-hour quintuple bypass operation.[126] The top US surgeon observing the operation said it was 'a complete success'.[127] When Major telephoned him on 23 December – Yeltsin's first day back in the office – the Russian president appeared 'a bit hoarse' and was reading partly from a script, but showed himself 'quite quick on the uptake'.[128] He voiced satisfaction ('Very good, John') that NATO's new members would not station nuclear weapons on their territory. But Kohl – who visited Yeltsin at his Zavidovo hunting lodge in early January – scotched any hopes that the Russian president would recover his former robustness. Kohl telephoned Clinton to tell him Yeltsin appeared five to ten years older than when he had seen him four months previously: 'There is virtually nothing left of his vitality.'[129]

Yeltsin was vigorous enough, according to Kohl, to reaffirm his opposition to NATO enlargement: 'He is afraid a new cold war is imminent and people won't understand.' Any Russian hopes that Kohl would use his influence to slow down enlargement were however illusory. Kohl told Yeltsin that, in this matter, he had no 'veto power'. Behind these words lay a momentous conclusion: in view of Yeltsin's fragility, NATO had to press on with enlargement, based on 'direct bilateral talks' with the Russian leadership, with a decision scheduled for the forthcoming summer NATO meeting.[130] In the immediate follow-up, Kohl summoned Talbott to an exceptionally fruitful Bonn meeting. The chancellor told the No. 2 in the state department he did not believe Yeltsin would last his term and mentioned on six occasions that time was running out.[131] In a similar vein to his sentiment over German unification, when he vowed to 'bring in the hay while the sun shines'[132] Kohl declared: 'We should make good use of the time remaining. If the chances are ever going to be good, it is now.'

Britain joined a combined effort to calm Russian nerves. Discussing in February a Russia–NATO rapport over enlargement, Major disingenuously told Primakov in London that 'if he were a Russian, he too would be concerned by the possibility that NATO might move up to Russia's borders'. But he was not a Russian, Major clumsily added, and he knew NATO had no intention of doing this. 'We had no wish to create political difficulties for the Russian government and were not seeking to box in Russia. NATO enlargement would happen, but it would be gradual, restricted and predictable.'[133] Primakov responded that, if Major were in his shoes, he would not like to hear of a 'gradual and predictable' increase in the number of missiles directed at Russia.

The diplomatic machinery rumbled on. The West's efforts were focused on winning Moscow's accord for a NATO–Russian Founding Act (signed in Paris in May) and at least tacitly accepting an enlargement timetable at a Madrid NATO summit in July. At breakfast in Paris, Tony Blair, Britain's new prime minister, met Yeltsin for the first time. Alastair Campbell, Blair's all-seeing, all-recording press secretary, portrayed the Russian leader as 'big, a bit clumsy, a bit gauche, larger than life'.[134]

Blair and others tried to persuade Yeltsin to attend the Madrid session.[135] But Yeltsin and senior Russian figures stayed away. Clinton understood the Russian leader's reluctance to give 'ammunition to the ultranationalists while they are working on ratification of START-II

[Strategic Arms Reduction Treaty]'.[136] Russian distaste at American 'pressure tactics'[137] over Moscow's assistance for Iran's nuclear weapons programme overshadowed the June 1997 G7 summit in Denver. Yeltsin was a prime guest, a landmark on the laborious journey to see the Group of Seven leading industrial countries converted into the G8. A British diplomatic note revealed Yeltsin's deterioration from his Blair breakfast meeting three weeks earlier – 'a "tan" closer to grey than bronze . . . no hamming it up as there had been in Paris . . . old and not 100% with us'.[138]

Complex multiple-cornered sparring over NATO coincided with fresh tension over the war in Kosovo. Contestants in the NATO jostling included the east European states, in particular, the Baltics, anxious to be included in the next-but-one enlargement round; a Congress that was manifestly split between pro- and anti-expansionists; European NATO allies, especially an ever-truculent Chirac; and a clutch of bipartisan US figures.[139] They recommended that European Union enlargement take precedence over NATO widening – a choice that European governments rejected.[140] Former senator Sam Nunn and Brent Scowcroft, George H.W. Bush's security advisers, drew comparisons with the years after the First World War. The 'central failure' of Versailles lay, they believed, in Keynes's critique from 1919 of 'the fatal miscalculation of how to deal with a demoralized former adversary'. This was an 'error we must not repeat'.[141]

Clinton and Yeltsin laboured once again to paper over the cracks. The Birmingham industrial country summit in May 1998 represented the culmination of the G7 to G8 conversion. In a studiedly genial bilateral session with Yeltsin, Clinton opined they were 'working with the stuff of history'. In twenty years 'when the Russian economy is booming, people will look back and say we were right . . . I just hope you get all the credit you deserve while you're still around.'[142] Yeltsin called the relationship 'more than just a friendship . . . co-leadership'.[143] But the bonhomie was showing fatal signs of fatigue. In the US, an active debate was starting on who was to blame for 'losing Russia'.[144] American scholar, author and cultural diplomat James Billington, a man with vast experience of the Soviet Union, wrote: 'Both the greatest opportunity and the greatest danger for the United States internationally may well still lie in Russia. If we do not soon seize the opportunity, the danger will increase – and could present us with the most serious threat to basic global stability since the end of the Cold War.'[145]

Russia's economic descent accelerated. The 1997–8 Asian financial crisis that started with the devaluation of the Thai baht in July 1997 spilled over in August 1998 into a collapse in credits to Russia, rouble devaluation and economic meltdown.[146] Amid renewed concerns about his health,[147] Yeltsin was largely sidelined.[148] Clinton warned him 'as a friend' that appointments in the new government under Primakov as prime minister 'raise concerns that Russia will return to the hyperinflation of 1992'.[149] A German official told the Americans that Yeltsin was suffering from dementia.[150]

NATO's eastern encroachment proceeded undaunted. In line with the Madrid timetable, Hungary, Poland the Czech Republic joined the alliance in March 1999. NATO bombing of Serbia between March and June 1999 dominated weeks of high-stakes diplomacy between Clinton, Yeltsin, vice president Al Gore, Prime Minister Sergei Stepashin (who had taken over in May from Primakov and would hand over in August to Putin) and their officials.[151] This was an ultimately successful NATO effort to constrain Serbian forces to withdraw from Kosovo – a severe test between Moscow and Washington. Yeltsin called the episode 'a military gamble [that] might have very grave consequences for the world at large and the Balkans'.[152] Stepashin said it was as serious as the 1962 Cuban nuclear missile crisis.[153] 'The majority of the Russian people and our political elite think that the US is trying to dictate to everyone else in the political and military spheres.' Like Yeltsin and others, he recalled the First World War.

> Several years after the war following its humiliating defeat and the armistice, Germany was engulfed by hysteria, which led to Hitler coming to power. The analogy with Russia today is obviously not exact. No Hitler will come to power here but the psychology is similar.[154]

The stand-off over Kosovo allowed an increasingly self-assured Putin to make his mark with Clinton's top officials. Heading both the FSB (successor to the KGB) and the national security council, he met Talbott in his Kremlin office,[155] and then, four days later, telephoned Samuel 'Sandy' Berger, national security adviser. The NATO onslaught intensified worries in Moscow that the alliance might next target Russia, on the grounds that there were 'many Kosovos' in Russia.[156] Putin glossed over the antipathy with aplomb. He elegantly outlined room for compromise over joint control of Pristina airport and for curbs on exports of sensitive 'dual technologies' to Iran.[157] He unveiled his ability to switch from rough language to the polished tones of international diplomacy. And he made conspicuous use of interlocutors' first names:

Sandy, if I may ask you that you could do me a favour? Could you make use of your very considerable authority and influence so that the question of sanctions does not arise all the time or only from time to time? Such threats are not conducive to the promotion of the Russian–American dialogue. Should any problems arise here, they would arise from lack of information. We could attempt to solve these problems quickly, maybe through the line of communication that we have established with you, Sandy.[158]

Putin suavely made no reference to the Washington summit the following month, commemorating NATO's fiftieth anniversary, when nine more countries were duly enshrined as NATO cooperation partners, primed to join the alliance in the next round.[159]

After Yeltsin sacked the hapless Stepashin and appointed Putin on 9 August, the fifth prime minister in sixteen months went quickly into action. He ordered air strikes against militants in Chechnya, told a TV interviewer that strikers sitting on railway tracks would be jailed, and set plans to reinforce his public profile.

According to UK ambassador Roderic Lyne,

For someone supposedly so boring, wooden and uncharismatic, he did a good job in his first TV interviews. He was wearing a pullover, sitting in an armchair, looking relatively relaxed. He had a down to earth attitude, not talking over people's heads, which was Gorbachev's problem. He deliberately used street language to make a point.[160]

In a telephone call with Berger on 12 August, Putin moved seamlessly into cloying mode: 'Sandy, I'm calling to express my gratitude . . . my cooperation with you has helped me a lot in my work.' He (not entirely comprehensibly) thanked the State Department for 'support to my naming as prime minister of Russia' and promised there would be 'no sharp changes' to the Cabinet or to foreign and domestic economic policy.[161]

With an anti-insurgency campaign in Chechnya that claimed massive numbers of civilian casualties, the hitherto barely known prime minister now ensconced as Russia's strongman attracted western condemnation but, at home, garnered increasing popular support. A spate of unexplained apartment bombings in Russia sparked a climate of fear and repression.[162] Clinton met Putin twice, at international summits in Auckland (September) and Oslo (November). The disturbed state of his own and Russia's health prompted Yeltsin to step down, six months early, on 31 December and hand over to Putin.[163] Putin obligingly implemented (on his first day as acting president) a decree to grant his predecessor an amnesty and immunity from prosecution.[164] In no uncertain terms, Yeltsin defined his legacy: 'The new century must begin with a new political era. The era of Putin.'[165]

A president was leaving who had been cajoled by Clinton, in his international stance, to carry out, in the words of Clinton's close friend Talbott, 'politically radioactive policies . . . He got him to do it because Yeltsin trusted him.'[166] Would the new man be as compliant?

During a twenty-minute New Year's Eve call, Yeltsin informed Clinton the Russian people now had three months to get used to Putin as acting president before the March elections. His designated successor was 'very strong, very intelligent' and 'with a big soul'. Yeltsin declared that Putin was a democrat. But some decisions, it seemed, were too important to be left purely to the ballot box. 'I am sure that he will be elected in the forthcoming elections,' he told Clinton. 'I am sure about that.'[167]

SEARCH FOR UTILITY

In advance of the March presidential election, knowing that Clinton would leave office the following January, Putin deduced that Tony Blair would be a key figure to support his western relationship-building. He invited the British prime minister to St Petersburg on 13 March. There was utility on both sides. As British ambassador Roderic Lyne put it,

'Putin chose Blair because he was the pre-eminent European leader and someone through whom he could deliver a message about his intentions both to other Europeans and to Washington.'[168] Blair was sympathetic. 'We were the same age and seemed to share the same outlook.'[169] Jonathan Powell, Blair's chief of staff, explained the 'calculated risk' of travelling to Russia. 'Putin wanted to build up an international profile as part of the election campaign. We cut him some slack over Chechnya.'[170] A month earlier, speaking to Blair's foreign secretary, Robin Cook, in Moscow, Putin had failed to show remorse over 'collateral damage' to civilians in Chechnya. Serving advance notice of the theme-switching 'what-aboutism' technique he would extensively use in coming decades to disarm western interlocutors,[171] he wrongfooted Cook by turning the conversation towards the Second World War. As a result of Anglo-American bombing, he said, 'German citizens had suffered extensively, but that had not stopped the Allies from fighting Hitler.'[172]

When Putin duly won the March presidential election, Clinton telephoned to congratulate him on 'a really historic milestone for Russia', calling the president-elect by his first name for the first time.[173] Putin responded: 'It is clear to the whole world that I am a person you can work with.' In fact, as the new leader's self-confidence grew, the West's faith in his credentials and character was starting to fall. Germany voiced doubts about Putin's 'democratic principles' and his apparent offer to bargain a constructive Russian approach on Yugoslavia at G8 meetings against western silence on the killing in Chechnya.[174] On the intriguing question of whether Russia might one day join NATO, Putin laid down a smokescreen. He reminded Clinton, on a visit to the Kremlin in June 2000, that he had already voiced theoretical support for Russian NATO membership[175] – not mentioning explicitly his crucial condition that NATO would first have to abandon its role as a military organisation.[176]

Talbott, as an astute student of Soviet and Russian affairs, and a Russian speaker, was keenly aware of Russia's sensitivities caused by the 'wounds' of 'collective humiliation'. He saw the struggle over Chechnya symbolising 'a more general sense of grievance and vulnerability after a decade of other difficulties and setbacks, real and imagined, most conspicuously the enlargement of NATO and the Kosovo war'.[177] As a result, Talbott was quicker than others to focus on growing problems with Moscow. He pointed out that Putin was 'walking a walk that is different from the talk he is talking'[178] – and was 'proving increasingly to be a problem'.[179] This was due to 'both his approach to issues and to his tactics', Talbott explained to Chris Patten, European commissioner in charge of external relations: 'Unlike the more direct, even confrontational style of Yeltsin, Putin tends to say "Yes" when he really means "No".'[180] Reflecting on Putin's unwillingness to engage with the US, Talbott told David Manning, Britain's designated ambassador to NATO, that Yeltsin had been seen in Russia as overly compliant with western wishes.[181] 'Putin has set himself up as a departure from Yeltsin.' Talbott suggested, 'The West might now be paying the price for seven years of successfully turning Yeltsin's Nyets into grudging OKs.'

During the US presidential election campaign, Condoleezza Rice, who later became national security adviser to President George W. Bush and later secretary of state, criticised Clinton for too 'romantic' a view of Yeltsin. At the outset of his administration, Bush kept a wary distance from Putin.[182] Opinion in Britain was split. In January 2001 an internal note entitled 'Putin's progress', drawn up for John Sawers, Blair's foreign-policy adviser, raised a variety of concerns, including those about a resurgence in Russian espionage activities.[183] Speaking in 2024, Sawers, who later become head of Britain's Secret Intelligence Service (MI6), played down the report. 'The intelligence people had made their assessment. They naturally saw the glass half empty and warned of the dangers. I didn't think that it made too much difference to Blair's thinking. It wasn't all that persuasive.'[184] Blair's contemporary messages were aligned with that view. He told Dick Cheney, Bush's vice president, in February 2001 (and partly repeated the message in March 2002), that Putin was a Russian patriot, sensitive to his country's 'loss of respect' in the world, deserving a seat at the 'top table' and with a similar 'mindset' to Charles de Gaulle.[185]

Blair undoubtedly played a role in Bush's discovery of a common wavelength with Putin in June 2001 when the US and Russian leaders met for the first time at the sixteenth-century castle of Brdo in Slovenia – scene of the celebrated Bush 'I looked the man in the eye' remark.

The 9/11 terrorist attacks on New York and Washington gave a multiple fillip to Putin's ever-inventive gamesmanship with the West.

He could, at least temporarily, put the relationship with the US onto an equal footing by showing sympathy to a country in distress.[186] He could label Russia's brutal war against Chechnyan separatists a helpful appendage to Bush's subsequent campaign against alleged centres of Islamic terrorism in Afghanistan and Iraq.[187] In assisting the American military with a route (for airborne and land forces) for an assault on Afghanistan, Putin wished to secure an important quid pro quo: western acquiescence over Russian aggression in Chechnya.[188] Furthermore, the aftermath of wrangling in the West over alleged 'weapons of mass destruction' in Iraq provided a welcome means of splitting the western allies.[189] Blair sealed an alliance with Bush on the 'war on terror', while France and Germany together with Russia came down on the side of neutral countries refusing to entertain armed conflict with Iraq unless specially sanctioned by the United Nations.[190] Reflecting earlier French outrage over Russian violence in Chechnya, Jacques Chirac, as Blair later explained, had given Putin 'something of a cold shoulder' at the beginning of Putin's tenue. 'In time that all changed,' Blair recorded, 'and their relationship became very close as mine waned.'[191]

Putin showed further tactical adroitness in attempts to outwit the US over Washington's long-running desire to abrogate the Anti-Ballistic Missile (ABM) treaty. However, he ended up bruised and resentful in episodic diplomatic sparring on an issue with a long history stretching back to the 1960s. The ABM treaty, signed in 1972,[192] was designed to uphold nuclear deterrence by preventing either superpower from implementing a national defence system that could overwhelm the other side's incoming missiles – and wreck the doctrine of 'mutually assured destruction' underpinning world peace. Starting with Ronald Reagan's exaggerated but politically effective belief in a high-tech defensive shield under the 1983 Strategic Defense Initiative – Star Wars – US politicians flirted with building 'national missile defense' during the 1980s and 1990s, a concept that effectively violated the treaty, and, three decades later, came back into vogue in Donald Trump's second term.[193]

As the end of Cold War lowered the need for defences against Russia, American experimental programmes gained favour providing 'theater missile defence' against shorter-range ballistic missiles from unstable and unpredictable countries like North Korea, Iraq, Iran and Libya. By Clinton's second term, the US was close to pressing ahead with National Missile Defence (NMD) systems to provide protection against so-called 'rogue states'. Clinton decided to leave a decision for the new administration. Bush and the Republicans, keen to capitalise on earlier Star Wars enthusiasm, seized the opportunity.

Bush told Putin at their first meeting in June 2001 that 'he intended to get out of the ABM treaty and would prefer to do it mutually'.[194] In a carefully phrased statement (which he said he had discussed 'with my friend President Vladimir Putin') Bush announced in December 2001 that America was withdrawing from the treaty to allow development of a national defence system.[195] Putin immediately declared that the move was 'erroneous'. But he said Russia would not be threatened by it, since his country had built up a sufficient nuclear arsenal to penetrate US defences.[196]

Germany, although not enamoured with a political move in the US that many believed would lower its European defence commitment, was struck by the possibilities for commercial partnership. Schröder made clear in his first meeting with Bush in March 2001 that Germany would be open to work with the US on NMD to maintain the country's technological edge.[197] But this was part of a careful balance of German economic interests where Russia played an important role. On Putin's first visit to Germany as president of Russia, in June 2000, Schröder helped lay the groundwork for a series of gas and energy deals that would cast an abiding shadow over the coming decades.[198]

REWARDS OF RISING OIL PRICE

As Putin's term in office lengthened, a series of developments hardened his approach to cooperation with the West. The economy improved substantially. Speaking in 2023, ex-ambassador Roderic Lyne explains: 'In 1998, the rouble had collapsed. The oil price recovered from $10 in 1998, to about $17 in 2000 and went steadily upwards until 2008, peaking above $100 a barrel. Russia's main export and budget revenues came from oil and gas. The economy started to grow again after the 1998 devaluation.'[199] As Bush put it, 'Over the course of eight years, Russia's newfound wealth affected Putin. He became aggressive abroad and defensive about his record at home.'[200]

Putin's self-confidence – and his belief that the West was treating him unfairly – rose with the oil price. In June 2001, at the memorable first Bush–Putin meeting in Slovenia, the Russian complained how Russia was burdened by Soviet debt.[201] Bush wrote, 'At that time oil was selling at $26 a barrel. By the time I saw Putin at the APEC [Asia-Pacific Economic Cooperation] summit in Sydney in September 2007, oil had reached $71 – on its way to $137 in the summer of 2008. He leaned back in his chair and asked how were Russia's mortgage-backed securities doing.'

Five key factors contributed to a progressive build-up of tension. First, the 'colour revolutions' in former Soviet states intensified Putin's fears about hostile encirclement. After the 'rose' revolution in 2003 in Georgia, with the deposition of Eduard Shevardnadze and replacement by Mikheil Saakashvili, came 'orange' in Ukraine in 2004–5, with the defeat of pro-Russia Viktor Yanukovich and election of Victor Yushchenko. Then followed, in 2005, 'pink' or 'tulip' in Kyrgyzstan, with the ousting of President Askar Akayev. Following high-profile American election campaign visits to Ukraine, Putin saw US and western influence every-where, speaking of 'a stab in the back' and claiming, 'They are stealing Ukraine from under me.'[202] Saakashvili's accession started the slippage towards a test of strength with Russia, culminating in Putin's decision to invade Georgia in August 2008 in sabre-rattling over disputed territories in South Ossetia and Abkhazia.[203] The short Russo-Georgian war had been foreshadowed in April 2002 when Putin told Blair, 'Suppose we act against Georgia, which is a base for terrorism against Russia. What would you say if we took Georgia out? Yet the Americans think they can do whatever they like to whomever they like.'[204]

Second, NATO expansion continued at a steady pace, with Bulgaria, Estonia, Latvia, Lithuania, Romania, Slovakia and Slovenia joining in March 2004.[205] Adhesion by the Baltic states marked the first entry by former constituents of the Soviet Union. This signified an important stage of the move towards a decision on Ukraine or Georgia member-ship – an issue which caused a major split in NATO at the Bucharest summit in April 2008.[206] Bush favoured Georgia and Ukraine applying for a Membership Action Plan (MAP) for NATO, but Merkel and Nicolas Sarkozy, France's new president, were against it. Under the resulting compromise, Georgia and Ukraine were denied an MAP but were stated to be joining at an unspecified date. Even though the would-be adherents were denied a fast track to access, Ukrainian and Georgian leaders were exultant.[207] In her memoirs, Merkel wrote in 2024 that Putin saw the general pledge of membership as 'a declaration of war'.[208] He told her in a later encounter: 'You won't be chancellor forever and then they'll become Nato members. And I'm going to prevent that.'[209]

Third, Anglo-American claims, pointedly not supported by France or Germany, about Sadam Hussein's alleged 'weapons of mass destruction', used to justify invading Iraq in March 2003, appeared to the Russians increasingly as a brazen attempt to solidify American advantage and undercut Russia. Blair's emotive 'moral imperialism' on Iraq[210] grated on Schröder,[211] strengthened the Paris–Berlin–Moscow axis[212] and emboldened Putin's 'Russia first' strategy. Britain and Blair came off worst. Rice affirmed that the US should treat Russia relatively lightly for siding with France and Germany in opposing the US-led invasion. She formulated the American response as 'Punish France, ignore Germany, forgive Russia'.[213] Well before the further souring of UK–Russian ties over the 2006 murder of Alexander Litvinenko, a former Russian intelligence agent who had fled to the UK,[214] Blair's moralising tone compromised the formerly propitious relationship with Putin. During an extraordinary scene at the Sea Island G8 summit in the US state of Georgia in 2004, Romano Prodi, European Commission president at the time, recalls Putin shouting at Blair: 'You are not God!'[215]

Fourth, western 'concessions' to Russia over NATO and other issues turned out to be mainly cosmetic. Putin saw NATO's strategy as undermining his popularity in Russia, where he was coming under pressure for appearing to give America undue support. In October 2002, Putin told Blair 'he was pretty much alone in the [Russian] leadership re pursuing a very pro-western policy, and he felt he was getting very little in return from the US'.[216] On the governance of the western alliance, the NATO–Russia Council,[217] established in May 2002 to build on the 1997 NATO–Russia Founding Act, fell well short of expectations.[218] The dialogue was designed to assemble the nineteen NATO then-member states and Russia on an equal basis, addressing Russia's complaints that it was perpetually shut out of debate.[219] But this modest innovation failed to make a difference. Putin displayed his anger when Blair visited Moscow in April 2003, not realising he was heading for a public relations trap. Putin coupled a mocking assault on the Anglo-American Iraqi weapons claims with an attack on America's post-9/11 worldview: 'The whole post-September 11 response was designed to show off American greatness. They don't care what anyone thinks.'[220]

Fifth, Putin grew increasingly discomfited by aggressive US moves on national missile defence. After initially parrying Bush's 2001 ABM announcement by declaring that Russia's atomic weaponry would overwhelm America's protective screens, Putin became alarmed by planned deployment of anti-missile systems in the new NATO and former Warsaw Pact members, allegedly targeted at missiles from 'rogue states'.[221] Bill Burns, US ambassador to Moscow in 1995–8, wrote, 'No amount of argument about the technological limitations of systems based in the Czech Republic and Poland against theoretical Russian targets, however soundly based, swayed Putin and his essentially suspicious military.'[222] Attempts to involve Russia in the exercise failed to make headway.[223] The Obama administration in 2009 reversed the planned deployment of radar systems in Poland and the Czech Republic,[224] but incited fresh hostility from Moscow by advancing with new anti-missile development in Poland and Romania.[225] One of Italy's most experienced diplomats, Pasquale Terracciano, had a ringside seat at the progressive deterioration of European–Russian relations from 2000 onwards.[226]

> The Russians offered a base for the radar equipment in Azerbaijan, which would have been closer to Iran and Iraq. The Americans said, 'No way'. This confirmed the Russians' feeling that it was aimed against them. Later on, the Americans started to deploy the equipment in Romania and the Czech Republic. This prompted Putin to start building an historical narrative to justify his own revanchism. The idea gained ground that Putin and Russia would never fit into the Atlantic community – playing into the hands of those on both sides who never wished to see Russia inside, and always thought we and they were inevitably enemies.[227]

'DRIFTING INTO VERY ROUGH WATERS'

Bill Burns, US ambassador to Moscow, wrote to secretary of state Condoleezza Rice in October 2006 that the US–Russian relationship was 'drifting into very rough waters'. Russia sensed that 'we are fundamentally uncomfortable with Russia's return as a Great Power and seek to constrain it'.[228] Five months later, in spectacular fashion, Burns's instinct was proven correct. Putin was gearing up for an assault on western pretensions of supremacy. In February 2007, speaking at the Munich Security Conference, with about five hundred delegates, Putin laid bare two decades of bruised pride and unveiled a monumental challenge to the West. His speech – vehemently duplicating and amplifying traditional messages of Kremlin Cold War resentment – veered between the bitterly aggressive and surprisingly sophisticated. He railed against America's 'unilateral and frequently illegitimate' military action in a 'unipolar world' where the US 'has overstepped its national borders in every way' and 'even more are dying than before'. A world 'in which there is one master, one sovereign . . . is pernicious not only for those within the system, but also for the sovereign itself, because it destroys itself from within.'[229] He accused the US of provoking a new nuclear arms race by developing ballistic missile defences, undermining international institutions, making the Middle East more unstable and trying to divide modern Europe. NATO expansion, he said, bore no relation to ensuring security in Europe. 'On the contrary, it represents a serious provocation that reduces the level of mutual trust. And we have the right to ask: against whom is this expansion intended? And what happened to the assurances our western partners made after the dissolution of the Warsaw Pact? Where are those declarations today?'

Underlining the need for 'multilateral diplomacy', Putin pointed out that India and China outweighed the US in combined economic size, measured in terms of purchasing-power parity. The gross domestic product of the BRICS countries – Brazil, Russia, India, China and South Africa – was greater than the European Union's. 'The economic potential of the new centres of global economic growth will inevitably be converted into political influence.'

In his follow-up speech, Robert Gates, the US defence secretary and former CIA chief, attempted a light-hearted touch to counter Putin. 'As an old cold warrior', he said Putin's speech 'almost filled me with nostalgia for a less complex time'.[230] To others in the audience, what shone through was not humour but anger. 'Putin was consumed with rage,' says Werner Hoyer, a leading foreign policy and security specialist from Germany's Free Democratic Party.[231]

Horst Teltschik, the long-serving adviser to Helmut Kohl, by 2007 a board member of the BMW motor group and chairman of the security conference, was sitting next to Putin. Merkel had spoken first – about present and future cooperation with Russia – but Putin pointedly ignored her. 'Putin was not paying attention to her speech but was working on his own text,' Teltschik recalls. 'He focused on the problems NATO expansion was causing for Russia, in particular the plans to station US anti-missile systems in Bulgaria and Romania.'[232]

Michael Stürmer, the German Cold War historian and veteran Russia-watcher, was seated six or seven rows behind Putin, optimally place for analysing Putin's body language.

He spent the whole time adjusting the manuscript, striking out and changing passages. He was visibly seething with anger. His message was that the West had deceived the Russians, had let him down. Eastern enlargement of NATO was the greatest humiliation for the Russian leadership. They had lost everything and got nothing. Putin wanted recognition for Russia. He did not wish to be ranked at the same level as Poland and Lithuania. The Russians need an element of triumph in their foreign policy. If they lose that, they lose everything.[233]

From his vantage point in Moscow, Burns wrote for his boss, Condoleezza Rice, an instant summary (as he admitted, 'an oversimplified version') of Putin's message for the West: 'We're back, and you'd better get used to it!'[234]

As the US–Russian dispute over anti-missile defence simmered on, the repercussions became clearer – part of a general build-up to events in Ukraine, a decade and more ahead. In August, Putin ordered Russian strategic nuclear bombers to resume regular long-range flights for the first time since the 1980s.[235] At the end of the year, Russia suspended adherence to the Treaty on Conventional Armed Forces in Europe.[236]

The divisive NATO summit in Bucharest in April 2008 was followed by Russia's invasion of Georgia in August. The George W. Bush administration, in its final months before the November 2008 election that brought Barack Obama to power, did not take seriously repeated Russian assertions strongly opposing Georgia and Ukraine joining

NATO.[237] Looking back, Jim Collins, the US diplomat who was chargé d'affaires when the Soviet Union collapsed and ambassador in 1997–2001, reflects on what he saw as the Bush administration's faulty view of the Russian status quo.

> They had not figured out that Russia was in a totally different place compared with the Soviet Union. They couldn't understand that this was not the same as the Allied victory over Nazi Germany. The Russians did not accept they had been defeated. They did not have the mindset of post-war Germany and Japan. America was treating the Russians as though they had lost the war. However, the Russians did not see it like that. They didn't want to be treated in that way.[238]

COUNTDOWN TO A CRESCENDO

The viewpoint of Rice, a major player in America's handling of Russia in the first decade of the twenty-first century, has shown some inflection over the years. At the 2008 Bucharest summit, when the US was urging NATO expansion to Ukraine and Georgia, she declared to NATO foreign ministers, 'Moscow needs to know the Cold War is over and Russia lost. We can't let it split the alliance.'[239] The phrase was a perhaps subconscious echo of Ronald Reagan, who expressed his approach to the Cold War in direct terms: 'We won and they lost.'[240] Speaking in 2024, she took a more emollient line, contradicting what she had affirmed nearly two decades earlier: 'No one was saying to the Russians: "You have lost the war and now we're going to treat you like a minor power." There was no sense that anyone was trying to put them down in any way, from Gorbachev all the way through to Putin.'[241]

Some authoritative America figures harbour a sense of mea culpa. In 2019, Bill Burns opined that the US had made fundamental mistakes in 2008 by pushing ahead with the NATO membership drive for Ukraine and Georgia. 'That fed Putin's narrative of "enemies at the gate", in particular the US, to justify what is a deeply repressive political system at home.'[242] The US–Russian relationship, Burns said, had been built on a dual illusion: the Russians believed that 'somehow they were going to be accepted, even though the power realities had changed enormously, as a peer, as a full partner'; the American illusion was that 'we could always maneuver over or around Russia'. The contradictions were untenable. Russian 'push back', the ambassador wrote, was inevitable.

The countdown to a crescendo over Ukraine proved Burns's point. In November 2013, under strong pressure from Russia, Ukrainian president Viktor Yanukovich refused to sign the 'association agreement' with the European Union under negotiation for seven years. This set off a chain of events via the Maidan revolution (named after the Independence Square in Kyiv where mass pro-EU demonstrations took place) and Yanukovich's subsequent ousting and exile.[243] Russia seized Crimea in February 2014 – without triggering a substantial western response – and an internal war started between the Ukraine military and pro-Russian separatists in Ukraine's eastern regions.[244]

The path to full-scale invasion eight years later was littered by misjudgement and miscommunication on both sides. The EU failed to heed warning signals from Russia about its readiness to retaliate over Ukraine's gradual move into the western orbit. A UK parliamentary committee found in 2015 that 'the EU, and by implication the UK, was guilty of sleep-walking into this crisis'. Member states, according to a British House of Lords report, displayed a 'worrying lack of political oversight' over the European Commission's negotiations with Ukraine on the association agreement.[245] Catherine Ashton, the British Labour Party politician who was the EU's foreign affairs supremo in 2009 to 2014 – designated 'high representative for foreign affairs and security policy' – disliked the 'sleep-walking' epithet but concedes the point: 'We should have looked harder for trouble and examined more closely the politics as well as the economics.'[246]

Many factors contributed to the miscalculations. As the hardworking, no-frills Ashton admits, in October 2012, Sergei Lavrov, the Russian foreign minister, at a meeting with EU foreign ministers in Luxembourg, was highly critical of the trade elements of the agreement. But she adds: 'The issue wasn't raised in the twice-yearly Russian summits until we moved closer to the signing.' Ashton and the Commission's foreign-policy arm, the European External Action Service (EEAS), were preoccupied with a nuclear deal with Iran and the aftermath of the Arab Spring pro-democracy protests in the Middle East.[247] Ashton says they lacked the 'bandwidth to stay on top of everything'.

Pierre Vimont, the French diplomat heading the EEAS, who worked closely with Ashton, agrees with the 'sleep-walking' phrase. He recalls Lavrov at the Luxembourg meeting saying Russia was not likely to accept the EU's agreement on Ukraine since it countered Russia's interests with its most important trading partner and would lead to significant trade losses for the Russian economy.[248] 'The Russians wanted to have a say in this' – a suggestion the Commission rejected. 'I thought this was shortsighted. But the Commission was intent on taking it one step at a time. The Commission was not used to dealing with geopolitics. It was not their natural playing field. They had a certain way of doing things in the trade sector and they were sticking to it.'

In view of Russian hostility, Vimont says he suggested to Herman Van Rompuy and José Manuel Barroso, presidents of the European Council and Commission, that they should discuss the association agreement with the Russians at the regular summits. 'They said that they had never heard Putin mention this issue so they did not try to talk about it.'[249]

Compartmentalisation of the EU's foreign-policy services meant that Štefan Füle, the commissioner for enlargement and neighbourhood policy, was in charge of the relationship with Ukraine and other former Soviet states. 'He was more aware of what was going on because, as a Czech, he knew the ground on which he was walking,' Vimont says.

> The EU was trying to extend European presence and influence in some of the former Soviet republics which Russia considered as its own sphere of influence. The Europeans should have been more cautious. There should have been more awareness that Europe did not have the leverage to prevent the Russians from striking back.

Füle oversaw the 'eastern partnership' programme established in 2009.[250] 'All the eastern countries had the same history and wanted to advance together. It was not aimed against Russia.' But he became aware in March 2013 of intensified antagonism. The problem was, Füle believes, that 'we had nothing similar to offer Russia. We had an ambitious and consensual policy towards the Eastern partnership countries, but we did not have an ambitious or a consensual policy towards Russia.'[251] As Füle explains, the EU's planned free-trade agreements with the eastern countries ran counter to new Russian integration efforts to form a customs union in the east, later the Eurasian Economic Union. 'It became clear, later, that countries which entered the European free trade agreements would not be able to be part of the Russian-led and -dominated customs union.'

At his meeting with the Russian government in March 2013, Füle realised that Moscow had reviewed the association agreement and free-trade plans 'and concluded that they would oppose our concept despite all the costs'. The Russians came to believe, according to Füle, that their previous strategy of opposition to NATO membership by former Soviet bloc states but openness to EU adherence had been 'a tragic mistake'. Allowing the post-Soviet countries to establish an increasingly closer relationship with the EU was not a secondary issue but 'the most powerful transformative instrument ever . . . The Russians realised that rather late. As soon as Putin realised this, Russia started its efforts to stop the process.'

Füle admits he and the Commission made an important strategic misstep.

> I should have gone to Moscow earlier to explain to them in 2012 what I told them in March 2013. We could have had a chance, maybe, to address these fundamental issues at the level of the EU–Eurasian Economic Union through exploring a possibility of a big treaty between the EU and the customs union. I had suggested going there earlier to Cathy Ashton but she reminded me that my responsibilities and portfolio covered Ukraine and other partners, not Russia.

John Herbst points out that, when he was US ambassador to Ukraine in 2003–6, Russia's ambassador (and later prime minister) Viktor Chernomyrdin repeatedly said Russia had no objections to Ukraine joining the EU. However, that emollience gave way later to a harder line.

As it became increasingly clear that Ukraine was going to conclude a trade agreement with the EU, Russia began to impose economic sanctions on Ukraine to kill the deal. Moscow's opposition to the trade deal – something far less than EU membership – was all about Russian influence: Russia's long-standing imperial tradition of claiming the right to dictate to its neighbors.[252]

At a meeting to discuss trade matters between Ukrainian, Russian and European leaders in Minsk in August 2014, Putin displayed ambivalence over territorial ambitions beyond Crimea. He told Ashton that his advisers had told him he should keep on going further into Ukraine, but he had chosen not to do so.[253]

As British prime minister between 2007 and 2010, Gordon Brown – the man responsible for sending Ashton to Brussels – witnessed Putin during a far less benevolent phase than his predecessor, Tony Blair. Brown opines: 'There was no doubt after 2005 that Putin was in the business of becoming more threatening. He derives strength from his perceptions of other people's weakness.'[254] Brown believes that the West's largely supine response to the seizure of Crimea set a pattern. It provided Putin with 'a form of carte blanche for further aggression'. The turbulent history of the previous two decades offered few indications that the Crimean incursion was likely to bring East–West enmeshment over Ukraine to a peaceable end. In fact, it marked the beginning of a new phase of escalation and danger – with effects spilling out into every corner of Europe.

6

HOLE AT THE HEART

Once, the Socialists believed they could abolish money. In any case the single currency would be very useful.
> Giuiliano Amato, prime minister, Italy, replying to French president François Mitterrand's complaint about the 'intolerable immorality' of speculation, 1992[1]

Financial conditions remain hostage to European developments. Europe continues to muddle through. The risk of a Lehman-style catastrophic financial event has not been eliminated. The European Central Bank needs to act as a backstop.
> Ben Bernanke, chairman, Federal Reserve, 2011[2]

From a political and social point of view, especially in view of the built-in strains in a monetary union among unequal economies but without a political union, Europe is more vulnerable than Japan. Japan can be stagnating and stable. If Europe stagnates it will not be stable.
> Indermit Gill, chief economist, World Bank, 2024[3]

The route to economic and monetary union and the institution at its apex, the European Central Bank, was sealed at Maastricht in the Netherlands in December 1991 by a dozen government leaders. Monetary union and the ECB combine ambiguous characterisations, implausible contradictions and spectacular transformations: a fusion of rationality and trauma.

EMU's birthplace is a location of appropriate singularity, an orderly town of antique shops, heritage sites and multilingual universities on the triple border between Germany, the Netherlands and Belgium. Fulfilling the old dream of a single currency to bind together a restless continent has been a relentless crusade of groundbreaking dimensions. Based on a blueprint worked out primarily between France and Germany, EMU was conceived as the foundation for post-Cold War Europe. For the premier player at Maastricht, Helmut Kohl, the outcome would determine the balance between 'war and peace'.[4] The second most important participant, François Mitterrand, regarded the goal as a form of nuclear disarmament: dismantling the German D-Mark, which the French president referred to as Germany's 'nuclear force',[5] now potentially still more lethal after the rapid expansion of the German state back almost to wartime size and potency.

The host, Dutch prime minister Ruud Lubbers, believed the currency project would be so attractive that it would lead to political union, the ultimate guarantor of continental stability. This was a mistaken view, as he admitted later.[6] A project borne of complex objectives symbolises, more than any other, a European unity that is fractious, piecemeal, vulnerable and prone to sporadic psychological upheaval.

Maastricht formed a historic staging post in a sinuous journey of European integration: a passage into a new world. The town's name is derived from a combination of the Meuse river it straddles and the classical Latin 'trajectus' (meaning ford, passage, crossing point). Was it a bridge too far? Might an alternative emblematic venue have been Vienna, the birthplace of Sigmund Freud, the father of psychoanalysis? Or Venice, spiritual home of the medieval Italian *commedia dell'arte*, a forerunner of English pantomime and modern burlesque? Where multiple permutations of caricature, comedy and conflict exist – and nothing is quite as it seems? For Indian academic and technocrat Rakesh Mohan, Maastricht as a university location embodies features that thirty years ago made Europe a beacon – one that is no longer shining. 'In 1993–4, I was in Maastricht for a year on leave from the Indian government, attempting to prepare a book on European industry and technology policy. Europe then was a role model: that is no longer the case.'[7] In an apt metaphor for EMU, Mohan's book was never finished.

The ECB is the one powerful central institution in a European Union that has otherwise become increasingly diffuse. So the story of the bank – and the plotting, politics and personalities behind it – is in many ways the story of Europe. The bank, set up in 1998, six and a half years after Maastricht and six months before the birth of the euro, is on most measures the world's second most important central bank after the US Federal Reserve. The euro is, after the dollar, the world's second reserve currency. Some fundamental economic criteria for the combined euro area – measurements of public debt, budget deficits and international trade balances – display a greater degree of stability than for the US and China.[8]

On this basis, if Europe manages a turnaround of the sort attempted in reaction to Trump 2.0 in 2025, the euro may build its importance as an international reserve currency and a challenger to the dollar.[9] But, by any historical yardstick, the bank is still a young and not fully tested institution, not least because of the continuous strain of maintaining a common monetary policy among differently performing separate sovereign states that do not form a common polity. It is owned, not by any European government, but by the central banks for the European Union, even those (like the Bank of England, before the UK left the EU in 2020) that are not part of the euro.[10]

As Joachim Nagel, president of the German Bundesbank, put it in 2025, 'We are not a fiscal union and not a political union. As long as this is not resolved, we are in a situation that from time to time will be tricky and complicated.'[11]

AMORPHOUS STRUCTURE

Housed since 2014 in a forty-five-storey intertwined double tower looming over unprepossessing eastern Frankfurt, the ECB symbolises the hole at the heart of an amorphous structure of political and economic decision-making. The appearance is one of solidity and order. Yet no one is fully in charge. One of Francois Mitterrand's more cerebral prime ministers, Michel Rocard, used to speak of central banks and governments intrinsically joined as the heart and lungs of the monetary system.[12] In the case of monetary union, the brain appears insufficiently connected to the limbs.[13] The ECB makes its decisions through the governing council, comprising six board members and heads of the central banks of the twenty countries that, as of 2024, had joined the bloc. The twenty-six-member body (as of early 2025, twenty-four men and two women) is more akin to a multinational parliament than a policy-making committee of the sort seen in other central banks.[14] As a sign of the increased influence of political factors at the ECB since its inception, the number of former finance ministers on the council has steadily increased over twenty-five years.[15] The ECB's iron-clad constitutional independence has a paradoxical effect. It raises the onus on euro member governments to choose, at a predetermined time of nomination, central-bank governors for membership of the council who are aligned with their own political leanings.[16]

The hole at the heart of monetary union is not an accident; it forms part of the basic design. The separation from any kind of overriding state system, in a framework where there is no European government, is a synonym for, and a consequence of, Europe's incompleteness. The ECB is owned, not by any European government, because there is none, but by the national central banks of the states of the Union – a uniquely complex governance structure.[17]

Disjunction from government, too, serves a fundamental purpose. As a result of successful Bundesbank experience, Germany believed that an independent central bank was the key towards maintaining low inflation and hence political stability. As an integral part of the grand bargain of monetary union, the rest of Europe went along with the idea that central-bank independence could be Europeanised. Felipe González, Spanish prime minister from 1982 to 1996, summed up the trade-off. Other countries were giving up their (limited) sovereignty over their own currencies; in return they were winning a share of what had become Germany's quasi-monopoly over European money.[18]

Niels Thygesen, the veteran professor at Copenhagen University, and a member of the committee established under European Commissioner Jacques Delors in 1988 to plan the single currency, explains:

> The Maastricht treaty deliberately separated the political and the monetary authorities to underpin ECB independence. There is today some effort of informing each other through minimal partici-

pation in the governing body of the other authority, but no real framework for coordination.[19]

Thygesen has frequently attended meetings between European finance ministers and the ECB in his capacity as chairman of the European Fiscal Board between 2016 and 2024. He points out an intriguing difference between Christine Lagarde, the former French economy and finance minister and IMF managing director who has headed the ECB since 2019, and her predecessor Mario Draghi:

The ECB talks quite openly in the economic councils about how governments should put their fiscal houses in order. Lagarde has been very firm in her language, more so than Draghi. In view of respect for the ECB's independence, there's not the same tough talk [from the finance ministers] in the other direction.[20]

With sovereign nation states setting up a new form of stateless money, the attempt to transcend nationhood appeared a harbinger of a post-modern Europe that would set aside past centuries' conflicts. According to Wim Duisenberg, the Dutchman who in June 1998 became the first president of the European Central Bank, the euro epitomised the 'mutual confidence at the heart of our community – the first currency that has not only severed its link to gold, but also its link to the nation-state.'[21]

Hans Tietmeyer, the one-time German economics and finance ministry official (and close ally of Helmut Kohl) who as Bundesbank president in 1993–9 helped lay the foundation for the new currency, spoke of 'denationalised money'.[22] But an organised monetary system which allows previously high-interest-rate countries very quickly to lower borrowing costs can suffer financial crises, as government or private-sector indebtedness in individual countries spirals out of control. In such conditions, governmental intervention is not a luxury: it is a necessity. This was what happened at the end of the first ten years of monetary union. A succession of further upsets following the global financial meltdown of 2007–8 showed that, in crisis conditions, the lack of a government behind a currency can become life-threatening.

At Maastricht, Dutch prime minister Lubbers was not the only leader who believed that political union was needed to maintain a successful euro. A month before the summit, Kohl postulated that it was 'absurd' to expect EMU to continue in the long run without political union.[23] Three weeks after the Maastricht gathering, he argued that political union would develop an irresistible momentum.[24] Others surmised that subsequent disappointments and failures in running the new currency would naturally result in government decisions to reinforce the euro's structure, in line with Monnet's famous dictum that Europe 'will be forged in crisis'.[25]

Otmar Issing, the generally sceptical Bundesbank economics supremo, became a pivotal figure behind the ECB's establishment as its first board member for economics. He suspended his doubts sufficiently to state, in 2001, 'the margin for erratic or profligate policies [in EMU] is small'[26] and, in 2006, 'for the time being EMU can proceed perfectly well without a political union'.[27] Years after he retired from central banking, Tietmeyer exhibited sceptical regret, pointing to the dashing of hopes, 'particularly in Germany', that Maastricht would act as a 'catalyst' for political integration. 'Up to now, there is little evidence of this catalytic effect.'[28]

What has ensued in the following three decades has been a collection of halfway-house measures. The EU has tightened up and centralised banking supervision. It has brought in more rigorous examination of state budgets, although with enforcement mechanisms that remain under the political control of states that, through majority decisions, tend to turn a blind eye to contraventions. All this falls a long way short of anything resembling a unified political structure. An ensuing breakdown of trust was the opposite of what EMU sought to achieve. In 2015, Issing, recalling that monetary union 'was supposed to propel Europe towards political union', wrote ruefully that 'the euro is no longer a strong common currency that reinforces a shared European identity'.[29]

To safeguard its prosperity and survival, monetary union requires reinforcement through some form of unity of governments and peoples. Yet progress to this goal is itself undermined by shortcomings and ambiguities in EMU's construction. A question of abiding virulence is whether the ECB and its shareholder central banks can use their collective balance sheets to shore up via the bond markets – in an overarching European interest – the finances of individual member states. This issue of government bond purchases – which, when deployed systematically, can be described by the technical term 'quantitative easing' (QE) – has been the greatest source of dispute in the ECB's twenty-five-year history.

Government bond-buying by the central bank seems to contradict one of the fundamental restrictions of the Maastricht treaty. At the insistence of Germany and 'hard money' EU members, individual states are obliged to stabilise their own finances and should have no recourse to bail out funding from other member states. But the sanctity of the 'no bailout' prohibition has itself been tested as a direct result of one of EMU's prime destabilising features.

Monetary union and its individual members are not shielded by the political protection of an all-compassing overarching state. So, at times of disequilibrium or crisis, they can suffer acute speculative pressure from financial market participants attacking not individual currencies, now fused together, but individual bond markets, linked by a common currency yet divided by the separate sovereignty of member states. Financial market interlinkages, conceived as a benevolent consequence of monetary union, can act as an instrument of the union's undoing.

Much more than differences over interest rates, divergences over whether, and under what conditions, the ECB and its national central-bank shareholders should buy bonds of member states has regularly generated antagonism across the euro area. During the 2010–15 crisis period, a representative of one of the world's leading sovereign funds asked a member of the ECB council visiting the fund's Asian HQ, 'How can I be expected to buy the bonds of your governments when you [the ECB] refuse to buy the bonds yourself?'[30]

European hesitancy during these periods of uncertainty has set off international repercussions. Christopher Smart, deputy assistant secretary of Treasury for Europe and Eurasia for part of the time, recalls:

We [the Obama administration] found irritating and unnecessary the European tendency of going to the cliff edge over stabilisation of the euro area. We were very eager to get on with the recovery. We wanted the markets to settle down, then the European crisis came along. One European official told me: 'We're asking the markets to trust us, but we have shown that we don't trust each other.'[31]

Partly because of the special conditions of the Covid pandemic, the EU has allowed higher government borrowing, partly facilitated by ECB purchases of member states' debt. All these measures increase government involvement in running the currency but fall well short of the political union desired by the system's architects.

More than a quarter-century after its inception, the euro remains a major currency without a firm political berth. It has been dogged by constant tension with governments over a central issue that goes to the core of Europe's struggle to find strength and status in a changing world. Should the ECB take on a more overt role as the guarantor of the euro, with a wider mandate to buttress government finances at a time of enormous – some would say existential – challenge? Or should it remain a secondary entity focused on its prime mandate of controlling inflation?

The more likely outcome is that the ECB will remain a last-resort instrument of defence, not on the front line. But these questions will not be definitively resolved, even as the ECB, reflecting existing and new tensions, becomes further drawn into the political fray. As Draghi accurately though quixotically stated in July 2012 when outlining steps to strengthen the euro, the single currency is 'a mystery of nature'.[32] The well-orchestrated but still fundamentally opaque Draghi rescue act will not be repeated in that inexact form. Europe is deadlocked by disparities too deep to resolve with more ECB 'whatever it takes'.[33] The ECB's constitution gives it independence but no jurisdictional power over European governments that have become progressively weaker, more disputatious and less likely to advance to full-scale European decision-making.

The hole at the heart of Europe looks set to remain.

UNPOPULAR COURSE

Among the roll call of Europe's early 1990s heavyweights gathered in the southern Dutch city, John Major was a newcomer. Britain's new prime minister was treated with avuncular fondness by Kohl on the grounds that he brought a boyish, almost puppy-like enthusiasm to the job – and was not Margaret Thatcher. Mitterrand, the master-illusionist – a man who during the Second World War had dextrously forged friendly relations with both the Nazi-supporting leadership and Resistance factions in German-occupied France[34] – supplied the essential choreography.

The most deity-like of Europe's grandees was normally last to arrive at any European gathering. This time he was over-punctual. By reaching Maastricht a day early, Mitterrand secured a pre-summit deal with Italian prime minister Giulio Andreotti for what both men regarded as an essential quid pro quo for reunification – locking the Germans into a firm timetable for the domestically unpopular course of giving up the D-Mark. One key Kohl adviser at the summit commented that the euro was a 'time bomb ticking under the chancellor'.[35]

Major, for his part, largely because of Kohl's benevolence, secured an enduring opt-out from any obligation for Britain to join the single currency. Major's tennis-playing press secretary, Gus O'Donnell (later UK Cabinet secretary and head of the civil service, and then, in active retirement, a board member of the All England Lawn Tennis Club that organises the annual Wimbledon tournament), claimed the Maastricht result was 'game set and match' to the British.

Maastricht ushered in a decade-and-a-half spell, under both Major and his successor, Tony Blair, when the UK garnered considerable influence on European policies – while for nearly all of that time maintaining its position outside a formal European currency framework. Yet the notion that the UK could play a role 'at the heart of Europe' (to use Major's phrase in 1991[36]), while not joining the single currency, was just one of the many Maastricht contradictions. For the British, and for some of the others, this was agreeable while it lasted – but, sooner or later, was bound to unravel.

Kohl believed that the City of London would quickly drive the UK government into monetary union. He agreed a wager (with the author) at a late-night press conference that the UK, despite the opt-out, would join in the first wave – as the treaty stipulated, in either 1997 or 1999.[37] Once it became clear, in 1998, that the UK would not be among the first adherents, he sportingly paid out the bet – six bottles of Palatinate wine from the chancellor's home region.

Kohl, who coined the phrase that a monetary union without a political union would be a 'castle in the air',[38] was aware of one principal, brutal lesson of history. The mantra had been drummed into him relentlessly by Bundesbank officials not keen to give up what they regarded as their benevolent monopoly on European money – that currency unions without a governing state at their centre normally collapse.[39] An indirect result of Maastricht was the commissioning of an internal Bank of England report (by Eddie George, governor from 1993 to 2003) that came to precisely that conclusion.[40] George was shocked by the findings, realising that, if the report was leaked, it would have an incendiary impact on Britain's decision over whether to join. Opponents of the project would regard it as evidence that it would inevitably fail. Supporters would say that, for it to succeed, Europe would have to proceed to a federal state – anathema to most of the UK population. The most secure option was to ensure that the report remained unread. On the governor's orders, the study was designated top secret and locked away where it would do no harm – in a Bank of England safe.

The technical objective of monetary union was to provide an essential ingredient for the single market in goods and services planned during the 1980s under European Commission president Jacques Delors, which came into effect in 1993. The prime political purpose was to prevent unified Germany from again becoming the dominant European power. A further aim was to build a globally important European currency that would hold its own against the dollar. This would imbue the Europeans with power and prestige – and above all shield them from the vicissitudes of frequently wayward American economic policies.

The interplay of politics, economics and emotion provides EMU with its binding force, yet imbues it, too, with hazardous internal characteristics that, unsuppressed, could lead to its implosion. A succession of economic crises soon revealed 'statelessness' as a source of weakness not strength. But, paradoxically and infuriatingly for the project's architects, these crises have also built in progressively higher obstacles towards any kind of state-like structure at EMU's core. Stable political unions require mutual confidence among their members; but crises, especially if their root causes remain unresolved, generate suspicion, not trust. Europe's interwoven monetary and financial arrangements represent a construct designed to bolster Europe's independence from the US. Yet one disquieting fact stands out. Periods of existential European crisis have been frequently generated by actions on the other side of the Atlantic. Moreover, remedial action has, more often than not, reflected solutions advocated not in Paris, Berlin or Brussels but in Washington and New York.

There was no shortage of EMU doubters in the German economic community. But Kohl's government had stuck solidly to the view in the 1990s that the new currency would be a Europeanised D-Mark: 'Our stability policy has become the Leitmotif for the future European monetary order.'[41] Gerhard Schröder struck a jarring note. Before he became chancellor in October 1998 (when he was forced to take a more statesmanlike line), he set out to counter Kohl's weighty pathos. The then German Opposition leader described the planned new currency as a 'premature sickly child' that would be weaker than the D-Mark, would increase German unemployment and would also raise Germany's economic dominance in Europe.[42] All three predictions were the opposite of what Kohl had forecast – and all came true.

Europe's politicians and monetary authorities believed that, by merging national currencies, they had forestalled the danger of economic upheaval. Internal currency fluctuations were no longer possible; they overlooked that upheavals could still take place on capital markets and in banking systems. The European Commission was caught unawares. In May 2008, marking the ECB's tenth anniversary, it published a glowing 328-page brochure on the bank's achievements.[43] Only two pages referred to the problems developing as the result of growing payments and budget deficits in the peripheral EMU members. Southern member states were using low interest rates inherited from the 1998–9 convergence of currencies to embark on borrowing sprees and live well beyond their means.

Mounting challenges in 2010–15 brought an unexpectedly brutal denouement. Problems over sharply deteriorating (and previously partly hidden) budget and current-account deficits in Greece rapidly spilled over to doubts over the creditworthiness of other countries which had seen rapid rises in ill-considered borrowing – Portugal, Spain, Ireland and Italy – leading to a succession of large-scale rescues and bailouts orchestrated by the International Monetary Fund and the EU.

Very little of this had been foreseen by the politicians and officials in notional charge of the project. On its website in 2009, the Commission denounced as a 'myth' the assertion that 'some euro area member states suffer from economic problems in others'.[44] Helmut Schlesinger, the Bundesbank president, had railed against the monetary union plan while in office up to 1993,[45] but became a sympathiser later, largely on the patriotic grounds that Kohl needed help in his endeavours to unite Europe.[46] Reflecting on the paucity of previous forecasts of how much would go wrong, he concluded later, 'No one had the imagination.'[47]

Economic divergence and wealth destruction on a hitherto undreamt-of scale were about to take place. Yet up to the last minute there was denial. As late as March 2010, a month before the IMF was called in to assist Greece, Klaus Regling, the German civil servant who became chief executive of Europe's emergency bailout European Financial Stability Facility (EFSF, later the European Stability Mechanism),wrote with co-authors, 'Thanks to the successful first decade of EMU, the euro area and its member states are today in a much better shape to weather these truly testing times than ever before.'[48] Just over a year later, Wolfgang Schäuble, the German finance minister, invited his Greek opposite number Evangelos Venizelos to dinner in a two-star Berlin restaurant and recommended that Greece leave monetary union.[49]

> I told him that Greece had used low interest rates within monetary union to make wealthy Greeks richer and drive Greece into debt. There was no way they can get out of this without debt rescheduling. Internal devaluation wouldn't work as it would be very painful. So I said they should leave the monetary union for a few years. Germany could be generous to them outside the monetary union. I said it would be better to have this shock, to get things over with. It could lead to a better outcome later.

Schäuble's views were shared by several European finance ministers – but not the French government, worried about the large Greek exposure of French banks. Venizelos rejected the advice. 'He said the Greeks wanted to make all efforts to stay in monetary union' – as did, more consequentially, Angela Merkel, who believed (along with the Obama administration) that Greek exit would lead to European monetary breakdown. Herman Van Rompuy, the scholarly former Belgian prime minister who, in 2010, became president of the EU's governing body, the European Council, admitted that the euro's relatively problem-free start after 1999 'was like some kind of sleeping pill, some kind of drug'.[50] In 2013, Draghi as ECB president accused 'all the actors' in monetary union of suffering from 'long, complacent amnesia'; they had ignored for years the risks that were building up.[51]

Delors, reflecting on the mishaps after his retirement, allocated a large portion of blame to European finance ministers. 'If the finance ministers had wanted to get a clearer picture of the situation, they could have seen Ireland's extravagant behaviour with its banks, Spain's equally extravagant behaviour with mortgage lending, Greece's dissimulation of its real statistics. But they turned a blind eye. That is why I have always considered, since the beginning of the crisis, that the Eurogroup was morally and politically responsible for the crisis.'[52]

A large part of the problems stemmed not from the fundamental state of government finances but from the banking sector, on account of large explicit and implicit state government guarantees to the banks – what became known as the bank–sovereign vicious circle or 'doom loop' mechanism. An authoritative 2016 report from Bruegel, the Brussels research institute, concluded, 'National authorities were ineffective in supervising banks adequately in the run-up to the crisis, and did not manage and resolve financial sector aspects of that crisis in an effective and timely manner. EU institutions, including the ECB, did not generally have the skills, experience or mandate that would have enabled them to offset the national authorities' shortcomings.'[53] The IMF, in a post-mortem report, wrote that its own surveillance staff, along with most other experts, 'missed the buildup of banking system risks in some countries.'[54] The IMF admitted that it had shared the 'widely held "Europe is different" mindset' that 'large imbalances in national current accounts were little cause for concern and that sudden stops [in capital flows] could not happen within the euro area'.

LONG AND TORTUOUS HERITAGE

Franco-German agreement has been the bedrock of EMU. When it breaks down, disharmony ensues. This is a long and tortuous heritage. France has constantly feared repression from overweening German ambitions. Well before Mitterrand coined similar phrases,[55] Charles de Gaulle's successor Georges Pompidou equated the D-Mark with France's independent nuclear arsenal.[56] The Banque de France in 1978 railed against 'the tyranny of the Mark'.[57] Valéry Giscard d'Estaing, for all his generally supportive stance on Germany and long friendship with Helmut Schmidt, believed monetary union was necessary to avoid 'preponderant influence by Germany'. French fears of a larger, untethered Germany were only partly assuaged by Kohl's compliance with Mitterrand's wishes for a speedy push towards a unified European currency.

Divergence was frequently on display. Four months before the fall of the Wall, a German finance ministry analysis by Hans Tietmeyer (shortly before he joined the Bundesbank) underlined fundamental differences in the French and German approaches towards monetary union.[58] In March 1990, four months afterwards, Franz Pfeiffer, the German ambassador to Paris, complained that doubts about Germany's 'basic political orientation' formed a 'constant' in French politics, with enduring questioning over Germany's attitudes towards a single currency. 'At regular intervals, France asks us for concrete evidence of our loyalty to Europe'[59] – a state of mind in Paris that has endured over the intervening decades.

In January 1991, a report on German unification by Alain Boublil, an adviser to Pierre Bérégovoy, the finance minister, concluded that France had chance to catch up during a forthcoming three-year phase of German weakness.[60] But the German embassy in Paris reported, with consternation, Boublil's warning that, if France failed to take advantage of this opening, Germany would end up stronger than before, with a negative effect on bilateral relations and European cooperation.[61] After receiving a copy, Tietmeyer (whom Boublil visited in Bonn in May 1990 for advice) wrote thanking him for his 'numerous profound reflections'.[62]

In September 1992, immediately before France's national referendum on the Maastricht treaty, and five days after the ejection of the British pound and the Italian lira from the exchange rate mechanism, France battled to avoid the franc suffering the same fate. In a bruising meeting in Washington with the top brass of Germany's monetary establishment, Jean-Claude Trichet, then head of the French Treasury, was pitted against Schlesinger, Tietmeyer and Otmar Issing of the Bundesbank together with finance minister Theo Waigel.[63] Trichet reacted angrily to Schlesinger's brusque suggestion that France should devalue. 'I am stupefied and indignant . . . This language is the language of break-down.' After telephonic intervention by Kohl (in a Parisian restaurant after meeting Mitterrand), the two other top Bundesbank officials outvoted Schlesinger and agreed a joint declaration of support to defend the franc parity.[64] Recalling the 'seminal and dramatic' incident more than thirty years later, Trichet says: 'It was a close call: Tietmeyer and Issing voted Yes against the No of Schlesinger. Had the vote been negative, the story of European monetary union would have been different.'[65]

The Washington meeting marked an opening skirmish in months of tussling culminating in a forced widening of the fluctuation bands of the exchange rate mechanism at the beginning of August 1993. At a crucial Bundesbank council meeting on 29 July, Schlesinger reacted with hostility to a strongly worded letter from Michel Camdessus, IMF managing director.[66] Camdessus, a former governor of the Banque de France and director of the French Treasury, called for 'a substantial reduction in the official discount rate', saying he feared 'the demise of the European Monetary System'.[67] The Bundesbank refused to back down. The 29 July meeting cut the Lombard rate by a larger than expected half-point, but it kept unchanged the discount rate on which Camdessus had focused his attention.

Prime Minister Edouard Balladur wrote a vitriolic protest letter to Kohl – and suggested to other European governments suspending the D-Mark from the ERM.[68] Hastily convened Franco-German crisis talks in Paris and emergency consultations between Schlesinger, Tietmeyer and Kohl at the chancellor's vacation residence in Austria marked the prelude to a frantic monetary bargaining session in Brussels. This ended with a past-midnight decision to widen the bands in the early hours of Monday 2 August.[69] Three weeks later, Klaus Kinkel, the German foreign minister (who took over from Genscher in May 1992), told Alain Juppé, his French counterpart, that Waigel and Schlesinger had been 'very upset' by the suggestion that the D-Mark should leave the ERM.[70] Juppé summed up the psychological state of play between the two countries, telling Kinkel that France had been 'traumatised' by the Bundesbank.

Two and a half decades after the Bundesbank ceded to the ECB its pivotal role in European money, the Franco-German relationship during the 2020s has been traversing another difficult period. Deep political differences have arisen over issues ranging from energy and defence policies to manufacturing electric vehicles and supporting Ukraine in the war against Russia. Poor personal chemistry between Macron and Scholz – mirroring the fraught relationship between Merkel and Nicolas Sarkozy during frequent past EMU strains – has added to the problems.[71] Macron regularly sought informal advice in Berlin on how to penetrate Scholz's near-unfathomable character.[72]

Emmanuel Moulin, director of the French Treasury from 2020 to 2024, and a close confidant of Macron, who became secretary general of the French presidency in April 2025, says German vulnerability has been an important factor behind overall European uncertainty.

> Germany realises it needs to reassess its overall economic and governance model. For security, it had become too dependent on US protection; Trump made the Germans think again. It had too much cheap energy emanating from Russia. It was over-reliant on exports to China. In all three cases geopolitics has intervened to change perceptions. Germany has to decide whether it wants to play a major role in Europe and in the world.[73]

Speaking in 2023, more than a year before Trump's second election victory and two years before the German government's change of tone on European nuclear policy, Moulin criticised Berlin's approach on energy. 'The Germans have always said they do not want nuclear energy at home. We have gone along with this since individual countries can choose their own energy mix. They are now going further by saying that nuclear energy should not be expanded in Europe as a whole. This is a big issue, given the fundamental importance of nuclear energy to France.'

Another French thinker concerned about Germany's vulnerability – and worried about what he sees as the 'renationalisation' of European policies – is Shahin Vallée, a former adviser to Macron at the economics ministry and to Van Rompuy in Brussels. Vallée is one of a group of experts behind a far-reaching March 2025 policy document recommending a much-expanded global role for the ECB in the face of a potential US retreat from the world finance and trading system.[74]

On energy, Vallée says, 'The French are upset about Germany's policies rejecting nuclear power, but in fact France's nuclear energy is in a shambles. This will add to France's long-term fiscal problems.'[75]

The mandates of both François Villeroy de Galhau at the Banque de France and Lagarde at the ECB are due to expire in November 2027, seven months after the French presidential election in April which will see Macron depart from the Élysée Palace after two five-year terms. There has been increasing speculation that Lagarde may leave early to take up a well-paid post at the World Economic Forum that runs the Davos economic conferences in Switzerland.[76] Macron played a key role in orchestrating Lagarde's ECB arrival in 2019. It would be consistent with French political preferences for him to have a crucial hand in steering through her successor – in coordination with Merz in Berlin – at the end of 2006 before he steps down from the presidency. As well as Lagarde, another three experienced members of the six-person ECB executive board – the vice president Luis de Guindos, board member for economics Philip Lane and Isabel Schnabel, the monetary operations specialist – will all leave in an eighteen-month spell between June 2026 and January 2028. Vallée highlights how Lagarde has 'changed a great deal in the decision-making processes. She acts as a chairwoman, not like a chief executive, as was the case with Draghi.'

A more collegiate ECB can be more adept in a crisis. The substantial personnel changes on the board in the next two years might make the bank more vulnerable to future political and economic buffeting.

'THE SYSTEM SQUEEZES THE BEST OUT OF EACH PERSON'

As Lagarde's role has shown, successive ECB presidents have each added to valiant efforts to keep monetary union under control. Former Bundesbank president Schlesinger in early 2022 provided a longer-term view of the underlying strains.

> I told the [German] constitutional court at the hearing in 1993, as I was stepping down from the Bundesbank, that setting up a common currency would succeed if the countries kept to the rules. The danger is now that a group of countries is no longer keeping to the European treaties. This group is led by Italy but also includes France. You have seen these problems getting bigger over time. Under Duisenberg, there were no problems. They became bigger under Trichet and they became most difficult under Draghi.[77]

A warning signal had been sounded more than a decade earlier. One of the prime architects of monetary union, Helmut Schmidt, speaking in late 2010, forecast that eventually the weaker states would split off from the stronger ones. 'Over the next 20 years, I think it is rather likely, at least 51 per cent likely, that a hard core of the Union will emerge. And it would comprise the French, the Germans, the Dutch – I'm not so sure about the Italians.'[78] Ominously, Schmidt forecast France could be the weak link. Would the French always side with Germany by remaining part of the inner circle of Europe? 'I am not a prophet. I don't know. It depends very much on the behaviour of the Germans.'

Yves Mersch, governor of the Luxembourg central bank when the ECB started in 1998, became a member of the ECB board in 2012, serving until 2020 – and so, uniquely, sat continuously on the decision-making ECB council for its first two decades. He describes the disparate characters of the four ECB presidents: 'The system squeezes the best out of each person.'[79] They have built robustness by adding successive, often politically and legally controversial instruments to the European monetary arsenal. The big question for coming years is whether the new 'toolkit' (as central banks refer to the implements of their trade) will be sufficient to meet ever more demanding requirements.

All of the four leaders apart from Lagarde (a lawyer) are economists who previously headed their countries' central banks. Duisenberg, a plain-speaking, lush-haired Dutchman who had also been his country's finance minister, guided the bank – not always sure-footedly – through a crucial build-up phase. He promoted consensus among the ECB representatives of the eleven-country monetary union starting group, earned a reputation for gaffes in dealing with the media and financial markets, and left many of the big decisions to Issing, as the ECB's first board member for economics.

Trichet, the most polished and probably hardest-working of any ECB chief, brought a much more determined leadership style. But his focused approach belied an usually broad interest in the cultural side of central banking, underlined by his passion for poetry, his epithet as 'the most cultivated civil servant in France',[80] and his occasional penchant for referring in speeches to Montaigne, Dante, Shakespeare and Goethe.[81] He took a studiedly bipartisan line on the ECB doctrine of monetary stability, saying in 2007 that its stemmed from a combination of Charles de Gaulle on the Right and Pierre Mendès France on the Left.[82]

His analytical qualities allowed him to counter – though not curb – the financial instability that built up below the surface in the euro's first decade and emerged fully as a disruptive force in 2010. Trichet's misfortune was to have presided over two sets of interest-rate increases – in July 2008 and in April and July 2011 – that with hindsight appear mistaken. Jürgen Stark, the German Bundesbank and finance ministry official who became the ECB's board member with responsibility for economics in 2006, exerted a powerful influence on these decisions. The first step, taken when the euro area was entering a recession, looks egregious.[83] The 2011 tightening, which the ECB reversed at the end of the year when Draghi took office, was more defensible.[84]

Under Trichet, in response to the post-2010 instability in Greece and other peripheral euro members, the ECB crossed the Rubicon of purchasing government bonds of problem countries – although only in relatively small and strictly defined quantities through the so-called 'securities markets programme' (SMP) that put the onus on governments themselves to take remedial action. After presiding successfully as Banque de France governor over a period of stable prices in France at the end of the 1990s, Trichet convincingly donned a Germanic anti-inflationary mantle. But when Delors in 2012 lambasted European policy-makers for failing to counter rising imbalances among euro members – 'They did not say anything; nobody said a word'[85] – he had in his sights not just the finance ministers but also the ECB governing council during Trichet's eight-year tenure.

Mersch comments on the differences between Duisenberg and Trichet: 'Duisenberg wanted everybody to be involved. There was a place for everyone; we were building up a new institution. Trichet wished to streamline the organisation.' Mersch describes how Trichet was occasionally 'upset' about 'parallel exchanges going on outside the centre which, Mersch says, 'were primarily for information purposes, not building voting positions in a particular direction. Peter Praet, a Belgian economist born in Germany, who became the ECB's board member in charge of economics in June 2011, earned Trichet's wrath when the bank's president learned of Praet's invitation to a clandestine offsite meeting of around half a dozen selected council members, mainly governors. The dinner was organised in September at the Bundesbank's training centre at Eltville on the Rhine by Jens Weidmann, freshly arrived in May as Axel Weber's successor as Bundesbank president. At a fraught time for monetary union, Trichet suspected (probably rightly) that the gathering represented an attempt to undermine his authority over stabilising the euro.[86]

Weber had turned down Merkel's half-hearted offer (in January 2011) of the ECB presidency, and then resigned prematurely from the Bundesbank to start a new career in commercial banking.[87] A strong factor behind Merkel's reticence over Weber (she told him that his presidency would make her life 'very difficult') was the implacable resistance of French president Sarkozy, who recorded in his memoirs in 2023. 'I wanted him on no account . . . He would have been even more rigid than Jean-Claude Trichet.'[88] Weidmann, formerly Merkel's economic adviser in Berlin and fortified by his previous experience of working at the Bundesbank, was determined to uphold German monetary orthodoxy.

Draghi took over from Trichet in November 2011. With a background at the Massachusetts Institute of Technology and Goldman Sachs, as well as the Italian Treasury and Banca d'Italia, Draghi was a central-bank leader of vast technocratic competence. He used to tell colleagues of his ability to get by with little nightly sleep because be preferred reading books.[89] Sarkozy regarded him, with favour, as an 'American' president (on account of his 'long association with Goldman Sachs'[90]) in contrast to the 'Germanic' Trichet – 'the perfect opposite'. In his account, Sarkozy writes: 'The first speaks only of growth, the second only of stability. Unnecessary to say that I shared the choice of Mario Draghi.'[91] After Weber turned down the job, Merkel transferred her allegiance to Erkki Liikanen, governor of the Bank of Finland: for Sarkozy, an 'unadventurous' choice who (he wrote) Merkel hoped 'would place himself under the protection of the Bundesbank'. Sarkozy stood up to Merkel and forced her acquiescence, writing later, with his well-known nonchalance about sticking too firmly to the facts: 'The Germans had no choice but to follow. His nomination was a complete success.'[92]

Sarkozy described Draghi's nomination in glowing terms. 'There was never any criticism of him. His action was welcomed unanimously from the beginning to the end of his mandate in 2019.' Wolfgang Schäuble gave a different – and more credible – verdict. 'Draghi's monetary policy helped the states to avoid reforms – exactly the state of affairs that led to the ECB's reaction. Draghi often emphasised that the ECB could never substitute for what the member states should do themselves. But as long as the member states didn't do this, the ECB, in the framework of its own limited mandate, had to do what it could.'[93]

For all his technocratic resonance within and beyond Europe, Draghi sometimes lacked the softer skills needed to manage his frequently fractious governing council.[94] He used his undoubted hold over the council in often overtly transactional fashion, dispensing smaller and larger favours to those backing him on key policy issues – and withdrawing support if positions changed.[95] He reached an unrepeatable career high point – the 'whatever it takes' speech in London in July 2012 credited with averting a euro break-up – through an economic and political conjuring trick whose full significance is still being debated.

At the end of his term in October 2019, Draghi left the ECB in psychological disarray after pushing through several decisions – notably on resuming quantitative easing through across-the-board purchases of government bonds the previous month – which drew hostile reactions from other leading figures on the governing council. The measures included an interest-rate cut as well as the QE restart. Klaas Knot, president of De Nederlandsche Bank, the Dutch central bank, issued an unusual immediate public denunciation of the September package, which he called 'disproportionate to current economic conditions' at a time when the European economy was running at full capacity.[96]

A fellow-member of the ECB council whose sympathies generally lie strongly with Draghi gives a scathing verdict on the September 2019 move. 'It was a wrong decision. In a sense, it was somewhat disrespectful to Lagarde. He wanted to create a convincing narrative for his successor.'[97]

Draghi subsequently became Italy's prime minister for twenty months, from 2021 to 2022 – although he failed at the end of that period in his aim of becoming Italian president.[98] A man who has known and worked with Draghi for forty-five years, Giuliano Amato, the most senior living former Italian prime minister, and latterly president of Italy's constitutional court, dissects key elements of Draghi's complex personality.

> He tends to be intolerant towards the bizarre negotiations that are frequent in politics, where anything can be negotiated with anything else. This is an intellectual advantage, but it can turn out as a limit when you have to move in a political context. Draghi deserved his success as prime minister, because his authority in envisaging and carrying out solutions with a strong technical profile was well recognised and accepted. When the arena became more purely political, he was the right man in the wrong place.[99]

According to Issing, 'Draghi is an outstanding economist and a man of firm views. Within the ECB during his presidency, if you did not follow his line of thinking, then you kept your opinions to yourself. This influenced the climate throughout the whole house. The nationality of the different officials started to play a stronger role.'[100] Mersch's acerbic judgment is: 'Trichet was very team-minded. Draghi preferred to work with a team he had chosen himself.'[101]

DIFFIDENCE IN THE TOP JOB

Although he had been a member of the governing council for eight years while heading the Banca d'Italia, Draghi showed remarkable diffidence when he started the top job. He began his eight-year term with two successive interest-rate cuts, in November and December 2011. But, as the new president, he did not seem fixated on rate cuts from the outset – they happened as much by accident as by design.

Trichet's controversial rate rises in April and July had been promulgated on the advice of Stark, the German board member responsible for economics. Aware that his orthodox views were falling out of favour, Stark announced his resignation in September 2011 after a dispute over what he saw as inappropriate bargaining between the ECB and the Rome and Madrid governments over purchasing Italian and Spanish bonds under the SMP initiative. A strong ancillary reason for Stark's departure (which he decided and communicated to Trichet early in

August) was that he believed Draghi would be impossible to work with.[102]

Patrick Honohan, the Trinity College Dublin professor who was governor of the Central Bank of Ireland during six turbulent years from 2009 to 2015, played a vital international and domestic role in stabilising the country's finances. Honohan's adroitness in the English language, in a decision-making group where communication is overwhelmingly in English even though the vast majority are not native speakers, earned him the sobriquet of 'the Bard of the Council'.[103] At the start of Draghi's presidency, Honohan says, the Italian gave mixed signals.

He was at first somewhat too casual, for example going in and out of meetings to make a phone call. This could be annoying for a council member about to make what he thought was a useful intervention only to realise that the president would not hear his view. In those early months, it wasn't always clear what Draghi wanted to achieve. An example was the council meeting where we lowered rates a second time in December 2011. I wonder if he really had this cut in mind. He seemed surprised to discover that there was a majority for a cut.

Honohan acted as a deft go-between bridging different ECB factions. He recalls a conversation with Stark in October 2011 after he had announced his resignation but before he left at the end of the year (a sequence which Stark now regrets, since it effectively left him powerless during his final ECB months). Honohan says, 'I respected his fear that the promise of the German government in the 1990s to the German people that the euro wouldn't become a transfer union now risked being betrayed.'[104] Although Honohan backed the SMP asset purchases, he describes Stark's opposition to the measures and his decision to resign as 'honest and honourable'.

Stark's resignation in the final weeks of Trichet's presidency hardened divergences on the council. Under Draghi, they were destined to intensify further. According to Honohan, 'Draghi wanted policy to move in a certain direction, and he seemed to become of the view that the so-called hawks on the council had become the opponents. They were chipping away at his position, not in a systematic or considered fashion, but in a way that was trying to send a message to their domestic audiences.'

Draghi, in techniques often ascribed to his Jesuit education,[105] used subtle but unmistakably hardline tactics in dealing with people of opposing views. Honohan recalls:

> There were just a couple of occasions when he took time out of the meeting to have individual informal discussions. As he settled in to being president, he could be very effective in steering the discussion. I was on the receiving end of this approach when I put forward a complicated initiative (in early 2012) regarding the resolution of the Irish banking debt. After I explained my plan Draghi said, rather pointedly: 'Does anyone support Patrick?', thereby making his position crystal clear and successfully discouraging any further discussion.

Christian Thimann formed a key part of the Draghi team as his chief adviser (until 2013), a position he had held under Trichet. He worked closely with Frank Smets, head of the ECB's economics department, and Massimo Rostagno, the long-time monetary director. Trichet was seeking 'collective wisdom and consensus', Thimann explains, through 'extensive crisis meetings with his board colleagues, senior management and expert staff'.[106] Draghi took a different line, consulting individually with board members and council members in his office and by telephone. 'He preferred small circles and short meetings,' Thimann says. 'He was looking for substantive advice and for majority decisions, and he exchanged views extensively with executives in financial markets.'

Christian Noyer, vice president of the ECB under Duisenberg between 1998 and 2002, remained a member of the council as governor of the Banque de France for twelve years between 2003 and 2015 – and can take a long-term view of the bank's vicissitudes. Noyer says that Draghi in 2011 started by maintaining the Trichet approach on assembling the council's 'collective wisdom'. But, later, confronted with strong opposition (above all from Weidmann) over monetary easing, 'he switched to preferring majority decisions'.[107] Draghi worked closely with Noyer to try to overcome (as it turns out, unsuccessfully) some of Weidmann's reservations about bond purchases before introduction of full-scale QE in March 2015. 'In discussions with some colleagues, I thought that we were close to a possible agreed concept. That was to consider QE as a legitimate instrument of monetary policy, but only in certain – or extreme – circumstances . . . Unfortunately, when the discussion came in the governing council, we could not achieve the same kind of balanced conclusion.'

A major difference under Draghi was the attitude towards market intervention. Noyer affirms:

> At the time of Trichet, in order to fight against the sovereign debt crisis that was paralysing the transmission of our monetary policy, we tended to use defined 'envelopes' for intervention [under the SMP], so only a certain volume of ammunition was available. Mario had a different view, which I shared. If you send the message that there is no limit, the market will not try to fight you, so you might not have to do anything. As they say in the US, 'You don't fight the Fed.'

To carry out his mission, Draghi needed political connections. Early on, he had been confronted with Merkel's conventionally Germanic monetary thoughts when (as governor of the Banca d'Italia) he attended a speech she gave in Berlin in June 2009. This was a period when she was still being advised by Weidmann, two years before he took over at the Bundesbank. She publicly castigated quantitative easing by the Federal Reserve and the Bank of England to combat the 2007–8 financial crisis, unprecedentedly citing both central banks by name in forthright terms. 'We must jointly revert to an independent central-bank policy and a policy of common sense. Otherwise in 10 years we will be at the same point again.'[108]

Only three years after her Berlin strictures, Merkel changed her mind, in characteristically enigmatic and understated fashion. Allowing the ECB to take, in 2012, a more energetic stance on bond purchases was, for her, less hazardous than the alternative, even more unpopular approach of calling for direct transfers to problem countries by German taxpayers.[109] Stefan Kornelius, perhaps the most assiduous of the many biographers who tried and failed to penetrate Merkel's near-impregnable carapace (and in May 2025 became her arch-rival Merz's chief spokesman), summed up in 2013 the psychological background to her tactical turnaround. 'The truth is that all sides fear the euro monster at the gates. They are all afraid of the moment when citizens will have to be told what their share of the bill is. The rational Merkel fears this too, but she hopes that by that time the figures will be sufficiently in her favour for her to say: 'I did my best, all the alternatives would have been worse for the country.'[110]

Through regular private conversations in Berlin and by telephone, unencumbered by the presence of officials, Draghi built up a close understanding with Merkel, sustained and shielded by their shared inscrutability. These backdoor channels – plus her growing conviction that the euro really was in trouble – enabled Draghi in 2012 to bring off the 'whatever it takes' feat without opposition from the German chancellor.

Benoît Cœuré, a senior French finance official who served on the ECB board from 2012 to 2019, with responsibilities that included market intervention, habitually accompanied Draghi to Berlin for regular consultations with Merkel and her top officials at the chancellor's office. Merkel and Draghi rounded off these sessions with separate bilateral exchanges from which all officials were excluded. 'Draghi didn't want to "lose" the Germans,' Cœuré says. 'However, he thought he could ruffle the feathers of the Bundesbank so long as he had Merkel.'[111] As his relationship with Merkel deepened, the once all-powerful Bundesbank gradually became expendable.

Of still greater significance – and prodigiously important for 'saving' the euro – were Draghi's frequent consultations with Tim Geithner, Obama's Treasury secretary during the first four years of his presidential term. Geithner was energetically leading the US campaign to persuade the Europeans to allow the ECB to assemble a Federal Reserve-like 'bazooka' (which the Americans also labelled a 'firewall') to protect the euro. He played a major role in stiffening Draghi's resolve to overcome German resistance to ECB support action, culminating in the 'whatever it takes' announcement in 2012.

Geithner and Draghi had built a durable relationship extending back to their spells from the 1990s onwards at their two countries' finance ministries and central banks (in 2003–9 Geithner had been president of the Federal Reserve Bank of New York, which handles the bulk of the Fed's international transactions). They shared a liking for dexterous financial footwork and distaste for Germanic monetary orthodoxy.

According to US Treasury records, Geithner during his four years in office interacted fifty-five times with Draghi in telephone calls (often very short ones, to be fitted into Geithner's punishing daily schedule) and meetings.[112] Testifying to Geithner's immense preoccupation with European affairs, according to the records, he interacted bilaterally on forty-one occasions with Trichet, seventy-four times with Lagarde (as French finance minister and then as IMF managing director after July 2011), fifty-nine times with Dominique Strauss-Kahn (IMF managing director until he quit in May 2011 after he faced sexual assault charges in New York) and thirty-four times with Wolfgang Schäuble. The official tally understates the full extent of Geithner's engagements, since it largely excludes encounters at multilateral gatherings and may not include all confidential exchanges.

Draghi and Geithner were in close touch during Draghi's six years as governor of the Banca d'Italia (when he was also chairman of the Financial Stability Board[113]), and intensified contacts after he became ECB president in November 2011. Draghi was the second foreign official Geithner spoke to by telephone (the first was Mervyn King, governor of the Bank of England) after being sworn in as Treasury secretary in January 2009. Geithner and Draghi spoke by phone for ten minutes in the morning (Washington time) on 2 November 2011, the new ECB chief's second day in the job. This formed part of a remarkable series of rapid-fire Geithner discussions with European officials and ministers, twenty-four hours before Draghi in Frankfurt presided over a landmark cut in the ECB's interest rates, and eleven hours before Geithner flew from Washington with Obama to the French Riviera for a Group of Twenty summit in Cannes overshadowed by the Greek financial crisis.[114]

There is no record of what Draghi and Geithner discussed on 2 November. But it is highly likely that they dwelled on two controversial issues raised in Cannes. These were a European plan to enlist US aid in a bid to unseat Italian prime minister Silvio Berlusconi (which Geithner says he persuaded Obama to reject – although Berlusconi did resign a week later[115]); and an American-led effort to persuade Merkel to force the Bundesbank to use its replenished reserves of special drawing rights (SDRs, the IMF's composite currency unit) to reinforce a Greek rescue fund. Reduced to tears at Cannes ('I have never seen her so upset,' Geithner recalled[116]), Merkel turned down the idea, saying, 'I will not commit suicide.' She pointed out that SDRs were the property of the Bundesbank, which owed its independence to the postwar settlement ordained by the US and its wartime allies.[117]

In her memoirs, Merkel provides a highly abbreviated account of the Cannes dispute, writing that she fought 'tooth and nail and even with tears' against 'huge pressure' for a 'bazooka' from Obama, Sarkozy, Berlusconi and other Cannes participants.[118] She underlines (hardly surprisingly) that her former adviser Weidmann, as the new Bundesbank president, though not at the meeting, supported her stand.[119] A participant in the meeting gives more detail:

> The men were ganging up to isolate her and force her to concede. The idea came from Geithner, whom Obama relied upon. He was very transactional. Merkel explained that she couldn't force the Bundesbank to do that. She was tearful. This was a misreading [by the Americans] of the legal and historical position. Obama took the rebuff a lot better than Trump would have done. Everyone was somewhat embarrassed. The meeting went on only for a short time afterwards.[120]

Geithner wrote in 2014, 'In Cannes we didn't make much headway on the European firewall or reform on the periphery. But I did have some promising talks about the use of overwhelming force with Mario Draghi'[121] – an important clue to what happened in July 2012.

ANOTHER POLITICAL STRUGGLE

Lagarde succeeded Draghi in November 2019 after another political struggle involving a German candidate. Undaunted by his bruising encounters with Draghi and other decision-makers, Weidmann allowed his name to go forward as a contender for the top job. His view was clear: his opposition to many monetary support measures during the

Draghi presidency strengthened rather than weakened his credentials.[122] Weidmann would indeed have made a credible figure at the ECB's helm, based on his evident monetary expertise and on his ability to reconcile Germany with a project many Germans still distrusted. Had he taken the job, however, he would have had to bend his principles to survive.

Ultimately, Weidmann's profile was out of kilter with the realpolitik of European central banking. His bid for the presidency was blocked by opposition from both Draghi and Macron, who combined successfully to push for Lagarde's (largely unexpected) nomination, confirmed by the European Council in July 2019.[123] The French president told Merkel months before the decision that her former adviser had no chance of getting the promotion he desired.[124] One ECB insider sums up the essential reason why Weidmann's candidacy was doomed: 'Merkel is a smart person. She may have put Weidmann's name forward, but she knew it wouldn't work. If you are the Bundesbank president, you have to take a certain position and you cannot put that position forward as the chairman of the council. Draghi was able to do that on behalf of Italy, but that's a very rare skill. He knew how to talk to Merkel.'[125]

Weidmann retired from the central banking fray at the end of 2021, two years after the rebuff, stepping down five and a half years before the end of his second eight-year term – the third successive Bundesbank president to leave early.[126] After a short but convoluted selection procedure, Nagel, Weidmann's long-time associate – a more convivial figure, combining deep knowledge of financial markets with an extrovert nature and pragmatic propensity to take risks and, from time to time, to change his mind – became Bundesbank president in January 2022.

Weidmann's persona was that of a deceptively quiet monetary crusader who often came across as an economic fundamentalist. Nagel's appointment signalled continuity with Weidmann's policies. But they were now promulgated in the more conciliatory style of an adept market operator rather than a missionary.[127]

Nagel had joined the Bundesbank in 1999 but departed in 2016 (above all because he failed to win the job of deputy president under Weidmann[128]), and did not anticipate returning to the top position. Up to his taking of the top job, the new Bundesbank chief and Lagarde had never previously met. But, in contrast to the traditional tension between the ECB and Bundesbank, they quickly established a personal bond, a relationship built on reciprocal bonhomie and recognition of each other's strengths and weaknesses. Perhaps this will be third time lucky for a German ECB candidate? Nagel has managed to tighten monetary policy in a fashion long desired by his predecessor. He is a leading contender – but by no means the only one – to replace Lagarde when she leaves. Yet making a German head of the ECB will be a fraught and heavily politicised undertaking.

With neat logic, Weidmann aligned his withdrawal at the end of 2021 with the ending of Merkel's sixteen-year chancellorship. Generously, and accurately, François Villeroy de Galhau says, 'He left when his influence was at its highest.'[129] Weidmann succeeded in concealing worries over what he foresaw as an impending conflict over a difficult period for the highly indebted larger nations of monetary union. EMU's built-in challenges caused by its diverse membership have been mitigated by Germany's economic stagnation in 2022–5, which has distracted attention from some fundamental disparities with France and Italy, especially over public debt levels. But German weakness does not auger well for EMU's strength. Internal European divergences can rapidly re-emerge as a factor behind external fragility.

In her spell at the ECB, Lagarde has had to cope with two monumental disruptions – the Covid-19 outbreak in 2020 which necessitated a new wave of government bond purchases, with wide-ranging consequences for overall economic stability, and Russia's full-scale invasion of Ukraine, which put monetary policy de facto onto a war footing. Of the two great tasks, the Russo-Ukrainian conflict – on account of its divergent effects on Europe and America, and among different European countries – has been the tougher to handle. Villeroy de Galhau, who underlines how the ECB has become 'ever more pragmatic' since the pandemic, says 'Covid in a sense made our lives still simpler. In just two hours we put together the most ambitious package in euro history.'[130]

Lagarde has used skills from her legal training both in marshalling her communications strategy and in countering criticism when she runs into difficulties. Lagarde was widely criticised in March 2020 for saying, at the outset of the Covid crisis, that the ECB's duty was not to close 'spreads' on euro area bond markets, which was blamed for a large sell-off of Italian bonds and led to a widening of bond-buying action through the 'pandemic emergency purchase programme' just six days later.[131] Her interest in a single currency was kindled in her early days at US law firm Baker McKenzie. Lagarde was the managing partner in Paris, handling corporate business across Europe.

> We were aware of the problems of currency fluctuations in contracts ... As I travelled across Europe, changing national currencies across borders was time-consuming and costly. I had to carry a bag with zip-fastener containers for the individual currencies. I did not have any strong feelings about the new European currency somehow rivalling the dollar. However, I did feel that, when we were invoicing in French francs, the reference currency was always the dollar. I looked favourably at the idea of a more balanced basket of currencies.[132]

Lagarde has compensated for her lack of formal economic education and central banking experience with political savvy and leadership acumen. In summer 2019, before moving to Frankfurt, she embarked on a successful charm offensive, including diplomatically timed lunch and dinner appointments, to soothe wounded feelings among council members troubled by Draghi's frequent off-handedness and verbal barbs.

Robert Holzmann, president of the Austrian National Bank from 2019 to 2025, one of the governing council's most outspoken members, says, 'Christine Lagarde is one of the most socially competent people I have ever met.'[133] Lagarde has shown great skill in dealing with Holzmann's outlier position as the archetypal 'hawk' on the council. As he explains: 'I habitually take up a stance that is more hawkish compared not only with the majority but also with Joachim Nagel or Klaas Knot. I am doing this not so much because I believe my suggestions will be implemented, but because that way I give the chance for the other more orthodox-minded members of the council to lead somewhat more from the centre.'

Once installed in Frankfurt, Lagarde reintroduced the tradition – discontinued by Draghi – of offsite council meetings to encourage social interaction and team spirit. She deploys her unusual background

– a one-time synchronised swimming champion as well as a non-economist – to reinforce her presence as a female leader in a male-dominated central banking world.

Observers' descriptions are habitually replete with natational metaphors: 'Navigating rough waters is Christine Lagarde's daily bread.'[134] Calling for more women in top economic positions, she both decries her exceptionalism and makes copious use of it by frequently defying norms. Whether in promoting gender diversity,[135] criticising a 'tribal clique' of economists,[136] warning (undiplomatically but accurately, ten months before his re-election) of a 'threat' from Trump's return to the White House,[137] or pondering her grandchildren's future in opining on climate change,[138] Lagarde has rewritten the rule book of central banking behaviour. Her biography on the ECB website records her past rankings as *Forbes* magazine's second 'most powerful woman in the world' as well as her 2016 'woman of the year and lifetime achievement award' from *Glamour* magazine.[139]

'I DON'T THINK HER MALE PREDECESSORS WOULD HAVE DONE IT'

One of the longest-running observers of the single currency's institutional development is Athanasios Orphanides, a former Federal Reserve official, governor of the Central Bank of Cyprus from 2007 to 2012, and for four years a member of the governing council (after Cyprus joined the euro 2008). Now a professor at the Massachusetts Institute of Technology, he says of Lagarde: 'She did admit her mistake when she said in March 2020 that the ECB was not there to close spreads. I admire her for that. I don't think her male predecessors would have done it.'[140]

Visco, the long-serving former governor of the Banca d'Italia, calls Lagarde 'a very determined woman, an experienced lawyer and a skilled politician'.[141] During her spells at the IMF and as French economy and finance minister, 'You have to deal with a permanent flow of new challenges. You can't just talk, you have also to know how to listen and advance informed proposals, while taking well thought decisions.' He adds: 'Draghi was MIT trained. Lagarde has had to learn quickly. The head of the central bank doesn't necessarily need to be an economist. Arthur Burns was one of the world's top economists but ended up as being seen as a weak central banker.' Burns, Richard Nixon's notoriously pliable Federal Reserve chairman who presided over a rise in inflation and the breakdown of the dollar's central international role in the 1970s, represents an apt benchmark.[142]

In the central key area of controlling inflation, Lagarde was slow in pushing for higher interest rates in late 2021 and early in 2022 to curb high inflation caused by the combined effects of large-scale quantitative easing, supply shocks after the end of Covid lockdowns, and the (later) effects of the Russian–Ukrainian war. One leading member of the governing council (from a northern European country) warned in March 2022 that she could become 'the Arthur Burns of European central banking'.[143] The warning, and others like it, hit home – and the timing was propitious. Nagel arrived on the governing council just as the credibility of Philip Lane, the ECB board member responsible for economics (who took over from Peter Praet in June 2019) was starting to wane.

A particular target for critics has been Lane's complacent monetary analysis ten days before the war broke out, when inflation in the euro area was already running at above 5 per cent.[144] 'Lane thought that inflation would come back to 2% without the need for the ECB to make any significant changes in monetary policy,' according to Otmar Issing. 'This was a grotesquely faulty forecast. It had an influence on the ECB's policies right up till the summer [2022]. Economists have to make forecasts and they must necessarily use models to do so. But in times of deep structural changes, it is unwise to rely on traditional models.'[145] Issing adds: 'Philip is an excellent economist. But it seems that he tends to be somewhat too much of a believer in traditional models which cannot themselves cope with deep structural changes – such as happened during and after the pandemic . . . Additional qualities of judgement and flexibility are required.'[146]

Lagarde was on the lookout for a new lodestar. Quick-witted Nagel, although a trained economist with an honorary professor title (which he does not use), can be irked by the academics' occasionally ponderous style. He was on hand to provide alternative navigational guidance. In his first speech as Bundesbank president he emphasised the risk of inflation (running at 6 per cent in Germany) remaining elevated for longer than forecast.[147] Nagel was given discreet backing by ex-president Schlesinger, who wrote to the Bundesbank board that, in his seventy years of experience, he had never witnessed central banks trying to combat high inflation with negative real (inflation-adjusted) interest rates.[148]

Lagarde's Lane-to-Nagel conversion brought mutual benefits. The new Bundesbank chief was seeking to fulfil a seemingly contradictory objective set by the German finance ministry: to bring about a sound ECB policy, while at the same time avoiding Weidmann's propensity to trap himself into a permanent minority position.[149] The Ukraine war – and Berlin-based classical-music maestro Daniel Barenboim – helped forge a meeting of minds. Lagarde's acquaintance with the star international conductor and her desire to show solidarity after the Russian invasion prompted her to ask Nagel to support a joint Bundesbank–ECB charity concert in Berlin under Barenboim's direction to support the humanitarian effort for Ukraine.[150] Nagel spontaneously agreed – earning her gratitude, buttressing his reputation for getting his priorities right, and setting the scene for full Lagarde–Nagel cooperation on ten successive increases in ECB interest rates from July 2022 onwards.

A pre-invasion misjudgement by Lane and the ECB on the 'transitory' nature of inflation (shared by other foremost central banks led by the Federal Reserve and Bank of England)[151] was crystallised in Lagarde's December 2021 statement: 'Under the present circumstances, it is very unlikely that we will raise interest rates in the year 2022.'[152] She used the quixotic setting of a 'Lunch with the *Financial Times*' interview in October 2023 to explain the miscalculation.[153] 'We initially handled that like a textbook case of a supply shock.' Referring to the ECB's earlier commitment not to start raising interest rates until it had stopped buying bonds through its pandemic-crisis QE programme (the phase-out came gradually over the first six months of 2022), she added: 'What I regret personally is to have felt bound by our forward guidance. I should have been bolder.'

Although the ECB takes decisions as a collective group, its missteps reverberated on the very public persona of the president – augmenting latent critical tendencies in the German media.[154] Nagel recognises Germany's sceptical institutional heritage.

Some of this was justified, but over time we have made the monetary union work better. One of my objectives is to complete the task of making the Bundesbank a fully integrated part of the Eurosystem.

We can do this in many ways, not least through the personnel and structural changes that we are putting into effect. This means modernising our set-up and making even better use of the many good ideas from within our ranks.[155]

Nagel's verdict on Lagarde is as 'an excellent team leader . . . incredibly good at getting on well with people, as you can see in many aspects of her professional life. She is a good monetary policy-maker with a clear commitment to our primary objective of maintaining price stability.'

For Nagel, internationalisation of central banking activities plays a prime role. 'Why do so many good German economists work abroad? Can we not bring some of them back to work with us in Germany – for example at the Bundesbank?' Nagel achieved a modest success in November 2024 by bringing into the bank its first female top economist, Fritzi Köhler-Geib – who joined as a board member from state financing entity KfW (where Nagel also worked from 2016 to 2020) after eleven years at the World Bank in Washington, where she had responsibilities for macroeconomics, specialising in Latin America.

Nagel's worldview affirms the value of cohesiveness: 'It is very important that all members of the governing council show commitment to what has been discussed and decided, and demonstrate their support of overall ECB objectives.'[156] Behind the scenes of the twenty-six-strong council, a new form of variable geometry is now in evidence. The traditional axis between Germany and France has been weakened and made more complicated by a large number of intersecting alliances among different countries with contrasting approaches. In addition to his personal rapprochement with Lagarde, Nagel has stepped up initiatives to strengthen relationships on the council extending to Spain and Italy as well as France and the Netherlands.[157]

The zenith of Nagel's monetary diplomacy came with his agreement in July 2022 to the 'transmission protection instrument' (TPI). The new form of safety net for higher-debt countries was agreed as a necessary condition for the ECB's larger than expected 0.5 percentage point increase in interest rates – the start of the euro area's long-overdue monetary tightening. Nagel knew he would face criticism in Germany that the TPI mechanism, laying down a path to potentially unlimited bond-buying to help hard-pressed momentary union members, could expose the Bundesbank to unfathomable political risks.[158] It was a gamble that his predecessor Weidmann would not have taken.[159] But, as the financial markets reacted with relative equanimity to a long period of monetary tightening, the aftermath of the announcement indicated that it was a risk worth taking.

CONTINUOUS STRANDS OF TENSION

The benefits, drawbacks and controversies of government bond purchases provide continuous strands of tension throughout the ECB's operational history. The dramatic peak was reached with Draghi's 'whatever it takes' initiative in July 2012. The repercussions stretched for years afterwards. They include political and economic consequences of large losses for the central banks of Germany and the Netherlands, the most solvent euro members, caused by large-scale purchases of low-yielding bonds from 2015 onwards – after the ECB had already moved to negative interest rates. As Banque de France ex-governor Noyer explains, these losses were not a surprise. From the beginning of quantitative easing, they were built into the ECB's internal calculations.

> Before general QE started in March 2015, we had a discussion involving risk-sharing – to determine whether central banks would buy bonds of other jurisdictions outside their own. Several members refused to do this, perhaps by fear that it could lead to a prohibited fiscal transfer. It was clear that it would mean the Bundesbank would take on low yielding or even negative yielding bonds on to its books and might therefore get into difficulties on its P&L.[160]

Lorenzo Bini Smaghi, an ECB veteran who was a board member from 2005 to 2011 and has been chairman of Société Générale since 2015, with his term ending in 2026, points to the paradox:

> By deciding negative rates and then QE, the Bundesbank made almost certain that they would be buying bonds at negative rates, increasing the potential for losses when inflation went up later. When German unification took place, many worried that Germany

would be dominating Europe and that everybody would have to become like the Germans. That has not happened. If you look at the position of the Bundesbank, they have become the first victims of the legacy of quantitative easing.[161]

The full political repercussions of these losses will probably take several years to emerge. Nout Wellink, De Nederlandsche Bank governor from 1997 to 2011, is among those who see the wider implications. 'This is a balancing act and you can make all kinds of arguments for why the losses have occurred. But there will be some ill-feeling in Germany that the Bundesbank appears to be making the biggest losses and that more indebted countries are protected by the higher rates of interest on the bonds in their national central bank portfolios.'[162]

A five-year countdown to massive ECB bond purchases started with the 'securities markets programme' announced in May 2010. The ECB started purchasing government bonds of Greece, Ireland and Portugal, expanded after August 2011 to Italy and Spain.[163] The programme got off to a difficult start when the Bundesbank's Weber at first signalled agreement with the SMP and then withdrew it, pondering resignation from the Bundesbank in the process (a step he took a year later). Trichet explains:

Weber was stretched between, on the one hand, recognition of the gravity of the situation, and, on the other, the spontaneous reaction of German public opinion. An important factor was the political promise made to the German people by eminent pro-European leaders like [Helmut] Kohl, [Theo] Waigel, and [Horst] Köhler that Germany was sharing its currency but that budgets remained strictly national. The SMP was perfectly legal of course. But purchasing Treasuries looked like transgressing against the political promise.[164]

A mismanaged meeting between Sarkozy and Merkel at the French Channel resort of Deauville in October 2010 was one of the factors leading up to 2012. The 'Deauville declaration' that future euro area bailouts would include forcing losses on private sector holders of EU government bonds sparked broader selling of European debt. One person close to Merkel explains her stand on so-called 'private sector involvement', which Sarkozy agreed in order to win a softening of German strictures on eventual fiscal union. 'There was an element of morality [in Merkel's stance], the idea that the bankers would have to pay something; they couldn't be allowed to get away with it.'[165] Trichet immediately rejected the accord, which he describes as 'catastrophic'.

> At a time when we were fighting against the speculators, it was rewarding speculation – those who were 'short' – and punishing those who had demonstrated confidence in the countries concerned – those who were 'long'. I expressed my total disagreement to Sarkozy and Merkel tête-à-tête. I told the European council that they should not adopt such a rule. And I maintained this position strictly until the European council of July 2011 which abandoned the Deauville agreement. The ECB interrupted activating the SMP after Deauville, to avoid throwing money out of the window.[166]

Transatlantic brinkmanship continued unabated, pitting the Obama administration and Federal Reserve against the German government and Bundesbank. Speaking on a G7 call in November 2010 from his holiday residence in Cape Cod,[167] Geithner joined Trichet in opposing the Deauville declaration. 'If you guys do that . . . all you will do is accelerate the run from Europe. No one will lend a dollar, a euro to a European government.' As he related (in unconventional but characteristically forceful terms) later, 'I was fucking apoplectic about it. I said, "If you're going to restructure Greece, you have to have the ability to in effect protect or guarantee the rest of Europe from the ensuing contagion." '[168]

The detailed archival records of Federal Reserve meetings in Washington in 2011–12 provide an incisive real-time account of American worries about Europe. The verbatim conversations show not only a forensic understanding of the factors separating differing factions on the ECB council. They also serve a foretaste of the measures eventually (after many exchanges with Geithner) propelled by Draghi, in Sarkozy's words, the 'American' president.

Dan Tarullo, the Fed governor responsible for bank supervision and regulation, told the rate-setting Federal Open Market Committee meeting in January 2011, 'The biggest short-term risk comes from the euro zone.' Europe was not using a period of relative calm 'to get ahead of the problem' through better backstops and bank recapitalisation schemes. Merkel's Christian Democrats 'faced coalition problems as German citizens resist the idea that they should pay for what they see as fiscal irresponsibility in the periphery.'[169]

Bill Dudley, Geithner's successor as president of the New York Fed, told the FOMC in June, 'We will avoid a catastrophe in the near term as Greece reluctantly agrees to do more and the private sector participates by rolling over some debt on a "voluntary basis". But even if we get this outcome, we should not be very comfortable with where we are.'

In six to twelve months, Dudley said he could 'easily imagine Greece falling short of its objectives . . . then we will have another episode, and at that point we actually could reach the end of the road.'[170] Thomas Hoenig, the Kansas City Fed president, told the same meeting, 'When a situation in a country the size of Greece has the world at risk, we know how fragile this economy of ours is, global and nationally.'[171]

In August 2011, with October's Deauville declaration ditched, the Securities Market Programme of limited bond-buying was reopened. The ECB council entered new territory by writing separate strongly worded letters to Silvio Berlusconi and José Luis Rodríguez Zapatero, the Italian and Spanish prime ministers, calling for 'pressing action' to ensure 'the sustainability of public finances', in each case spelling out detailed recommendations. The letters – signed by Trichet and, respectively, Draghi and Miguel Ángel Fernández Ordóñez, governors of the two central banks – effectively and controversially set conditions for the ECB to carry out purchases of the two countries' bonds under a widened SMP.[172] Trichet explains the position in characteristically nuanced terms: 'The letters contained no conditionality, there was not a quid pro quo, but expressed which orientations in our view could and would help the country counter successfully the speculation at a very difficult time. There are substantial similarities between the SMP and the TPI, decided by the ECB in July 2022. The wheel has turned full circle.'[173]

The SMP episode, against the backdrop of continuing high-publicity manoeuvring over Greek debt, prompted Stark to leave the ECB (he decided to go in early August but announced the decision only in September, and departed at the end of the year[174]). It accelerated

Zapatero's progressive withdrawal from politics and, most significantly, led to Berlusconi's resignation in November and replacement by Mario Monti.[175]

Steve Kamin, the Federal Reserve's international director, explained to the Federal Open Market Committee (FOMC) in September 2011 that Stark's resignation underscored 'deep division within the ECB itself'. The ECB was the sole institution with the resources to head off a 'systemic run on the debt of European sovereigns'. Yet it had been reluctant to 'get ahead of the political process' by expanding sovereign bond purchases. 'With the crisis in Europe deepening and financial markets extremely jittery, any number of events, such as a disorderly Greek default, could trigger a chain reaction of events that would be very difficult to control.'[176]

The Federal Reserve laid down a blueprint for ECB action. On 2 November, Bernanke highlighted Europe's 'fundamental misconception' in not allowing the ECB to lend to 'a bank or some facility' that was using sovereign debt as collateral. 'The ECB is effectively the only institution that can provide unlimited firepower . . . It's not clear that this is going to work. Moreover, it's going to get harder and harder, because Europe is slowing . . . We are innocent bystanders, but we are very severely affected by what's happening there.'[177]

Three weeks later Bernanke reported to FOMC members 'fairly discouraging' conversations with European central-bank governors and finance ministers on a G7 Thanksgiving Day conference call on 24 November.[178] The ECB was in 'a very delicate position . . . although they talk about legalities, they view their main constraints as political. Essentially, what will the Germans allow the ECB to do?'

Bernanke termed as 'kind of perverse' that the ECB was directly buying Greek debt, as opposed to lending to an institution such as the European Investment Bank to pass on funding to the Greek government. Although he emphasised the risk of a 'Lehman-style catastrophic financial event' in Europe, Bernanke in December held out hopes of compensatory benefits. 'Stress in Europe lowers US Treasury yields, leads funds to flow into US banks, and may give US banks new opportunities to gain global market share.'[179]

The Fed chairman treated the FOMC to a scholarly exposition of game theory.

You've got two sides – call them North and South – who have very different objectives. On the one hand, both North and South would like to see the euro continue. They'd like to avoid a financial crisis. On the other hand, the North – Germany and its close neighbors – are most interested to avoid making any fiscal transfers or being responsible for providing any financial support to what they view as profligate Southerners . . . What we've seen here is a game of chicken where both sides are threatening a crisis essentially in order to get as good a deal as they can for themselves.

After Draghi signalled a fresh tilt to dovish policies with interest-rate cuts in November and December, the January 2012 FOMC session discussed the new ECB president's tactics. Minneapolis Fed president Narayana Kocherlakota asked whether markets were quieter because they believed Draghi would play a more active role.[180]

Dudley said Draghi had been careful not to step into 'the fiscal space' by expanding bond purchases. Bernanke opined that Draghi was 'playing a careful game. He has actually been very hawkish fiscally.' The purpose might be 'to give comfort to the Germans in particular, in the hope that they will, given these reassurances, be more forthcoming themselves.' The FOMC in June discussed at length whether Greece might leave EMU. Dudley stated: 'The problems go far beyond Greece . . . I see this as likely to get worse as opposed to get better.' The Europeans were caught 'in a series of very bad dynamics'.[181] Dudley emphasised the need for a 'broad leap to much greater political and fiscal integration'; however, 'there is no stomach for that politically'.[182]

Offsetting the general gloom, Europe was making progress on the important issue of banking union. Monti, an urbane and well-regarded former European commissioner, after taking over from Berlusconi in November 2011, immediately set about righting Italy's fraught relationship with France and Germany. He regarded the ECB's demands on Italian fiscal tightening in the August letter as unduly restrictive. And he believed the ECB was overstepping its mandate. But Monti realised that peace on the European front was a necessary condition for Italian stability.[183]

Monti used his first meeting in Strasbourg with Merkel and Sarkozy to agree what he called a 'symmetrical silence': the three main euro members would cease making interest-rate recommendations to the ECB. After Berlusconi's boorishness, Monti's gentlemanly sophistication was, for Merkel, a relief. 'I believe I did get through to her inner soul,' Monti recalls. 'Obama was most interested in her economic point of view, and asked me what I thought was a good way to approach her.'[184]

TOWARDS A *COUP DE THÉÂTRE*

In frequent telephone calls, Geithner sought to push Draghi towards a *coup de théâtre* on a muscular bond-purchasing programme – the 'over-whelming force' that the two men had discussed nine months previously on the French Riviera. 'I told Draghi that there was no way any plan that could actually work would get Bundesbank support. He had to decide whether he was willing to let Europe collapse.'[185]

Parts of Draghi's celebrated passage – 'Within our mandate, the ECB is ready to do whatever it takes to preserve the euro. And believe me, it will be enough' – had been practised in advance (including on the flight from Frankfurt to London).[186] But the construct as a whole was ad-libbed at the last moment.[187] An official ECB document describes it as 'off the cuff'.[188]

But there had been exhaustive efforts to lay the groundwork. Some ran along ill-coordinated parallel lines. On 17 June, the ECB held an emergency Sunday meeting to discuss the different options, including a close bond-purchasing relationship with the European Stability Mechanism, the successor to the EFSF bailout fund.[189]

In an important part of the build-up, at the end of June, EU leaders at a summit meeting in Brussels opened the way to a 'single supervisory mechanism' for euro area banks that would rectify some of the key causes of the financial instability that had rocked Europe during the past five years, affirming, 'It is imperative to break the vicious circle between banks and sovereigns.'[190] Furthermore, they proclaimed: 'We affirm our strong commitment to do what is necessary to ensure the financial stability of the euro area.'[191]

Pressure by Italy, France and Spain, aided by behind-the-scenes persuasion by Obama, 'tore down the German straitjacket', according to Monti, and paved the way for Draghi's 'whatever it takes' statement by providing 'political coverage at the highest level'.[192] Luis de Guindos,

Spain's minister of economy and competitiveness between 2011 and 2018, who was on the front line of Spanish economic firefighting in 2012 and has been the ECB's vice president under Lagarde since 2018, concurs with Monti's assessment. 'The decision to create the banking union at the European Council in June was a game changer. Without that, Draghi's words would not have had the same effect.'[193]

According to Cœuré, 'In July we had lots of discussions on the board about what to do. There were lots of avenues. One question was whether the support would be unlimited. Many balls were up in the air. The key point was to mark a difference compared with the SMP.'[194]

Diversity of approaches led to intra-European strife. The Banca d'Italia under Draghi's successor, Visco, had been carrying out studies on a similar scheme to the one Draghi eventually unveiled. Visco discussed this with Monti, who subsequently passed the information on to Obama. The US president spoke to Merkel, who was annoyed at not having been informed.[195] For his part, Draghi voiced irritation after discovering the soundings via Monti. Neglecting to indicate his own frequent interactions with the US Treasury secretary, Draghi believed (probably rightly) that interplay with the Italian prime minister would damage his efforts to portray the initiative to the Bundesbank and others as a non-political manoeuvre.

In trademark sibylline manner, Draghi did not clear his London statement with the ECB board or council. By not writing it down in advance, Draghi removed both requirement and mechanism for approval. In near-mythological terms, the speech later took on the hallmark of greatness. Yet its content was ambiguous, its delivery impro-vised and its setting incongruous: an international gathering of business people and functionaries at Lancaster House, an ornate early Victorian-era government hospitality centre.

Ewald Nowotny, president of the Austrian National Bank and member of the council at the time, describes Draghi's selective consul-tative style.

I believe Draghi made contact with the big banking players before the speech. What impressed me is how quickly his speech in London worked. He changed the way that markets were thinking. He planted very firmly the idea that the ECB was going to buy government bonds. The Germans objected. He didn't talk to the governing council about it. But I believe that he did speak to other people.[196]

Another council member frames the matter more bluntly. 'He spoke to Geithner, but he didn't speak to me.'[197]

'DRAGHI'S COMMENTS HAD CLEARLY NOT BEEN VERY PRECISELY PREPARED'

British prime minister David Cameron, self-described as a 'practical Eurosceptic', had convened the Lancaster House gathering at the start of the London Olympic Games to solicit investment into the UK. Mervyn King, the owlish governor of the Bank of England, a man of courtly demeanour and implacable Eurosceptic tendencies, was charged with moderating a panel of three central-bank governors: Agustin Carstens of the Bank of Mexico, Alexandre Tombini of the Central Bank of Brazil, and Draghi. King recalls: 'Draghi's comments had clearly not been very precisely prepared. There was no draft of the speech. It was not released at the time to the media. It had to be put together afterwards. It is a myth that he knew exactly what was going on. He rushed off quickly afterwards. He was very nervous after the speech about what the impact would be.'[198]

The next day, Merkel and French president François Hollande backed the Draghi line – an intervention of crucial significance.[199] Draghi's words – later moulded into conceptual shape with the 'outright monetary transactions' (OMT) mechanism painstakingly assembled by the ECB in ensuing weeks – pulled off a striking feat in stabilising the euro, even though the OMT was never activated (and probably never will be).[200] But one important reason for the success reflected a bizarre misunderstanding.

At the end of his ten-minute opening statement introducing the three speakers, the Bank of England governor asked innocuously: 'After the two great sporting superpowers, who is going to win the coveted third spot in the Olympic medals table? Could it be Brazil, or could it be Mexico or perhaps even the euro area?'[201]

According to one of his closest ECB confidants, Draghi, sitting on the stage preparing for his speech and only half-listening to King's opening lines, misinterpreted the Bank of England boss's awkward but clearly good-humoured remark – regarding it as a veiled barb against the euro.[202] This reinforced Draghi's perception of the 'darkness' at the conference about prospects for the European currency[203] – and prompted him to add emphasis to supplement the statement's impact. Years after the event, Draghi still displayed some private irritation about King's superficially harmless Olympic allusion.[204] Remarkably, King, a committed doubter on the euro, may unwittingly have helped its durability.

Draghi's stress in London on 'within our mandate' (intriguingly, he uttered the phrase twice, leaving some to believe that he didn't quite believe in the avowed conditionality) reflected the advice of Yves Mersch. As ECB board member in charge of legal affairs, the ex-Luxembourg central-bank chief was responsible for protecting the ECB from the depredations of the German constitutional court and the higher juridical entity, the European Court of Justice (ECJ). 'I had made that clear to him all along that these words would be needed in discussion of any new instrument. I had told him: "If we lose at the ECJ, we are dead." '[205]

In previous weeks, Draghi had held an elliptical exchange with Merkel in a partial rehearsal of his London performance. He did not discuss details because there were none.[206] A well-placed ECB insider explains:

> Draghi made a prior trip to Berlin for a meeting with Merkel. No advisers were present, so only Draghi and Merkel know what went on. The Draghi statement was premeditated but not preconcerted. He wanted to give the impression that the euro was too important a project to fail. The political will was not there to go full-scale towards the goal of fiscal union, so the only solution was to allow the ECB to take the lead.[207]

Former ECB board member Issing confirms the Merkel approach: 'She preferred the ECB to take the strain rather than to resort to taxpayers' money for direct support for euro area member countries.'[208] Trichet – who held frequent consultations with Merkel during his eight years as Draghi's predecessor – is well aware of the chancellor's cautious style: she would not have given 'specific advance backing', he says. 'What remains true is that the decision of the European Council on banking union was a clear, powerfully symbolic signal that governments of the euro area were determined to support it.'[209]

The 27 July Merkel–Hollande statement supports this interpretation. According to former Irish central-bank governor Honohan,

> Draghi squared it [the basic content] with Merkel beforehand. He knew that she was not going to protest. She must've realised that the euro was in trouble in summer 2012. It was not clear whether it would survive . . . Merkel and Draghi would have met informally. People told me such a meeting took place. Such a meeting to give assurances and guidance doesn't need to be formal, it could have been on the margins of a more formal session. She would've said: 'I don't like any of this stuff. But do what you have to do.'[210]

Holzmann of the Austrian National Bank, states: 'Draghi was such a dominant figure that he was able to make an announcement that calmed the markets. It would not have been possible without a supporting environment. Merkel thought it was wise not to get down in history as the leader who was responsible for breaking up the euro.'[211]

Orphanides, the former president of the Central Bank of Cyprus, believes – somewhat puristically – that governmental concertation by Trichet and Draghi damaged the ECB's independence. 'Both of them consulted regularly with the governments of the two largest member states' – which he calls 'disproportionate'.

> On one occasion, during a governing council meeting in July 2011, Trichet was invited to Berlin where the German chancellor and French president had a meeting that same day. He informed the council, asked for views, and subsequently left the meeting. Would he have considered such a request if the leaders of two small states had asked him? That's not the way an independent central bank should behave.[212]

Draghi's speech, even after the Merkel–Hollande intervention, was insufficient to bring a lasting truce. On 30 July, four days after Draghi's London intervention, Geithner made a flying visit to Schäuble on the holiday island of Sylt in the North Sea. 'I left Sylt more worried than ever. He told me that there were many in Europe who still thought kicking the Greeks out of the euro was a plausible – even desirable – strategy.'

On the same day, Geithner stopped in Frankfurt to see Draghi. 'It wasn't clear yet what they [the ECB] were actually prepared to do. When I got back to Washington I told the president [Obama] I was deeply worried and he was too.'

Addressing the FOMC the next day, Dudley said: 'I take some joy from Mario Draghi's remarks that the ECB is now prepared to do more.'[213] But he confessed to being 'a little confused' . . . 'I wonder about the intersection between what Mario would like to do and what he is allowed to do under the ECB charter and what the Germans would actually agree to.' The ECB's agreement on the OMT programme – based on beneficiary governments agreeing policy conditionality – brought some relief.[214]

At the FOMC September session, Dudley said that Fed deputy chair Janet Yellen and he had met European central bankers in Basel over the weekend, recording their view that the ECB did 'the best that they could accomplish'.[215] Noting that the ECB council had agreed OMT with a 22 to 1 vote, 'with only Weidmann of the Bundesbank dissenting', and that the German government 'at least for now' seemed supportive, Dudley recorded: 'the Bundesbank's opposition is somewhat marginalized'. But he added: 'You still have a very bad feedback loop from the austerity programs to the economy, to fiscal performance, and the state of the banking system . . . and there's still no road map as to where we're actually going in terms of the ultimate destination: What does greater fiscal union in Europe look like?'

By December the Europeans had made sufficient progress for Dudley to issue a cautious 'all-clear': 'The situation is a long way from being fixed, so I'm not really optimistic about the longer term, but it's probably not going to go off the rails in the near future.'[216] On the ECB board, Weidmann's opposition to the OMT did, however, have a longer-lasting effect – weighing on both his own and his country's credentials. As Cœuré put it, 'It was not so bad that he voted against OMT. He took responsibility for it. There was transparency. It was well managed. What was bad was the Bundesbank's action in speaking against the ECB in the course of the hearing [at the German constitutional court in 2013]. It gave ammunition to those suggesting that the German government and Bundesbank were taking their distance from monetary union.'[217]

NEVER-ENDING BATTLE OF WITS

Judging by the lessons of the past, current strains and the panoply of challenges ahead, the ECB is likely to remain in permanent crisis mode, perpetually watching for upsets that may lie close at hand and erupt at almost any moment.

Yannis Stouranas, governor of the Bank of Greece since 2014, and previously the country's finance minister, is a man battle-hardened by Greek economic upheavals. He says the ECB is now a much 'more modern and flexible central bank', having 'enhanced its decision-making as part of corrective action on the Greek crisis'.[218] Greece has been the 'midwife of history', Stouranas opines, since the crisis enabled the Europeans to bring in the European Stability Mechanism as a multi-billion euro credit tool to assist cash-strained governments, a system of macroprudential banking supervision and a more modern set of instruments for monetary policy. 'But Europe faces higher monetary and economic risks than the US because it is not a federal state. We do not have a full banking union. We don't have a fiscal union or a capital markets union. This makes our task more difficult. The US has major advantages because it is an energy exporter. And it has the world's supreme reserve currency.'

Stouranas says the ECB has more independence than the Fed, since it is enshrined in an intergovernmental treaty. Yet the bank has less flexibility, 'because the tasks of the ECB are set by the European treaties, with the primary mandate achieving price stability, whereas the Fed has a dual mandate' – to maintain price stability and maximise employment.

Pablo Hernández de Cos, governor of the Banco de España from 2018 to 2024, who took over as general manager of the Bank for International Settlements in summer 2025, takes a similar view.

Mario Draghi and Christine Lagarde have both been outstanding leaders in very different ways and in very different circumstances. Both have delivered in the face of unprecedented challenges . . . The ECB is now a genuine peer of the Federal Reserve, with a similar set of tools and a similar reaction function. No one can now credibly say that the ECB cannot or does not live up to its responsibilities. We have proved it. And that extra credibility makes us more effective.[219]

There is a darker side. The original concept of monetary union operating 'stateless money' is accurate, solely to the extent that a central European government neither exists nor is likely to materialise. Yet the central bank and individual European governments are engaged in continual interplay – a never-ending battle of wits. The ECB's policy stance partly depends on whether or not governments' fiscal policies are in harmony with the rules set down by the European Commission, which were reformed and supposedly simplified in 2022–3. Doubts regularly surfacing at the ECB over the plausibility of the Commission's framework can further complicate the fiscal–monetary policy equation.

According to Vítor Constâncio, a former Portuguese finance minister and governor of the Banco de Portugal, who was ECB vice president from 2010 to 2018, the ECB and European governments must go much further in advancing common action. 'One of the euro system's flaws has been the lack of decisive measures to provide financial assistance to countries or to address liquidity crises in the national sovereign bonds.'[220]

Beyond the creation of the NGEU and TPI, Constâncio backs a 'European Stabilisation Fund' to respond to recessions, along the lines proposed in an IMF discussion document in 2018.[221] The NGEU will not be used in its entirety, Constâncio forecasts: instead of the planned €750 billion, he believes the fund will end up dispersing only €450 billion. 'The countries concerned would have to increase their budget deficits, and that goes against the constraints of the stability pact [limiting member states' borrowing]. So there is a mechanical contradiction.'

The perturbations of the debt crisis have left wounds. The greatest peril for the ECB arises when it is drawn into a conflict between upholding anti-inflation discipline, on the one hand, and, on the other, depressing interest rates on bond markets to maintain the euro's existence.

The sharpest conflict of interest emerged when the ECB became part of the 'troika' – together with the IMF and the European Commission – lending to the overindebted governments of Cyprus, Greece, Ireland and Portugal in 2010–15. As former US Treasury official Christopher

Smart puts it, 'The troika was a very awkward and ultimately ill-advised structure. The ECB was sitting uncomfortably on both sides of the table, supplying funding for the troubled states, but also likely to have to step in to bear the brunt of the crisis if things went wrong.'[222]

Once started, aggressive monetary action raises the likelihood that central banks will be constrained to continue easy-money policies out of fear of the painful consequences if they were to withdraw. Noyer recalls telling Draghi in 2019 that the ECB was being 'trapped by the markets into policies that were too accommodative' – including resumption of the asset purchase programme in September 2019.'[223]

Luis de Guindos, vice president of the ECB since 2018, summarises the shortcomings:

> We have a single monetary policy, single bank supervision and resolution framework (although more limited). However, we have no fiscal union, no capital markets union, no common deposit insurance system. Because of the lack of a fiscal facility, whenever there is a crisis, the ECB has been asked to step in, and it becomes overburdened. This asymmetric framework is the original sin.[224]

Visco, the former governor of the Banca d'Italia, elaborates on the euro's vulnerability:

> The euro is a symbol, not just a means, of establishing Europe as a balancing force in the world economy. The euro is part of the whole. If left alone, it will be difficult for Europe to survive to fulfil that vision. A money without a state is very difficult to manage. For the euro to have survived the crises of the last 20 years is a great achievement. But we must go beyond that. We need more unity in public finances, we need to get to better consolidated public solutions.[225]

INTERNAL AND EXTERNAL SHOCKS

Surveying the ECB's performance in its first twenty-five years, a variety of US experts agree it has more leeway to introduce innovative policies than the Federal Reserve. But the lack of political cohesion brings permanent exposure to internal and external shocks. According to former Federal Reserve chairman Ben Bernanke,

> It is well run, has an excellent staff, and is an intellectual leader in the central banking community. Its decisions have important effects on the world economy, as well as in Europe, and its actions are closely watched by financial market participants. Partly because of fewer legal constraints the ECB has more policy tools (and potential policy tools) than the Fed, although in deploying those tools it has to walk a fine political line given the sometimes diverging interests of member countries.

Bob Zoellick, president of the World Bank in 2007–12, and one of the most ardent pro-Europeans in the German reunification team of George H.W. Bush, praises European ability to learn from setbacks: 'The establishment of the euro as the second reserve currency must be recognized as a significant achievement. The flaws were known from the beginning – setting up a currency without a political union and without a process for fiscal transfers. Mario Draghi saved it – but this is an ongoing process of experimentation.'[226] But Zoellick criticises the ECB's hesitant strategic approach – epitomised by its efforts to hinder US suggestions for using in Ukraine's defence $300 billion in Russian assets frozen at the outset of the Ukrainian war.[227]

> The ECB should be the crown jewel but it has been in some disarray. It has not been able to take on a more effective overall role in shaping Europe. You can see this in its attitude over the freezing of Russian assets. The euro's international role should be a source of strength not weakness. The ECB was worried that the freezing of assets could lead other countries such as China selling their euro-denominated bonds. If that was going to happen then the ECB could've said it's going to buy them. The ECB should not allow itself to be black-mailed by other countries.[228]

Tim Geithner emphasises how the ECB has to be permanently on guard:

Monetary union is bound to face bouts of instability from time to time throughout the cycle. This requires what you might call a form of insurance provided by the central bank. It is better for this to be explicit and priced in, but with discretionary power. It's OK to have some ambiguity built into the system. If, as in the US, you have to go to parliaments each time to get authorization, then the reaction will be slow and late. And because action is delayed, you end up with greater economic costs and higher fiscal costs.[229]

The US economic expert with the longest experience of front-line dealing with Germany is Fred Bergsten, assistant Treasury secretary for international affairs in the administration of Jimmy Carter. Bergsten, a long-time Keynesian supporter of German fiscal stimulus to help Europe build momentum, founded the Washington Institute for International Economics (which became the Peterson Institute in 2006), and led it until 2021.

He says the euro area has been handicapped by Germany's unwillingness to finance the weaker countries. This reliance makes the currency system prone to semi-permanent disruption. Bergsten retains the firm view that Germany 'will never allow the euro to break up . . . When the crunch comes, they will always write a cheque.'[230] Having campaigned already in 2014 for Germany to modify the constitutional 'debt brake' limiting public borrowing, Bergsten believes Germany's reluctance to follow strategically appropriate economic policies has been a major factor behind Europe's disappointing growth.[231] He welcomes the shift towards higher spending on defence and infrastructure orchestrated by Friedrich Merz's government-in-waiting in March 2025.

This is better late than never. If they can pull it off, then it's good for Germany, good for Europe, good for the world. Probably there will be strains on national bond markets and therefore the next step may be for Germany to move toward backing pan-European borrowing, not just for items like defense but for overall macroeconomic purposes. Merz has shown impressive pragmaticism over reforming the debt brake. I suspect he will do the same now on European borrowing.[232]

Larry Summers, Bill Clinton's Treasury secretary in 1999–2001, was intensively involved with the Europeans during the euro's birth. From the beginning, when he was deputy Treasury secretary responsible for international monetary affairs (in 1995–8), he was a sceptic. 'I felt that the countries that would enter the euro would not form an optimal currency area. There was a lack of flexibility and mobility. And I thought there was an absence of a consolidated approach to standing behind domestic financial systems.'

Summers relates how he made himself unpopular at a meeting of 'Working Party 3', the group of officials at the Organisation for Economic Cooperation and Development dealing with international macroeconomic and balance-of-payments issues. He raised an issue about cross-border banking, which became virulent during the 2007–8 financial crisis – '"What would happen if a major bank in a non-German European country failed? Who would take responsibility for orchestrating the rescue? Frankfurt, Brussels, the local capital, or what?" There followed angry chaos among Europeans.'[233]

This is a question that remains acute two decades later, highlighted by the unresolved debate about the mooted takeover of Commerzbank, Germany's No. 2 private bank, by Italy's largest lender, UniCredit, in 2024.[234] Lorenzo Bini Smaghi confirms that the issue of 'lender of last resort in Europe' is still an open question. 'Who decides if a bank is solvent or not? It used to be a national decision. But now the ECB is responsible for banking supervision, there will have to be a European decision on this. Even though the money will come mainly from national resources.'[235]

Summers remains unconvinced by the euro's merits.

These have been years of moderate comity among European countries, given all the difficulties and strains. Maybe, by binding Germany into a major institution, the euro contributed to that comity. I don't minimize that. But I would say these have been pretty disastrous years for Europe economically. If you look at Europe's share of global stock market wealth compared to the US, it is shockingly low.[236]

At a country level, Summers focuses on Greece and Italy. 'If things go smoothly from here, Greece will restore its 2009 level of

GDP sometime in the early 2030s. And in many respects, Italy is worse off than Greece.' Summers sums up: 'Relative to any kind of counterfactual, the European economy has to be judged a failure. That is true whether your aspirations are for growth and employment, or for financial strength and fiscal control.' Summers foresees an uncomfortable future: 'Europe has done enough to make it unlikely that the union will fissure. But it has not done enough to assure that it will be an optimal currency area or avoid doing substantial regional economic damage.'

Some of sceptical Summers's misgivings about Europe's 'halfway house' arrangements are shared by Constâncio, a full-hearted supporter of European integration.

> Countries have refused to pool their financial interests. It has been difficult to reach agreement among the technocratic structures of different national capital market authorities, and regretfully, the governments have not compelled them to agree, as they did with the central banks for a monetary union. Following the UK departure from the EU, different European financial centres are competing with each other. This is to the detriment of Europe as a whole.[237]

Constâncio adds:

> It's a setback that we have not had further developments with banking union. The deposit insurance scheme would be good to have, although it became less essential given the great improvement of European banks' robustness. The European deposit guarantee scheme creates great political difficulties for Germany given the position of the co-operative and savings banks which pay very little for their present mutual protection.

However, like Bergsten, he is reasonably sanguine about Germany's 2025 change of heart on borrowing.

> I'm not worried about the differential effect on other countries' capital markets outside Germany. Provided that inflation does not

go up significantly as a result, this increased German borrowing will be easily absorbed by markets. The Americans are shooting themselves in the foot over the dollar. An improved assessment of European investments will help to booster the euro's standing. If there is a peace deal over Ukraine this will boost valuations in Europe. This will be effective in helping with European financing, whatever the terms of the deal.[238]

Steve Cecchetti, the former Bank for International Settlements economist, suggests that the ECB – once again – is approaching a turning point.

The project of monetary union and the ECB does not look as though it is getting more cohesive – contrary to what might have been expected 25 years ago. Member states are hanging on to national financial systems and fiscal operations. The ECB and the overall European system have not brought completion of the banking union with European deposit insurance, allowing more cross-border banking mergers, or enabled Europe permanently to issue large volumes of joint debt.[239]

Cecchetti concludes: 'There is reason for doubt how long Europe can carry on like this.'

The future, as always the case with the euro, remains beguilingly open.

7

THE TROUBLE WITH BRITAIN

Britain does not dream of some cosy, isolated existence on the fringes of the European Community. Our destiny is in Europe, as part of the Community.

Margaret Thatcher, 1988[1]

What happened over the exchange rate mechanism was not just an economic difficulty for the UK. It was an economic and political disaster and one that we believed was avoidable.

John Major to Helmut Kohl, September 1992[2]

I always thought that the Leave side would win the referendum. Britain had been saying for 40 years it was not a full supporter of the European Union. So when the British had a chance to leave, I thought they would take it.

Jean-Claude Juncker, former European Commission president, 2023[3]

Sealed by zealotry and culminating in catharsis, Britain's departure from the European Union has been a misfortune that marked an epochal shift – not just for the UK but for the continent as a whole. The referendum decision in 2016 and its chaotic aftermath led to political and trade barriers between the UK and the rest of Europe just when maximum solidarity was required to face multiple upsets ranging from Covid-19 to the rise of an antagonistic Russia. A plan which many believed would never happen, and for whose outcome no one was prepared, culminated, after many twists and turns, with the political destruction of its main progenitors in the Conservative Party.

Geography and history – sea and the centuries – have always made Britain a nation apart.[4] Yet, for all the domestic infighting and sporadic rebuffs to British pride and ambition, the UK's forty-seven-year EU membership brought direction, rather than disorder, more success than setbacks. In the years since the referendum and formal exit in 2020, the UK's departure has been, on balance, a failure. The realities of interdependence have flooded into UK political life – with substantial lessons for the rest of Europe and further afield. Withdrawal was the climax of a fifty-year ideological battle over national sovereignty, European influence and Britain's place in the world. It saddled the UK economy with regulatory burdens and impediments to investment at precisely the wrong time, coinciding with radical uncertainty in world politics and economics. This has not only made Britain a poorer and more unequal country than it would, arguably, otherwise have been: it also coincided with, and helped to spur, a sense of political malaise across the continent.

Britain is not alone in sensing defects and deficiencies in European integration. Similar tussles over European ideology and its practical effects are in train in many other parts of the continent; Britain has gone further than anywhere else by taking these disagreements to their logical conclusion. Reversal is unlikely. Whatever happens with a sought-after European rapprochement under Keir Starmer's government, there is no possibility of fully fledged EU re-entry in the foreseeable future.[5] For the outcome, no one is free of responsibility. Chronic shortcomings in the UK coincided with failings in judgment, communication and performance among European governments. The 'Union' with which the Labour government is attempting to build a new relationship is a less reliable, more fractured and less powerful global force than the entity Britain quit. Concerns about the sociological and economic effects of large-scale immigration – a key factor behind the UK vote – have come to a head as a severe political factor in many countries. In a sense, the British decision furnished an early indication of what was due to happen in other parts of the continent. Reflecting the disturbed state of Europe, as well as the intermingled convulsions of the 2007–8 financial upheaval, the Covid-19 pandemic and the Ukraine war, it is too early for a definitive analysis of the longer-term effects of departure.[6] They were always likely to be less fear-reaching than the protagonists' projections. As Meghnad Desai of the London School of Economics pointed out immediately after the vote in June 2016, 'We can ignore the miracles promised by the Brexiteers or the dire predictions of the Remainers.'[7] But there is little doubt that the UK decision reinforced the EU's downwards spiral.

One common feature of the past serves as a warning for the future. In dealing with European partners and neighbours over past decades, Britain has repeatedly demonstrated fundamental flaws. The trouble with Britain has been a persistent tendency to overestimate its strengths, and underemphasise or misunderstand those of other Europeans. This frequently recurring pattern of miscalculation – stretching back to the UK's refusal to take part in European integration efforts in the 1950s – has left a legacy that both sides must try to overcome. The residue of problems for Britain's reputation and influence has been extended by more recent missteps, notably by David Cameron, and particularly Boris Johnson and Liz Truss.

In terms of the shorter-term consequences, sentiment in the UK and further afield has coalesced around the assessment already advanced by most mainstream forecasters before the 2016 vote. Denigrated as 'Project Fear' by Brexiters, the prediction was that departure would be economically harmful[8] – an appraisal that has, on the whole, been vindicated, although less spectacularly than excessively pessimistic forecasters had surmised.[9]

The British public agrees: two-thirds think it has damaged the economy, while even among Leave voters only one in five thinks the impact has been positive. According to a major study on the effects of departure, published in January 2025 on the fifth anniversary, the overall impact has been an economic 'slow puncture', rather than a car crash.[10] A shift in the months after the vote towards a 'hard Brexit', encompassing departure from the single market and customs union,[11] guaranteed that the adjustment as well as the pain would be greater.

Brexiters, too, used scare-mongering tactics that have since been disavowed. The most notorious claim was that leaving the Union would save £350 million a week which the government could channel into strengthening the National Health Service. Jacob Rees-Mogg, a leading Johnson supporter among Conservative MPs, admitted the Leave campaign was 'over-egging the pudding . . . It was not a good idea to stretch the truth to gain attention.'[12]

One issue is clear: Brexit has not helped living standards; but neither has it had the unduly deleterious effect, relative to the country's peers, often ascribed to it by Remainers. The UK's economic performance over the decade and a half straddling the period before and after the referendum has remained in the middle-to-lower ground of the Group of Seven leading industrial countries.[13] The Bundesbank, the German central bank, which normally refrains from commenting on other countries' politics, somewhat unguardedly threw its weight behind a judgement that quitting the EU had made the UK much worse off.[14] On the eve of the 2024 general election which saw the Conservative Party's parliamentary representation plummet to the lowest in its 200-year history, 56 per cent of voters indicated they believed leaving had been economically disadvantageous, compared with 12 per cent who termed it beneficial.[15] The balance of British public opinion on whether Britain should rejoin has shifted in favour of UK accession, but by a smaller margin.[16]

Whether or not this negative sentiment persists is unclear. There are two mitigating features. Britain's place outside the EU almost certainly augmented Europe's ability to react quickly and effectively to the Russian invasion of Ukraine in 2022. The UK acting by itself was able to react more speedily and decisively than had it been part of a communal exercise. Furthermore, had the UK still been in the EU, Europe would have faced much greater difficulties in deciding and deploying a joint borrowing programme in June 2020 to offset the effects of the Covid-19 pandemic.

Taking all considerations into the balance sheet, it appears that the negative repercussions for the continent as a whole have outweighed the positive effects by a wide margin. But, in view of the intervening Covid pandemic and the list of other significant international factors influencing economic performance, drawing up a convincing analysis of cause and effect during that period will probably take another decade.

WAS DEPARTURE PREORDAINED?

Britain ranks roughly equal with France as the second most important economy in Europe after Germany. Departure marked the first time that any member state had left the grouping Britain joined in 1973 as the European Economic Community. 'Brexit' was, on paper, the biggest blow to integration since postwar European reconstruction started with the Treaty of Rome in 1957.[17] As the tale has unfolded, rather than producing emulators, it has acted as a significant deterrent, at least for the time being, to other countries tempted to follow suit. A welling up of anti-EU sentiment in key countries across the continent has made the Union more quarrelsome and less effective but not so far less numerous.[18] Dissent has been channelled into internal disarray, rather than triggering escape routes. Indeed, the EU intends to get bigger, not smaller: plans for further EU expansion into the western Balkans, together with the planned adhesion of the still more problematic aspirants Ukraine and Georgia, underline both the scale and pitfalls of the EU's ambitions.

Was departure preordained? Would fate and circumstance make Britain 'a stranger in Europe'?[19] Winston Churchill wrote in 1930, 'We are with Europe, but not of it.'[20] After the Second World War, Churchill believed in a united Europe, not least to keep Germany in check, with the British helping to supervise the new construct from the sidelines. A united Europe was 'the only solution' to a two-sided problem: 'to restore the economic life of Germany and revive the ancient fame of the German race without exposing their neighbours and ourselves to any rebuilding or reassertion of their military power of which we still bear the scars.'[21] The British decision to stay outside the Community in the 1950s was founded on the belief that the country's history was more glorious, its constitution more stable, and its people less willing to be led astray than elsewhere.[22] Jean Monnet, a principal architect of the peaceful postwar alignment between France and Germany in the original European Economic Community, told a British television interviewer the 'price of victory' in the war was the 'illusion' that the UK could stay outside the new construct in the 1950s – so that 'you could maintain what you had, without change'.[23]

An important landmark, second in significance only to the 1973 EEC adhesion, came, after years of dithering, when Britain signed up in 1990 to a central element of western European unity, the exchange rate mechanism of the European Monetary System. The ERM was a technical currency stabilisation scheme, with immense constitutional and political implications. Its contradictory purposes proved fatal for the British. It was simultaneously the 'waiting room' for a monetary union about which Britain (and especially Margaret Thatcher, prime minister until November 1990) were greatly sceptical; a badge of virtue symbolising stable and constructive European policies; and a mechanism for reducing both the UK's stubbornly high inflation rate and interest rates – especially household mortgages.

A major impulse for postwar western European integration was the unsettled state of divided Germany. So there is a certain mournful symmetry in Britain's announcement of ERM membership just two days after the 3 October 1990 formalisation of German reunification. Britain became a member of the scheme on 8 October – just at the time when the Bundesbank was weighing up an overdue tightening of monetary policy to counter the inflationary impact of unification. In joining the monetary mainstream, the British were, uncomprehendingly, entering the maelstrom.[24] With the fall of the Berlin Wall and the dissolution of the Soviet empire, the circumstances that had drawn western Europe together after 1945 were starting to lose traction. They were changing force and character in a way that few could recognise, let alone understand. Many British monetary decision-makers in the Treasury and Bank of England, despite a decade and a half of British adhesion to the European Community, were still highly insular in their approach. Antennae to pick up the new messages were sorely lacking.

There is room for debate whether the ERM denouement – sterling's forced departure on 'Black Wednesday',[25] 16 September 1992 – ranks as the 'first Brexit'. The schism can be traced back to Henry VIII's 1530s break with the Church of Rome, or even the departure of Roman legions from England around AD 400.[26] However viewed, the ERM exit was a gigantic inflection point, with consequences spreading far beyond the UK's borders.

The events of September, followed by further European currency turbulence in summer 1993, concentrated on France and Germany, triggered a stream of developments which raised the probability, sooner or later, of a full British departure. It underlined the fundamental limitations of Britain's efforts to adapt its own domestic priorities to align with European polices. It had a major impact on the decision by the post-1997 Labour government – after some initial hesitation by Tony Blair – to keep sterling out of the euro. The evident shortcomings of the ERM/EMS construct accelerated the European venture towards a much further-reaching, highly risky goal – completing the long-conceived journey to a single currency, an idea with which the British were manifestly out of favour. Another longer-run consequence of the upheavals was to weaken the Bundesbank's resistance to Europe's monetary unification[27] – adding to well-founded suspicions in Britain and elsewhere that the single currency would be established with undue haste and without sufficient thought for the longer-term consequences.[28]

Furthermore, as a result of the Black Wednesday flare-up and a string of associated devaluations of other currencies, the D-Mark became significantly overvalued on the foreign exchanges. This caused an economic contraction in 1993 which impeded Germany's task of meeting the most sensitive of the chosen entry conditions for monetary union – limiting public sector budget deficits. Their own difficulties in fulfilling the 'convergence criteria' weakened the Germans' capacity for imposing stringent conditions – providing a strong reason for Europe's collective failure to prevent serious design flaws becoming ingrained in the fabric of monetary union. The shortcomings were obscured for a while by the euro's relatively problem-free technical introduction after 1999. However, when intractable difficulties started to emerge with full realisation of the Greek economic malaise from 2010 onwards, the euro required growing support through intervention measures, assembled through laborious political compromises of ever greater complexity – a huge reversal from the euro's original ideals of a self-regulating economy. To enable the single currency's survival, the EU had to move towards greater political integration and more generous economic burden-sharing. This was destined to appear unpalatable and perhaps, too, over a longer period, unworkable – not just to the British but also to a growing share of the continental population.

Cameron, who became prime minister in 2010 (and made a brief comeback as foreign secretary under Rishi Sunak in 2023–4[29]), famously warned his party conference as leader in 2006 against 'banging on' about Europe.[30] In an ill-starred statement a few months before he won victory over Gordon Brown in the May 2010 election, he declared, 'I don't want Europe to define my premiership.'[31] On the other hand, he recognised that efforts to counter the forces of destabilisation across the single currency area were moving Europe in a direction inimical to Britain.

Among the first to spot the trend was a man with vastly greater experience in foreign policy, David Owen, who at the age of thirty-eight took up a two-year tenure as foreign secretary in 1977 under prime minister James Callaghan. Owen wrote in June 2012, 'The euro crisis is driving the European Union to a point when it can no longer be ambivalent about the two basic models for Europe. One is the present one: a union of self-governing nations with a separation of powers between the supranational and the intergovernmental. The other is the model we may have in the future: a fiscal union within the euro area.'[32]

That was a line reproduced in Cameron's speech in January 2013 announcing the EU referendum: 'The European Union that emerges from the Eurozone crisis is going to be a very different body. It will be transformed perhaps beyond recognition by the measures needed to save the Eurozone.'[33]

He was also aware that pressure for an in/out referendum was rising from the Eurosceptic wing of his own party and the UK Independence Party – and might soon become irresistible.

LIMITS OF OPT-OUTS

Simon McDonald is an archetypal civil servant figure who – after ambassadorships in Israel and Germany, and working as foreign policy adviser for Prime Minister Gordon Brown – became head of the Foreign Office in 2015–20. Working with Boris Johnson when he became foreign secretary in 2016, and playing a piquant role in his downfall as prime minister in July 2022,[34] McDonald was a front-line observer of the structural shifts that were progressively pushing Britain away from the EU's centre ground. Over the years the UK had 'managed to get various deals and opt-outs which gave Britain an almost totally bespoke membership'.[35] But following the euro's launch, 'it became obvious that, because Britain was not in monetary union and didn't want to be, we had made a firm choice to be separate. So the others would meet and make decisions without us. That was a watershed moment.'

The rules of the European 'club' changed, too, in another way, under the Lisbon treaty in 2009, with the introduction of a mechanism for

member countries to withdraw if they wished.[36] In view of the historical and cultural background, if any country was going to leave, in an
attempt (however motivated) to turn back the clock and rediscover a
new vitality, Britan was always, by a wide margin, the likeliest member
to attempt such an experiment.

There was, too, a deadly inevitability in the leaden-footedness of
British efforts to untangle the relationship. Cameron announced the
referendum in 2013, and implemented it in 2016, believing the exercise would be relatively straightforward.[37] A man who in his dealings
with other Europeans never attempted to conceal his basically
Eurosceptic views, Cameron thought the vote would overcome, not
exacerbate, divisions in his party.

Cameron defines himself as 'a practical Eurosceptic – I haven't
changed my mind'.[38] As evidence of what he says is an underlying positive stance backing European ideals, he says: 'In my year off in 1985 I
travelled to the Soviet Union. The seminal moment was in 1989–90
when communism collapsed. I wanted these countries [that had been
part of the Soviet empire] to have the chance to join the EU.'

Ken Clarke, an opponent of the referendum, a pro-European
Conservative MP from 1970 to 2019, and minister in the administrations of Thatcher, Major and Cameron,[39] saw the innate contradictions.

> I had a row with Cameron about it. He did it to try to pacify the
> backbenchers, to stop them from banging on about Europe. He
> didn't think he was going to lose it. Since he was trying to find a way
> of appeasing them, he didn't talk too much about the virtues and
> the merits of Europe. His view was, 'The EU is a dreadful arrange-
> ment. But I'm a tough prime minister, I can sort them out. We are
> going to reform it; it won't be a problem winning the referendum.'[40]

Cameron has never been known as a conviction politician.[41] This
applies in particular to matters European. Charles Moore, a leading
Conservative writer, Brexit supporter and close follower of Cameron,
says, 'He gave the impression of never having taken Europe seriously
enough. He did just enough to stay in the saddle. He was balancing being
a Eurosceptic by doing just enough to appear to be a Europhile.'[42]
According to Richard Balfe, a Roman Catholic trade unionist and long-

time member of the European parliament, who became Cameron's adviser on trade unions in 2008 (and warned him in 2014 of the perils of holding a referendum), 'Cameron did not feel much empathy on Europe. He was not so much untouched by foreign influence as somewhat impervious, as one often finds in people from his class and background.'[43]

A similar view comes from David Frost, a career Foreign Office civil servant whose aversion to the European Commission took root in Brussels in the 1980s, and who joined Johnson's side in 2016, becoming his chief EU adviser and negotiator in 2019–21.[44] Frost says, 'Cameron saw Europe as a slightly annoying part of the prime minister's job – having to go around speaking to foreigners who were telling you all kinds of irritating things that you don't care very much for.'[45]

There was plenty of this in store. In a nine-month spell in 2015–16, when the prime minister embarked on 'the biggest diplomatic tour in recent history'[46] attempting to win concessions from his European partners, particularly on immigration, Cameron's relationship with Angela Merkel was crucial. As the long-serving leader of Europe's biggest economy, she set the tone for the rest of the Union. Benefiting from strong trade and investment links with Germany, the British government believed – exaggeratedly – it had an important hold over the Germans, since the UK's relatively liberal economic policy views were generally aligned with German industrial interests.[47]

By controversially espousing in 2015 an 'open borders' policy towards asylum-seekers from conflict-ridden parts of the Middle East and Africa, Merkel helped stoke widespread fears of untrammelled immigration across Europe. Unwittingly, she fuelled overdone projections of vast population flows into Britain from countries with unstable histories such as Turkey – a factor that loomed large in the propaganda battle over the British referendum.[48]

Never short of self-confidence, Cameron believed he had more leeway over the German chancellor than was the case. A central misunderstanding in the pivotal relationship at the heart of Europe had fatal consequences for Britain and the rest of the continent. Merkel gave every impression of equanimity. But beneath the superficial bonhomie there was no meeting of minds and, at the end, very little mutual trust.

Ivan Rogers, Britain's permanent representative (ambassador) to the EU in the crucial period from the end of 2013 until January 2017 –

whose acerbic and largely valid criticisms of the UK's post-referendum policies antagonised many Brexiters – says of the German chancellor: 'She found him entertaining, but annoying, with a lack of seriousness. There was a certain frustration on her side. It was never a trusting relationship. He came across as somewhat cavalier and full of himself.'[49] An important example of Cameron's misjudgement of their relationship came at a crucial bilateral session in London in February 2013, shortly after the referendum announcement. After the meeting (excluding officials), 'He came to us in a very good mood saying: "I think that went very well." He thought he had got a greater measure of agreement about the way forward, including, at that point, on potential treaty change options, than I believed he had. She had a tendency to leave him, like many others, believing he had heard more than she had actually ever committed to.'

McDonald provides a similar assessment. 'Merkel liked Cameron's company. He was charming, a good and humorous talker. But she wouldn't make a concession just because she liked him; I don't believe she ever gave a signal that she would allow the UK an exemption from free movement.'[50]

The German chancellor's quiet modesty and refusal to make elaborate statements – in direct contrast to the barnstorming Cameron approach – may have given the prime minister a false sense of security. Merkel confided in him, in 2012, before the announcement of the referendum plan, 'Without you in the EU, I don't know what is going to happen.'[51] But, by the time of their 2015–16 interactions, the relationship had become hollowed-out. A Merkel aide who played an important behind-the-scenes role in EU parleying, says Cameron's 'very British way of negotiating' grated on the chancellor.

> Cameron gave her a list of what he wanted [in the area of freedom of movement]. He said, 'I want these things – Number 1, Number 2 and Number 3.' He set out his red lines and then he didn't get them. She would not negotiate like that. She would not set out red lines. He was completely the opposite to her. If you are in a dominant position, you can maybe practise that kind of policy. It is the kind of thing the Americans do all the time. However, Britain was not in a dominant position. So he somewhat misjudged his capabilities.[52]

Another politician at the heart of Europe is Mario Monti, Italy's prime minister in 2011–13. His priest-like manner derives partly from his earlier decade-long stint as European commissioner in charge of Europe's single market and, later, competition. Monti regards Cameron as a man embodying Britain's missed opportunities. He says he tried to persuade Cameron to 'engage' with the EU to drive forward liberalisation and the single market, claiming that this would complete the work of Margaret Thatcher.[53] 'He could have championed opening up the cross-EU services market, where Britain has a very strong position.'

Monti however failed to realise – as Ivan Rogers explains – that Cameron's agenda had shifted towards loosening integration, not deepening it, which had become 'a negative, not a goal, for the Conservatives'.[54] Pondering the differences in support for the EU between England, Scotland and Northern Ireland in the 2016 referendum, Monti's verdict on Camero is a sobering one: 'He could have been the hero of this period – at a time when many European member states – Sweden for example – favoured liberalisation and market-orientated policies. Instead, he might go down in history as the person who triggered some disintegration, if not within the EU, perhaps eventually within the UK.'[55]

PARALLELS FROM THE PAST

Cameron's negotiating blind spots showed uncanny parallels to other misadventures, most notably Britain's disastrous departure from the ERM under his Conservative predecessor, John Major. Measured against the gigantic constitutional and historical implications, the Conservatives' approach to the 2016 referendum was amateurishly ill-prepared. The process embodied an ethereal, almost fairy-tale quality. Like many fairy tales, it did not end happily. Cameron's device to unify his party laid down a trail to the July 2024 vote, the Conservatives' biggest electoral calamity.

Cameron had good reason to doubt (even though he denied it later) whether the ploy might ever be implemented – on the grounds that his pro-European post-2010 coalition partners, the Liberal Democrats, would prevent him from carrying it out.[56] The referendum loomed large only after Cameron emancipated himself from the Lib Dems by winning an unexpected absolute majority in the 2015 general election.[57] Cameron's government came out in favour of Remain, based above all on an economic assessment. But the prime minister and his hopelessly split team of key ministers failed to campaign effectively to counter the central preoccupations – focused on 'control' and 'sovereignty' – that were uppermost in the minds of the Leavers.

The referendum process was marked by incongruity and confusion at every stage. Cameron's expectation that he would win was shared by rebels within his own party, led by the capricious and unpredictable Johnson,[58] who decided to back the Leave campaign at the last moment. The decision was less for ideological reasons, more because Johnson thought it would further his political career.[59] The former journalist and mayor of London, who became a Tory MP in 2016, believed that, by going down fighting at the helm of the Leavers,[60] he would reinforce his status with grass-roots Conservative supporters. Finishing as a vanquished gladiator on the losing side would put him in a superior position to George Osborne, Cameron's long-time friend and chancellor of the exchequer, Johnson's icily uncharismatic Remainer rival. And that, Johnson reasoned, would improve his chances of leapfrogging into 10 Downing Street when Cameron eventually stood down.

Neither side made any attempt to plan for departure. The vote, though formally non-binding on parliament, was regarded as decisive. No one had given serious thought about how, under what safeguards, and within which timeframe such a far-reaching decision would be implemented. A parliamentary committee accused Cameron of 'gross negligence' for declining to make contingency plans for the eventuality of the Leave side winning.[61] Cameron said before the referendum he would stay on if he lost,[62] yet announced his resignation a few hours after the vote – and was gone within three weeks. Cameron's decision to quit immediately brought in the interregnum of Theresa May as a compromise candidate for the Tory leadership and premiership. Then followed her fateful decision to make Johnson foreign secretary, from which he was catapulted to prime minster. For both jobs he was thoroughly ill-equipped – as underlined by a range of views from people nominally on his side of the political divide.

Charles Moore, author of an acclaimed three-volume biography of Thatcher, who knows Johnson well (and attended his sixtieth-birthday party in June 2024) describes his mix of characteristics: 'For all his amazing faults, he is the man who can make the weather. This has to be set against the negative traits of unreliability, casualness and indecisiveness.'[63]

He will often say, on the spur of the moment, that he agrees with you, without really thinking about it, and then admit later that he's changed his mind.'[64] David Frost describes him as 'a Shakespearean character brought down by flaws', adding, not wholly credibly, 'Boris as PM with a ten-year term would've been very different.'[65] More realistically, Andrew Gimson, a sympathetic biographer, wrote: 'In the end even his own colleagues felt there was too much to forgive.'[66]

The comparisons with Thatcher are instructive. Charles Powell, Thatcher's long-term foreign-policy adviser, opines, 'Thatcher would make jibes about Europe – the quips about feeling sorry for the other Europeans in being isolated 11 to 1 against her – but I believe she commanded respect. There is a big difference compared with the attitude shown by Boris Johnson, who has been a fool, acting shamefully in his policies on Europe.'[67]

David Davis, a senior Conservative MP, a down-to-earth Eurosceptic with his own maverick style of doing business, whom Theresa May in 2016 appointed the minister in charge of exiting the EU, says, 'If you presented a case to Thatcher, she would go through it in forensic detail – that's something Boris could not do.'[68] Christopher Tugendhat, a Conservative MP in 1970–7, then a member of the European Commission, has been a Conservative member of the House of Lords since 1993 and has known Johnson since he was a boy. He says, 'I don't have a good word to say about him.'[69]

Ken Clarke became aware of Johnson's shortcomings in the mid-1990s, during his period as chancellor of the exchequer, when Johnson was the *Daily Telegraph* correspondent in Brussels.

He can be fun, good company, he would've been a good TV personality, but he should never have become prime minister.[70] I saw him in Brussels when I used to go to summit meetings. We would have a drink in the bar afterwards. I would say to him, 'In your last column, you wrote about something in our last finance ministers' meeting which wasn't even on the agenda. You were sitting in a room like this and you made it up.' He did what he always did, giggled, ruffled his hair, grinned and said something like he wouldn't see it quite that way. The truth is that he wrote fictitious columns.[71]

The only UK public institution ready for the 2016 shock was the Bank of England under Mark Carney. He says: 'We [the Bank of England] had done a lot of work in advance. The civil service was not allowed to make contingency plans, but that didn't apply to the Bank. That is the advantage of being operationally independent.'[72] The thoughtful though frequently short-tempered Canadian-born governor, one of the few authoritative figures emerging with any credit from the Brexit saga, enraged Brexiters with repeated forecasts of the ill-effects of a Leave vote.[73] In his victory speech after winning the election in April 2025 that confirmed him as prime minister of Canada, Carney spelled out the adage he had already displayed at the Bank of England in 2016: 'One of the responsibilities of government is to prepare for the worst, not hope for the best.'[74]

Carney's plain speaking brought him into the realm of politics – never an optimal outcome for a supposedly independent central bank governor, and one which, at the time of the referendum, may have helped strengthen the forces to which he was opposed. According to Clarke, 'Carney set off the right wing of the Tory party. So, in some ways, his stance was counter-productive.'[75] Osborne, Cameron's hapless chancellor of the exchequer – an opponent of the referendum plan, as he frequently told the prime minister – threatened a punitive tax-raising 'Brexit budget' in case of 'Leave', an economically illiterate concept that disappeared from the policy landscape as speedily as its instigator.[76] Taking over from Cameron, May, a lukewarm Remainer, who had been a brisk but uninspiring home secretary for six years, did not trust David Davis, the minister she put in charge of negotiating a withdrawal deal. The Brussels officials facing him and British mandarins, individually and severally, were considerably more adept at European bargaining.

Martin Selmayr, chief of staff for Jean-Claude Juncker, European Commission president in 2014–19, played a prominent role in the post-referendum stand-off.

We had been expecting tough and professional negotiations, which was the British reputation. However, they took a long time to get back to us. For many months, there was no ambassador in Brussels. No ministers came to Brussels. David Davis was never as much on top of the file as Michel Barnier, our Commission negotiator. Many at the political level of the post-referendum governments didn't realise the complexity of unravelling 40 years of membership.'[77]

Johnson quickly became sidelined. 'Theresa May didn't trust him,' says McDonald. 'How can it work if the prime minister doesn't trust the foreign minister?'

Fellow EU foreign ministers made clear they were not happy to deal with him. McDonald recalls walking up the grand staircase in the Victorian splendour of the Foreign Office with Frank-Walter Steinmeier, on his first visit to London after the referendum. The German foreign minister, later Germany's federal president, 'was very angry; he turned to me and said: "Europe has been the central project of my life and this man has just despoiled it."'[78] A fairly typical view of Johnson from the German business community comes from industrialist Gerhard Cromme: 'Boris Johnson is a despicable character. It was a scandal that, as an act of political opportunism, he exposed his country to great harm.'[79]

Britain formally withdrew from the EU in January 2020. But a further three years elapsed before a final settlement was worked out in February 2023, under prime minister Sunak, over thorny issues of trade with Northern Ireland. Sunak reaped no benefit from the deal. Victim of multiple Conservative missteps for which he was only partly to blame, Sunak lost the election to the Labour Party by a record margin in July 2024. The *Daily Mail*, a best-selling pro-Brexit newspaper, gave him a disdainful send-off: 'What made Rishi think he was fit to be PM?'[80] Frost – author of some of the most authentic articulations of the Brexiters' case[81] – says the Conservative defeat was inevitable.

The PM [Sunak] had given up defending Brexit, the government seemed to regard it as a natural disaster. The government never talked up the advantages of leaving. They never pushed back against the popular perception that it had all been an error with trade collapsing and the economy going downhill. The country was fed up with the Conservatives and wanted to give them a kicking.[82]

'WORM IN THE APPLE'

In his 2022 book *The Worm in the Apple*, Christopher Tugendhat describes a symbiotic process in which his party and a significant section of the electorate turned against British membership. This coincided with the EU becoming a more political and less purely trade-orientated grouping, particularly with the birth of EMU in 1999. This development 'destabilised British foreign policy, corroded the body politic, and destroyed several of the party's leaders'.[83]

After examining changes in his party and the country over the past half a century, Tugendhat says: 'I don't think future historians will be so surprised that we left the EU. What will surprise them is that Britain should have taken a such a huge step with so little preparation, so little consideration of the implications and no plan. This was a recipe for chaos.'[84] Speaking in February 2023, Tugendhat correctly foresaw that the former prime minister and his party were heading for the exit. 'The Conservative Party is ungovernable. It has lost any sense of cohesion and mutual loyalty.' This was four months before a damning report from a House of Commons committee found Johnson 'deliberately misled' parliament, resulting in his resignation as an MP.[85]

Pasquale Terracciano, one of Italy's most respected diplomats, ambassador to the UK between 2013 and 2018, and then for three years Italian ambassador in Moscow, spots some similarities with Russia.

In both countries, there is a certain pathology of mourning for a lost Empire. We saw this in the UK before the referendum among different categories of people: those in the northern, less wealthy parts of England, who feel upset about being left behind, some of the wealthier people in London and south England, and also those in other more fringe areas like Cornwall which benefit from EU contributions. You see examples where the loss of what was thought to be 'great power status' played a subliminal role in the rejection of the EU.[86]

Jacques de Larosière, France's elder statesman of money, is the most courtly of interlocutors, but he displays a waspish tone over British withdrawal.

They are a nationalistic country. I always thought the French were chauvinistic, but that is nothing compared with the British. They are sure that they are the best. We had an English nanny when I was a child in the 1930s. She brought us up to believe that the English are the most intelligent and best behaved in the world. She told us children that we were appalling and did not know how to behave. We would have to change our ways if we were to go to England. We believed her. She was so sure of the superiority of her country. You see exactly that behaviour in the British attitude on departing the European Union.[87]

An insider's account of the reasons why the outcome has not lived up to Brexiters' expectations comes from Mark Carney, governor of the Bank of England during the Brexit period. He re-emerged in July 2024 as an adviser to Rachel Reeves, Starmer's chancellor of the exchequer, before entering Canadian politics in January 2025 and succeeding Justin Trudeau as prime minister in March.

Speaking in 2023, Carney underlined changes in 'the geopolitical environment which influenced the referendum result' – changes which have become still more marked with Trump's entry in 2025. 'The liberalised, globalised framework of the 1980s and 1990s has given way to a very different environment. Globalisation is being restrained, free trade has much less significance, trade deals are harder to conclude. Within this new international framework, the Brexit model was and is unlikely to prosper.'[88]

Carney recounts a pre-referendum conversation with Johnson: 'I was explaining to him the likely outcome of a vote to leave. I could see there might be issues of identity, sovereignty and so on. I would leave those questions to him as a politician and concentrate on the economics. I told him there would be no net economic benefit from leaving the EU.'

Carney spelled out that Johnson's espousal of a 'cold shower approach' – introducing an external economic constraint to bring down the size of the state and slash regulation – would not necessarily lead to desired rises in productivity, growth and living standards. The Bank governor told Johnson that 'he would have to judge whether it was politically sustainable given the UK's revealed preference for public health care, state education, and a medium-sized social safety net'.

Yet all is not completely lost. Britain's track record of consistently standing back from European advances is not a good omen, but dislocation since 2016 has sharpened both British and European minds about the necessary priorities in a future relationship. The crisis-ridden premierships of Johnson and Truss, and Sunak's speedy ejection, left Britain with its economic equilibrium, institutional structures and international standing in need of repair. Under Sunak, Britain took a more pragmatic approach than under the disorganised and ideologically driven premierships of his two immediate predecessors. This includes the sensitive field of Northern Ireland trading arrangements, where a further series of technocratic solutions was enacted in line with an improved political relationship with Europe.

Rose-tinted views of the future benefits of trade and investment with large developing countries have been heavily scaled down as a result of changed geopolitical realities. These stem both from the Russian–Ukrainian war and the dislocation of the Trump tariffs. China and the BRICS group are no longer regarded as providing Britain's economic nirvana. The combined result of Trump and Putin has been to cast Britain's capabilities in security and defence, and its positioning within NATO, as important benefits in bargaining over the future EU relationship.

The UK's experience and expertise, across industry, finance and research, in the fight against climate change have, in a similar way, emerged as a significant benefit. A more rational reappraisal of the balance of European risk, reward and opportunity is under way. Britain's worldview, institutional solidity (despite the episodic strains inflicted by Johnson and Truss) and strategic clout could still be of great value for a Europe seeking fresh direction.

According to Wolfgang Schäuble, Germany's most experienced contemporary politician, speaking eleven months before he died in 2023, 'Britain will not be in the core group for currency and economic matters, but it is important for defence and security.'[89] The co-architect of the 'concentric circles' model of European integration, laid down in 1994,[90] outlined his vision of a future British role.

I believe we will be able to achieve co-operation with the British in the future, thanks to variable geometry. I do not accept that, because of a run of mediocre prime ministers, Britain's reputation with the EU has been durably damaged. The UK will be able to win back its position relatively quickly. It is idiotic for some people in France and

Brussels to say that it was a good thing for the UK to leave. We need the UK in Europe especially in defence, security, foreign policy and migration. We need to do things together. This can be carried out in a 'coalition of the willing' among individual member states, provided electorates are basically in favour.

Labelling Cameron's decision to hold the referendum a 'mistake which led to the catastrophe we have now,' Schäuble opined, 'Even if the Remain side had won the referendum, which I thought would happen, this would not have resolved the "in" versus "out" problem.'

With the wounds of Brexit still far from healed, Britain's status in Europe seems likely never to be more than semi-detached. This need not necessarily be detrimental to overall European interests. If intelligent management is brought to bear, and the overall direction of the European Union turns more pragmatic in coming years, then Britain's Churchillian position, 'with but not of Europe', may still end up benefiting both sides. But – particularly in view of the baleful influence of Trump in the White House – it will be an uphill struggle, prone to periodic setbacks and misfortune.

DYSFUNCTIONAL DECISION-MAKING

Striving for a benevolent future, all sides need to take account of the past. In the litany of missteps, Britain's decision to join Europe's exchange rate mechanism in October 1990, and the manner of its departure, twenty-three months later, set in train an enduring pattern. Britain's propensity to overestimate its own position, and misjudge or ignore that of other Europeans, was put on ample display during the next three decades of dysfunctional decision-making. Thacher had briefly considered membership in 1980, in a gesture to Helmut Schmidt.[91] Within the depths of 10 Downing Street, Thatcher was weighing up the risks of ERM adhesion in 1985, a period when she did her best to stop Chancellor of the Exchequer Nigel Lawson in his semi-clandestine manoeuvrings on membership.[92] John Redwood, her economic adviser, told Thatcher not to heed Lawson, warning that Britain would lose sovereignty if sterling joined. 'British monetary policy, the level of interest rates, the amount of the reserves spent on intervention in foreign exchange markets, and, in turn, growth and inflation themselves, will be to a great extent be determined by German policy rather than by the British Treasury.'[93]

Even after thirty-five years, some features of ERM entry remain unclear and controversial. In early October 1990, after months of cajoling by ministers, led by John Major (chancellor of the exchequer, replacing Thatcher less than two months later), the PM – her grip weakening noticeably after nearly eleven and a half years in power – consented to British membership.[94] She set the crucial condition that interest rates should be cut at the same time. When she relayed the decision to her top Downing Street aides on 5 October – breaking off a surreal discussion over using a parrot-featuring *Monty Python* TV sketch (which she did not understand) to lambast the Liberal Democrats at the forthcoming Conservative Party conference – she glossed over the act of joining, emphasising, 'We've got the cut in interest rates.'[95] She told confidants that Britain was not entering a straitjacket: sterling could be adjusted within the system if the need arose[96] – an erroneous judgement, as informed officials admit.[97] Robin Leigh-Pemberton, Bank of England governor, told Thatcher in a stern formal missive (kept secret for decades) on the eve of entry that the simultaneous cut in interest rates was a mistake that possibly 'we would have to reverse'.[98]

Pleading the risk of leaks, Major avoided discussing ERM entry with the Cabinet: the decision was taken by a small group of officials and ministers. 'They made me do it,' Thatcher told Redwood.[99] At the first Cabinet meeting (on 18 October) after Britain joined, Major was highly economical with the truth, telling ministers the Bank of England governor 'supported the move',[100] skating over Leigh-Pemberton's disapproving letter. European finance ministers and central bankers were upset that Britain selected the central DM 2.95 exchange rate without discussion. Karl Otto Pöhl, the Bundesbank president, told Major the rate was too high.[101] Philippe Lagayette, a former chief of staff of French finance minister Jacques Delors, and deputy governor of the Banque de France, was part of the European central-bank group parlaying with the British.[102] He was adamant that the lack of consultations contravened the spirit of membership. Recalling the episode three and a half decades later, Lagayette says, 'The British have always over-estimate the strength of demand for their presence. They act as if they are greatly needed. So they are surprised if Europe can function quite well without them.'[103]

An early indication of what would go wrong came at a German embassy dinner in London on 28 November given by Hermann von Richthofen, the urbane German ambassador.[104] Earlier in the day Thatcher finally relinquished the prime ministership, forced out in a Conservative Party revolt. Franz Scholl, head of the Bundesbank's foreign department, told his British dinner guests, including officials from the Treasury and Bank of England, bankers and industrialists, that sterling was overvalued within the ERM. Beneath the opaque language of von Richthofen's four-page report on the encounter, relayed to Bonn and Frankfurt a week later, lay an ominous Bundesbank warning.[105] Scholl's message – destined to be fully vindicated less than two years later – was that the ERM framework rested 'on very unstable foundations' and was 'unsustainable in the longer term'.

Once in No. 10, Major had the chance to greatly improve relations with the Germans. The Bonn foreign office described the new incumbent as a politician 'of most humble upbringing', noting archly that, with a circus artist as a father, 'the average Briton can identify [with him] more easily than with his predecessor'.[106] Chancellor Kohl saw the forty-seven year old – the youngest British prime minister of the century – as 'more moderate and Europhile' – although still disinclined to bring the UK into the mooted European single currency.[107] On Major's first visit to Bonn, in March 1991, he spoke of Britain 'at the very heart of Europe'.[108] The improved Anglo-German meteorology paid off a year later when Major secured substantial concessions from Kohl at the Maastricht summit in the Netherlands that set Europe on the path to monetary union. But the mood quickly darkened after Denmark's electorate in June 1992 rejected the Maastricht treaty in a referendum in June 1992 – setting off a 'grumbling volcano' on foreign-exchange markets.[109]

The road to Black Wednesday was paved with British and German warnings that both sides chose to ignore. Major wrote Kohl a series of entreating letters in July and August to try to persuade him to persuade the Bundesbank to cut interest rates.[110] An important issue, as Major correctly noted to Kohl, was the dollar's weakness against European currencies which had pushed up sterling to $2 – 'an absurd level' – but had made the D-Mark still stronger, straining the ERM'S permitted currency bands.[111] Major urged Kohl to 'press these points [for lower interest rates] on the Bundesbank council'. Norman Lamont, the luckless chancellor of the exchequer (chief secretary to the Treasury under Major, and the manager of Major's successful Tory party leadership campaign), had inherited membership of an exchange rate scheme of which he was innately suspicious. Lamont tried in vain to engage the prime minister about a pre-emptive move to suspend ERM membership: Major refused any discussion. A 1 September note from the German foreign office described Germany's entrapment.[112] Any cut in interest rates to resolve the impasse was ruled out by the 'stability objective' of the Bundesbank. The report accurately predicted that the ERM could suffer several realignments under the weight of the 20 September referendum called by President Mitterrand to win France's backing for the Maastricht treaty. This would lead to a 'secular overvaluation' of the D-Mark 'with painful consequences for German export competitiveness', the report concluded.

The UK, too, was caught in an intractable dilemma. It did not wish to devalue sterling unilaterally but was unable to organise an overall exchange rate realignment because France desperately wished to maintain the franc's parity to avoid rejection of the Maastricht treaty in the September plebiscite.[113] The Treasury and Bank of England in August–September 1992 were aghast at negative remarks from German officials reported in the press and on news agency wire services on the pound's overvalued ERM position.[114] Lamont chaired a bad-tempered meeting of European finance ministers and central-bank governors on 4 September in Bath, when he repeatedly and fruitlessly called on the Bundesbank to cut rates. He ran into robust opposition from Helmut Schlesinger, a fiercely orthodox economist wedded to the central bank's anti-inflation principles, who had taken over as Bundesbank president in August 1991, and promptly raised German interest rates, after the mercurial Pöhl resigned following a dispute with Kohl over conditions for German unification. Strongly criticised for his remarks from the chair, Lamont claimed afterwards he was speaking, too, on behalf of other countries, 'particularly Piero Barucci and Bertie Ahern [the Italian and Irish finance ministers]'.[115] According to Jean-Claude Juncker, attending the Bath meeting as Luxembourg's finance minister, 'Schlesinger reacted badly to the pressure, threatening at one time to leave the meeting. For me this was another sign of Britain's habitual failure properly to understand the Germans.'[116] Once he discovered the upset caused to the Germans, Major was furious that Lamont had dramatically overplayed his hand.[117]

But Major was on shaky ground. His July–August series of letters to the German chancellor underlined his own role in the mishap. He was the principal instigator spurring Lamont on in the ultimately fruitless strategy of goading the German into cutting rates.[118] And, as further developments would emphasise, Major greatly exaggerated his personal ability to change the policies of the Chancellor of German Unity. Both Theo Waigel, the German finance minister (complaining about America's unwillingness to support the dollar), and Schlesinger advocated changing ERM exchange rates at the Bath meeting, according to a detailed Treasury memorandum.[119] Schlesinger told the gathering: 'People must realise the interest rates alone might not work, and action on exchange rates might help to improve the position on interest rates.'[120] A similar view came from Wim Kok, Dutch finance minister (later prime minister). Another attendee, Mario Draghi, then Italy's Treasury director, opined, with trademark irony, that the likelihood of an alignment increased with the frequency of finance ministers' statements ruling it out.[121]

Terry Burns, the soft-spoken yet insistent permanent secretary at the British Treasury, who was originally not intended to attend the monetary meeting, was despatched to Bath in the late afternoon, receiving a call while on a South London golf course. Burns – who had got on well with Schlesinger during the 1980s at international economic meetings in Paris – could have played a role as a peace-maker, but arrived too late to make any difference to the acerbic outcome. He later said he lacked information from the Bank of England. 'The Bank did not report adequately on what was going on at the Bundesbank. I thought they didn't really do their job very well. They had all these bankers' meetings in Basel, but they didn't make the necessary deductions.' Bath made him wish he had been in contact with Schlesinger beforehand.

I spent some time talking to Helmut Schlesinger, both at the pre-dinner drinks and the following morning at breakfast. I learnt more from Schlesinger than I had from all the briefings at the Bank of England. He made it clear that the Bundesbank had no option but to keep money tight in view of the strains of German unification and the cost of integrating East Germany. In a fixed rate system, they could not take any other position than the one they took. If other countries agreed any changes in exchange rates, then they would look at their interest rate position.[122]

On the day of acrimony, Kohl wrote to Major saying he 'understood' the prime minister's concerns about the economy but 'emphatically' countered Major's attempt to blame German reunification for high interest rates.[123] Showing growing animosity with Frankfurt, Lamont wrote to Schlesinger on 10 September that he was 'very disturbed . . . that sources at the Bundesbank were reported as saying that a devaluation of sterling was inevitable.'[124]

OBSESSION WITH SECRECY

Nigel Wicks, previously Thatcher's principal private secretary, a dapper functionary who by 1992 had become second permanent secretary in the Treasury, was ranked as the UK's supreme monetary diplomat. A strikingly pro-European figure at the Treasury, who took pains to ensure that Treasury documents were not overly sceptical of European integration efforts,[125] he later became chairman of the European monetary committee, highly regarded by his European peers, at the focal point of European central banking and finance ministry arrangements. But Wicks's overall approach to crisis management, especially his well-known obsession with secrecy, contributed to the gravity of the September turbulence.[126] As Burns emphasises, sharper intelligence about continental discord and intrigue would have enabled the Treasury and Bank to refine tactics on sterling foreign-exchange intervention – and could have avoided the indignity of Britain running out of currency reserves on 16 September. Wicks showed complacency in masterminding an emergency $14 billion international bank loan for the Treasury that had to be repaid at a loss after the subsequent sharp decline in sterling.[127] He failed to discover the details of a damaging impasse between the French, German and Italian monetary authorities on the weekend of 12–13 September – when the Italian lira was devalued but other currencies were left unchanged.[128] Neither he nor others at the Treasury appear to have a strategic rationale for a fruitless mission he organised on 14 September for the Treasury's Alan Budd and the Bank of England's Mervyn King to visit the Bundesbank and the German finance ministry to argue (in vain) that sterling was correctly valued.[129]

The limits to Wicks's influence were brutally revealed on 14 September. Reuters news agency carried a report citing an unnamed German finance ministry official drawing attention to sterling's vulnerability. The episode underlining the lack of German sympathy for the UK position is revealed by UK Treasury files, dormant for three decades.[130] Attempting to profit from his good connections to Bonn, Wicks faxed a letter to Horst Köhler, state secretary at the finance ministry (and future German federal president), asking him 'to do all you can to prevent any further damaging reports'.[131] In a brief formal reply the next day, Köhler said Wicks's letter 'has promoted me once again to remind my collaborators that we have absolutely no interest in public discussion about realignments'. But he omitted any undertakings about future statements and, in a barely concealed invitation for the British to devalue sterling, stated, 'You will know that the EMS rules do provide for adjustments of the central rates if necessary.'[132]

At head-of-government level, a supreme example of miscommunication came in a telephone conversation between Major – staying with Queen Elizabeth at Balmoral on 13 September – and Giuliano Amato, the Italian prime minister. While reports about the conversation have circulated for many years, the secret UK government briefing document on the matter has not hitherto surfaced.[133] Major's principal private secretary wrote to Lamont's office that Amato told Major he had received a personal assurance from Chancellor Kohl that he was pressing for a Bundesbank rate cut and realignment – and required an Italian devaluation to accompany it. Amato denies having received any such message.[134] Schlesinger – who turned 100 in September 2024 and died three months later[135] – was adamant that Kohl, who visited the Bundesbank by helicopter the previous Friday (11 September) to discuss the Italian lira's escalating difficulties, did not put the central bank under pressure on interest rates.[136] The chancellor told the Bundesbank: 'Do what you can.'[137]

This depiction seems plausible. For Kohl to have belaboured Schlesinger on interest rates, in a late-night meeting in the presence of his finance minister and senior officials, would have been an extraordinary act by a German chancellor firmly favouring Bundesbank independence. Major may have somewhat embroidered the story, included in his memoirs (published in 2000), to reinforce his arguments on British rectitude and German wrong-headedness.[138]

Italy agreed to devalue the lira on 12–13 September. The British maintained sterling's central rate, believing they could ride out the storm. The Bundesbank cut interest rates on 14 September by 0.5 per cent for its symbolic discount rate and 0.25 per cent for the operationally more important Lombard rate – the minimum expected. The Treasury initially showed relief.[139] The denouement came after Schlesinger's clumsily handled (although painfully honest) newspaper interview with the *Wall Street Journal* and *Handelsblatt*, circulated by news agencies in abridged and 'unauthorised' form on the evening of 15 September, emphasised how sterling was exposed after the Italian devaluation.[140] The pound (together with the lira) was forced to leave the ERM the next day after an international tide of sterling-selling triggered massive Bank of England intervention that emptied the UK's official stock of foreign currency.

At 2.15 p.m., Major telephoned Kohl for fifteen minutes: a grandiose example of governments speaking past each other. Major sounded the alarm: in an apparent mix of negligence, ignorance and apathy, Kohl was unmoved. Major told the chancellor, 'We are in a crisis of enormous proportions.' Schlesinger's overnight remarks had caused 'absolute mayhem on the foreign exchange markets'.[141] In a studiously brief response,[142] Kohl said he was 'somewhat surprised at the reaction of the UK to Schlesinger because his remarks had not played in Germany the role they had in the UK. He would concert with his staff to see what could be done.'[143] The answer was – not much. The die was cast in a parallel conversation (the second of three so-called 'concertations' that day) among the Bank of England and European central banks, coinciding with the Kohl–Major telephone call.[144] The continent's money men were unsympathetic. Hans Tietmeyer, Schlesinger's deputy, urged intervention and interest rate changes. De Larosière invited the British to consider that Sweden had raised rates to 500 per cent to defend its currency. The message was that Britain had to play by the rules. The all-powerful European monetary committee met in Brussels shortly before midnight to rubber-stamp sterling's ERM suspension that Lamont had already announced at 7.30 p.m.[145]

The affair severely strained Anglo-German relations, inflamed by media leaks and accusations of blame between the two sides. Fighting back against fierce criticism of the Bundesbank in the UK press, von Richthofen wrote to his government complaining of 'spectacular action' from 10 Downing Street to pin responsibility on the Bundesbank for 'homemade' British problems.[146] On 30 September Kohl telephoned Major to attempt to return to his 'close personal friendship'. Kohl ran into further complaints about Britain's 'economic and political disaster' and 'a long and detailed list of remarks' by German officials that had damaged sterling.[147] The same day, Lamont told Michel Rocard, a former French prime minister, during a London visit that the Bundesbank had 'behaved appallingly'.[148] But the wounds were starting to heal. Schlesinger had been 'inept rather than deliberately unhelpful'. According to the meeting note, 'It was all over now and [Lamont] did not want to dwell on it.' Years later, looking back at this episode, Lamont termed the Bath meeting 'the last resort. I was not sympathetic to or contemptuous of Schlesinger. In his situation I might have behaved in a similar way.'[149] In his memoirs, he wrote, 'In my heart I thought attempts to persuade Dr Schlesinger to cut interest rates were probably in the end unlikely to succeed.'[150]

ESCAPING THE TRAP

The political fall-out for Major's government, which limped on until election defeat in 1997 at the hands of Tony Blair's Labour, was punishingly negative. A decade later, Alan Budd, in 1992 the Treasury's chief economic adviser, delivered a cruel summary: 'we went into the ERM in despair and left in disgrace'.[151] The ERM had been a trap for the British government. Now, pushed by the Bundesbank, it had escaped.[152] In perhaps the most accomplished account of the economic effects, Budd concluded that the ERM experience – although it brought recession – had been worth it. A gradualist approach would not have succeeded in squeezing out inflation.[153] Lamont – with some justification, considering his hands were tied by Major's intransigence – is adamant that he acted correctly: 'If I had it not been for Helmut Schlesinger's comments [on 15 September] we could have remained in the ERM.[154] Twenty-five years later Schlesinger apologised for the incident (possibly the first time the Bundesbank has ever apologised for anything) though in careful tones: 'I regret to this day that a general remark by myself, not focused especially on the pound, should have played a role in aggravating sterling's position.'[155]

Kenneth Clarke – Lamont's successor as chancellor of the exchequer, when Major in 1993 eventually engineered the resignation of the man who had once been a close confidant[156] – takes a scathing view of Major's tactics. 'He couldn't raise interest rates, and therefore the Germans had to cut theirs. He thought Germany would understand. But why would Helmut Kohl mess up his own policy to help John Major out of a political problem?' Major did not understand the German psyche, Clarke says. 'You couldn't expect Kohl to go to the Bundesbank and ask him to cut interest rates. They would say, "The old man has lost it." They would laugh at him.'[157]

In the aftermath of Black Wednesday, Clarke gained respect among fellow European Community finance ministers. In a direct follow-on to the autumn upsets, the French franc came heavily under pressure in summer 1993 when the French government tried to cut interest rates. At an emergency Sunday European finance ministers meeting on 1 August 1993, Clarke was the key figure holding the group together, avoiding ERM break-up and allowing a compromise widening of the fluctuation bands.

One of the most experienced operators in European deal-making, Luxembourg's Jean-Claude Juncker, says: 'This was a central moment in European monetary history. And we owe it to Ken Clarke that he saved the day.'[158] Clarke's view three decades afterwards is that the 'wider bands' approach, employed in September 1992, could have enabled sterling to stay in the ERM. 'However, no one thought of that at the time.' Clarke draws wider parallels.

John [Major] thought that, once we were in the ERM, we didn't need to bother too much. He thought the Germans and French would look after us. He thought he could carry forward the fiscal expansion in the 1992 manifesto. He believed Germany would be obliged to change its monetary policy to help us. This was similar to David Cameron when running the EU membership renegotiations. He thought he was the only person in Europe who counted, and he could run the whole show.[159]

In the economic sphere, with the government free to set (as Lamont put it immediately after Black Wednesday), 'a British monetary policy and a British exchange rate policy',[160] the Treasury and Bank of England were responsible for a series of positive and relatively long-lasting monetary policy innovations. Lamont set in place in October 1992 an inflation-targeting regime which, helped by external circumstances, proved far more successful than previous stratagems. The new monetary policy laid down the path to the decision in 1997, under Lamont's and Clarke's successor, Gordon Brown, to make the Bank of England operationally independent.

Britain staged a dramatic economic recovery which put largely moribund continental economies in the shade.[161] Britain patched up the relationship with Germany, aided by two damage-repairing European summit meetings at Birmingham and Edinburgh. As Roderic Lyne – who became Major's foreign policy adviser in 1993 – put it, 'We didn't kid ourselves that we could enjoy the same standing as France. We couldn't put ourselves between France and Germany, so we were trying to get on with both of them.'[162] Major understood the transactional roots to Kohl's political approach. 'You could trade with Kohl. If he asked for a personal favour, then you knew that he owed you one.'

Detente was signalled by an exchange of letters at Christmas and a convivial springtime visit to Kohl's favourite Austrian spa resort, intended as a symbolic mark of the chancellor's favour.[163] The German and British leaders were united by a visceral dislike of Thatcher – Kohl's resentment driven by baleful memories of her anti-reunification stance, Major's by her disruptive support for Tory backbenchers rebelling against Maastricht ratification. At a jovial lunch at Chequers a year later, they indulged in pantomimic banter at Thatcher's expense, as Major's adviser Lyne relates.

> Major said to Kohl: 'Have I told you the story about how I was having lunch at this table with Margaret Thatcher? I said to her: "Do you know what Winston Churchill said about the Royal Navy?" "No," she said, "What did Winston say?"' Major recounted: 'Churchill said: "The Royal Navy ran on three traditions: rum, sodomy, and the lash." Margaret Thatcher then replied: "But I don't like rum!"' Dorothea Kaltenbach [the official German government interpreter]

was convulsed with laughter at that point and couldn't carry out the translation. Kohl got really angry about this and asked her to translate. When she eventually did get the words out, the result was like an earthquake. His huge frame was shaking with laughter. The whole room was reverberating.[164]

Britain's economic prowess outside the ERM made Major a star in Europe. Lyne recalls: 'Many European summits were dreary affairs, but at the informal Majorca meeting in 1995, hosted by Felipe González on the economic future of Europe, Major was asked to lead off the conversation. He was the most savvy on economics. The British economy was doing much better after Black Wednesday. And he was saying something they wanted to hear.'[165] For all the rebuilding of his international reputation, Major was widely expected to lose the next election (eventually taking place in 1997). During the run-up, the concept of Bank of England independence started to gain traction. Lamont had already started to muse that independence – rapidly becoming the norm in Europe based on the model of the Bundesbank and the mooted new European central bank – might help buttress UK economic stability. Major strongly opposed the idea. Lamont recalls, 'He wanted to avoid political trouble by making interest rate cuts. As soon as we had made one cut, he wanted another one. On one occasion Major rang the Treasury from India ordering me to cut rates.'[166] Once ensconced as Lamont's successor, Clarke took a similar view to Lamont. 'Bank of England independence was, in my view, an essential step, with the aim never again to have hyperinflation.'[167]

Independence was enacted only after Labour's victory in May 1997. The groundwork was laid in a clandestine series of European encounters by the still-in-opposition Labour Party. Ed Balls, a former *Financial Times* journalist who in 1994 became an adviser to Gordon Brown, then shadow chancellor of the exchequer, was given crucial help by the Treasury.[168] Acting under guidance from cabinet secretary Robin Butler, Nigel Wicks, well connected as chairman of the European monetary committee, set up meetings for Balls in Frankfurt, Bonn and Paris in February 1996.[169] Brown and Balls went a month later to Germany, Brussels and Paris.[170] Theo Waigel, the German finance minister, was supportive of the independence plan, saying, 'It is useful to have an independent central bank because you could blame them when interest rates went up.'

This febrile European activity stood in stark contrast to a complete absence of public discussion. 'Brown made a speech in 1995, on the case for independence. Apart from that we barely mentioned it.'[171] Brown and Balls discussed the subject with Lamont before the election, but not with Clarke. Consultation within the Labour Party was minimal. Balls records: 'We joked that Gordon seemed to spend more time talking to former chancellors of the exchequer than he did his own cabinet.' When Brown made the announcement, on 6 May 1997, just five days after the election, it was a welcome surprise, buoying the pound on the foreign exchanges – as well as sparking a fierce dispute with the Bank of England about removal of its bank supervision responsibilities. Richard Lambert, editor of the *Financial Times*, asked the chancellor why he had not mentioned the planned move during the election campaign. Brown replied gruffly, 'No one asked me.'[172]

Blair, like Major seven years previously, was given a warm welcome in Bonn. But Kohl, making heavy weather of his final term and less than eighteen months away from losing office to Gerhard Schröder, was in a much-weakened state. The balance of strength was underlined by secret British–German deliberations on delaying the start of EMU. Following a visit by the Bank of England's Mervyn King to Hans Tietmeyer at the Bundesbank, Christopher Meyer, Britain's ambassador in Bonn, told London: 'EMU is in trouble. Many serious players are talking about postponement, some publicly ... We are beginning to hear the suggestion that the prime minister should intervene with Kohl to ensure a "controlled" postponement.'[173] Meyer counselled caution. The case for British intervention 'might look seductive, but it is extremely dangerous'. Although the UK had made 'dramatic progress' following Blair's landslide victory, 'we do not enjoy a position with Kohl to be prime mover for a postponement'. The chancellor might see this as a 'reversion to wrecking tactics and a clumsy intervention in German politics'. Blair scribbled on the note 'agreed', suggested a meeting with Kohl during the summer, and returned the idea of a 'controlled postponement' to the realm of theory rather than practice.

CONSEQUENCES OF STAYING OUTSIDE

Starting monetary union without the UK was – in view of the legacy of 1992 – well-nigh inevitable. But the Blair government kept open for six years whether it might join later. After a laborious process examining if Britain had met five UK government-set economic performance tests to justify adhesion – it turned out that it didn't – Gordon Brown formally reaffirmed in 2003 Britain would stay outside the bloc.[174] In view of the financial crisis that erupted in 2007–8, joining the euro would probably have led not to more European commonality, but to less, according to Ed Balls, a key architect of 'stay out'.

> If UK had joined the monetary union in 2003, or in any period before that, given the size of economy, and given the condition the Union was in, without having made many advances in governance, the strains on the system would have been so large that we would have left the euro by September 2007. This huge destabilisation probably would have led to Britain leaving the European Union. As a consequence there is no way that we would have got through to a referendum of the sort that took place in 2016. Britain's membership would have blown up already.[175]

Balls refutes the argument that, had the UK joined earlier, it would have helped improve the euro area's crisis-fighting capacity. Without the outbreak of the financial crisis, EU governments would not have been ready to take steps to free constraints on the ECB to buy government bonds and prop up the economy. 'Britain would not have been stronger inside EMU,' Balls says. 'The government would have been weaker because it would not have been able to take the necessary steps to tackle the financial crisis. We would not have been able to use the Bank of England and the government balance sheet. That was outside what was feasible in Europe at the time. So Britain would have broken loose.'

The EMU episode formed an important landmark in the run-up to the referendum drama, which started well before Cameron became prime minister after unseating Brown in the 2010 election. To win the Eurosceptics' support for his campaign to become party leader in 2005, Cameron pledged to withdraw the Conservatives from the European parliament's centre-right European People's Party (EPP) grouping, on the grounds of divergence on key issues such as Europe's 'federalist' agenda.[176] Enactment in 2009 took the party away from the European mainstream towards the fringes.[177]

According to McDonald, 'This was a crucial moment. It incensed Merkel.[178] The Conservatives made no bones about showing contempt for the established Conservative parties in Europe. The decision demonstrated the smallness and shortsightedness of British actions, and how they were driven by domestic political factors rather than wider issues.'[179]

David Davis, himself a Eurosceptic,[180] who was defeated in the 2005 leadership contest against Cameron, gained notoriety as May's minister in charge of exiting the EU in 2016–18 – a job which brought little success.[181] Davis maintained during the 2005 leadership tussle that the Conservatives should stay in the EPP to nurture political links with Europe's principal leaders – particularly Germany's Merkel. During the contest Davis phoned Cameron and said: 'Don't do this, whatever happens, we're in opposition for the next four years. [Staying in the EPP] is your only way of getting to meet the Merkels and so on.'[182]

Cameron was given a similar warning, more than a year before he became prime minister, from José Manuel Barroso, president of the European Commission, and a former EPP vice president. He told the British prime minister in Brussels: 'If you leave the EPP, you will become eccentric in the two meanings of the term.' To accommodate the Conservative Party, Barroso offered to tone down the integrationist overtones in the EPP's statutes.[183] Cameron, for his part, says he was always sceptical about the EPP–European Democrats alliance, which formed the repository for the British Conservatives' participation in the European parliament.

> I was afraid that the Conservative Party was giving one message at home and one in Brussels. This was intensified by the start of monetary union which I always thought Britain should never join. If we had stayed within the EPP, it would have over-stretched the Conservative position. The EPP membership wanted to deepen the European Union for all EU members, to make monetary union work. That was not the Conservative Party's position. Nor did I ever want it to be.[184]

Accepting Barroso's EPP proposal in 2009 'was not a practical alternative', Cameron says. 'We would not have been able, from within, to reform the EPP over time. The EPP wanted more integration, more Europe. We did not.'

VULNERABILITY AND PRESSURE

As it turned out, the Conservatives' EPP withdrawal was a powerful factor contributing both to British vulnerability and to pressure for an in–out referendum. After Cameron won the 2010 election, a crucial test with Europe loomed over the EU's plans for new instruments to shore up monetary union through the so called 'fiscal compact'. But the catalyst was the crisis in the euro bloc as financial markets reacted badly to belated recognition of unsustainable policies in highly indebted southern countries led by Greece. Merkel and Sarkozy sought changes in the European treaties to reinforce the monetary system's institutional structures through bold new measures supporting budgetary discipline and strengthening convergence.[185] Treaty change could take place only if agreed by all twenty-seven EU states (the membership total then, before Croatia's accession in 2013). Cameron's attempt to maximise leverage from outside the currency bloc, but without inside knowledge of how to manage the process, was a high-risk strategy – and it failed.

Cameron had already raised hackles by lecturing the euro members from the sidelines on ways to solve the euro crisis through a 'big bazooka' approach of massive central-bank intervention.[186] Kim Darroch, Blair's chief European adviser in 2004–7, who then became Britain's permanent representative to the European Union – he spanned Gordon Brown's prime ministership as well as Cameron's first eighteen months in power – pinpoints what he sees as the new PM's early mistakes over the euro crisis.

> During the financial crisis sparked off in Greece, the Europeans were desperate to find money for various rescue actions. They wanted to raid funds which included British money. Cameron was adamant about not allowing this. Blair would have come up with some kind of gesture, this could have been used as a bargain in exchange for something else. Cameron never went down that path.

Instead he used very strong language to say Britain would not be part of any bailout action. This created bad blood. Being helpful and generally supportive can win you a great deal of solidarity. Otherwise it's a zero-sum game, you lose influence. This can be significant when the next crisis comes along.[187]

Cameron, for his part, maintains that the 'big bazooka' strategy was correct. 'I accept that by going public, I did put some people's backs up.'[188] He says his arguments were eventually taken into account with the European Central Bank action after Mario Draghi's 'whatever it takes' intervention in July 2012. 'I did speak to Draghi about this regularly including at summit meetings. The euro area's economic weakness was affecting our economy, so it was legitimate for me to take up this issue.' Cameron acknowledges that the German government and Draghi were getting the same advice from the US government, in the shape of Tim Geithner. 'It was more acceptable for the Europeans to hear this from the US Treasury secretary than from a British Eurosceptic.'

A further milestone came in bargaining over the 'fiscal compact' changes the EU wished to enact in 2011, in a Europe-wide treaty change to protect the euro by solidifying state finances throughout the bloc. The UK said it would back the measures (requiring a majority decision) only if the other countries agreed to safeguard the UK's position outside the euro. In particular, Britain wanted support for the City of London by allowing concessions on and exemption from financial market regulation. The British stratagem collapsed in an acrimonious summit in December 2011, two days after Merkel, Sarkozy and other leaders met, without the British, at a separate EPP conclave in Marseilles.

The gathering confirmed a legally contorted means to circumnavigate British objections by formulating a side-deal treaty covering the other twenty-six EU members states, not requiring British ratification.[189] Jon Cunliffe, Cameron's EU adviser, who subsequently became Britain's permanent representative in Brussels and then a deputy governor of the Bank of England, was in charge of a series of negotiating ploys. The chances of UK success were always slim and then shrunk to zero.

Ivan Rogers, the European specialist who took over as Cameron's European adviser after the December summit before succeeding Cunliffe in Brussels in November 2013, says the December events turned the tide:

'This is when Britain got screwed – the start of the end-game.'[190] Rogers left government service in a blaze of publicity in January 2017 after his strong criticism of May's handling of Brexit negotiations was leaked to the press.

Rogers says Cameron was slow to realise he was on a path to defeat. 'The UK put forward a package of six demands for multiple treaty amendments, in complicated Treasury/Bank of England language, three of which involved rolling back shifts to majority-voting back to a unanimity provision.' The proposals were destined for rejection, Rogers says. 'Key euro players interpreted the demands as the UK attempting to exploit a moment of existential risk for the euro to its own advantage on key financial services issues.'

Cameron explains:

> The three issues were not matters that would have made the tabloids but they were all important questions. I accept that there was a diffi-culty over when to put forward our proposals. It is very difficult to get the timing right in these negotiations. You either table your proposals early, and you know they're going to get leaked. Or you bring them in late – and then you get accused of forcing the hand of your partners, and are prone to have some last-minute deals done against you. That is what happened in 2011.

He adds:

> I tried very hard to persuade the other countries. The other Europeans said initially they did not want treaty change [for the fiscal compact] but in the end they did make extensive treaty changes. Therefore it was right that the British should get some-thing in exchange. They said that the EFSF [bailout mechanism that turned into the European Stability Mechanism] was not going to be used again, but it was. They also changed the legal basis, regarding the possibility that a treaty could be agreed and fully implemented by the other 26 members. Right at the last moment, the Commission gave legal advice that this course was institution-ally lawful and feasible, reversing the EU's earlier position.[191]

The 2011 collision was an accident waiting to happen. As Rogers explained later, monetary union and its problems had 'radically changed the dynamics of the Union', and thus the intrinsic balance between the EU and the UK. 'There could be no case for the UK outside monetary union, and dealing, alone, with its own extraordinary banking crisis, participating in any way, at further taxpayer cost, in the resolution of the euro crisis.'[192]

The prime minister turned the setback to short-term advantage by presenting the UK treaty veto as a policy triumph.[193] But Paddy Ashdown, a leading Lib Dem figure, immediately saw the larger consequences: 'We have lost control of the European agenda and the prime minister has lost control of demands for a referendum.'[194]

Cameron, in the immediate aftermath, insisted that Britain's membership of the EU would not be jeopardised, telling parliament, 'We are in the European Union and we want to be.'[195] The prime minister told the House of Commons. 'I believe in an EU with the flexibility of a network, not the rigidity of a bloc.' In reality, the fiscal-compact saga marked a major point of divergence, as Cameron admits:

> My vetoing of the treaty was welcomed by the Conservative Party and by part of the UK press. But it was a false victory. I did not succeed in my aim. And we saw this as proof that the long-term nature of Europe was changing radically, as the result of the establishment of EMU and the measures needed to safeguard it. And this would radically change the relationship with the UK. This was the turning point. It set us on the path towards the referendum.[196]

BATTLE AGAINST THE ODDS

Cameron's advisers agonised until the last moment over the timing and wording of his speech announcing the referendum, which came on 23 January 2013.[197] He declared that the British people 'will have their say' after a process in which Britain would 'address the changes we need in a negotiation with our European partners. It will be a relationship with the single market at its heart.'[198] Despite the support for 'Remain' from broad swaths of the British establishment as well as most of the UK's foreign partners, it was a battle against significant odds. As a self-avowed long-time sceptic on Europe, Cameron was overwhelmed by the task of engineering changes in EU rules that would go far enough to win support of anti-European forces in the UK, but not so far as to breach fundamental, non-negotiable Union principles.

Preparing for the speech, Cameron was given a strong warning of how far he could go in a phone call shortly beforehand with Brussels Commission chief Barroso. 'When he [Cameron] told me about the referendum, I said: "You will be trying to win some changes, before the referendum. What will they be?" He said: "I am going to ask for exemptions on freedom of movement." I said: "You are not going to get that. Ask for anything else, and there may be a chance. But not freedom of movement." '[199]

Cameron recalled in 2024: 'I was well aware that not contravening one of the four founding principles was an important issue. It was important for Barroso to say that to me. It wasn't so important for me to hear it, because it was something I was aware of.'[200]

At the time, however, Cameron appeared to exude greater confidence that he could move the Union on key issues of 'free movement' that would make a difference to the British electorate. According to McDonald, at the Foreign Office nerve centre, Angela Merkel was never going to shift far enough to make a difference.

> She did not, I judge, believe that concessions big enough to change UK opinion could be compatible with the integrity of the EU. She never promised to seek such concessions from other heads of state and government. If anyone in Downing Street or elsewhere thought that Merkel had given assurances that she would secure concessions big enough to change the UK political assessment of the EU, and then somehow let us down, then this is based on a complete misunderstanding.[201]

Between the referendum announcement and the start of membership renegotiations came an important personnel interlude – and another British setback. In 2014, Cameron attempted to block the appointment of Jean-Claude Juncker as Barroso's successor. Cameron felt that the Luxembourg prime minister – 'the wrong candidate, with the wrong views, at precisely the wrong time'[202] – symbolised a backward-looking 'federalist' agenda. Cameron fell out with Merkel, who first supported him, and then changed her mind,[203] accusing her of bad faith.[204]

Somewhat superciliously, Cameron described Juncker in his memoirs as 'convivial' and 'amazingly tactile – a big hugger and kisser – often with a strong aroma of his trademark scent of brandy and cigarette smoke'.[205]

Cameron recalled in 2024: 'I was really confident that we would not get Juncker. Merkel thought it was a bad idea and she said that.'[206] Cameron however, as so often, was viewing only one aspect of a multi-faceted picture. Martin Selmayr, the German civil servant who managed Juncker's presidency campaign, points out how Merkel gave Juncker early backing for the May 2014 European parliamentary election over his EPP rival Michel Barnier because 'he was much stronger on the substance of EU policy matters, and she believed that he – being very eloquent in German and French – would be able to win against the socialist candidate Martin Schulz'.[207]

Cameron persisted with his anti-Juncker campaign even though he knew he would lose the nomination vote (only Hungary sided with the UK): 'I did not change my mind on Juncker though I could see we were heading for defeat. I would've been thought of as a soft touch.'[208] As with the 2011 Brussels summit veto, Cameron's forthright anti-Juncker stance was well received by Conservative-supporting UK newspapers. The press reports delivered a strong message that Britain might be nearing the end of the EU road.[209]

Cameron's election victory in May 2015 started the countdown to the plebiscite. On his long-running European renegotiation tour, Cameron's charm was on full display – as was his propensity to place the most favourable interpretation of what was said to him. One positive aspect was that Juncker bore no visible resentment over Cameron's campaign: 'I don't feel my attitude disadvantaged us in the renegotiation. Juncker was one of the more helpful leaders, probably more than Barroso might have been. He was a fixer and he knew the Germans very well.'[210] Timing was an important, frequently overlooked issue. Rogers and Cunliffe both made clear to Cameron, in 2012–13, that the referendum had to be mid-2016 at the latest to allow sufficient time for political negotiation before the impending French and German elections.[211] Accompanied by Tom Scholar – who had become his European and global adviser, taking over from Rogers when he moved to the EU job – and other officials, Cameron flew around the capitals. Rogers carried out informal debriefings in Brussels, seeing all twenty-seven delegations, and passing on to Whitehall a comprehensive view of where Britain stood. Rogers spotted gaps in the Whitehall accounts of what Cameron thought he was achieving.

> Clearly when Cameron went to see various prime ministers, they were not rude to him. I heard from the delegations a more down to earth and brutally realistic version of events. Of course, London – senior ministers or cabinet secretaries – often does not want to hear such realism. It is more comforting to think that when other leaders pull their punches with the PM, that must be the 'real' national position, not the one articulated by the key officials when they are in Brussels. But the reality is always the reverse.[212]

Juncker regarded the UK's complicated procedures as exposing the difficulties that the British would later encounter in preserving government unity. 'Cameron said he could not agree various matters, because they would be in opposition to Theresa May as home secretary. May said she could not agree because she was worried about Johnson. And then Johnson put forward conditions based on what others had said.'[213] The deal that Cameron eventually achieved from other EU leaders in February 2016 – and which he said he would back as the kernel of the Remain campaign – was hard-won. It contained some genuine concessions to the UK, reinforcing Britain's earlier opt-outs on the single currency, ending the much-reviled treaty commitment to 'ever closer union' and introducing a 'social brake' to restrict welfare payments to EU immigrants.[214] According to McDonald at the Foreign Office, 'Cameron didn't think that Remain would lose, and that confidence conveyed itself to European leaders who saw no need to make concessions which weren't really needed for a Remain victory.'[215] Cameron agrees: 'The deal produced some very helpful advances for the British position. But it was not sufficiently transformative. One of the reasons why we couldn't get a better deal was that the other Europeans thought that the Remain side would win anyway, therefore there was not enough pressure for them to make concessions. They did not want to give too much away because it might encourage others to ask for more.'[216]

'I SHOULD HAVE ADJUSTED EXPECTATIONS'

The technical modifications in fact played practically no role in the referendum campaign. At the heart were emotions – allied to grass-roots principles largely untouched by Britain's renegotiation, notably the fundamental questions of laws, immigration and money that were particularly important to voters outside metropolitan centres. Cameron was in no position to focus on these issues. He acknowledged in 2024, 'I should have adjusted expectations against thinking that we would get transformational change.'[217]

It was anyway, arguably, too late. Peter Sedgwick, a long-time UK Treasury official who was a vice president of the European Investment Bank (EIB) in 2000–6, travelled extensively in the UK at that time in connection with EIB funding for infrastructure projects, especially school and hospitals. 'Most people I met were very keen to access cheap EIB finance. But hardly anyone I met during those six and a half years was very enthusiastic about EU membership.'[218]

David Davis underlines the depth of feeling outside the cosmopolitan mainstream. A decorator working at his house in Yorkshire related how he was voting Leave because Bulgarian and Polish workers had used opportunities to carry out their trade in the UK – with the result that he had not had a pay increase for ten years. He told Davis: 'I don't blame them for coming here. I blame you for letting them in.'[219] A builder, on hearing that Osborne had said leaving would cost British families £4,000 each, said: 'Tell Mr Osborne from me, Mr Davis, £4,000 pounds for my freedom, cheap at the price!' Davis adds: 'If you walked around the House of Commons, most people would be Remainers. But if you talk to the staff, almost 100 per cent were not. The wage competition divide was much more important than people thought.'

A British official at the heart of the process says: 'A more logical move would have been to spend several years building up the idea that EU membership was fundamentally a good thing for the UK – and vote on that basis. But this option was plainly impossible to realise. And therefore was not put forward.'[220]

Cameron's inner doubts were conveyed through subtleties that were not lost on well-connected *Daily Telegraph* writer Charles Moore:

He arranged to ring me up after the [February 2016] summit in the way that politicians like to talk to journalists. I had been briefed about the [British renegotiation] deal, a complicated set of arrangements. I thought he wanted to talk about the deal, but he started talking about something different, asking me to agree that, if the UK agreed to stay in the EU, it would be helpful for European security. I realised then that he knew that the deal was not very convincing, so he thought it was better not to talk about it.[221]

Cameron realised by that stage that the core changes sought by arch-Eurosceptics were impossible to achieve.[222] And his own opinions seem to have been advancing towards a difficult-to-sell notion: that Britain should vote to stay in not because he had changed the nature of the Union, but because he had secured acceptance that the UK would be a halfway-house member.[223]

Jacob Rees-Mogg underlines a fundamental point: 'Cameron's failure to get more in terms of restricting free movement of people represented a very important reason for voting Leave in the referendum. This showed that, for the EU, sticking to the overall principle of freedom of movement was more important than keeping a very important member state in the EU.'[224] Another Eurosceptic complaint comes from David Frost: 'Cameron wore out a lot of shoe leather but he was not ambitious enough. His view was that it was sufficient to have been very active and to say: "I got what I can." But he should've achieved much more to move the EU towards a two-speed Europe.'[225]

Mervyn King, the Eurosceptic governor of the Bank of England in 2003–13, says Cameron – after failing to get required changes on immigration – should have ignored arguments about colliding with the French and German elections and postponed the referendum by a year, seeking two objectives: 'Greater devolution on decision-making on immigration towards national governments. And recognition that there will be two types of membership, one within the euro and another outside. Non-euro countries outside the euro would not take part in financial mechanisms geared to keeping the system together.'[226] King believes Cameron should have told the EU that, unless it agreed these changes, Britain would hold the referendum, but with the prime minister voting for Leave. 'That would have had a salutary effect on EU thinking.'

Cameron had threatened on numerous occasions before the referendum to campaign against EU membership unless he reached a satisfactory deal.[227] In his memoirs, Cameron says that, after the referendum, he 'agonised' whether he should have stopped discussions and postponed the vote until 2017. One key official says: 'He pushed as far as humanly possible something the EU had previously rejected [the social brake]. They all had serious doubts about it, and whether it would prove to be legally valid, it might have unravelled in the courts. That might have been one of the reasons they went along with it. So he applied himself fully, but it was the wrong strategy with the wrong plan.'[228] In 2024, Cameron explained his position with greater clarity:

> I could've stopped the clock and gone back to negotiate in the autumn. I discussed this with advisers and we decided against it. There was never a meeting with ministers when we made a formal decision on 'stopping the clock'. I have thought a lot about what I might've done differently. If I had told the other leaders that I would be likely to vote against staying in, unless they gave me sufficient concessions, it would've looked like brinkmanship. I don't think it would have improved my position.[229]

Once he had achieved a deal over which he himself had doubts, and the Remain campaign started in earnest ahead of the 23 June vote, Cameron's energy levels seemed to fall. He largely declined to go to parts of the country which were decidedly anti-EU. Pasquale Terracciano, Italy's ambassador during the referendum period, says:

> Cameron seemed to believe that he could win the referendum once he started his campaigning shortly before the referendum in June. He never gave the faintest impression that he could fail. I saw him in April [2016] with [prime minister Matteo] Renzi. He had a somewhat messianic view. I saw it somewhat as the traditional English public school essay crisis when pupils prepare for an exam right at the last moment. Behind a charming character lay a rather shallow personality.[230]

A week before the poll, the assassination in Yorkshire of Jo Cox, a pro-EU Labour MP, by a right-wing terrorist appeared to raise the probability of a vote to stay in. 'Number 10 was gloomy about the outcome of the referendum immediately before the murder of Jo Cox,' recalls McDonald.[231] 'They hoped that a shocking murder might lead waverers to vote Remain. But it is clear now, with hindsight, that the momentum [towards Leave] was already too great to reverse.' In the early hours of 24 June, Charles Moore was at Leave HQ in London with Johnson and Michael Gove, the Brexiter environment secretary. On realising that Leave had won, by a margin of 52 per cent to 48 per cent, 'they were in a daze. They didn't believe that they would win, especially after the Jo Cox murder.'[232]

Mark Carney was in charge of Bank of England staff who had trained for possible upsets, as he says, 'just like you might before a big match'. He was chauffeured to his office at 2.30 a.m. after the first indication, from TV exit polls, that Leave might win. 'The big moves in foreign exchange occurred after midnight. We had prepared for the worst-case scenario and were asking the right questions, such as the functioning of the gilts market and the foreign exchanges.' Osborne rang at around about 7 a.m. to say Cameron was going to resign, and would make a statement, asking Carney to do the same, which he did – a substitute for the chancellor's conspicuous absence from the scene of disturbance.[233] Disruption reverberated well beyond the UK. A fortnight before the referendum, Wolfgang Schäuble, the German finance minister, foresaw a watershed for European integration. 'If the British vote to leave, we cannot simply answer by calling for more European integration. Many would ask if we politicians have still not got the message.'[234]

UNDULATIONS, U-TURNS AND INTRIGUE

Once Theresa May became prime minister, her quixotic appointment of Boris Johnson as a caricaturally unsuitable foreign secretary set the scene for four years of undulations, U-turns and intrigue before the UK eventually quit the EU. May called an election in 2017 which, disastrously for her, resulted in a reduced Conservative majority. In July 2019, she handed dover Downing Street to Johnson, who won a sound victory in the December election.

As Davis summarises: 'The party put itself into a terrible mess at the tail end of the May regime. Collective responsibility collapsed. They couldn't deliver things through the House of Commons. And the party thought it needed a shock, something dramatic, and so they threw the dice. The dice came up sixes for Boris.'[235] Moore's verdict is: 'May made people feel she couldn't be trusted to carry out her decision. She was after all a Remainer. Johnson won the trust of people to get it done. If he had become leader immediately [after Cameron] he would have called an election straightaway, which he would have won. We would've had the same development as in 2019, only a couple of years earlier.'

John Redwood says that May, in her first period, 'followed a reasonably sound pro Brexit course'.[236] This changed after the poorly managed 2017 election and her move to bring in civil servant Olly Robbins, opposed by many Brexiters, to work with (and control) Davis in the EU exit ministry. 'Brexiteers disliked what they saw as a sell-out, seeking to keep more of the features of our membership of the EU at high price to national independence. Johnson played a blinder to win the election where we just basically had to win the referendum a second time. The election was won on the simple slogan, "Get Brexit done".'

Johnson, a manifestly unhappy and unsuccessful foreign secretary, 'became frustrated very quickly', McDonald says. 'He was obsessed by the Cabinet minutes which appeared to show that he didn't count in the government. Therefore he was always trying to get the minutes amended to record a greater number of his thoughts and priorities.'[237]

Gavin Barwell, May's chief of staff, and a former Conservative MP, had got to know Johnson well, and regarded him as a friend, during his spell as mayor of London, when Johnson would frequently visit Barwell's Croydon constituency to provide down-to-earth electioneering support. But the period as foreign secretary damaged the relationship. 'He wasn't on top of it. He didn't enjoy the job. He often came across in meetings with her [May] as not fully briefed. Theresa would ask him something about African policy and he would reply with the usual verbiage. She found him difficult.'[238]

Most important were the philosophical differences. 'Theresa believed that, because the referendum margin had been very close, and had pitted different factions in Britain against each other, the deal with the EU had to be a compromise which would give something to all sides.

Johnson's view was that there could be no compromise, Britain had to go as far as possible to remove itself from the EU, otherwise it may as well not bother. This was an unbridgeable chasm.'

Barwell, like others, highlights how Johnson refused to engage with 'the most intractable part of the problem – Northern Ireland'. Eventually Johnson accepted a deal 'which he knew was deeply flawed': Great Britain [the mainland of the UK] would depart both the customs union and the single market, but Northern Ireland would remain under EU jurisdiction – introducing a border in the Irish Sea between different parts of the UK. 'He believed he would find some way to wriggle out of it down the line, but the deal he agreed did profound damage to the Good Friday institutions [established by the April 1998 peace deal] and the governance of Northern Ireland. His efforts to wriggle out of it did profound damage to the reputation of the UK.'

Johnson's nadir came with his August 2019 attempt – overturned by the UK supreme court a month afterwards – to prorogue (suspend) parliament to prevent MPs scrutinising the final passage of the agreement on departing the EU.[239]

When the ploy was struck down by an 11 to 0 vote in the UK's highest court, one of the most apposite reactions came from José María Roldán, president of the Spanish banking association: 'I have recovered my lost faith in UK democratic institutions. You have had some kind of unwritten constitution since the 17th century. We were beginning to wonder if it works. And now we know it does. Politicians who play with fire may get burnt.'[240] No stratagem could stand in greater contradiction to Johnson's avowals of the primacy of parliament[241] nor better illustrate his lack of forethought. Johnson's friend David Frost delivers what amounts to a political epitaph: 'Boris was never aware of the amount of ammunition he was giving to enemies. He once said to me: "I never realised how much people dislike me." '[242]

LESSONS FROM BRITISH EXCEPTIONALISM

In European dealings over the decades, self-awareness has not been Britain's strongest suit. A major test of a Conservative government's ability to consider the consequences of its actions took place in September–October 2022, under Johnson's successor Liz Truss. The exercise ended, quickly, in failure – with lessons not just for the UK but also for the rest of Europe. The ill-fated 23 September 2022 'mini-budget' introduced by Truss and Kwasi Kwarteng, her chancellor of the exchequer, proposed £45 billion in largely unfunded tax cuts, 50 per cent more than indicated during her campaign to become Conservative Party leader.[243]

According to the dry official account of the UK's Debt Management Office, the episode brought, for the government bond market, 'a period of unprecedented stress and volatility ... which led to intervention by the Bank of England to help stabilise the market'.[244] Like the referendum outcome six years earlier, this was a landmark gesture of independence: the ultimate extension of a high-risk exercise in British exceptionalism.[245]

The denouement – with Truss forced to stand down after forty-nine days, the shortest tenure in UK prime ministerial history – set off events diametrically contradicting her intentions. It bolstered the power of the British Treasury, safeguarded Andrew Bailey, the Bank of England governor she had wanted to depose, and contributed significantly to the Labour Party's landslide victory (and her own demise as an MP) at the July 2024 general election. The saga reverberated beyond the UK's borders. It drew unusually intense criticism from government and monetary authorities abroad, including a rebuke from the International Monetary Fund and the French, German and Spanish finance ministers.[246]

One leading European central banker erupted in anger at Kwarteng's 'fiscal hooliganism'. The European Central Bank claimed it represented a wake-up call against fiscal profligacy.[247] It had a major impact on a new Italian government, conferring an unforeseen spirit of caution onto Giorgia Meloni, who became prime minister in November 2022, following the September election victory of her right-wing populist Brothers of Italy party.[248]

Truss is a former Liberal Democrat party member who voted to stay in the EU in 2016, but subsequently took on the trappings of an ardent Brexiter. Having advanced to foreign secretary under Johnson, she was elected Conservative leader at the beginning of September 2022 after a hard-fought contest with her rival, Rishi Sunak. Chancellor of the exchequer for a two-and-a-half-year spell in Johnson's administration, Sunak eventually succeeded Truss in October 2022 before giving way to Starmer after the July 2024 election. Sunak had raised taxes to their highest level in seventy years to try to correct imbalances after the Covid-19 pandemic. Truss wanted to do things differently – in line with her iconoclastic style during previous government jobs. Kim Darroch, Britain's ambassador to the US in 2016–19, recalls her ministerial visits to Washington.

> She came across as a bit weird. Her conversation consisted of asking you questions. You would say something and it was clear from her look that she didn't like the answer, but then she simply moved onto the next question. There was also a lack of intellectual curiosity. She didn't seem interested in having a breakfast with Washington pundits, which most ministers enjoyed doing. Most politicians in similar positions who came to Washington were Americophiles with some sort of background understanding of or interest in the US. She wasn't in that category.[249]

By the time she became prime minister on 6 September, Truss regarded herself as bearing Margaret Thatcher's tax-cutting heritage.[250] The die was cast during the run-up to the move to 10 Downing Street. At a preparatory meeting with Kwarteng and a small group of Conservative-leaning economists (some of whom she barely knew) at the foreign secretary's official country residence of Chevening in Kent on Bank Holiday Monday, 29 August, Truss asked: 'If I sack the governor of the Bank of England, will there be a sterling crisis?'[251] She was told she did not have the power to dismiss him, and even if she had, it would not be a wise way to start her premiership.

Two days later, Gerard Lyons and Julian Jessop, two of the sympathetic economists, received an invitation to return the following Saturday; they wrote a paper for her (subsequently leaked to the *Guardian* and *Financial Times*) which stated, 'The markets are nervous about the UK and about policy options. If immediate economic policy announcements are handled badly then a market crash is possible.'[252]

Jessop comments, 'She was made more vulnerable by her recklessness. And she combined that with extreme haste in thinking that the entire growth agenda had to be delivered within two years. As it happens, the fallout from the mini-budget meant she lasted less than two months.'[253] Queen Elizabeth died on 8 September, two days into the Truss premiership, disrupting her start-up phase and especially preparation for the first tax cuts. According to Jessop,

> Without the death, there would've been a second meeting the following weekend, probably at Chequers [the prime ministerial country residence], and that could have made a lot of difference, in terms of presentation of the tax cuts in the direction of more caution. As it was, I had no further contact with Liz Truss during her time as PM. Budget secrecy also made it next to impossible to reach Kwasi Kwarteng.

But even before the royal death, Truss displayed the impatience that was to be her undoing. Irritated that she could not unseat Bailey, the novice prime minister forced Kwarteng – as soon as he arrived at the Treasury building on 6 September – to sack Tom Scholar, the department's experienced and well-regarded permanent secretary, who at the beginning of the 2000s had been Britain's executive director at the IMF in Washington.

Ejecting the top Treasury civil servant on the first day of a new government is unparalleled in modern British history. It set the scene for a fatally flawed administration. Kwarteng arrived at around 7.30 in the evening to carry out briefings with key staff. He called Scholar to see him. The following conversation ensued:

> Kwarteng: We would like a fresh start. You are aware that there are views in the Conservative Party that the Treasury was against the growth plan and had not been supporting the government's policies. You are in charge of the Treasury. Therefore, I'm going to have to ask you to leave.
> Scholar: There are number of serious questions to deal with, including the international situation and the domestic economy. You are going to need some time to get settled in. The budget needs to be prepared. Therefore, I would suggest we give it a month, allow me to get on with my job and then, in a month's time, if you want me to go, I will do so.
> Kwarteng: I don't see how I can go back and tell her that.[254]

John Redwood, a Truss supporter, says that, before she became prime minister, he had advised her to enact 'a reasonably radical three-part budget, containing tax cuts, spending reductions and supply side measures including transport and energy capacity and amended business regulation to speed growth. She clearly felt it was not radical enough.'[255]

Redwood says sacking Scholar without lining up a replacement was Truss's 'biggest single mistake'. One of the reasons for the defenestration was Truss's personal pique, a residue of slights she felt she had suffered during her previous job as chief secretary to the Treasury. She blamed Scholar for having kept her out of meetings with Philip Hammond, chancellor of the exchequer in 2016–19. In fact, Scholar showed traditional civil service punctiliousness in all his dealings with her. In ensuring she was kept away from certain meetings, Scholar was simply implementing the then chancellor's wishes. Hammond regarded her contributions as no more than nuisance value.[256]

With political idiosyncrasies that could border on the obsessive, Truss continued to harbour grudges against Scholar – in this case, in her eyes, being in league with Washington's liberal institutional elite.[257] She told aides on 30 September, just before the Conservatives' annual party conference that was overshadowed by the financial crisis: 'It's Tim Scholar and his fucking mates at the IMF who are responsible for all the fuss.'[258]

'WE HAD A GUN TO OUR HEADS AT THE BANK OF ENGLAND'

In view of the shortage of financial market expertise at 10 Downing Street and lack of contact between Truss and Andrew Bailey (they never met during her premiership), Scholar's removal was supremely unhelpful for the new government's mini-budget preparations. Truss and Kwarteng refused to have the measures assessed by the independent financial watchdog set up in 2010 by George Osborne, the Office for Budget Responsibility.[259] The effect was compounded by an ill-judged Kwarteng TV interview on 25 September, immediately after the fiscal announcement, when he proclaimed: 'There's more to come.'[260]

The turmoil led to sharp falls in government bonds and sterling. It sent market interest rates soaring, at a speed and scale not seen in the UK since the 1970s,[261] forcing the Bank of England into groundbreaking action – a £65 billion exercise on 28 September to stabilise a highly volatile market in gilt-edged stock. Bailey, governor since March

2020, was already under pressure when Truss arrived in Downing Street, reflecting both poor relations with the Conservatives as well as a series of communications lapses. Bailey said four months later:

> People forget that it was not just the government that was under pressure. We had a gun to our heads at the Bank of England, because it was a very reactive market. Our market intelligence told us that the market was going to blow up by Wednesday morning [28 September] unless we came in to intervene. So the pressure for us to calm the markets by buying gilts became extremely large.[262]

The Bank's officials lined up to explain to the public, financial markets and parliament what they termed a temporary, targeted programme of government bond purchases.[263]

Bailey explained the thinking behind an ultra-high-risk operation. A time limit was needed to avoid 'moral hazard'. The Bank had to explain that it was not reversing monetary policy and restarting quantitative easing. And it had to move fast. 'All these factors led to us deciding a timeframe of 2½ weeks to get it done and then to stop. None of this had anything to do with keeping the government in office or otherwise. I've always been clear that the Bank of England is not there to either prop up governments, or to get rid of them. That is not part of our job. There are no hidden criteria.'[264]

But Bailey acknowledges voices in the Trump camp alleging some form of anti-government conspiracy. 'The [critical] IMF statement did not help. This was not coordinated with the UK. I believe it represented unhappiness by the IMF about the action of a G7 country. The idea of the G7 is to lead by example. The IMF and the G7 spend a lot of time telling emerging market economies how to behave. And here you had a major economy carrying out the opposite of that advice.'

Truss and her ministers attempted a series of damage-limitation exercises to reverse important parts of the 23 September measures. After running into fresh criticism at the annual meetings of the IMF and World Bank in Washington on 13 October, Truss forced Kwarteng to fly back and resign the chancellorship on the next day. One victim was not, however, sufficient. After three weeks of financial market upsets, Truss finally lost the confidence of Conservative MPs and resigned on

20 October, triggering the second Tory party leadership contest in four months.[265]

British exceptionalism had comprehensively, in the eyes of the world, run into the buffers.[266]

Nick Macpherson, Scholar's predecessor as head of the Treasury, forcefully criticised Truss in a speech in Edinburgh shortly after she stepped down.[267] Truss had attacked the Treasury as 'an easy target' in an effort to seek 'new dragons to slay'. But 'failed Treasury orthodoxy is now back with a vengeance', he proclaimed – the exact opposite of Truss's intention. Macpherson added that government incompetence would exert an overall negative effect on the UK economy because of the need to recover credibility – 'hard won and easily lost' – on international financial markets.

Liberty comes with limits. The bold plan to exploit post-Brexit freedoms ended in disorderly retreat. The episode was a big factor behind the caution in the budget plans of Britain's new Labour government after July 2024.[268] It sent ripples across the Atlantic.[269] In view of the precariousness of the US budget deficit, the Truss turbulence provided a benchmark for the disruptive policy acrobatics of Trump's second administration.[270] Britain's failed experiment showed with renewed intensity that no country, not even America as the global leader, can shield itself from the consequences of ill-thought-out economic actions. In Europe and the world, this is a lesson that will run on.

8

DREAMS, REALITY AND THE FUTURE OF POWER

*If some demagogue on horseback gained control of the efficient
Russian miliary machine . . . he could play havoc with European peace
for a while.*
Harry Truman, US president, 1945[1]

*Well, I think it's a very bad situation. I think this man's gone crazy. He
is simply inventing any means whatever to knock us out.*
Harold Macmillan to John F. Kennedy,
referring to Charles de Gaulle, 1963[2]

*Europe will need a different architecture. In the past, leaders stuck to a
script that commercial union comes first, followed by monetary union,
and then on to fiscal union, which would require some kind of political
union. Geopolitics is likely to demand an inversion in that sequential
thinking because European security is unlikely to be able to rely so
heavily on Washington.*
Paul Tucker, former deputy governor, Bank of England, 2024[3]

In the four central issues at stake for the future of Europe – energy,
defence, industry and money – the continent faces a high-wire balancing act of epic proportions. A weakening of the political centre in
many countries is feeding fragmentation and lowering cohesion. In its
struggle to maintain relatively high living standards, hold its own in
international competition, and secure a climate-friendly future, Europe

has to come to terms with the US and China as they jostle for advantage in a world split by binary superpower duelling. Exploiting European weakness, the US under Trump 2.0 is entering a new phase of bombast. In spite of the vaunted checks and balances in the American constitution, it will be difficult to prevent a deterioration of the post-Second World War order that spurred and protected the European recovery. The task of European statecraft is to prevent a complete breakdown.

According to the celebrated analogy put forward by Harold Macmillan, Britain's studiedly Edwardian prime minister of the 1960s, Britain sixty years ago took the role of the 'Greeks in this American empire'.[4] Judging by Trump's early bellicosity over defence, trade and economics, Europe may end up, in the relationship with today's Trumpian American Romans, as not Athens but Carthage – the ancient North African city state destroyed in the Punic wars.[5] The continent which was the first to industrialise faces the risk of being eclipsed in coming decades by faster-growing economies elsewhere – from both North America and Asia.

By failing to make sufficient reforms in combining economic prowess with social welfare, Europe has sacrificed leadership. In aspiring for sustainable economic systems, Europe knows that, through its own direct actions, it can make only a modest difference to the world's carbon output. It has sought an enhanced role in the ecological field for a mixture of reasons. One aim – a legitimate element of 'soft power' – is to gain leverage in international discussions by setting a positive example for other countries. Another element – much emphasised by Emmanuel Macron and by Friedrich Merz – is to promote Europe's own industries to the top league of environmental technology. But drawbacks will be palpable in joint ventures and other collaboration agreements where European entities will be junior partners with better-capitalised American or Asian firms likely to dominate any such tie-ups.

In mapping out a route between dreams and reality, Europe has in the past all too often embarked upon a path of delusion, witnessed above all in the first ten years of economic and monetary union. A series of world events starting with the financial upsets of 2007–8 and the Fukushima nuclear disaster of 2011, accompanied by the progressive ascent of China, has brought in a new age of hard-headedness.

The development and denouement of the European debt crisis, Britain's EU exit referendum, the Covid-19 pandemic, the outbreak of the Russo-Ukrainian war, and Trump's renaissance have swollen further the tide of adversity. The fast-changing cavalcade of European leaders, and the faction-ridden domestic coalitions they have strove (and often failed) to control, navigated these hazards only with huge difficulty. Tests which ten years ago might have been viewed as merely problematic now are close to unmanageable. In their preoccupation with home-made concerns, the Europeans have become more prone to navel-gazing – and less aware that their major anxieties, for example over Russia's designs on Ukraine (and indeed on other parts of the continent), are of only negligible importance to the majority of the Global South.[6]

Anxieties which were paramount after the fall of the Berlin Wall have been turned on their head. Speaking in the year he died, Wolfgang Schäuble – one of the few genuinely European elder statemen of the past few decades – put this change into perspective.

> When Germany was reunified, there was fear in foreign countries that we might become too strong. You could excuse Thatcher and even Mitterrand for believing that. The only leader in Europe not to harbour anxieties was González in Spain. Now it is the opposite. The belief is that the Germans, in the defence and military sphere, are too weak. The Germans have to learn that freedom and peace need to be defended. This is not just a question of money. There has to be a willingness for expenditure in lives and blood.[7]

Schäuble recalled asking Tim Geithner, then US Treasury secretary, in 2014, 'If Estonia was attacked, would the Americans be willing to come to their side under Article 5 of the Nato treaty?'[8] Geithner replied: 'Yes, the Americans would be willing to expend blood' – an opinion that, by 2025, might have become more fluid. Schäuble's view in 2023 was: 'Germany now backs away from this, we have become very pacific. The Germans do not wish to go to war. We have been living well for 40 years under American protection. We are a very moralistic people who like to give others advice on how to behave. Perhaps this is now changing slowly.'

The redrawing of Europe's psychological map after in the wake of Russia's aggression and Trump's 2025 volte-face has compounded the

complexities of confronting the continent's social, economic and industrial challenges. Setting up structures to alleviate these problems is beset
by a proliferation of fault lines within the EU and by the political and
economic weakness of the countries at its centre – France and Germany.
Inevitably, the future constellation will move towards the structure
of 'variable geometry' favoured by Jacques Delors. But the geometry is
becoming ever more variable, less geometric – and ever less likely to
generate the economic and social gains on which European stability
depends.

Furthermore, the framework of democracy in western societies –
social inclusion, civil liberties and the balance of entrepreneurial
freedom and regulatory constraint – is being undermined by the
increasing frailty of many of these societies' economic foundations.

Mario Draghi has summarised Europe's vulnerability.

We are the most open: our trade-to-GDP ratio exceeds 50 per cent,
compared with 37 per cent in China and 27 per cent in the US. We
are the most dependent: we rely on a handful of suppliers for critical
raw materials and import over 80 per cent of our digital technology.
EU companies face electricity prices two to three times higher than
those in the United States and in China. We are severely lagging
behind in new technologies. And we are the least ready to defend
ourselves: only 10 member states spend more than or equal to 2 per
cent of GDP on defence, in line with NATO commitments.[9]

Draghi spelled out the likely outcome – one that Donald Trump, in
his own manner, has also grasped: 'Over time, we will inexorably
become less prosperous, less equal, less secure and, as a result, less free
to choose our destiny.' Europe's future depends on successful international cooperation both within and beyond the continent. But the
upsurge of populist politics, powered by declining governance standards in wildly proliferating social media, is likely to impede genuine
burden-sharing and encourage renationalisation of European policies
and priorities. Conflicts of interest will multiply as Europe battles to
find an equilibrium between manifold extremes: shorter- and longer-
term rewards, appeasing and antagonising the Trump administration,
and supporting and disappointing the centre-ground of the electorate.

Nowhere are the conflicts sharper than in the environmental field. And nowhere, for the coming years, are the stakes higher. A stream of influential voices has warned over the past decade of the linkages between ecological damage – including the cost of major climate-related disasters – and the wider financial and economic system. Yet an important backlash has come from organisations supporting fossil fuels around the world, ranging from pro-coal lobbies in China to Trump-backing American senators castigating fund-management companies for discriminating against fossil-fuel companies. In 2015, Mark Carney, as governor of the Bank of England, ten years before he became Canadian prime minister, was one of the first senior people within the financial system to pinpoint the looming longer-term financial risks.

> The catastrophic impacts of climate change will be felt beyond the traditional horizons of most actors – imposing a cost on future generations that the current generation has no direct incentive to fix . . . The horizon for monetary policy extends out to 2–3 years. For financial stability it is a bit longer, about a decade. Once climate change becomes a defining issue for financial stability, it may already be too late.[10]

In 2023, Janet Yellen, a former chair of the Federal Reserve and Treasury secretary in the Biden administration, pointed to a fivefold increase in annual billion-dollar disasters over the past five years, compared to the 1980s, after considering inflation.[11] As David Callaway, a California-based climate commentator, stated,

> From the deep freeze in Texas and wildfires in California to sunny-day flooding in Florida, these disasters are reflected in higher insurance premiums, or worse, a withdrawal by insurers from certain volatile areas . . . Investors and professional asset managers don't see climate risk as a 'woke' pathway to imposing cultural ideologies on Americans, as some red state leaders charge. They simply see it for what it is – risk.[12]

There are opportunities, too. All European countries wish to develop world-class environmental technology and sustainable energy industries and services which can secure jobs in a competitive environment. Politicians have spotted merit in combining international development policy with sustainability – but there are also pitfalls. European plans to reward developing countries for taking better care of their environment have a long pedigree. German chancellor Helmut Kohl proposed at the Venice economic summit in 1988 forgiving debt for third-world countries that took steps to protect their tropical rainforests[13] – but this can sometimes be equated with a new form of economic colonialism.[14] European leaders wish to respond to home-grown political pressures for 'greener' economies – although they are mindful that changing industrial structures normally destroys jobs before it creates them.

The political movements that are pushing towards climate-friendly policies can spawn forces impeding these goals.[15] Supporters of radical solutions face revolt when ordinary voters are confronted with policies that seem to discriminate against them. The war in Ukraine, pressures on Russian energy supplies, and the subsequent relaxation of plans to phase out coal-fired power stations were all significant mechanisms weakening commitments to ambitious zero-carbon targets. Espousal of secure and sustainable but costly alternative forms of heating or transport to wean countries away from traditional fossil-fuel systems can spur fears of an 'eco dictatorship'. At the centre of attention, with hundreds of thousands of jobs at risk throughout the continent's industrial heartlands, lies the automobile industry.[16] The Italian and German government joined forces in late 2024 to back the European automotive industry in calling for relaxation of CO_2 emissions standards for cars, softening the planned ban on sales of new petrol and diesel models by 2035.

Macron in France never recovered from the 'gilets jaunes' episodes in 2018–20 when demonstrators in yellow high-visibility vests took to the streets and online media to protest against rising oil and fuel prices and the high general cost of living.[17] The UK witnessed unrest over plans to extend fees for driving polluting vehicles in London, seen as discriminating against motorists in areas relatively ill-served by public transport.[18] In Germany, Robert Habeck, the high-profile Green economics minister in Scholz's battered coalition, suffered a near-terminal collapse of political esteem in 2023 over poorly prepared policies to bring in costly heat pumps to replace gas- and oil-fired systems in homes and commercial premises.[19] Quarrels over the heat-pump debacle represented a primary reason for the collapse of the Berlin coalition in November 2024.

MODEST GROUNDS FOR HOPE

Europe's problems run deep. Yet there are modest grounds for hope that the continent may, in the mid- to late 2020s, have traversed the position of peak pessimism – and be ready to take its future into its own hands. In the four big areas that count for the future, there is an array of actions that Europe can enact to improve its straitened circumstances.

In the energy field, Europe will have to shift gear towards a more stable and sustainable resource mix. Europe's undue dependence on Russian gas has been exposed as one of the most important policy setbacks since the Second World War. France and Germany have started to take steps to repair their discord over the fundamental merits of nuclear power – a fault line across the Rhine that has deepened over the years. Nuclear energy will need to find its place. With the new German government under no illusions about the scale of energy-policy missteps over the past twenty years, Germany will require a new policy of energy pragmaticism which might even encompass a cautious reopening towards small-scale nuclear reactors.

Europe must apply a much more effective risk-management approach to guard against future energy mishaps. The combined forces of the EU, together with other countries within a potential 'union' of partnerships, including Switzerland, Norway and Britain, hold the key to vital technologies in many spheres of the future energy mix, including hydro, wind and solar energy as well as the all-important hydrogen question. Europe's financial institutions, although fragmented compared with their American counterparts, can marshal substantial resources in this field, backed up by government spending.

The 'Next Generation' EU initiative can prove of significant value, especially if it can be combined intelligently with funding via the European Investment Bank and other European institutions. Investors – both at the retail end of the spectrum and also large private-sector entities such as insurance companies and pension funds – are integrating the precepts of environmental, social and governance concepts in their investment strategies. This is one area where 'concentric circles' and variable geometry can make a difference. Europe is aware that it makes up only a small part of the world in terms of energy use and carbon emissions. But if it can bring off an exemplary performance in this sphere, and additionally muster better financing possibilities for countries in Asia, Africa and Latin America likely to be most affected by climate-linked disruption, Europe could end up with a far stronger position at the world bargaining table. At the same time, a shift towards energy-saving technologies, renewable energy sources and more efficient means of energy transmission has come into view. In many high-tech fields, ranging from carbon capture and storage and generation of green hydrogen to battery technology and energy-saving data centres, Europe has significant trump cards at its disposal. That could help tip the balance – against all the odds – towards a more favourable energy and climate picture in the 2030s.

In defence, a two-pronged strategy will be required. Continued reliance on the US nuclear umbrella – which will require acceptance of US-imposed conditions for NATO operability – has to be combined with higher spending on conventional armaments towards the 3.5 to 5 per cent of gross domestic product that has become a new NATO target.[20] Already ten months before the November 2024 election, European members of NATO were preparing for a possible Trump return. As a report from the German Marshall Fund pointed out, 'Europeans can't determine the outcome of the US elections, but they can begin to prepare for the worst.'[21] The report emphasised how plans for increased European defence spending, prompted by Trump's threats during his first term, had fallen well short of earlier pledges.[22]

During 2024, Europe made some progress in bridging this gap – but by no means enough. Extending this further presents a challenge of exceptional severity for budget-strapped governments. And it comes at a time when the Russo-Ukrainian war, and the terms for its ending, have enhanced America's position of strength. The US military and intelligence establishment has used the war to gain ground on three fronts.[23] It has taken the opportunity to improve its real-time assessment of Russia's military capabilities, accomplishing considerable intelligence insights into the workings of the Moscow military apparatus.[24]

It has been able to carry out a major examination of its own defence capabilities – together with allies, a key test of NATO resilience for further conflicts. And the boost in arms deliveries by top American companies has provided a further shot in the arm to the US economy.[25] As politicians like Merz have indicated, Europe may have no choice in future but to attempt to harness American technological and military power to joint advantage – perhaps through combined European procurement.[26] This will be an uphill journey, and a vocal one, probably accompanied by White House invective which will weigh heavily on the transatlantic relationship.

In industry, America's defence prowess represents a large and growing obstacle to meaningful intra-European cooperation. As Éric Trappier, the head of France's Dassault Aviation which makes the Rafale jet fighter, has put it, European countries' temptation to 'buy American' casts considerable doubts over EU pledges to boost joint arms production.[27] Trappier's warning on Europe's tendency to buy from the US finds confirmation in the dominant share of US equipment purchased under Germany's special €100 billion off-budget military-procurement fund set up after the Russian invasion in 2022.[28] This applies in particular to thirty-five F-35 fighter aircraft Germany acquired at a cost of €10 billion.

Several mooted Franco-German defence projects have run into severe difficulties.[29] The European defence industry landscape has been complicated, but also potentially enriched, by a UK–German defence agreement in October 2024.[30] The arrangement is designed to boost joint procurement between the two countries – it could be enhanced further, although possibly at the expense of France, by the landmark increase in defence spending heralded by the Merz government.

Attempts to kick-start industrial investment across Europe will continue to be impeded by competition with grants and subsidies enacted by the Biden administration, continued in different forms under Trump.[31] Implementing the recommendations of the Draghi report, in particular increasing cross-border cooperation in technology and innovation, and promoting more measures to overcome economic fragmentation, will be a necessary requirement for generating prosperity.[32]

In areas where Europe is relatively undeveloped compared with the US – high-speed computing, artificial intelligence, materials science – Europe will have to find new ways of cooperation, both internally and with America. Both in high-level decision-making and in implementation, Europe will have to both streamline and speed up its processes for bringing technology advances to market. Draghi's recommendations encompass a stream of promising proposals for better financing for 'disruptive' innovation, start-ups and scale-ups. These ideas include expanding incentives for business 'angels' and private/public seed-capital investors. These are all areas where Anglo-American investment expertise can be combined with home-grown European industrial and technological prowess.

The Draghi report favours enhancing the firepower of the European Investment Bank and national development banks to mobilise public–private funds and co-investments. In addition, promoting the mobility of researchers, extending the 'Erasmus+' educational programme, developing a European framework to facilitate private-sector fundraising for public universities, and reinforcing research and technology infrastructure through a 'research and innovation union' are all further-reaching Draghi ideas. The scope of all of these measures would be greatly increased if the UK could be brought into the framework – an area where much work and commitment will be needed in the coming years.

Finance and innovation are closely linked. As far as monetary union is concerned, Europe must face up to reality. The euro bloc will either turn into a transfer union, where more efficient and solvent member states pool fiscal resources in favour of the weaker states, in particular to strengthen financial buffers against crisis, or it is likely to wither and perhaps even die. In parallel to stepping up efforts to drive forward capital markets union – now increasingly termed a union for 'savings and investment'[33] – Europe will have to find ways of extending the Next Generation EU fund beyond the 2026 deadline, reducing annual funding but prolonging it across a lengthier period.

Beyond these technical issues, EU leaders must accept some basic facts. The long-running experiment to set up EMU as 'stateless money' has not borne fruit. The 'independence' model of the German Bundesbank worked so long as it applied solely to one country. The ECB's task in maintaining stability by keeping inflation under control and improving the international standing of the euro will be immeasurably helped if the EU can return to moderately successful economic growth. If these measures do not succeed, then Germany – with an economically orthodox Christian Democrat chancellor, and the anti-euro AfD party placed second in the February 2025 parliamentary election – will be highly cautious about approving any kind of budgetary largesse for weaker states.

The ECB will not be able to repeat the Draghi 'whatever it takes' rescue act of 2012. Much depends on politics in France. There is a real chance that the cooperation at the centre of monetary union could break down. In the run-up to the French presidential election in April 2027, Germany will come under increasing pressure from Emmanuel Macron to launch more growth-enhancing European initiatives, including common borrowing – undertakings that would confront Chancellor Merz with sizeable domestic opposition. Splitting monetary union asunder might appear an extreme scenario. The chances of this happening over the next ten to fifteen years are modest, but they cannot be ignored. The unpublished 1997 Bank of England paper shows that, if they are not accompanied by political union, monetary unions, sooner or later, tend to collapse. The more Europe lags in economic performance, the greater the likelihood that the unpalatable becomes plausible.

A PANOPLY OF CONTRADICTIONS

A panoply of contradictions – with widespread implications for the Old Continent – was on acute display at the beginning of 2025. In the fortnight before Trump's second inauguration, an extraordinary sequence of events, centred on the US, set the scene for future strife. As wildfires caused incontestably by climate change raged in Los Angeles suburbs, reducing some wealthy townscapes to ashes, the forty-seventh president was about to take office, committed to scale back America's decarbonisation efforts and step up oil and gas production. 'The images are out of a Mad Max movie, bordering on apocalyptic,' wrote Richard Haass, a veteran American diplomat and national security official. 'This country is overdue for a serious conversation about climate change, land use, and insurance availability, but our ability to have one is alas questionable.'[34]

On 9 January, at the Washington funeral of Jimmy Carter, the thirty-ninth president, who died in December aged 100, mourners heard eulogies of the politician who in his generally unsuccessful presidency contributed to pioneering solar energy in the US.[35] On the same day, BlackRock, the world's largest money manager, whose founder and chief executive, Larry Fink, in 2020 had publicly backed Biden over Trump,[36] pulled out of an important 'net zero' initiative because of legal and regulatory concerns raised especially by the Republican party.[37] In what appeared a late-stage move to counter antagonism of soon-to-be-president Trump towards institutionalised climate mitigation, BlackRock took this step knowing that it was likely to cause dissension among its large group of European clients who wish the firm to maintain efforts in promoting sustainable investments. Carter's funeral coincided with two other sombre landmarks. Official EU data revealed that 2024 was the hottest on record.[38] Munich Re, alongside Swiss Re one of the top two global reinsurance companies, announced that natural catastrophes, in many cases linked to climate change, caused $320 billion worth of damage in 2024 – on an inflation adjusted basis, $34 billion more than 2023.

In Vienna, Herbert Kickl, leader of Austria's right-wing populist Freedom Party (FPÖ), a man of pronounced pro-Russian sympathies, started talks on forming a government after the FPÖ won 29 per cent of votes in September's election.[39] This raised the prospect that Austria would soon be led by a far-right government for the first time since the Second World War – and would join Hungary and the Czech Republic in a triple alliance of EU members from central and eastern Europe generally favourable to Putin and opposing the EU's supportive line on Ukraine.

Eventually the Austrian parties settled on a three-party coalition without the FPÖ.[40] But formation of such a bloc in the future could have a major impact on overall EU decision-making. Without qualified majority voting in major decisions, Brussels' ability to establish 'strategic autonomy' will be fatally underlined by countries which once made up the Austro-Hungarian empire.

In a further note of incongruity, Elon Musk, the billionaire entrepreneur reputed to be the richest man on earth, embarked on a high-profile social media campaign to destabilise governments in both Berlin and London,[41] earning rebukes from both countries' prime ministers. Musk's flurry of publicity backing the far-right AfD met a tide of countervailing news articles pointing out that the AfD had campaigned against Musk's Tesla electric vehicle plant south of Berlin on the grounds that the factory and its products polluted the environment.[42]

Trump's pre-inauguration press conference at his Florida residence of Mar-a-Lago, in which he refused to rule out using force to push through territorial claims in Greenland, Canada and Panama,[43] was met by a chorus of disapproval, led by Germany and France. Scholz – about to be eclipsed in the February 2025 German election – underlined Europe's 'incomprehension' about 'statements from the US' which appeared to undermine 'fundamental principles of constitutional law'.[44]

Scholz's intervention, in which he indicated America might be harbouring aggressive intent like Putin's Russia, was denounced by the opposition Christian Democrats as bringing 'anti-Americanism' into the German election campaign.[45] However, subsequent events confirmed that Scholz was right: America has tilted towards neo-imperialism.[46]

Standing up to Trump will require a combination of European political forces. Across a heterogeneous continent, assembling a workable coalition of different governments with a common policy on Trump will be a difficult task. The highest profile European to cross Trump's pre-inauguration path was not Scholz but the prime minister of Italy, Giorgia Meloni, leader of the far-right Brothers of Italy. She pulled off a coup by travelling to Florida for a five-hour encounter. Underlining how she may become a pivotal European player under Trump 2.0, the president-elect praised her for 'really taking Europe by storm'.[47]

Giuliano Amato, Italy's most senior living ex-prime minister, whose first term in office started when Meloni was fifteen years old, speaks highly of the country's first female government chief. He praises her dexterity – as leader of the then Opposition party, the far-right – in dealing with Prime Minister Draghi before the general election in September 2022 which brought her to power.[48]

Amato believes she can play a strong role in what he sees as Europe's mission in the next four years. 'We must do whatever we can to preserve the transatlantic relationship and to keep the West alive. However, the selfish America that Trump wants can be quite an obstacle.' Of Meloni, he says:

She is a clever woman . . . she speaks remarkably good English. She is well aware of what needs to be done and what can be done, not least in view of the budgetary restraints. She wants to play her cards in the mainstream of the Union, not at the borders. She is moving towards the political centre, which is not a bad thing for Italy. But it might be difficult for her to preserve her support in the sphere of her party where the fascist (or neo-fascist) roots are much stronger. Developments in the Italian centre-right might be beneficial for Europe, where strong leaders are not abundant.

Italy's ascent puts Germany's weakness into perceptive. And it throws into sharp relief the overall strength of the populist far-right AfD – with lessons for the whole of Europe. Bernd Lucke, a mild-mannered and scholarly economics professor from Hamburg, who founded the party in 2013 (and departed in 2015 after it moved much further to the right), puts the AfD's emergence in the context of the one-time narrowness of Germany's post-1945 political spectrum. And he ascribes its rise since 2015, at least initially, wholly to the pro-immigration stance of Angela Merkel.[49]

The AfD, with many members (like Lucke) who had previously belonged to mainstream parties, was established to register protest over euro policies. 'I had been in favour of the euro when it was introduced in 1999, but with the euro crisis, it had taken the wrong track with faulty policies and a failure to maintain the agreed stability criteria.' The German media portrayed AfD as a right-wing nationalist party long before this was true, Lucke says.

> Over time, this led moderate party members to become increasingly concerned about their reputation, prompting many to leave. New members joined, mistakenly expecting the party to align with the image portrayed in the media. These newcomers aggressively pushed issues such as German sovereignty, migration, Islam, and US influence onto the agenda, accelerating the exodus of centrist-minded members. Gradually, the initial majority of euro-critical members melted away, allowing nationalist forces to gain dominance. The media portrayal became a self-fulfilling prophecy.

When the party convention in July 2015 moved to the hard right, 6,000 liberal-conservative members, including Lucke, left the AfD.

'This might have been a fatal blow, had not, just three months later, the refugee crisis invigorated the AfD as a right-wing anti-migratory party.'

The AfD has gained ground partly because of a trend predicted in a German foreign ministry document in 1990: resentment that Germany has given up power to European institutions, particularly the European Central Bank. Klaus-Jürgen Citron, head of the ministry's planning staff, wrote – with alarming prescience:

> It is questionable whether the Germans will be able to transform their economic strength into political power and international influence. This reflects pooling of central areas of economic policy, the operational independence and increasing Europeanisation of banks and corporations, and the extreme export dependence of the German economy, resulting in vulnerability amid intensive world market competition.[50]

This shift is likely to continue in coming years – especially if strengthening EMU requires a form of pooling of fiscal resources. Bundesbank and ECB veteran Otmar Issing points out that the relevant commissioners in Brussels are almost universally on the side of the most highly indebted nations. He adds:

> High government debt is the sword of Damocles hanging over the monetary union. This is the main reason why I believe we are on our way to a transfer union. Whatever people say about the German political landscape turning against this, I do not believe German politicians in the end will be able to say No. Future parliamentarians and ministers will be afraid of being identified as taking the risk of a collapse of a member country, not to say the collapse of EMU.[51]

Immediately after unification, France was preoccupied about binding Germany to Europe to keep it under control. In recent years, the mood has shifted. As Dominique Moïsi wrote in 2021, 'The fear of an overtly strong Germany dominating Europe has been replaced with fears of a weak German leadership, unable to fulfil the international role now expected of it. We have moved from the anxiety of "too much" Germany to "less" Germany, which would also mean "less Europe".'[52]

The prospect of a weakened Germany fearful of transferring to its neighbours prized elements of national wealth in the cause of European unity makes that objective neither more probable nor more secure.

RISK MANAGEMENT IN DEMAND

The dilemma of western governments is that they seldom have sufficient time to put into place necessary but unpopular reforms encompassing shifting financial and social benefits and often imposing higher taxes and levies on ordinary voters. Well before any longer-term advantages feed through, the disadvantages become evident via electoral distaste for inevitable shorter-term hardships. The reform process grinds to a halt, at progressively higher levels of dissatisfaction and dislocation. After monetary policy was tightened to cope with higher inflation, Europe used up the breathing room provided by huge financial hand-outs during the Covid outbreak. Europe manifestly needs a comprehensive risk-management approach running across all spheres of public policy. During the good times, the European culture of social welfare has traditionally provided such a risk-abatement framework, making Europe more resilient to changing economic patterns. But the costs of the 'European way of life' have spiralled just as the economic system that sustains it is being progressively undermined. The ensuing clash of need and vulnerability goes to the heart of Europe's malaise – and opens it up to large sources of risk.

How should Europe cope? Guidelines for the future can be deduced by examining Europe's response to a range of conundrums. Iain Conn, one of Europe's foremost energy experts, with a long career as board member of oil giant BP and chief executive of energy company Centrica, recounts the story of Russian gas and the Ukraine war. In view of Russia's perceived reliability throughout the Cold War, 'It seemed like a pretty safe option. Europe has got to import hydrocarbons from somewhere. For a petrostate like Russia it appeared to be in that country's interest that it should carry on exporting to proximate markets, and once pipelines are built the economics normally mean they flow for decades. The problem was exposed as a singular low-probability very high-impact risk. However low-probability the risk appeared to be, the consequences would be material.'[53]

Shortly after the full-scale Russian invasion of Ukraine, Conn was part of an expert group on natural gas convened by Ursula von der Leyen, the European Commission president, to establish whether Europe could get through the winters of 2022–3 and 2023–4. He wrote much of the analysis, concluding that Europe would indeed make it, with the help of a rebalancing of gas supply and demand including demand curtailment. 'Markets are amazing things.' He forecast that 'Europe would be able to achieve a lot through a combination of factors, and this has turned out to be exactly what happened and broadly in the proportions we esti-mated'.[54]

One priority for the future, according to Conn, is to make changes in the 'plumbing' of gas supplies, so that central and eastern Europe, once almost wholly dependent on Russian gas, can turn to supplies from the west. 'Europe's pipelines mainly flow from east to west. They need to change direction.' Despite some progress in this sphere, the overall picture is not reassuring.

> The US has become self-sufficient in energy. Europe doesn't have as broad and deep an economy. The US has a much stronger federal system and a reserve currency. And Europe has a social system that places a burden on business. Europe is an energy deficit region. It must develop local sources of energy. Otherwise it will be exposed to hydrocarbon markets where it will be vulnerable to pressure from other regions which may be run by unsavoury leaders or dictators.

Jörg Kukies, the top Berlin economics official and former Goldman Sachs banker who became Germany's finance minister in the last unhappy phase of the Scholz government, provides an intriguing anal-ysis of two offsetting sources of risk for Europe's largest economy.[55] On the one hand, gas from Russia was at an 'artificially cheap price [which] did not take into account the costs to the environment'. Germany further benefited in the short term by deciding not to take out 'insur-ance' against a curtailment of Russian supplies: for example, through building liquified natural gas terminals. On the other hand, Kukies says, the country's stubbornness in sticking to economic orthodoxy has given it leeway to relax fiscal policy at times of stress. 'I am convinced that, in the grand coalition [between the Christian Democrats and

Social Democrats] before and after 2018, had we not carried out the stance of fiscal solidity, we would not have had the fiscal strength and power to unleash the bazooka as we did under Covid and following the invasion of Ukraine.'

Energy will remain tantalisingly crucial to Germany's future with Russia. One of the best equipped to look ahead is Bernd Pfaffenbach, former economic adviser to Merkel and Schröder.

> At least one of the lines of Nord Stream 2 will come into use eventually, as part of the settlement over Ukraine, probably after Putin has left office. Perhaps in 10 years. It would otherwise be a huge waste of expensive infrastructure. More importantly, Germany and Russia are drawn to each other by history, geography and economics. Assuming a settlement to the Ukrainian war, it would be impossible to believe that there should not be some kind of economic cooperation between the two countries.[56]

ENERGY, ECOLOGY AND FINANCE

A sizable influence on the future stems from an admixture of energy, ecology and finance. A man whose job intersects these factors is Frank Elderson, a Dutch lawyer and former board member of Nederlandsche Bank, now board member responsible for sustainability at the European Central Bank. He says:

> We take a risk-management approach to the climate and environment crises in our banking supervision . . . Through our strict focus on banks' risk management practices, as prudential supervisors we exert leverage on all European banks – which the banks subsequently exert on their clients to ensure that climate-related and environmental risks are managed appropriately. So, as supervisors, we indirectly influence, across a very wide area, what is happening in the real economy. This is a very powerful channel.[57]

From a purely legal point of view, Elderson sees risks for the system emerging more from under-appreciation of environmental risks rather than over-zealousness. Pointing to more than 2,000 climate litigation cases outstanding, he says: 'We are in a litigious environment and yet no one has sued the supervisors for exceeding their mandate on this issue . . . There might be a greater chance of being sued for doing too little than for doing too much.'[58] However, central banks' actions face limits. 'The power of central banks is that we are independent and therefore can put forward views and policies independently of the political process. Our weakness is that we can be accused of going beyond our mandate. It is a thin dividing line.'

Elderson draws attention to 'climate mitigation through climate litigation' – stemming from the Dutch supreme court judgement that the Netherlands government is obliged to reduce emissions on the basis of human rights considerations.[59] A cascade of lawsuits can be expected against the state, companies, banks and bank supervisors. 'All these actors, including central banks, are potentially vulnerable to lawsuits aiming to commit them to take stronger action to meet the Paris targets. These legal processes may well have repercussions around the world, beyond the specific jurisdiction of litigation.'

Anne Simpson, a long-serving practitioner of long-term economic thinking in finance – an Englishwoman based in San Diego in California – is global head of sustainability at Franklin Templeton, one of the world's largest asset managers. She has helped forge commonality in sustainability policies among a large and influential group of public- and private-sector asset managers and owners including some of the world's leading sovereign investors.

She believes that, despite the backlash against decarbonisation policies in the US, 'There is great potential for a community of interest, bringing together the providers of the money and those who are investing it. This will ultimately provide the economic case for integrating sustainability factors into finance.'[60] Simpson describes how a central force in world financial markets – the demographics of retirement – is increasing the leverage of private savings. Europe will retain leadership in sustainable economics, Simpson believes, because of the widespread understanding across the continent that finance will inevitably flow to areas where risk and return are in the most favourable balance. She is unperturbed about the sway of those espousing climate change denial. 'When physics meets finance, economics will be the decisive factor.'[61]

On the economic front, the shortcomings of monetary union add up to the most important internal risk to Europe's stability. Pablo Hernández de Cos, the new head of the Bank for International Settlements, says: 'The unfinished business of EMU produces a drag in European growth and impairs our ability to manage crises and shocks as efficiently as other economies like the US.'[62]

Alongside measures to complete the banking union and build capital markets union, Hernández de Cos calls for 'a central fiscal capacity that can be used to smooth out shocks. Certainly, Europe has made some progress in this direction as a response to the exogenous and dramatic shock posed by the COVID pandemic with the Next Generation EU Funds. But these are temporary; a permanent stabilising mechanism is needed.' In a similar vein, Mario Centeno, Portuguese finance minister from 2015 to 2020 who then became governor of the country's central bank, says:

> The EU still has not learned how to deal with risk. Europe has spent much of the past 15 years in crisis-fighting mode. We now need mechanisms for making Europe more secure from crises on a longer-term basis. We have spent a lot of time discussing risk reduction and risk sharing. We need to link these processes together by bringing an overall risk management approach through a policy of integration and solidarity.[63]

At the time of the pandemic, Centeno says, 'Europe was able to combine monetary, fiscal and regulatory measures in a highly constructive way.' Europe now needs to embark on further steps, he says, such as increasing the issuance of common safe assets through enhanced borrowing by the Next Generation EU fund. 'Even if Europe doesn't become a unified sovereign state, we can develop the capacity to make sovereign-like policies at the overarching state level.' Centeno welcomes the 2025 steps by the German government to substantially raise borrowing to boost infrastructure and defence spending. 'But I would be happier if this was inscribed into a European institutional framework for public investment and reform under what we set up in 2019 for the "convergence and competitiveness" process.'[64]

Suggestions for more pan-European borrowing from Centeno and other advocates from southern member states are certain to face strong opposition from traditionally 'hard money' northerners, especially in view of the rapid rise of the anti-euro far-right in these countries. The parlous state of the German economy in 2024–5 could bring a glimmer of hope for further financial integration. As Charles Goodhart of the London School of Economics points out:

> One of the main obstacles to greater fiscal union has been German objection to a fiscal transfer system. But if the German model of energy imports from Russia and sales of machinery to China has now completely broken, it is possible that Germany could decline so much relative to the rest of the EU that it might perceive the need to get some inwards transfers itself and cease to object to a transfer union. The fragmentation of the world could assist the unification of Europe.[65]

On the other hand, a fresh deterioration in the German economy nd forced recourse to EU largesse would almost certainly coincide with a further strengthening of the AfD – which would greatly constrain the political appetite for big changes in cross-border financing.

Linked to these fundamental issues, the governance of monetary union requires considerable improvement. Transparency and account-ability, perhaps inevitably, lags well behind that in other, less compli-cated jurisdictions. Luis de Guindos, the former Spanish finance minister who became ECB vice president in 2018, favours lifting the ban on releasing details of voting behaviour.

> I personally think publishing the names of the members of the governing council regarding voting behaviour would help to make central bankers more responsible. There are arguments against this. In my view, they are outweighed by those in favour. It is sometimes said that publication would make the governors subject to domestic political pressure. However, in view of the ECB's very strong statu-tory independence, I don't think that should pose a problem.[66]

Athanasios Orphanides, the former Cyprus central banking chief, now a professor at MIT in Massachusetts, backs de Guindos. 'Transparency is essential for accountability and this is sorely lacking.

The ECB must start providing more details regarding its deliberations, including a record of votes, creating an environment for better decision-making.'[67]

TOWARDS AN AGE OF RESILIENCE

Europe's greatest task is to turn high-blown phraseology – 'The EU has strengths on which it can build – and it has a plan to fix its weaknesses'[68] – into concrete action and verifiable implementation. In any deliberations on Europe and its future, the UK will be a key variable. Post-referendum disputes have impeded growth in the UK, but have also had a dampening effect on continental Europe. Britain is struggling to achieve the aim of improving its economic structure and citizens' prospects outside the EU. But the departure of an economy with strong positions in finance, defence, business services and some high-tech industries has represented a net loss for the EU. The UK and EU need to find a constructive modus vivendi: 'variable geometry' will be crucial. Otherwise, the whole of Europe will be the poorer. The initial reaction to the Brexit vote was for Europe to draw closer together – a mood that has continued throughout the turbulence of the pandemic and the Russo-Ukrainian war. But the underlying forces triggered by Britain's departure have been centrifugal not centripetal. The shift, exemplified by wins for populist parties, could intensify depending on the war's trajectory and aftermath.

In view of the size of the Labour majority at the 2024 election, Keir Starmer has every chance of remaining in office until 2029. If he plays his political cards right, and (an even bigger if) the economics turn out propitiously, Britain could over that time become Europe's pivotal player. Post-Brexit freedoms in trade, financial market and budgetary matters, if they can be used to buttress home-grown sources of dynamism from scientific and technological expertise, could turn out to be a winning constellation. In a positive scenario, this could be combined with constructive trade and investment relations with both China and the US. But conditions for genuine rapprochement with the EU will be hard to achieve. Replicating the degree of exceptionalism of Britain's arrangements with the EU when it was a member will be impossible.[69] The awkward reality is that the UK will be taken seriously by Brussels and other European capitals only if it resurrects a reputation for economic prowess. But alleviation of inevitable constraints on trade and investment with the EU – and the economic improvement that would ensue – will come about only if the UK builds up negotiating clout in Brussels and elsewhere. Breaking through this innate contradiction will take much more political skill than Britain was able to muster in post-referendum negotiations – and, indeed, during its often accident-strewn European dealings spanning the entire post-1945 period.

As Peter Foster, one of the most assiduous commentators on Britain's Brexit-related industrial and trade dilemmas has pointed out, 'Even quite substantial upgrades to the EU–UK Trade and Cooperation Agreement will have limited overall economic impact. For as long as current political red lines rule out membership of a customs union with the EU and the EU single market, the UK will remain structurally disadvantaged.'[70] Generally welcome changes in the post-Brexit trading regime with the EU, agreed in May 2025 as part of a wider 'reset' in relations, do not make much difference to these underlying realities.[71] Domestically generated economic growth thus becomes even more important. As Foster says, this requires painful reforms in areas like tax, land use and education, and an end to 'wishful thinking'.

On the other hand, the EU's phase of economic doldrums, as well as post-invasion convulsions in the security landscape, may benefit the UK in Brussels bargaining. The celebrated 1994 German position paper that established ideas for a differentiated approach to European integration emphasises the symbiotic character of Britain's relationship with the EU. Wolfgang Schäuble and his co-author Karl Lamers – writing at a time when UK prime minister John Major was underlining the UK's post-Thatcherite European commitment – set out a possible framework: 'Suggestions for forming a core Europe and strengthening German–French cooperation do not mean abandonment of hope for Britain to take its role in the heart of Europe, at the core. The further development of Europe is the best way of clarifying Britain's relationship to Europe and its willingness to take part in further integration.'[72]

Three decades later, 'core Europe' as a concept has fallen into disrepair. Monetary union has been established, but has endured a decade of travails. The Franco-German relationship has broken down. Far from finding its place 'at the heart' of Europe, as Major once affirmed,[73] the

UK has drawn the consequences of what Schäuble and Lamers termed 'the future development' of the EU – and is no longer in it. Most important of all, the Trump administration has served notice that eighty years of Euro-Atlanticism may be may be drastically changing its shape.

Quizzed about this in 2023, eleven months before he died, and two years before Trump's second inauguration, Schäuble expertly sketched out the general context.

> Building up European defence is a key part of the strategy. This is not an alternative to NATO but a contribution to strengthening it. We are all very dependent on what happens in the US. Three countries in mainland Europe are the most important for defence: France, Germany and Poland. It is very important that Poland is part of this group. We will not be able to build Europe wholly with the Brussels institutions. We will continue to need to co-operate with Britain, even after Brexit.[74]

Central to Schäuble's vision of a 'coalition of the willing' with the British is the issue of financial integration. As finance minster, Schäuble, like his one-time boss Helmut Kohl, showed an almost mystical belief in the prowess of the City of London. Pier Carlo Padoan, chairman of Unicredit, the largest Italian bank – permanently striving for improved cross-border banking linkages in Europe – says the UK will be crucial for a better-performing European financial industry. He wants to fuse 'banking union' and 'capital markets union' into a quest for 'financial union' to add political momentum. He asks: 'How will the UK financial industry react to coming back to Europe in some form when it is clear that the British are needed to help to complete the union?'[75]

The phraseology of a past British prime minister – speaking at one of the bleaker junctures of Britain's post-1945 relations with Europe, after de Gaulle had vetoed the UK application to join the European Economic Community – provides an apt historical counterpoint. Harold Macmillan, in a radio broadcast in January 1963, castigated France for 'looking backwards'.[76] De Gaulle's view was that 'one nation can dominate Europe'. Equally wrong, in Macmillan's view, was the Gaullist notion that 'Europe can or ought to stand alone'. The reality,

Macmillan opined, was the opposite: 'Europe cannot stand alone. She must cooperate with the rest of the Free World, with the Commonwealth, with the United States in an equal and honourable partnership.'

Another politician whose premiership was wrecked over European engagement, David Cameron, outlines a future setting along similar lines. He draws conclusions both from the failures of his premiership as well as from his brief period as foreign secretary in 2023–4, during the final months of the Biden administration. His experience of the so-called Group of Five was generally positive: 'Building a bridge between Britain, France, Germany and Italy, and the US – it worked well and this can still be an important instrument for the future, also with Donald Trump in the White House.'[77]

The later stages of the journey are a long way from being settled. Bob Zoellick, the former World Bank president who has written a solid history of two centuries of US diplomacy and foreign policy, issues this assessment of the Trump policy switch over Europe: 'It's big, it's significant. I don't see us going back to the old pattern. But the course of history doesn't move in a straight line, it depends on events and these can be unpredictable. I see this moving via a series of discontinuities.'[78]

Zoellick adds a cautionary note on Trump, based both on his personality and on the repercussions of a peace deal in Ukraine.

It's sometimes overlooked that he built his career as a reality TV host. He needs to control the narrative. There has to be a hero in the story, with many ongoing episodes. If Putin dominates a rump Ukrainian state, this will be an ongoing security risk for Europe and this will be a gain for Putin. But if he overplays his hand and the US seems to be losing security as a result, this will weaken Trump. There is a positive side to the transatlantic relationship, there's a lot of existing [military] infrastructure tied up in NATO and the US. People in America generally don't like Putin. They like NATO and they don't want to concede to Putin.

As a result of diverse pressures, Britain and Europe need to move – alongside the enhanced NATO spending targets – to supply immediate support cover for Ukraine. In addition, a commitment is required for security guarantees via European or United Nations troops on the ground in the aftermath of the fighting. Longer-term goals should encompass defence readiness and combat support at present provided primarily by the US.[79] If defence procurement in Europe is to be revolutionised, Britain will have to play a full part, along with Turkey and Norway, two other non-EU NATO member countries with sizable defence commitments. In view of the stupendous costs for both sides, and the need to present a common front to both Trump and Putin, it is encouraging that France and Britain in July 2025 under the 'Northwood declaration' sealed a far-reaching accord on the two countries' so-called independent nuclear deterrents. To 'deepen their nuclear cooperation and coordination', the two countries are setting up a joint Nuclear Steering Group 'to provide political direction'.[80] It would be important to coordinate planning on nuclear targeting, as well as in programmes for joint future military systems. Germany's role as a pivotal player in European defence, yet a non-nuclear weapons state, makes it imperative that Berlin is drawn still closer into European and NATO nuclear planning with both France and the UK – a move facilitated by a separate (but linked) Anglo-German defence and security agreement (the 'Kensington treaty') sealed shortly after the Northwood accord.[81]

Fault lines across the euro bloc, widely acknowledged at the start of EMU, since then only partly corrected, are still a major impediment to Europe's development. Profiting from London's status as Europe's largest financial centre, the UK, though outside both EMU and the EU, can play a role in stabilising monetary union during what may be another difficult period in the long series of challenges since the single currency's foundation. That attempt to provide a new equilibrium – requiring an element of financial and fiscal transfers among continental European countries – will involve many painful dilemmas. Success will be in the interest of Britain as well as the rest of Europe.

Linked to this, the Trump administration's drive to use technologically generated developments in digital assets to help drive a large pool of hitherto untapped world savings into US Treasury bonds, thus helping finance an otherwise unsustainable US budget deficit, creates an enormous incentive for the UK and the rest of Europe to work together. Stablecoins are a fast-growing form of digital assets designed to remain stable by pegging their price to a reserve asset, usually the dollar – offering a fast-track route to maintaining the US currency's international supremacy.[82] What is needed is a joint European response – in terms of financial management, market regulation and product innovation – to what amounts to a remarkable attempt at American monetary colonisation.[83]

Helping the EU's common funding drive – whether through the Next Generation Fund or other initiatives – would make considerable sense for all concerned. The UK could make use of European borrowing schemes to fund defence procurement projects under the à la carte arrangements it is seeking with Germany and other countries. All these schemes will become acutely more important in a new European defence framework that seeks to make the continent less dependent on America.

Two countries with well-developed financial markets, Britain and Switzerland, although both outside the EU and EMU, can help the EU organise an improved form of capital market integration that will buttress the continent's position in the world. Under agreements that will need to pay due regard to defence and security imperatives, working with China on common trade and investment projects – especially in the energy and environmental fields – can be propitious for the UK and other European countries. Anglo-German cooperation over China could mitigate competitive problems, bring mutual advantage in the fields of finance and technology, and help offset political complications with Trump's Washington.

Europe together with the UK has to face up to some home truths over China. It is best that they do that together. China is already taking a leading position in AI and related areas. In many technology fields, in terms of price and quality, China has moved comprehensively and probably irreversibly ahead. China has shown itself well prepared for the Trump tariff conflict – and has the financial and commercial resources to ride out future squalls.

In the system of regionalised trading blocs likely to open up in coming years, European countries will need to strengthen their trade relations and cross-border investments with Asia. The Association of Southeast Asian Nations (ASEAN) plus three – China, Japan and Korea – will be building a 'managed free trade zone', with the possible participation of Australia and New Zealand (as well as, at the fringes, India).

Europe, counting, too, non-EU UK, can seek to cooperate with all these countries to help craft production, service and supply lines to make the best of the fragmented global trading regime that seems likely to represent one of Trump's many unsettling legacies.

Over Russia and Ukraine, the interests of the UK and the rest of Europe are again intermingled. Putin has transmuted over twenty-five years from talisman into tyrant; as a result of a range of influences another metamorphosis in Moscow may before too long come into view. Britain can play a role, under very different conditions, but in some ways comparable to patterns seen under Gorbachev and Yeltsin, in helping shape Europe's response to whatever Russia brings forth.

With America, and the second Trump administration, upheaval and drama are inevitable. Europe and the world will not be able to escape the dilemma of the US remaining 'the indispensable nation'[84] which rarely misses the opportunity to proclaim that Europe is losing the battle to rival the US and China[85] – and whose 'every whim'[86] needs constantly to be analysed, indulged, guided, parried and acted upon. Working with rather than against America must be the order of the day. The Europeans have survived worse depredations than Trump's return. It will be an uphill journey and a long haul. But for Europe, this does not have to be an age of acrimony: it can be an age of resilience.

NOTES

INTRODUCTION

1. George Washington, farewell speech, 19 September 1796. Avalon Project, Lillian Goldman Law Library, Yale Law School. https://avalon.law.yale.edu/18th_century/washing.asp.
2. Emmanuel Macron, speech, Sorbonne University, Paris, 25 April 2024. https://www.elysee.fr/en/emmanuel-macron/2024/04/24/europe-speech.
3. Vladimir Putin, statement on Rossiya-1 state TV, RIA Novosti, 2 February 2025.
4. Helmut Kohl, *Erinnerungen, 1982–1990* (Munich: Droemer, 2005), pp. 964–76 – containing a description of the drama of 9 November and the immediate aftermath. Further accounts are in AAPD 1989, Documents 353–5, pp. 1505–13; DESE, Documents 76–93, pp. 492–540, containing a far wider selection of accounts of meetings and telephone calls with leaders from East and West in reaction to the events of 9 November. See also Mary Elise Sarotte, *The Collapse: The Accidental Opening of the Berlin Wall* (New York: Basic Books, 2014), p. 123.
5. Eduard Ackermann was Kohl's long-time confidant and communications chief, dubbed by the chancellor 'Count Carbonara' on account of his fondness for Italian cuisine.
6. Rudolf Seiters, Kohl's chancellery minister, was the first to tell him, by telephone, that the East German leadership had announced at seven o'clock that it was granting visas for East Germans wishing to depart for the West, effectively opening the Berlin Wall.
7. Kohl met a group of journalists – including the author – in 'Ballroom C' of the Marriott hotel. Horst Teltschik, *Die 329 Tage zur deutschen Einigung: Das vollständige Tagebuch* [*329 Days to German Unification: The Complete Diary*], ed. Michael Gehler (Göttingen: Vandenhoeck & Ruprecht, 2024), pp. 96–7.
8. Teltschik, *329 Tage, Innenansichten der Einigung* [*329: Internal Account of Unity*] (Berlin: Siedler, 1991), p. 16, and *Die 329 Tage zur deutschen Einigung*, p. 93. Teltschik's account in both the original and enlarged book goes somewhat further than the official rendering 'Kohl conversation with Wałęsa, Warsaw, 9 November 1989', which says the Solidarity leader 'doubted' whether the Wall would exist in one or two weeks. In both accounts Kohl tries to allay Wałęsa's forebodings by saying that East German demonstrations had been peaceful and the East Germans were not in a revolutionary frame of mind.
9. *Gazeta Wyborcza*, 10 November 1989. Recognising the risks of damaging further Polish sensitivities, Kohl stayed in Warsaw on Friday morning for a further session with Mazowiecki before flying (via a circuitous route in view of post-1945 travel restrictions) to Berlin and then Bonn on Friday evening. He spoke reassuringly by telephone to Margaret Thatcher in London and George H.W. Bush in Washington. On Saturday he telephoned François Mitterrand in Paris and Egon Krenz, the new East German leader, in East Berlin,

chaired a special Cabinet meeting, took a friendly call from Felipe González, the Spanish prime minister, and then spoke to Mikhail Gorbachev in Moscow before returning to Poland to resume discussions on Sunday with Wojciech Jaruzelski, Poland's now reform-minded communist president.

10. David Marsh, 'Marching in the vanguard of history', *Financial Times*, 11 November 1989.

11. Frank Gardner, 'Trump–Putin call lowers the temperature but at Ukraine's expense', BBC, 12 February 2025. https://www.bbc.co.uk/news/articles/c2k5wyqqlq0o. Stephen Collinson, 'Trump's rush for a deal with Putin leaves Ukraine and Europe scrambling', CNN, 18 February 2025. https://edition.cnn.com/2025/02/18/politics/trump-putin-deal-ukraine-analysis/index.htm. The Putin–Trump closeness over Ukraine illustrates general political and psychological similarities. As one of Trump's greatest critics over Russian policies, Michael McFaul, ambassador to Russia under President Obama in 2012–14, described it in 2018: 'In addition to supporting pro-Kremlin policies, Trump's ideological orientation overlapped with many of Putin's views.' Michael McFaul, *From Cold War to Hot Peace: An American Ambassador in Putin's Russia* (New York: Houghton Mifflin Harcourt, 2018), p. 432

12. Friedrich Merz, statement, Berlin, 14 March 2025. https://www.bbc.co.uk/news/articles/cvgd3d427kqo.

13. Jim Tankersley and Christopher F. Schuetze, 'Germany is lifting a foot off its debt brake. Here's why', *New York Times*, 18 March 2025. https://www.nytimes.com/2025/03/18/world/europe/germany-debt-brake.html.

14. Armin Steinbach and Jeromin Zettelmeyer, 'Germany's fiscal rules dilemma. Without further reform, European Union fiscal rules could stop Germany from using the new fiscal space it has freed up for itself', Bruegel, 24 April 2025. https://www.bruegel.org/analysis/germanys-fiscal-rules-dilemma.

15. Merz spelled out his intention for a more positive stance towards France at an OMFIF briefing in London in February 2020, five years before he won the chancellorship in the February 2025 election. David Marsh, 'Merz's hurdles on German leadership path', OMFIF, 10 February 2020. A well-publicised Merz visit to the Élysée Palace in December 2024, two months before he won Germany's 23 February 2025 election, paved the way for a 'reset'. On 26 February, Macron and Merz, in a renewed Paris meeting, proclaimed a 'new start'. Michaela Wiegel, 'Die Übereinstimmungen waren noch größer als erwartet' ['Alignments were even bigger than expected'], *Frankfurter Allgemeine Zeitung*, 27 February 2025. https://www.faz.net/aktuell/politik/ausland/friedrich-merz-bei-emmanuel-macron-diese-agenda-wurde-schon-umrissen-110323975.htmlart. The change in Germany's nuclear energy stance was signalled in a joint German–French position paper on 7 May 2025, coinciding with Merz's first visit to Paris after his Bundestag election as chancellor on 6 May, when the two leaders pledged that energy policy would be based on 'climate neutrality, competitiveness and sovereignty'. 'Emmanuel Macron et Friedrich Merz: Il faut remettre à plat les relations franco-allemandes pour l'Europe' ['We need to reset Franco-German relations for Europe'], *Le Figaro*, 7 May 2025. Strong opposition to Merz's backing of a 'non-discriminatory' stance on nuclear energy at the EU level was voiced later in May by his Social Democrat coalition partners.

16. Gideon Rachman, 'Trump, Putin, Xi and the cult of the strongman leader', *Financial Times*, 31 October 2016. Fiona Hill, 'The Kremlin's strange victory', *Foreign Affairs*, November/December 2021. Michael Gold, 'In rambling interview, Trump blames Zelensky, not Putin, for Ukraine war', *New York Times*, 17 October 2024. Michael McFaul, 'The tragic success of global Putinism – How the West underestimated an ideology's animating force', *The Atlantic*, 10 March 2025. Trump's earlier real-estate dealings in Russia have sparked speculation that the US president has had connections with the Russian underworld in which Putin is held to be a leading figure. 'Donald Trump is a "Russian asset" owned by the Mafia, author claims in new book', *Newsweek*, 17 August 2018, reporting on Craig Unger, *House of Trump, House of Putin: The Untold Story of Donald Trump and the Russian Mafia* (London: Bantam Press, 2018). For encounters before their 15 August 2025 Alaska meeting – a Putin public-relations victory – see 'The surreal history of Donald Trump and Vladimir Putin's private meetings', *Financial Times*, 12 August 2025.

17. 'The president says the US has been "pillaged, raped and plundered" for years by international trade partners', BBC, 2 April 2025. https://www.bbc.co.uk/news/articles/cm257z1y2q9o.
18. 'The U.S. set the global order after WWII. Trump has other plans', NPR Politics, 1 May 2025. https://www.npr.org/2025/05/01/nx-s1-5369457/truman-trump-foreign-policy.
19. Rebecca Patterson, 'America's economic exceptionalism is on thin ice', *New York Times*, 21 March 2025. https://www.nytimes.com/2025/03/21/opinion/trump-economy-us-exceptional.html.
20. For an account of Europe's interlinked problems and the 'five Ds', see Boris Vujčić, governor, Croatian National Bank, 'Future of inflation', lecture, London, 18 November 2024, and subsequent discussion with OMFIF, 19 November.
21. Consolidated version of the Treaty on European Union, Protocol No. 12 on the excessive deficit procedure, Official Journal 115, 9 May 20008, pp. 279–80. https://eur-lex.europa.eu/eli/treaty/teu_2008/pro_12/oj/eng. See Jan Priewe, 'Why 3 and 60 per cent? The rationale of the reference values for fiscal deficits and debt in the European Economic and Monetary Union', *European Journal of Economics and Economic Policies*, September 2020. https://www.elgaronline.com/view/journals/ejeep/17/2/article-p111.xml.
22. OECD Economic Outlook, October 2024. https://www.oecd.org/content/dam/oecd/en/topics/policy-sub-issues/economic-outlook/eo116/EO116_Annexes_E.pdf. IMF World Economic Outlook. https://www.imf.org/en/Publications/SPROLLS/world-economic-outlook-databases#sort=%40imfdate%20descending.
23. Gravity model: 'workhorse model' of international trade for more than fifty years. See Scott Baier and Samuel Standaert, 'Gravity models and empirical trade', Oxford Research Encyclopaedias, Economics and Finance. https://oxfordre.com/economics/display/10.1093/acrefore/9780190625979.001.0001/acrefore-9780190625979-e-327. For a view of how this applies to the service economy, see Benjamin Fraser, 'Services trade modelling', DIT Analysis Working Paper, 2021. https://assets.publishing.service.gov.uk/media/612363ee8fa8f53dcd3ae89f/dit-analysis-services-trade-modelling-gravity-working-paper.pdf.
24. Strobe Talbott, 'Mikhail Gorbachev and George Bush: The summit goodfellas', *Time*, 5 August 1991.
25. 'Obama, in dig at Putin, calls Russia "regional power"', Reuters, 25 March 2014.
26. Simona Mocuta, chief economist, State Street Global Advisors, SSGA-OMFIF seminar, London, 15 May 2025. Mocuta, like other economists, had been backing a looser German fiscal stance for several years. She points to the irony that the catalyst for a change came not from within Europe but from the US.
27. There is a vast literature on the links between government credit and military power. For the war-connected origins of the Bank of England, see, among many other historical accounts, David Kynaston, *Till Time's Last Stand: The Bank of England 1694–2013* (London: Bloomsbury, 2017), Prologue, pp. 1–8 and subsequent. Referring to the Nine Years' War with France that started in 1688, he quotes Sir John Clapham, in his earlier history (1944): 'Had the country not been at war in 1694, the government would hardly have been disposed to offer a favourable charter to a corporation which proposed to lend it money.' Also cited is political economist Charles Davenant's contemporary observation that 'the whole Art of War is in a manner reduced to Money', so that 'that Prince, who can best fund Money to feed, cloathe, and pay his Army, not he that has the most Valiant Troops, is surest of Success and Conquest'. Around ninety years later, Alexander Hamilton, as a military aide to George Washington, eight years before he became the first US Treasury secretary (1789–95), made an identical point. Hamilton suggested setting up a national bank to reinforce the fledgling US's finances and counter the enemy British in the War of Independence: ' 'Tis by introducing order into our finances – by restoring public credit – not by gaining battles that we are finally to gain our object.' Hamilton regarded the British as supported by 'a vast fabric of credit . . . 'Tis by this alone that she menaces our independence.' Hamilton, letter to superintendent of finance Rupert Morris, 30 April 1781. Quoted in Ron Chernow, *Alexander Hamilton* (New York: Penguin, 2004), p. 156. See also Nuno Palma and Patrick O'Brien, 'The wartime power of central banks: Lessons from

the Napoleonic era', VoxEV-CEPR, 12 March 2022. https://cepr.org/voxeu/columns/wartime-power-central-banks-lessons-napoleonic-era.

28. Edward Fishman, Gautam Jain and Richard Nephew, 'How Trump could dethrone the dollar. The world's reserve currency may not survive the weaponization of US economic power', *Foreign Affairs*, 8 April 2025. https://www.foreignaffairs.com/united-states/how-trump-could-dethrone-dollar.

29. David Marsh, 'Getting serious about euro internationalisation', OMFIF, 22 April 2025. https://www.omfif.org/2025/04/getting-serious-about-euro-internationalisation/.

30. The proposition in 2007 of Michel Rocard, Mitterrand's prime minister in 1988–91 – a rival, and therefore given the post only in the president's second seven-year term – may prove prophetic. 'Independence of the central bank is a means to an end, to win Germany's approval for monetary union, but it is not the end of the story. We will not be able to escape a situation taking place where the government will have to give orders to the central bank. This could take place in a war, or as a result of an American financial collapse. If the American financial tsunami explodes – $12,000 billion in external debt and $2 billion in new borrowings every day – then European governments and the European Central Bank will have to act in concert.' David Marsh, *The Euro: The Battle for the New Global Currency* (New Haven/London: Yale University Press, 2009), p. 212. Interview with author, Paris, 24 May 2007. By the end of 2024 US external debt had more than doubled to $26 trillion.

31. 'Whether it's Trump or Biden, some in Europe see the US as an unreliable ally', CNN, 23 April 2023. See also Xi's speeches in favour of 'just global development and governance', 'inclusiveness' and 'shared future for humankind', G20 meetings, Rio de Janeiro, *China Daily*, 20 November 2024. See Xi Jinping, World Economic Forum, Davos, 17 January 2022. https://www.weforum.org/stories/2017/01/full-text-of-xi-jinping-keynote-at-the-world-economic-forum/.

32. Hugo Dixon, 'Trump's America First revival could backfire', Reuters Breaking Views, 11 November 2024.

33. Shakespeare, *Macbeth*, Act III, Scene 4, lines 1439–42.

1 THE RECKONING

1. Allan Bullock (ed.), *The Twentieth Century* (London: Thames and Hudson, 1971), p. 78.

2. Angela Merkel, speech, Bundestag, Berlin, 29 June 2012. https://www.euractiv.com/wp-content/uploads/2014/02/BK_Merkel_Regierungserklaerung_2012Juni29.pdf.

3. Larry Summers, interview with author (video), Scottsdale–London, 30 January 2024.

4. Kohl, press conference, Moscow, 26 October 1988. Kohl made the statement in reply to a question from the author. Later he qualified the remark (resorting to the ambiguities of the German word 'erleben') by saying he meant he did not think he would live to see reunification as chancellor. Kohl, interview with author, Bonn, 17 December 1990. David Marsh, *Germany and Europe: The Crisis of Unity* (London: Heinemann, 1994), p. 26.

5. James Baker, US secretary of state under President George H.W. Bush. https://www.nytimes.com/1990/07/21/opinion/to-make-europe-whole-and-free.html. For an interpretation of how the US reaction was predicated on policies after the Second World War, see Robert Zoellick, *America in the World: A History of U.S. Diplomacy and Foreign Policy* (New York: Twelve, 2020).

6. Louis J. Halle, *The Cold War as History* (London: Chatto & Windus, 1967), p. 2.

7. Germany's public-debt-to-GDP ratio was 63.1 per cent in 2007 and 62.7 per cent in 2024; France's rose from 64.7 per cent in 2007 to 112 per cent in 2024. IMF, World Economic Outlook database, 2024.

8. Niels Thygesen, interview with author, London, 5 March 2025.

9. IMF Working Paper, 'Macroeconomic consequences of tariffs', January 2019. An IMF analysis of tariffs in 151 countries from 1963 to 2014 indicates that tariffs lead to lower output and productivity and higher unemployment, exchange rate appreciation and inequality.

10. David Cameron, interview with author, London, 11 November 2024.

11. For a discussion of the usage of the phrase 'iron curtain' see Martin Gilbert, *Winston S. Churchill*, vol. VIII: *Never Despair, 1945–1965* (Boston, MA: Houghton Mifflin Company, 1988), p. 7. Count Schwerin von Krosigk, the German foreign minister, in a broadcast to the German people on 2 May 1945, said: 'In the East the iron curtain behind which, unseen by the eyes of the world, the work of destruction goes on, is moving steadily forward.' In 1918 Vasily Rozanov, a Russian émigré philosopher, wrote: 'With a rumble and a roar, an iron curtain is descending on Russian history.'

12. For an account of China's globalisation drive from the beginning of the 1980s, see Jianyong Yue, *China's Rise in the Age of Globalization: Myth or Reality?* (London: Palgrave Macmillan, 2018). 'The World Bank in China', 2024. https://www.worldbank.org/en/country/china/overview

13. 'China's double threat to Europe: How Beijing's support for Moscow and quest for EV dominance undermine European security', Liana Fix and Heidi Crebo-Rediker, *Foreign Affairs*, 5 September 2024.

14. Evan Medeiros, Georgetown University, 'US–China relations will depend on which Trump shows up', *Financial Times*, 13 November 2024.

15. Wendy Cutler, 'Trump wants a trade deal, not a trade war. He may get one', *New York Times*, 31 January 2025.

16. For differing interpretations of the outcome, see Paul Taylor, European Policy Centre, 'Why Donald Trump's return is a disaster for Europe', *Guardian*, 7 November 2024 and Nathalie Tocci, Istituto Affari Internazionali, 'For Europe, Trump's victory could be a blessing in disguise', *Prospect*, 7 November 2024.

17. Stephen Moore, statement, 16 November 2024.

18. Pascal Lamy, interview, *Observer*, 18 November 2024.

19. Xi–Starmer meeting, Rio de January, G20 summit, Xinhua state news agency, 18 November 2024.

20. 'EU strategic autonomy 2013–2023: From concept to capacity', European parliament think-tank, 8 July 2022. José Ignacio Torreblanca, European Council on Foreign Relations, 'Onwards and outwards: Why the EU needs to move from strategic autonomy to strategic interdependence', Madrid, 24 August 2023.

21. Max Bergmann, 'The United States now wants European strategic autonomy', Center for Strategic and International Studies, Washington, 8 November 2024.

22. Jean-Claude Trichet, 'Putin and Trump will drive Europe together', speech, London, 12 November 2024.

23. Liana Fix and Michael Kimmage, 'Trump's threat to Europe: His first term tested the transatlantic relationship—but his second would break it', *Foreign Affairs*, 22 March 2024. Steven Erlanger, 'Trump will test European solidarity on NATO, Ukraine and trade', *New York Times*, 7 November 2024.

24. Summers, interview with author, Scottsdale–London, 21 April 2025.

25. Martin Wolf, 'The EU must build on past successes', *Financial Times*, 17 December 2024.

26. Maddison Project statistics. https://www.rug.nl/ggdc/historicaldevelopment/maddison/

27. EMU started in 1999 with eleven of the then fifteen members of the European Union – Austria, Belgium, Germany, Finland, France, Ireland, Italy, Luxembourg, the Netherlands, Portugal and Spain. Of the remaining four, Greece joined two years later, while Britain, Denmark and Sweden remained permanently outside.

28. See Josephine Quinn, *How the World Made the West: A 4,000-Year History* (London: Bloomsbury, 2024). See also Meghnad Desai, *Hubris: Why Economists Failed to Predict the Crisis and How to Avoid the Next One* (New Haven/London: Yale University Press, 2015), p. 262.

29. Halle, *The Cold War as History*, p. 5.

30. Heather Conley, interview with author, Washington, 2 June 2023.

31. 'Merkel warns on cost of welfare', *Financial Times*, 12 December 2012. https://www.ft.com/content/8cc0f584-45fa-11e2-b7ba-00144feabdc0.

32. For example, Kohl, conversation with Edouard Balladur, French prime minister, Paris, 22 April 1993. AAPD 1993, Document 127, pp. 514–19.
33. Kohl, speech, Königswinter, 8 April 1994.
34. François Heisbourg, interviews with author, Paris, 24 April 2023 and London, 16 May 2023.
35. Kishore Mahbubani, interview with author (video), London–Hong Kong, 29 August 2024.
36. Jin Liqun, interview with author (video), Beijing–Redda, 19 September 2024.
37. For challenges surrounding the 2030 enlargement plan, see 'The EU is finally rebooting the enlargement machine', *The Economist*, 28 September 2023. https://www.economist.com/europe/2023/09/28/the-eu-is-finally-rebooting-the-enlargement-machine.
38. Trump, statement, Morristown, New Jersey, 20 June 2025. After European diplomats met the Iranian foreign minister in Geneva, Trump said, 'Iran doesn't want to speak to Europe. They want to speak to us.' Twenty months previously, Israel launched an invasion of Gaza on 27 October 2023 following the 7 October Hamas attack on northern Israel. Peter Wittig, former German ambassador to the US and UK, wrote in December 2023: 'The US is again the only power which can exert decisive influence on the region.' *Tagesspiegel*, 7 December 2023.
39. Trump's Middle East initiatives are also aimed at outweighing Chinese clout in the region. See Frederick Kempe, 'Trump's remarkable Middle East tour is all about striking megadeals and outfoxing China', Atlantic Council, 13 May 2025. https://www.atlanticcouncil.org/content-series/inflection-points/trumps-remarkable-middle-east-tour-is-all-about-striking-megadeals-and-outfoxing-china/.
40. 'MBS: Middle East can be the "new Europe"', statement, Riyadh, 25 October 2018, and subsequent. https://www.arabnews.com/node/1393491/saudi-arabia#:~:text=RIYADH%3A%20The%20Middle%20East%20can%20be%20the%20%E2%80%9Cnew,he%20vowed%20to%20see%20the%20region%20thrive%20economically.
41. Putin, Valdai International Discussion Club meeting, Sochi, 5 October 2023.
42. Merkel, interview, Reuters, 18 November 2021. 'Maybe initially we were rather too naive in our approach to some cooperation partnerships. These days we look more closely, and rightly so.' German exports to China quintupled in 2005–20 to just under €100 billion, about 3 per cent of GDP. *The Economist*, 16 July 2020.
43. In April 2024, NATO officials estimated that the Russian military had grown by 15 per cent since its 2022 invasion of Ukraine. Much of this growth was attributed to Beijing's support.
44. Jeromin Zettelmeyer, 'What does German debt brake reform mean for Europe?', Bruegel, 31 March 2025. https://www.bruegel.org/newsletter/what-does-german-debt-brake-reform-mean-europe.
45. 'The German far right and the scars of reunification', Guy Chazan, *Financial Times*, 6 September 2024. For a view shortly after reunification, see David Marsh, 'Brothers, but strangers in their own land. Why so many east Germans feel like second-class citizens of their newly united country', *Financial Times*, 1 June 1991. For an up-to-date account from a historical perspective, see Heinrich August Winkler, 'Ein Triumph, von dem Putin kaum zu träumen wagte' ['A triumph that Putin could scarcely dare to dream'], *Der Spiegel*, 28 September 2024.
46. Conley, interview with author, Washington, 2 June 2023.
47. Heisbourg, interviews with author, Paris, 24 April 2023, London, 16 and 23 May 2023.
48. Karl Lamers and Wolfgang Schäuble, 'Überlegungen zur europäischen Politik' ['Reflections on European politics'], CDU policy paper, Bonn, 1 September 1994.
49. Pessimistic commentaries on Europe in 2003–4 include the Bundesbank monthly report, June 2003. 'Weak growth of the German economy since the mid-1990s is marked by loss of confidence among investors and consumers, falling capacity utilisation, rising unemployment and protracted restraint in investment.' The central bank called for 'comprehensive structural reform' to take account of 'demographic strains and high non-wage labour costs' – foreshadowing measures by Gerhard Schröder's government.

50. Delors, interview, *The Economist*, 12 February 2004.
51. Charles Grant, 'Ten reflections on Jacques Delors', point 10, 'Delors' ideas are not redundant', *CER Insight*, 4 January 2024, citing the Conclusion of Charles Grant, *Delors: Inside the House That Jacques Built* (London: Nicholas Brealey, 1994). In 2000 Delors wrote an article for the CER criticising the drafting of a European constitution, since, he wrote, constitutions belonged to nation-states. His 'vision' for an enlarged Europe was that of 'a geopolitical entity bringing together a wider Europe – "the Union" – and an *avant-garde* . . . overtly organised into a federation of nation-states'.
52. 'Europe splits on Trump's call to dramatically boost defense spending', Politico, 8 January 2025. https://www.politico.eu/article/donald-trump-tells-allies-spend-5-percent-gdp-defense-nato/.
53. Johann Wadephul, Germany's CDU foreign minister, backed the idea first, although without the support of the SSPD coalition partners. 'Germany split on NATO 5% defence push as Wadephul backs Trump plan', DPA, 15 May 2025. Merz approved 5 per cent as the objective by 2032 during a visit to Lithuania a week later. Politico, 23 May 2025. The 3.5 and 5 per cent goal (by 2035) was agreed at a NATO summit in The Hague attended by Trump on 25 June 2025.
54. Jacques Poos, statement, May 1991, ahead of negotiations on trying to end a ten-day war in Slovenia, *New York Times*, 29 June 1991. https://www.nytimes.com/1991/06/29/world/conflict-in-yugoslavia-europeans-send-high-level-team.html. See also Radek Sikorski, Poland's foreign minister, 'Europe's real test is yet to come: Will the continent ever get serious about its own security?', *Foreign Affairs*, 20 June 2023.
55. Hans-Friedrich von Ploetz, interview with author, Berlin, 18 January 2023.
56. Britain's tally of eight prime ministers over the last twenty years is only one fewer than the number of chancellors of Germany (counting West Germany up to 1990) in the seventy-five years after the postwar state was founded in 1949.
57. The Conservatives' share of the vote fell especially sharply in Leave-voting constituencies. Compared with 2019, support for the Conservatives fell 12 points in seats where fewer than 45 per cent voted Leave in 2016. In contrast, support for the party fell 27 points in seats where more than 65 per cent voted Leave. John Curtice, BBC, 4–5 July 2024. https://www.bbc.co.uk/news/articles/c2x0g8nkzmzo.
58. Michael Portillo, 'Cameron shouldn't fear the EU wolf', *Financial Times*, 14 February 2012.
59. See Kerstine Appunn, 'The history behind Germany's nuclear phase-out', Clean Energy Wire, 9 March 2021. https://www.cleanenergywire.org/factsheets/history-behind-germanys-nuclear-phase-out#.
60. Gerhard Schröder, *Entscheidungen: Mein Leben in der Politik* [*Decisions: My Life in Politics*] (Hamburg: Hoffmann & Campe, 2006), p. 246. For a critical summary of Germany's Russian policies over the past half-century, see Bastian Matteo Scianna, *Sonderzug nach Moskau: Geschichte der deutschen Russlandpolitik seit 1980* [*Special Train to Moscow: The History of Germany's Russian Policy since 1980*] (Munich: C.H. Beck, 2024).
61. Putin convinced Schröder to take over the chairmanship in a telephone call in December 2005, when Putin told him: 'If you cannot carry this out, then who can?', Schröder, interview with author, Hanover, 27 January 2011. Schröder claimed that he was motivated by overriding European considerations. 'It should be just as normal in German public opinion to work for a German–Russian project as for a German–French or German–American one. But the opposite was the case. The public debate following my decision exceeded any darker visions I might have envisaged.' Schröder, *Entscheidungen*, p. 461. See also Katrin Bennhold, 'The former chancellor who became Putin's man in Germany', *New York Times*, 23 April 2022: 'Gerhard Schröder, who is paid almost $1 million a year by Russian-controlled energy companies, has become a pariah. But he is also a symbol of Germany's Russia policy.' In the interview, Schröder said the phone call took place in the evening of 9 December 2005, seventeen days after he stepped down from the chancellorship. Schröder used the interview to back the widely held view that, sooner or later, Germany's business ties with Russia would regain momentum. 'When this war is over, we will have to go back

to dealing with Russia. We always do.' https://www.nytimes.com/2022/04/23/world/europe/schroder-germany-russia-gas-ukraine-war-energy.html.

62. Schröder's work for Russian state-owned companies and his refusal to break off Putin ties in 2022 attracted considerable criticism from the SPD as well as elsewhere. 'Gerhard Schröder sues German parliament for shutting down his office', *Financial Times*, 12 August 2022. https://www.ft.com/content/9e247df5-9066-4fca-85e7-bf5f3aabb00b. Signs of a thaw came in October 2024 during the run-up to the February 2025 general election. https://www.politico.eu/article/german-social-democratic-party-spd-gerhard-schroder-vladimir-putin-ukraine-waar/.

63. Angela Merkel, Freiheit: *Erinnerungen 1954–2021* (Cologne: Kiepenheuer & Witsch, 2024). The English edition, published at the same time along with editions in nearly thirty other languages, is *Freedom: Memoirs 1954–2021* (London: Macmillan, 2024).

64. For example, Helen Thompson, 'Europe is headed for one thing . . . The European Union cannot now be led. No one is going to become the new Ms. Merkel', *New York Times*, 26 October 2021.

65. Nord Stream consists of two double pipelines able to deliver a total 110 billion cubic metres of gas to Europe each year from Russia to Germany via 1,224-kilometre pipes through the Baltic Sea. The first pair, Nord Stream 1, established in 2005, started operations in 2011–12. The second, Nord Stream 2, was agreed in 2015, completed in 2021, but never received an operating permit. Undersea explosions in September 2022 hit both lines of Nord Stream 1 and one of Nord Stream 2, leaving the other line intact. Some western officials have suggested that Moscow was responsible, while Russia has blamed the US, Britain and Ukraine. All claims have been denied. Nord Stream is a consortium 51-per-cent owned by Russian state oil company Gazprom. According to the Nord Stream website (https://www.nord-stream.com/about-us/, last updated in November 2022) the other shareholders are Wintershall Dea and PEG Infrastruktur (E.on), each with 15.5 per cent, and Dutch natural gas infrastructure company Nederlandse Gasunie and French energy provider ENGIE, each with 9 per cent. Wintershall Dea, formerly owned by BASF, is now owned by Harbour Energy. 'Gas pipeline Nord Stream's long way back to Europe', Reuters, 7 March 2025. Anglo-Dutch oil company Shell earlier backed Nord Stream 2 with a loan for 10 per cent of the total €9.5 billion construction cost, but announced on 28 February 2022 it was pulling out. In May 2025, Nord Stream, headquartered in Zug in Switzerland, was rescued from insolvency under a Swiss court judgement, opening the way for a debt rescheduling, but was preparing for procedures on EU sanctions. 'The EU is close to restricting the Nord Stream 2 pipeline in a new round of sanctions as Russia refuses a ceasefire in its war against Ukraine', Bloomberg, 23 May 2025.

66. Michael Bauchmüller, Georg Ismar, Georg Mascolo and Nicolas Richter, 'Macht euch keine Sorgen! Brisante Akten aus dem Bundeskanzleramt zeigen, wie vehement sich Angela Merkel dafür engagierte, das Gasgeschäft mit Russland trotz aller politischen Bedenken zu erweitern und die Pipeline Nord Stream 2 durchzusetzen' ['No cause for concern! Controversial documents from the chancellor's office show Angela Merkel's forceful engagement for widening gas business with Russia and pushing through the Nord Stream 2 pipeline despite all political concerns'], *Süddeutsche Zeitung*, 16 May 2025. A cache of sixty-three government files from the chancellor's office released to the newspaper under Freedom of Information Act procedures applied for in 2024 and granted in 2025 underlined Merkel's involvement in the geopolitics of Nord Stream 2. This contrasted with her public claim that the pipeline was a private, commercial endeavour. The official files emphasised the relaxed view of Merkel and leading Berlin officials in a landmark energy asset swap between Gazprom and Wintershall agreed in 2015 alongside an accord on Nord Stream 2 after three years of negotiations. The energy asset swap, giving Gazprom a hold over German domestic energy supplies in return for Wintershall gaining upstream Russian assets, was not seen as raising Germany's vulnerability to a Russian energy squeeze, even though it was agreed one year after Russia's annexation of Crimea. According to the released files, only in 2021 did German officials become perturbed that Gazprom's control over facilities such gas storage exposed Germany to potential Russian political pressures. The

documents show Berlin was more concerned about opposition to the Russian deals from Ukraine, Poland and the Baltic states than about possible domestic supply vulnerabilities. According to the *Süddeutsche Zeitung*, 'The 63 hitherto unknown documents show how intensively the chancellor's office was occupied with questions concerning Russian gas business, particularly the Nord Stream 2 pipeline, during the chancellorship of Angela Merkel.' https://www.sueddeutsche.de/projekte/artikel/politik/gas-nordstream-russ-land-merkel-e107357/. The revelations were followed up by many foreign media. See for example Derek Scally, 'Nord Stream saga shows German leaders' magical thinking and economical approach to the truth', *Irish Times*, 23 May 2025: 'Files show how Merkel chancellery officials worked steadily and silently to smooth Nord Stream 2's political path, against considerable political opposition from the European Commission and Germany's eastern neighbours'. https://www.irishtimes.com/world/europe/2025/05/23/nord-stream-saga-shows-german-leaders-magical-thinking-and-economical-approach-to-the-truth/.

67. Olaf Scholz was rejected by SPD members in December 2019 when he stood for the party chairmanship in SPD on a joint ticket with Klara Geywitz. Instead, the joint party chair was taken by the uninspiring combination of Norbert Walter-Borjans and Saskia Esken.

68. Kurt Georg Kiesinger's three-year chancellorship was a fragile interregnum encompassing West Germany's first postwar recession in 1967 – although with a strong recovery thereafter – overshadowed by the legacy of the long 'hate-envy' relationship between the two previous CDU chancellors, Konrad Adenauer and Ludwig Erhard. Daniel Koerfer, *Kampf ums Kanzleramt: Erhard und Adenauer* (Stuttgart: Deutsche Verlags-Anstalt, 1987). For an appreciation of Kiesinger on the 100th anniversary of his birth, see Philipp Gassert, Ceremonial Lecture, Albstadt, 2 April 2004. https://www.kas.de/de/einzeltitel/-/content/kurt-georg-kiesinger-eine-wuerdigung.

69. 'German AfD party grows parliamentary clout, sparking concern', *Deutsche Welle*, 1 March 2025.

70. 'AfD räumt im Osten ab', ZDF Heute, 24 February 2025. https://www.zdf.de/nach-richten/politik/deutschland/afd-wahlergebnisse-bundestagswahl-2025-100.html.

71. Michael Kretschmer, Saxony prime minister, interview, *Der Spiegel*, 17 April 2025.

72. David Marsh and Andreas Meyer-Schwickerath, 'Germany gets ready – after a wait – for Merz as leader', OMFIF, 7 November 2024. https://www.omfif.org/2024/11/germany-gets-ready-after-a-wait-for-merz-as-leader/. The advantages accruing to Merz as a result of his opposition to Merkel policies, for example over building up gas supplies from Russia, were evident on Merz's first visit to Trump at the White House in June 2025. 'Germany's chancellor cracks the Trump code, but to what end?', *New York Times*, 6 June 2025.

73. Olaf Scholz, *Hoffnungsland: Eine neue deutsche Wirklichkeit* [*Land of Hope: A New German Reality*] (Hamburg: Hoffmann und Campe Verlag, 2017), p. 200.

74. Friedrich Merz, *Neue Zeit – Neue Verantwortung: Demokratie und Soziale Marktwirtschaft im 21. Jahrhundert* [*New Times – New Responsibility: Democracy and Social Market Economy in the 21st Century*] (Berlin: Econ Verlag, 2020), pp. 176–82.

75. Charles Goodhart and Manoj Pradhan, *The Great Demographic Reversal: Ageing Societies, Waning Inequality, and an Inflation Revival* (London: Palgrave Macmillan, 2020).

76. Kohl, speech, Vienna, 18 May 1993.

77. For an attempt to construct an index of political polarisation in Europe, and to link it to macroeconomic factors, see Sebastian Müller and Gunther Schnabl, 'A Database and Index for Political Polarization in the EU', Leipzig University, Institute for Economic Policy, 29 December 2021.

78. Ulle Ellemann-Jensen, interview with author, Copenhagen, *Financial Times*, 19 September 1992.

79. Joachim Gauck, speech, Berlin, 22 February 2013. https://www.bundespraesident.de/SharedDocs/Reden/EN/JoachimGauck/Reden/2013/130222-Europe.html.

80. 'European Union borrowing costs rise after global index compiler excludes its bonds', Reuters, 13 June 2024.

81. Scholz, interview, *Die Zeit*, 20 May 2020.

82. George Calhoun, 'Europe's Hamiltonian moment – What is it really?', Forbes, 26 May 2020. https://www.forbes.com/sites/georgecalhoun/2020/05/26/europes-hamiltonian-moment--what-is-it-really/. For a full appreciation, see Chernow, *Alexander Hamilton*, Prologue, pp. 1–6 and subsequent.

83. Gunther Schnabl and Sebastian Müller, Leipzig University, 'The Brexit as a Forerunner: Monetary Policy, Economic Order and Divergence Forces in the European Union'. https://www.ifo.de/en/cesifo/publications/2018/working-paper/brexit-forerunner-monetary-policy-economic-order-and-divergence.

84. Marsh, 'AfD surge brings fresh ECB hurdles', OMFIF, 3 September 2019. As one Berlin government official said, 'There has been general disenchantment in the east on how the population has been treated. There is a feeling that the region is run by other people who tell the east Germans how to behave, and on top of this put negative interest rates on bank deposits.' https://www.omfif.org/2019/09/afd-surge-brings-fresh-ecb-hurdles/.

85. The six leading European economies in 1989 had a combined GDP of $4.8 trillion (current prices), against a mere $450 billion for the remaining six countries, Belgium, Denmark, Greece, Ireland, Luxembourg and Portugal.

86. Mitterrand was in office for fourteen years between 1981 and 1995. Kohl stayed for sixteen years, from 1982 to 1998. Thatcher, who became prime minister in 1979, had already been in Downing Street for ten years, although she was deposed in October 1990. Andreotti was on his third premiership, having taken office in July 1989, and served already in 1976–9 and 1972–3.

87. James Baker (with Thomas M. DeFrank), *The Politics of Diplomacy: Revolution, War and Peace, 1989–1992* (New York: G.P. Putnam's Sons, 1995), p. 172. The phrase came from Rick Burt, a former US ambassador to Germany.

88. Macron became president in 2017; Sanchez became prime minister in 2018; Johnson, 2019; Draghi, February 2021; Scholz became chancellor in December 2021. Rutte's VVD party lost ground badly to finish third place in the Dutch general election in November 2023. Rutte stayed on as caretaker prime minister pending formation of a new government.

89. With a background at the French tax inspectorate and as an investment banker at Rothschilds, Macron had spent two years as economy minister in 2014–16 but had never held elected office before he won the presidency in 2017. At thirty-nine, he was France's youngest-ever head of state.

90. Philip Zelikow, author of two seminal books on the political upheavals at the time of German unification

91. Zelikow, interview with author (video), Stanford–London, 4 December 2023.

92. John Burn-Murdoch, 'Democrats join 2024's graveyard of incumbents', *Financial Times*, 7 November 2024.

93. Carney was the second G7 central-bank governor to become prime minister, following Mario Draghi who was Italy's premier in 2021–2.

94. 'Mark Carney's Liberals have won. What now?', *Globe and Mail*, 29–30 April 2025. https://www.theglobeandmail.com/politics/federal-election/article-mark-carney-liberal-victory-canada-election-2025-explainer/.

95. 'Trump goes for the jugular with his Canada threats', *Independent*, 14 March 2025. https://www.independent.co.uk/news/world/americas/us-politics/trump-canada-annex-greenland-b2714806.html.

96. 'Anthony Albanese and Labor Party sweep federal election 2025 with large majority after shock swing against Coalition', Sky News Australia, 3 May 2025. https://www.skynews.com.au/australia-news/politics/federal-election-2025-anthony-albanese-and-labor-party-sweep-federal-election-2025-after-shock-swing-against-coalition/news-story/00119875068ae509c3a510608b521ed6.

97. 'Fears of global instability drive Singapore voters into ruling party's arms', BBC, 3 May 2025. https://www.bbc.co.uk/news/articles/cly505gqwwpo. 'US allies say no at the ballot box to Trump's tariff bullying', Nikkei Asia, 10 May 2025. https://asia.nikkei.com/Opinion/US-allies-say-no-at-the-ballot-box-to-Trump-s-tariff-bullying.

98. 'What will the EU election results mean for Europe?', Centre for European Reform, 11 June 2024.
99. 'Michel Barnier devient le premier ministre le plus éphémère de la Vième République' ['Michel Barnier becomes the shortest-tenured prime minister of the Fifth Republic'], *Le Figaro*, 4 December 2024.
100. French presidents are limited to two terms in office. Macron, at the helm of a political movement he founded only in 2016, has appeared unlikely to bequeath a sound political berth to whatever candidate his party chooses to succeed him.
101. 'Marine Le Pen attacks five-year ban from running for public office as "political decision"', BBC, 31 March 2025. https://www.bbc.co.uk/news/live/cwyewv8xdp7t.
102. 'Farage's Reform UK Party wins mayoral and parliamentary post in surge of support', Reuters, 2 May 2025. https://www.reuters.com/uk/nigel-farages-reform-uk-party-ahead-by-four-votes-key-election-race-2025-05-02/
103. Enrico Letta, interview, *Politico*, 5 January 2024.
104. In March 2025, Austrian conservatives, Social Democrats and Liberals formed a coalition to prevent the far-right from coming to power despite its electoral victory. 'Austria swears in new government, ending five-month political crisis', *Politico*, 3 March 2025.
105. 'Right-wing strikes deal to lead new government', *Deutsche Welle*, 31 January 2025.
106. Dan, the pro-EU mayor of Bucharest, unexpectedly won the presidential election in Romania on 18 May. 'Pro-EU centrist wins Romania's tense presidential race over hard-right nationalist', AP News, 19 May 2025. In Portugal, on the same day, the anti-immigration Chega party tied with the Socialists for second place as the governing Democratic Alliance won most seats. 'Far right surges in Portugal as moderate conservatives win election', *Financial Times*, 19 May 2025.
107. 'Conservative historian wins Polish presidential vote', BBC, 2 June 2025. https://www.bbc.co.uk/news/articles/cx27897vedno.
108. World Economic Outlook, IMF database, April 2024. Germany's GDP in the seven years from 2018 to 2024 grew by an annual average of 0.4 per cent. During this period, the population was rising. So GDP per capita on a constant price basis was unchanged – €38,693 in 2018, against €38,666 in 2024.
109. For a timely account of the economic malaise, see Wolfgang Münchau, *Kaput: The End of the German Miracle* (London: Swift Press, 2024).
110. 'China's trade surplus reaches a record of nearly $1 trillion . . . China's vast exports in 2024 exceeded its imports on a scale seldom seen anywhere except during or immediately after the two world wars', *New York Times*, 12 January 2025.
111. Bundesbank, monthly report, January 2024.
112. 'Germany confronts a broken business model', Guy Chazan and Patrica Nilsson, *Financial Times*, 6 December 2022. Markus Steilemann, head of the VCI, the German chemicals trade body, said Germany risks 'turning from an industrial country into an industrial museum'. Responding, Robert Habeck, the economy minister, told the *Financial Times* the dire state of affairs partly reflects industry's own errors. 'They didn't diversify their energy supply but relied on Russian gas.'
113. Jean-Claude Juncker, interview with author, Brussels, 29 November 2023. 'Many parts of Luxembourg's culture, literature and philosophy have been strongly influenced by France, but in monetary and economic questions the Germane has often been greater. The memory of two sets of German occupation in the First and Second World Wars remains in people's minds. There is no country in Europe that is so torn between these two countries. This condition of psychological and historical conflict [*Zerrissenheit*] is unique to Luxembourg.'
114. Juncker's assessment is fully borne out by the *Süddeutsche Zeitung*'s revelations in May 2025 of Merkel's part in the Nord Stream 2 build-up. One the reasons she put forward for pressing ahead with the pipeline is that she believed this would give her the opportunity to negotiate with Putin over Crimea. Nicolas Richter, 'Angela Merkel hat drei große Fehler gemacht. Dass sie es bestreitet, ist der vierte' ['Angela Merkel made three big mistakes. The fourth one is that she denies it'], *Süddeutsche Zeitung*, 18 May 2025.

115. Summers, interview with author (video), Scottsdale–London, 30 January 2024.
116. Schröder's statements underline the personal nature of his agreements to work for Russian state-controlled companies. In his interview with the *New York Times* on 23 April 2022, Putin's phone call with Schröder on 9 December 2005 is framed as a direct personal request: ' "Are you afraid to work for us?" Mr Putin had joked.'
117. José Manuel Barroso, interview with author (video), London–Munich, 7 September 2023.
118. Conley, interview with author, Washington, 2 June 2023.
119. For an account of the setting up of the stability and growth pact, and its chequered aftermath, see https://economy-finance.ec.europa.eu/economic-and-fiscal-governance/stability-and-growth-pact_en. Jan Priewe, 'The new EU stability and growth pact', *European Journal of Economics and Economic Policies*, September 2024. https://www.elgaronline.com/view/journals/ejeep/aop/article-10.4337-ejeep.2024.0143/article-10.4337-ejeep.2024.0143.xml.
120. 'Europe's economic laggards have become its leaders – more than a decade after painful austerity, Greece, Portugal and Spain have been growing faster than traditional power-houses like Germany', *New York Times*, 30 April 2024.
121. David Marsh, 'German budget disarray sends out powerful ripples beyond Berlin', OMFIF, 20 November 2023. https://www.omfif.org/2023/11/german-budget-disarray-sends-out-powerful-ripples-beyond-berlin/.
122. Thomas Matussek, interview with author, Hardenberg, 15 September 2023.
123. Michael Stürmer, interview with author, Munich, 20 January 2023.
124. Uwe Corsepius, interview with author, Berlin, 24 May 2023.
125. Klaus Borger, Fritzi Köhler-Geib and Philipp Scheuermeyer, 'Wettbewerbsfähigkeit – vom kranken Mann Europas zum Superstar und zurück: Wo steht die deutsche Wirtschaft?' ['Competitiveness – from the sick man of Europe to superstar and back: Where does Germany's economy stand?'], KfW Research, no. 461, 17 May 2024.
126. Lars-Hendrik Röller, interview, *Financial Times*, 1 October 2023. 'If we'd known then what we know now, we would of course have acted differently . . . It helped to deliver us strong growth rates that paid for things we otherwise wouldn't have had, for a period of 10–15 years.' Röller insisted that Merkel had little choice but to rely on Russian gas after deciding to phase out nuclear energy. 'You can argue whether that was the right thing to do, but it was the consensus in society at the time.'
127. Röller, interview with author, Berlin, 19 February 2024.
128. https://de.wikipedia.org/wiki/Fortune_Global_500#1990.
129. Edzard Reuter died on 27 October 2024.
130. Reuter, interview with author, Stuttgart, 6 September 2023.
131. Julius Betschka and Veit Medick, 'Amtsantritt in den USA' ['Entering office in the USA'], Stern, 16 January 2025.
132. According to German opinion polls, over several years Merz has consistently suffered from a lower popularity rating in eastern Germany compared with the (already relatively low) score in the west. For example, according to a poll by the Forsa survey agency for the RTL/n-tv broadcasting group in December 2024, Merz was ahead nationwide with an approval rating of 25 per cent, followed by Robert Habeck (Greens) with 20 per cent, Olaf Scholz (SPD) 17 per cent, and Alice Weidel (AfD) 16 per cent. However, including only east Germans, Merz performed significantly worse. Weidel came in first place with 31 per cent, followed by Scholz at 23 per cent, Merz 16 per cent and Habeck 9 per cent. 'Im Osten unbeliebt: Umfrage offenbart Merz' großes Problem' ['Unloved in the East: Poll shows Merz's big problem'], t-online, 11 December 2024. https://www.t-online.de/nachrichten/deutschland/innenpolitik/id_100549216/im-osten-unbeliebt-umfrage-offenbart-merz-grosses-problem.html. Following his move into the Chancellery in May 2025, there were signs of an improvement in Merz's ratings.
133. In view of the reduced hold of establishment parties, Germany's so-called 'grand coalition' that took office in May 2025 between the CDU/CU and the SPD has a majority of just twelve seats in the Bundestag. By comparison, the first of post-1945 Germany's hitherto

four 'grand coalitions' in 1966 had a 210-seat majority. An ominous sign of trouble came in the first round of voting in Merz's Bundestag election as chancellor on 6 May 2025. He received only 310 votes, below the required 316 in the 630-seat parliament, so the vote had to be repeated. This was the first time in the Federal Republic's history that a chancellor had not been confirmed in the first round of Bundestag voting. See 'Protokoll eines Fehlstarts' ['Account of a false start'], *Der Spiegel*, 10 May 2025.

134. Stefan Kornelius, 'Merkels Mängel' ['Merkel's shortcomings'], *Süddeutsche Zeitung*, 26 November 2024.

135. Stefan Kornelius, 'Europas Hoffnung auf eine starke Regierung in Deutschland wurde von den Wählern nicht erfüllt' ['Europe's hopes for a strong government in Germany have not been fulfilled by the voters'], *Süddeutsche Zeitung*, 24 February 2025.

136. 'SZ-Ressortchef wird Regierungssprecher' ['Head of Department named government spokesman'], *Süddeutsche Zeitung*, 29 April 2025.

137. Mario Draghi, 'The future of European competitiveness', Brussels, 9 September 2024. https://commission.europa.eu/topics/eu-competitiveness/draghi-report_en.

138. Market capitalisation of top global banks, 2024: in September 2024, the market capitalisation J.P. Morgan was €540 billion, against a total of €545 billion for the top twelve euro-area lenders, ranging from BNP Paribas, Santander and Intesa (each around €70 billion to €75 billion) to Commerzbank and Société Generale (€18 billion each).

139. J.P. Morgan's valuation at the end of November 2024 was $700 billion.

140. https://www.statista.com/statistics/262742/countries-with-the-highest-military-spending/.

141. Draghi, 'The future of European competitiveness', p. 3.

142. Dominique Moïsi, interview with author, Paris, 10 October 2023. Macron's first Sorbonne speech was on 26 September 2017.

143. Marek Belka, interview with author, Brussels, 29 November 2023.

144. Sylvie Kauffmann, 'Europe urgently needs a dose of Franco-German couples therapy', *Financial Times*, 14 October 2024. https://www.ft.com/content/73049759-3871-457a-a665-49e18736ccb9.

145. See 'Szenen einer Entfremdung' ['Scenes of an estrangement'], *Der Spiegel*, 2 November 2024.

146. François Villeroy de Galhau, interview with author, Paris, 14 February 2022.

147. Jens Weidmann and Villeroy de Galhau wrote a symbolically important joint article in 2016 promoting a common European treasury and finance ministry – an objective that both knew was highly unlikely to prove feasible in the foreseeable future. 'Europa braucht mehr Investitionen' ['Europe needs more investment'], *Süddeutsche Zeitung*, 8 February 2016.

148. Villeroy de Galhau, 'The reawakening of Europe and the Franco-German engine', lecture, Frankfurt School of Finance and Management, 12 December 2023.

149. '25 Jahre Euro', Stiftung Geld und Währung, 7 June 2024. https://www.bundesfinanzministerium.de/Monatsberichte/Ausgabe/2024/06/Inhalte/Kapitel-2-Fokus/25-jahre-euro-pdf.pdf?__blob=publicationFile&v=4.

150. Otmar Issing, statement, conference on '25 years Euro', Berlin, 7 June 2024. Macron's second Sorbonne speech was on 24 April 2024.

151. Mitterrand statement, TV debate, September 1992.

152. Florian Toncar, statement, conference, '25 years Euro', Berlin, 7 June 2024. A week previously, Standard & Poor's rating agency had downgraded France from 'double A' to 'double A minus' because of higher than planned deficits and political fragmentation. Giorgio Leali, 'France hit by ratings downgrade despite spending-cuts crusade', *Politico*, 1 June 2024. https://www.politico.eu/article/france-hit-by-ratings-downgrade-despite-spending-cuts-crusade/.

153. The sole other triple A borrowers, outside the EU, are Australia, Canada, Hong Kong, Liechtenstein, Norway, Singapore.

154. ECB press release, 21 July 2022. https://www.ecb.europa.eu/press/pr/date/2022/html/ecb.pr220721~973e6e7273.en.html.

155. Marsh, *The Euro*. See Chapter 7.

156. The combined GDP in 2024 of Croatia (accession 2023), Estonia (2011), Latvia (2014) and Lithuania (2015) was $261 billion ($488 billion in international dollars, PPP basis). The combined GDP of Cyprus (2008), Malta (2008), Slovakia (2009) and Slovenia (2007) was $272 billion ($463 billion, PPP basis). The combined GDP of the eight newcomers was therefore $533 billion ($951 billion, PPP basis). With Greece, the combined GDP of the nine countries was $790 billion ($1.4 trillion, PPP basis). Austria's GDP in 2024 was $521 billion; Bulgaria's $112 billion. Argentina, Malaysia and the Philippines each generated GDP on a PPP basis of $1.4 trillion in 2024; the figures were $1.7 trillion for Vietnam and $1.8 trillion for Thailand. IMF World Economic Outlook, Database, April 2025.

157. The five outside are Poland (No. 6), Sweden (7), Denmark (11), Romania (12) and the Czech Republic (13).

158. Europe's top sixteen economies (not counting Russia) measured by GDP, ranked in order on a PPP basis, are Germany, the UK, France, Italy, Spain, the Netherlands, Poland, Switzerland, Romania, Belgium, Ireland, Sweden, Austria, Czech Republic, Portugal and Norway. IMF WEO Database, October 2023.

159. Draghi, speech, Global Investment Conference, London, 26 July 2012. The ECB president termed the euro as 'a bumblebee . . . it shouldn't fly'. He took for his opening statement a phrase used in a *Financial Times* editorial: 'Happy 10th anniversary, Emu'. 'European monetary union is a bumble-bee that has taken flight', *Financial Times*, 25 May 2008.

160. Ben Bernanke, interview with author, email, 29 December 2023.

161. Nout Wellink, 'ECB must provide explanations on bond programmes', OMFIF, 19 August 2022.

162. Tim Geithner, *Stress Test: Reflections on Financial Crises* (New York: Crown, 2014), provides an account of long-running travails with the Europeans over Greece and other problem countries. On 11 November 2014 the *Financial Times* revealed the following episodes, based on transcripts of preparatory interviews Geithner gave to assistants: 1) Geithner describes a G7 finance ministers' meeting in the remote Canadian town of Iqaluit in February 2010, at the start of the euro debt crisis. He recalls 'complete carnage [on financial markets] because of people [who] were saying: crisis in Greece, who's exposed to Greece?' The Europeans 'came into that meeting basically saying: "We're going to teach the Greeks a lesson."' He recalls saying: 'You can put your foot on the neck of those guys if that's what you want to do. But you've got to make sure that you send a countervailing signal of reassurance to Europe and the world that you're going to hold the thing together and not let it go.' 2) Geithner records his furious reaction to the October 2010 'Deauville declaration' by Merkel and Sarkozy that future euro area bailouts could include forcing losses on holders of EU government bonds – a move which sparked broader selling of European debt. During a G7 call during a US holiday, Geithner joined with Trichet in opposing the declaration: 'If you guys do that . . . all you will do is accelerate the run from Europe. No one will lend a dollar, a euro to a European government.' 3) Geithner recounts his frosty reception at a meeting of EU finance ministers in Poland in September 2011, when he urged stronger action to protect the euro area. 'They asked me to come to the fucking meeting. I call them in advance and say: "You really sure you want me to come? It's kind of a sensitive thing for me to come to your meeting." They turn to me in their meeting, they ask me for my views . . . and a bunch of their ministers go walk out afterwards and say: "Who's Geithner to tell us what to do?" Very disparaging, like quite disrespectful from their peripheral ministers.' 4) Geithner relates a plan by EU leaders to deny financial aid to Italy unless Silvio Berlusconi, then Italian prime minister, resigned, which Geithner told Barack Obama not to enact at a November 2011 G20 summit in Cannes. He told Obama: 'We can't have blood on our hands.' He adds: '[T]o be sympathetic to them, the Germans' experience has been every time they buy a little bit of calm [on the] markets and the Italian spreads start to come down, Berlusconi reneges on anything he committed to do. So they were just paranoid that every act of generosity was met by sort of a "fuck you" from the establishment of the weaker countries in Europe.' 5) Geitner adds background to the impromptu nature of the 'whatever it takes' speech in July 2012, based on a discussion with Draghi afterwards. 'He was in London at a meeting

with a bunch of hedge funds and bankers. He was troubled by how direct they were in Europe, because at that point all the hedge fund community thought that Europe was coming to an end.'

163. Geithner, *Stress Test*, p. 82.
164. Richard McGregor, 'Euro crisis reveals limits of US leadership, White House frustrated and helpless', *Financial Times*, 2 November 2011. 'Mr Obama has made numerous personal phone calls to European leaders, Angela Merkel and Nicolas Sarkozy, in particular. Tim Geithner, the Treasury Secretary, has likewise logged long hours on the issue.' There is little doubt that the report was based on a briefing by Geithner, who met Lionel Barber (editor) and McGregor in the 'Secretary's Small Conference Room' at 12.45 to 1.20 p.m. on 1 November, according to Treasury records.
165. Geithner, *Stress Test*, p. 438.
166. Geithner, interview with author (video), New York–London, 12 June 2023.
167. Joachim Nagel and Villeroy de Galhau, 'Franco-German dialogue is needed now more than ever', *Frankfurter Allgemeine Zeitung* and *Le Monde*, 22 November 2024.
168. The central bank governors called for a deepening of Europe's single market, a 'savings and investments union' to integrate capital markets, less bureaucracy to drive innovation and more cooperation in defence.
169. China made up 18.8 per cent of the world economy on a purchasing-power parity (PPP) basis in 2022–3, up more than fivefold from 3.7 per cent in 1988. Over that period France's share fell from 4 per cent to 2.2 per cent, Germany's from 5.7 per cent to 3.2 per cent, and Italy's from 4.3 per cent to 1.8 per cent. The US share fell by a smaller amount, from 22 per cent to 15.5 per cent.
170. In 1985 to 1989, France achieved real GDP growth of 3.2 per cent, Germany and Italy 3 per cent, the Netherlands 3.4 per cent, Spain 4.4 per cent and the UK 3.8 per cent. The figures for these six countries from 2017 to 2021 were, respectively, 1.0 per cent, 0.8 per cent, 0.2 per cent, 1.8 per cent, 0.5 per cent and 0.4 per cent.
171. Average euro area GDP compared with the US has fallen sharply by 10 percentage points. According to the World Bank, inflation-adjusted GDP in the euro area was 60.3 per cent of the American figure in 2023, against 70.4 per cent in 2008.
172. Jacques de Larosière, email exchange with author, 5 September 2024.
173. Jacques de Larosière, *France's Decline: Is It Reversible?* (Paris: Odile Jacob, 2024), pp. 9, 141.
174. Tim Adams, interview with author, Washington, 2 June 2023.
175. Gordon Brown, interview with author, London, 28 September 2023.
176. Jürgen Stark, interview with author, Frankfurt, 15 December 2023.
177. Christian Sewing, speech, AFME–OMFIF conference, Frankfurt, 23 May 2023. See also 'Searching for growth: the future of EU capital markets', *New Financial*, September 2024. https://www.newfinancial.org/reports/searching-for-growth%3A-the-future-of-eu-capital-markets.
178. European parliament website, Lisbon, European Council 23 and 24 March 2000 Presidency Conclusion.
179. Europe 2020 strategy with foreword by José Manuel Barroso, 3 March 2010. https://ec.europa.eu/eu2020/pdf/COMPLET%20EN%20BARROSO%20%20%20007%20-%20Europe%202020%20-%20EN%20version.pdf. See Chapter 2.
180. 'The future of European competitiveness', Draghi report, Brussels, 10 September 2024. The document makes limited reference to previous efforts at rectifying a long-perceived problem: 'Europe has been worrying about slowing growth since the start of this century. Various strategies to raise growth rates have come and gone, but the trend has remained unchanged.'
181. Ravi Menon, interview with author (video), Singapore–London, 27 August 2024.
182. Of total global funding for AI start-ups, 61 per cent goes to US companies, 17 per cent to China and 6 per cent to the EU. The EU's share of global technology revenues dropped from 22 per cent in 2013 to 18 per cent in 2023, while the US share rose from 30 per cent to 38 per cent. Draghi recorded: 'There is no EU company with a

market capitalisation over €100 billion that has been set up from scratch in the last 50 years, while all six US companies with a valuation above €1 trillion have been created in this period.' Draghi, 'The future of European competitiveness'.

183. Of the top 20 highest-capitalised stock-market-quoted companies in the world in 2023, fifteen were from the US, with two from Europe, and one each from Saudi Arabia, Taiwan and China. American firms made up twenty-three of the top thirty. For a list of 1990 companies ranked by turnover, see https://archive.globalpolicy.org/component/content/article/221-transnational-corporations/47187-the-worlds-100-largest-corporations.html. For a 1989 list based on stock market value, see https://www.cnbc.com/2014/04/29/what-a-difference-25-years-makes.html. For 2023 updates, see https://www.statista.com/statistics/263264/top-companies-in-the-world-by-market-capitalization/.

184. The German DAX-40 market capitalisation was $1.9 trillion in March 2025.

185. Øystein Olsen, interview with author, Stavanger, 5 June 2024.

186. Ana Botin, discussion at Banco Santander international banking conference, Madrid, 31 October 2023.

187. For further background, see Yasmeen Serhan, 'Boris Johnson shattered Britain's political norms. Ultimately, that was his undoing', *Time*, 3 September 2022, quoting Andrew Gimson on Johnson's impact on the Leave campaign. https://time.com/6210260/boris-johnson-legacy-british-politics/.

188. Christine Lagarde, interview with author, Frankfurt, 25 April 2023.

189. After his resignation from parliament, Johnson resumed his former profession as a journalist, writing a well-paid weekly column in the *Daily Mail*. He produced his memoirs *Unleashed* (London: William Collins) in 2024.

190. Dominic Grieve, interview with author, London, 13 July 2023.

191. Pasquale Terracciano, interview with author, Rome, 9 March 2023.

192. Kenneth Clarke, interview with author, London, 2 May 2023.

193. 'Johnson has thrown US ambassador under the bus, say top Tories', *Guardian*, 10 July 2019.

194. Kim Darroch, interview with author, London, 3 April 2023. Johnson told Darroch in a phone call that he was 'sorry' that his failure to support him had led to Darroch's decision. 'There was a certain tension in the atmosphere,' Darroch recalls, 'but our parting words were amicable.' Darroch, *Collateral Damage: Britain, America and Europe in the Age of Trump* (London: William Collins, 2020), p. 261.

195. Jacob Rees-Mogg, interview with author, London, 16 May 2023.

196. George Parker, Sebastian Payne and Laura Hughes, 'The inside story of Liz Truss's disastrous 44 days in office', *Financial Times*, 8 December 2022. https://www.ft.com/content/736a695d-61f6-4e84-a567-fb92ed2a3dca.

197. Ignazio Visco, governor, Banca d'Italia, lecture, London, 20 April 2023. Commenting on UK financial market upheavals after unfunded tax cuts on 23 September 2022, Visco said, 'We have learnt from that.' This was an allusion to the hitherto orthodox economic policies followed by Giorgia Meloni, heavily influenced by the negative response to the UK fiscal measures, which led to the ousting of Prime Minister Liz Truss. 'Ignazio Visco warns euro area against going too far with tightening', OMFIF, 21 April 2023. https://www.omfif.org/2023/04/ignazio-visco-warns-euro-area-against-going-too-far-with-tightening/.

198. Corsepius, interview with author, Berlin, 24 May 2023.

199. Issing, 'Separating fact from illusion – British EU departure would strengthen protectionism,' OMFIF, 2 March 2016.

200. Issing, interview with author, Würzburg, 5 April 2023.

201. Zoellick, interview with author, telephone, Washington–Berlin, 27 July 2023.

202. Bob Kimmitt, interview with author (video), Washington–London, 3 July 2023.

203. Bob Kimmitt, interview with author, Washington, 26 April 2025.

204. Richard Clarida, interview with author (video), New York–London, 15 August 2024.

2 BETWEEN THE SUPERPOWERS

1. Churchill, telegram to Truman, 12 May 1945. UKNA, CAB 120/186. https://www.nationalarchives.gov.uk/education/resources/cold-war-on-file/churchill-post-yalta/. See Gilbert, *Winston S. Churchill*, vol. VIII, p. 7.
2. Memorandum, Mao Zedong–Helmut Schmidt conversation, Beijing, 20 October 1975, AAPD 1975, Document 323, pp. 1495–9.
3. Trump, press conference with Ursula von der Leyen, European Commission president, Turnberry, Scotland, 27 July 2025. https://www.youtube.com/watch?v=lFyqK3x2CyQ.
4. China had a GDP of $35 trillion in 2024 according to IMF data, on a PPP basis (adjusting for exchange rate distortions) against $29 trillion for the US and $28 trillion for the EU. Using current dollars, the figures are: China and EU each $19 trillion, US $27 trillion.
5. Lisbon European Council, Presidency conclusions, 23 and March 2000. 'The Lisbon strategy five years on', European Central Bank monthly bulletin, July 2005. The ECB recorded, 'The results are at best mixed.'
6. 'A global strategy for the European Union's foreign and security policy', European high representative for foreign affairs and security policy, 14 November 2016.
7. Nicole Koenig, 'The geopolitical Commission and its pitfalls', Hertie School/Jacques Delors Centre, 2 December 2019.
8. Josep Borrell, high representative/vice president-designate, European parliament, 7 October 2019.
9. Letter, Borrell to EU foreign ministers, December 2019. https://www.politico.eu/article/on-foreign-policy-josep-borrell-urges-eu-to-be-a-player-not-the-playground-balkans/.
10. 'How the EU succumbed to Trump's tariff steamroller', *Financial Times*, 27 July 2025. https://www.ft.com/content/85d57e0e-0c6f-4392-a68c-81866e1519c3.
11. Richard von Weizsäcker, speech on the fortieth anniversary of Germany's constitution, Bonn, 24 May 1989.
12. Draghi, 'The future of European competitiveness'.
13. 'The inconvenient truth about Ursula von der Leyen', *Politico*, 2 July 2019.
14. 'The EU's plan for critical technologies ends up as a shadow of the promised sovereignty fund', *Science Business*, 15 February 2024.
15. 'Russia puts Estonian prime minister Kaja Kallas on wanted list', *Guardian*, 13 February 2024.
16. Kaja Kallas, 'Wir müssen stark bleiben' ['We must remain strong'], interview, *Süddeutsche Zeitung*, 14 December 2024.
17. Kallas, statement, Brussels, 16 December 2024.
18. See, for a diverse range of effects: 'China says Trump's crackdown on Harvard "will only damage" US', CBS News, 23 May 2025. https://www.cbsnews.com/news/trump-harvard-international-students-china-says-crackdown-will-damage-us/; James Crabtree, 'Trump could make China great again', *Foreign Policy*, 18 February 2025. https://foreignpolicy.com/2025/02/18/trump-us-china-hawks-pivot-asia-pacific-europe-russia-nato/; Ryan Hass, 'Why Trump will blink first on China', *Time*, 25 April 2025. https://time.com/7279900/trump-xi-us-china-trade-war/; and Yun Sun, 'How China would tackle a second Trump term', Brookings, 31 May 2024. https://www.brookings.edu/articles/how-china-would-tackle-a-second-trump-term/.
19. Juncker, interview, *Der Spiegel*, 30 November 2024.
20. Harriet Clarfelt and Kate Duguid, 'Investors shift away from US bond market on fears over Donald Trump's policies', *Financial Times*, 23 May 2025. See also Barry Eichengreen, 'Can the dollar remain king of currencies?', *Financial Times*, 22 March 2025.
21. For a range of views on the tariff question, see 'Economists offer differing views on Trump's tariffs and trade war', PBS News, 30 April 2025. https://www.pbs.org/newshour/show/economists-offer-differing-views-on-trumps-tariffs-and-trade-war.
22. Conley, interview with author, Washington, 23 June 2023.
23. Nathan Sheets, statement at OMFIF seminar, Washington, 26 October 2024.

24. Richard Baldwin, 'China is the world's sole manufacturing superpower: A line sketch of the rise', CEPR, 17 January 2024. https://cepr.org/voxeu/columns/china-worlds-sole-manu-facturing-superpower-line-sketch-rise.

25. 'Trump announces sweeping new tariffs to promote US manufacturing, risking inflation and trade wars', Associated Press, 2 April 2025.

26. 'Trump may have just ended globalization as we know it', *Washington Post*, 4 April 2025, quoting Carmen Reinhart, former chief economist of the World Bank, now a Harvard professor. https://www.washingtonpost.com/business/2025/04/04/trump-tariffs-plan-economic-policy-free-trade/.

27. Colin Grabow, Scott Lincicome and Kyle Handley, 'More about Trump's sham "reciprocal" tariffs', Cato Institute, 3 April 2025. https://www.cato.org/blog/more-about-trumps-sham-reciprocal-tariffs.

28. 'Trump announces tariffs at "Make America Wealthy Again" event, United Press International, 2 April 2025. https://www.upi.com/Top_News/US/2025/04/02/trump-tariffs/8981743623481/.

29. Trump, inauguration speech transcript, *Politico*, 20 January 2017. https://www.politico.com/story/2017/01/full-text-donald-trump-inauguration-speech-transcript-233907.

30. 'Making America wealthy: A brief history on William McKinley, the "Napoleon of Protection"'. https://www.stateoftheunionhistory.com/p/making-america-wealthy-brief-history-on.html.

31. US Global Investors, 28 February 2025. https://www.usfunds.com/resource/president-mckinleys-tariff-mishap-could-be-a-warning-sign-for-trumps-trade-war/. Nathan Carden, 'Donald Trump and William McKinley: What can the past tell us about the political risks of tariffs?', University of Birmingham, 4 April 2025. https://www.birmingham.ac.uk/news/2025/donald-trump-and-william-mckinley-what-can-the-past-tell-us-about-the-political-risks-of-tariffs.

32. Pascale Riché, 'Trump doesn't know it, but his protectionist hero, McKinley, ended up changing his stance', *Le Monde* (international), 3 April 2025. https://www.lemonde.fr/en/opinion/article/2025/04/03/trump-doesn-t-know-it-but-his-protectionist-hero-mckinley-ended-up-changing-his-stance_6739804_23.html. Douglas Irwin, 'Why Trump's trade hero turned away from tariffs', CNN/Econbrowser, 15 September 2024. https://econ-browser.com/archives/2024/09/doug-irwin-on-cnn-mckinley-and-tariffs.

33. McKinley, speech, Pan-American exposition, Buffalo, 5 September 1901. https://archive.org/stream/lastspeechofpres00mcki/lastspeechofpres00mcki_djvu.txt. See also Zoellick, *America in the World*, p. 222.

34. 'President Donald J. Trump declares national emergency to increase our competitive edge, protect our sovereignty, and strengthen our national and economic security', White House statement, 2 April 2025. https://www.whitehouse.gov/fact-sheets/2025/04/fact-sheet-president-donald-j-trump-declares-national-emergency-to-increase-our-competitive-edge-protect-our-sovereignty-and-strengthen-our-national-and-economic-security/.

35. 'S&P 500 down over 10% in 2 days as Trump upends the global order', *New York Times*, 4 April 2025. https://www.nytimes.com/live/2025/04/04/business/trump-tariffs-stocks-economy.

36. Jerome Powell, speech, Washington, 4 April 2025. https://www.federalreserve.gov/newsevents/speech/powell20250404a.htm.

37. Richard Haas, 'Cry havoc', 4 April 2025. https://richardhaass.substack.com/p/cry-havoc-april-4-2025. Haas was president, US Council on Foreign Relations, 2003–23.

38. A constant refrain from Chinese policy propagandists has been that US tariff policy will prove counterproductive. See, for example, 'Washington's extreme tariff strikes will back-fire', *China Daily*, 27 April 2025. The article claimed the US strategy was 'not just short-sighted – it's self-sabotaging'. https://www.chinadaily.com.cn/a/202504/27/WS680d6b0da3104d9fd3821c4f.html.

39. Gideon Rachman, *Financial Times*, 22 July 2009, quoting Reginald Dale (a former *Financial Times* journalist): 'According to the late Peter Rodman, who knew him well, the saying is apocryphal.' Henry Kissinger was 'fed up' with having to deal with an 'incompe-

tent and ineffective' president of the Council. Kissinger was 'seeking to divide and rule in Europe, rather than be restricted to a single voice on the telephone'.

40. Willam Wallace and Jan Zielonka, 'Misunderstanding Europe', *Foreign Affairs*, 1 November 1998.

41. John F. Kennedy, press conference, Washington, 10 August 1961. John F. Kennedy Library. https://www.jfklibrary.org/archives/other-resources/john-f-kennedy-press-conferences/news-conference-15.

42. Statement by Admiral William Crowe, chairman, joint chiefs of staff, in Michael R. Beschloss and Strobe Talbott, *At the Highest Levels: The Inside Story of the End of the Cold War* (Boston, MA: Little, Brown, 1993), p. 76.

43. Robert Gates, *Duty: Memoirs of a Secretary at War* (New York: Alfred A. Knopf, 2014), pp. 193–4.

44. Obama: statement, Hanover trade fair, 25 April 2016; press conference, Warsaw, 3 June 2014; press conference, Rome, 27 March 2014.

45. Mike Pence, speech, Munich Security Conference, 17 February 2017.

46. J.D. Vance, speech, Munich Security Conference, 14 February 2025.

47. Daniel Friedrich Sturm, 'Die Deutschen ohne Joe Biden', *Tagesspiegel*, 30 July 2024.

48. Bruce Stokes, 'All is not well in the transatlantic relationship', *Politico*, 10 January 2022.

49. James E. Hewes, Jr., 'Henry Cabot Lodge and the League of Nations', *Proceedings of the American Philosophical Society*, vol. 114, no. 4 (20 August 1970).

50. John H. Maurer, 'Forced into the shade: Winston Churchill and America's naval challenge', *Diplomacy & Statecraft*, vol. 35, issue 3, 2024. Christopher M. Bell, 'Thinking the unthinkable: British and American naval strategies for an Anglo-American War, 1918–1931', *International History Review*, vol. 19, no. 4 (November 1997).

51. R.J. Reinhart, 'Gallup vault: U.S. opinion and the start of World War II', 29 August 2019. https://news.gallup.com/vault/265865/gallup-vault-opinion-start-world-war.aspx. 'The great debate', National WWII Museum, New Orleans. https://www.nationalww2museum.org/war/articles/great-debate.

52. Wayne S. Cole, 'The America First committee', *Journal of the Illinois State Historical Society*, vol. 44, no. 4 (Winter 1951), pp. 305–22.

53. 'Lend-Lease and military aid to the Allies in the early years of World War II', Office of the Historian. https://history.state.gov/milestones/1937-1945/lend-lease.

54. https://history.blog.gov.uk/2021/07/28/whats-the-context-signature-of-the-atlantic-charter-14-august-1941/. https://avalon.law.yale.edu/wwii/atlantic.asp.

55. Benn Steil, *The Marshall Plan: Dawn of the Cold War* (New York: Simon & Schuster, 2018), p. 3. 'Home alive by '45': Operation Magic Carpet', National WWII Museum, New Orleans, 2 October 2020. https://www.nationalww2museum.org/war/articles/operation-magic-carpet-1945. John Lewis Gaddis: 'The US had made no commitment to reverse its long-standing tradition of remaining aloof from European affairs – Roosevelt had even assured Stalin at Tehran [November–December 1943] that American troops would return home within two years after the end of the war.' John Lewis Gaddis, *The Cold War* (New York: Penguin, 2005), p. 9, citing Warren F. Kimball, *The Juggler: Franklin Roosevelt as Wartime Statesman* (Princeton, NJ: Princeton University Press, 1991), pp. 97–9. Roosevelt advised Churchill on 18 November 1944: 'You know, of course, that after Germany's collapse I must bring American troops home as rapidly as transport problems will permit.' Herbert Feis, *Churchill, Roosevelt, Stalin* (Princeton, NJ: Princeton University Press, 1957), p. 472.

56. Martin Gilbert, *Churchill: A Life* (London: William Heinemann, 1991), pp. 843–4.

57. Churchill, telegram to Truman, 12 May 1945. UKNA, CAB 120/186. https://www.nationalarchives.gov.uk/education/resources/cold-war-on-file/churchill-post-yalta/. His public allusion to an 'iron curtain' came in a celebrated speech in Fulton, Missouri, on 6 March 1946. See Gilbert, *Winston S. Churchill*, vol. VIII, p. 7.

58. Field Marshal Alanbrooke, diary entry, 27 July 1944, quoted in Arthur Bryant, *Triumph in the West, 1943–1946* (London: William Collins, 1959), p. 242. Anne Deighton, *The*

Impossible Peace: Britain, the Division of Germany, and the Origins of the Cold War (Oxford: Clarendon Press, 1990), p. 20.

59. Zoellick, *America in the World*, p. 240.
60. Harry S. Truman, address to Congress, Washington, 12 March 1947. https://www.archives.gov/milestone-documents/truman-doctrine.
61. George C. Marshall, speech, Harvard, 5 June 1947. https://www.marshallfoundation.org/the-marshall-plan/speech/.
62. Forest C. Pogue, *George C. Marshall: Statesman, 1945–1959* (New York: Viking, 1987), pp. 194–6, citing Charles E. Bohlen, *Witness to History, 1929–1969* (New York: W.W. Norton, 1973), p. 263. See also Zoellick, *America in the World*, p. 267.
63. Andrew Adonis, *Ernest Bevin: Labour's Churchill* (London: Biteback, 2021), p. xiv.
64. Orme Sargent, permanent undersecretary, British foreign office, in Anne Deighton, *The Impossible Peace: Britain, the Division of Germany and the Origins of the Cold War* (Oxford: Clarendon Press, 1990), p. 73.
65. Victor Gollancz, *In Darkest Germany: The Record of a Visit* (London: Gollancz, 1947).
66. Steil, *The Marshall Plan*, p. 12.
67. Central Intelligence Agency, 'Review of the world situation as it relates to the security of the United States', 26 September 1947, Box 203. See also A.P. Central, 'Cold War and global hegemony, 1945–1991'. https://apcentral.collegeboard.org/series/america-on-the-world-stage/cold-war-and-global-hegemony-1945-1991.
68. 'Suez crisis: key players', BBC, 21 July 2006. http://news.bbc.co.uk/1/hi/in_depth/5195582.stm.
69. 'Nixon and the end of the Bretton Woods system, 1971–1973', Office of the Historian. https://history.state.gov/milestones/1969-1976/nixon-shock.
70. Ksenia Demidova, *European Integration and the Atlantic Community in the 1980s*, Chapter 4: 'The deal of the century: The Reagan administration and the Soviet pipeline' (Cambridge: Cambridge University Press, 2013). https://www.cambridge.org/core/books/abs/european-integration-and-the-atlantic-community-in-the-1980s/deal-of-the-century-the-reagan-administration-and-the-soviet-pipeline/07A6DC112C2148F61BD8EE190EA394F4.
71. 'Merkel criticises US over crisis', *Financial Times*, 26 November 2008.
72. 'Geithner's "succinct" message irks Europeans', Reuters, 16 September 2011. https://www.reuters.com/article/world/uk/geithners-succinct-message-irks-europeans-idUSTRE78F4FF/.
73. Dwight Eisenhower, conversation, 6 February 1956, in Geir Lundestad, *'Empire' by Integration: The United States and European Integration, 1945–1997* (New York: Oxford University Press, 1998), p. 6.
74. NIC is an agency that forms part of the Office of the Director of National Intelligence, Washington.
75. Alex Barker, 'Europe: A hobbled giant', *Financial Times*, 21 November 2008. https://www.ft.com/content/5b2bb216-01cc-3983-bb38-93e34e2aca40. John Wyles, 'How ageing and the Russian mafia will add to the EU's woes', Politico, 26 November 2008. https://www.politico.eu/article/how-ageing-and-the-russian-mafia-will-add-to-the-eus-woes/.
76. William I. Hitchcock, *The Struggle for Europe: The Turbulent History of a Divided Continent, 1945–2002* (New York: Doubleday, 2003), pp. 463–4.
77. 'An economic "friendship" that could rattle the world', *Financial Times*, 14 May 2024.
78. 'A steadfast constructive force in a changing world', Wang Yi, Chinse foreign minister, speech, Munich Security Conference, 14 February 2025.
79. 'Europe should get its own house in order', *China Daily*, 3 March 2025. '[Europe's] reliance on Nato and that organisation's expansionism and relentless roll towards Russia's border . . . has been a principal factor in triggering the conflict.'
80. 'EU businesses warned of China challenge', EU Chamber of Commerce in China report, *Financial Times*, 10 May 2024.
81. US productivity per head has advanced by roughly double the pace in Europe since 2000.

82. 'Europe's economy poised to fall further behind US, IMF warns', Financial Times, 24 October 2024. https://www.ft.com/content/7d431fd6-3146-462f-aafb-f687 30fd6c0c.

83. Ian Bond et al., 'Can Europe navigate Trump-2?', Centre for European Reform, 8 November 2024.

84. Sarang Shidor, 'The quiet development shaking America's power', New York Times, 11 November 2024.

85. Barry Eichengreen, 'Resetting US–China economic relations', Project Syndicate, 10 September 2024.

86. Marco Rubio, remarks, Senate Foreign Relations Committee, Washington, 15 January 2025.

87. Christoph Heusgen, interview with author (video), Munich–Stuttgart, 6 September 2024. Establishment of a National Security Council was one of the foreign policy features of the coalition agreement for Germany's Merz-led government unveiled in April 2025. 'The CDU/CSU and SPD coalition treaty: What it contains', Deutschlandfunk, 10 April 2024. https://www.deutschland.de/en/topic/politics/coalition-treaty-new-federal-government-germany-overview.

88. Merkel, Freedom, p. 586.

89. Merkel, Freedom, p. 588.

90. Jürgen Hambrecht, interview with author, Neustadt an der Weinstrasse, 21 December 2022.

91. Robert Habeck, speech, Bundestag, Berlin, 16 December 2024.

92. For a historical analysis, see Otmar Emminger, 'The D-Mark in the conflict between internal and external equilibrium, 1948–75', no. 122, Essays in International Finance, Princeton University, June 1977.

93. Haizhou Huang statement, OMFIF meeting, London, 5 November 2024.

94. Zoellick, interview with author, Berlin–Washington, 27 July 2023.

95. Reuter, interview with author, Stuttgart, 6 September 2023.

96. Ola Källenius, interview, Süddeutsche Zeitung, 15 December 2024.

97. Clarke, interview with author, London, 2 May 2023.

98. 'How national security has transformed economic policy', Financial Times, 4 September 2024.

99. Draghi, speech, Rome, 6 May 2013.

100. Ignazio Visco, speech, Rome, 15 November 2019.

101. Draghi, 'The future of European competitiveness', report, Brussels, 9 September 2024.

102. 'Brussels explores Draghi option of extending up to €350bn in EU debt', Financial Times, 12 September 2024.

103. Christian Lindner statement, X, 9 September 2024.

104. Draghi, press conference, Brussels, 9 September 2024.

105. Juncker, 'Completing Europe's economic and monetary union', 2015, in cooperation with Donald Tusk, Jeroen Dijsselbloem, Mario Draghi and Martin Schulz.

106. Draghi, press conference, Brussels, 9 September 2024.

107. 'Can Trump do a "reverse Nixon" and break China and Russia apart?', Times of India, 21 February 2025. http://timesofindia.indiatimes.com/articleshow/118455140.cms?utm_source=contentofinterest&utm_medium=text&utm_campaign=cppst. For a view on China's background role in Trump's policies at the start of in his first term, see Ariel Cohen, 'Beyond the Trump–Putin warmth, tough decisions lurk', Financial Times, 6 December 2016. https://www.ft.com/content/418aa2d5-f9f5-31a5-89f4-4567afb470bb.

108. Sanshiro Hosaka, 'Why the "Reverse Nixon" strategy will fail: The illusion of decoupling', International Centre for Defence and Security, 1 March 2025. https://www.jstor.org/stable/resrep68500?seq=1. Michael McFaul and Evan Medeiros, 'China and Russia will not be split: The "Reverse Kissinger" delusion', Foreign Affairs, 4 April 2025.

109. Robert Dohner, Atlantic Council, former deputy assistant secretary, US Treasury, conversation with author, Washington, 25 April 2025. See also 'Böses Amerika, gutes China' ['Bad America, good China'], Der Spiegel, 5 April 2025, p. 8.

110. Norbert Tofall, 'Trump's two grave geostrategic errors: Trump making Russia and China the beneficiaries of his Ukraine and European policy completely undermines US interests', Global Ideas Center, Berlin, *The Globalist*, 26 March 2025. https://www.theglobalist.com/russia-china-united-states-europe-geopolitics-ukraine-war-donald-trump-vladimir-putin/.
111. Klaas Knot, 'China may start selling its products to Europe at discounted rates if the US starts a trade war by imposing new tariffs', interview, *Volkskrant*, 30 December 2024. https://www.bnnbloomberg.ca/business/international/2024/12/30/ecbs-knot-says-trade-war-could-export-china-deflation-to-europe/.
112. Deutsche Bundesbank, monthly report, January 2024.
113. 'Can Europe go green without China?', *Financial Times*, 21 September 2023.
114. Garret Martin, 'Playing the China card? Revisiting France's recognition of Communist China, 1963–64', *Journal of Cold War Studies*, vol. 10, no. 1 (Winter 2008), pp. 52–80.
115. Memorandum, Mao–Schmidt conversation, Beijing, 20 October 1975. The official German transcript of the conversation states that the three female interpreters often had great difficulty deciphering Mao's statements. AAPD 1975, Document 323, pp. 1495–9.
116. Letter, Schmidt to Schröder, 28 October 1999, in Gregor Schöllgen, *Gerhard Schröder: Die Biographie* (Stuttgart: Deutsche Verlags-Anstalt, 2015), p. 455.
117. Schröder, interview, *Der Spiegel*, 27 December 1999.
118. Merkel, *Freiheit*, p. 709. In the English translation, *Freedom*, pp. 677–8.
119. Burns, statement, *Financial Times* Festival, London, 7 September 2024.
120. Liana Fix and Heidi Crebo-Rediker, 'China's double threat to Europe: How Beijing's support for Moscow and quest for EV dominance undermine European security', *Foreign Affairs*, 5 September 2024.
121. In 2019, the EU approved a strategy document declaring that China was at the same time a partner, competitor and systemic rival. The EU has maintained that nomenclature since then, but now places more emphasis on the systemic rivalry. In December 2020, China and the EU agreed on the text of a 'Comprehensive Agreement on Investment', to facilitate investment between them. Germany's then chancellor, Angela Merkel, pushed strongly for the treaty.
122. As examples of China's increased activity, it has raised the stakes in its dispute with Japan over the Senkaku/Diaoyu islands, displayed increasing amounts of military force near Taiwan, built artificial militarised islands to reinforce its claims in the South China Sea, and sanctioned Lithuania for allowing Taiwan to open a representative office in Vilnius.
123. For example, the Switzerland peace summit in June 2024 where neither Russia nor China was represented.
124. Nathaniel Sher, 'Behind the scenes: China's increasing role in Russia's defense industry', *Carnegie Politika*, 6 May 2024.
125. Sher, 'Behind the scenes'. Despite the sensitivity around dual-use trade with Russia, China's General Customs Administration continues to report bilateral transactions, even in areas subject to western export controls. In 2023, China was responsible for roughly 90 per cent of Russia's imports of goods covered under the G7's high-priority export-control list.
126. Xi–Putin talks in Moscow, 23 March 2023. The expression finds resonance in China because Xi is paraphrasing a well-known statement by a nineteenth-century Chinese mandarin who, after the Opium wars forced China to open, spoke of 'changes not seen in 3,000 years'. The author is grateful to Philip Short for pointing this out.
127. 'China's Xi Jinping likens "US hegemony" to "fascist forces" ahead of Vladimir Putin summit', *Financial Times*, 8 May 2025.
128. 'US widens sanctions on Russia to discourage countries such as China from doing business with Moscow', AP News, 12 June 2024.
129. Fix and Crebo-Rediker, 'China's double threat to Europe'.
130. Kurt Campbell, US deputy secretary of state, media briefing, Brussels, 10 September 2024. According to Campbell, the new technologies for Beijing would endanger not just to the US, but also India, Australia, Japan and South Korea. Campbell's allegations came

two weeks after US national security adviser Jake Sullivan undertook his first trip to Beijing.

131. IMF World Economic Outlook, October 2024.
132. Pierre-Olivier Gourinchas, interview with author, Washington, 21 September 2023.
133. Noah Barkin and Gregor Sebastian, 'China in an era of zero-sum competition', Rhodium Group, 15 February 2024.
134. Sebastian de Quant, Sander Tordoir and Shahin Vallée, 'Caught in geopolitical fragmentation: How to de-risk Germany's economic model', Forum for a New Economy, Berlin, 26 January 2024. https://newforum.org/en/studie/caught-in-geopolitical-fragmentation-how-to-de-risk-germanys-economic-model/.
135. 'Why competition with China is getting tougher than ever', Alexander Al-Haschimi, Lorenz Emter, Vanessa Gunnella, Iván Ordoñez Martínez, Tobias Schuler and Tajda Spital, European Central Bank blog, 3 September 2024. https://www.ecb.europa.eu/press/blog/date/2024/html/ecb.blog240903-57f1b63192.en.html.
136. 'Trump imposes 34% reciprocal tariffs on Chinese imports as part of Liberation Day package', *South China Morning Post*, 2 April 2025. https://www.scmp.com/news/us/diplomacy/article/3304971/trump-announced-34-reciprocal-tariffs-chinese-goods-part-liberation-day-package.
137. 'EU industry chief pushes "buy European" in response to Donald Trump', *Financial Times*, 21 May 2025. https://www.ft.com/content/cd3b82a6-49dd-431e-98aa-91ce-46d2aa2c.
138. According to the Draghi competitiveness report, owing to fast innovation, low manufacturing costs and state subsidies four times higher than in other major economies, China dominates global exports of clean technologies. 'Significant overcapacity is expected: by 2030 at the latest, China's annual manufacturing capacity for solar photovoltaic is expected to be double the level of global demand, and for battery cells it is expected to at least cover the level of global demand. Production of EVs is expanding at a similar pace.'
139. Statements by Chinese think-tank representatives to visiting European economists, summer 2024.
140. Charles Grant, CER Annual Report, 18 February 2004. The EU argues that its rising trade deficit with China – almost €400 billion in 2022 compared to €165 billion in 2019 – reflects China's relatively closed markets. 'Meanwhile Europe has become increasingly worried about reliance on China for green technologies, such as solar panels and electric vehicle batteries, as well as for many rare earths.'
141. Joerg Wuttke, interview with author, Washington–London, 20 August 2024.
142. According to International Energy Agency projections, mineral demand for clean-energy technologies is expected to grow four- to sixfold by 2040. However, the supply of CRMs is highly concentrated in a handful of providers, especially for processing and refining, which creates risks of price volatility and exposure to use of CRMs as a geopolitical weapon. 'China is the single largest processer of nickel, copper, lithium and cobalt, accounting for between 35 and 70% of processing activity, and has shown willingness to use its market power for overall political purposes'. Draghi, 'The future of European competitiveness'.
143. In June 2024, the Australian government ordered funds linked to Yuxiao Fund and four associates to reduce or dispose of their stakes in Northern Minerals, a western Australian rare-earths developer, to protect Australian national interest and comply with the country's foreign investment framework.
144. China plans to double the ownership of overseas mines containing critical minerals by Chinese companies. Draghi, 'The future of European competitiveness'.
145. Jin Liqun, interview with author (video), Beijing–Redda, 19 September 2024.
146. Rakesh Mahon, interview with author, Delhi–London, 16 October 2024.
147. 'Nvidia's chief says US chip controls on China have backfired', *New York Times*, 21 May 2025. https://www.nytimes.com/2025/05/21/business/nvidia-china-washington-chip-controls-failure.html.
148. Hambrecht, interview with author, Neustadt an der Weinstrasse, 21 December 2022.

149. 'Chinese auto suppliers ponder US production to grow under Trump', *Nikkei Asia*, 9 January 2025.

150. Paul Triolo, interview with author (video), Washington–London, 30 October 2024. See also Triolo, 'The evolution of China's semiconductor industry under US export controls', *American Affairs*, 22 November 2024.

151. For example, the EU currently has no foundry producing below 22nm process nodes and relies on Asia for 75 per cent to 90 per cent of wafer fabrication capacity (as does the US). Europe has become dependent on non-EU countries for chip design, packaging and assembly as well. Dependencies are also acute for other advanced tech. The EU's AI industry relies on hardware produced largely by one US-based company for the most advanced processors. Similarly, Europe's dependence on cloud services developed and run by US companies is massive. For quantum computing platforms, the EU suffers from six critical dependencies across seventeen key technologies, components and materials. China and the US hold technological leadership in most of these critical areas. Draghi, 'The future of European competitiveness'.

152. BRICS group membership was expanded in 2024 to include Egypt, Ethiopia, Iran and the United Arab Emirates. Argentina and Saudi Arabia were invited to join. Argentina later declined the invitation, and Saudi Arabia did not decide immediately whether to accept. Fyodor Lukyanov, chair, Council on Foreign and Defence Policy (Russia), 'BRICS as diversification of the world order', Council of Councils global memo, 7 November 2024. 'An unusual community that does not bear the hallmarks of a traditional international institution. So far, it is a rather amorphous club with a single unifying principle: creating a space for interaction that bypasses Western states and institutions. An overtly anti-Western policy will not prevail in the BRICS, as the overwhelming majority of states there are not interested in aggravating relations with the West. But they are eager to have different options for building political and economic ties, free of US and EU guidance and mechanisms.'

153. Martin Mühleisen, 'The Bretton Woods institutions under geopolitical fragmentation', Atlantic Council, Washington, 9 October 2023. James David Spellman, 'Why the world needs a Bretton Woods 2.0', *South China Morning Post*, 8 May 2024. Alexander Gale, 'China's multilateral influence-building strategy: Threats to an open and stable international order', UK parliament committees, London, 10 February 2024. https://committees.parliament.uk/writtenevidence/128511/pdf.

154. 'US anger at Britain joining Chinese-led investment bank', *Guardian*, 12 March 2015.

155. Like the AIIB, an institution sometimes regarded as its sister, the New Development Bank set up in Shanghai in 2015 and owned by the BRICS countries is a firmly dollar-based bank.

156. Herbert Poenisch, OMFIF commentary, 29 October 2024. Mark Sobel, OMFIF commentary, 2023.

157. Subrahmanyam Jaishankar, interview, *Die Zeit*, 21 February 2024.

158. Kishore Mahbubani, 'It's time for the west and the rest to talk to each other as equals', *Financial Times*, 13 December 2023.

159. Menon, interview with author (video), Singapore–London, 27 August 2024.

160. Jude Blanchette, 'China is in denial about the war in Ukraine', *Foreign Affairs*, 13 August 2024. A series of experts are cited who have seen their sense 'punctured . . . that China, more than any country besides the US, enjoys the capacity to decide the trajectory of the global economy and world events'.

161. This would have stark implications for China: in October 2022, one researcher at China's central bank warned that China must be ready to defend against a US effort 'replicating this financial sanction model against China' if tension rises over Taiwan.

162. Röller, interview with author, Berlin, 19 February 2024.

163. Jörg Kukies, interview with author, Berlin, 6 February 2023.

164. Daleep Singh, interview with author (video), Washington–London, 5 September 2023.

165. For a description of West Germany's leverage over the US and the rest of the West caused by fears of a 'drift to the East, to neutralism', see Marcell von Donat, 'Neutralism in Germany', in *Government and Opposition*, vol. 21, no. 4 (Autumn 1986), pp. 406–19.

166. Hans-Georg Wieck quoted in David Marsh, 'Illusion makes way for reality', *Financial Times*, 28 August 1991.

167. Kissinger, speech, 7 September 2015. See also https://www.henryakissinger.com/remembrances/memorial-remarks-for-egon-bahr.

168. Otto-Axel Herbst, German foreign office director for trade and development policies, memorandum, 20 January 1970, AAPD 1970, Document 23, p. 86. An accord between Ruhrgas and Mannesmann for delivery of gas to Germany and supply of 1.2 million tonnes of pipes had been secured in November–December 1969.

169. Herbst, memorandum, 27 June 1969, AAPD 1969, Document 213, pp. 740–2.

170. Conley, interview with author, Washington, 2 June 2023.

171. Fred Bergsten founded the International Institute for International Economics in 1981 (later Peterson Institute for International Economics), which he ran until 2012.

172. Fred Bergsten, 'The United States and Germany: The imperative of economic bigemony', Brookings Institution, Bonn, 1974.

173. G.H.W. Bush, speech, Mainz, 31 May 1989.

174. Remarks by President Biden on the End of the War in Afghanistan, White House, Washington, 31 August 2021.

175. Author's private information.

176. Martin Selmayr, interview with author, Vienna, 23 January 2023.

177. Richard Burt, interview with author, Bonn, in Marsh, *Germany and Europe*, p. 127.

178. There are echoes of Heinrich Heine's lines: 'Deutschland ist noch ein kleines Kind / Doch die Sonne ist seine Amme / Sie säugt es nicht mit stiller Milch / Sie säugt es mit wilder Flamme' ['Germany's still a little child / And the sun's his nursing maid / She suckles him not on placid milk / But on wild flames unstayed'].

179. Gavin Barwell, interview with author, London, 13 March 2023.

180. Summers, interview with author (video), Scottsdale–London, 28 January 2024.

181. John Kornblum, interviews with author, Berlin, 2022–3. 'Germany has undergone a lot of change over the past 120 years. The East Germans have lived in six different countries: the German empire, the Weimar Republic, the Third Reich, the occupation regime, the German Democratic Republic and now the Federal Republic. This is one of the reasons why, when things change, the Germans like to see it happening slowly. When change does occur, people say things have always been like this. Precisely because of the depth of the changes over the last century, there is a leaning towards orthodoxy and conservatism.'

182. Schmidt, 'Progressive Governance' summit, podium discussion, Berlin, *Guardian*, 13 October 2022.

183. Judy Dempsey, 'German president quits over remarks on military', *New York Times*, 31 May 2010. https://www.nytimes.com/2010/06/01/world/europe/01germany.html. In the radio interview on 22 May, Horst Köhler said a country of Germany's size and reliance on foreign trade 'must be aware that military deployments are necessary in an emergency to protect our interests, for example, when it comes to trade routes, for example, when it comes to preventing regional instabilities that could negatively influence our trade, jobs and incomes.' In his resignation statement he said he regretted his remarks and the way he said they were misunderstood, adding that intense criticism and loss of confidence made it impossible to remain in office.

184. Köhler, interview with author, Berlin, 13 November 2023.

185. Kimmitt, interview with author, Washington, 25 April 2025.

186. Andrew Small, 'The meaning of systemic rivalry: Europe and China beyond the pandemic', European Council on Foreign Relations, 13 May 2020.

187. EU–China Relations fact sheet, EU External Action Service, 7 December 2023. https://www.eeas.europa.eu/eeas/eu-china-relations-factsheet_en.

188. 'China rejects WHO criticism and says Covid lab-leak theory "ruled out"', *Financial Times*, 31 March 2021.

189. European Commission, press release, 30 December 2020. https://ec.europa.eu/commission/presscorner/api/files/document/print/en/ip_20_2542/IP_20_2542_EN.pdf.

190. Schäuble, interview with author, Berlin, 18 January 2021. 'It was a mistake for the EU to agree the China investment deal before the American president. This was the will of Merkel – She wanted to deliver this during the German presidency.'

191. 'EU reaffirms readiness for trade war with China to protect domestic jobs', *Guardian*, 7 May 2024.

192. James Crabtree, 'Why Xi thinks he got the better of Biden', *Foreign Policy*, 1 December 2023. Commenting on the meeting between Xi and Biden in San Francisco on 15 November, Crabtree wrote: 'The summit may have calmed relations, but don't expect that state to last.' He pointed out: 'The decision of countries like the Philippines to move closer to the United States is in large part a response to repeated aggressive behaviour from China. Yet these allies and partners rarely want a worse relationship with China than the United States itself is willing to bear.'

3 RUSSIA, GERMANY AND THE EUROPEAN HOME

1. Memorandum, Charles de Gaulle–Willy Brandt conversation, Paris, 15 December 1966, AAPD 1966, Document 398, pp. 1637–9.

2. Memorandum, Leonid Brezhnev–Helmut Schmidt conversation, Bonn, 23 November 1981, AAPD 1981, Document 334, p. 81.

3. Jörg Kukies, interview with author, Berlin, 6 February 2023. For an account of the role of Kukies and other key players in the Russian asset freeze, see Edward Fishman, Chokepoints: American Power in the Age of Economic Warfare (New York: Portfolio/Penguin, 2025), pp. 338–42.

4. Putin, interview with Keir Simmons, NBC, 11 June 2021. For a view that Putin is likely to remain in power into the 2030s, see Michael Kimmage and Maria Lipman, 'Forever Putinism', *Foreign Affairs*, 13 March 2024.

5. Fiona Hill, 'Are we indulging Putin?', interview with Institute of Art and Ideas, February 2024. https://www.youtube.com/watch?v=pJ7DWLWAsGM.

6. Alastair Campbell, *Diaries*, vol. 3: *Power and Responsibility, 1999–2001* (London: Hutchinson, 2011), 17 May 2000, p. 291, reporting on Putin's talk in London with Prime Minister Tony Blair.

7. Vladimir Putin, *First Person* (New York: Public Affairs, 2000), pp. 78–81. A seminal moment, which Putin and others may later have exaggerated for effect, came on 5 December 1989, when peaceful East German demonstrators converged on the local office of the KGB in Dresden. Putin, concerned about the threat to Soviet authority and the fate of confidential papers in the building, telephoned for armed support from Soviet military forces in the city. The request was rejected since no one in the Soviet chain of command could approve it. Putin's interlocutor explained: 'Moscow is silent.' Putin turned back the protesters by threatening to shoot, then organised a mass burning of incriminating papers. The phrase haunted Putin, he wrote later, as a portent of coming Soviet collapse. 'I got the feeling that the country no longer existed.' See Philip Short, *Putin: His Life and Times* (London: Bodley Head, 2022), pp. 116–18 and Mary Elise Sarotte, *Not One Inch: America, Russia, and the Making of the Post-Cold War Stalemate* (New Haven/London: Yale University Press, 2021), pp. 19–20. In *Putin*, Short says he may have overplayed the episode, pointing out that Soviet forces arrived within half an hour.

8. Putin, 'Russia on the threshold of the new millennium', later known as the 'Millennium Message', Russian government website, 29 December 1999. Fiona Hill and Clifford G. Gaddy, *Mr Putin: Operative in the Kremlin* (Washington, DC: Brookings Institution Press, 2013), pp. 39–40. In late 2024, Putin repeated that Russia had moved back 'from the brink of the abyss' when he assumed power. Press conference, Moscow, 19 December 2024. https://www.bbc.co.uk/news/live/cpw2yw0nr7qt.

9. Sarotte, *Not One Inch*, using an array of sources.

10. Bernd Pfaffenbach, interview with author, Berlin, 17 January 2023.

11. Rolf Martin Schmitz interview, *Der Spiegel*, 25 June 2002. Schmitz was RWE chief executive from 2016 to 2021. https://www.spiegel.de/international/business/anatomy-of-

germany-s-reliance-on-russian-natural-gas-decades-of-addiction-a-ad156813-3b24-424f-a51e-3ffbd7b6385c.

12. The author is grateful to Josef Joffe for pointing out Bismarckian continuity. But Joffe points out the exceptions: the German invasions of 1918 and 1941. Joffe, interview with author (video), 9 August 2023. The 'Draht nach St Petersburg' concept emerged with Bismark's 'Reinsurance treaty' with Russia in 1887.

13. A taste of personal bargaining over the pull-back of Soviet forces from eastern Germany came in a telephone call between Kohl and Gorbachev in September 1990. Kohl offered DM 8 billion for the overall costs of bringing back the Red Army east of the Elbe, recommending that most of this should be spent on homes for returning soldiers. Gorbachev replied 'pointedly', according to the German archives, 'This number leads to a dead end.' Pointing out that the German Democratic Republic's integration into united Germany would cost DM 500 billion over ten years, Gorbachev said Kohl's offer 'undermined the joint work carried out so far'. Memorandum of Kohl–Gorbachev telephone conversation, 7 September 1990, DESE, Document 415, pp. 1527–30.

14. UK briefing document on Boris Nikolaevich Yeltsin (1994, otherwise undated). UKNA, PREM 19/4964. The document highlighted Yeltsin's weaknesses – 'painful spinal damage and occasional bouts of heavy drinking'.

15. John Lough, *Germany's Russia Problem: The Struggle for Balance in Europe* (Manchester: Manchester University Press, 2021), pp. 2–3.

16. Letter, Christopher Mallaby to Geoffrey Howe, foreign secretary, 'The Federal Republic of Germany – How reliable an ally?', Bonn, 10 April 1989. Mallaby wrote, correctly, 'It would be hard to find any responsible observer in the Federal Republic, German or foreign, who sees any prospect of the Federal Republic leaving the Alliance or of an early move to achieve reunification. But there is a debate about how far there is a danger that the lure of detente or the prospect of reunification could one day weaken Federal German alignment in in the West.' UKNA, PREM 19/2691, DBPO, series III: 1960–, vol. VII: German Unification, 1989–1990, No. 1, pp. 1–8.

17. Stürmer, interview with author, Munich, 20 January 2023.

18. William Taubman, Gorbachev: *His Life and Times* (London: Simon & Schuster, 2017), pp. 1, 5, 693.

19. Gorbachev referred to Lenin as a 'special genius'. Victor Sebestyen, *Lenin: The Dictator* (London: Weidenfeld & Nicolson, 2017), p. 2. See Mikhail Gorbachev, *Memoirs* (Berlin: Siedler, 1995), p. 783 for Gorbachev's reference to Lenin's importance for 'perestroika' (reform) – replacement of a revolutionary approach, 'in the sense of a direct and complete break with the old', by 'an entirely different approach of a reformist type'.

20. Vladislav Zubok, *Collapse: The Fall of the Soviet Union* (New Haven/London: Yale University Press, 2021), p. 21.

21. Gail Sheehy, Gorbachev: *The Making of a Man Who Shook the World* (London: Heinemann, 1991), p. 2.

22. 'The Mystery of Mikhail Gorbachev's Ambiguous Legacy', *Der Spiegel* (international), 18 August 2011. https://www.spiegel.de/international/world/the-mystery-of-mikhail-gorbachev-s-ambiguous-legacy-a-781043.html. Short, *Putin*, p. 223.

23. Putin, annual address to the Federal Assembly, 25 April 2005, www.kremlin.ru/events/president/transcripts/22948. Putin first publicly opined on the 'tragedy of the collapse of our state' in a TV interview in 1992, just six weeks after the demise of the Soviet Union. Short, *Putin*, p. 223.

24. 'Schäuble vergleicht Putins Vorgehen mit Hitlers' ['Schauble compares Putin's behaviour with Hitler's'], *Die Welt*, 31 March 2014.

25. Schäuble, interview with author, Berlin, 16 January 2023. For another comparison between Hitler and Putin, over the Ukraine war, see Timothy Garton Ash, *Homelands: A Personal History of Europe* (London: The Bodley Head, 2023), p. 322.

26. Winston Churchill, 'The truth about Hitler', *Strand*, 1935, republished (with some modifications) as 'Hitler and his choice', *Great Contemporaries* (London: Thornton Butterworth, 1937).

27. William J. Burns, Ditchley lecture, 1 July 2023. See also CNBC interview, 22 July 2022. Burns coined the expression in 2019. 'I always saw Putin as a combustible combination of grievance and ambition and insecurity . . . The insecurity part is not something that he likes people to see easily, because he projects this kind of bare-chested persona . . . But there is, and it has roots in Russian history, this sense of insecurity about threats from the outside and threats from within his own society.' Burns, interview with Isaac Chotiner, 'A diplomat compares the foreign-policy establishment with Donald Trump', *New Yorker*, 19 March 2019.

28. William J. Burns, Memorandum to Condoleezza Rice, 26 June 2006, *The Back Channel: American Diplomacy in a Disordered World* (London: Hurst & Co., 2021), p. 209.

29. Burns, *Back Channel*, p. 413.

30. Robert M. Gates, *Duty: Memoirs of a Secretary at War,* 2014 (New York: Alfred A. Knopf, 2014), p. 532.

31. Halle, *The Cold War as History*, p. 17.

32. Halle, *The Cold War as History*, p. 50.

33. Feis, *Churchill, Roosevelt, Stalin*, p. 655.

34. Richard Moore, head of Britain's MI6 intelligence agency, 'I've never seen the world in a more dangerous state . . . Russia would not stop if it wins in Ukraine.' Sky News, 29 November 2024.

35. Stürmer, interview with author, Munich, 20 January 2023. The search for allies in Europe follows similar historical trends. 'To understand what is at stake, you have to go back into history, to the wars that ushered in the 18th century. Russia has always tried to find a western partner to back up its territorial and political ambitions in Europe. It has always had the idea of pushing its boundaries towards the Atlantic. It was not an accident that the Great Northern War and the War of Spanish Succession took place at around the same time. Louis XIV wanted a European empire, the Russian Tsars wanted an empire extending to the Baltics. They combined forces against the Habsburgs. Russia achieved its ambition of becoming a great European power.'

36. A reference to Alexander I's victory over French forces in 1814, the first time a foreign army had taken the French court for nearly four hundred years. V.M. Berezhkov (Stalin's interpreter), *Riadom so Stalinym* [*Next to Stalin*] (Moscow: Vagrius, 1998), p. 371, quoted in Oleg V. Khlevniuk, *Stalin: New Biography of a Dictator* (New Haven/London: Yale University Press, 2015), p, 9. See also Stephen Kotkin, 'Russia's perpetual geopolitics: Putin returns to the historical pattern', *Foreign Affairs*, May/June 2016, pp. 2–9.

37. Gaddis, *The Cold War*, 2005, p. 14, citing Ralph B. Levering, *Debating the Origins of the Cold War: American and Russian Perspectives* (Lanham, MD: Rowman & Littlefield, 2002), p. 174.

38. Gaddis, *The Cold War*, p. 11.

39. 'Putin resists western pressure as testy G20 closes', *France 24*, 16 November 2014.

40. Selmayr, interview with author, Vienna, 21 January 2023. Merkel's advisers were not allowed into the chancellor's meeting, which was held, in accord with the usual pattern of Merkel–Putin encounters, in a mixture of Russian and German. Selmayr joined the meeting at around 1.30 a.m. as a dispute had arisen on the legal status of the Budapest memorandum, and Selmayr's legal expertise was required. Selmayr explains: 'Putin figured out that I was German and spoke German, so he allowed me to stay on.' The episode caused mild resentment among Merkel's key advisers Lars-Hendrik Röller and Christoph Heusgen, who had to stay outside and wait for their leader while eating takeaway pizzas.

41. According to Selmayr, 'I did not pay a lot of attention to this at the time, but only understood later that he did this in case the paper in the hotel had been laced with poison. Years later, I checked later with a protocol officer of a member State, who confirmed that Putin always travelled with his own toilet paper.'

42. 'Threats, insults, and Kremlin "robots": How Russian diplomacy died under Putin', BBC, 3 September 2023.

43. Finland has a 1,340km (830 miles) border with Russia, which more than doubled NATO's pre-existing border with Russia.

44. The Russian army remains alive to a Chinese military threat. 'How Russia war-gamed a Chinese invasion', *Financial Times*, 29 February 2024.

45. Short, *Putin*, pp. 670–1.

46. Tatiana Stanovaya, 'Putin's Age of Chaos: The dangers of Russian disorder', *Foreign Affairs*, 8 August 2023.

47. Putin TV address on the launch of Russia's 'special military operation', 24 February 2022. https://www.aljazeera.com/news/2022/2/24/putins-speech-declaring-war-on-ukraine-translated-excerpts.

48. Yulia Tymoshenko, leader of the 2004 Ukraine 'Orange' revolution and twice prime minister, described Putin as 'determined to go down in Russian history alongside Stalin and Peter the Great . . . driven by this idea of historic mission'. *Guardian*, 8 June 2022. For historical factors guiding Putin, see Lynne Hartnett: 'The long history of Russian imperialism shaping Putin's war', *Washington Post*, 2 March 2022. Jane Burbank: 'The ardor and content of Mr Putin's declarations are not new or unique to him. A revitalized theory of Eurasian empire informs Mr Putin's every move,' 'The grand theory driving Putin to war', *New York Times*, 22 March 2022. Shahzada Rahim Abbas, 'Russia's Eurasian union dream: A way forward towards multipolar world order', *Journal of Global Faultlines*, vol. 9, no. 1 (January–February 2022), pp. 33–43. https://www.jstor.org/stable/48676221?seq=2. Masha Gessen, 'Vladimir Putin's guide to world history', *New York Times*, 30 September 2015. Figures such as Aleksandr Dugin, an unconventional philosopher whose book *Foundations of Geopolitics* (Moscow: Arktogeja, 2000) has been adopted as a textbook in both the Russian military academy and state school system, have provided Putin with cultural and ideological bedrock. See Stephen Pittz, 'A civilisational war?', *City Journal*, 27 March 2022. https://www.city-journal.org/article/a-civilizational-war. For a review of the historical and contemporary factors behind the war, see Keith Gessen, 'Was it inevitable?', *Guardian*, 11 March 2022. https://www.theguardian.com/world/2022/mar/11/was-it-inevitable-a-short-history-of-russias-war-on-ukraine.

49. For a full account of Putin's unremarkable early life, see Short, *Putin*, pp. 17–68.

50. Rodric Braithwaite, *Across the Moscow River: The World Turned Upside Down* (New Haven/London: Yale University Press, 2002), p. 333.

51. Barbara Hay, interview with author, London, 3 July 2023. In her diary for 1991–2 (quoted in Short, *Putin*, p. 163), Hay describes Putin as 'lugubrious', looking 'tired and sick', 'nondescript, not tall, with thin, lank hair, pasty-faced'. On the rare occasions when he attended a diplomatic reception, 'he didn't circulate, he didn't work the room. He never appeared to really want to be there: it was a chore. Not even a duty, a chore.'

52. Pierre Morel, interview with author, Paris, 24 April 2023. Putin's early period was as international adviser, at the St Petersburg Committee for External Relations.

53. Yeltsin in March 1988 replaced Viktor Chernomyrdin with Sergey Kiriyenko, who lasted until August. There followed Chernomyrdin again (to September 1998), Yevgeny Primakov (to May 1999) and Sergei Stepashin (replaced by Putin in August).

54. Letter, Tim Barrow, private secretary to Robin Cook (foreign secretary), to Michael Tatham, private secretary to Tony Blair (prime minister), 9 August 1999. PREM 19/496. Putin joined the KGB in 1975 and resigned in August 1991. He was stationed in East Germany between 1985 and 1990.

55. Memorandum, Bill Clinton–Boris Yeltsin conversation, 8 September 1999, CPL, Declassified per EO 13525, 2015-0782-M-2 (1.49).

56. '29 times Donald Trump did what Putin wanted', *Politico*, 21 February 2025.

57. Fiona Hill, 'The Kremlin's strange victory', *Foreign Affairs*, 27 September 2021.

58. During Trump's first term (2017–21), the US may have had the world's largest military structure, a position that was later taken by China.

59. Putin–Schröder telephone conversation, 19 August 2005, in Schöllgen, *Gerhard Schröder*, p. 854. Schöllgen writes that Putin's decision to attend the signing ceremony – in a deal between German private companies and Russian gas monopoly Gazprom – was 'a sign of friendship that Schröder did not forget.' See *Deutsche Welle* report, 8 September 2005: 'The timing of the Russian president's brief visit to Berlin is seen by observers as Putin's

attempt to boost the flagging re-election campaign of his good friend, German Chancellor Gerhard Schröder.' Vladislav Belov, from the Russian Academy of Science, said Putin was supporting Schröder even though 'all the signs are that the Schröder era is at an end'. The article added: 'Significantly, [the pipeline] does not pass over Ukraine, upsetting that country and Poland, which receive considerable transit fees from Gazprom for allowing its current pipelines to pass over their territory . . . Schröder has pushed for Germany to lessen its dependence on oil and gas from the Gulf and the US'. https://www.dw.com/en/putin-and-schr%C3%B6der-to-seal-gas-deal/a-1703205.

60. Schröder, *Entscheidungen*, p. 457.
61. Putin speech, Berlin, 25 September 2001. According to Norbert Röttgen, a Christian Democratic Union deputy, who became head of the Bundestag's foreign affairs committee, 'Putin captured us.' The voice was quite soft, in German, a voice that tempts you to believe what is said to you. Roger Cohen, 'The making of Vladimir Putin', *New York Times*, 26 March 2022. Sergei Guriev, dean of London Business School since 2024, a rector at Moscow's New Economic School in 2004–13, who met Putin ten to twenty times in small groups or panels before he left Russia in 2013, says: 'His experience as a KGB officer has helped his ability to take account of the type of conversation and interlocutor to adapt accordingly his voice and intonation.' Guriev, interview with author (video), Paris–London, 11 July 2023.
62. Condoleezza Rice, interview with author (video), Stanford–London, 23 May 2024. Announcement of Schröder's appointment at Nord Stream 2 was on 9 December 2005.
63. David Owen, interview with author, London, 27 March 2023.
64. Russia joined the Group of Eight in 1997. Putin and Dmitry Medvedev, Russian president during Putin's renewed prime ministership in 2008–12, took part in Group of Twenty meetings after heads of government started convening in 2008. Russia was expelled from the G8 in 2014 but carried on as a member of the G20.
65. Mikhail Khodorkovsky, the former Yukos oil tycoon jailed by Putin for a decade in 2003–13, said in 2016: 'Putin orients himself very precisely to a person . . . If he wants you to like him, you will like him.' Cohen, 'The making of Vladimir Putin'.
66. Hans von Ploetz, interview with author, Berlin, 18 January 2023.
67. Rolf Nikel, interview, *Der Spiegel*, 7 September 1993.
68. Michael Thuman, *Die Zeit*, podcast, 26 March 2025. https://www.zeit.de/politik/2025-03/wladimir-putin-praesidentschaft-russland-nachrichtenpodcast.
69. Roderic Lyne, interview with author, London, 9 June 2023.
70. Barrack Obama, *A Promised Land* (New York: Crown, 2020), pp. 459, 466.
71. Barroso, interview with author (video), Munich–London, 7 September 2023.
72. Christopher Meyer, *DC Confidential: The Controversial Memoirs of Britain's Ambassador to the US at the Time of 9/11 and the Iraq War* (London: Weidenfeld & Nicolson, 2005), p. 178. Meyer, British ambassador to the US in 1997–2003, was reporting on exchanges in February 2001 between Blair and Bush at Camp David. 'Bush peppered Blair with questions on international issues, especially Russia . . . Blair clearly found this flattering. He had taken something of a gamble by cultivating Vladimir Putin very early on'. See Campbell, *Diaries*, vol. 3, Friday, 23 February 2001, p. 534. '[Bush] clearly hadn't warmed to Putin and TB was urging him to give him a chance, also speaking up for [Gerhard] Schröder.'
73. George W. Bush, press conference, Brdo castle, near Ljubljana, Slovenia, 16 June 2021. https://georgewbush-whitehouse.archives.gov/news/releases/2001/06/20010618.html. John M. Evans, an official in the State Department's Bureau of Intelligence and Research for Russia and the Former Soviet States (1999–2002), and director of the Office of Russian Affairs (2002–4), points to a possible source for Bush's remark on Putin's 'soul'. Since 'that's not the way George Bush from Texas talks about people generally . . . he must have . . . picked that up from some staffer who might have advised him and it might have been national security advisor Dr [Condoleezza] Rice. Somebody had talked about the "Russian soul" and that was the last thing that stuck in his head.' ADST Oral History Project, October 2009. https://adst.org/2015/10/putin-the-early-years/.
74. George W. Bush, *Decision Points* (New York: Crown, 2010), p. 196.

75. Condoleezza Rice, *No Higher Honor: A Memoir of My Years in Washington* (New York: Simon & Schuster, 2011), p. 63. Rice later said: 'It was just a phrase that occurred to him [Bush], he was being asked some difficult questions, if he trusted Putin. When he said that, I thought, "That's going to be trouble [for us]." I don't think he meant it in any particular way. He was just trying to say something that suggested that they had a good meeting and he had confidence in Putin.' Rice, interview with author (video), Stanford–London, 24 May 2024.

76. John McCain, 'I looked into Mr Putin's eyes and saw three letters, a K, G, and a B.' Statement during presidential TV debate with Barack Obama, 27 September 2008. British ex-ambassador Roderic Lyne: 'I noticed Putin's very cold, small piggy eyes – and his cynical, somewhat coarse sense of humour. He had been known to make racist remarks including about the Chinese. He showed homophobia in some ways, although not antisemitism . . . Putin has a cunning intelligence, full of suspicion and vindictiveness.' Lyne, interview with author, London, 8 June 2023. Simon McDonald, a long-service British diplomat who at the time was foreign policy adviser to Prime Minister Gordon Brown, recalls his impression of Putin when they met at the Bucharest NATO meeting in 2008. 'He is quite a small man and this was perhaps a factor in his apparent discomfort when dealing with Brown, a tall and somewhat dominant figure. I noticed his cold blue eyes; if someone had told me that he could remove my heart with a spoon, I would've believed him.' A striking description, noting Putin's powers of transformation, comes from Robert Andrew, a former US soldier who joined the foreign service and became a political-military official in America's Russian embassy. He was in the welcoming group when Putin travelled to the VIP section of Vnukovo airport on 15 November 2006 to greet President George W. Bush on a brief Moscow visit. 'I made eye contact with him, and I felt this icy cold glare . . . This is like the Godfather has just walked in, or a KGB intel agent or something that felt incredibly criminal. He's sizing me up, along with everyone else in the room . . . I even checked my wallet to make sure it was still in my pocket. After this intense and icy stare around the spacious VIP terminal, his aides scurry him off to this room. About 10 minutes before Air Force One lands, Putin and his then-wife Ludmilla walk out of this room . . . It's like a cocoon has turned into a butterfly. The president of Russia emerges from this room. He's smiling, his eyes are sparkling, he's shaking hands. If there had been a baby in there, I'm sure he would have gone and kissed it . . . He's transformed himself, and he's now the president of a great country.' 'Vladimir Putin's "icy cold glare" ', ADST Oral History Project, April 2021. https://adst.org/2023/01/vladimir-putins-icy-cold-glare/?mc_cid=edd48999c6&mc_eid=494b962d16.

77. The circumstances of the baptismal-cross story are not clear. It seems likely that it formed part of a Putin ploy to win over Bush. Rice wrote that Putin related it after Bush 'asked about a cross that the Russian was wearing'. Rice, *No Higher Honor*, p. 63. Bush depicts the episode differently, in an overblown version that appears less authentic. 'After a few minutes I interrupted his presentation with a question: "Is it true that your mother gave you a cross that you had blessed in Jerusalem?" A look of shock washed over Putin's face.' Bush says Putin told him how a firefighter recovered the cross from his dacha after a fire. Bush claims he then said: 'Vladimir, that is the story of the cross. Things are meant to be.' Bush then felt 'the tension drain from the meeting room'. Bush, *Decision Points*, p. 196.

78. Rice, interview with author (video), Stanford–London, 23 May 2024.

79. Steve Witkoff, podcast with Tucker Carlson, 'Putin said he prayed for "his friend" Trump after 2024 assassination attempt, U.S. envoy says', NBC News, 22 March 2025. https://tuckercarlson.com/tucker-show-steve-witkoff.

80. Juncker, interviews with author, Brussels, 29 November 2023 and 24 January 2024. Luxembourg held the EU presidency at the time of the fifteenth EU–Russia summit, 10 May 2005. https://www.consilium.europa.eu/uedocs/cms_data/docs/pressdata/en/er/84811.pdf.

81. Barroso, interview with author (video), Munich–London, 7 September 2023.

82. Claude Blanchemaison, *La Croix*, 30 September 2019. https://www.la-croix.com/Monde/Europe/Comment-sest-nouee-relation-entre-Vladimir-Poutine-Jacques-Chirac-2019-09-30-1201050986.

83. Putin interview, *Financial Times*, Moscow, 26 June 2019. https://www.ft.com/content/878d2344-98f0-11e9-9573-ee5cbb98ed36.

84. Lamberto Dini, interview with author (video), Rome–London, 3 April 2004. Dini went from fifteen years as director general of Banca d'Italia to become Treasury minister in 1994–6 and then prime minster before becoming foreign minister. He remained chairman of the Senate foreign policy commission until 2013.

85. Dini, interview with author (video), Rome–London, 3 April 2004. 'Putin always mastered his brief without needing to bring a dossier of papers.'

86. Michel Camdessus, interview with author, Paris, 10 October 2023. He was taking part in the G8 summit as personal representative for Africa on behalf of France.

87. Camdessus, interview with author, Paris, 10 October 2023.

88. 'Tony Blair said Putin should be on "top table"', Document on Blair visit to Washington, 23 February 2001. UKNA, BBC, 30 December 2022. According to Kim Darroch, Blair's principal European affairs adviser in 2004–7 (before becoming the UK's permanent representative to the EU), Blair appeared to favour a relationship with Putin that could match Margaret Thatcher's well-documented build-up of ties with Mikhail Gorbachev. 'Putin looked like a guy we could do business with. Blair opined: "Mrs Thatcher found Gorbachev, I'll have Putin."' Darroch, interview with author, 3 April 2023.

89. Tony Blair, *A Journey: My Political Life* (London: Hutchinson, 2010), pp. 244–5.

90. Letter, 'Note on Iraq', Blair to Bush, July 2002, Chilcot inquiry, July 2016. https://www.theguardian.com/uk-news/2016/jul/06/with-you-whatever-tony-blair-letters-george-w-bush-chilcot.

91. Blair, *A Journey*, p. 451.

92. Jonathan Powell, interview with author, London, 12 September 2023.

93. Ralph Bollmann, *Angela Merkel: Die Kanzlerin und ihre Zeit* [The Chancellor and Her Time] (Munich: C.H. Beck, 2021), p. 303. Bollmann says this was their first meeting; in fact, according to Merkel, this took place when the Russian leader visited Berlin in 2000. Of both encounters, she says (characteristically) in her memoirs, she has no memory. Merkel, *Freiheit*, p. 376.

94. Merkel's memoirs contain eighty-two references to breakfast, lunch or dinner with various interlocutors.

95. Merkel, *Freiheit*, p. 708. Noting well-known aspects such as Putin's thin-skinned nature and propensity to keep interlocutors waiting, she limits her analysis to banalities such as: 'It would be a mistake to underestimate Putin.' Her cautious, non-confrontational style of diplomacy reflects a self-protective 'listening mode' mindset stemming from her earlier life in East Germany.

96. Merkel, interview, *Der Spiegel*, 23 November 2024. Merkel says Putin's soft-spoken German reminded her of the language of East German state-security officers.

97. Merkel would make contributions in Russian, at which she showed great proficiency at school. In her memoirs she underlines her lack of fluency.

98. Merkel, *Freiheit*, pp. 379–80. There have been reports that the main element of the Sochi residence was demolished in 2024. 'The mystery of the missing palace: Why has Putin demolished his residence on the Black Sea?', *Neue Zürcher Zeitung*, 14 October 2024.

99. Merkel, *Freiheit*, p. 380.

100. Merkel, *Freiheit*, p. 451.

101. Christoph Heusgen, *Führung und Verantwortung: Angela Merkels Außenpolitik und Deutschlands künftige Rolle in der Welt* [*Leadership and Responsibility: Angela Merkel's Foreign Policy and Germany's Future Role in the World*] (Berlin: Siedler, 2023), pp. 171–6.

102. The Merkel–May bond partly reflected their shared background as clergymen's daughters as well their tacit alliance in standing up to Trump's routine political misogyny during his first term.

103. Barwell, interview with author, London, 13 March 2023.

104. Horst Teltschik, interview with author, Tegernsee, 20 January 2023. For another (innocuous) Koni recollection see João Vale de Almeida, *The Divorce of Nations: A Diplomat's Inside View as the Global Order Collapses* (London: Flint Books, 2025), p. 27.

105. Putin, 'Überfall auf die Sowjetunion: Offen sein, trotz der Vergangenheit', *Die Zeit*, 22 June 2021.
106. With Valentin Falin, Soviet ambassador to West Germany in 1971–8, Kvitsinsky proposed the doctrine that Russia's military influence on former socialist countries in eastern Europe should be replaced by extending the dependence of these countries on Russian gas and oil supplies.
107. Yuli Kvitsinsky, 'Talking points for the Prague International Conference on the Future of European Security', Prague, 25–6 April 1991. PAAA, B 42/214/156457.
108. Mikhail Gorbachev, speech in Prague, April 1987. Milan Svec, 'The Prague Spring: 20 years later', *Foreign Affairs*, Summer 1988.
109. Jim Hoagland, 'Europe's destiny', *Foreign Affairs*, 1989–90. See also G.H.W. Bush, 'A Europe whole and free', speech, Mainz, 31 May 1989. https://usa.usembassy.de/etexts/ga6-890531.htm.
110. Leonid Brezhnev, conversation with Helmut Schmidt, Bonn, 23 November 1981. AAPD 1981, Document 334, p. 81.
111. Arthur Sullivan, 'Russian gas in Germany: A 50-year relationship', *Deutsche Welle*, 9 March 2022. https://www.dw.com/en/russian-gas-in-germany-a-complicated-50-year-relationship/a-61057166.
112. Brandt greatly disliked the word *Wiedervereinigung* (reunification). Interview with author, Bonn, October 1986
113. The celebrated Brandt expression seems to have stemmed from a combination of statements and interviews. See for example SFB-Mittagsecho, *Berliner Morgenpost*, 10 and 11 November 1989. 'Rede vor dem Rathaus Schöneberg zum Fall der Berliner Mauer' ['Speech at Schöneberg town hall on the fall of the Wall'], 10 November 1989. https://dokumente-online.com/deutsch-interpretation-rede-von-willy-brandt-10-11.html. Hoagland, 'Europe's destiny'. https://beruhmte-zitate.de/zitate/126542-willy-brandt-jetzt-wachst-zusammen-was-zusammengehort/.
114. Egon Bahr, memorandum, 25 July 1969. AAPD 1969, Document 245, pp. 857–8. Through the Ruhrgas deal, 'German industry has an additional durable foundation for supplying the Russian market,' Bahr recorded. 'East–West economic association is in our interest.'
115. Henry Kissinger, memorandum for the president, 'Brandt's eastern policy', 16 February 1970.
116. Later in his life, Kissinger revised his view of Bahr. From Kissinger's speech at Bahr's funeral: 'Ein langer Weg bis zur bleibenden Freundschaft' ['A long road to lasting friendship'], 7 September 2015, in Peter Brandt, Hans-Joachim Gießmann and Götz Neuneck, '. . . aber eine Chance haben wir': Zum 100. Geburtstag von Egon Bahr [*On the 100th Birthday of Egan Bahr*] (Bonn: J.H.W. Dietz Nachf, 2022).
117. Roger Jackling, 'The implications of Herr Brandt's Ostpolitik', Diplomatic report 343/70, Bonn, 29 June 1970. UKNA, FCO 160/115/3.
118. Telegram, no. 55 to Foreign and Commonwealth Office (no author name), Paris, 17 August 1970.
119. Horst Blomeyer-Bartenstein, memorandum, Paris, 10 June 1970. AAPD 1970, Document 258, pp. 942–3. 'We are repeatedly being asked what advantages we are hoping for.'
120. Hans-Hellmuth Ruete, memorandum, Paris, 23 July 1970. AAPD 1970, Document 331, pp. 1230–1.
121. Memorandum, Willy Brandt–Alexei Kosygin conversation, Moscow, 12 August 1970. AAPD 1970, Document 387, pp. 1441–3. Geological investigations had shown that for 'all commodities – iron ore, gas, coal and wood and so on – we have confirmed reserves covering needs for 40 to 50 years.' The Soviet side offered a market for German equipment, chemical products and consumer goods. 'We have to find interesting areas for both sides. Neither you nor we are charitable organisations. Cooperation must bring utility.'

122. Memorandum, Brandt– Kosygin conversation, 12 August 1970. AAPD 1970, Document 387, pp. 1443–4. Trust and practical cooperation, Brandt told Kosygin, depended on both sides remaining 'loyal to their own alliance'.

123. Peter Merseburger, *Willy Brandt 1913–1992: Visionär und Realist* [*Willy Brandt 1913– 1992: Visionary and Realist*] (Munich: Pantheon, 2013), p. 612.

124. Memorandum, Brandt–Brezhnev conversation, Moscow, 12 August 1970. AAPD 1970, Document 213, 388, pp. 1453–5. Brezhnev castigated Walter Scheel, Brandt's foreign minister – a member of the Free Democratic Party, with traditionally close links to the US – for having told the TASS news agency that the implementation of the treaty depended on a positive solution for the status of Berlin. He said this was a matter for the four Allied powers, and that he would not allow the US to have a veto on ratification. 'The US could torpedo the treaty and dominate the Federal Republic further . . . That would be a tragedy.'

125. With remarkable flattery, Brezhnev termed the Federal Republic a geopolitical partner. 'The Federal Republic should use his influence on security and cooperation in Europe . . . If both our states show political will and demand that the position in Europe becomes more healthy, then no one in the world can counter our joint conclusions.'

126. Kohl, interview with *Newsweek*, 'Kohl to Reagan: "Ron, be patient"', 27 October 1986. 'I'm not a fool: I don't consider him to be a liberal. He is a modern communist leader who understands public relations. Goebbels, one of those responsible for the crimes of the Hitler era, was an expert in public relations, too.'

127. Julij A. Kwizinskij [Yuli Kvitsinsky], *Vor dem Sturm: Erinnerungen eines Diplomaten* [*Memoirs of a Diplomat*] (Berlin: Siedler, 1993), p. 416.

128. Hans-Dietrich Genscher conversation with Eduard Shevardnadze, Soviet foreign minister, Moscow, 24 October 1988. AAPD 1986, Document 301, pp. 1572–3.

129. Helmut Kohl, *Erinnerungen 1982–1990* (Munich: Droemer, 2005), p. 451.

130. Teltschik, memorandum to Kohl, Bonn, 30 October 1986. AAPD 1986, Document 308, p. 1591.

131. Teltschik's poor relations with Genscher's foreign ministry were legendary. See Helmut Kohl, *Erinnerungen 1990–1994*, pp. 420–1. 'Teltschik was a thorn in the flesh to the Bonn foreign ministry officials, and the chemistry between him and the ministry never worked. In short: Teltschik was far superior to most of the grandees of the foreign office, and would easily have earned the position of a state secretary. Horst Teltschik blamed me for many years for not calling him to a higher position, but Genscher's resolute refusal made this impossible.' Teltschik's inability to rise beyond the position of a ministerial director was one of the reasons why the possibility of his becoming defence minister was never properly considered. Kohl did not seem to consider making Teltschik state secretary within the chancellor's office.

132. Teltschik, memorandum to Schäuble and Kohl, 30 October 1986. AAPD 1986, Document 308, pp. 1590–2. Teltschik worried that Moscow might use the fracas to undermine 'favourably developing German–Soviet relations' and influence German elections in January. Suggesting that Kohl should write a personal letter to Gorbachev, Teltschik affirmed that the Social Democratic Party (SPD) opposition should not be given the chance to 'exploit the affair for their benefit'.

133. Anatoly Kovalev, conversation with Hermann von Richthofen, Moscow, 30 October 1986. AAPD 1986, Document 301, pp. 1598–1602.

134. Von Richthofen, memorandum, Moscow, 3 November 1986. AAPD 1986, Document 313, pp. 1612–1.

135. On a visit to Moscow in March 1987, Teltschik was told by Yuri Vorontsov, first deputy foreign minister, that the new 'dynamism' of the Soviet Union's foreign policy was not being properly considered by the West. Teltschik report on meetings in Moscow of Bergedorfer group, 27–8 March 1987. Memorandum, Mitterrand–Kohl conversation, Chambord, 28 March 1987. AAPD 1987, Document 89, p. 437, n. 22.

136. Memorandum, Mitterrand–Kohl conversation, Chambord, 28 March 1987. AAPD 1987, Document 89, p. 436.

137. Genscher was a frequent user of the phrase about the 'dead Germans'. 'Die Heckenschützen feuern noch immer' ['The snipers are still firing'], *Der Spiegel*, 14 June 1987. https://www.spiegel.de/politik/die-heckenschuetzen-feuern-noch-immer-a-fa41b636-0002-0001-0000-000013523956.

138. Memorandum, Mitterrand–Kohl conversation, Chambord, 28 March 1987. 'After the first nuclear weapons had been fired, there will be revolutions everywhere. If Hamburg were destroyed, the Soviets would destroy three or four French cities in retaliation. If the French then reacted by hitting Kyiv, the Soviets would then perhaps destroy Paris, Toulouse, Bordeaux and Lyon.'

139. Von Rihthofen, memorandum, Bonn, 17 June 1987. AAPD 1987, Document 177, p. 888.

140. The author was present among the accompanying journalists watching Kohl's arrival at the Kremlin and his far-from-amiable initial greeting by Gorbachev.

141. Gorbachev, interview, *Der Spiegel*, 24 October 1988, p. 30. (Formal written text.)

142. Gorbachev, interview, *Der Spiegel*, 24 October 1988, p. 22. (Authorised spoken interview.)

143. Gorbachev, interview, *Der Spiegel*, 24 October 1988, p. 28. (Formal written text.)

144. Kohl, speech, Moscow, 24 Oktober 1988. https://www.bundeskanzler-helmut-kohl.de/seite/24-oktober-1988/. See also *Erinnerungen*, p. 768.

145. Charles Mitchell, 'Kohl, Gorbachev cross swords over reunification', United Press International, 24 October 1989. https://www.upi.com/Archives/1988/10/24/Kohl-Gorbachev-cross-swords-over-reunification/3255593668800/.

146. Anatoly Chernyaev, diary entry, 2 May 1989, trans. Vladislav Zubok. Cold War International History Project, Documents and Papers (CWHIP). https://worldhistorycommons.org/excerpt-anatoly-chernyaevs-diary.

147. 'In the event of a Soviet attack, the Americans envisaged going nuclear straightaway, with extensive use of short-range missiles and Atomic Demolition Mines pre-positioned in areas like the Fulda Gap. It was a tripwire strategy, because they, and we, believed that the Russians would have overwhelming conventional superiority: NATO exercises assumed that if deterrence failed the Red Army would be on the Rhine within three days. But the Germans were naturally uneasy about the prospect of a nuclear exchange killing millions, most of them Germans.' John Kerr, interview with author, London, 8 September 2023.

148. Kerr, interview with author, London, 8 September 2023. Two other predictions, Kerr admits, he was happy to get wrong: on the possibility of Soviet troops leaving East Germany within Kerr's working lifetime, and on the likelihood that states from within the Soviet Union (such as the Baltics) would be allowed to leave the USSR.

149. Hans-Dietrich Genscher, West German foreign minister, set the tone (not initially welcome in conservative circles inside and outside Germany) when he said at the Davos World Economic Forum in January 1987. 'We should take Gorbachev at his word.' Genscher, speech, Davos, 1 February 1987. Hans-Dietrich Genscher, *Erinnerungen* (Berlin: Siedler, 1995), pp. 516, 526–7. 'Unsicher wie jedermann' ['Uncertain as everyone'], *Die Zeit*, 28 February 1992.

150. Gorbachev, press conference, Bonn, 15 June 1989. Archive of the Gorbachev Foundation. Published in Mikhail Gorbachev, *i germanskii vopros. Sbornik dokumentov 1986–1991* [The German Question: Documents] (Moscow: Ves' Mir, 2006), trans. Svetlana Savranskaya for the National Security Archive. https://mronline.org/wp-content/uploads/2021/04/1989-06-1520Gorbachev20press-conference20Bonn.pdf.

151. Günter Schabowski, *Der Absturz* [The Collapse] (Berlin: Rowolt, 1991), p. 123.

152. David Marsh, 'Changes in the magnetic pull of East and West', *Financial Times*, 15 February 1988.

153. Schabowski, *Der Absturz*, p. 157.

154. Otto Reinhold, statement, East German radio, 19 August 1989. See Philip Zelikow and Condoleezza Rice, *Germany Unified and Europe Transformed: A Study in Statecraft* (Cambridge, MA: Harvard University Press, 1995), p. 38.

155. 'Reagan may have publicly called on Gorbachev to get rid of the wall. But in negotiations with the Russians he set other priorities and certainly did not put into question the division of Germany.' Zelikow and Rice, *Germany Unified and Europe Transformed*, p. 20. Willy Brandt, *Erinnerungen* (Frankfurt: Propyläen, 1989), p. 55.

156. 'The NATO summit', Scowcroft memorandum to Bush, 20 March 1989. The document was written by Philip Zelikow and Robert Blackwill. On 26 March Bush noted to Scowcroft that he had 'read this with interest'. The 'commonwealth of nations' phrase was introduced in Bush's Mainz address, 31 May 1989 – along with the concept of a 'Europe whole and free'. https://usa.usembassy.de/etexts/ga6-890531.htm. Zelikow and Rice, *Germany Unified and Europe Transformed*, p. 28.

157. 'Treaty on conventional armed forces in Europe'. https://www.osce.org/files/f/documents/4/9/14087.pdf.

158. Beschloss and Talbott, *At the Highest Levels*, p. 41.

159. Zoellick, *America in the World*, pp. 426–35.

160. Letter, Bush to Kohl, undated, handed over personally by US embassy on 12 May 1989. DESE, Document 35, quoting Bundesarchiv (BA) B 136/29806.

161. 'Wiedervereinigung' ('reunification') entered into common political parlance only relatively late in the process, in September 1989, driven by Volker Rühe, general secretary of Kohl's CDU, who later became defence minister and an early advocate of NATO enlargement.

162. Gorbachev travelled to Washington to see President Reagan in December 1987.

163. Kohl, interview with author, Bonn, *Financial Times*, 7 February 1989. 'The idea – the vision – is that we want the political unity of Europe and that freedom is more important than boundaries.' Kohl was anxious to play down any suggestion that West Germany would be an unreliable ally. 'The Federal Republic is part of the western world. I said this to Gorbachev. There is no price at which we could be, so to speak, bought out.'

164. Teltschik, interview, June 1992, in Zelikow and Rice, *Germany Unified and Europe Transformed*, p. 35.

165. Benjamin Fischer, CIA historian, and panellists, conference proceedings, 'Vernon A. Walters: Pathfinder of the intelligence profession', 3 June 2004. https://archive.org/details/DTIC_ADA511754/page/n5/mode/2up. Walters wrote a book about his German experience, *Die Vereinigung war voraussehbar* [*Reunification Was Foreseeable*] (Berlin: Siedler, 1994).

166. George Ward, testimony, conference proceedings, 'Vernon A. Walters, Pathfinder of the intelligence profession'. 'There was a clash of styles in which Walters's flamboyance contrasted with the lawyerly approach of the State Department.'

167. The FDP had switched sides from Helmut Schmidt's SPD-led coalition in 1982, bringing Kohl to power.

168. Kohl, interview with author, Bonn, *Financial Times*, 7 February 1989.

169. Braithwaite, memorandum to Douglas Hurd, foreign secretary, Moscow, 11 November 1989.

170. Gorbachev, *Memoirs*, p. 677.

171. The author was standing below the podium where Gorbachev, Honecker and other eastern bloc leaders were reviewing the parade. Honecker, holding up a bunch of bedraggled daffodils, looked unenthusiastic.

172. Schabowski, *Der Absturz*, p. 180.

173. The exact formulation remains a matter for conjecture. *Die Welt*, 6 October 2014. https://www.welt.de/geschichte/article132968291/Gorbatschow-hat-den-beruehmten-Satz-nie-gesagt.html. See Gorbachev, *Memoirs*, p. 677. Taubman, *Gorbachev: His Life and Times*, p. 485.

174. Alexandra Ritchie, *Faust's Metropolis: A History of Berlin* (London: HarperCollins, 1999), p. 833. The letters 'Egon' formed the basis of a chant: 'Er geht oock noch' – 'He will be going too'.

175. Memorandum, Mikhail Gorbachev–Egon Krenz conversation, Moscow, 1 November 1989. Note dated 1 December 1989: 'Top Secret, to all members and candidates of the

Politburo', signed Egon Krenz. 'Making the History of 1989, Item 435'. https://nsarchive2.gwu.edu/NSAEBB/NSAEBB293/doc09.pdf. The convertible currency deficit was put at $12.1 billion (income: $5.9 billion against outgoings of $18 billion). The GDR needed $4.5 billion to make interest payments, amounting to 62 per cent of export earnings.

176. The East German broadcaster Mitteldeutscher Rundfunk (MDR) reported later that Gerhard Schürer, the East German planning chief, had deliberately overstated East Germany's foreign debt. 'Wie pleite war die DDR?' ['How bankrupt was the GDR?'], 9 September 1991. https://www.mdr.de/geschichte/ddr/wirtschaft/pleite-gerhard-schuerer-staatliche-plankomission-100.html. For a further account of Schürer's attempts to explain the true economic position to the GDR leadership, see Schabowski, *Der Absturz*, pp. 121–4.

177. Memorandum, Gorbachev–Krenz conversation, Moscow, 1 November 1989.

178. Gorbachev, telephone conversation with Vyacheslav Kochemasov, 6 November 1989. Igor Maximychev, 'Possible "Impossibilities"', *International Affairs*, no. 6 (June 1993), pp. 112–13. Zelikow and Rice, *Germany Unified and Europe Transformed*, p. 98, n. 109.

179. Walter Ulbricht, East German party leader, said 'No one has the intention to build a Wall', 15 June 1961.

4 TURNING POINTS

1. Honecker, statement, East Berlin, 19 January 1989. 'Honeckers "mutige" Vorhersage – Auf dem Weg zur Deutschen Einheit' ['Honecker's "courageous" statement – on the way to German unity'], Die Bundesregierung. https://www.bundesregierung.de/breg-de/schwerpunkte-der-bundesregierung/deutsche-einheit/honeckers-mutige-vorhersage-459118.

2. Chernyaev, diary entry, 10 November 1989, trans. Anna Melyakova, ed. Svetlana Savranskaya. GWU-NSA. https://nsarchive2.gwu.edu/NSAEBB/NSAEBB275/1989%20for%20posting.pdf.

3. Norman Lamont, interview with author, 14 February 2023.

4. Sobel interview with author, telephone/email, 24 June 2023.

5. Blair, A Journey, p. 451.

6. Romano Prodi, interview with author, Bologna, March 2023.

7. The literature on NATO's eastern expansion is immense. See Marie Elise Sarotte, 'Not one inch eastward? Bush, Baker, Kohl, Genscher, Gorbachev and the origins of Russian resentment toward NATO enlargement in February 1990', Diplomatic History, vol. 34, issue 1 (January 2010), pp. 119–40. As one example, Ron Asmus, a State Department official under President Bill Clinton, 'remembers being continually confronted by these claims: Moscow firmly believed that it had received assurances from the US, France, and the UK that NATO enlargement would go no further than eastern Germany'.

8. Germany as a state effectively did not exist in 1945–90. The 1987 Random House Dictionary of the English Language described Germany as 'a former country in central Europe'. The corollary was that East Germany was described in a book published in the UK in 1988 as 'perhaps the most stable socialist state in Eastern Europe'. Mike Dennis, German Democratic Republic: Politics, Economics and Society (London: Pinter, 1988). See also Marsh, Germany and Europe, p. 24.

9. 'Record of conversation between Mikhail Gorbachev and James Baker', 9 February 1990. GWU-NSA. 'NATO Expansion: What Gorbachev Heard', US Department of State, FOIA 199504567. https://nsarchive.gwu.edu/sites/default/files/documents/4325680/Document-06-Record-of-conversation-between.pdf. Gorbachev, Memoirs, p. 683. Sarotte, Not One Inch, p. 55.

10. Zelikow and Rice, Germany Unified and Europe Transformed, p. 197.

11. Beschloss and Talbott, At the Highest Levels, p. 186.

12. Memorandum of conversation between George Bush and Alexander Yakovlev, 19 November 1991. George H.W. Bush Presidential Library. https://bush41library.tamu.edu/files/memcons-telcons/1991-11-19--Yakovlev.pdf. See also Sarotte, Not One Inch, p. 127.

13. George H.W. Bush, address to Congress, Washington, 29 January 1992. 'Communism died this year . . . By the grace of God, America won the Cold War.' https://www.nytimes.com/1992/01/29/us/state-union-transcript-president-bush-s-address-state-union.html.

14. Prodi, interview with author, Bologna, 10 March 2023.

15. Zubok, *Collapse*, pp. 22–3. Soon after coming to power in 1985, Gorbachev listed the economic and social problems he wanted to address: '1) Quality, 2) Struggle against drinking, 3) People in need, 4) Land for orchard and gardens, 5) Medicine'. The list did not include the pressing issues his deceased mentor Yuri Andropov had raised about macroeconomic stability. Gorbachev relied greatly in his reform programme on his key associate Alexander Yakovlev, a member of the Politburo from 1985 to July 1990, as well as earlier advice from Andropov. A mammoth speech to the Soviet party congress in February 1986, which finished with a crescendo urging fulfilment of the 'farewell wishes of the great Lenin', drew substantially on Yakovlev's efforts.

16. Lamont, interview with author, London, 14 February 2023. 'Gorbachev told me once he was against privatisation as it would make rich people richer. As a matter of fact, that turned out to be right, but for reasons that have got nothing to do with the basic principles of privatisation.' See also Norman Lamont, *In Office* (London: Little, Brown, 1999), p. 68.

17. Morel, interview with author, Paris, 24 April 2023.

18. Lyne, interview with author, London, 9 June 2023.

19. Memorandum, 'Further developments in Russia – domestic and foreign policies', Klaus Neubert, 4 March 1993. AAPD 1993, Document 77, pp. 304–9.

20. Valentin Falin memorandum to Mikhail Gorbachev, 18 April 1990. 'Summing up the past six months, one has to conclude that the "common European home", which used to be a concrete task the countries of the continent were starting to implement, is now turning into a mirage.' NSA-GWU. https://nsarchive.gwu.edu/document/16130-document-16-valentin-falin-memorandum-mikhail.

21. Brent Scowcroft, interview with Fred Kempe, 'Freedom's Challenge', Atlantic Council, November 1989. https://www.atlanticcouncil.org/blogs/new-atlanticist/brent-scowcroft-on-the-fall-of-the-berlin-wall/.

22. Letter, John Weston (Foreign Office political director) to Christopher Mallaby, 17 September 1990. Reflecting on psychological and political change in Germany, the poetry-loving Weston concluded his letter with two lines from T.S. Eliot's *Four Quartets*, indicating that the German people now were embarking on the political equivalent of a railway journey during which they were likely to adopt a new national character – an observation that has been neither proved nor disproved in the ensuing thirty-five years. DBPO, series III: 1960–, vol. VII: German Unification, 1989–1990, No. 238, pp. 466–71.

23. 'What Gorbachev Heard', 12 December 2017. Analysis of declassified US, Soviet, German, British and French documents, GWU-NSA. 'Numerous declassified documents showed that multiple national leaders were considering and rejecting central and eastern European membership in NATO as of early 1990 and through 1991, discussions of NATO in the context of German unification negotiations in 1990 were not at all narrowly limited to the status of East German territory, and that subsequent Soviet and Russian complaints about being misled about NATO expansion were founded in written contemporaneous memcons and telcons at the highest levels.' https://nsarchive.gwu.edu/briefing-book/russia-programs/2017-12-12/nato-expansion-what-gorbachev-heard-western-leaders-early. Backing this up, Christoper Mallaby, a Soviet specialist who was Britain's ambassador to West Germany (later united Germany) and France in the period during and after German unification, wrote his memoirs, 'The remarks of Baker and Major [on NATO enlargement] were not binding, but the Russian resentment at NATO's enlargement is understandable.' Christopher Mallaby, *Living the Cold War* (Stroud: Amberley, 2017), p. 233.

24. Scowcroft, 'Freedom's Challenge'.

25. Press conference, Moscow, October 1988.

26. Kohl, interview with author, Bonn, *Financial Times*, 7 February 1989.

27. Comment by Kohl, meeting with aides, Chancellor bungalow, Bonn, 23 November 1989. The timing estimate was recorded by Teltschik in *329 Tage* (p. 52) as 27 November 1989.

28. Kohl, conversation with Christopher Mallaby, British ambassador to West Germany. Charles Moore, *Margaret Thatcher*, vol. 3: *Herself, Alone* (London: Allen Lane, 2019), pp. 507–8. See also Mallaby, *Living the Cold War*, p. 214.
29. Kohl–Mitterrand conversation, Paris, 24 April 1991. AAPD 1991, Document 137, p. 549. Kohl was reporting on a visit to Bonn by Elena Bonner, Andrei Sakharov's widow. Many of the most intimate documents pertaining to German unification are still held by Kohl's widow.
30. Zubok, *Collapse*, p. 6. Frank Kennan, *The Kennan Diaries*, ed. Frank Costigliola (New York: W.W. Norton, 2014), p. 199.
31. James Collins, interview with author (video), Washington–London, 14 May 2024.
32. 'NATO enlargement at twenty-five: How we got there and what it achieved', Atlantic Council, 6 March 2024. https://www.atlanticcouncil.org/blogs/new-atlanticist/nato-enlargement-at-twenty-five/. See also 'NATO enlargement: Sweden and Finland', House of Commons Library, 11 Match 2024. https://commonslibrary.parliament.uk/research-briefings/cbp-9574/.
33. Assurances by the West were made at the time of German unification, when NATO enlargement to the states of the Warsaw Pact was not on the agenda. Gorbachev as well as Boris Yeltsin and other Russian leaders (including Putin) made clear in later statements that they recognised the principle that states could join the alliances they chose.
34. Juncker, interview with author, Brussels, 29 November 2023.
35. Von Ploetz, interview with author, Berlin, 18 January 2023.
36. Teltschik, interview with author, Tegernsee, 20 January 2023.
37. Brathwaite interview with author, Wimbledon, 30 April 2023. He cites in particular the agreement by America, Britain, France and Germany in March 1991 that the east Europeans would be offered neither membership nor security guarantees.
38. Merkel, *Freedom*, pp. 669, 675.
39. Merkel, *Freedom*, p. 448.
40. Braithwaite, interview with author, Wimbledon, 30 April 2023, and email exchanges.
41. Bérégovoy was a fierce proponent of Britain joining the European monetary union 'so that France would not be left alone with the Germans'.
42. Pierre Bérégovoy, TV interview, 1992.
43. Kohl, *Erinnerungen 1990–1994*, pp. 59, 61.
44. Moore, *Thatcher*, vol. 3, pp. 470, 855. Mallaby: 'I do not think Margaret Thatcher's attitude was a considered view. Rather it was a gut feeling which dated from the Second World War.' Mallaby, *Living the Cold War*, p. 208.
45. Peter Ruggenthaler, 'The 1952 Stalin note on German unification', *Journal of Cold War Studies*, vol. 13, no. 4 (Fall 2011), pp. 172–212.
46. Margaret Thatcher, *The Downing Street Years* (London: HarperCollins, 1993), p. 814.
47. John Fretwell, minute, 14 November 1989. DBPO, series III: 1960–, vol. VII: German Unification, 1989–1990, No. 45. See also Douglas Hurd, Thatcher's foreign secretary, 'The French may be with us in their hearts, but we must expect them to play a very canny game in talking to the Germans.' Hurd speaking note, enclosure to DBPO, series III: 1960–, vol. VII: German Unification, 1989–1990, No. 45, 14 November 1989.
48. Yakovlev, press briefing, 'The US, Britain and France do not want reunification of Germany and hope the Soviet Union will forestall such a development.' Zelikow and Rice, *Germany Unified and Europe Transformed*, p. 117.
49. Taubman, *Gorbachev*, pp. 686–7.
50. Kohl, *Erinnerungen 1982–1990*, p. 984. Kohl referred to a NATO summit declaration in 1970, based on Article 7 of the 1955 Germany treaty.
51. Jacques Attali, *Verbatim III* (Paris: Fayard, 1996), 18 November 1989. French and German accounts (including Kohl's memoirs, which for the dinner on 18 November, seem to draw heavily on the text in Attali's *Verbatim III*), appear to back Thatcher's own various assessments of Mitterrand's thoughts.
52. David Manning, interview with author, London, 12 June 2023. See also Thatcher, *The Downing Street Years*, p. 792. Shortly before the fall of the Wall, she told Gorbachev,

'Although NATO had traditionally made statements supporting Germany's aspiration to be reunited, in practice we were rather apprehensive.'

53. Letter, Michael Alexander to Patrick Wright, Brussels, 18 September 1989. Report of a conversation with Robert Blackwill at the IISS Conference in Oslo, in which Blackwill said that Bush was increasingly concerned about 'how to manage the Germans'. DBPO, series III: 1960–, vol. VII: German Unification, 1989–1990, No. 12, pp. 31–3.
54. Charles Powell, conversation with author, London, 28 February 2023.
55. Strategic Defense Initiative (SDI), 1983, US Department of State archive. https://2001-2009.state.gov/r/pa/ho/time/r/104253.htm.
56. 'Reagan and Gorbachev: The Reykjavik Summit', transcript of Gorbachev–Reagan talks, GWU-NSA. Final Meeting, 12 October 1986. https://nsarchive.gwu.edu/document/22397-document-2-transcript-gorbachev-reagan.
57. Kerr, interview with author, London, 8 September 2023. Kerr adds: 'Reagan really admired Thatcher. When she was doing her full Bette Davis routine, explaining why what he'd just said was shocking, totally misconceived, and a betrayal of all our two nations hold dear, I'd see him nudge [George] Bush, or [Roger] Macfarlane, [George] Shulz or [Casper] Weinberger, and the nudge clearly meant "Gee she's a class act", as well as "Your turn to answer all this. I've used all my cue cards already."'
58. Charles Powell, interview with author, London, 28 February 2023.
59. Jonathan Powell, minute to Robert Cooper, 22 November 1989. DBPO, series III: 1960–, vol. VII: German Unification, 1989–1990, No. 55.
60. Kohl, 'Erklärung vor dem Deutschen Bundestag: Zehn-Punkte-Programm zur Deutschlandpolitik' ['German Bundestag statement: Ten-point programme on Deutschlandpolitik'], 28 November 1989. https://www.bundeskanzler-helmut-kohl.de/seite/28-november-1989/.
61. Kohl, *Erinnerungen 1982–1990*, p. 996.
62. Teltschik, interview with author, Tegernsee, 6 September 2023.
63. Teltschik, *329 Tage*, pp. 42–5. Teltschik, *Die 329 Tage zur deutschen Einigung*, pp. 34–45, 140–6, pp. 680–5. A facsimile of Portugalov's seven-page document – divided into an 'official' and 'unofficial' part – is published in Teltschik's second account. It reveals that Portugalov suggested that a unified Germany might wish to consider departing from both the European Community and from NATO. The Portugalov document forms the centrepiece of a note by Teltschik to Kohl on 6 December 1989, 'The Soviet Union and the German Question', produced after announcement of the 10-point plan, with the aim of showing that the plan 'rests on major considerations of the Soviet leadership'. Teltschik underlines an important reason for Kohl's 10-point announcement – to prevent him from being wrong-footed by prior publication of the Soviet Union's own unification proposals. DESE, Documents 112 and 112A, pp. 616–18. See a (not-100-per-cent-accurate) English translation: https://nsarchive2.gwu.edu/NSAEBB/NSAEBB296/doc06.pdf.
64. Teltschik, interview with author, Tegernsee, 6 September 2023.
65. Genscher, *Erinnerungen*, p. 670.
66. Author's private information.
67. Mallaby, memorandum to Douglas Hurd, 27 November 1989. DBPO, series III: 1960–, vol. VII: German Unification, 1989–1990.
68. Memorandum, Bush–Kohl telephone call, Robert Hutchings–Robert Blackwill to Scowcroft, 'The President's telephone call to Chancellor Kohl', 28 November 1989. Zelikow and Rice, *Germany Unified and Europe Transformed*, p. 123.
69. Memorandum, Bush–Kohl telephone conversation, 28 November 1989. George H.W. Bush and Brent Scowcroft, *A World Transformed* (New York: Alfred A. Knopf, 1998), p. 195.
70. Author's private information.
71. Memorandum, Teltschik to Kohl, Bonn, 30 November 1989. DESE, Document 102, pp. 574–7.
72. Memorandum, Fran Lambach to Jürgen Sudhoff (state secretary), Bonn, 1 November 1989. DE, Document 25, pp. 147–53.

73. Von Richthofen, memorandum, Genscher–Thatcher conversation, London, 29 November 1989. DFDE, Document 10, pp. 49–51.

74. Memorandum, Hurd–Genscher conversation, dinner, 29 November 1989. AAPD 1991, Document 388, pp. 1650–2.

75. Franz Pfeiffer, memorandum, Genscher–Mitterrand conversation, Paris, 30 November 1989. Determined to sow doubts in the Anglo-Saxon camp, Mitterrand told Genscher that Thatcher's position on unification was 'much more reserved' than his. Mitterrand said he doubted whether the Bush administration would ultimately support unification 'because conservative governments tend to reject ground-breaking changes'. DFDE No. D 11, p. 58.

76. In Rome, Gorbachev urged a summit meeting for thirty-five members of the Conference on Security and Cooperation in Europe in 1990. He emphasised the philosophy of perestroika: 'We have abandoned the claim to have a monopoly on truth . . . We have now decided, firmly and irrevocably to base our policy on the principle of freedom of choice.' Zelikow and Rice, *Germany Unified and Europe Transformed*, p. 127. *Pravda*, 2 December 1989.

77. 'The Soviets and the German question', Scowcroft memorandum to Bush, 29 November 1989. Zelikow and Rice, *Germany Unified and Europe Transformed*, pp. 125–6.

78. Zelikow and Rice, *Germany Unified and Europe Transformed*, p. 130.

79. Bush–Kohl conversation, dinner, Brussels, 3 December 1989. Bush and Scowcroft, *A World Transformed*, p. 199.

80. Dieter Kastrup, memorandum, Gorbachev–Genscher conversation, Moscow, 5 December 1989. DFDE No. 13, pp. 73–80.

81. Memorandum, Mitterrand–Gorbachev conversations, Kyiv, 6 December 1989. Attali, *Verbatim III*, part 1, pp. 452–62.

82. Kohl, *Erinnerungen 1982–1990*, p. 1011.

83. Thatcher took out of her handbag and brandished maps of Germany's borders before and after the Second World War. Pointing to Silesia, Pomerania and East Prussia, she told Mitterrand: 'They'll take all of that, and Czechoslovakia too.' Thatcher, *The Downing Street Years*, p. 796. Attali, *Verbatim III*, 8 December 1989. For a reference to the map in Thatcher's handbag, see also Bush and Scowcroft, *A World Transformed*, p. 192.

84. Attali, *Verbatim III*, 8 December 1989.

85. Kohl, *Erinnerungen 1982–1990*, p. 1020. Kohl's remark was made to Rudolf Seiters, his chancellery minister.

86. Kohl speech, Dresden, 19 December 1989, Die Bundesregierung. https://www.bundesregierung.de/breg-de/service/bulletin/rede-des-bundeskanzlers-auf-der-kundgebung-vor-der-frauenkirche-in-dresden-790762.

87. Karl-Dieter Paschke, memorandum, 12 January 1990. 'The US administration is not attempting to describe publicly or test plainly the supposed Soviet pain barrier.' AAPD 1990, Document 8, pp. 31–42. See also 'The American Jews and the question of overcoming German division', Jürgen Ruhfus (German ambassador to Washington) memorandum, 22 January 1990. DE, Document 42, pp. 217–20.

88. Sarotte, *Not One Inch*, p. 45.

89. Sarotte, *Not One Inch*, p. 47. Chernyaev diary, entry 25 January 1990. GWU-NSA. https://nsarchive2.gwu.edu/NSAEBB/NSAEBB317/chernyaev_1990.pdf.

90. Teltschik, memorandum to Kohl, Bonn, 29 January 1990. DESE, Document 150, pp. 722–6.

91. Genscher, *Bild am Sonntag*, 28 January 1990. AAPD 1990, Document 25, p. 106, n. 15. Genscher pointedly foresaw a continued role for the Warsaw Pact. Existing miliary alliances would become 'building blocks for cooperative security structures for the whole of Europe'. The idea did not meet with approval in the chancellor's office. Teltschik noted: 'How can this work in practice: a unified Germany, of which two-thirds is in NATO, one-third outside?' Teltschik, *329 Tage*, p. 117.

92. Genscher, speech, Protestant Academy, Tutzing, 31 January 1990. AAPD 1990, Document 25, pp. 106–7, n. 17. 'Ideas that the part of Germany which today forms the

German Democratic Republic would be integrated into the military structure of NATO would block German–German rapprochement.' Genscher's motivation was above all to pay attention to Gorbachev's vulnerability. Frank Elbe, Genscher's key aide, later recalled how 'nervous' Genscher was, fearing even that the commitment to NATO was 'on thin ice'. Zelikow and Rice, Germany Unified and Europe Transformed, pp. 175–6. Richard Kiessler and Frank Elbe, Ein runder Tisch mit scharfen Ecken: Der diplomatische Weg zur deutschen Einheit [A Round Table with Sharp Edges: The Diplomatic Route to German Unity] (Berlin: Nomos, 1993), p. 80.

93. Bush and Scowcroft, A World Transformed, p. 237. 'Genscher had not made clear just what NATO's relationship to the territory of the GDR would be, and when, or even if, NATO was to pick up its defense. The role of the Bundeswehr was not covered, nor did he mention the future of US troops in Germany.'

94. Klaus Blech, memorandum, 6 February 1990. AAPD 1990, Document 27, p. 115. German diplomats regarded as positive that themes such as 'neutrality' and 'demilitarisation' had played no role in recent Soviet commentaries.

95. Letter, 'Internal situation in East Germany', Charles Powell, letter to Stephen Wall (private secretary to Majo), 31 January 1990. Gorbachev's statement came at a press conference with Hans Modrow, the vising East German prime minister. DBPO, series III: 1960–, vol. VII: German Unification, 1989–1990, No. 111, p. 233.

96. Von Ploetz, memorandum, Brussels, 9 February 1990. He underlined that there had been no military objections within NATO to the Tutzing speech. Genscher's dual rejection both of any change in West Germany's membership of the western alliance, and of enlargement NATO territory to the east, had attracted large and generally positive interest among alliance partners. He recognised, however, the drawback that 'for a certain time Soviet troops would be stationed on the present GDR territory'. AAPD 1990, Document 32, p. 136.

97. Genscher told Baker, 'There was a need to assure the Soviets that NATO would not extend its territorial coverage to the area of GDR nor anywhere else in Eastern Europe for that matter.' Knowing that Genscher would probably not convey the content of his meeting to the chancellor's office, Baker instructed Vernon Walters, the US ambassador to Bonn, to provide Teltschik with a report of his 2 February talk with Genscher. Sarotte, Not One Inch, p. 49, quoting State Department documents and news reports. Teltschik conversation with Walters, Bonn, 4 February 1990. DESE, Document 159, pp. 756–7.

98. Kohl–Mitterrand telephone conversation, 5 February 1990. DESE, Document 160, p. 757.

99. Hurd, memorandum to Mallaby, London, 6 February 1990. DBPO, series III: 1960–, vol. VII: German Unification, 1989–1990, No. 129, pp. 261–4.

100. The announcement of an internal German currency union – of monumental significance for the whole of Europe – was accelerated after Teltschik received news that Lothar Späth, prime minister of Baden-Württemberg and an arch-rival to Kohl within the CDU, was due to propose the move in the Stuttgart parliament on 7 January. Teltschik, 329 Tage, pp. 129–30.

101. David Marsh, 'Now is the time to jump', Financial Times, 15 May 1991. Marsh, The Euro, p.152, n. 78.

102. Pöhl, statement, Bundesbank council meeting, 15 February 1990. Verbatim report, HADB, B 330/ZBR, 20054.

103. The travel plans were initially uncoordinated. Washington was surprised by news that the German duo were planning to visit Gorbachev. Teltschik told Scowcroft that Bonn had discovered Baker's intention to get there first. The two sides then agreed that Robert Gates, Scowcroft's deputy, would find a way to brief Kohl just before his meeting with Gorbachev.

104. Memorandum, Shevardnadze–Baker conversation, Obsobuyak Guest House, Moscow, 9 February 1990. https://nsarchive.gwu.edu/media/16115/ocr. Baker backed the 'Two plus Four' arrangement on the grounds that 'the use of the four-power mechanism alone would be deeply resented by the German people or opposed by them. Indeed, it would probably produce a resurgent nationalism in Germany.' On the question of neutrality,

proposed publicly by Hans Modrow, East German prime minister, on 1 February, following his visit to Gorbachev on 30 January, Baker said: 'We think that would be a mistake. I think that if you just look at the history, you can see it would be a mistake. A neutral Germany would undoubtedly acquire its own independent nuclear capability; however, a Germany that is firmly anchored in a changed NATO, by that I mean a NATO that is far less of a military organisation, much more of a political one, would have no need for independent capability. There would, of course, have to be iron-clad guarantees that NATO's jurisdiction or forces would not move eastwards. And this would have to be done in a manner that would satisfy Germany's neighbours to the east.' See also GWU-NSA, 'NATO Expansion: What Gorbachev Heard'. US Department of State, FOIA 199504567. https://nsarchive.gwu.edu/sites/default/files/documents/4325680/Document-06-Record-of-conversation-between.pdf.

105. Memorandum, Gorbachev–Baker conversation, Moscow, 9 February 1990. Zelikow and Rice, *Germany Unified and Europe Transformed*, p. 181, citing 'Memcon of meeting with President Gorbachev at the Kremlin'. The document exists in various other forms, including in Russian. See 'Archive of the Gorbachev Foundation', Fond 1, Opis 1. Sarotte, *Not One Inch*, p. 55, n. 67. Gorbachev, *Memoirs*, p. 683. Letter, Baker to Kohl, 10 February 1989. This contains the same basic message but differs in other important respects For example, Baker's memoirs contain only one page on the meeting with Gorbachev on 9 February and diplomatically avoid his references to German militarism or nuclear weapons or on any kind of 'assurances' to Moscow on NATO. DESE, Document 173, pp. 793–4. Baker, *The Politics of Diplomacy*, p. 205.

106. Zelikow and Rice, *Germany Unified and Europe Transformed*, p. 181.

107. 'Record of Conversation between Mikhail Gorbachev and James Baker', 9 February 1990. GWU-NSA, 'NATO Expansion: What Gorbachev Heard'. US Department of State, FOIA 199504567. https://nsarchive.gwu.edu/sites/default/files/documents/4325680/Document-06-Record-of-conversation-between.pdf.

108. For an account of why Gorbachev did not ask for a written guarantee, see Taubman, *His Life and Times*, p. 547.

109. Gorbachev added: 'The technological and industrial potential allows Germany to do this. If it will exist within the framework of European structures, this process could be prevented.' Archive of the Gorbachev Foundation, Fond 1, Opis 1. A parallel conversation between Robert Gates and Vladimir Kryuchkov, the KGB chief, took place on 9 February at the KGB's Lubyanka headquarters. Gates told him 'We support the Kohl/Genscher idea of a united Germany belonging to NATO but with no expansion of military presence to the GDR.' He asked what Kryuchkov thought of the Kohl–Genscher proposal under which a united Germany would be associated with NATO, but in which NATO troops would move no further east than they now were. Kryuchkov replied that German unification was especially sensitive for the Soviet public and suggested that the Germans should offer the Soviet Union guarantees. 'We can't exclude that a reborn united Germany might become a threat to Europe. We would hate to see the US and the USSR have to become allies again against a resurgent Germany.' George H.W. Bush Presidential Library, NSC Scowcroft Files, Box 91128, Folder 'Gorbachev (Dobrynin) Sensitive'.

110. Letter, Baker to Kohl, 10 February 1990. 'I mentioned that it was unrealistic to assume that a big, economically significant country like Germany would be neutral. And then I put the following question to him. Would you prefer to see a unified Germany outside of NATO, independent and with no US forces, or would you prefer a unified Germany to be tied to NATO, with assurances that NATO's jurisdiction would not shift one inch eastward from his present position? He answered that the Soviet leadership was giving real thought to all such options and would be discussing them soon, "in a kind of seminar". He then added, "Certainly any extension of the zone of NATO would be unacceptable." (By implication NATO in its current zone might be acceptable.)' The summary was handed over by Klaus Blech, West German ambassador to Moscow, on Kohl's arrival on 10 February. DESE, Document 173, pp. 793–4. Gorbachev's version of the conversation contains the message from Baker, on the unacceptability of NATO extension, 'We agree with that.'

111. Letter, Bush to Kohl, 9 February 1990. DESE, Document 1970, p. 784. The letter was Scowcroft's suggestion, indicating he was unhappy that Baker had gone too far in his meeting with Gorbachev and Shevardnadze. Bush and Scowcroft, *A World Transformed*, pp. 240–1. The formulation 'special military status' was taken from a speech by Manfred Wörner, NATO secretary general and a former West German defence minister.

112. Teltschik, memorandum, Kohl–Gorbachev conversation, Moscow, 10 February 1990. The meeting took place, as was habitual in restricted meetings of heads of government, without Genscher. As well as two interpreters, the only other person present, according to the German record, was Anatoly Chernyaev. DESE, Document 174, pp. 795–807.

113. Kohl press conference, Moscow, 10 February 1990.

114. Teltschik, *329 Tage*, pp. 140–1. Gorbachev's agreement to determine the outcome in a six-state negotiating process without preconditions – 'no demand for a price and no threat' – was 'a sensation', Teltschik recorded. On the eve of Kohl's departure to Moscow, Teltschik had prepared the ground for the visit in an off-the-record briefing for journalists in Bonn. In answer to questions, he stated that East Germany was close to economic collapse, making headlines in the German press on 10 February and undoubtedly confirming the suppositions of the Kremlin. Teltschik's briefing statement to the press, where he was not named as the source, caused consternation in the German foreign office. For more details on the context, see Zelikow and Rice, *Germany Unified and Europe Transformed*, p. 200.

115. A Bonn government statement on 19 February laid down that no Bundeswehr troops, whether assigned or non-assigned to NATO, would be stationed in East Germany. Teltschik termed this 'a public concession to the Soviet Union which up to then had not been requested', Teltschik, *329 Tage*, p. 152. Antony Acland, memorandum to FCO, recording 'Americans concerned by Kohl statement [of 19 February]', Washington, 24 February 1990. DBPO, series III: 1960–, vol. VII: German Unification, 1989–1990, No. 154, p. 307. See n. 6 on disagreements within the West German government.

116. Bush and Scowcroft provide this summary: 'Kohl insisted that only a unified German government could agree to any de jure change in the 1937 borders, which had included substantial portions of what was now Poland. His ambiguous statements on the issue worried many who feared the behavior of a future Germany, lending support to the arguments of those concerned about unification, such as Margaret Thatcher.' Bush and Scowcroft, *A World Transformed*, p. 247.

117. This was the first time a German chancellor had been invited to the US presidential retreat. Genscher was pointedly not invited, even though Baker, his opposite number in Washington, took part. Conspicuously emphasising the informal nature of the proceedings, Baker met Kohl and his small delegation (including his wife Hannelore and Teltschik) at Dulles airport dressed in a red flannel shirt and Texan hat.

118. Bush statement, Bush and Scowcroft, *A World Transformed*, p. 250.

119. Bush and Scowcroft, *A World Transformed*, p. 248. Thatcher, *The Downing Street Years*, pp. 789–99. 'I stressed the importance of ensuring that a united Germany stayed within NATO and that US troops remained there.' Letter, Charles Powell to Stephen Wall on 'Prime Minister's talk with President Bush', 24 February 1990. DBPO, series III: 1960–, vol. VII: German Unification, 1989–1990, No. 155, pp. 310–11. Thatcher said she was grateful to Bush for proposing discussions on unification in NATO. She added: 'Looking to the future, we should also need a broader political framework in which to discuss Europe's security, and this must include the Soviet Union as well as the US. The best course would be to strengthen and build on the CSCE framework. Not only would this help avoid Soviet isolation, it would help balance German dominance in Europe.'

120. Thatcher, *The Downing Street Years*, pp. 798–9. 'President Bush, as I afterwards learnt, failed to understand that I was discussing a long-term balance of power in Europe rather than proposing an alternative alliance to NATO. It was the last time that I relied on a telephone conversation to explain such matters.' She wrote that the call took forty-five minutes, whereas Bush recorded that it went on for an hour.

121. Bush and Scowcroft, *A World Transformed*, pp. 250–6. Bush overcame a crucial moment during the meeting when Kohl toyed with imitating France in not joining NATO's full military integration. Furthermore, Teltschik succeeded (via his close relationship with Scowcroft) in persuading Baker no longer to use the word 'jurisdiction' when speaking about GDR territory, to avoid weakening NATO's commitment to the defence of the whole of a future united Germany (a theme that would prove controversial at the final signing of the unification treaty in Moscow in September 1990). According to Bush, quoting Teltschik's 'critical' argument: '"Jurisdiction" affected the underlying alliance responsibility (which we did not wish to compromise), while the location of forces did not. Baker agreed. "I used the term 'jurisdiction' before I realised it would impact upon Articles 4 and 5 of the North Atlantic Treaty," he admitted.' The otherwise successful Camp David session ended on a sour note. The Americans showed disquiet that Kohl ducked the issue of the Polish border at a closing press conference. This attracted the hostility of France, too, made clear when Bush telephoned Mitterrand the next day. Jürgen Ruhfus, German ambassador to Washington (who, much to the annoyance of the German foreign office, was not present at the Camp David meeting), reported complaints from ethnic Polish and Jewish organisations about the 'lack of credibility' of Kohl's ambiguity on Poland which had quickly become 'a top-ranking domestic policy theme in the US'. Rufus, memorandum to Foreign Office,1 March 1990. AAPD 1990, Document 57, pp. 241–5.

122. Bush and Scowcroft, *A World Transformed*, p. 253. See also Memorandum of Bush–Kohl conversation, 24 February 1990 (first meeting). Brent Scowcroft collection, George H.W. Bush library, GWU-NSA. The German DESE memorandum of the meeting notes the 'ghosts of the past' reference and adds Bush's description that Thatcher was 'living in history' ('in der Geschichte'). Kohl is recorded as saying of Thatcher, 'One cannot change the attitude of Prime Minister Thatcher', with a further passage about her redacted from the published German account. DESE, Document 192, p. 866. The US account includes these (slightly contradictory) sentences from Kohl: 'I can't understand her. The Empire declined fighting Germany – she thinks the UK paid this enormous price, and here comes Germany again.' In his innermost thoughts, Bush was genuinely greatly more relaxed than Thatcher about the prospect of a larger Germany. 'I don't think we can be naïve about history,' he wrote in his diary two days after the Camp David meeting with Kohl. 'But I don't think we need to let history and the problem with WWI and WWII control Germany's fate in the future. Perhaps it's different when we're this far away, but there is a certain insult to the Germans suggesting that they will give up democracy and give way to some new Hitler once they're unified, or that they will immediately want to expand their borders.' George H.W. Bush unpublished diary, 26 February 1990. Bush private collection. Moore, *Margaret Thatcher*, vol. 3, pp. 520–1.

123. Memorandum, Bush–Kohl conversation, Camp David, 24 February 1990. DESE, Document 192, pp. 861, 865. The US account of the meeting records the 'deadly' epithet as applying to Kohl's statement on neutrality, whereas in the German account (which is more likely to be accurate in relation to the chancellor's statement) he is clearly referring to Germany's potential acquisition of nuclear weapons.

124. Memorandum, Bush–Kohl conversation, Camp David, 24 February 1990. DESE, Document 192, p. 869. Bush and Scowcroft, *A World Transformed*, p. 253. See also Teltschik, *329 Tage*, pp. 158–61.

125. Two days after the Camp David meeting, Gorbachev's key German adviser, Valentin Falin, confirmed to British ambassador Braithwaite in Moscow, the dual importance of a continuing American presence in Europe: US troops would help keep not just the Soviets but the Germans under control. 'Pan-European structures' were necessary 'as a form of insurance' against the danger that, in ten years, 'Germany could break loose of its own accord from the ties of NATO and the Community'. Memorandum, Braithwaite–Falin conversation, Moscow, 19 July 1990. UKNA, PREM 19/3183.

126. Memorandum, 'Four political directors talks in London', 28 February 1990. AAPD, Document 54, pp. 218–29.

127. Memorandum, Dieter Kastrup–Anatoly Adamishin (deputy Soviet foreign minister) conversation, Geneva, 3 March 1990. AAPD, Document 61, pp. 258–9.

128. Memorandum, Teltschik–Portugalov conversation, Bonn, 28 March 1990. Teltschik, *329 Tage*, pp. 186–7. Portugalov put forward a further ploy to blur the demarcation between eastern and western armed forces. Germany would withdraw from the military aspects of NATO, which would allow 'overarching structures' with the Warsaw Pact; the Soviet Union might even join a new version of NATO (an idea that, more than a decade later, Putin put forward in the early years of his presidency).

129. Zelikow and Rice, *Germany Unified and Europe Transformed*, pp. 245–6.

130. Zubok, *Collapse*, p. 160.

131. Bush and Scowcroft, *A World Transformed*, p. 367.

132. Teltschik, *329 Tage*, pp. 231–5.

133. Charles Powell, interview with author, London, 28 February 2023.

134. Letter, Kohl to Gorbachev, 22 May 1990. DE Document 284, pp. 1136–7.

135. Teltschik, *329 Tage*, report on White House meeting, 17 May 1990, pp. 236–8. During the wider delegation meeting, Kohl asked Bush to consider Gorbachev's requirement for a positive 'psychological climate' for his forthcoming visit. Kohl therefore asked Bush to keep demonstrators away from the White House. Report on delegation meeting, Kohl–Bush, Washington, 17 May 1990. DE, Document 281, pp. 1126–31.

136. Memorandum, Gorbachev–Mitterrand conversation, Moscow, 25 May 1990. *Mikhail Gorbachev i germanskii vopros* [*Mikhail Gorbachev and the German Question*,], ed. Alexander Galkin and Anatoly Chernyaev (Moscow: Ves' Mir, 2006), pp. 454–66. Trans. Anna Melyakova for the National Security Archive. GWU-NSA. https://nsarchive.gwu.edu/document/16133-document-19-record-conversation-between.

137. Zubok, *Collapse*, pp. 118–20.

138. Zelikow and Rice, *Germany Unified and Europe Transformed*, pp. 276–9.

139. Bush told Gorbachev: 'We all in the West are united in one [concern]: the main danger lies in separating Germany from the community of democratic states, in trying to impose some special status and humiliating conditions on her. It is precisely this kind of development of events that could lead to a revival of German militarism and revanchism – which is exactly the concern you have.' Record of Gorbachev–Bush conversation, Washington, 31 May 1990. Gorbachev Foundation Archive, Moscow, Fond 1, Opis 1. 'NATO Expansion: What Gorbachev Heard', 12 December 2017. GWU-NSA. https://nsarchive.gwu.edu/document/16135-document-21-record-conversation-between.

140. A strong motivation for the concession seems to have been Gorbachev's desire for a free-trade agreement with the US. As Baker put it, 'From Gorbachev's perspective, progress required that he return to Moscow with tangible economic benefits – and this meant the trade agreement.' Shevardnadze told Baker, 'We just can't go home without it.' Baker, *The Politics of Diplomacy*, p. 254.

141. Zelikow and Rice, *Germany Unified and Europe Transformed*, pp. 276–7. The authors were unable to locate a US memorandum for the conversation. Their published version draws on Russian sources, especially from Chernyaev, as well as interviews with participants. See also Valentin Falin, *Politsche Erinnerungen* (Munich: Droemer Knaur, 1993), pp. 492–3, and letter, Bush to Kohl, 4 June 1990. DE, no. 299, p. 1178.

142. Transcript, Bush–Gorbachev press conference, 3 June 1990. https://www.washington-post.com/archive/politics/1990/06/04/transcript-of-bush-gorbachev-news-conference/9e85ac99-3ffb-44b6-b2e3-ebb0ea4b9d36/.

143. Kohl declaration, Bonn, 17 July 1990. Teltschik, *329 Tage*, pp. 313–42.

144. Memoranda of Gorbachev–Kohl conversations, Moscow and Archys (Stavropol area), 15–16 July 1990, including preparation of Soviet–German treaty on partnership and cooperation. DESE, Documents 350–4, pp. 1340–67.

145. Scowcroft agreed: Zubok, *Collapse*, p. 143.

146. Baker, *The Politics of Diplomacy*, pp. 1–16.

147. John Weston, political director at the UK foreign office, played a critical role in stiffening resistance to weakening western terms, earning complaints (especially from Frank Elbe,

Genscher's chief aide) that the British were holding up the process. Before departing for Moscow, Weston took advice from Charles Powell to assure himself of Thatcher's backing on a crucial point over the continued foreign military presence in Berlin, determining that this would be solely on the request of the unified German government, giving the Germans (rather than the 1945 victor powers) control over the question. Once in Moscow, in the early evening of 11 September, he phoned Powell again to ensure he could hold out over NATO forces 'crossing the line' before Douglas Hurd, the foreign secretary, arrived later in the day.

148. Braithwaite, memorandum to Foreign Office, 12 September 1990. 'The thorny issue of movement by non-German armed forces into East Germany after Soviet withdrawal had to be resolved personally by Foreign Ministers. The UK and US argued strongly against accepting arrangements which would extend limitations on East Germany beyond non-stationing and thus constrain Alliance options . . . Shevardnadze was finally brought to agree that, although after Soviet withdrawal foreign forces would not be stationed or deployed in East Germany, questions regarding the application of the word "deployed" would be decided by the government of Germany.'

5 PATH TO BREAKDOWN

1. Memorandum of Kohl–Gorbachev conversation, Meseroye (near Kiev), 5 July 1991. AAPD 1991, Document 235, p. 964. See also, for this and other exchanges, translations of Kohl's meetings with Gorbachev. Wilson Center Digital Archive. https://digitalarchive. wilsoncenter.org/document/chancellors-helmut-kohls-meeting-soviet-president-gor-bachev-friday-5-july-1991-meseroye. Kohl, Erinnerungen 1990–1994, p. 346.
2. Fritz Stern's sentiments at dinner, Columbia University, November 1996, after a meeting of the Harriman Institute at which Talbott spoke upholding Clinton's policy on NATO enlargement. The dinner guests spoke mainly against enlargement, led by George Kennan. According to Talbott, Stern was the only participant in favour. The paraphrase of his comments comes from a January 1997 conversation from which Talbott quotes Kohl as making the same argument as Stern two months earlier. Strobe Talbott, The Russia Hand: A Memoir of Presidential Diplomacy (New York: Random House, 2002), pp. 220, 226. Memorandum, Kohl–Talbott conversation, Bonn, 15 January 1997. US Department of State, F-2017-13804, Document C06702796D.
3. Rice interview, 14 April 2022. SMU Center for Presidential History.
4. Description by Lyne, interview with author, London, 9 June 2023.
5. Scowcroft interview with Zelikow, 10–11 August 2000. University of Virginia Miller Center, Presidential Oral Histories. Transcript released after Scowcroft's death in August 2020.
6. Chernyaev, diary entry, 23 October 1990. GWU-NSA.
7. Chernyaev, diary entry, 15 November 1990. GWU-NSA.
8. Chernyaev, diary entry, 25 February 1991. GWU-NSA.
9. Memorandum, Bush–Kohl conversation, 23 February 1991. George H.W. Bush Presidential Library, Brent Scowcroft Collection, Presidential Telcon Files, FOIA 2009-0275-S.
10. 'Yeltsin, criticizing failures, insists that Gorbachev quit', New York Times, 20 February 1991.
11. Nixon, 'A superpower at the abyss', Time, 22 April 1991.
12. Braithwaite, diary entry, 5 March 1991. GWU-NSA. https://nsarchive.gwu.edu/document/16142-document-28-ambassador-rodric-braithwaite-diaryc.
13. Memorandum, 'Quadripartite meeting of political directors, Bonn, 6 March: Security in central and eastern Europe.' UKNA, PREM 19/3326. See also Memorandum, Jürgen Chrobog, Political Directors Consultations, 6 March 1991, Bonn – relating a nine-page British foreign office paper which stated inter alia 'No NATO membership will be considered for individual central and eastern European states'. AAPD 1991, Document 83, pp. 322–32.

14. Memorandum, Genscher–Gorbachev conversation, Moscow, 18 March 1991. AAPD 1991, Document 103, p. 411.
15. Memorandum, Hans-Dietrich Genscher–Alexander Bessmertnykh conversation, 19 March 1991. PAAA, BI ZA 971/178930.
16. Memorandum following Vaclav Havel's visit to NATO, 21 March 1991. PAAA, 214/TSE 156457.
17. Von Ploetz memorandum, Wörner visit to Bonn, 19 April 1991. AAPD 1991, Document 136, pp. 536–45.
18. Chrobog memorandum, political directors meeting, London, 24 April 1991. AAPD 1991, Document 138, p. 557.
19. Memorandum on Kohl–Gorbachev telephone conversation, 30 April 1991. AAPD 1991, Document 149, pp. 606–9.
20. For German priorities on the matter, Strobe Talbott's reflections are important. 'The European Union, if it was going to expand, would bring into its bosom countries that had been marginalized and brutalized and deprived of all of these positive influences for the fifty years, if not longer, of being under one totalitarian regime or another. But it was quite clear in the minds of the principal European leaders, first and foremost Helmut Kohl, that that wasn't going to happen. That is, central Europe wasn't going to be brought into Europe and the EU wasn't going to expand unless NATO expanded. And NATO wasn't going to expand unless the US made it expand.' Warren Christopher and Strobe Talbott Oral History, interview, Clinton Presidential Oral History Project, 15–16 April 2002.
21. Genscher–Baker conversation, Washington, 10 May 1991. AAPD 1991, Document 159, pp. 649–50. Baker stated: 'I agree we can rule out the possibility of NATO membership by the Baltic states. However, for the countries of central and eastern Europe, we cannot demand from them that they permanently desist from a decision on alliance membership. These countries should not at the current time press for NATO membership, but this cannot be ruled out for the future.'
22. German–French ambassadors conference, Weimar, 16–17 May 1991. AAPD 1991, Document 165, pp. 671–3.
23. Von Ploetz memorandum on NATO summit, Copenhagen, 6 June 1991. AAPD 1991, Document 190, pp. 772–80.
24. National Security Council. Meeting on US–Soviet relations, White House situation room, 3 June 1991. NSC Burns files, Box 2, OA/ID CF010308-008.
25. Bush and Scowcroft, report on 20 June meeting in Oval Office, in *A World Transformed*, pp. 504–5. The Americans passed on a message from Jack Matlock, the US ambassador to Moscow, who had received the news that Gorbachev would be overthrown the next day. 'Yeltsin discounted the rumor entirely, saying there was no way it would happen.'
26. Memorandum of Kohl–Gorbachev conversation, Meseroye (near Kyiv), 5 July 1991. AAPD 1991, Document 235, pp. 964–72.
27. German press and information office documents, message from Department IIIB5 to Dr Zickerick, 9 July 1991, and associated documents on 'Das Nordatlantische Bündnis: Eine Allianz für den Frieden' ['The North Atlantic Alliance: An alliance for peace']. PAAA, B14 ZA/151142.
28. Zubok, *Collapse*, p. 252, citing Savranskaya and Balton (eds), *The Last Superpower Summits: Gorbachev, Reagan, and Bush. Conversations That Ended the Cold War* (Budapest: Central European University Press, 2016), pp. 852–3 and other sources. On the '$100bn for a war', Scowcroft writes: 'I don't think he understood that the Gulf countries, Japan and others . . . had dug deeply to defray the cost of the war.' Bush and Scowcroft, *A World Transformed*, p. 507.
29. Bush and Scowcroft, *A World Transformed*, p. 509. Gorbachev related this joke to other leaders at 10 Downing Street. 'Two Russians were complaining as they stood waiting in line to buy vodka. One declared impatiently that the line was too long, and he was going to go and shoot Gorbachev. After disappearing for a couple of hours, the man returned to his friend, who asked, "Well, did you shoot him?" The man shook his head. "No, the line over there was longer than this one."'

30. Beschloss and Talbott, *At the Highest Levels*, p. 407.
31. Zubok, *Collapse*, p. 254.
32. Baker, *The Politics of Diplomacy*, p. 529.
33. Memorandum, Mitterrand–Kohl conversation, Bad Wiessee, 23 July 1991. AAPD 1991, Document 250, pp. 1038–47.
34. Shortly after taking office in January 1993, Clinton, Talbott's fellow Rhodes Scholar (as students they shared a house in Oxford), invited him to become ambassador to Moscow. Talbott, a journalist specialising on Soviet and East–West issues, made his name with *Time* magazine in the 1970s and 1980s. Although he turned the offer down, Talbott soon afterwards accepted a request from Clinton's secretary of state, Warren Christopher, to help manage relations with the ex-Soviet CIS. After a year, he took over as deputy secretary of state. In 2016, Talbott described his switch to government: 'A guy that I had shared a house with in Oxford and who used to literally cook breakfast for me, and it was usually scrambled eggs, while I was working on the Khrushchev memoirs . . . called after he was elected president and said I'm coming to Washington and I'd like to talk to you. And I said great, and I went over to his hotel and he said, "How'd you like to be my ambassador to Moscow?" I said I'd love it but I can't because my wife has got a job and my kids are in school and he said, "Well, okay, too bad. Thanks, all right. Have a nice day."' Association for Diplomatic Studies and Training, interview, Foreign Affairs Oral History Project, 26 July 2016.
35. 'Mikhail Gorbachev and George Bush: The summit Goodfellas – How Mikhail Gorbachev and George Bush developed one of the most extraordinary yet subtle collaborations in history, using their personal rapport to facilitate the Soviet Union's capitulation', *Time*, 5 August 1991. Talbott's article focused particularly on Gorbachev's abandonment of long-held Soviet claims on arms control and acceptance of many parts of America's negotiating position. 'In all three treaties that have been concluded since he came to power – Intermediate-Range Nuclear Forces (INF) in 1987, Conventional Forces in Europe (CFE) in 1990, and START this week . . . the US–Soviet dialogue has been rewritten . . . Today George Bush worries less about whether the USSR will start World War III than whether it will slide into a civil war.'
36. Sarotte, *Not One Inch*, p. 125. Memorandum, Bush–Wörner conversation, 11 October 1991. George H.W. Bush Presidential Library.
37. Memorandum, Gorbachev–Genscher conversation, Moscow, 9 September 1991. AAPD 1991, Document 297, pp. 1201–4.
38. Memorandum, Yeltsin–Genscher conversation, Moscow, 10 September 1991. AAPD 1991, Document 300, pp. 1207–11.
39. Memorandum, Kohl–Mitterrand conversation, Bonn, 18 September 1991. Mitterrand commented witheringly that John Major, Britain's new prime minister, had visited him in Paris a few days earlier. He had not understood the president's ironic reference to solving the Yugoslav problem (as in the First World War) by Germany, Turkey and Hungary sending troops to protect Croatia, with Britain, France and the Soviet Union intervening on the side of Serbia. AAPD 1991, Document 315, pp. 1256–61.
40. Memorandum, 'NATO Perspectives – Central and Eastern Europe including Soviet Union', for Genscher, Hans-Bodo Bertram, Bonn, 19 September 1991. AAPD 1991, Document 319, pp. 1271–5.
41. 'The alliance must prepare itself for increasing requests about this possibility [of membership] by the states of central and eastern Europe (Poland, the Czech-Slovak Federation, Hungary).'
42. Memorandum, ministerial discussion with Kohl, Genscher, Theo Waigel and Gerhard Stoltenberg, Bonn, 1 October 1991. AAPD 1991, Document 329, pp. 1304–8.
43. Memorandum, Hans-Dietrich Genscher–Boris Pankin telephone call, 11 October 1991. Pankin: 'I have the impression that these three states [Czech-Slovak Federation, Hungary, Poland] believe their chances of joining NATO are now greater.' Genscher: 'That is absolutely not the case. We are therefore not speaking of membership in NATO, rather of developing orderly relationships with NATO.' PAAA, BI ZA 971/178930.

44. Memorandum, Shevardnadze–Genscher conversation, Moscow, 26 October 1991. AAPD 1991, Document 364, pp. 1461–7.

45. Memorandum, Bush–Yakovlev conversation, 19 November 1991. George H.W. Bush Presidential Library. https://bush41library.tamu.edu/files/memcons-telcons/1991-11-19--Yakovlev.pdf.

46. 'Draft Options Paper – US Relations with Russia and Ukraine', 22 November 1991. Quoted in Sarotte, *Not One Inch*, p. 127.

47. Memorandum, Kohl–Yeltsin conversation, Bonn, 21 November 1991. AAPD 1991, Document 392, pp. 1573–80.

48. Memorandum, Waigel remarks to Yeltsin, wider Kohl–Yeltsin exchanges, Bonn, 21 November 1991. AAPD-1991, Document 393, p. 1583.

49. The agreement was signed on 8 December at Viskuli, a hunting estate in Belovezhskaya Pushcha, Belarus, on 8 December 1991.

50. Memorandum, Bush–Yeltsin conversation, 8 December 1991. GWU-NSA. https://nsarchive.gwu.edu/document/22495-3-memorandum-telephone-conversation-bush.

51. Boris Yeltsin, *Midnight Diaries* (London: Weidenfeld & Nicolson, 2000), p. 253. 'It was easier to break with the revolution [of 1917] abruptly than to drag it out.'

52. Memorandum, Bush–Yeltsin telephone conversation, 23 December 1991. National Security Archive. https://nsarchive2.gwu.edu/NSAEBB/NSAEBB447/1991-12-23%20Memorandum%20of%20Telephone%20Conversation%20between%20President%20Bush%20and%20President%20Yeltsin.PDF.

53. Gorbachev, *Memoirs*, p. 864.

54. Memorandum, Bush–Gorbachev telephone conversation, 25 December 1991. GWU-NSA. https://nsarchive.gwu.edu/sites/default/files/documents/10-Memorandum-of-Telephone-Conversation-Gorbachev.pdf.

55. Gorbachev, *Memoirs*, pp. 866–7.

56. Chernyaev, diary entry, 27 December 1991. GWU-NSA.

57. Chernyaev, diary, 'Afterword to 1991'. GWU-NSA.

58. Braithwaite, interview with author, Wimbledon, 30 April 2023, and further Braithwaite notes to author.

59. Yegor Gaidar was first vice premier of economics and economic minister in 1991–2 and finance minister and acting prime minister for brief periods in1992 until parliament rejected him, and Viktor Chernomyrdin was chosen as a compromise. In 1993, Yeltsin again appointed him first vice premier under Chernomyrdin.

60. Anatoly Chubais became a minister in November 1991, in charge of the committee for managing state property that handled Yeltsin's oligarch-enriching privatisation. He was deputy prime minister for economic and financial policy from November 1994 to January 1996.

61. Serge Schmemann, 'A secret cable and a clue to where U.S.–Russia relations went wrong', *New York Times*, 28 January 2025.

62. 'The long telegram of the 1990s: "Whose Russia is it anyway? Toward a policy of benign respect"', E. Wayne Murray, NSA, 18 December 1993. https://nsarchive.gwu.edu/briefing-book/nato-75-russia-programs/2024-12-18/long-telegram-1990s-whose-russia-it-anyway-toward.

63. Morel, interview with author, Paris, 24 April 2023.

64. The First Chechen war took place between December 1994 and August 1996. The prelude was the battle of Grozny in November 1994, when Russia sought to overthrow the Chechen government.

65. Klaus Neubert, memorandum, German–Ukraine relations, 25 January 1993. AAPD 1993, Document 27, pp. 94–100.

66. Von Ploetz, memorandum, NATO foreign ministers meeting, Brussels, 26 February 1993. AAPD 1993, Document 68, pp. 259–65.

67. 'Ukraine agrees to give up its nuclear arsenal, Clinton says', *Los Angeles Times*, 11 January 1994. 'January 14 trilateral statement', Clinton–Yeltsin Moscow summit, 25 January 1994. GWU-NSA. https://nsarchive.gwu.edu/document/30922-document-10-january-

14-trilateral-statement-january-14-1994. Putin signed the December 1994 Budapest memorandum guaranteeing Ukraine's territorial integrity in exchange for giving up the Soviet-era nuclear weapons on its soil. https://policymemos.hks.harvard.edu/files/policy-memos/files/2-23-22_ukraine-the_budapest_memo.pdf?m=1645824948.

68. 'Bill Clinton saw Putin's Ukraine campaign as "just a matter of time" in 2011', *Financial Times*, 5 May 2023. Clinton said in New York that Putin had told him in 2011 that he rejected Yeltsin's agreement to respect Ukraine's territory in exchange for Kyiv relinquishing its nuclear arsenal. Clinton said, 'I knew from that day forward it was just a matter of time.'

69. Memorandum, Yeltsin–Kohl conversation, Moscow, 3 March 1993. AAPD 1993, Document 75, pp. 292–7.

70. 'Personal message of the federal chancellor to President Clinton, President Mitterrand and Prime Minister Major', Bonn, 5 March 1993. PAAA, 213 321.00 Russ, additional document.

71. Memorandum, 'Discussion on NATO enlargement', Hermann von Richthofen, Brussels, 2 June 1993. AAPD 1993, Document 174, pp. 729–6.

72. 'Yeltsin "understands" Polish bid for a Role in NATO', *New York Times*, 26 August 1993. https://www.nytimes.com/1993/08/26/world/yeltsin-understands-polish-bid-for-a-role-in-nato.html.

73. Yeltsin's foreign minister recorded: 'Wałęsa invited him to a private dinner in a "simple and friendly" format, one-on-one. Well after midnight, a call from the president woke me, which was unusual. When I walked into Yeltsin's apartment, it was clear that he was almost unable to speak. He finally said that he had agreed with Wałęsa to insert a new paragraph into the prepared text of a political declaration scheduled for the assigning ceremony the following morning. He handed me a piece of paper with ragged handwriting on it, but was not in any condition to discuss anything.' The Polish leader had resorted to 'a trick' played by Kazakh leader Nursultan Nazarbayev and other CIS [Commonwealth of Independent States] bosses, who habitually submitted Yeltsin to 'friendly toasts' after which they would persuade him to make promises and sign papers on concessions, mostly on trade and financial matters. Andrei Kozyrev, *Firebird: The Elusive Fate of Russian Democracy* (Pittsburgh, PA: University of Pittsburgh Press, 2019), p. 215.

74. Retranslated letter, Yeltsin to Clinton on NATO expansion, 15 September 1993. The letter stated: 'In the long run, it should probably not be ruled out that even we [Russia] would join NATO, but for the time being this is a theoretical position.' US Department of State, M-2006-01499.

75. Partnership for Peace (PfP) remains in existence, with thirty-four members, although Russian and Ukrainian membership is suspended.

76. The NACC was launched on 20 December 1991, linking the sixteen NATO members and nine states of central and eastern Europe including the Soviet Union. As the final communiqué was being agreed, the Soviet ambassador announced that the Soviet Union had dissolved during the meeting and that he now represented only the Russian Federation. This was a day before the 21 December signing of the Alma-Ata protocols, formally ending the USSR and establishing the CIS. Foreign ministers of the Czech-Slovak Federation and Romania used the occasion to state their wish to join NATO. Yeltsin sent a message to the signing ceremony stating: 'Today we [Russia] are not raising the question of Russia's membership in NATO, but we are ready to regard it as a long-term political aim.' Von Ploetz memorandum on first meeting of NACC council, 20 December 1991. AAPD 1991, Document 439, pp. 1764–9. See also NATO documentation: https://www.nato.int/cps/en/natohq/topics_69344.htm.

77. A comprehensive account of diplomatic papers published on these issues, focused on the US, is contained in 'NATO expansion: What Yeltsin heard', 16 March 2018. GWU-NSA. https://nsarchive.gwu.edu/briefing-book/russia-programs/2018-03-16/nato-expansion-what-yeltsin-heard. See also James Goldgeier, 'Promises made, promises broken – What Yeltsin was told about NATO in 1993 and why it matters', *War on the Rocks*, 12 July 2016.

78. See Josha Shifrinson, 'Deal or no deal? The end of the Cold War and the U.S. offer to limit NATO expansion', *International Security*, vol. 40, no. 4 (Spring 2016), pp. 7–44. Shifrinson

argued that the US was playing a double game in 1990, leading Gorbachev to believe NATO would be subsumed in a new European security structure, while working to ensure hegemony in Europe and the maintenance of NATO.

79. 'Strategy for NATO's expansion and transformation', 7 September 1993. Department of State, 7 July 2004, 199904515. The State Department document laid down a calendar including admission of Ukraine, Belarus and Russia in 2005, after the central and eastern Europeans and the Baltic states. The document drew attention to possible divergence in the German government. 'German Defence Minister [Volker] Ruhe has been outspoken on this question [enlargement] and the fact that he has not been reined in by Chancellor Kohl suggests he may be a stalking horse.'

80. For a general description of the Zavidovo meeting, see Sarotte, *Not One Inch*, p. 178. Christoper described Yeltsin as 'stiff, almost robotic' and 'emanating heavy alcohol fumes'. Warren Christopher, *Chances of a Lifetime: A Memoir* (New York: Simon & Schuster, 2001), p. 280. The encounter was prefaced by Christopher telling the Russian foreign minister Kozyrev in Moscow, 'We [the US] were sensitive to the Russian position and that we had developed a proposal that balanced various objectives and interests. There would be no immediate provision for new [NATO] memberships and no associated memberships; no one would be excluded.' Christopher said, 'Eventual alliance membership would be based on performance and other factors; for now, the door to future membership would be open to all on an equal basis.' The State Department document cited Kozyrev asking 'pointedly, whether there would not be two or three new members now?' Christopher answered, 'No . . . We were emphasising Partnership for Peace which would involve training and exercises in dealing with security questions.' The aim to 'develop a habit of interoperability and cooperation'. Memorandum, Christopher meeting with Foreign Minister Kozyrev, 22 October 1993. US Department of State, 11 March 2023, 200001030.

81. James 'Jim' Collins, the US chargé d'affaires in Moscow (who became ambassador in 1997–2001), warned Christopher before his Moscow trip in October 1993, the NATO issue 'is neuralgic to the Russians. They expect to end up on the wrong side of a new division of Europe if any decision is made quickly. No matter how nuanced, if NATO adopts a policy which envisions expansion into central and eastern Europe without holding the door open to Russia, it would be universally interpreted in Moscow as directed against Russia and Russia alone – or "neo-containment".' Further, the document stated, 'NATO expansion could damage the foundation of Yeltsin's policies.' US Department of State, 4 May 2000, 200000982.

82. Memorandum on Secretary Christopher's meeting with President Yeltsin, 22 October 1993, Moscow. US Department of State, 8 May 2000, 200000982.

83. Kozyrev, *Firebird*, p. 221. An account of the 22 October meeting by Strobe Talbott, Christopher's key aide, who accompanied him to the meeting, indicated that Yeltsin heard only what he wanted to hear, not giving the Americans the time to explain that the real message was, 'PfP today, enlargement tomorrow.' Talbott, *The Russia Hand*, p. 101.

84. Memorandum, Kozyrev's European security plan, to Tony Lake (Clinton's national security adviser) from Strobe Talbott, ambassador-at-large and special adviser (1993–4) to Secretary of State Christopher, who became deputy secretary of state in 1994–2001. The paper criticised Kozyrev's plan, published in a German newspaper the previous weekend, for a five-step approach on European security which would place NATO, the western European Union and the Commonwealth of Independent States under the coordinating authority of the North Atlantic Cooperation Council, and the Conference on Security and Cooperation in Europe. This would 'severely hamstring NATO's ability to act'. The paper concludes that Kozyrev was moving to a 'tougher more nationalistic line', guided by his own personal interests and Russia's 'backlash against reform and the West' evident in elections on 12 December. NSA-GWU, US Department of State, F-2017-13804, Doc No. C06689721.

85. Memorandum, 'Further developments in Russia – domestic and foreign policies', Klaus Neubert, 4 March 1993. AAPD 1993, Document 77, pp. 304–9.

86. Memorandum, telephone conversation between Douglas Hurd and Klaus Kinkel, UK and German foreign ministers, 14 December 1993. UKNA, FCO 176/336.

87. Memorandum, British embassy, Bonn, on Kinkel's visit to Russia, 19 December 1993. UKNA, FCO 176/336.

88. Memorandum, 'The President's meeting with Czech leaders', 11 January 1994: 'Russia is not a near-term threat ... But if historical trends do reassert themselves, we will have organized ourselves so that we could move quickly not only to NATO membership but other security relations that can serve as a deterrent.' According to the US account, 'Given sensitivities of the population here, he [Havel] must emphasise that the PFP is a first step leading to full NATO membership. The President expressed full agreement.' William J. Clinton Presidential Library. Clinton spelled out the PfP insurance policy.

89. The President's luncheon plenary meeting with the heads of state and government of Poland, Hungary, Slovakia and the Czech Republic, Prague, 11 January 1994. William J. Clinton Presidential Library.

90. Clinton press conference, Prague, 12 January 1994. https://www.govinfo.gov/content/pkg/WCPD-1994-01-17/pdf/WCPD-1994-01-17-Pg41.pdf. Clinton's statement was seized on by proponents of NATO expansion in Washington to indicate this was the real goal behind PfP. James M. Goldgeier, *Not Whether But When: The U.S. Decision to Enlarge Nato* (Washington, DC: Brookings Institution Press, 1999), pp. 57–8, 62–76.

91. Memorandum of conversation, 'One-on-one meeting with President Yeltsin of Russia [and President Clinton]', Moscow, 13 January 1994, GWU-NSA, CPL.

92. 'There is still an enormous amount of respect for you among the leaders with whom I deal, but there is an underlying theme. "Yeltsin is a great man. But he is fighting a losing battle against the forces of history." It would be helpful for them to see that you don't believe that. I don't believe it. We don't want people to have a stereotype of Russia that is frozen in the past.' Memorandum of conversation, 'One-on-one meeting with President Yeltsin of Russia [and President Clinton]', Moscow, 13 January 1994, GWU-NSA, CPL. Clinton's attempted reassurance show an intriguing similarity to Kohl's words to Gorbachev in a telephone conversation on 30 April 1991. Kohl spoke of a 'diffuse mood' in Washington, which he said was partly caused by the Soviet Union itself. 'The talk there goes along the following lines: "The man [Gorbachev] is good, but he probably won't make it." The Chancellor told Gorbachev: "It is psychologically important to counter such versions." Kohl added he would do be doing that himself.' Memorandum on Kohl–Gorbachev telephone conversation, 30 April 1991. AAPD 1991, Document 149, pp. 606–9.

93. Putin was head of the St Petersburg Committee for External Relations until 1996. Among other appointments, in March 1994 he became first deputy head of the city administration. He gained a reputation as 'the most closed figure in the city government'. Short, *Putin*, p. 199.

94. Bergerdorf Discussion Group, meeting, St Petersburg, 26–7 March 1994. Account from Körber Foundation archive.

95. Statement by Ingeborg Fleischhauer, professor at St Petersburg State University.

96. Memorandum, Clinton–Yeltsin telephone conversation, 5 July 1994. GWU-NSA, US Department of State, F-2017-13804, Document C06838158. Clinton said: 'I would like us to concentrate on efforts on the Partnership for Peace programme so we can achieve a united Europe.'

97. Clinton speech to Polish parliament, Warsaw, 7 July 1994.

98. Janusz Reiter, telephone interview with author, Warsaw–London, 2 April 2024. Reiter, who was speaking with Kohl at the St Petersburg guest house ahead of his foreign minister's official conversation, at first denied Kohl's claim, but after Kohl pressed his argument admitted that the chancellor's point was correct. Olechowski's visit was on 8 July 1994.

99. Richard Holbrooke, about to become assistant secretary of state, was the chief architect of an address by Al Gore, Clinton's vice president, which stressed that NATO was 'the best hope for stability and security' for central and eastern Europe. Rühe reinforced the message, criticising the vagueness of the PfP proposition as 'the highest possible degree of ambiguity'. Ceremony to mark western troop withdrawals, Berlin, 9 September 1994.

100. Revelling in his 'bulldozer' reputation, Holbrooke succeeded in taking over a new Talbott-inspired interagency working group (IWG) on NATO policy. Talbott had begun advising Christopher that an expanded NATO could help manage post-Cold War conflicts like disintegration in Yugoslavia. He wanted to keep the initiative quiet: as he put it, 'NATO expansion will, when it occurs, by definition be punishment, or "neo-containment", of the bad Bear.' The preparatory papers for the first IWG meeting, on 22 September 1994, stated: 'The goal is to achieve NATO expansion.' The US needed to develop 'a sense of inevitability', as with German unification. M.E. Sarotte, 'How to enlarge NATO: The debate inside the Clinton administration, 1993–5', quoting 'Preparatory papers for IWG meeting', NATO Expansion: Concept and Strategy, 17 September 1994, DS-OIPS.

101. The briefing paper stated that Washington had to consider 'the impact of [the] momentum of the expansion discussion on Ukraine's progress on nuclear weapons dismantlement, and NPT [i.e. its plans to accede to the Nuclear Non-Proliferation Treaty].' Russian objections were secondary. 'We should not be deterred by whether a rationale for expansion can be sold to the Russians or others. They won't buy it now under any circumstances.'

102. Clinton–Yeltsin conversation, Washington, 28 September 1994. GWU-NSA, US Department of State F-2017-13804, Document C06838462. Talbott, *The Russia Hand*, p. 136.

103. North Atlantic Council communiqué, Brussels, 1 December 1994. https://www.nato.int/docu/comm/49-95/c941201a.htm.

104. Primakov built up his position under Yeltsin as a prime member of the anti-West faction and a rival to Kozyrev. 'In November 1993, Primakov published a report that NATO was still a threat to Russia.' Later, 'Primakov told Yeltsin that Clinton deceived him to get NATO approval and that the PfP was a trick to draw East Europeans into NATO, leaving Russia in the cold. The Russian press increasingly shared this suspicion.' Andrei Kozyrev, 'Russia and NATO enlargement: An insider's account' in Daniel S. Hamilton and Kristina Spohr (eds), *Open Door: NATO and Euro-Atlantic Security After the Cold War* (Washington, DC: Transatlantic Leadership Network, 2019), pp. 449–58.

105. Kozyrev, *Firebird*, pp. 280–1.

106. Clinton letters to Yeltsin, 28 November and 2 December 1994. Yeltsin letters to Clinton, 30 November and 3 December 1994. GWU-NSA.

107. Bill Clinton, *My Life* (New York: Alfred A. Knopf, 2004), p. 637. 'I had no advance warnings about Yeltsin's speech, and he spoke after I did.' Clinton wrote that he had no opportunity to respond. 'Apparently Yeltsin's advisers had advised him that NATO would admit Poland, Hungary and the Czech Republic in 1996, just when he would be running for re-election against the ultra-nationalists, who hated NATO expansion, and I would be running against the Republicans, who supported it.'

108. Yeltsin speech at CSCE conference, Budapest, 5 December 1994. 'History demonstrates that it is a dangerous illusion to suppose that the destinies of continents and of the world community in general can somehow be managed from one single capital.' https://www.latimes.com/archives/la-xpm-1994-12-06-mn-5629-story.html. Pondering the reasons for the Yeltsin outburst in 2002, Talbott stated: 'The Russians were aghast at the results of the '94 election,' citing the Republicans' desire for early enlargement of NATO. 'The Russians concluded, or at least feared, that they were no longer dealing merely with Clinton, but that it was all but lame ducked by the '94 elections.' Warren Christopher and Strobe Talbott, interview, Clinton Presidential Oral History Project, 15–16 April 2002.

109. Nick Burns, note to Talbott, 5 December 1994. 'The President reacted very strongly to Yeltsin's Budapest speech. In fact, he was really pissed off and his anger grew when we returned to Washington to see how the evening news treated it.' Clinton 'felt that Yeltsin showed him up by criticizing not only our NATO policy in such strong and unexpected terms but also his criticism of the US role in the world.' He declared 'he did not want to be used any more as a prop by Yeltsin'. GWU-NSA, US Department of State, Case No. F-2017-13804, Document C06838501.

110. Kissinger, 'Expand NATO now', *Washington Post*, 19 December 1994. https://www.washingtonpost.com/archive/opinions/1994/12/19/expand-nato-now/f1f0b4ed-56ee-4e5b-84ba-ae19a07a9997/?utm_term=.aefe7342e870.

111. Lamers and Schäuble, 'Überlegungen zur europäischen Politik'.

112. Clinton speech, White House conference on trade and investment in central and eastern Europe, Cleveland, 13 January 1995.

113. Memorandum, Clinton–Yeltsin meeting, Moscow, 10 May 1995. https://nsarchive.gwu.edu/document/27172-doc-18-memorandum-conversation-between-president-clinton-and-president-yeltsin. Freedom of Information lawsuit, US Department of State Case No. F-2017-13804 Doc No. C06698826. Clinton insisted that NATO expansion would be 'gradual, steady, measured . . . You can say you don't want it speeded up – I've told you we're not going to do that – but don't ask us to slow down either, or we'll just have to keep saying No.' Clinton added he would not support any change 'that undermines Russia's security or redivides Europe'. The two leaders agreed that any NATO expansion would be delayed until after the 1996 presidential elections (in both countries). At a further Clinton–Yeltsin meeting in June 1995 at Halifax, Nova Scotia, Clinton applauded Russia's agreement finally to join PfP. Yeltsin said he had 'no doubt about our partnership . . . for the sake of world peace' but added: 'There should be no rapid expansion of NATO.'

114. Memorandum of Clinton–Yeltsin telephone conversation, 21 February 1996. https://nsarchive.gwu.edu/document/16826-document-06-memorandum-telephone-conversation. NSA-GWU, CPL, Declassified per EO, 13526, 2015-0732-M-1 (1.29). After they dealt swiftly with contentious points over Chechnya, Ukraine, Bosnia and the START II disarmament treaty, Yeltsin hesitantly asked Clinton whether 'individual dialogue' with central and eastern European states contravened the May 1995 agreement that there would be a one-year 'hiatus' on the NATO issue. Clinton denied any 'recommendations for timetables', though there had been 'conversations'. Yeltsin quicky moved on to Russia's request for a $9 billion loan from the International Monetary Fund, asking for Clinton's help in raising it to $13 billion 'to deal with social problems in this very important pre-election situation and help the people'. Clinton immediately affirmed backing. The IMF agreed a $10 billion loan in March, without onerous conditions. 'IMF approves three-year EFF credit for the Russian Federation', IMF, 26 March 1996.

115. Sarotte, *Not One Inch*, p. 247.

116. Hill and Gaddy, *Mr Putin*, p. 23.

117. The list of claims, encompassing points about armaments including nuclear weapons as well as the September 1990 Two plus Four agreement, was part of Primakov's combative diplomatic style. Contrasting him with his predecessor Kozyrev, Talbott recorded how the new foreign minister, in Moscow in March 1996, 'put on a jaunty display of cynicism and self-confidence. He was relaxed, jovial, and absolutely dismissive of any chance that our diplomatic initiatives would be successful.' Talbott, *The Russia Hand*, p. 193.

118. 'Russian assertions about Two-Plus-Four Agreement', 23 February 1996. John Kornblum, a future ambassador to Germany, was assistant secretary of state for Europe. John Herbst, a future ambassador to Ukraine, was at the State's Department's office dealing with the Newly Independent States (NIS). The two termed the Russian claims about NATO as 'specious' and 'unfounded'. The memo stated that the Germany unification treaty's prohibition on NATO forces in east Germany 'does not apply to territory outside Germany . . . We should remind Moscow that its 2+4 involvement in internal German affairs . . . was unique, arising from the postwar settlement, and did not set any legal or political precedents. Russia does not have a similar right to define or dictate the security arrangements of other sovereign states.' The memo stated that the treaty and related provisions 'contain no references to exercises involving foreign forces on eastern German territory. The decision whether to hold such exercises remains the prerogative of a sovereign, united Germany. Holding firm on the difference between "stationing", "deployment", and "exercises" was in fact a key final point in the 2+4 negotiations.' GWU-NSA, US Department of State, F-2008-02356.

119. Talbott, *The Russia Hand*, p. 196.
120. Clinton visit to St Petersburg, 18–19 April 1996. Talbott, *The Russia Hand*, p. 200. Putin was standing inconspicuously behind Clinton during the US president's short address upon arrival at St Petersburg airport. https://www.youtube.com/watch?v=nxCTEJTQLco.
121. Memorandum of Clinton–Yeltsin conversation, Kremlin, 21 April 1996. CPL, Declassified per EO, 13526, 2015-0782-M-1 (1.31), Talbott, *The Russia Hand*, pp. 202–3.
122. Memorandum on Clinton–Yeltsin telephone conversation, 5 July 1996. Yeltsin told Clinton he had spoken to Kohl and Chirac to find a way forward on NATO 'without putting you in an uncomfortable position'. CPL, Declassified per EO, 13526, 2015-0782-M-2 (1-06).
123. Talbott, *The Russia Hand*, p. 210.
124. Letter, Talbott to Christopher, 16 July 1996, including memorandum of Talbott–Primakov talks on 15 July 1996. US Department of State, M-2017-11926/ C06570196. *Cold War History*, vol. 23, issue 1 (2023). https://www.tandfonline.com/doi/full/10.1080/14682745.2023.2162329.
125. Kennan published an article in the *New York Times*, 5 February 1997, saying expansion 'would be the most fateful error of American policy in the entire post-cold-war era'. He said his view was 'shared by a number of others with extensive and in most instances more recent experience in Russian matters . . . Such a decision may be expected to inflame nationalistic, anti-Western and militaristic tendencies in Russian opinion; to have an adverse effect on the development of Russian democracy; to restore the atmosphere of the cold war to East–West relations, and to impel Russian foreign policy in directions decidedly not to our liking.' He added it might impede or prevent the Duma ratifying the START II agreement and achieving further nuclear disarmament. https://www.nytimes.com/1997/02/05/opinion/a-fateful-error.html.
126. 'Yeltsin has 7-hour heart surgery and doctors say it was a success', *New York Times*, 6 November 1996.
127. Michael E. DeBakey, the American heart surgery pioneer, had consulted on the Yeltsin case.
128. Memorandum, Major–Yeltsin telephone conversation, 23 December 1996. UKNA, PREM 19/6243.1.
129. Memorandum, Clinton–Kohl telephone conversation, 6 January 1997. 'He [Yeltsin] still has a very good memory. He still reacts logically and his remarks are to the point, but he is much stiffer in his performance. He is more static and he seems to have slowed down significantly.' Kohl reported that Yeltsin was still against NATO enlargement, which he saw as 'unnecessary and fraught with enormous psychological problems'. Kohl said he told him he had no veto: it was an objective that 'we all want to bring about together'. CPL, Declassified per EO 13526, 2015-0776-M (1.36). https://clinton.presidentiallibraries.us/items/show/101472. Talbott reported on a conversation with Joachim Bitterlich, Kohl's security adviser, who telephoned him on 6 January, relating the contrast with Yeltsin's appearance when the chancellor visited him four months previously. Talbott added an excerpt from the Kohl–Yeltsin conversation that Bitterlich had diplomatically not mentioned. According to Javier Salona, NATO secretary general (with whom Talbott spoke on a separate call), Yeltsin, at his meeting with Kohl, 'openly expressed bitterness towards the US and Clinton personally'. Why, he kept asking, had 'our friend Bill' unleashed 'this monster'? NATO's image as an enemy was so deeply etched in Russia's political psyche that it could not be erased overnight.' Talbott, *The Russia Hand*, p. 224.
130. The alternative, Kohl said, would cause 'great irritation in prospective members, Poland, Hungary and others'. He specifically invoked involvement by Major and Chirac in future conversations with Yeltsin to offset Russian sensitivities about a German–American initiative.
131. Memorandum, Kohl–Talbott conversation, Bonn, 15 January 1997. Kohl said: 'The situation in Russia is getting more difficult all the time, both concerning NATO and in other areas. New waves of nationalism are mounting . . . Seventy years of dictatorship has left

Russians in total ignorance of the world around them.' US Department of State, No. F-2017-13804, C06702796 D.

132. Kohl expression used in February 1990. Marsh, *Germany and Europe*, p. 54.

133. Philip Barton, memorandum, 'Call by the Russian foreign minister', London, 27 February 1997. UKNA, PREM 19/6243.1. Primakov complained that 'a new geopolitical situation was being created'. Major affirmed, 'We were not anticipating that nuclear weapons would move forward. Neither would air, land or naval forces. There would be some infrastructure, but no more than that.' 'NATO enlargement would go ahead. He suspected that the Russians knew this. Gradualism did not mean that there would be something nasty at a later stage. We needed to go through the issues one by one to identify areas of agreement, rather than disagreeing in more general terms.'

134. Campbell described how Yeltsin had a finger missing. (In fact, two were amputated after a wartime accident with a grenade.) Alastair Campbell, *Diaries*, vol. 2: *Power and the People, 1997–1999* (London: Hutchinson, 2011), 27 May 1997, pp. 36–7. The British interpreter's description was of Yeltsin being 'collected and articulate' with no sign of 'thickness of speech, chestiness and hoarseness of tone or tendency to lose full control of his thoughts . . . I should note in full a particularly flattering and unprompted statement that Yeltsin made to the PM: "You have good eyes and a clear mind. Your age is right and you have good experience."' K.A. 'Tony' Bishop, memorandum, 'Some personal impressions of Yeltsin at today's working breakfast with the prime minister in Paris', 27 May 2027. UKNA, PREM 49/159.

135. John Holmes, memoranda, Blair–Yeltsin breakfast meeting, Paris, 27 May 1997. UKNA, PREM 49/159.

136. Memorandum, Clinton–Chirac conversation, Denver, 20 June 1997. CPL, 2017-0775-M.

137. Primakov's description of US policies towards Russia over Iran. This followed a comment by Madeleine Albright, Clinton's second-term secretary of state, that the Iran problem was 'about to go critical on us' and would probably replace NATO enlargement as the most divisive issue between the US and Russa. Talbott, *The Russia Hand*, pp. 255–6.

138. Bishop, 'Note on Yeltsin's appearance and performance at Denver', 21 June 1997. UKNA, PREM 49/159.

139. Robert McNamara, former defence secretary, Jack Matlock, former ambassador to Russia, former senator Sam Nunn and Brent Scowcroft, George Bush's German unification adviser, called for a pause or halt to NATO expansion. The so-called 'Eisenhower group', organised with the help of presidential granddaughter Susan Eisenhower, published an open letter on 26 June 1997 stating that Clinton's 'open-ended' enlargement was unnecessarily risky. Nunn's and Scowcroft's call for a delay was in the *New York Times*, 4 February 1998.

140. Schröder rejected the proposal when Clinton put it to him at the June 1999 Cologne G8 summit. For a description of Europe's contrasting policies on widening and deepening, see Roger Cohen, 'The new Europe: United and divided; Shiny, prosperous "Euroland" has some cracks in façade', *New York Times*, 3 January 1999. https://www.nytimes.com/1999/01/03/world/new-europe-united-divided-shiny-prosperous-euroland-has-some-cracks-facade.html. See also Lucas Schramm, 'Navigating widening and deepening: The European Council, geopolitical motives, and Union enlargement', *Journal of European Integration*, 31 January 2025. https://www.tandfonline.com/doi/full/10.1080/07036337.2025.2457007.

141. Nunn and Scowcroft wrote that analogies with the 'shadow of Versailles', alleging that 'resistance to NATO enlargement would be comparable to Senate rejection of the League of Nations', were misplaced. Nunn and Scowcroft, 'NATO: A debate recast', *New York Times*, 4 February 1998. https://www.nytimes.com/1998/02/04/opinion/nato-a-debate-recast.html.

142. Memorandum, Clinton–Yeltsin conversation, Birmingham, 17 May 1998. NSA-GWU, CPL, Declassified per EO, 13526, 2015-0782, M-2 (1.40). https://nsarchive.gwu.edu/document/16838-document-12-memorandum-conversation.

143. Yeltsin enthused: 'We've had the fundamental convictions, courage and stamina to abandon old stereotypes.' Memorandum, Clinton–Yeltsin conversation, Birmingham, 17 May 1998.

144. William Safire, 'Who's losing Russia?', *New York Times*, 28 May 1998. https://www.nytimes.com/1998/05/28/opinion/essay-who-s-losing-russia.html. On a flight to Moscow with Clinton in August 1998, Talbott heard Clinton remark for the first time, 'If we lose Russia.'

145. James Billington, 'Russia between a dream and a nightmare', *New York Times*, 17 June 1998. Billington, professor of history at Princeton University and a former director of the Woodrow Wilson International Center for Scholars, was Librarian of Congress in 1998, a post he ended up holding for twenty-eight years under five American presidents.

146. Brian Pinto, Homi Kharas and Sergei Ulatov, 'An analysis of Russia's 1998 meltdown: Fundamentals and market signals', Brookings Papers on Economic Activity, 2001, no. 1.

147. John Schmid, 'Kohl challenger casts doubt on Yeltsin's ability to rule', *International Herald Tribune*, 12 September 1998.

148. Michael Wines, 'Moscow memo: Yeltsin and crew are sinking like the rouble', *New York Times*, 22 August 1998.

149. Memorandum, Clinton–Yeltsin telephone conversation, 12 September 1998. CPL, Declassified per EO, 13526, 2015-0782 M-2 (1.45).

150. Samuel 'Sandy' Berger (Clinton's national security adviser) memorandum for the president, 'Message to President Yeltsin of Russia'. Undated (apparently 22–3 June 1999). 'Michael Steiner, my German counterpart, told Strobe [Talbott] today that Yeltsin performed poorly in yesterday's meetings-[at Cologne G8 summit]. He appeared to be suffering from dementia.' CPL, Declassified per EO, 13526, 2016-0620-M (1.03).

151. NATO's bombing action, hotly opposed by Yeltsin and his prime minister Primakov, lasted from 24 March to 10 June 1999. NATO members countries' attempts to gain authorisation from the UN Security Council were blocked by China and Russia, so the campaign was launched without UN approval, on the grounds it was a humanitarian intervention to prevent Serbian 'ethnic cleansing' in Kosovo.

152. Memorandum, Clinton–Yeltsin telephone conversation, 5 October 1998. CPL, Declassified per EO, 13625, 2016-0620-M (1.02). Yeltsin told Clinton on 20 June at the G8 meeting in Cologne, 'Our co-operation came to the brink of collapse with Kosovo.' Memorandum, Clinton–Yeltsin conversation, 20 June 1999. CPL, Declassified per EO, 13526, 2015-0782-M-2 (1.47).

153. Stepashin, conversation with Talbott, Moscow, 10 June 1999. Talbott, *The Russia Hand*, p. 334.

154. Talbott commented, 'It was a variation of something we've been hearing from Russians of different stripes for years. You're dealing with a confused, angry, screwed up country; don't overplay your strong hand with us; give us a break, otherwise we might do something crazy.' Talbott, *The Russia Hand*, p. 334.

155. A Russian effort to establish a military foothold within Kosovo after the bombing ceased led to an intense last-minute flurry of negotiations on 10–12 June. During this hectic period Talbott met Putin for the first time, at his Kremlin office. At their first meeting, on 11 June, Talbott was 'struck by his ability to convey self-control and confidence in a low-key, soft-spoken manner. He was physically the smallest of the men at the top – short, lean and fit, while all the others were taller and most of them were hefty and overfed.' When, after a drama-filled twenty-four hours of alarms and about-turns on Russian troop movements, Talbott saw him again at the Kremlin on 12 June, Putin 'set about explaining – slowly, calmly, in a voice that was sometimes barely audible – why what he'd promised wouldn't happen [twenty-four hours previously, when he had pledged '100% cooperation and coordination' between the Russian and NATO militaries] had now happened. It's all politics, he said.' Talbott, *The Russia Hand*, pp. 332–45.

156. Igor Ivanov, Russia's foreign minister, told Albright in a phone conversation in winter 1998–9: 'Madeleine, don't you understand we have many Kosovos in Russia?' The

Russians saw in Kosovo an analogy to Chechnya. Kosovo was a Muslim-majority province on the southern border of a state with a Slavic orthodox majority, and both Chechnya and Kosovo were consumed by nationalist passions. Talbott, *The Russia Hand*, pp. 300–1. See also Memorandum, 'Talbott briefing to North Atlantic Council', 29 April 1999. Talbott reiterated that Russia was worried about the possibility of a permanent protectorate in Kosovo run by NATO and about the 'many Kosovos' in the former Soviet Union and Russia. US Department of State, F-2017-13804, C06814702.

157. Putin conveyed to Berger 'best wishes from Mr [Andrei] Kokoshin' (his predecessor on the national security council). He emphasised that Russia had established a 'command control system' over thirty-seven Russian enterprises to counter nuclear proliferation. Memorandum, Putin–Berger telephone conversation, 12 August 1999. CPL, Declassified per EO, 13526, 2017-0222- M (1.06).

158. Memorandum, Putin–Berger conversation, 12 August 1999. CPL, Declassified per EO, 13526, 2017-0222- M (1.06).

159. Albania, Bulgaria, Estonia, Latvia, Lithuania, Romania, Slovakia, Slovenia and the former Yugoslav republic of Macedonia.

160. Lyne, interview with author, 'A biography was produced showing the new figure to the Russian population. The television stations ran by Boris Berezovsky and Vladimir Gusinsky helped Putin become much better known.'

161. Memorandum, Putin–Berger telephone conversation, 12 August 1999. CPL, Declassified per EO, 13526, 2017-0222- M (1.06).

162. In September 1999, explosions hit four apartment blocks in Buynaksk, Moscow, and Volgodonsk, killing more than three hundred and injuring more than a thousand. The bombings, together with the invasion of the republic of Dagestan, triggered the Second Chechen War.

163. Yeltsin communicated his decision to Putin on 14 December 1999, five days before elections to the Duma which resulted in the rightist Unity party that Putin supported finishing slightly behind the Communists. Yeltsin told his prime minister, who was at first taken aback, 'I want to step down this year.' Yeltsin, *Midnight Diaries*, p. 6.

164. Yeltsin denied a 'deal' with Putin under which he stepped down early in exchange for an amnesty and immunity, calling the hypothesis 'ridiculous' since 'no decree can secure any kind of immunity'. Yeltsin, *Midnight Diaries*, p. 365.

165. Yeltsin, *Midnight Diaries*, p. 6.

166. Talbott, interview, 25 February 2010, Clinton Presidential Oral History Project. Asked whether Clinton's famous empathy misdirected Yeltsin in foreign policy, Talbott said the opposite was true. 'Clinton got Yeltsin to do stuff that was politically radioactive for Yeltsin to do.' Yeltsin's view of Clinton was, Talbott believed, that 'Bill, my friend Bill, won't see it my way but he's not going to screw me'.

167. Memorandum, Clinton–Yeltsin telephone conversation, 31 December 1999. CPL, Declassified per EO, 13526. 2015-0782-M-2 (1.51).

168. Lyne, interview with author, London, 9 June 2023. 'There was of course kudos in it for Blair as the visit attracted huge media attention.'

169. Blair, *A Journey*, pp. 243–5. 'I met him just before he took over as president in 2000, when others at the time, including Jacques Chirac, gave him something of a cold shoulder . . . in time that all changed and their relationship became very close as mine waned. Back then Putin wanted Russia to orient towards Europe, and our first meeting was at St Petersburg, the most European of all Russian cities. We met at the Mariinsky theatre . . . Putin had chosen the opera, carefully – *War and Peace*.'

170. Jonathan Powell, interview with author, London, 12 September 2023. Powell added, 'After the erratic figure of Yeltsin, Putin appeared a chance for a new start, a moderniser. He looked like a grey accountant, a bureaucrat.'

171. Putin's tactic had been long in the making. 'The key to his personality is not so much his KGB background – I have met a number of KGB generals who can be reasonably straightforward interlocutors – but his childhood. A small boy who grows up in a tough neighbourhood in Leningrad, and is subject to bullying – he learns judo so he can throw his

opponents off balance. This underlines that he is a tactician not a strategist.' Jonathan Powell, interview with author, London, 12 September 2023.

172. Memorandum, George Krol, political affairs minister-counsellor, US embassy, Moscow, 24 February 2000, reporting on Robin Cook's visit to Moscow. Briefing by UK ambassador Roderic Lyne. US Department of State, F-2017-13804, C06815109.

173. Memorandum, Clinton–Putin telephone conversation, 27 March 2000. CPL, Declassified per EO, 13526.2017-0222-M (1.21).

174. Memorandum, Talbott–Steiner conversation, Washington, 8 August 2000. Michael Steiner was Germany's national security adviser. US Department of State, F-2017-13804, C06814951 D.

175. Memorandum, Clinton–Putin conversation, Moscow, 4 June 2000. Matching his interlocutor's ambiguity, Clinton told Putin, 'I am serious about being ready to discuss NATO membership with Russia. I recognize that domestic considerations with Russia will prevent this for now, but over time Russa should be part of every organization that holds the civilized world together.' CPL, Declassified per EO, 13526. 2016-0014-M (1.30).

176. Memorandum, Talbott–Berzins (Indulis Berzins, Latvian foreign minister) conversation, 6 March 2000. Referring to Putin's earlier comments on Russia's willingness to join NATO, Talbott said 'Putin wants Russia to be in a NATO when it is no longer a military alliance.' Berzins responded, 'We should use this statement as an argument with Russia not to object to Baltic membership.' US Department of State, F-2017-13804, C06814976.

177. Talbott, speech, All Souls College, Oxford, 21 January 2000. Talbott acknowledged his debt to Isiah Berlin, the Russian-British political philosopher, whom Talbott interviewed at Oxford in summer 1968 while working as a summer intern in the London bureau of *Time* magazine.

178. Memorandum, Talbott–Meyer conversation, Washington, 14 March 2000, containing briefing on UK prime minister Tony Blair's visit to Russia.

179. Memorandum, Strobe Talbott–Chris Patten conversation, 11 September 2000, US Department of State, F-2017-13804, C06815162. Talbott had benefited from having met Putin already three times in 1999, before he became president. At a meeting in Moscow at the Russian White House in December, just after the parliamentary elections, Putin reprimanded the West for pushing Russia eastwards through its criticism over Chechnya. 'Every Russian citizen rejects this criticism as being fundamentally dishonest. When the rebels carried out a terror campaign, killing women and children, there was a real genocide of Russians in Chechnya.' Memorandum, Putin–Talbott conversation, Moscow, 22 December. US Department of State, M-2017-11844, C06551526.

180. Talbott added: 'Putin's discourses on the Balkans have been a mixture of denial about what's really happening in the region and deceit over Russia's approach, with a view to maximizing Russian options and minimizing commitments.'

181. Memorandum, Talbott–Manning conversation, Washington, 7 November 2000. US Department of State, F-2017-13804, C06815050.

182. 'Soul gazing', *New York Times*, 9 February 2004.

183. 'Putin's progress', document for John Sawers, Blair's foreign-policy adviser, January 2001, UKNA, 30 December 2022. 'The Russian intelligence presence in the UK is at Cold War levels, and they continue to try to post active and hostile officers to work against British interests worldwide.' The document gives a list of assurances from Putin to Blair during international summits, which turned out to be false. They included backing for the West's tough line on dealing with Iraqi dictator Saddam Hussein and pledges that Moscow would stop supplying Iran's nuclear programme.

184. Sawers, interview with author, London, 18 June 2024.

185. 'Tony Blair said Putin should be on "top table" ', document on Blair visit to Washington, 23 February 2001. UKNA, BBC, 30 December 2022. Alastair Campbell, *Diaries*, vol. 4: *The Burden of Power: Countdown to Iraq* (London: Hutchinson, 2012), Monday, 11 March 2002, p. 187.

186. Putin was the first foreign leader to telephone Bush to offer support after the attacks. He did not get through to the president and spoke to Condoleezza Rice instead. Simon

Shuster, 'How the war on terrorism did Russia a favor', *Time*, Monday, 19 September 2011. Nick Lockwood, 'How the Soviet Union transformed terrorism', *The Atlantic*, 23 December 2001.

187. Putin TV address, 11 September 2001. He described the attacks as 'an unprecedented act of aggression on the part of international terrorism . . . an event that 'goes beyond national borders'. He declared: 'Russia knows first hand what terrorism is. So, we understand as well as anyone the feelings of the American people.' See John O'Loughlin, Gearóid Ó Tuathail and Vladimir Kolosso, 'A "risky westward turn"? Putin's 9–11 script and ordinary Russians', *Europe–Asia Studies*, vol. 56, no. 1 (January 2004), pp. 3–34.

188. Putin, ABC News interview with Barbara Walters, 7 November 2001. Putin said his support for Bush in the telephone call on 11 September was 'not just out of emotional influences, but out of pragmatic considerations' regarding 'the efforts of the international community in fighting terrorism'. https://abcnews.go.com/2020/story?id=123996&page=1.

189. Bush wrote: 'Putin was wily. As a quid pro quo for supporting Jacques Chirac and Gerhard Schröder in their efforts to counterbalance American influence in Europe, Putin convinced them to defend his consolidation of power in Russia.' Bush, *Decision Points*, p. 433.

190. 'Russia sides with France and Germany on Iraq', *EU Observer*, 11 February 2003. 'France and Russia ready to use veto against Iraq war', *New York Times*, 6 March 2003.

191. Blair, *A Journey*, pp. 243–5.

192. The ABM treaty formed part of the SALT-1 accords signed by Richard Nixon and Leonid Brezhnev. See Ivanov, 'The missile-defense mistake: Undermining strategic stability and the ABM treaty', *Foreign Affairs*, September/October 2000, 1 September 2000.

193. Trump, address to Congress, Washington, 6 March 2025. https://www.whitehouse.gov/remarks/2025/03/remarks-by-president-trump-in-joint-address-to-congress/. 'Fact Sheet: President Donald J. Trump directs the building of the Iron Dome missile defense shield for America', Washington, 27 January 2025. https://www.whitehouse.gov/fact-sheets/2025/01/fact-sheet-president-donald-j-trump-directs-the-building-of-the-iron-dome-missile-defense-shield-for-america/.

194. 'Calmly, Putin said that he could never agree to that [ABM treaty abrogation] but did not threaten any retaliation. They agreed to see if they could find a non-confrontational way forward.' Rice, *No Higher Honor*, p. 62. Bush emphasises a different aspect: 'I told Vladimir I planned to give him the required six months' notice that America would withdraw from the ABM treaty . . . He made clear that this wouldn't make me popular in Europe.' Bush, *Decision Points*, p. 432.

195. Bush announcement, Washington, 13 December 2001. 'I have concluded the ABM treaty hinders our government's ways to protect our people from future terrorist or rogue state missile attacks.' https://www.nytimes.com/2001/12/13/international/bush-pulls-out-of-abm-treaty-putin-calls-move-a-mistake.html?searchResultPosition=1.

196. Putin, nationwide TV address, Moscow, 13 December 2001. 'As is well known, Russia and the US, unlike other nuclear powers, have for a long time possessed effective means to overcome missile defences. Therefore, I fully believe that the decision taken by the president of the US does not pose a threat to the national security of the Russian Federation.' As Talbott wrote, the statement effectively demolished a central pillar of three decades of nuclear strategy. 'In a single sentence, Putin had repudiated the numerous presentations I'd heard in 1999 and 2000 form General Nikolai Zlenko, who, with the aid of maps and charts, had argued vociferously and implacably that an American anti-missile system would neutralize Russia' strategic deterrent,' Talbott, *The Russia Hand*, p. 419.

197. Memorandum, German embassy in Washington on Schröder–Bush visit, 29 March 2001. Schöllgen, *Gerhard Schroeder*, pp. 507–8, n. 338, BKG/ZA, GV, A-B.

198. Projects worth DM 4 billion were agreed between Gazprom and a series of German energy companies led by Wintershall and Ruhrgas covering storage facilities, pipelines and energy saving. For political background, see Gerold Büchner, 'Schröder strebt

Neuanfang im Verhältnis zu Moskau an' ['Schröder seeks new beginning in Moscow relationship'], *Berliner Zeitung*, 15 June 2000. https://www.berliner-zeitung.de/archiv/finanzfragen-praegen-berlin-besuch-von-praesident-putin-schroeder-strebt-neuanfang-im-verhaeltnis-zu-moskau-an-li.1322153.

199. Lyne, interview with author, London, 9 June 2023. Lyne emphasised the importance of reformers Putin brought into his administration: Mikhail Kasyanov, German Gref, Alexei Kudrin, Andrei Illarionov.

200. Bush, *Decision Points*, p. 432.

201. Bush, *Decision Points*, 431. John Lough, NATO's first representative in Russia, commented in 2014: 'The oil price rose exponentially, and Russia became a wealthy country, relative to what it had been when Mr Putin came to office in 1999–2000. As a result of that wealth, a degree of confidence returned. The adrenaline started to course through the system, and it seems in a very bizarre way, despite the greater confidence about Russia's place in the world, to have reactivated a sense of grievance about the way the Cold War ended and what happened to Russia: the trauma that Russia lived through with the amputation of some of the former Soviet republics.' Lough, evidence EU subcommittee on external affairs, 'The EU and Russia: Before and beyond the crisis in Ukraine', London, 24 July 2014. https://www.parliament.uk/globalassets/documents/lords-committees/eu-sub-com-c/EU-Russia/EU-Russia-EvidenceFINAL.pdf.

202. Short, *Putin*, p. 395, citing multiple sources. See Ian Traynor, 'US campaign behind the turmoil in Kiev', *Guardian*, 26 November 2004. Peter Dickinson 'How Ukraine's Orange Revolution shaped 21st century geopolitics', Atlantic Council, 22 November 2020. Leah Morris, 'US intervention in the Orange Revolution in Ukraine and how technology influences democracy', *Manchester Historian*, 9 February 2024.

203. The conflict between Georgia and a combination of Russia and the two breakaway republics precipitated a Russian invasion of Georgia on 8 August after Russia accused Georgia of 'genocide' in the region. A ceasefire was negotiated on 12 August after the intervention of French president Nicolas Sarkozy. There was a strong link with the West's earlier decision to recognise independent Kosovo. Ron Asmus, a Caucasus specialist from the State Department, wrote, 'Moscow's terminology and rhetorical line of defense were almost a mirror image of the West's rationale on Kosovo . . . It was payback time for a grievance Putin had borne against the West for nearly a decade.' Ron Asmus, *Opening NATO's Door: How the Alliance Remade Itself for a New Era* (New York: Columbia University Press, 2002), p. 109. See also Yuri Zarakhovich, 'Russia cashes in on Kosovo fears', *Time*, 8 March 2008. 'By splitting the West and the wider international community, the US-backed declaration of independence by Kosovo has given Russia an opening.' Russia withdrew most of its troops from the undisputed areas of Georgia by early October.

204. Blair, *A Journey*, p. 452.

205. Later joiners were Albania and Croatia in 2009, Montenegro in 2017 and North Macedonia in 2020. Putin regularly said nations had the right to choose their foreign policy and had earlier affirmed that the Baltic states joining was 'not a tragedy'. But with equal regularity called he called enlargement a mistake and cast doubt on its strategic significance. His equanimity stood in inverse proportion to the individual country's geographical and historical proximity to the core of Russa. See Putin statement, Kremlin press conference, 24 June 2002. 'We don't think that the expansion of NATO improves anybody's security, either the security of those countries that want to join it or the security of the organisation itself.' Radio Free Europe, archive. https://www.rferl.org/a/1100074.html.

206. NATO summit communiqué: 'NATO welcomes Ukraine's and Georgia's Euro-Atlantic aspirations for membership in NATO. We agreed today that these countries will become members of NATO.' Bucharest, 3 April 2008. https://www.nato.int/cps/en/natohq/official_texts_8443.htm.

207. Mikheil Saakashvili, president of Georgia from 2004 to 2013, said: 'We received more than we hoped for.' Mze TV, Tbilisi, 3 April 2008. Victor Yushchenko spoke of 'an exceptional victory'. *Interfax-Ukraine*, 3 April 2008. Short, *Putin*, p. 426.

208. Merkel, *Freedom*, p. 435.

209. Merkel writes she 'cannot recall the precise details' – incongruously in a book where she annotates times of aeroplane departures and arrivals. *Freedom*, p. 435.

210. Margaret Hodge, a minister in Labour administration up to 2010, coined the phrase 'moral imperialism' in 2006 when she became the first Labour government member openly to attack the Iraq war. *Guardian*, 17 November 2006.

211. Schröder wrote that his initial view of working with Britain to form a 'triangle' with France on European policies turned out an 'illusion'. 'For the foreseeable future there will be no European impulses from the UK. On the contrary, the country will try to promote its intermediary role in transatlantic relations even if this is to the detriment of the European unification process.' Schröder, *Entscheidungen*, p. 319.

212. Schöllgen, *Gerhard Schröder*, pp. 650–1 and 696–7.

213. Rice, *No Higher Honor*, pp. 212–13. After the Iraq invasion, the Bush administration was trying to restore some 'normalcy' to relations. Rice believed, like Bush, that the Russians, 'having at least been straightforward about their opposition to the war', should be treated relatively lightly compared with France and Germany. Rice 'uttered what I thought was a clever quip in what I thought was a private moment with the President and a couple of aides standing in the Oval Office . . . We all laughed but I was horrified to see that someone had passed on this titbit to the press.' The phrase was revealed by Jim Hoagland, 'Three Miscreants', *Washington Post*, 12 April 2003. See Elisabeth Bumiller, 'For Condoleezza Rice, discipline is a constant', *New York Times*, 18 November 2004. Philip H. Gordon, ' "Punish France, ignore Germany, forgive Russia" no longer fits', Brookings Commentary, September 2007. https://www.brookings.edu/articles/punish-france-ignore-germany-forgive-russia-no-longer-fits/.

214. Alexander Litvinenko had been part of the Russian Federal Security Service (FSB) and its predecessor, the KGB. In 1998, Litvinenko and other Russian intelligence officers said they had been ordered to kill businessman Boris Berezovsky. In exile in Britain, Litvinenko worked with British intelligence. On 1 November 2006, he was poisoned and later hospitalised. He died on 23 November, the first confirmed victim of polonium-210-induced radiation syndrome.

215. Prodi, interview with author, Bologna, March 2023. Bush and Blair, Prodi adds, 'both saw democracy as a method of bringing in Christianity'. This was in relation to Blair's tendency to take a moralising stance over the Iraq war. 'He had a missionary attitude.'

216. Campbell, *Diaries*, vol. 3, Friday, 11 October 2002, p. 326. 'If there was something the Americans were worried about, they expect the whole world to share their concerns and drop everything . . . He was clearly getting pretty pissed off. Putin's rhetoric cranked up during the day . . . Blair was saying we have to get the Americans on to a more multilateral track. On Iraq, VP said to TB: "Do you really think that Iraq is more dangerous than this fundamentalism? Course not." '

217. The NRC was designed to replace the Permanent Joint Council, a forum for consultation and cooperation created by the Founding Act.

218. The die had already been cast early in Bush's first term. When Condoleezza Rice asked Sergei Ivanov, secretary of the Russian security council (later defence minister), how far Russia wanted to go in integrating with NATO, he rolled his eyes and told her: 'Condi forget it, we're not going to join an alliance where our vote is the same as a country like Latvia. You needn't ask me that again.' Short, *Putin*, p. 378, quoting interview with Daniel Fried.

219. 'NATO–Russia dialogue and the future of the NATO–Russia Council', European Council on Foreign Relations, 5 July 2016.

220. Campbell, *Diaries*, vol. 3, Tuesday, 11 April 2002, pp. 554–9. 'Putin told Blair, "There are bad people in the administration and you know it." Blair thought a lot of it was driven by Russia no longer being seen as a superpower . . . They were angry and humiliated and needed to let out the anger.'

221. Sheryl Gay Stolberg, 'Putin presents Bush with plan on missile shield', *New York Times*, 7 June 2007. Vladimir Rukavishnikov, 'The US–Russian dispute over missile defense', *Connections*, vol. 7, no. 4 (Fall 2008), pp. 81–94.

222. Burns, *Back Channel*, p. 231.
223. Ivan Konovalov, 'America's ABM shield in Europe and Russia's response', Elcano Royal Institute, 21 September 2007.
224. 'Obama scraps Bush missile defense plan', ABC News, 17 September 2009.
225. Andrew E. Kramer, 'Russia calls new U.S. missile defense system a "direct threat"', *New York Times*, 12 May 2016.
226. Terracciano had spells at Italy's NATO permanent representative office in Brussels as well as at the Rome ministry of foreign affairs, followed by ambassadorships in Spain (from 2006), Britain (from 2013) and Russia (from 2018).
227. Terracciano, interview with author, Rome, 9 March 2023.
228. Memorandum, Burns to Rice, 17 October 2006. US Department of State, Case No. MP-201607420. Carnegie Endowment for International Peace, 'The Back Channel'. https://carnegieendowment.org/features/back-channel?lang=en.
229. Putin speech, Munich, 10 February 2007. http://en.kremlin.ru/events/president/transcripts/24034.
230. Robert Gates speech, *New York Times*, 11 February 2007. Gates spoke the following day. 'Many of you have backgrounds in diplomacy or politics. I have, like your second speaker yesterday, a starkly different background – a career in the spy business. And, I guess, old spies have a habit of blunt speaking.'
231. Werner Hoyer, interview with author, Berlin, 22 April 2024.
232. Teltschik, interview with author, Tegernsee, 20 January 2023.
233. Stürmer, interview with author, Munich, 20 January 2023.
234. Memorandum, Burns to Rice, 16 February 2007. US Department of State, Case No. MP-2015-07420. Carnegie Endowment for International Peace, 'The Back Channel'. https://carnegieendowment.org/features/back-channel?lang=en.
235. 'Russia to revive long-range bomber patrols', NBC, 17 August 2007.
236. 'Putin suspends implementation of CFE agreement', *US–Russia Relations*, December 2007. https://usrussiarelations.org/2/timeline/after-the-fall/100.
237. Short, *Putin*, p. 502.
238. Jim Collins, interview with author (video), Washington–Berlin, 22 May 2024. Collins recalls a conversation with Donald Rumsfeld, Bush's defence secretary, in July–August 2001. 'What struck me from the meeting was the message that Russia was a declining secondary power, getting weaker, not much more than a regional actor. The administration's view was "Russia was Clinton's thing. We are not sure whether we should even be bothering with Russia. We have other priorities, and we are going to pursue them."'
239. Rice, *No Higher Honor*, p. 674.
240. Richard Allen, Presidential Oral Histories, Miller Center of Public Affairs, University of Virginia. https://millercenter.org/the-presidency/presidential-oral-histories/richard-allen-oral-history.
241. Rice, interview with author (video), Stanford–Berlin, 23 May 2024. 'If you've lost the war, maybe you feel people are treating you as if you lost the war, even if they are trying to treat you as if you didn't.'
242. Burns, interview with Isaac Chotiner, 'A diplomat compares the foreign-policy establishment with Donald Trump', *New Yorker*, 19 March 2019.
243. 'Ukraine uprising: He has gone', *Independent*, 23 February 2014. https://www.independent.co.uk/news/world/europe/ukraine-uprising-he-has-gone-he-has-gone-glory-to-our-brave-heroes-as-president-yanukovych-flees-to-the-east-his-beleaguered-people-taste-freedom-9146885.html.
244. For a review the Crimea invasion, see John Simpson, 'Russia's Crimea plan detailed, secret and successful', BBC, 19 March 2014. https://www.bbc.co.uk/news/world-europe-26644082.
245. House of Lords EU Sub-Committee on External Affairs, 'The EU and Russia: Before and beyond the crisis in Ukraine', statement by Christopher Tugendhat, chairman of the committee, 20 February 2015.
246. Catherine Ashton, *And Then What? Despatches from the Heart of 21st-Century Diplomacy* (London: Elliott & Thompson, 2023), p. 182.

247. The EEAS role in foreign policy is described in 'The Diplomatic Service of the EU'. https://www.eeas.europa.eu/eeas/structure-and-organisation_en.
248. Pierre Vimont, interview with author, Paris, 3 October 2023.
249. Putin took part in European meetings as prime minister in 2008 to 2012, a period when Dmitry Medvedev was president.
250. The partnership started with six countries – Armenia, Azerbaijan, Belarus, Georgia, Moldova and Ukraine. According to Štefan Füle, this represented 'a clear reaction to these countries' ambitions. Moving closer to the EU, they would strengthen their reform and transformation potential.' Füle, interview with author (video), Prague–London, 31 October 2023.
251. Füle, interview with author (video), Prague–London, 31 October 2023.
252. Herbst, interview with author, Washington, 21 September 2023.
253. Ashton, email to author, 9 February 2025. See also 'Putin reveals why he didn't launch full invasion of Ukraine in 2014', Newsweek, 19 March 2023. https://www.newsweek.com/putin-reveals-why-he-didnt-launch-full-invasion-ukraine-2014-1788767.
254. Brown, interview with author, London, 28 September 2023.

6 HOLE AT THE HEART

1. Amato, conversation with Mitterrand, Paris, 10 November 1992. Mitterrand's argument was: 'If there wasn't this interplay among European currencies, speculation wouldn't exist. There is no reason why the policy of a state should be at the mercy of volatile capital which does not represent any real wealth, or creation of real goods.' 'Elysée Palace transcript, Institut François Mitterrand, Paris. Amato email exchange with author, 28 June 2025.
2. Bernanke, statement to Federal Open Market Committee meeting, 13 December 2011. FRBT.
3. Indermit Gill, interview with author (video), Washington–London, 4 October 2024.
4. Kohl's frequently applied epithet was countered by one of the most prominent American sceptics of the European currency plan. See Martin Feldstein, 'EMU and international conflict', *Foreign Affairs*, 1 November 1997. 'Instead of increasing intra-European harmony and global peace, the shift to EMU and the political integration that would follow it would be more likely to lead to increased conflicts within Europe and between Europe and the United States.'
5. Mitterrand, statement to Council of Ministers, IFMS, p. 355. Paris, 17 August 1988. Attali, *Verbatim III*, 17 August 1988.
6. Ruud Lubbers, interview with author, Amsterdam, 24 March 2011.
7. Rakesh Mohan, interview with author (video), Delhi–London, 16 October 2024.
8. The euro area in 2024 ran an overall government budget deficit of 3.1 per cent of GDP and a current account surplus of 2.6 per cent of GDP. Gross government debt was 88.1 per cent of GDP. The corresponding figures for the US were 7.6 per cent (deficit), 3.3 per cent (deficit) and 121 per cent (debt) and for China 7.4 per cent (deficit), 1.4 per cent (surplus) and 90.1 per cent (debt). IMF World Economic Outlook, October 2024. https://betadata.imf.org/en/Data-Explorer?datasetUrn=IMF.STA:COFER(6.0.0).
9. The euro makes up around 20 per cent of world foreign-exchange reserves against 57 per cent for the dollar and 2 per cent for the renminbi. IMF, 'Currency composition of official foreign exchange reserves (COFER)'. https://data.imf.org/?sk=E6A5F467-C14B-4AA8-9F6D-5A09EC4E62A4&sId=1442948906947. See Gary Smith, 'Which currencies will benefit from dollar erosion?', OMFIF, 17 January 2025. https://www.omfif.org/2025/01/which-currencies-will-benefit-from-dollar-erosion/.
10. 'ECB's subscribed capital to remain steady after Bank of England leaves the European System of Central Banks', ECB statement, 30 January 2020. https://www.ecb.europa.eu/press/pr/date/2020/html/ecb.pr200130_2~59d6ffffe1.en.html.
11. Nagel, statement, Frankfurt, 12 March 2025.
12. Rocard, interview with author, Paris, 29 May 2007.
13. Charles Goodhart, email exchange with author, 18 April 2025.

14. Steve Cecchetti, former head of monetary and economics department, Bank for International Settlements, interview with author, telephone, New York–Boston, 22 October 2024. Cecchetti is now a professor at Brandeis University.

15. The ECB council included seven ex-finance ministers in early 2025.

16. Angela Merkel described in her memoirs Jens Weidmann, president of the Bundesbank from 2011 to 2021, as 'Germany's representatives on the ECB council'.

17. Most central banks around the world were originally set up as private companies, many in the nineteenth century or previously, but are now owned by national governments. There are many examples – not least in European cases like Italy, Belgium and Switzerland – where private shareholders remain alongside government shareholders. The US Federal Reserve possesses some similar qualities to the ECB, although its structure is that of a single state and not a multinational polity.

18. David Marsh, *Europe's Deadlock: How the Euro Crisis Could Be Solved – And Why It Won't Happen* (New Haven/London: Yale University Press, 2013), p. 66. See also González, interview with author, Madrid, *Financial Times*, 11 October 1993.

19. Thygesen, interview with author, London, 15 June 2023.

20. Thygesen, interview with author, London, 5 March 2025.

21. Wim Duisenberg, speech, Charlemagne prize ceremony, Aachen, 9 Mary 2022.

22. Hans Tietmeyer, speech, Österreichisch-deutsche Kulturgesellschaft, Vienna, 27 November 1997.

23. Kohl, speech, Bundestag, Bonn, 6 November 1991. The chancellor was taking up a position long advocated by the Bundesbank, whose decision-making central council published statements in 1990 and 1992 forcefully restating Germany's traditional line that political union was needed to make monetary union a success. See also Tietmeyer's conclusion in 1991: 'Monetary union cannot live for a long time without a broader basis of political union.' Tom Redburn and Richard E. Smith, 'Political accord "before monetary": Germany cautious on union', *International Herald Tribune*, 6 November 1991. See also Tietmeyer, 'Zur politischen Fundierung des monetären Integrationsprozesses in Europa' ['Towards a political foundation for the monetary integration process in Europe'], Festschrift for Dr. Ulrich Everling, 26 June 1996. HADB, N8/49.

24. Kohl, *Handelsblatt*, 31 December 1991. André Szász, *The Road to European Monetary Union* (London: Palgrave Macmillan, 2000), p. 163.

25. Jean Monnet, 'L'Europe se fera dans les crises et elle sera la somme des solutions apportées à ces crises' ['Europe will be forged in crisis, and will be the sum of the solutions adopted for those crises']. *Mémoires* (Paris: Fayard, 1976), p. 488.

26. Issing, paper for the European Society for the History of Economic Thought, 2001. https://www.ecb.europa.eu/press/key/date/2001/html/sp010223.en.html.

27. Issing, 'A currency without a state', speech, Helsinki, 24 March 2006. https://www.ecb.europa.eu/press/key/date/2006/html/sp060324.en.html.

28. Hans Tietmeyer, *Herausforderung Euro* [*The Challenge of the Euro*] (Munich/Vienna: Hanser, 2005), p. 307.

29. Issing, *Handelsblatt*, 20 October 2015.

30. Author's private information.

31. Christopher Smart, interview with author (video), Boston–London, 14 June 2023.

32. Draghi, speech, Global Investment Conference, London, 26 July 2012.

33. Marsh, '10 reasons why there'll be no Draghi moment', OMFIF, 21 April 2020.

34. In his early twenties, when his ambition turned to becoming a writer, the young Mitterrand joined a youth movement linked to an extreme nationalist group, the Croix-de-Feu. Pierre Péan, *Une jeunesse française: François Mitterrand, 1934–1947* [*François Mitterrand: Early life in France 1934–1947*] (Paris: Fayard, 1994), p. 33. François Mitterrand, *Mémoires interrompus* [*Interrupted Memories*] (Paris: Odile Jacob, 1996), quoted in Hubert Védrine, *Les mondes de François Mitterrand* [*The Worlds of François Mitterrand*] (Paris: Fayard, 1996), p. 122. François Mitterrand, 'Pèlerinage en Thuringe' ['Pilgrimage to Thuringia'], *France, revue de l'État nouveau*, November 1942, quoted in Péan, *Une jeunesse française*, p. 234; Védrine, *Les mondes de François Mitterrand*, p. 124.

35. Dietrich von Kyaw, conversation with author, Maastricht, 10 December 1991.
36. Major, speech, Konrad Adenauer Foundation, Bonn, 11 March 1991.
37. Exchange of letters, Kohl and Marsh, Bonn–London, 13 September 1993, 22 September 1993, 3 February 1997.
38. Kohl, speech, Jouy-en-Josas, 3 December 1991.
39. Bundesbank statement on monetary union, Monthly report, October 1990. https://www.bundesbank.de/resource/blob/691220/b9a8d31ad2e89d5bebc5c31e38d44888/472B63F07 3F071307366337C94F8C870/1990-10-monatsbericht-data.pdf. Marsh, *The Euro*, p. 153.
40. Jagjit Chadha and Suzanne Hudson, 'A Short Survey of Monetary Unions', unpublished Bank of England paper, 1997. This was part of a series of internal studies on whether the prospective monetary union was an optimal currency area. The historical research showed that monetary unions are typically not an OCA so a political union is required for sustainability.
41. Waigel, interview, *Europa*, December 1991. 'We are bringing the D-Mark into Europe. The treaty on Economic and Monetary Union, agreed after long and intense negotiations, bears the German hallmark.'
42. Schröder, interview, *Bild-Zeitung*, 26 March 1998.
43. For a shorter version, see European Commission, *Quarterly Report on the Euro Area*, vol. 7, no. 2 (2008). https://ec.europa.eu/economy_finance/publications/pages/publication12808_en.pdf.
44. European Commission, Economic and Financial Affairs, 'Myths and facts: Is it true . . .?', 30 April 2009. http://ec.europa.eu/economy_finance/emu10/myths_en.htm.
45. David Marsh, *The Bundesbank: The Bank That Rules Europe* (London: Heinemann, 1992), p. 236. For an indication of Schlesinger's thinking shortly before he left the Bundesbank, see Brandon Mitchener, 'Schlesinger questions Maastricht treaty timetable', *International Herald Tribune*, 17 September 1993. https://www.nytimes.com/1993/09/17/business/worldbusiness/IHT-schlesinger-questions-maastricht-treaty-timetable.html.
46. Helmut Schlesinger, 'Money is just the start', *The Economist*, 21 September 1996.
47. Schlesinger, interview with author, Oberursel, 11 May 2023.
48. Klaus Regling, Servaas Deroose, Reinhard Felke and Paul Kutos, 'The euro after its first decade: Weathering the financial storm and enlarging the euro area', ADBI Working Paper Series, no. 205, Asian Development Bank Institute, Tokyo, March 2010. Although the report called for better economic coordination and more structural reforms to overcome the post-financial-crisis recession, it concluded, 'The crisis has also made the euro more attractive, and most EU countries that are not yet members of EMU are expected to join during the next decade.'
49. Schäuble, interview with author, Berlin, 18 January 2021. The dinner with Evangelos Venizelos took place at the Tim Raue restaurant on 6 July 2011. See 'Euro-Zone: Schäuble soll Griechenland 2011 den Euro-Austritt nahegelegt haben' ['Euro area: Schäuble said to have suggested Greek withdrawal in 2011'], *Frankfurter Allgemeine Zeitung*, 4 January 2015. Schäuble describes the episode in his posthumously published memoirs. 'We discussed [leaving the euro] lengthily and openly. What I said seemed to spoil his appetite. At any rate [Venizelos] ate hardly anything.' Schäuble suggested that the European Commission should take control as a trustee of the Greek government 'to implement the measures without consideration of parliamentary majorities . . . a deep intervention into Greece's sovereignty which Venizelos, who would have preferred to become prime minister himself, immediately rejected.' Wolfgang Schäuble, *Erinnerungen: Mein Leben in der Politik* [*Memories: My Life in Politics*] (Stuttgart: Klett-Cotta, 2024), p. 499.
50. Herman Van Rompuy, 'Strong euro hid crisis, says EU chief', *Financial Times*, 14 June 2010.
51. Draghi, speech, Rome, 6 May 2013.
52. Delors, speech, Brussels, 28 March 2012.
53. Nicolas Véron, 'The IMF's role in the euro-area crisis: Financial sector aspects', Bruegel, 29 August 2016. https://www.bruegel.org/policy-brief/imfs-role-euro-area-crisis-financial-sector-aspects.

54. 'The IMF and the crises in Greece, Ireland, and Portugal', IMF Independent Evaluation Office, 28 July 2016.
55. See also Attali, Mitterrand's foreign policy and security adviser. 'The German atom bomb . . . I mean the D-Mark.' Marsh, *The Euro*, pp. 120–1.
56. Stürmer, 'Sie haben die Deutschmark, wir unsere kleine Bombinette' ['You have the D-Mark, we have our little [nuclear] bomb'], *Die Welt*, 17 May 2017.
57. 'Les chances de réintégration du franc dans le serpent monétaire européen' ['The chances of reintegrating the franc in the European monetary snake'], Banque de France foreign directorate, February 1978. BFA, 1489200205, Box 273.
58. Tietmeyer, memorandum on Kohl–Mitterrand meeting, Paris, 14-16 July 1989. HADB, Tietmeyer archive. The meeting established that, as part of a policy of fostering 'social progress', France wished to set up a European 'monetary identity' with defensive barriers externally; Germany favoured international cooperation and 'joint responsibility' for the worldwide monetary system and world trade.
59. Pfeiffer, memorandum, 'German–French government consultations 25–6 April', 16 March 1990. AAPD 1990, Document 73, pp. 296–301.
60. Alain Boublil, 'Les conséquences économiques de l'unification de L'Allemagne' ['The economic consequences of German unification'], Paris, 20 November 1990 (finalisation), published January 1991. Cited in René Lasserre, 'L'unification économique de l'Allemagne: bilan et perspectives' ['German economic union: Status and perspective'] in 'Matériaux pour l'histoire de notre temps' ['Documents on history in our time'], 1991, pp. 14–18. https://www.persee.fr/doc/mat_0769-3206_1991_num_23_1_404062. See also Alain Boublil, 'Les trois maux de l'économie allemande' ['The threefold malaise of the German economy'], AB-2000.com, 28 September 2015. https://ab-2000.com/fr/archives/2015/09/28/les-trois-maux-de-leconomie-allemande/.
61. Memorandum, German embassy, Paris, 21 January 1991. HADB, Tietmeyer archive.
62. Letter, Tietmeyer to Boublil, Frankfurt, 25 January 1991. HADB, Tietmeyer archive.
63. Document sent with Trichet cover letter to Mitterrand, 31 December 1993. Institut François Mitterrand, Paris. Marsh, *The Euro*, pp. 173–4.
64. Marsh, *The Euro*, p. 174.
65. Trichet, interview with author, Paris, 10 October 2023.
66. Report, Bundesbank council meeting. HADB, 29 July 1993. Schlesinger complained about leaking of an IMF executive board discussion in which several countries urged a cut in Bundesbank interest rates. 'Raising of such expectations, which are subsequently disappointed, is an independent factor leading to foreign-exchange market unrest, for which those who produce such expectations must be held responsible.'
67. Letter, Camdessus to Schlesinger, 27 July 1993. HADB, B 330/24953. Letter, Schlesinger to Camdessus, 12 August 1993. HADB, N 8/14. Schlesinger complained to the Bundesbank council meeting about leaking of an IMF executive board discussion urging that the Bundesbank ease credit, saying it would lead to 'foreign exchange market unrest . . . Those who generate such expectations must be held responsible.' He wrote back to Camdessus complaining about what he viewed as an unprecedented attempt to put pressure on the Bundesbank.
68. Marsh, *The Euro*, pp. 178–81.
69. The fluctuation bands were widened to 15 per cent either side of a central rate. This was in line with a suggestion made by the Germans (and rejected by France) ten days earlier.
70. Report, Kinkel–Juppé conversation in Dresden, 24 August 1993. AAPD 1993, Document 252, p. 1050.
71. Anton Hofreiter, a Green member of the Bundestag, head of the Europe committee: 'This isn't a Franco-German problem – it's a Macron-Scholz problem. But it still has a massive impact on everything else.' *Financial Times*, 15 March 2023. Hofreiter's remark is symptomatic of the many statements on the poor personal chemistry between the French and German leaders.
72. Author's private information.
73. Emmanuel Moulin, interview with author, Paris, 24 April 2023.

74. 'Europe's policy options in the face of Trump's global economic reordering', Monetary Dialogue Papers, for European parliament ECON committee, March 2025. The recommendations include that the ECB should drive the euro as the most important reserve currency, extend bilateral swap lines to a broad range of countries, and play the role of lender- and market-maker of last resort to a much broader range of financial counterparties.

75. Vallée, interview with author (video), Paris–London, 1 May 2024.

76. 'Christine Lagarde discussed leaving ECB early to head WEF, says Klaus Schwab', *Financial Times*, 28 May 2025. https://www.ft.com/content/6bd1bd41-0ede-45a6-9a7e-d9efae75 d309.

77. Schlesinger, interview with author, Oberursel, 11 January 2022.

78. Schmidt, interview with author, Hamburg, 5 November 2010.

79. Yves Mersch, interview with author, Luxembourg, 4 October 2023.

80. Ralph Atkins, 'Trichet navigates choppy waters: Cultivated polymath with a sure hand on the financial tiller of Europe', *Financial Times*, 23 December 2007. https://www.ft.com/content/af1a4d9e-b1ba-11dc-9777-0000779fd2ac.

81. Trichet, 'European identity', Vincent Lecture, Vincent van Gogh bi-annual award for contemporary art in Europe, Maastricht, 10 September 2004. https://www.ecb.europa.eu/press/key/date/2004/html/sp040910.en.html. Trichet, 'Europe – cultural identity – cultural diversity', CFS Presidential Lecture, Center for Financial Studies, Frankfurt, 16 March 2009. https://www.bis.org/review/r090317a.pdf?noframes=1.

82. Trichet, interview with author, Paris, 4 April 2007.

83. Ashok Mody, *Euro Tragedy: A Drama in Nine Acts* (New York: Oxford University Press, 2016), pp. 211–12.

84. Underlining how the then Banca d'Italia governor had favoured tighter money in early 2011, Draghi said publicly in late March 2011 that monetary policy 'has been expansionary for a long time' and voted in favour of the rate rise the following month. Draghi 'repeated Trichet's scenario of a wage-price spiral'. Mody, *Euro Tragedy*, pp. 292–3.

85. Delors, speech, Brussels, 28 March 2012.

86. Author's private information. See also 'Bundesbankpräsident sucht Partner im EZB-Rat' [Bundesbank president seeks partners in ECB council], *Frankfurter Allgemeine Zeitung*, 21 September 2011.

87. 'Germany's Axel Weber to quit as Bundesbank boss', BBC, 11 February 2011. https://www.bbc.co.uk/news/business-12434447 Weber was chairman of the board of UBS Group from 2012 to 2022. An ancillary reason for Weber's discomfiture over the ECB nomination process was his belief that Merkel had contacted Philipp Hildebrand, president of the Swiss National Bank in 2010–11, about a possible European post.

88. Nicolas Sarkozy, *Le Temps des Combats* (Paris: Fayard, 2023), p. 446.

89. Author's private information.

90. Draghi was a vice chairman and managing director at Goldman Sachs International from 2002 to 2005, helping set European strategy and working with European governments and corporations. His association, as Sarkozy indicates, continued after he left the firm. Greece joined the euro in 2001 partly as a result of manipulation of Greek debt figures masterminded by Goldman Sachs. Charles Dallara, a former senior official at the US Treasury and IMF, and former managing director of the Institute of International Finance, wrote, 'Greece resorted to a now rather infamous currency swap, with the engagement of Goldman Sachs, to reduce the national debt.' Dallara, *Euroshock: How the Largest Debt Rescheduling in History Helped Save Greece and Preserve the Eurozone* (New York: Rodin Books, 2024), p. 81.

91. Sarkozy, *Les Temps des Combats*, p. 446.

92. Sarkozy, *Les Temps des Combats*, p. 447.

93. Schäuble, *Erinnerungen*, p. 507.

94. Draghi showed some resemblance to Karl Otto Pöhl, Bundesbank president from 1980 to 1991, who was widely acclaimed outside Germany but gradually lost control of the often fractious Bundesbank council made up of the heads of the state (*Land*) central banks. In

monetary policy reaction, Draghi – reflecting his academic and banking background – was much better equipped technically than Pöhl.

95. Author's private information.
96. 'Dutch central bank chief criticises ECB interest rate cut to stimulate growth', Dutch News, 13 September 2019. https://www.dutchnews.nl/2019/09/dutch-central-bank-chief-criticises-ecb-interest-rate-cut-to-stimulate-growth/.
97. Author's private information.
98. 'Anyone but Draghi – how an Italian presidential bid fell flat', Reuters, 3 February 2022. https://www.reuters.com/world/europe/anyone-draghi-how-an-italian-presidential-bid-fell-flat-2022-02-02/.
99. Giuliano Amato, interview with author, Rome, 7 March 2023.
100. Issing, interview with author, Würzburg, 5 April 2023.
101. Mersch, interview with author, 4 October 2023.
102. Author's private information.
103. Some on the governing council believed the allusion would have been more aptly applied to James Joyce rather than Shakespeare. Somewhat mischievously, Honohan occasionally used his linguistic adroitness and familiarity with the finer points of Irish politics to allow modest technical imperfections to stand uncorrected in ECB statements as camouflaged signals of subtle dissent.
104. Patrick Honohan, interview with author (video), Dublin–London, 4 July 2023.
105. Draghi studied at the Massimiliano Massimo Institute, a Jesuit school in Rome.
106. Christian Thimann, interview with author (video), Frankfurt–London, 23 July 2024.
107. Christian Noyer, interview with author, Paris, 3 October 2023.
108. Merkel, speech, Berlin, 2 June 2009.
109. Wolfgang Proissl, a former head of communications at the European Stability Mechanism (ESM) and journalist at *Financial Times Deutschland* and *Die Zeit* who in 2021 became the head of the ECB's communication department, wrote in 2010 that Merkel was 'restrained in her ability to exercise leadership – unlike in previous years it no longer pays in Germany to be seen a Europe's driving force'. Proissl, 'Why Germany fell out of love with Europe', Bruegel Essay and Lecture series, Brussels, July 2010, p. 11.
110. Stefan Kornelius, *Angela Merkel: The Authorized Biography*, trans. Anthea Bell (London: Alma Books, 2013), pp. 275–6.
111. Benoît Cœuré, interview with author, Paris, 4 October 2023. He became head of Autorité de la concurrence, the French competition authority, in 2022, after a spell at the Bank for International Settlements.
112. Analysis of Geithner calendar, January 2009–January 2013, US Treasury website. Some of Geithner's exchanges are redacted for reasons of political or personal sensitivity – a practice to which successors Jack Lew, Steven Mnuchin and Janet Yellen also made recourse.
113. The Financial Stability Forum was set up in 2006 to improve cooperation among the national and international supervisory bodies and international financial institutions. It became the Financial Stability Board in 2009. Draghi chaired both bodies until he became ECB president in November 2011.
114. Treasury records give the following timings for Geithner's calls with European officials: 1 November, Lagarde 8.30 to 8.40 a.m.; Schäuble, 9.30 to 9.45 a.m.; Klaus Regling (EFSF head), 9.55 to 10.00 a.m.; François Baroin (French finance minister), 11.40 to 11.50 a.m. Geithner had twelve further recorded appointments and interactions before dinner with Bill Dudley, his successor as New York Fed president, 7.00 to 8.00 p.m. On 2 November, the timings were: Draghi, 8.30 to 8.40 a.m.; Lagarde, 8.40 to 8.50 a.m. Geithner had twenty-four further appointments before flying to Nice with Obama at 7.15 p.m.
115. 'Silvio Berlusconi bows out after Italian MPs vote for savage cuts', *Observer*, 12 November 2011.
116. Geithner, *Stress Test*, p. 476.
117. Peter Spiegel, 'How the euro was saved', *Financial Times*, 11 May 2014. The details in the report have been largely confirmed by officials with knowledge of the gathering at Cannes

on the evening of 3 November 2011. See also the other two articles in the three-part *Financial Times* series, 'Inside Europe's Plan Z', 14 May 2014, 'If the euro falls, Europe falls', 15 May 2014.

118. Merkel, *Freedom*, p. 411.
119. Merkel describes Weidmann, in the German-language edition of her memoirs, as 'the German representative on the ECB council'; this is erroneously translated in the English edition as 'on the ECB board'. The passage indicates Merkel's negligence or ignorance regarding the legal position: national central bank governors on the ECB council are deemed to represent the interests of Europe as a whole, not of their respective countries.
120. Author's private information
121. Geithner, *Stress Test*, p. 476.
122. Claire Jones, 'Jens Weidmann on Draghi and the ECB': 'The hawkish Bundesbank president on how he would find common ground if he landed the top job in European finance', *Financial Times*, 23 February 2018. The article, based on an interview with Weidmann in the weekend 'Lunch with the FT' series, raised controversy in Frankfurt, reflecting (unfounded) suspicions that it was deliberately edited to reduce the chances that Weidmann would get the top job.
123. Author's private information.
124. Author's private information.
125. Author's private information.
126. Weidmann became chairman of the supervisory board of Commerzbank in 2023. Ernst Welteke resigned in 2005, falling foul of disclosures in *Der Spiegel* magazine over a disputed Adlon hotel bill in Berlin during a celebration to mark the entry of euro bank coins and notes. Weber left in 2011 one year before expiry of his mandate, after he turned down the top ECB job.
127. Marsh, 'Nagel, convivial central banking heavyweight, takes Bundesbank helm', OMFIF, 20 December 2021. https://www.omfif.org/2021/12/nagel-convivial-central-banking-heavyweight-takes-bundesbank-helm/.
128. Claudia Buch became deputy president in 2014, an example of the importance of the quest for gender balance in top institutional positions.
129. Villeroy de Galhau, interview with author, Paris, 14 February 2022.
130. Villeroy de Galhau, interview with author, Paris, 14 February 2022.
131. Lagarde statement, Frankfurt, 12 March 2020. 'Close' could mean either 'narrowing' the spreads or reducing them to zero – possibly justifying the ambiguity in Lagarde's language. The pandemic emergency programme was decided and announced on 18 March 2020. For more background see Jana Randow and Piotr Skolimowski, 'Christine Lagarde's $810 Billion coronavirus U-turn came in just four weeks', Bloomberg, 7 April 2020.
132. Lagarde, interview with author, Frankfurt, 12 January 2022.
133. Holzmann, interview with author, Vienna, 14 March 2024.
134. Minouche Shafik, contribution to 'The *FT*'s 25 most influential women of 2024', 6 December 2024.
135. As of March 2025, the ECB had seventeen males and fourteen females in director/director general and chief service officer positions. This compares with male/female ratios of 16/2 in 2010, 22/4 in 2017 and 17/8 in 2019.
136. Lagarde statement, Davos, 18 January 2024. '[They] are among the most tribal scientists that you can think of. They quote each other. They don't go beyond that world.'
137. Lagarde, interview, France 2 TV station, 12 January 2024.
138. Lagarde, statement, Davos, 2 September 2021.
139. ECB website, 31 December 2024. https://www.ecb.europa.eu/ecb/decisions/html/cvla-garde.en.html.
140. Athanasios Orphanides, interview with author, Vienna, 11 June 2024.
141. Visco, interview with author, Rome, 14 June 2022.
142. Arthur Burns, 'The anguish of central banking', Per Jacobssen lecture, Belgrade, 30 September 1979.
143. Author's private information.

144. Philip Lane, 'Bottlenecks and monetary policy', ECB 'blog' statement, 14 February 2022. https://www.ecb.europa.eu/press/blog/date/2022/html/ecb.blog220210~1590dd90d6.en.html.
145. Issing, interview with author, Würzburg, 5 April 2023.
146. Issing's strictures – and complaints by other well-known orthodox figures – may have been a factor behind Lagarde's scepticism about economists' models voiced at Davos in January 2024, when she said a broader range of disciplines was needed to study the impact of pandemics, climate-change-induced weather events and sudden supply shortages. She said that before becoming ECB president she warned the governing council and analysts to 'beware of models'.
147. Nagel, inaugural speech, 11 January 2022. https://www.bis.org/review/r2201 12c.pdf.
148. Author's private information.
149. Author's private information.
150. 'Charity concert for Ukraine at Berlin State Opera', Bundesbank statement, 2 March 2022. The concert took place on 6 March.
151. Lane, 'The 2021–2022 inflation surges and monetary policy in the euro area', ECB statement, Frankfurt, 11 March 2024. Bill English, Kristin Forbes and Ángel Ubide, 'Monetary policy responses to the post-pandemic inflation: Challenges and lessons for the future', CEPR, 14 February 2024.
152. Lagarde, press conference, Frankfurt, 16 December 2021.
153. Martin Arnold, 'Christine Lagarde: "I should have been bolder"', *Financial Times*, 27 October 2023. The article is notable for vocabulary which would not have been used in an interview with a male central banker. 'Christine Lagarde hands over a small white paper bag with something surprisingly heavy inside after sweeping through the restaurant with her customary assured elegance. Taking off her black leather gloves before shaking hands, she explains: "It is marmalade I made with grapefruits from our garden in Corsica … I've been eating a grapefruit a day since about 45 years ago," says the European Central Bank president, flashing a bright smile that sets off her cropped silver bob, white silk blouse, monochrome floral scarf and pearl earrings. "It gives you vitamin C and a little pep in the morning."'
154. 'German tabloid attacks ECB chief Lagarde as "Madam Inflation"', Reuters, 30 October 2021. 'Germany's best-selling tabloid *Bild* scathingly criticised European Central Bank President Christine Lagarde, accusing her of destroying the earnings and savings of ordinary people by tolerating a rise in inflation. The article, echoing a *Bild* attack on Lagarde's predecessor Mario Draghi in 2019, may signal fresh hostility towards the ECB on the part of the German public, which has for a decade been sceptical of the bank's ultra-easy policy.'
155. Nagel, interview with author, Frankfurt, 30 August 2023.
156. Nagel: 'The "one person one vote" system is a particular characteristic of the group – something we need to uphold and value. Europe's great strength is its diversity, the diversity of its countries and people. Each country in Europe makes an important contribution to our common effort. We all benefit from learning about other countries' background, history and culture.'
157. A landmark was the forging of an agreement in 2024 between Nagel and new Banca d'Italia governor Fabio Panetta for occasional joint board meetings between the two central banks as well as collaboration on academic and research links.
158. 'Bundesbank-Präsident verteidigt Beschlüsse der EZB: Der Prozess der Zinserhöhungen muss weitergehen' ['Bundesbank president defends ECB decisions: The interest rate cutting process can continue'], Nagel, interview, *Handelsblatt*, 22 July 2022.
159. Author's private information.
160. Noyer, interview with author, Paris, 3 October 2023.
161. Lorenzo Bini Smaghi, interview with author, Paris, 10 October 2023.
162. Nout Wellink, interview with author (video), The Hague–London, 14 July 2023.
163. The SMP, announced on 10 May 2010, was 'intended to ensure depth and liquidity in malfunctioning segments of the debt securities markets and to restore an appropriate

functioning of the monetary policy transmission mechanism'. https://www.ecb.europa. eu/pub/pdf/other/mb201006_focus01.en.pdf. See also Ariel A. Smith, 'The European Central Bank's securities markets program', Yale School of Management, Yale Program on Financial Stability Case Study, 15 March 2019. Ansgar Belke, 'Driven by the markets? ECB sovereign bond purchases and the securities markets programme', *Intereconomics*, vol. 45, no. 6 (2010), pp. 357–63. The SMP was announced a day after EU leaders agreed to create the European Financial Stability Facility (EFSF) 'to preserve the financial stability of Europe's monetary union by providing temporary financial assistance to member states if needed', with commitments of €780 billion.

164. Trichet, interview with author, Paris, 10 October 2023.
165. Author's private information.
166. Trichet, interview with author, Paris, 10 October 2023.
167. According to the Geithner calendar the conference call took place on Friday 26 November 2010. US Treasury website.
168. Spiegel, 'Draghi's ECB management: The leaked Geithner files', *Financial Times*, 11 November 2014.
169. Dan Tarullo, statement, FOMC meeting, 25–6 January 2011. FBRT.
170. Dudley, statement, FOMC meeting, 21–2 June 2011. FBRT.
171. Thomas Hoenig, statement, FOMC meeting, 21– June 2011. FBRT.
172. ECB governing council, confidential letters to Italian and Spanish prime ministers, 5 August 2011. Later released as part of 'public access regime' and published on ECB website.
173. Trichet, interview with author, Paris, 11 October 2023.
174. Stark's resignation was announced on 9 September 2011.
175. 'Italy crisis: Silvio Berlusconi resigns as PM', BBC, 13 November 2011. https://www.bbc. co.uk/news/world-europe-15708729.
176. Steve Kamin, statement, FOMC meeting, 20–1 September 2011. FBRT. He added, 'The European EFSF rescue fund was still well below the $1 trillion needed to backstop Italy and Spain as well as Greece.'
177. Bernanke, statement, FOMC meeting, 2 November 2011. FBRT.
178. Bernanke statement, FOMC conference call, 28 November 2011. FBRT.
179. Bernanke statement, FOMC meeting, 13 December 2011. FBRT.
180. Discussion, FOMC meeting, 24–5 January 2012. FBRT.
181. Dudley, statement, FOMC meeting, 19–20 June 2012. FBRT. First, fiscal austerity lowered economic performance, worsening budgetary slippages, undermining fiscal sustainability and eroding political support. Second, Dudley said, 'private claims are increasingly being replaced by public claims', with remaining private claims viewed as subordinate to the public claims, 'which increases the incentive for the private-sector investors to withdraw further'.
182. Dudley explained, 'It would require countries to give up their sovereignty in terms of their budgets and the regulation of their banking systems. Moreover, it would require the core countries, such as Germany, to be explicit to their populations about the fiscal burden that they have to take on for the rest of the euro area . . . In absence of relief, I don't really see what stops these poor dynamics from continuing.'
183. Mario Monti, interview with author, Rome, 8 March 2023. 'As I wrote in the *Corriere della Sera* at the time. It was for the Commission and the Council, not the central bank, to issue such recommendations. In addition, although many of the measures made sense, the macroeconomic thrust was overly restrictive and definitely procyclical. Italy alone, among all euro area countries, was requested to bring forward from 2014 to 2013 the objective of a zero structural deficit. It was clear that this was going to contribute to an unnecessarily high degree of restriction – and recession.'
184. Monti, interview with author. 'As I said to him [Obama], Merkel was not so different to most German politicians from the Christian Democrats and Christian Social Union, but also the Liberals and many Social Democrats. They believe economics is still part of moral philosophy. Growth is an outcome that comes from carrying out ethically correct behaviour.'

185. Geithner, *Stress Test*, p. 468.
186. Author's private inflation.
187. For further background on the speech – which however excludes key issues focused on Geithner and Merkel, as well as the detailed context of the speech itself – see Jana Randow and Alessandro Speciale, '3 words and $3 Trillion: The inside story of how Mario Draghi saved the euro', Bloomberg, 2 November 2018. https://www.bloomberg.com/news/features/2018-11-27/3-words-and-3-trillion-the-inside-story-of-how-mario-draghi-saved-the-euro?embedded-checkout=true.
188. Massimo Rostagno et al., 'A tale of two decades: the ECB's monetary policy at 20', Working Party Series, no. 2346, p. 200.
189. Rostagno et al., 'A tale of two decades', p. 199. The meeting was chaired by Benoît Cœuré.
190. EU summit declaration, 29 June 2012. 'The Commission will present proposals on the basis of Article 127(6) for a single supervisory mechanism shortly. We ask the Council to consider these proposals as a matter of urgency by the end of 2012.'
191. The EU summit emphasised readiness to use 'the existing EFSF/ESM instruments in a flexible and efficient manner in order to stabilise markets'.
192. Monti, interview with author, Rome, 8 March 2023.
193. Luis de Guindos, interview with author, Frankfurt, 20 March 2024.
194. Cœuré, interview with author, Paris, 4 October 2023.
195. Author's private information.
196. Ewald Nowotny, interview with author, Vienna, 15 March 2024.
197. Author's private information.
198. Mervyn King, interview with author, London, 1 November 2023. Separately, King recalled: 'As he stood up to make his remarks, I noticed that, unusually, he did not intend to read from a prepared text.' King, *The End of Alchemy: Money, Banking and the Future of the Global Economy* (London: Little, Brown, 2016), p. 227.
199. 'Politicians back Draghi's aggressive stance', *Financial Times*, 27 July 2012. https://www.ft.com/content/a105046a-d7fd-11e1-80a8-00144feabdc0.
200. For a review of OMT see David Marsh, '10 reasons why there'll be no "Draghi moment"', OMFIF, 21 April 2020. 'The OMT was a hastily engineered sleight of hand – brilliantly effective because it was never used. It was neither monetary nor outright nor did it lead to any transactions.' https://www.omfif.org/2020/04/10-reasons-why-therell-be-no-draghi-moment/.
201. King, statement, Global Investment Conference, London, 26 July 2012. https://www.youtube.com/watch?v=pbTlFI18L7w&list=PLF61D25D758656755&index=3.
202. Author's private information.
203. Geithner, *Stress Test*, p. 482.
204. Author's private information.
205. Mersch, interview with author, 4 October 2023.
206. Merkel writes in her memoirs that Draghi did not previously discuss the statement with her. Since the speech was not formally written down until after he had made it, this claim contains an element of truth, but it falls well short of providing an accurate representation. In view of the intensive consultations with Geithner and other international interlocutors, her assertion that Draghi 'acted in his independent capacity as president of the ECB' is a glibly truncated version of a much more complex reality. Merkel, *Freiheit*, p. 436; *Freedom*, p. 413.
207. Author's private information.
208. Issing, interview with author, Würzburg, 5 April 2024.
209. Trichet, interview with author, Paris, 10 October 2023.
210. Honohan, interview with author (video), Dublin–London, 4 July 2023.
211. Holzmann, interview with author, Vienna, Vienna, 14 March 2024.
212. Orphanides, interview with author, Vienna, 11 June 2024.
213. Dudley, statement, FOMC meeting, 31 July 2012 (first day of two-day meeting). FBRT.

214. ECB OMT statement, 6 September 2012. https://www.ecb.europa.eu/pub/pdf/other/mb201209_focus01.en.pdf.
215. Dudley statement, FOMC meeting, 12–13 September 2012. FRBT.
216. Dudley statement, FOMC meeting, 11–12 December 2012. FRBT.
217. Cœuré, interview with author, Paris, 4 October 2023.
218. Yannis Stouranas, interview with author (video), Athens–London, 16 April 2024.
219. Pablo Hernández de Cos, interview with author, Madrid, 11 January 2024.
220. Vitor Constâncio, interview with author (video), Lisbon–London. 4 August 2023. See also Constâncio, 'Completing the Odyssean journey of the European monetary union', speech, Frankfurt, 16 May 2018. 'Aside from a single currency and a fiscal brake, the initial EMU's architecture was minimalist: the governance of economic and financial policies firmly remained a national competence and there was no fiscal policy at the European level, no crisis management mechanisms of financial assistance to states and no European financial supervision.'
221. 'A central fiscal stabilization capacity for the euro area', IMF staff discussion note, 22 March 2018.
222. Smart, interview with author (video), Boston–London, 14 June 2023. See also Mody, *Euro Tragedy*, p. 243 and subsequent.
223. Noyer, interview with author, Paris, 3 October 2023.
224. De Guindos, interview with author, Frankfurt, 20 March 2024.
225. Visco, interview with author, Rome, 6 June 2022.
226. Zoellick, interview with author (video), Washington–Berlin, 27 July 2023.
227. Summers, Zelikow and Zoellick, 'Why Russian reserves should be used to help Ukraine', *The Economist*, 27 July 2023. https://www.economist.com/by-invitation/2023/07/27/lawrence-summers-philip-zelikow-and-robert-zoellick-on-why-russian-reserves-should-be-used-to-help-ukraine. Zoellick, 'How Trump can help Ukraine without offering security guarantees', *Washington Post*, 25 March 2025. https://www.washingtonpost.com/opinions/2025/03/25/trump-ukraine-security-guarantees/s.
228. Zoellick, interview with author (video), Washington–London, 24 March 2025.
229. Geithner, interview with author (video), New York–London, 12 June 2023.
230. Bergsten, interview with author (video), Washington–Berlin, 19 and 28 February 2024.
231. Bergsten, speech, American Academy, Berlin, June 2014. https://www.international-economy.com/TIE_Sp15_Bergsten.pdf.
232. Bergsten, interview with author (video), Washington–Berlin, 14 March 2025.
233. Summers, interview with author (video), Scottsdale–London, In the period immediately before the euro's advent in 1999, Summers, along with Alan Greenspan, Fed chairman, a pronounced sceptic on the European currency, was persuaded to veer away from an overly acerbic public line. Summers' compromise line became, 'We support monetary union and if it works for Europe it will work for the US.'
234. 'UniCredit lifts Commerzbank exposure to 28%', *Financial Times*, 18 December 2024.
235. Bini Smaghi, interview with author, Paris, 10 October 2023.
236. Summers, interview with author (video), Scottsdale–London, 30 January 2024.
237. Constâncio, interview with author (video), Lisbon–London, 4 August 2023.
238. Constâncio, interview with author (telephone), Lisbon–London, 26 March 2025.
239. Cecchetti, interview with author (video), Boston–New York, 22 October 2024.

7 THE TROUBLE WITH BRITAIN

1. Thatcher, speech, College of Europe, Bruges, 20 September 1988. Thatcher Archive, COI transcript, later issued as a pamphlet by the 10 Downing Street press office. https://www.margaretthatcher.org/document/107332.
2. Wall, letter to Christoper Prentice, FCO, on Kohl–Major telephone call, 30 September 1992. UKNA, PREM 19/3751/2.
3. Juncker, interview with author, Brussels, 29 November 2023. Juncker had a bet with Jonathan Hill, the British European commissioner, with a stake of £1/€1. 'And so I received a pound from Jonathan after the referendum vote.'

4. For an essay on the political impact of Britain's maritime traditions, drawing inter alia on writings by Ernst Junger, see Thomas Kielinger, 'Ein Volk von Seefahrern' ['A seafaring people'], *Die Welt*, 25 June 2016. https://www.welt.de/print/die_welt/politik/article15655 4043/Ein-Volk-von-Seefahrern.html.

5. Keir Starmer declared on the eve of the 4 July election that the UK would not re-enter the single market or the customers union in his lifetime. *Guardian*, 3 July 2024.

6. For an analysis of the effects on trade, see Emily Fry, 'Britain's post-Brexit trade patterns are finally emerging in the data', Resolution Foundation, 28 February 2024. 'By the end of 2023, goods trade had shrunk to levels not seen since 2015 . . . few expected non-EU trade to be hit as hard as that with the EU. The equally feeble performance across the UK's trade partners means that in 2023, the EU share of goods imports and exports had returned to its pre-Brexit level. Services trade, which has grown rapidly in importance (accounting for 56 per cent of UK exports) has, by contrast, been booming, growing 14 per cent between 2019 and 2023.' Fry points out that the shifts have been to the detriment of manufacturing workers. 'It is the highly paid bankers, lawyers and consultants who are now in view.' For a take on the positive effects of departure, see John Redwood's Diary, 'Great Brexit wins', 23 June 2024, highlighting Britain's advance to become the world's No. 2 exporter of services. https://johnredwoodsdiary.com/2024/06/23/great-brexit-wins/.

7. Meghnad Desai, 'The future: Neither paradise nor perdition', OMFIF, 27 June 2016. Desai wrote that, had the UK reported to the time-honoured approach of setting up a royal commission rather than a referendum to guide decision-making, 'the UK would have had a more balanced, nuanced account of the costs and benefits'.

8. Fear was a factor in both sides' campaigns. Chris Grayling, the Brexit-backing leader of the House of Commons, claimed on the eve of the poll that the EU was moving towards removing the UK and France from their permanent seats on the United Nations Security Council and was considering allowing EU citizens to vote in British general elections. 'EU to grab more powers, warns Leave camp', *Sunday Times*, 12 June 2016. This coincided with lurid claims that, if Britain stayed in the EU it would be forced to open borders to Turkish citizens.

9. In a poll of more than a hundred economists for the *Financial Times* at the start of 2016, more than three-quarters thought Brexit would adversely affect the UK's medium-term economic prospects, against 8 per cent who thought the economy would benefit. 'Three futures for a Britain outsider the EU', *Financial Times*, 23 February 2016. Other studies have come to similar conclusions. See accounts of Centre for Economic Performance, CBI/ PwC and Oxford Economics, *Financial Times*, 22 March 2016, and Office for Budgetary Responsibility. George Osborne, chancellor of the exchequer, said in May 2016 that leaving the single market would be 'catastrophic for people's jobs, their incomes and their livelihoods'. A total of 1,285 business leaders said in a letter to *The Times* that Brexit would damage the economy. 'FTSE chiefs join forces in huge vote for Remain', *The Times*, 22 June 2016.

10. 'The Brexit Files: From referendum to reset', UK in a Changing Europe, 28 January 2025, p. 84. https://ukandeu.ac.uk/reports/the-brexit-files-from-referendum-to-reset/.

11. Theresa May, October 2016 Conservative party conference speech, *Financial Times*, 3 October 2016. 'From reluctant Remainer to iron-willed Brexit enforcer – Prime minister tells delegates, "We are going to be a fully independent, sovereign country." '

12. Rees-Mogg, interview with author, London, 16 May 2023. 'I thought it was not strictly speaking necessary. It would not make that much difference to the voting: after all, £150 million a week would also be a large figure. I did put my views at the time to some of the organisers of the campaign: Matthew Elliot, for example, but I believe it was a [Dominic] Cummings decision.' But he says: 'On the other hand, if you are supporting a campaign, you cannot make a large issue out of an item like this, you have to show solidarity. It was important after the referendum that we did put an equivalent amount of extra money into the NHS, as I told Simon Steven [NHS chief executive 2014–21].'

13. Britain's rise in GDP per capita in the seven years between 2016 to 2023 was the third lowest in the G7 grouping, according to the IMF World Economic Outlook database,

April 2025. In the seven proceeding years it was the third highest. The seven-year 2006–23 rise was 2.7 per cent for Germany, 3.5 per cent for Canada, 3.9 per cent for the UK, 4.9 per cent for Japan, 10 per cent for Italy and 13.6 per cent for the US. In the seven years before the vote, 2009–16, Italy's per capita GDP fell by 1 .9 per cent. GDP per capita rose 4.7 per cent in France, 7.9 per cent in Canada, 8.9 per cent in the UK, 11.0 per cent in Japan, 11.3 per cent in the US and 14.4 per cent in Germany. https://www.imf.org/en/Publications/WEO/weo-database/2025/april.

14. Joachim Nagel, Bundesbank president, 'The United Kingdom's withdrawal from the single market may have reduced the country's GDP by 6 per cent so far, a recent study suggests', speech in Munich, 15 February 2024, citing a 2024 Cambridge Econometrics report. https://www.bundesbank.de/en/press/speeches/stability-and-prosperity-in-europe-924914. Nagel gave a somewhat misleading, abbreviated account of the study, which projected that Gross Value Added (GVA: an alternative to GDP in calculating the size of the economy) would be 10.1 per cent lower in 2035 than if withdrawal had not occurred. Elsewhere the report cited the National Institute of Economic and Social Research suggesting that GVA was 2–3 per cent lower in 2023 than had Brexit not occurred, with the negative impact expected to gradually increase to 5–6 per cent by 2035.

15. 'Starmer's growth plan doomed without access to EU markets, warn economists', Opinium poll, *Observer*, 23 June 2024. Of those surveyed, 62 per cent believed Brexit had contributed to higher shop prices, against 8 per cent who thought it had the opposite effect.

16. In a YouGov opinion poll on the in/out question in August 2024, 59 per cent of respondents said they wanted to rejoin, with 41 per cent saying they were against.

17. Four territories of EU member states have withdrawn: French Algeria, in 1962, when Algeria became independent; Greenland, a semi-autonomous territory of Denmark, in 1985, following a referendum; Saint Pierre and Miquelon, 1985; and Saint Barthélemy, in 2012. The last three became 'overseas countries and territories of the European Union'.

18. Eurobarometer opinion polls for the European Commission have shown little impact on overall European support for the Union. Forecasts that a British Leave vote might encourage others to follow came, among others, from Philip Hammond, UK foreign secretary, in February 2016, speaking of fears that 'contagion would spread'. *Financial Times*, 19 February 2016.

19. Stephen Wall, *A Stranger in Europe: Britain and the EU from Thatcher to Blair* (Oxford: Oxford University Press, 2008), pp. vii–viii. Wall, a former UK permanent representative to the European Commission, working closely with John Major, and later EU adviser to Tony Blair, wrote that Ted Heath was probably the only UK leader to have shared the view of the original Six that the European Community's destination might one day be a federation. Wall, *A Stranger in Europe*, p. 3.

20. Churchill added: 'We are linked, but not comprised. We are interested and associated, but not absorbed.' See Helene von Bismarck, 'With Europe but not of it: An exclusively British attitude?', 15 June 2012. https://www.helenevonbismarck.com/wp-content/uploads/2017/12/With-Europe-but-not-of-it.pdf.

21. Churchill, speech, Congress of Europe. The Hague, 7 May 1948. Somewhat hopefully, Churchill termed a united Europe 'a solution which can be implemented without delay'.

22. William Keegan, David Marsh and Richard Roberts, *Six Days in September: Black Wednesday, Brexit and the Making of Europe* (London: OMFIF Press, 2017), p. 27.

23. Michael Charlton, *The Price of Victory* (London: BBC Books, 1983), p. 307.

24. Keegan, Marsh and Roberts, *Six Days in September*, p. 72.

25. Given some of the benevolent (for the UK) economic outcomes of the exit, some commentators immediately coined the epithet 'White' Wednesday. See Anatole Kaletsky, 'White Wednesday', *The Times*, 17 September 1992.

26. See, for example, Steven Castle, 'Britain, breaking up with E.U., looks to an expert: Henry VIII', *New York Times*, 30 March 2017.

27. Helmut Schlesinger, Bundesbank president in 1991–3, showed considerable scepticism about the prospects for monetary union during his time as Karl Otto Pöhl's vice president and for most of his turbulent period at the helm. He mildened conspicuously at the end of

his mandate. In retirement, Schlesinger gave signals of approval for the project – partly on the grounds that he saw it as his patriotic duty to support Helmut Kohl. See for example, Schlesinger, 'Money is just the start', *The Economist*, 21 September 1996. Otmar Issing, the Bundesbank's director for economics in 1990–8, who in 1998 later took on the same job at the European Central Bank, was another hawk who changed his tune. 'The decisive moment came with the currency crises of 1992–3. The status quo was not tenable.' Issing, conference, Hamburg, November 2007.

28. Hans Tietmeyer, a member of Kohl's Christian Democratic Union, Bundesbank president in 1993–9, maintained a barrage of demands over the conditions needed for monetary union. Yet, reflecting underlying complicity with Kohl, Tietmeyer eventually saw it as part of his duty to prepare for EMU – even on weaker conditions.

29. Cameron was given generally high marks for his performance as foreign secretary, reinforcing the more serious note Sunak was trying to strike on foreign policy circles after the fiascos of the Johnson and Truss premierships.

30. Cameron, speech, Conservative party conference, Bournemouth, 1 October 2006. http://news.bbc.co.uk/1/hi/uk_politics/5396358.stm.

31. Cameron, interview, Anthony Seldon and Peter Snowdon, *Cameron at 10: The Verdict* (London: William Collins, 2015), p. 165. With the 2009 Lisbon treaty enacted, Whitehall specialists had told Cameron that the EU would settle down to a quiet period. 'We didn't expect Europe to form a big part of the agenda.' In his memoirs, Cameron wrote that the coalition formed in 2010 expected 'five relatively Europe-free years'. David Cameron, *For the Record* (London: William Collins, 2019), p. 320.

32. David Owen, 'Why Europe must be restructured: EMU can survive only with closer union', OMFIF Bulletin, June 2012. Owen's plan for a remodelled Europe aimed to move from 'Existing Europe', made up of NATO, the European Economic Area, the EEC/EU and the euro area, to 'Restructured Europe', made up of NATO, the Single Market/European Community (including Turkey) and the EU/ euro area. According to Owen, the latter would consist of Austria, Belgium, Bulgaria, Croatia, Cyprus, Estonia, Finland, France, Germany, Hungary, Latvia, Lithuania, Luxembourg, Malta, Poland, Slovakia and Slovenia. See David Owen, *Europe Restructured? The Eurozone Crisis and Its Aftermath* (London: Methuen, 2012).

33. Cameron, speech, Bloomberg HQ, London, 23 January 2013. In his memoirs, Cameron writes: 'Britain was in danger of being left in an organisation whose future was being dictated to by an integrationist core, those for whom the euro was their currency.' Cameron, *For the Record*, p. 400.

34. Simon McDonald published a letter correcting the prime minister's untruths about an alleged sexual assault by Chris Pincher, a former junior foreign office minister. McDonald, interview, Cambridge, 6 July 2023. 'The man who brought down Boris Johnson: "I just wanted Number 10 to tell the truth"'. https://inews.co.uk/news/politics/simon-mcdonald-man-brought-down-boris-johnson-number-10-truth-1960984.

35. McDonald, interview with author, Cambridge, 6 July 2023.

36. The Lisbon treaty entered into force on 1 December 2009.

37. For an account of Cameron's mistakes in analysing and negotiating with the other European countries, and the lessons these hold for Keir Starmer, see Simon Nixon, 'Will Starmer fall into the Cameron trap?', *New European*, 28 September 2024. 'The former Tory PM had no idea what he was doing on Europe. If the present PM hasn't learned from the mistakes of the past, he is doomed to repeat them.' https://www.theneweuropean.co.uk/simon-nixon-will-starmer-fall-into-the-cameron-trap/?utm_source=substack&utm_medium=email.

38. Cameron, interview with author, London, 11 November 2024.

39. Clarke was justice secretary and lord chancellor from 2010 to 2012 and minister without portfolio from 2012 to 2014.

40. Clarke, interview with author, London, 2 May 2023.

41. According to Derek Laud, a long-time associate whom Cameron approached to become mayor of London, Cameron 'rarely expressed any strong views in his life'. Michael Ashcroft

and Isabel Oakeshott, *Call Me Dave: The Unauthorised Biography of David Cameron* (London: Biteback Publishing, 2016), p. 95.

42. Charles Moore, interview with author, London, 25 June 2024. Cameron defines himself as a 'pragmatic Eurosceptic'. Cameron, *For the Record*, p. 321.

43. Richard Balfe, interview with author, London, 4 July 2024.

44. During David Frost's spell in Brussels, 'I had a rather naive view of Europe. People who go to Brussels see their views either reinforced or weakened. I reacted against Europe. I was irritated by the self-righteousness in the European Commission, the opinion that we were all heading in one direction. I would wonder to myself how people like Arthur Cockfield had the right to say what they did about decisions needed to set up the single market under the 1992 project.'

45. Frost, interview with author, London, 23 July 2024. Cameron backs up this impression, commenting to Anthony Seldon on his relationships with EU counterparts, 'Nothing I did beforehand gave me any preparation for them.' Seldon and Snowdon, *Cameron at 10*, p. 169.

46. Cameron, *For the Record*, p. 637.

47. See Tim Bale and Karl Pike, 'Hopes will be dashed: Brexit and the "Merkel myth"', *Journal of European Integration*, 4 September 2023.

48. As an example of 'false claims' on Turkish accession, 'Vote Leave launched a poster warning: "Turkey (population 76 million) is joining the EU", next to a picture of a British passport.' The campaign 'drowned out' Cameron's statement the previous day: 'At Turkey's current rate of progress, it would probably join the EU in the year 3000.' Cameron, *For the Record*, p. 669.

49. Ivan Rogers, interview with author, London, 30 June 2023.

50. McDonald, interview with author, Cambridge, 6 July 2023.

51. Merkel conversation with Cameron at Downing Street, November 2012. Seldon and Snowdon, *Cameron at 10*, pp. 261–5. Kornelius, *Angela* Merkel, pp. 257 and 264–5.

52. Anonymous Berlin official, interview with author, May 2024.

53. Monti, interview with author, Rome, 8 March 2023.

54. Rogers, interview, Britain in a Changing Europe, 27 November 2020. https://ukandeu.ac.uk/brexit-witness-archive/ivan-rogers/. Rogers told Italian interlocutors in 2012–13: 'You think that we want more powerful and more rigorous enforcement mechanisms, both on competition policy and the single market. That's the last bloody thing we want: we are much less keen than we once were on driving forward and deepening market integration. So one kept on having to explain: Look, you're not dealing with an old generation of Tories who believe in any of that stuff. Cameron does want to find a way to stay in. But he needs a looser relationship, not a deepened one.'

55. Monti, interview with author, Rome, 8 March 2023.

56. The Liberal Democrat position on a European referendum had fluctuated. Although staunchly opposed to the UK leaving the EU, it was the first major political party to call for an in/out referendum. Jo Swinson, then Liberal Democrat leader, said in parliament in 2008 that the party 'would like to have a referendum on the major issue of whether we are in or out of Europe'. In his memoirs, Cameron writes: 'The accusation that I decided to make the referendum pledge because I didn't believe I'd actually have to hold one is absolutely false . . . I didn't believe the Liberal Democrats would block it.' Cameron, *For the Record*, p. 399.

57. Brexiters had in fact argued for exactly that outcome; announcing an intended referendum in the Conservative party's 2015 election manifesto would, they reasoned, raise the likelihood of a clear majority which would clear the way for the European poll to take place. John Redwood, interview with author, Wokingham, 22 June 2024.

58. Cameron wrote in his memoirs: 'Whichever senior Tory politician took the lead on the Brexit side – so loaded with images of patriotism, independence and romance – would become the darling of the party . . . [Johnson] was certain that the Brexit side would lose. So opting to back it bore little risk of breaking up the government that he wished to lead one day.' Cameron, *For the Record*, p. 654.

59. One version of Johnson's decision-making process is that he came to the view of backing Brexit over a game of tennis. Rachel Johnson (Johnson's sister), *Mail on Sunday*, 28 February 2016.

60. For accounts of Johnson's range of views on the matter and Cameron's surprise at his decision to back Leave see Tom Bower, *Boris Johnson: The Gambler* (London. W.H. Allen, 2020), pp. 256–67.

61. House of Commons foreign affairs committee, 20 July 2016.

62. Cameron interview with Andrew Marr, BBC TV, 10 January 2016. Kenneth Clarke, ever realistic, had earlier given notice that Cameron 'would not last 30 seconds' if he lost the referendum. 'Brexiteers and EU braced for messy divorce', *Financial Times*, 7 June 2016.

63. Another of Johnson's character defects is the incapacity to think through the consequences of his actions. 'Throughout the interviews one consistent theme emerged: Johnson resists the idea that he has to bother with the consequences for his actions that normal people have to continue with. "Maybe there is something deep in his personality that resists the idea that he has to face up to the same reality as the rest of us," one colleague said.' Sebastian Payne, *The Fall of Boris Johnson: The Full Story* (London: Macmillan, 2022), p. 258.

64. Moore, interview with author, London, 25 June 2024.

65. Frost, interview with author, London, 23 July 2024.

66. Andrew Gimson, *Boris Johnson, The Rise and Fall of a Troublemaker at Number 10* (London: Simon & Schuster, 2022), p. 412.

67. Charles Powell, interview with author, London, 28 February 2023.

68. David Davis, interviews with author, London, 19 April and 17 May 2023.

69. Tugendhat, interview with author, London, 15 February 2023.

70. Examples abound of Johnson's lack of depth and seriousness. One of many was when he was reprimanded by Andrew Tyrie, chairman of the Commons Treasury committee, in March 2016 for his 'busking, humorous approach to a very serious question for the United Kingdom': 'Boris Johnson skewered over Brexit', *Financial Times*, 24 March 2016.

71. Clarke, interview with author, London, 2 May 2023. For accounts of Johnson's period in Brussels, see Bower, *Boris Johnson*, pp. 44–7, quoting Johnson's father, Stanley, a former Commission official, defending his son's propensity to make up stories: 'Exaggeration is OK, because Boris has to ask: "How do I make my mark?"'

72. Mark Carney, interview with author (video), Toronto–London, 23 October 2023.

73. See, for example, letter, Carney to MPs, April 2016, warning of a weaker exchange rate, higher prices and lower growth if Britain were to quit the EU. 'Carney warns of fall in sterling from Brexit', *Financial Times*, 28 April 2016. Carney's energetic communication style on the EU vote has made his successor, Andrew Bailey, highly cautious about revealing preferences on Britain's European policies.

74. Carney, victory speech, Ottawa, 29 April 2025. https://globalnews.ca/news/11154593/canada-election-mark-carney-victory-speech/.

75. Clarke, interview with author, London, 2 May 2023. Jacob Rees-Mogg was a key Carney critic. 'Mark Carney's mistake was to have got involved in the politics of the referendum. He should've been studiously neutral. You can't be an independent central bank and start to take sides on political issues. He overstepped the mark.' Rees-Mogg, interview with author, London, 16 May 2023.

76. On 15 June, a week before the vote, Osborne announced that if the UK chose to leave he would carry out an emergency budget to plug the £30 billion hole Brexit was likely to generate – raising income and inheritance tax, petrol and alcohol duties, and cutting health, defence and education spending. Looking back, Cameron described the unenacted 'punishment budget' as 'over the top'. Cameron, *For the Record*, p. 673. Rather than introducing austerity measures, Britain brought in fresh monetary stimulus to counter what Carney called 'economic post-traumatic stress'. *Financial Times*, 1 July 2016.

77. Selmayr, interview with author, Vienna, 23 January 2023.

78. McDonald, interview with author, Cambridge, 6 July 2023. For an account of the antipathy to Johnson of Merkel and Steinmeier, who regarded him as a 'clown', see Bower, *Boris Johnson*, p. 309.

79. Gerhard Cromme, former chief executive and supervisory board chairman, ThyssenKrupp, and former supervisory board chairman, Siemens, Axel Springer and Saint-Gobain, interview with author, Berlin, 15 November 2023.

80. Stephen Glover, *Daily Mail*, 6 July 2024.

81. Frost, 'Reflections on the revolutions in Europe', speech, Brussels, 17 February 2020. 'It is good for a country and its people to have its fate in its own hands and for their own decisions to matter.'

82. Frost, interview with author, London, 23 July 2024.

83. Christopher Tugendhat, *The Worm in the Apple: A History of the Conservative Party and Europe from Churchill to Cameron* (London: Haus, 2022), p. 1.

84. Tugendhat, interview with author, London, 15 February 2023.

85. Johnson announced his resignation from the House of Commons after being sent an advance copy of a report by the House of Commons privileges committee, which was eventually published on 16 June 2023. https://www.bbc.co.uk/newsround/65913600.

86. Pasquale Terracciano, interview with author, Rome, 9 March 2023.

87. De Larosière, interview with author, Paris, 23 April 2023.

88. Carney, interview with author (video), Toronto–London, 23 October 2023.

89. Schäuble, interview with author, Berlin, 16 January 2023.

90. Lamers and Schäuble, 'Überlegungen zur europäischen Politik'.

91. Marsh, *The Euro*, p. 115.

92. In November 1985, Thatcher convened a top-level meeting at 10 Downing Street with Nigel Lawson, Robin Leigh-Pemberton (Bank of England) and Geoffrey Howe (foreign secretary). The prime minister ended the meeting abruptly: 'If you join the EMS, you will have to do so without me.' Nigel Lawson, *The View from No. 11: Memoirs of a Tory Radical* (London: Bantam, 1992), p. 499.

93. John Redwood, memorandum ('secret') to prime minister, 27 September 1985. Redwood warned presciently of 'great pressures against the pound' and a future devaluation that would be a 'visible national humiliation under the EMS system'. He favoured 'a more pragmatic approach', as Britain had followed hitherto, 'at times taking care of the exchange rate and other times placing more reliance on monetary targets'. This was, he wrote, 'politically much more sensible; keeps our destinies in our own hands and not in those of the Germans; and still leaves us free to try to track the DM exchange rate if we wish to do so and if it suits us.' UKNA, unknown file number.

94. Redwood says: 'By the end of her time in office she had become antagonistic to the ambition to move towards ever closer union and so on. Despite this she became progressively worn down by the forces behind European integration. She didn't want to have a battle with the people who wished to take Britain into the ERM [Howe, Lawson, Hurd, etc.]. She started to think that signing up to the ERM might be better than agreeing a single currency, and it would enable Britain to avoid some of the other unpleasant aspects of Europe.' Redwood, interview with author, Wokingham, 14 April 2023.

95. John Whittingdale, Thatcher's political secretary, diary entry, 5 October 1990. Moore, *Margaret Thatcher*, vol. 3, p. 630. The cut in interest rates was the first line in the Treasury press statement. This was a strong signal that domestic monetary policies would take precedence over international commitments. The message became fully apparent twenty-three months later.

96. Kenneth Baker, Conservative Party chairman, opposed ERM entry and tried to dissuade Thatcher from joining. She told him, 'We will be able to adjust the value of sterling. I have been assured that we will have that flexibility.' Baker, *The Turbulent Years: My Life in Politics* (London: Faber & Faber, 1993).

97. John Kerr, Britain's permanent representative to the European Community in Brussels, was by chance in the chancellor of the exchequer's office in October 1990 when John Major came back from No. 10, having secured Thatcher's agreement to joining the ERM. Kerr says: 'He knew, indeed it was obvious, that the rate at which she had insisted sterling should join was too high. He asked my advice: "Could a rate, once set, be changed?" I said, "Yes," and described the realignment process I'd witnessed. I fear I hadn't spotted the extent

to which the ERM had, following the Delors Report, become a glide-path to monetary union, less flexible than in the early 1980s. It would have been better to talk Thatcher into agreeing a more sensible rate, and Major had tried: it was in any case not right for us to decide, and announce, our joining rate unilaterally.' Kerr, interview with author, London, 8 September 2023.

98. Letter, Leigh-Pemberton to Thatcher, 4 October 1990. The letter bore the imprint of his deputy and eventual successor, Eddie George (who was highly sceptical about joining the ERM). BoE, 14A /99/1.

99. In October 1990, Redwood was considering resigning from his Downing Street post in protest against the decision. 'Instead of arguing with me and saying I was wrong, instead of saying, "You've got a nice job, why don't you keep it?", she did the only thing that could've persuaded me to stay: she became very defensive and apologetic and asked me to understand her position.' Redwood argues that the DM 2.95 central rate for sterling was too low at the beginning of ERM membership, but too high towards the end. 'They [the supporters of ERM] didn't see how inflationary it was, as it was in the early stages, as well as imposing a deflationary threat, as it did later on.' Redwood, interview with author, Wokingham, 14 April 2023.

100. Conclusions of Cabinet meeting, 18 October 1990. UKNA, CAB 128/97.

101. Keegan, Marsh and Roberts, *Six Days in September*, pp. 68–9.

102. 'Governor's bilateral with chancellor of the exchequer', 6 September 1990. BoE 14A/99-1.

103. Official UK minutes of European consultations played down the discord among Karl Otto Pöhl, Bundesbank president, and Jacques de Larosière at the Banque de France and his combative deputy Philippe Lagayette. Lagayette, interview with author (video), Paris–London, 13 June 2024.

104. As a great-nephew of Manfred von Richthofen, the First World War flying ace known as the 'Red Baron', the German foreign service veteran was a media favourite in the UK, as demonstrated by headlines such as 'The *Sun* meets the Hun'.

105. Letter, von Richthofen to German finance and economic ministries (Bonn) and the office of Hans Tietmeyer, Bundesbank (Frankfurt), 5 December 1990. Lecture by Bundesbank director Franz Scholl on current economic and monetary policy questions, London, 28 November 1990. The pound had risen more than 20 per cent in real (inflation-adjusted) terms since the last exchange rate realignment, making British exports too expensive. 'If the exchange rate policy leads to a lasting loss of price competitiveness, industry is losing ground on foreign and domestic markets and businesses have to be closed,' Scholl said. Treasury and Bank of England representatives at the dinner displayed 'muted reaction but no contradiction'. Richard Evans, chief executive of British Aerospace, also present, pointedly supported Scholl's remarks, according to von Richthofen's report, complaining about the high sterling exchange rate depressing the company's competitiveness. PAAA, B 224 ZA 168549.

106. Norwin Leutrum von Ertingen report to state secretary, Bonn, 30 November 1990. PAAA, B31 ZA 178054.

107. Kohl, *Erinnerungen 1990–1994*, p. 285. John Major wrote, 'I took to Helmut Kohl from the first and we became firm friends and, on occasion, allies.' John Major, *The Autobiography* (London: HarperCollins, 1999), p. 267.

108. Major, *Autobiography*, p. 269. See also Stephan Kieninger, 'At the very heart of Europe': New Evidence on John Major's Foreign Policy', Wilson Center, 1 March 2019. https://www.wilsoncenter.org/blog-post/the-very-heart-europe-new-evidence-john-majors-foreign-policy.

109. Leigh-Pemberton speech, Tokyo, 8 October 1992.

110. In a telephone call with Major on 25 August 1992, in which the British prime minister voiced his concerns about German monetary policies, Kohl requested a letter on currencies and interest rates (Major's second, following an earlier missive on 14 July). The same day, 25 August, Major sent the letter, expressing the possibility that the UK, France and Italy would have to raise interest rates, with negative political and economic conse-

quences. The letter had already been prepared in draft form on 24 August. In the telephone call, 'Chancellor Kohl listened to all this with frequent interjections of "Ya" [sic], although an "Mm" when the Prime Minister referred to the need for the Bundesbank to cut its Lombard rate.' Kohl said, 'he would very much welcome it if the Prime Minister could set out his arguments in a letter.' Letter, Alex Allan, principal private secretary to Major, to Jeremy Heywood, Norman Lamont's private secretary, 25 August 1992. UKNA, T 668/177. A third letter to Kohl was sent on 28 August. Major, *Autobiography*, pp. 320–5.

111. Letter, Major to Kohl, 25 August 1992. UKNA, T 668/177. Major, *Autobiography*, p. 320.

112. Klaus Barth report for Klaus Kinkel, 'Influence of dollar development on European Monetary System', Bonn, 1 September 1992. AAPD 1992, Document 272, pp. 1091–7. Schlesinger explained further the nature of the trap in an interview with *L'Expansion* in late September. UKNA, T 702/1010/2.

113. On multiple occasions France made known its rejection of a realignment involving the franc. During the mission to Paris by Köhler and Tietmeyer on 12 September, Michael Sapin, the French finance minister, reaffirmed France's rejection of a realignment and instead raised the issue of lower German interest rates. Report, Central Bank Council meeting, 14 September 1992, p. 4. HADB.

114. A list prepared for Lamont on 16 September 1992 includes four episodes in August–September as well as earlier in the summer.

115. Lamont, interview with author, London, 19 May 2023.

116. Juncker, interview with author, Brussels, 29 November 2023.

117. Author's private information.

118. Anthony Seldon, one of Major's biographers, wrote that Lamont's 'arm-twisting' of Schlesinger was 'with Major's agreement, urging even'. Anthony Seldon, *Major: A Political Life* (London: Orion, 1997), p. 310. Lamont recorded in 1999, that, pre-Bath, he had discussed the situation 'at length' with Major. 'Far from urging caution, he was one of the keenest that I should put maximum pressure on Dr Schlesinger and throughout that weekend in Bath I received several messages from the PM reminding me that it was essential to put pressure on the Germans to cut interest rates. I agreed completely. It was a long shot but it was not entirely without hope.' Lamont, *In Office*, pp. 233–4.

119. Waigel told the meeting it was important that US–European interest rate differentials should not rise further. 'The Germans had already done their bit with both Schlesinger and Tietmeyer having said that German rates had peaked.' Schlesinger 'gently reproved' Waigel for saying that interest rates had reached a peak. 'People fell off summits.' 'Record of initial table round at Bath informal Ecofin meeting', 4 September 1992. Paul Gray, 'Secret and personal' letter to Nigel Wicks, 11 September, noting, 'Would copy recipients [six names] please ensure this record is treated with due discretion.' UKNA T671/85. The Treasury note directly contradicts Lamont's firm denial in his memoirs of reports that a realignment was offered at the Bath meeting. '[F]rankly I am baffled by these suggestions. No suggestion was ever made to me, either at the meeting or any other time, and all my officials at the Treasury denied that any such approaches were made to them.' Lamont, *In Office*, p. 262.

120. Schlesinger was recorded as saying: 'The ERM system was a fixed one but there could be realignments. Indeed, there had been 12 and we had now had a five-year gap since the last one.' Inflation differentials had been growing, 'with 6 to 7 per cent gaps developing on cost and price performance'. Gray, 'Record of initial round table at Bath informal Ecofin meeting', 4 September 1992. UKNA, T 671/85.

121. Heywood, 'Bath informal Ecofin: Talk of realignments', 12 September 1992. UKNA, T 671/83.

122. Burns, interview with author (video), Berlin–London, 2 October 2023.

123. Letter, Kohl to Major, 4 September 1992, replying to Major letters of 25 and 28 August. 'We should not forget that reunification produced a tremendous impetus for growth from which our European partners in particular have benefited.' UKNA, T 671/83.

124. Letter, Lamont to Schlesinger, 10 September 1992. For a finance minister to write such a letter to the governor of a foreign central bank is highly unusual. UKNA, T668/177. The letter was discussed in draft form in a meeting on 10 September between Heywood and Leigh-Pemberton. BoE, 9A376/2. See Harold James, *Making a Modern Central Bank: The Bank of England 1979–2003* (Cambridge: Cambridge University Press, 2016), p. 295.

125. Author's private information.

126. Wicks, whose previous job had been as Britain's executive director at the IMF, had little background in economics and financial markets, which was held against him by other senior Treasury officials, and raises the question of why he was appointed to such a senior role. He was taken aback by the market pressures that materialised in the ERM. Greater openness within the Treasury (and Bank) could have offset somewhat his lack of expertise and opened his mind to alternative approaches.

127. The loan, for 10 billion European currency units ($14 billion), was meant to mark a commitment to the UK's European economic goals. The British seemed insouciant or unaware of misgivings on international borrowing that were voiced privately by Italian officials who were wary about raising loans in a currency that, in view of what they considered was likely to be an impending devaluation of the lira, would probably be revalued shortly against their own currency. Wicks's complacency was sharply criticised by Alan Budd, the Treasury's chief economic adviser. The Treasury was unaware that, at the time of borrowing, the relatively unknown hedge fund run by George Soros was marshalling an equivalent massive loan in sterling which it would sell to bet on a sterling devaluation. Soros commented later: 'When Norman Lamont said just before the devaluation that he would borrow nearly $15 billion to defend sterling, we were amused because that was about how much we wanted to sell.' Anatole Kaletsky, 'How Mr Soros made a billion by betting against the pound', *The Times*, 26 October 1992. Only after Black Wednesday did Wicks start to ponder the extra cost of paying back borrowed foreign currency in devalued sterling. Treasury note on 'the cost of intervention', Evershed to Wicks, 9 September 1992. A month later (on 11 October) Wicks wrote by hand on a copy of the earlier document: 'Mr Collins' note attached shows the "cost" to the Buba [Bundesbank] is likely to be quite high. Can Mr Collins give an estimate assuming say an average repayment exchange rate of DM 2.55?' UKNA, T 671/85.

128. Note, Wicks (handwritten), undated (probably from 14 September), after the German interest rate cut, refers to some of the scrambled Treasury–Bank meetings over the weekend. UKNA, T 668/178. Wicks explicitly asked his personal assistant to 'save this paper', possibly indicating his belief that the document would help provide justification for his work during the crisis. 'We had always made clear that we were not seeking a realignment involving just the lira and the pound. We were told on the Saturday evening about the proposed Italian realignment and the German interest rate cuts. I held a meeting early on Sunday morning at which the decision not to realign with the Italians was reaffirmed. This was made clear to the Italians. We received no request during the weekend from the German authorities that the pound should realign with the lira and that, if we had, the cuts in the German interest rates would have been higher.' The memorandum further records notes from a conversation with the 'chairman of the monetary committee' (Trichet). 'I had a request of [*sic*] Buba under pressure because of high interventions. Meeting approved to try to get broad alignment. Went to France and Rome, no official request in public. Officially did not ask.'

129. The 14 September mission – which Budd referred to later as 'one of the great wasted journeys' – is not mentioned in any of the contemporaneous Treasury notes in September–October 1992 listing the chronology of the foreign exchange crisis. UKNA, T 668/178. For years afterwards, the mission remained shrouded in secrecy, perhaps reflecting above all Treasury and Bank embarrassment about how little it accomplished. Norman Lamont writes in non-committal fashion in his memoirs: 'Arrangements had been made for a visit on Monday 14 September of senior Treasury and Bank of England officials to the German

Ministry of Finance and the Bundesbank'. Lamont, *In Office*, p. 265. In a 2004 account, Budd referred to the visit obliquely: 'Let us assume, for the moment, that such a visit did take place.' Alan Budd, Wincott lecture, London, 2004, published as *Black Wednesday: A Re-examination of Britain's Experience in the Exchange Rate Mechanism* (London: Institute of Economic Affairs, 2005), p. 25. In 2007, Budd went further by terming it 'one of the great wasted journeys'. Marsh, *The Euro*, p. 164; Budd, interview with author, London, 25 September 2007. King's verdict, in 2023, more than thirty years later, is impressively excoriating: 'I never thought [the visit] would go anywhere. It was a foolish mission and it made no difference to the ultimate outcome of events. We had no systematic arguments to back the view that DM2.95 was, somehow, the "right" rate. The right rate depends on the conditions affecting the market. This was underlined by the fact that sterling did return to DM2.95 eventually, following a reversal of the initial fall in the currency after we left the system.' King does say, however, that Bundesbank officials Helmut Schlesinger, Hans Tietmeyer and Otmar Issing were 'very nice' to him and Budd. King, interview with author, London, 1 November 2023.

130. Letter (fax), Wicks to Horst Köhler, 14 September 1992, and the reply (fax) from Köhler, dated 15 September. The German finance ministry official was quoted by Reuters as not ruling out another realignment of European exchange rates in the period up to 1997 (the first deadline for permanently fixing currency rates in monetary union). UKNA, T 668/178.

131. Wicks termed the damning final sentence of the Reuters report as 'particularly unhelpful' – 'There is no tension between the franc and the mark, but concerning the British pound we will just have to wait and see.' Letter (fax), Wicks to Horst Köhler, 14 September 1992. UKNA, T 668/178.

132. The state secretary, in his reply on 15 September, said Wicks's message 'has prompted me once again to remind my collaborators that we have absolutely no interest in public discussions about realignments'. Letter (fax), Köhler to Wicks, 15 September 1992. UKNA, T 668/178.

133. Letter, Alex Allan, Major's principal private secretary, to Heywood, Lamont's private secretary, 13 September 1992. The note starts off: 'NO further copies should be made of this letter, and it should be made available ONLY to other Ministers and officials with a strict need to know of its contents.' Wicks had difficulty finding a record of the Amato conversation. An internal Treasury note to him on 9 October, part of the post-mortem into Black Wednesday, records: 'You asked if there were a record of the prime minister's conversation with Amato. I have established that it exists but the Treasury copy is held in the chancellor's office and may not be copied further.' In handwritten comments on a separate Treasury briefing document, on 9 October, Wicks wrote, 'In no event should the PM's conversations with Amato be referred to.' UKNA, T 668/178.

134. Amato, email to author, 14 April 2023. Although he had received no personal message from Kohl, Amato said it was 'obvious' that 'if you accept devaluation, rates will be lower afterwards'.

135. David Marsh and Olaf Storbeck, 'Helmut Schlesinger, former Bundesbank president, 1924–2024', *Financial Times*, 27 December 2024. https://www.ft.com/content/f56fe64d-03d7-415f-849b-08746f473d73.

136. The details of the German response to the ERM crisis are laid out in 'Chronologie der Erreignisse im Zusammenhang mit Realignment vom 13. September 1992 (Abwertung der Lira)' ['Chronology of events connected to realignment of 13 September 1992 (devaluation of the lira)'], Bundesbank internal note, 23 September 1992. On Friday 11 September, following an earlier telephone call at 10.20 a.m. between Schlesinger, Waigel and Carlo Ciampi, governor of Banca d'Italia, Schlesinger and Tietmeyer met Kohl, Waigel, Horst Köhler and Gert Haller (finance ministry) and Joahnnes Ludwig (chancellor's office) between 9 p.m. and 11 p.m. at the Bundesbank's guesthouse in the central bank's grounds in north-west Frankfurt. HADB, B330/28186.

137. Schlesinger, interview with author, Oberursel, 26 July 2024; telephone call, 12 August 2024; handwritten note to author, 9 August 2024.

138. Recording that 'Helmut Kohl had sent a personal message to Giuliano saying he was pressing for this [a cut in interest rates]', Major added, 'As Helmut had aways told me that German interest rate policy was solely a matter for the Bundesbank, I smiled somewhat wryly at this development.' Major, *Autobiography*, p. 327.

139. David Cameron, Treasury adviser, later prime minister, 'Note for the record', 14 September 1992. Lamont said, 'We should stress that this is the first cut in German rates for five years and we are in no way disappointed by the extent of the cut.' UKNA, T 668/178.

140. The message relayed by *Handelsblatt* to news agencies on 15 September (using reported speech, but firmly attributed to Schlesinger), said, 'It cannot be ruled out that, after the realignment and the German interest rate cut, one or two currencies could come under pressure before the referendum in France. In a conversation with the *Handelsblatt* and *Wall Street Journal*, he [Schlesinger] commented that the measures taken up to now have, naturally, not definitely resolved the problems. A more comprehensive realignment would have had a greater effect in alleviating EMS tensions.' See also meeting note, Owen Barber, 'Deputy governor telephone conversation with Hans Tietmeyer', 13 September 1992. Schlesinger's message directly contradicted the Bank of England's firmly stated wishes. In the call with Tietmeyer, Eddie George, deputy governor, said, 'It would be very useful if Tietmeyer could make a statement to accompany the announcement of the realignment saying that, in the view of the Bundesbank, it was unnecessary for there to be further exchange rate adjustments within the ERM.' Tietmeyer said he 'understood' George's concerns and 'would discuss with Schlesinger what could be said to meet them'. UKNA, T 668/178. The Germans pointed out, accurately but not completely relevantly, that, in the full version of the *Handelsblatt* article that appeared on 17 September (by which time the damage had been done and sterling had left the ERM), Schlesinger's remarks were supportive of sterling. Robin Leigh-Pemperton, governor of the Bank of England, wrote to Schlesinger acknowledging that 'your interview reproduced in the Handelsblatt of 17 September 1992 "expressly excluded the UK currency from being endangered". But as you are aware from our conversation on the evening of 15 September, it was the version of your remarks released to the wire services that evening which did such great damage to sterling.' Letter, Leigh-Pemberton to Schlesinger, London, 30 September 1992. HADB, B330/28186.

141. Letter, Wall to Heywood, on telephone conversation, Kohl–Major, 16 September 1992. Major said the UK had been forced to put up interest rates from 10 to 12 per cent and had spent '20 billion [currency unstated]' from its reserves without any effect. 'We could extinguish all our foreign exchange reserves by tomorrow morning.' A further interest rate increase (to 15 per cent) had been announced. If this did not work, Britain would 'step outside' the ERM until after the French referendum. Complaining that 'the ERM was meant to shelter us against speculation, but the scale was such that it was not working', Major again called for lower interest rates. He 'could not ask the Bank of England to go on spending the Reserve, which had been built up painfully over the years.' UKNA, T 671/83.

142. Brevity was not Kohl's usual speaking style: the tactic was reserved for conversations in which he had little or no interest.

143. Kohl said he had just been informed that the Bundesbank had intervened 'to the tune of 25 billion [currency unstated]'. Major retorted that he knew that but 'that was of course our money: we had to pay it back'. Kohl said he knew it was 'a very dangerous situation'. Major said, 'We would need a decision within the hour' – although it was far from clear what he expected Kohl to do. Letter, Wall to Heywood, 16 September 1992. UKNA, T 671/83.

144. Note for record, 'Concertation with EC governors', Paul Tucker, private secretary to Leigh-Pemberton, London, 16 September 1992. UKNA, T 671/83.

145. The meeting agreed to suspend the lira's membership, while Spain's peseta was devalued 5 per cent.

146. Von Richthofen, memorandum, London, 17 September 1992. He opined that City analysts believed that the pound had been 15 per cent overvalued. AAPD 1992, Document 290, pp. 1168–71.

147. Wall, letter to Prentice, on Kohl–Major telephone call, 30 September 1992. The closely typed five-page minutes reveal that this was a constructive conversation that helped to repair bruised feelings. Kohl's negative comments about Lamont's well-known antipathy to ratifying the Maastricht treaty were excised for the final version of Wall's note. UKNA, PREM 19/3751/2.

148. Memorandum, Norman Lamont–Michel Rocard conversation, 30 September 1992. Lamont said Schlesinger had been 'inept rather than deliberately unhelpful. It however was all over now and he did not want to dwell on it.' UKNA, T 671/85.

149. Lamont, interview with author, London, 13 July 2007.

150. Lamont, *In Office*, p. 234.

151. Budd, *Black Wednesday*, p. 33.

152. William Keegan, 'Full marks to the Bundesbank', *Observer*, 20 September 1992. Keegan suggested that Schlesinger be awarded a knighthood for apparently having brought about the collapse of the government's economic strategy, which, he wrote, 'has done the country a great service'. A framed copy of the article was presented to Schlesinger on his 100th birthday on 4 September 2024.

153. 'While we remained a member we were forced to adopt a policy that prolonged a recession. Those extra two years brought inflation down to levels that we have been able to maintain ever since. I do not believe that, in the circumstances of the time, the same effect could have been achieved by other means.' Budd, *Black Wednesday*, p. 32.

154. Lamont, interview with author, London, 15 May 2023. 'Our policy was simple: interest rates in Germany were not coming down, and they needed to, in both Germany's and other countries' interest.'

155. Schlesinger, 'A system and its limits', Foreword, in Keegan, Marsh and Roberts, *Six Days in September*, pp. iv–vi.

156. In his resignation statement in the House of Commons, ten days after he left office, Lamont recognised how, in choosing to stay on as chancellor after Black Wednesday, he had partly acted as a shield for the prime minister. 'He [Major] emphasised that he regarded the attacks on me as coded attacks on himself, so I decided that my duty and loyalty was to the prime minister and that I should remain in office.' Lamont's bitterness showed through: 'Since the war only two Conservative chancellors have been responsible for bringing inflation down to below 2 per cent. Both of them were sacked.' Memorably, he declared that Major's term as prime minister gave the impression of being 'in office but not in power' and was over-prone to 'short-termism . . . Unless this approach is changed, the government will not survive.' Lamont, *In Office*, p. 382.

157. Clarke, interview with author, London, 2 May 2023.

158. Juncker, interview with author, Brussels, 29 November 2023.

159. Clarke, interview with author, London, 2 May 2023. 'The reason why the ERM operation was successful was that if France had left it would've been a catastrophe. Britain by contrast had been a bloody nuisance and the other countries on the whole were not displeased we left. I didn't come back from the meeting and tell my colleagues in London how persuasive I had been in helping to save the ERM. If I had done, perhaps John Major wouldn't have spoken to me for six months.'

160. Lamont, BBC Radio, 17 September 1992.

161. The contrast with the period immediately before Black Wednesday – and with other European economies – was extraordinary. British GDP growth fell to -1.1 per cent from 0.7 per cent in 1991, and rose anaemically by 0.4 per cent in 1992, while German GDP grew 5.7 per cent in 1990 and 5 per cent in 1991, and by 1.5 per cent in 1992. The longer-term aftermath can be divided into three periods, delineated by the 1999 birth of the euro and the 2008–9 crisis. In each of the three periods, UK output outperformed that of the two major continental economies, while unemployment was on the whole also lower. In the periods 1992–9, 2009–9 and 2009–16, UK GDP rose by an annual average of 2.7 per cent, 2.5 per cent and 1.2 per cent respectively, compared with 1.4 per cent, 1.6 per cent and 1.0 per cent in Germany and 2.0 per cent, 1.9 per cent and 0.6 per cent in France. Unemployment in 1992–9, 2009–9 and 2009–16 was 8.2 per cent, 5.2 per cent

and 7.0 per cent in the UK, 8.4 per cent, 9.0 per cent and 5.6 per cent in Germany, and 10.5 per cent, 8.5 per cent and 9.8 per cent in France. Inflation was comparable in all three periods.

162. Lyne, interview with author, London, 9 June 2023.

163. Kohl went with a minimal entourage on a low-diet visit to the Bad Hofgastein spa resort each spring, inviting selected European leaders to visit him for informal private conversations. The 1993 visit took place on 6 April.

164. Lyne, interview with author, London, 9 June 2023. The Chequers visit took place on 27 April 1994.

165. Lyne, interview with author, London, 9 June 2023. See also Major, *Autobiography*, pp. 523–4.

166. Lamont, interview with author, London, 19 May 2023. 'As I observed Nigel Lawson develop the case for independence I became increasingly convinced, and it was strengthened by my own experiences as chancellor. I put forward a plan for independence on two occasions, both before and after the UK left the ERM. When we were in the ERM, the external influence came effectively from the Bundesbank. After we left the ERM, I felt such a policy would have been effective in adding to the government's policy credibility.' See also Lamont, *In Office*, pp. 321–5.

167. Clarke, interview with author, London, 2 May 2023.

168. Ed Balls, interview with author (video), London, 20 June 2023.

169. Balls met the finance ministry's Jürgen Stark and the Bundesbank's Otmar Issing.

170. Brown and Balls met Waigel, German finance minister, Tietmeyer, Bundesbank president, and Trichet, governor of the Banque de France, with members of the Bank's monetary committee. Robert Peston, *Financial Times* political correspondent, came on the European trip with Brown and Balls, although he did not attend the confidential meetings.

171. One of the reasons for discretion was that, in the public dialogue between Eddie George, the Bank's governor, and Clarke, the chancellor of the exchequer, George habitually backed higher interest rates. Balls: 'This was one of the reasons why we kept silent on the issue during the election campaign We had no interest in mentioning giving independence to the Bank in a way that would cause people to believe that they'd be voting for higher mortgage rates.'

172. Richard Lambert, interview with author, London, 14 June 2007. 'As the *FT* editor, I did the first interview with Gordon Brown after the 1997 election. I sensed something was up because the TV cameras were there.'

173. Memorandum, 'Conversation with Mr Mervyn King, Bank of England, 24 June', Meyer, 24 June 1997. UKNA PREM 49/72. King had been to see Otmar Issing, his opposite number at the Bundesbank. 'The Bundesbank were very fearful that if a single currency were launched on the present timetable, it would not work . . . The Bundesbank believed that the only rational solution was to postpone the launch of the Euro, possibly with a view to still bring in notes and coins by 1 January 2002 . . . The problem was that Kohl would not face up to the economic reality of the situation . . . Tietmeyer saw a possible highly influential role for the UK in this situation. He hoped that we would have a quiet word with Kohl to put the case for postponement.' See also 'EMU, Germany and Britain', Meyer to John Coles, permanent undersecretary, Bonn, 30 June 1997. UKNA, T 49/71. Christopher Mallaby, previously Britain's ambassador to France and, before, to Germany, visited Tietmeyer on 26 June, who told him ('not to be quoted') of his preference for delay. Michael Jay, UK ambassador to Paris, wrote on 22 July, 'We should not allow ourselves to be manoeuvred into advocating delay first . . . Let the French and Germans compete for that parcel of odium.'

174. 'Britain not ready to join euro: Four of five economic tests failed – Only financial services test met', *Guardian*, 9 June 2003.

175. Balls, interview with author (video), London, 20 June 2023.

176. 'David Cameron explains his party's approach to Europe', *Daily Telegraph*, 14 July 2006. 'I made a pledge that Conservative MEPs should leave the EPP . . . While the British Conservatives and Continental parties in the EPP agree on many things, such as open

markets and deregulation, we don't share their views about the future direction of the European Union.' See also 'David Cameron has kept his promise on the EPP grouping. Power needs to be repatriated from Brussels, not surrendered further', *Daily Telegraph*, editorial, 22 June 2009.

177. For an account of the importance of the EPP decision and its effect on both Merkel and France's Nicolas Sarkozy, see Ashcroft and Oakeshott, *Call Me Dave*, pp. 498–500.

178. Merkel withdrew the head of the Konrad Adenauer Foundation from London. Seldon and Snowdon, *Cameron at 10*, p. 165.

179. McDonald, interview with author, Cambridge, 6 July 2023.

180. Davis was minister for Europe in 1994–7 under foreign secretary Douglas Hurd. He relates that because he'd been a whip (party manager) in the House of Commons, manoeuvring the Maastricht treaty through parliament in 1990–2, Major thought, erroneously, he believed in the Maastricht treaty. 'Major said, "I want you to be minister for Europe." I said, "You must be fucking joking." He sent me off to sit in the study while he tried to find somebody else to do the job. And eventually I had a telephone call from William Waldegrave who was my existing boss, chancellor of the Duchy of Lancaster. He said, "What's going on?" I said, "I've been offered this bloody silly job. I don't want to do this. I don't believe in this." And he said, "Well, Douglas won't accept anybody else." ' Davis, interviews with author, London, 19 April 2023, and 17 May 2023.

181. For a full account see Davis, interview, Institute of Government, 22 September 2022.

182. Davis, interview with author, 19 April 2023.

183. Barroso, interview with author (video), Munich–London, 7 September 2023. Cameron came to Brussels on 5 December 2008. See also 'UK's clout in EU will fall under Tories', *Independent*, 17 March 2009.

184. Cameron, interview with author, London, 11 November 2024.

185. The Treaty on Stability, Coordination and Governance in the Economic and Monetary Union was agreed at the EU summit of 30 January 2012. See ECB description. https://www.ecb.europa.eu/pub/pdf/other/mb201203_focus12.en.pdf

186. ' "Time short" for eurozone, says Cameron', *Financial Times*, 9 October 2011. 'David Cameron has urged European leaders to take a "big bazooka" approach to resolving the eurozone crisis.' Cameron's message was very close to that of Barack Obama and Tim Geithner. Cameron writes in his memoirs, apparently misreading Merkel's thoughts, 'Privately Angela Merkel initially seemed to welcome our intervention,' then adds, 'But all German politicians – right, left and centre – are allergic to activist monetary policies and interventionist central banks.' Elsewhere in his memoirs Cameron admits that Obama had told him that the other Europeans would not open up in front of him 'after what I had said in the *FT* urging the "bazooka" approach'. Cameron, *For the Record*, pp. 330, 342. Rogers, when he became Cameron's European adviser at the end of 2011, told him to stop talking publicly about the 'big bazooka', opining: 'You might well be right but it's only going to be viewed as a hostile act encouraging more market turbulence at their cost.' Rogers, interview with author, London, 30 June 2023.

187. Darroch, interview with author, London, 3 April 2023.

188. Cameron, interview with author, London, 11 November 2024.

189. For a full account of the December 2011 summit, see Seldon and Snowdon, *Cameron at 10*, pp. 173–7, and 'Q&A: David Cameron and the EU summit on the eurozone', BBC, 2 February 2012.

190. Rogers, interview with author, London, 30 June 2023.

191. Cameron, interview with author, London, 11 November 2024.

192. Rogers, lecture, Hertford College, Oxford, 24 November 2017. 'There was simply no reputable alternative position to the one Cameron took on these issues. And this is why the Union of 2012 was so different from the Community of pre-Maastricht years, and why much criticism of the UK supposedly absenting itself from a central role is so misplaced.'

193. Rogers, lecture, Hertford College, Oxford, 24 November 2017. 'Cameron seldom – probably never – had a warmer reception on a European issue from his own benches. Poll

ratings bounced sharply, and he was lionised for having forced the Eurozone players to go another route.'

194. 'David Cameron blocks EU treaty with veto, casting Britain adrift in Europe', *Guardian*, 9 December 2011. The article quoted Ashdown: 'The foreign policy priorities of this country for the past 40 years has gone down the plughole in a single night. That foreign policy has now been hijacked by the Eurosceptics in the Conservative Party aided by a prime minister who was not prepared to stand up for the national interest.'

195. Cameron, statement, House of Commons, 12 December 2011.

196. Cameron, interview with author, London, 11 November 2024.

197. The date was postponed at the last moment to avoid a clash (which his team realised only late) with the date (22 January) of the fiftieth anniversary of the signing of the Élysée treaty enshrining postwar Franco-German entente. Seldon and Snowdon, *Cameron at 10*, pp. 260–1.

198. Cameron, speech, Bloomberg, London, 23 January 2013.

199. Barroso, interview with author (video), Munich–London, 7 September 2023.

200. Cameron, interview with author, London, 11 November 2024.

201. McDonald, interview with author, Cambridge, 6 July 2023.

202. Cameron, *For the Record*, p. 518.

203. Merkel changed her mind because of domestic German politics, with the Christian Democratic Union and Christian Social Union parties backing Juncker as part of the EPP grouping's claim on the presidency – reinforced by the EPP's strong showing in the May 2014 European parliament elections.

204. Cameron, *For the Record*, pp. 518–19. 'I pointed out to Merkel's team, only partly joking, that the time between a Merkel promise and a Merkel promise being broken was getting shorter – "the half-life of a Merkel promise".' According to McDonald, 'The British thought that they could block Juncker, as in the case of Jean-Luc Dehaene [under Major in 1994], the former Belgian prime minister, even though the rules had changed and no country had a veto.' McDonald, interview with author, Cambridge, 6 July 2023.

205. Cameron, *For the Record*, p. 518. The description of Juncker appeared an unnecessarily cavalier depiction from a man who (as short-lived foreign secretary) found himself back on the diplomatic circuit in 2023–4.

206. Cameron, interview with author, London, 11 November 2024.

207. Selmayr, interview with author, Vienna, 23 January 2023.

208. Cameron, interview with author, London, 11 November 2024. The vote came at the leaders' summit on 27 June 2014. Seldon and Snowdon, *Cameron at 10*, pp. 435–6.

209. The *Times* headline was 'Britain nears EU exit', whereas the *Daily Telegraph* ran: 'One step closer to quitting Europe'.

210. Cameron, interview with author, London, 11 November 2024.

211. The French presidential election was set for April 2017, the German federal election for September 2017. Cameron, *For the Record*, p. 626. 'A theoretical way forward would've been to say [in 2013] that the referendum could be held sometime in the next seven years, but Cameron felt that would have been impossible to defend in the Party and the country. So, once the commitment to an in/out referendum was made, the window for any negotiation to change and entrench in primary law a changed status for the UK was exceptionally tight, and that in itself militated against seeking excessive numbers of radical changes. There was no way 27 other leaders would have unanimously agreed more radical change than we got.' Rogers, interview with author, London, 30 June 2023.

212. Rogers, interview with author, London, 30 June 2023. Cameron was exasperated by the divergent reactions. 'If I was finding the leaders hard work, their officials were even worse. To them, I was a dangerous heretic stamping on their sacred texts. Often I would report back to Ivan [Rogers] or Tom [Scholar] after a tête-à-tête with a fellow prime minister, only to be told that their officials refused to accept what had been agreed.' Cameron, *For the Record*, p. 640.

213. Juncker, interview with author, Brussels, 29 November 2023.

214. The social brake idea emerged in the autumn of 2014, after several months of debate on immigration numbers and control. Rogers, lecture, Hertford College, Oxford, 24 November 2017.
215. McDonald, interview with author, Cambridge, 6 July 2023.
216. Cameron, interview with author, London, 11 November 2024.
217. Cameron, interview with author, London, 11 November 2024.
218. Peter Sedgwick, email to author, 2 September 2024.
219. Davis, interview with author, 19 April 2023.
220. Interview, anonymous British official, April 2023.
221. Moore, interview with author, London, 25 June 2024.
222. Lynton Crosby, his campaign adviser, was clear that the terms Cameron achieved were not sufficient to impress the electorate. Seldon and Snowdon, *Cameron at 10*, p. 546.
223. According to Ivan Rogers, 'The more [Cameron] reflected on [the differences], the more he thought, "Well, quite a lot of the agenda that I would actually like to pursue as pan-European, they don't support me on. So I want to tilt this more towards entrenching British exceptionalism. To demonstrate to the public that we are not going on the journey that the vast bulk of the others – or at least their political establishments – want to.' Rogers, 'UK in a Changing Europe', London, 27 November 2020.
224. Rees-Mogg, interview with author, London, 16 May 2023.
225. Frost, interview with author, 23 July 2024. Another indication of Cameron's changed analysis stems from comparison of two speeches. Cameron said at Bloomberg in January 2013 the EU's 'main, overriding purpose' was 'not to win peace, but to secure prosperity'. He stressed a British 'settlement' seven times. On 9 May 2016, in a speech at the British Museum, Cameron offered no hint of any forthcoming positive changes, emphasising far more the security, defence and economic risks of upsetting the status quo. In January 2013, Cameron mentioned 'security' twice and 'war' three times; in his May 2016 address there were twenty references to 'security' and six to 'war', and none to 'settlement'. David Marsh, 'Consequences of a non-settlement: Prime minister's miscalculations in EU strategy', OMFIF, 1 June 2016.
226. King, interview with author, London, 1 November 2023.
227. 'Seven times Cameron and Osborne suggested they might vote Leave', Mark Wallace, *Conservative Home*, 19 April 2016. https://conservativehome.com/2016/04/19/seven-times-cameron-and-osborne-suggested-they-might-vote-leave/.
228. Author's private information.
229. Cameron, interview with author, London, 11 November 2024.
230. Terracciano, interview with author, Rome, 9 March 2023.
231. McDonald, interview with author, Cambridge, 6 July 2023.
232. Moore, interview with author, London, 25 June 2024.
233. Carney, interview with author (video), Toronto–London, 23 October 2023. Osborne did not make a statement until the following week. 'Osborne lies low post-Brexit as allies take soundings on his future', *Financial Times*, 27 June 2016.
234. Schäuble interview, *Der Spiegel*, 10 June 2016.
235. Davis, interview with author, 19 April 2023.
236. Redwood, interview with author, Wokingham, 14 April 2023.
237. 'The minutes were sent back constantly to the prime minister/cabinet secretary from the foreign secretary's office.' McDonald, interview with author, Cambridge, 6 July 2023.
238. Barwell, interview with author, London, 13 March 2023.
239. See, among many other references, Lisa James and Meg Russell, 'Five things you may not know about Parliament and Brexit', *UK in a Changing Europe*, 23 March 2003. https://ukandeu.ac.uk/five-things-you-may-not-know-about-parliament-and-brexit/.
240. José María Roldán, interview with author, Madrid, 23 September 2019. See David Marsh, 'UK judgment "victory for rule of law"', OMFIF, 24 September 2019. https://www.omfif.org/2019/09/uk-judgment-victory-for-rule-of-law/. 'The forceful rebuke – and the court's statement that "the effect upon the fundamentals of our democracy was extreme" – adds up to an unparalleled governmental setback. The reassuring effect on

Britain's standing in the world looks likely significantly to outlive the memory of a prime minister who may go down as the most ill-fated in history.'

241. For example, Boris Johnson, 'There is only one way to get the change we want: Vote Go', *Daily Telegraph*, 22 February 2016. The article underlines the need 'to assert the sovereignty of parliament' against 'some of the more federalist flights of fancy of the Court and the Commission'.

242. Frost, interview with author, London, 23 July 2024.

243. 'The inside story of Liz Truss's disastrous 44 Days in office', describing 'the most ambitious and disastrous budget in modern British history', *Financial Times*, 9 December 2022.

244. Debt Management Office, annual report and accounts 2022–3, p. 9. https://assets. publishing.service.gov.uk/media/64b7eaa806f78d000d7424f5/DMO_DMA_2022-2023__20230710__-_Website__accessible_.pdf.

245. David Marsh, 'Britain's failed attempt at monetary and fiscal exceptionalism', De Gruyter Brill, 22 June 2023. https://www.degruyterbrill.com/document/doi/10.1515/ev-2023-0021/html.

246. 'IMF openly criticises UK government tax plans', BBC, 28 September 2022. https://www.bbc.co.uk/news/business-63051702.

247. Isabel Schnabel, ECB board member, speech, London, 19 May 2023.

248. The party has its roots in postwar incarnations of Italy's fascist movement, with supporters including some modern-day admirers of 1930s and 1940s dictator Benito Mussolini. There was general disquiet about the potential effect of Giorgia Meloni's policies on international financial markets.

249. Darroch, interview with author, London, 3 April 2023. 'Further evidence . . . At the Conservative Party conference on 5 October – just a fortnight before she resigned as prime minister – Truss had associated the Treasury with an alleged "anti-growth" coalition she blamed for slowing Britain's economic dynamism. After her forced departure, she returned to the theme in a widely publicised 4,000-word newspaper article assailing the UK economic "establishment" which she accused of a "left wing drift".' Marsh, 'Britain's failed attempt at monetary and fiscal exceptionalism'.

250. Truss was not impressed by reminders that Thatcher's first budget, in 1979, raised rather than lowered taxes to balance the books. 'The 1981 budget: Background and documents', Margaret Thatcher Foundation. https://www.margaretthatcher.org/archive/1981. Anthony Seldon with Jonathan Meakin, *Truss at 10: How Not to Be Prime Minister* (London: Atlantic, 2024), pp. 80–3.

251. Author's private information.

252. Gerard Lyons and Julian Jessop, 'UK policy issues', 2 September 2022. See Larry Elliot, 'Liz Truss ignored economists' stark warnings over mini-budget', *Guardian*, 21 October 2022. The paper suggested the best policy option for the UK was higher interest rates from the Bank of England to curb inflation, and tax cuts and spending increases from the Treasury to mitigate recession risks.

253. Jessop, interview with author, London, 14 October 2024.

254. Author's private information. The account is consistent with Seldon, *Truss at 10*, p. 114 – based partly on an interview with Kwasi Kwarteng.

255. Redwood, interview with author, Wokingham, 14 April 2023.

256. Darroch, interview with author, London, 3 April 2023. 'On her performance as international trade secretary, she got credit for sealing several trade deals on her watch. But most were carbon copies of those deals Britain had had under their membership of the EU. The main new trade deal was with Australia. And this agreement, as stated by some of her former ministerial colleagues, was downright disastrous.'

257. Truss may have been unconsciously expressing fear of the power of credit discovered by Alexander Hamilton in his campaign against the British 240 years earlier: 'America could defeat the British in the bond market more readily than on the battlefield.' Chernow, *Alexander Hamilton*, p. 156.

258. Seldon, *Truss at 10*, p. 219.

259. Seldon, *Truss at 10*, pp. 194–5.

260. Kwarteng, interview, BBC TV, 25 September 2022.

261. The market turmoil resulted in two daily increases in thirty-year gilt yields of more than 35 basis points. Hitherto, the biggest such two-day increase (according to data going back to 2000) had been 29 basis points. Measured over a four-day period, the increase in thirty-year gilt yields was more than twice as large as the largest move since 2000, which occurred during the 'dash for cash' in 2020. The 130-point rise was more than three times larger than any other historical move. Jon Cunliffe, Bank of England deputy governor, letter to Treasury Select Committee, 5 October 1992. https://www.bankofengland.co.uk/-/media/boe/files/letter/2022/october/letter-from-jon-cunliffe-ldi-5-october-2022. George Parker, 'Seven days that shook the UK', *Financial Times*, 30 September 2022.

262. Andrew Bailey, interview with author, London, 14 February 2023.

263. The operation appeared a substantial reversal in Bank policy. 'There may appear to be a tension here between tightening monetary policy as we must, including so-called quantitative tightening, and buying government debt to ease a critical threat to financial stability.' Bailey, interview with author, London, 14 February 2023. By the time the bond purchases ended, on 14 October, the Bank had succeeded in stabilising yields through purchases of £19.3 billion of gilts, three-quarters of which took place in the final week of operations – much lower than the maximum £65 billion committed at the outset. Close-knit liaison with market practitioners helped spur the move from 11 October to extend Bank purchases to index-linked gilts, a major technical innovation involving fast-paced large-scale work by the Bank's IT department. This turned out be a 'game-changer', according to Bailey.

264. Bailey, interview with author, 14 February 2023.

265. Liz Truss resignation speech, BBC, 20 October 2022. https://www.bbc.co.uk/news/uk-63328000.

266. Marsh, 'Britain's failed attempt at monetary and fiscal exceptionalism'. See also John Ryan, 'British exceptionalism causes Brexit conundrum', De Gruyter Brill, 7 December 2019. https://www.degruyterbrill.com/document/doi/10.1515/ev-2019-0020/html.

267. Macpherson, speech, Strand Group, Edinburgh, 1 November 2022. Macpherson was Treasury permanent secretary in 2005–16 under three chancellors, one of the longest spells of service since the post was established in the 1860s.

268. Darren Jones, chief secretary to the Treasury, 'Investors' reaction to budget "very different" to Truss', BBC, 31 October 2024. https://www.bbc.co.uk/news/articles/cx2n0eeep90o.

269. 'US faces Liz Truss-style market shock as debt soars, warns watchdog', *Financial Times*, 26 March 2024. https://www.ft.com/content/dd751b97-7485-4457-aaae-c632062f0976. Mark Chandler, 'Is this America's Liz Truss moment?', *New York Times*, 8 April 2025. https://www.nytimes.com/2025/04/08/world/europe/trump-tariffs-markets-liz-truss.html.

270. Ruchir Sharma, 'The end of American exceptionalism goes way beyond Trump', *Financial Times*, 24 March 2025. https://www.ft.com/content/dd751b97-7485-4457-aaae-c632062f0976. For a wider view see Daniel W. Drezner, 'The end of American exceptionalism', *Foreign Affairs*, 12 November 2024. https://www.foreignaffairs.com/united-states/end-american-exceptionalism.

8 DREAMS, REALITY AND THE FUTURE OF POWER

1. Harry Truman, 'Truman at Potsdam: His secret diary', 30 July 1945. NSSA-GWU. https://nsarchive.gwu.edu/document/28466-document-47-trumans-potsdam-diary.

2. Transcript, John F. Kennedy–Harold Macmillan telephone call, 19 January 1963. John F. Kennedy Presidential Library. https://www.jfklibrary.org/asset-viewer/archives/jfkpof. See also Alistair Horne, *Harold Macmillan*, vol. 2, *1957–1986* (London/New York: Penguin, 1989), p. 446.

3. Paul Tucker, interview with author, London, 8 February 2024.

4. D.R. Thorpe, *Supermac: The Life of Harold Macmillan* (London: Pimlico, 2011), p. 170. See also David Reynolds, 'A "special relationship"? America, Britain and the international order since the Second World War', *International Affairs*, vol. 62, no. 1 (Winter 1985–6), pp. 1–20. https://www.jstor.org/stable/2618063.

5. The three Punic wars were fought from 264 to 146 BC between the victorious Roman Republic and the Carthaginian (Punic) empire.

6. See, for example, 'Ukraine war exposes splits between Global North and South', *France-24*, 17 February 2023, underlining differences in perceptions between Europe and a wide range of developing and emerging market economies. https://www.france24.com/en/europe/20230217-ukraine-war-exposes-splits-between-global-north-and-south.

7. Schäuble, interview with author, Berlin, 16 January 2023.

8. Geithner, *laudatio* for Schäuble, Jewish Museum, Berlin, 9 November 2014. https://www.jmberlin.de/auszeichnung-fuer-bundesfinanzminister-wolfgang-schaeuble-und-verleger-hubert-burda.

9. Draghi, speech, European parliament, Strasbourg, 17 September 2024.

10. Carney, 'Breaking the tragedy of the horizon: Climate change and financial stability', speech, Lloyds of London, 29 September 2015.

11. 'Yellen warns climate change could trigger asset value losses, harming US economy', Reuters, 7 March 2023.

12. 'Yellen's climate warning ties rising disasters in U.S. to systemic financial risk', *Callaway Climate Insights*, 9 March 2023. https://www.callawayclimateinsights.com/p/yellens-climate-warning-ties-rising?.

13. The World Bank Group, Summary Proceedings, 26–8 September 1988, p. 7. https://documents1.worldbank.org/curated/en/447651468146055033/pdf/534240BR0board11Offic ial0Use0Only10.pdf.

14. See, for example, Radhika Desai, Michael Hudson and Ann Pettifor, 'Colonialism or sovereignty? How the global financial system traps countries in debt', *Geopolitical Economy*, 11 July 2023. https://geopoliticaleconomy.com/2023/07/11/colonialism-sovereignty-financial-system-debt/.

15. 'Hard truths about green growth', *The Economist*, 1 July 2023.

16. 'Italy, Germany join carmakers in call to rethink internal combustion engine ban', *Euronews*, 25 September 2024. This followed a U-turn by the German government in March 2023. The move led to French calls for Berlin to submit to its own demand to have nuclear energy accepted as a 'green' source of energy. *Politico*, 24 March 2023.

17. 'Macron cancels fuel tax increase after gilets jaunes protests', *Financial Times*, 5 December 2018.

18. 'Ulez expansion: Sadiq Khan "faces political backlash" against plan to extend zones across Greater London', *Evening Standard*, 11 March 2022. https://www.standard.co.uk/news/transport/ulez-expansion-sadiq-khan-backlash-greater-london-tory-mp-b986959.html.

19. 'How the humble heat pump pushed Germany to the far right', *Daily Telegraph*, 22 February 2025. https://www.telegraph.co.uk/money/net-zero/how-humble-heat-pump-pushed-germany-far-right/?msockid=1e894a1c20fb63da29755ebd21ee62be. 'How heat pumps exploded Germany's ruling coalition', *Politico*, 7 September 2023. https://www.politico.eu/article/heat-pumps-exploded-germany-ruling-coalition-green-law/.

20. Trump, 'They can all afford it, but they should be at 5 percent, not 2 percent', press conference, Palm Beach, 7 January 2025. Trump was referring to the percentage of gross domestic product NATO members should commit to spend on defence.

21. Bruce Stokes, 'How Europe can start Trump-proofing', *Politico*, 11 January 2024. https://www.politico.eu/article/how-europe-leaders-can-start-trump-proofing-security-us-elections-transatlantic-relations.

22. 'Most NATO countries are still spending less than 2 percent of GDP on defence. And 20 out of the 28 European NATO members currently spend more on personnel than on major equipment, maintenance, research and development, operations, and infrastructure.' Stokes, 'How Europe can start Trump-proofing'. See also 'Defence expenditure of

NATO countries (2014–2024)', NATO, Brussels, June 2024. https://www.nato.int/nato_static_fl2014/assets/pdf/2024/6/pdf/240617-def-exp-2024-en.pdf.

23. 'U.S. Saw an opportunity while it pushed to arm Ukraine', *New York Times*, 9 January 2025.

24. Adam Entous and Michael Schwirtz, 'The spy war: How the C.I.A. secretly helps Ukraine fight Putin', *New York Times*, 25 February 2024. Joshua C. Huminski, 'Russia, Ukraine, and the future use of strategic intelligence', National Defense University Press, 7 September 2023.

25. Eric Lipton, Michael Crowley and John Ismay, 'Military spending surges, creating new boom for arms makers', *New York Times*, 18 December 2022. 'The prospect of growing military threats from both China and Russia is driving bipartisan support for a surge in Pentagon spending, setting up another potential boom for weapons makers that is likely to extend beyond the war in Ukraine.' See Kiel Institute Ukraine war tracker. https://www.ifw-kiel.de/topics/war-against-ukraine/ukraine-support-tracker/.

26. 'Merz fordert gemeinsame EU-Rüstungseinkäufe in den USA' ['Merz calls for joint EU armaments purchases from the USA'], *Handelsblatt*, 21 January 2025. https://www.handelsblatt.com/politik/deutschland/verteidigung-merz-fordert-gemeinsame-eu-rues-tungseinkaeufe-in-den-usa/100102234.html.

27. 'Dassault chief warns Europe's defence industry will take decades to build', *Financial Times*, 6 March 2024.

28. 'German firm sees U.S. getting lion's share of 100 billion euro military fund', Reuters, 4 July 2023. https://www.reuters.com/business/aerospace-defense/german-firm-sees-us-getting-lions-share-100-bln-euro-military-fund-2023-07-04/.

29. Shahin Vallée, 'Franco-German disagreements on defense', Geoeconomics Substack, 10 January 2023. https://geoeconomics.substack.com/p/franco-german-disagreements-need.

30. 'UK and Germany sign "landmark" defence agreement', BBC, 22 October 2024. https://www.bbc.co.uk/news/articles/cy808e4p9j9o.

31. 'EU struggles to counter Joe Biden's big green push', *Financial Times*, 12 December 2022.

32. Draghi, 'The future of European competitiveness', Part B: 'In-depth analysis and recommendations', p. 247.

33. Noyer, report, 'Developing European capital markets to finance the future', French Treasury, 25 April 2024. https://www.tresor.economie.gouv.fr/Articles/2024/04/25/developing-european-capital-markets-to-finance-the-future.

34. Richard Haass 'Apocalypse now', 10 January 2025. https://richardhaass.substack.com/p/apocalypse-now-january-10-2025.

35. Stephen Collinson, 'Carter's funeral captures the American story at a fraught political moment', CNN, 9 January 2025. See also 'Jimmy Carter raised climate change concerns 35 years before the Paris Accords', Associated Press, 7 January 2025. Thomas L. Friedman, 'What if Reagan had been more like Carter?', *New York Times*, 30 December 2024.

36. 'Power brokers lose their grip on US politics', Reuters, 5 November 2024.

37. 'BlackRock quits climate group in latest green climbdown', *Financial Times*, 9 January 2025. BlackRock said it had quit Net Zero Asset Managers, a global group committed to reduce to zero greenhouse gas emissions by 2050 or sooner. It said it took the step because of 'confusion regarding BlackRock's practices [which] subjected us to legal inquiries from various public officials'.

38. 'World temperatures overshoot 1.5°C Paris deal limit for first time', *Guardian*, 9 January 2025. The data came from the EU's Copernicus Climate Change Service (C3S).

39. Sam Jones, 'Herbert Kickl, Austria's far-right leader eyeing the chancellorship', *Financial Times*, 11 January 2025.

40. A new government in Vienna was sworn in on 3 March 2025, headed by Chancellor Christian Stocker, the first tripartite coalition since 1949.

41. Elon Musk endorsed the Reform party in the UK, which according to opinion polls in early 2025 was running ahead of the Opposition Conservative Party in public popularity. He called for Keir Starmer, the prime minister, to stand down. In Germany, Musk said he supported AfD, the far-right populist party gaining rapidly in the opinion polls. He carried out a live interview on his social media platform X with Alice Weidel, the AfD chancellor candidate in the 23 February 2025 election.

42. 'Tesla-Chef Elon Musk wirbt für die Anti-Tesla-Partei' ['Tesla chief Elon Musk campaigns for anti-Tesla party'], *Handelsblatt*, 9 January 2025.

43. Trump, press conference, Palm Beach, 7 January 2025.

44. Scholz, statement, Berlin, 8 January 2025.

45. 'CDU empört über Scholz' Trump-Kritik' ['CDU indignant over Scholz's criticism of Trump'], *Frankfurter Allgemeine Zeitung*, 9 January 2025.

46. Franklin Foer, 'Emperor Trump's new map', *The Atlantic*, 23 January 2025. 'The president who built his fan base on isolationism is pivoting to a kind of imperialism the US hasn't seen in decades.'

47. 'Giorgia Meloni meets Donald Trump in flying visit to Mar-a-Lago', *Guardian*, 5 January 2025. See also Peter Rough and Daniel Kochis, 'Trump and Meloni: A promising friendship', *Wall Street Journal*, 13 November 2024.

48. Amato, interview with author, Rome, 7 March 2023. Amended/extended 12 January 2025.

49. Bernd Lucke, interview with author, London, 27 November 2023.

50. Klaus-Jürgen Citron, note for Genscher, 18 January 1990. AAPD 1990, Document 11, p. 52.

51. Issing, interview with author, Würzburg, 5 April 2023.

52. Moïsi, 'Rising fears of a weakened Germany', Institut Montaigne, 16 September 2021. https://www.institutmontaigne.org/en/expressions/rising-fears-weakened-germanyMoisi.

53. Iain Conn, interview with author, London, 13 December 2023.

54. The shortfall was made up partly by increased liquid natural gas (LNG) supplies from the US, and more pipeline imports from Africa, Azerbaijan and Norway. The slowing China economy left more global LNG for Europe. New Norwegian production entered the market. Europe was able to curtail demand materially. Before the invasion, Europe had imported 150 billion cubic metres per annum of Russian gas (15 billion LNG, 135 billion through pipelines). The volume was made up by a combination of the following (roughly one-third each): additional pipeline supplies from Africa and Azerbaijan, and LNG from US and Norway production; LNG acquired in competition from the rest of world, through taking market share from China, Korea and Taiwan; higher efficiency and cuts in demand.

55. Jörg Kukies, interview with author, Berlin, 6 February 2023.

56. Pfaffenbach, interview with author, Berlin, 23 April 2024.

57. Frank Elderson, interview with author, Frankfurt, 30 August 2023.

58. For example, if a bank is blindly building up business in projects likely to end up as stranded assets, or assembling portfolios of office buildings which neglect energy efficiency, or financing housing in flood-prone areas without considering the risks, then the banks (and possibly even the supervisors, if they had consistently failed to draw attention to the sound management of such risks) could potentially be vulnerable to lawsuits.

59. 'Urgenda v. State of the Netherlands: Lessons for international law and climate change litigants', London School of Economics, 10 December 2019. https://www.lse.ac.uk/granthaminstitute/news/urgenda-v-state-of-the-netherlands-lessons-for-international-law-and-climate-change-litigants/.

60. Anne Simpson, interview with author, London, 22 April 2024.

61. Simpson, interview with author, London, 7 November 2024.

62. Hernández de Cos, interview with author, Madrid, 11 January 2024.

63. Mario Centeno, interview with author (video), Lisbon–London, 22 April 2024.

64. Centeno, interview with author (video), Lisbon–London, 11 April 2025.

65. Goodhart, email exchange with author, 18 April 2025.

66. De Guindos, interview with author, Frankfurt, 20 March 2024.

67. Orphanides, interview with author, Vienna, 11 June 2024. 'The ECB should learn from the Fed. The current ECB practice, waiting thirty years before it publishes details of its decision-making, is not helpful for improving policy and learning from past policy errors. The Fed publishes the transcripts of FOMC meetings and briefing materials after five years. The ECB could agree to publish these papers after eight years – the length of service of board members.'

68. Christine Lagarde and Ursula von der Leyen, 'Europe has got the message on change', *Financial Tines*, 31 January 2025.

69. 'We had managed to get ourselves effectively the best of both worlds: the advantages of membership, absent the obligations we didn't like, and with a special discount on costs.' Darroch, *Collateral Damage*, p. 62.

70. Peter Foster, *What Went Wrong with Brexit: And What We Can Do About It* (London: Canongate, 2023), p. 168.

71. Foster, 'UK–EU post-Brexit reset: The key points', *Financial Times,* 19 May 2025. https://www.ft.com/content/47adc80f-ab03-49a1-9f7e-1a5962e71b83.

72. Karl Lamers and Wolfgang Schäuble, 'Überlegungen zur europäischen Politik' ['Reflections on European politics'], CDU policy paper, 1994. https://www.thefederalist.eu/site/index.php/en/documents/2592-reflections-on-european-politics.

73. Major, speech to Conservative general council, Southport, 23 March 1991.

74. Schäuble, interview with author, Berlin, 16 January 2023.

75. Pier Carlo Padoan, interview with author, Rome, 7 March 2023.

76. Macmillan, BBC broadcast, 30 January 1963. Horne, *Harold Macmillan*, vol. 2, p. 448.

77. Cameron, interview with author, London, 11 November 2024.

78. Zoellick, interview with author (video), Washington–London, 24 March 2025.

79. 'Defending Europe with less America', European Council on Foreign Relations. https://ecfr.eu/publication/defending-europe-with-less-america/. 'Paradoxically, such a deliberate approach to overcoming institutional challenges and strengthening Europe's defence capabilities may be the best way to preserve a strong transatlantic relationship and a degree of US commitment.' Claudia Major, Carlo Masala, Christian Mölling and Jana Puglierin, 'Wie ein neuer Krieg in Europa noch zu verhindern ist' ['How to avoid a new war in Europe'], *Der Spiegel,* 18 February 2025. https://www.spiegel.de/ausland/ukraine-krieg-ein-sofortprogramm-gegen-die-ausweitung-des-krieges-a-98528458-9eb0-4584-8656-c02372b65bca.

80. UK–France Northwood agreement, 10 July 2025. https://www.gov.uk/government/news/northwood-declaration-10-july-2025-uk-france-joint-nuclear-statement. For an overview of Anglo-French nuclear cooperation possibilities see 'Could Britain and France's nuclear weapons protect Europe?', Chatham House, 14 July 2025. https://www.chathamhouse.org/publications/the-world-today/2025-06/data-could-britain-and-frances-nuclear-weapons-protect-europe. For a longer-term perspective for Anglo-French nuclear cooperation, see David Owen, former UK foreign secretary: 'The urgent priority now is for the two West European nuclear powers – France and the UK – to work ever more closely with Germany and Poland.' Owen, speech, Paris, 12 May 2025.

81. UK–Germany Kensington agreement ('Friendship and bilateral cooperation treaty'), 17 July 2025. https://www.gov.uk/government/news/friendship-and-bilateral-cooperation-treaty-the-17-projects-the-uk-and-germany-will-deliver-together. See Timothy Garton Ash, 'Britain is great at muddling through. But imagine if its leaders knew where they were heading', *Guardian,* 19 July 2025.

82. Sandy Carter, 'How stablecoins and tokenization are rebuilding global finance', Forbes, 28 April 2025. https://www.forbes.com/sites/digital-assets/2025/04/28/how-stablecoins-and-tokenization-are-rebuilding-global-finance/.

83. The European Central Bank has been intensifying warnings over stablecoin adoption, arguing that launching a central bank digital currency could help preserve the euro area's monetary sovereignty. See Piero Cipollone, ECB board member, opining that a potential digital euro 'would limit the potential for foreign currency stablecoins to become a common medium of exchange within the euro area'. ECB statement, 8 April 2025. https://www.ecb.europa.eu/press/key/date/2025/html/ecb.sp250408~40820747ef.en.html.

84. Madeleine Albright, US secretary of state, interview, NBC-TV, 19 February 1998. https://1997-2001.state.gov/statements/1998/980219a.html.

85. Jamie Dimon, chief executive, J.P. Morgan, statement, Dublin, 10 July 2025.

86. Churchill said, 'No lover ever studied every whim of his mistress as I did those of President Roosevelt.' Gilbert, *Winston S. Churchill*, vol. VIII, p. 415, quoting John Colville, *The Fringes of Power: 10 Downing Street Diaries, 1939–1955* (London: Hodder & Stoughton, 1985), entry for 2 May 1948, pp. 623–4.

AUTHOR INTERVIEWS

All citations in the text based on these interviews have been checked and authorised by the interlocutor. Many interlocutors agreed with the author that some or all of their statements, at their own discretion, would be off the record. The location and date of the interview are given at the end of the entries.

Adams, Tim President and Chief Executive Officer, Institute of International Finance (2013–); Under Secretary for International Affairs, Treasury Department, US (2005–7): Washington, 2 June 2023

Amato, Giuliano Member, Constitutional Court, Italy (2013–23; President in 2022); Prime Minister, Italy (1992–3, 2000–1); Interior Minister, Italy (2006–8): Rome, 7 March 2023

Armellini, Antonio Permanent Representative to OECD, Italy (2008–10); Ambassador to India, Italy (2004–8): London, 7 February 2025

Ashton, (Baroness) Catherine High Representative of the European Union for Foreign Affairs and Security Policy (2009–14); European Commissioner for Trade (2008–9): London, 24 July 2023

Bailey, Andrew Governor, Bank of England (2020–); Chief Executive Officer, Financial Conduct Authority, UK (2016–20): London, 14 February 2023

Balfe, (Lord) Richard Trade Union Adviser to David Cameron, Prime Minister, UK (2010–16); Member, European Parliament (1979–2004): London, 4 July 2025

Balls, Ed Shadow Chancellor of the Exchequer, UK (2011–15); Secretary of State for Children, Schools and Families, UK (2007–10): London, 20 June 2023*

Barroso, José Manuel President, European Commission (2004–14); Prime Minister, Portugal (2002–4): London–Munich, 7 September 2023

Barwell, (Lord) Gavin Chief of Staff to Theresa May, Prime Minister, UK (2017–19); Minister of State for Housing and Planning, UK (2016–17): Member of Parliament, Croydon Central, UK (2010–17): London, 13 March 2023

Baukol, Andy Acting Under Secretary for International Affairs, Treasury Department, US (2021–2); Deputy Assistant Secretary for Middle East and Africa, Treasury Department, US (2015–21): Washington, 2 June 2023

Belka, Marek Member, European Parliament (2019–24); President, National Bank of Poland (2010–16); Prime Minister, Poland (2004–5): Brussels, 29 November 2023

Bernanke, Ben Distinguished Senior Fellow, Brookings Institution (2014–); Chairman, Board of Governors, Federal Reserve (2006–14); Member, Board of Governors, Federal Reserve (2002–5); Chair, Department of Economics, Princeton University (1996–2002): Washington–London, 22 October 2023E

Bergsten, Fred Emeritus Director, Peterson Institute for International Economics (formerly Institute for International Economics) (2012–), Director (1981–2012), US; Assistant Secretary for International Affairs, Treasury Department, US (1977–81): Washington–London, 19 February 2024, 28 February 2024, 18 March 2025*

Bindseil, Ulrich Director General, Market Infrastructure and Payments, European Central Bank (2019–25); Director General, Market Operations, European Central Bank (2012–19): Frankfurt, 20 March 2024

Bini Smaghi, Lorenzo Chairman, Société Générale (2015–26); Member, Executive Board, European Central Bank (2005–11): Paris, 10 October 2023

Bond, Ian Director, Foreign Policy, Centre for European Reform, UK (2013–); Berlin–London, 2 August 2023

Braithwaite, (Sir) Rodric Ambassador to Soviet Union, then Russia, UK (1988–92); Chairman, Joint Intelligence Committee, UK (1992–3): London, 30 April 2023, 9 May 2024

Brown, Gordon United Nations Special Envoy for Global Education (2012–); Prime Minister, UK (2007–10); Chancellor of the Exchequer, UK (1997–2007): London, 28 September 2023

Burns, (Lord) Terence Chairman, Ofcom, UK (2018–20); Chairman, Santander UK (2002–12); Permanent Secretary, Treasury, UK (1991–8); Chief Economic Adviser, Treasury, UK (1980–91): London–Berlin, 2 October 2023

Burns, William 'Bill' Director, Central Intelligence Agency, US (2021–5); Deputy Secretary of State, US (2011–14); Ambassador to Russia, US (2005–8): Washington, 24 April 2025

Camdessus, Michel Managing Director, International Monetary Fund (1987–2000); Governor, Banque de France (1984–7); Director, Treasury, France: Paris, 10 October 2023

Cameron, (Lord) David Secretary of State for Foreign, Commonwealth and Development Affairs, UK (2023–4); Prime Minister, UK (2010–16): London, 11 November 2024

Carney, Mark Prime Minister, Canada (2025–); Member, National Wealth Fund Taskforce, UK (2024–5); Chairman, Bloomberg Inc (2023–5); Chairman, Brookfield Asset Management (2020–5); United Nations Special Envoy on Climate Action and Finance (2020–2); Governor, Bank of England (2013–20); Governor, Bank of Canada (2008–13): Toronto–London, 27 October 2023, 25 January 2024

Centeno, Mario Governor, Banco de Portugal (2020–); President, Eurogroup of European finance ministers (2018–20); Finance Minister, Portugal (2015–20): Lisbon–London, 22 April 2024, 11 April 2025*

Clarida, Richard 'Rich' Professor of Economics and International Affairs, Columbia University (2016–18, 2022–); Global Strategic Advisor, PIMCO (2022–); Vice Chairman, Board of Governors, Federal Reserve (2018–22); Assistant Secretary of the Treasury for Economic Policy, US (2002–3): New York–London, 15 August 2024*

Clarke, (Lord) Kenneth Lord Chancellor, UK (2010–12); Chancellor of the Exchequer, UK (1993–7); Home Secretary, UK (1992–3); Member of Parliament for Rushcliffe, UK (1970–2023): London, 14 March 2023, 2 May 2023

Coeuré, Benoît President, Competition Authority, France (2022–); Head, Innovation Hub, Bank for International Settlements (2020–2); Member, Executive Board, European Central Bank (2012–19): Paris, 4 October 2023

Collins, James 'Jim' Senior Fellow, Carnegie Endowment for International Peace (2007–); Ambassador to Russia, US (1997–2001): Washington–London, 14 May 2024, 22 May 2024

Conley, Heather President, German Marshall Fund of the US (2021–4); Senior Vice President for Europe, Eurasia, and the Arctic, Center for Strategic and International Studies (CSIS) (2009–21): Washington, 2 June 2023

Conn, Iain Senior Advisor, Blackstone Group (2020–); Chief Executive, Centrica (2015–20): London, 13 December 2023

Constâncio, Vítor Professor, University of Navarra (2018–); Vice President, European Central Bank (2010–18); Governor, Banco de Portugal (1985–6, 2000–10); Finance Minister, Portugal (1978): Lisbon–London, 4 August 2023*

Corsepius, Uwe European Adviser to Angela Merkel, Chancellor, Germany (2015–21); Secretary, European Council, Brussels (2011–15): Berlin, 5 May 2023, 24 May 2023

Cromme, Gerhard Chairman, Siemens (2001–7); Chairman, ThyssenKrupp (1999–2001): Berlin, 15 November 2023

Cunliffe, (Sir) Jon Permanent Representative, European Union, UK; Deputy Governor, Financial Stability, Bank of England (2013–23): London, 2 November 2023

Darroch, (Lord) Kim Ambassador to the US, UK (2016–19); National Security Adviser, UK (2012–15); Permanent Representative to European Union, UK (2007–11): London, 3 April 2023

Davis, (Sir) David Member of Parliament for Goole and Pocklington (previously Haltemprice and Howden), UK (1997–); Secretary of State for Exiting the European Union, UK (2016–18); Minister of State for Europe, UK (1994–7): London, 9 April 2023, 15 May 2023

Desai, (Lord) Meghnad Professor Emeritus, London School of Economics and Political Science (2003–): London, 9 October 2023

Dhingra, Swati Member, Monetary Policy Committee, Bank of England (2022–); Associate Professor of Economics, London School of Economics and Political Science (2016–): London, 17 April 2023

Dini, Lamberto Senator for Tuscany & Lazio, Italy (2001–13); Foreign Minister, Italy (1996–2001); Prime Minister, Italy (1995–6); Treasury Minister, Italy (1994); Director General, Banca d'Italia (1979–94): Rome–London, 3 April 2024*, 8 April 2024*

Dudley, William 'Bill' Senior Research Scholar, Princeton University (2019–); President, Federal Reserve Bank of New York (2009–18); Partner and Managing Director, Goldman Sachs (1986–2007): New York–London, 8 January 2024*

Elderson, Frank Board Member, European Central Bank (2020–); Executive Director, De Nederlandsche Bank (2011–20): Frankfurt, 30 August 2023

Franco, Daniele Minister of Economy and Finance, Italy (2021–3); Director General, Bank of Italy (2020–1): Rome–London, 2 February 2024*; Rome, 11 March 2024

Fratzscher, Marcel President, DIW Berlin (2013–); Head of International Policy Analysis, European Central Bank (2001–13): Berlin, 9 January 2023

Frost (Lord) David Minister of State, Cabinet Office, UK (2021–2); Chief Negotiator for Exiting the European Union, UK (2019–20); Europe Adviser to Boris Johnson, Foreign Secretary, UK (2016–19): London, 23 July 2024

Füle, Stefan European Commissioner for Enlargement and European Neighbourhood Policy (2010–14); Czech Permanent Representative to NATO (2005–9); Minister for European Affairs, Czech Republic (2004–5): Prague–London, 8 September 2023, 31 October 2023

Geithner, Timothy 'Tim' President, Warburg Pincus (2014–); Secretary of the Treasury, US (2009–13); President, Federal Reserve Bank of New York (2003–9): New York–London, 12 June 2023*

Giavazzi, Francesco Economic Adviser to Mario Draghi, Prime Minister, Italy (2021–2); Professor of Economics, Bocconi University (1989–): Milan, 10 March 2023

Goodhart, Charles Emeritus Professor of Economics, London School of Economics and Political Science (2002–), Professor (1985–2002); External Member, Monetary Policy Committee, Bank of England (1997–2000): London, 30 April 2025**E**

Gourinchas, Pierre-Olivier Economic Counselor and Director, Research Department, International Monetary Fund (2022–); Professor of Economics, University of California, Berkeley (2003–22): Washington, 21 September 2023, 23 April 2025

Grieve, Dominic Member of Parliament for Beaconsfield, UK (1997–2019); Attorney General for England and Wales, UK (2010–14); Shadow Secretary of State for Justice, UK (2009–10): London, 12 July 2023

de Guindos, Luis Vice President, European Central Bank (2018–); Minister of Economy, Industry and Competitiveness, Spain (2011–18); Secretary of State for Economic Affairs, Spain (2002–4): Frankfurt, 20 March 2024, 12 March 2025

Guriev, Sergei Dean, London Business School (2024–); Provost, Sciences Po, Paris (2022–4); Scientific Director, Sciences Po (2019–22); Chief Economist, European Bank for Reconstruction and Development (2016–19); Rector, New Economic School, Moscow (2004–13): London–Paris, 12 July 2023

Hambrecht, Jürgen Chairman, Supervisory Board, BASF (2014–20); Chief Executive Officer, BASF (2003–11); Member, Supervisory Board, Daimler (2008–14): Neustadt/Weinstrasse, 21 December 2022

Haskel, Jonathan, Professor of Economics, Imperial College Business School, Imperial College London (2018–); External Member, Monetary Policy Committee, Bank of England (2018–24): London, 30 March 2023

Hay, Barbara Consul-General, Los Angeles, UK (2009–13); Consul-General, Istanbul, UK (2004–9); Ambassador to Uzbekistan and Tajikistan, UK (1995–9); Consul-General, St Petersburg, UK (1991–2, 2000–4): London, 3 July 2023

Heisbourg, François Senior Adviser, International Institute for Strategic Studies (2006–); Chairman, International Institute for Strategic Studies (2001–6); Director, Fondation pour la Recherche Stratégique (1998–2005): Paris, 24 April 2023; London, 16 May 2023

Herbst, John Director, Eurasia Center, Atlantic Council (2014–); Coordinator for Reconstruction and Stabilization, Department of State, US (2006–9); Ambassador to Ukraine, US (2003–6): Washington, 21 September 2023

Hernandez de Cos, Pablo General Manager, Bank for International Settlements (2025–); Governor, Banco de España (2018–24); Director General, Economics, Statistics, and Research, Banco de España (2015–18): Madrid, 11 January 2024

Heusgen, Christoph Chairman, Munich Security Conference (2022–5); Permanent Representative of Germany, United Nations (2017–21); Foreign Policy Adviser to Angela Merkel, Chancellor, Germany (2005–17): Munich–Stuttgart, 6 September 2023*

Holzmann, Robert Governor, Österreichische Nationalbank (2019–25); Senior Adviser, World Bank (1992–2019): Vienna, 14 March 2024

Honohan, Patrick Non-resident Senior Fellow, Peterson Institute for International Economics (2016–); Governor, Central Bank of Ireland (2009–15); Professor, Trinity College Dublin (2007–9): Dublin–London, 4 July 2023*

Hoyer, Werner President, European Investment Bank (2012–23); Minister of State, Foreign Ministry (Deputy Foreign Minister), Germany (2009–11, 1994–8); Member of Bundestag (1987–2012): Berlin, 22 April 2024

Issing, Otmar President, Center for Financial Studies (2006–23); Board Member, European Central Bank (1998–2006); Board Member, Deutsche Bundesbank (1990–8): Würzburg, 5 April 2023

Jessop, Julian Economics Fellow, previously Chief Economist, Institute of Economic Affairs: London, 14 October 2024

Jin Liqun Chairman, Asian Infrastructure Investment Bank (2015–26): Chairman, China International Capital Corporation (2013–14); Chairman, Supervisory Board, China Investment Corporation (2008–13); Vice President, Asian Development Bank (2003–8); Vice Minister of Finance, China (1998–2003): Beijing–Radda, 19 September 2024*; London, 2 October 2024

Joffe, Josef Member, Board of Editors, *Die Zeit* (2000–23); Foreign Editor, *Süddeutsche Zeitung* (1985–2000): Hamburg–London, 9 August 2023*

Juncker, Jean-Claude President, European Commission (2014–19); Prime Minister, Luxembourg (1995–2013); Finance Minister, Luxembourg (1989–2009): Brussels, 29 November 2023, 24 January 2024

Kamin, Steve Senior Fellow, American Enterprise Institute (2021–); Director, International Finance Division, Federal Reserve (2011–20); Senior Adviser, Federal Reserve (2007–11): Washington–London, 4 January 2024*

Kannan, Prakash Chief Economist (2019–), Head, Total Portfolio Management (2012–), GIC, Singapore: Singapore–London, 29 August 2024*

Kerr, (Lord) John Deputy Chairman, Scottish Power (2005–12); Permanent Under-Secretary, Foreign & Commonwealth Office, UK (1997–2002); Ambassador to US, UK (1995–7); Permanent Representative to EU, UK (1990–5): London, 7 September 2023

Kimmitt, Robert 'Bob' Senior International Counsel, Wilmer Hale (2010–); Deputy Treasury Secretary, US (2005–9); Managing Director, Lehman Brothers (2001–5); Ambassador to Germany, US (1991–3); Under Secretary of State for Political Affairs, US (1989–91): Washington–London, 3 July 2023*, 8 January 2024*; Washington, 25 April 2025

King, (Lord) Mervyn Governor, Bank of England (2003–13); Deputy Governor, Bank of England (1998–2003): London, 1 November 2023, 24 November 2023*

Knot, Klaas President, De Nederlandsche Bank (2011–25): The Hague, 29 March 2022; Amsterdam, 28 June 2023, 12 April 2024, 11 February 2025

Köcher, Renate Managing Director, Allensbach Institute (2010–): Berlin, 22 February 2023

Köhler, Horst Federal President, Germany (2004–10); Managing Director, International Monetary Fund (2000–4); President, European Bank for Reconstruction and Development (1998–2000); President, German Savings Banks Association (1993–8); State Secretary, Finance Ministry, Germany (1990–3): Berlin, 13 November 2023, *d. 1 February 2025*

Kornblum, John Senior Counselor, Noerr LLP (2009–21); Ambassador to Germany, US (1997–2001); Assistant Secretary of State for European and Canadian Affairs, Department of State, US (1994–7): Berlin, 25 February 2022, 23 September 2022, 1 December 2022, 25 January 2023, *d. 21 December 2023*

Kukies, Jörg Finance Minister, Germany (2024–5); State Secretary, Chancellor's Office, Germany (2021–4); State Secretary for Financial Market Policy and European Policy, Federal Ministry of Finance, Germany (2018–21); Co-Head, Goldman Sachs Germany (2014–18): Berlin, 6 February 2023

Lagarde, Christine President, European Central Bank (2019–); Managing Director, International Monetary Fund (2011–19); Minister of Economy, Finance and Industry, France (2007–11): Frankfurt, 12 January 2022, 25 April 2023

Lagayette, Philippe Chairman, Fondation de France (2005–17); President, JP Morgan France (1997–2005); Director General, Caisse des depots et consignations (1992–7); Deputy Governor, Banque de France (1984–92); Director of office of Jacques Delors, Finance and Economy Minister, France (1981–4): Paris–London, 13 June 2024*

Lamont, (Lord) Norman Chancellor of the Exchequer, UK (1990–3); Member of Parliament for Kingston-upon-Thames, UK (1972–97): London, 14 February 2023, 19 May 2023

de Larosière, Jacques Adviser to Chairman, BNP Paribas (1998–2008); President, European Bank for Reconstruction and Development (1993–8); President, Banque de France (1987–93); Managing Director, International Monetary Fund (1978–87); Director, Treasury, France (1974–8): Paris, 24 April 2023, 3 October 2023

Liddle, (Lord) Roger Chair, Policy Network (2008–); Special Adviser, President of the European Commission (1997–2004): London, 25 July 2023

Lucke, Bernd Professor of Macroeconomics, University of Hamburg (2003–); Co-Founder and Federal Chairman, Alternative for Germany (2013–15); Member of European Parliament (2014–19): London, 27 November 2023

Lyne, (Sir) Roderic Ambassador to Russia, UK (2000–4); Private Secretary to John Major, Prime Minister, UK (1993–6): London, 7 June 2023

Lyons, Gerard Chief Economic Strategist, Netwealth (2019–); Chief Economic Adviser to Boris Johnson, Mayor of London (2013–16); Chief Economist, Standard Chartered Bank (1999–2012): London, 6 September 2022, 20 November 2022, 14 December 2023

McDonald, (Lord) Simon Master, Christ's College, Cambridge (2021–); Permanent Under-Secretary, Foreign & Commonwealth Office, UK (2015–20); British Ambassador to Germany (2010–15): Cambridge, 6 July 2023

Macpherson, (Lord) Nicholas 'Nick' Chairman, C. Hoare & Co. (2016–); Permanent Secretary, Treasury, UK (2005–16): Edinburgh, 2 December 2023; London, 7 December 2023

Mahbubani, Kishore Distinguished Fellow, Asia Research Institute, National University of Singapore (2017–); Dean, Lee Kuan Yew School of Public Policy (2004–17); Singapore Permanent Representative, UN (1984–9): Singapore–London, 14 June 2024*; Hong Kong–London, 29 August 2024*

Manning, (Sir) David Ambassador to US, UK (2003–7); Foreign Policy Adviser, Prime Minister Tony Blair, UK (2001–3); Ambassador to Israel, UK (1995–8): London, 12 June 2023

Matussek, Thomas Ambassador to India, Germany (2009–11); Permanent Representative, United Nations, Germany (2006–9); Ambassador to UK, Germany (2002–6): Hardenberg, 15 September 2023

Menon, Ravi Chairman, Global Finance and Technology Network (2024–); Ambassador for Climate Action, Singapore (2024–); Managing Director, Monetary Authority of Singapore (2011–24): Singapore–Frankfurt, 27 August 2024*

Mersch, Yves Member, Executive Board, European Central Bank (2012–20); Governor, Central Bank of Luxembourg (1998–2012); Director, Treasury, Luxembourg (1989–98); Council Member, Luxembourg Monetary Institute (1983–98): Luxembourg, 4 October 2023; Luxembourg–London, 27 October 2023*

Merz, Friedrich Chancellor, Germany (2025–); Chairman, Christian Democratic Union (2022–): London, 4 February 2020+, 21 September 2021+

Micossi, Stefano Director General, Assonime (2002–23); Director General for Industry, European Commission (1994–8): Rome, 11 March 2024

Moïsi, Dominique Senior Adviser, Institut Montaigne (2016–); Visiting Professor, Harvard University (2010–11); Deputy Director, French Institute of International Relations (1991–2011): Paris, 10 October 2023

Monti, Mario President, Bocconi University (1994–); Prime Minister, Italy (2011–13); European Commissioner for Internal Market & Services, then Competition (1999–2004): Rome, 8 March 2023

Moore, (Lord) Charles Editor, *Daily Telegraph* (1995–2003); Editor, *Spectator* (1984–90): London, 25 June 2024

Morel, Pierre European Union Special Representative for Central Asia (2006–12); Ambassador to Russia, France (1992–6); Deputy Permanent Representative to United Nations, France (1989–92): Paris, 24 April 2023

Mosdorf, Siegmar Member of Bundestag, Germany (1998–2002); Parliamentary State Secretary, Federal Ministry of Economics and Technology, Germany (1998–2002): Berlin, 13 November 2023

Moulin, Emmanuel Secretary-General, Elysée Palace, France (2025–); Chief of Staff, Prime Minister's office, France (2024); Director General, Treasury, France (2020–4); Chief of Staff, Minister of Finance, France (2017–20); Deputy Chief of Staff, President of France (2012–17): Paris, 24 April 2023

Nagel, Joachim President, Deutsche Bundesbank (2022–); Board Member, Deutsche Bundesbank (2010–16); Deputy Director General, KfW Group (2016–20); Deputy Head of Banking, Bank for International Settlements (2021–2): Frankfurt, 30 August 2023

Nakao, Takehiko Chairman, Mizuho Research Institute (2020–); President, Asian Development Bank (2013–20); Vice Minister of Finance for International Affairs, Japan (2011–12): London, 20 June 2024

Nowotny, Ewald President, Austrian Foreign Policy Association (2020–); Governor, Österreichische Nationalbank (2008–19): Vienna, 14 March 2024, 23 May 2025

Noyer, Christian Chairman, Bank for International Settlements (2010–15); Governor, Banque de France (2003–15); Vice President, European Central Bank (1998–2002): Paris, 3 October 2023

O'Donnell, (Lord) Gus Cabinet Secretary and Head of the Civil Service, UK (2005–11); Permanent Secretary, Treasury, UK (2002–5): London, 15 February 2023

Olsen, Øystein Governor, Norges Bank (2011–); Director General, Statistics Norway (2005–11); Executive Director, International Monetary Fund (2000–4): Stavanger, 5 June 2024

Orphanides, Athanasios Professor of Practice, MIT Sloan School of Management (2012–); Governor, Central Bank of Cyprus (2007–12); Senior Advisor, Federal Reserve Board (1999–2007): Vienna, 11 June 2024

Owen, (Lord) David Secretary of State for Foreign & Commonwealth Affairs, UK (1977–9); Member of Parliament for Plymouth Devonport, UK (1966–92): London, 21 April 2023

Padoan, Pier Carlo Chairman, UniCredit (2020–); Economy and Finance Minister, Italy (2014–18); Deputy Secretary-General, OECD (2007–14): Rome, 7 March 2023

Pfaffenbach, Bernd State Secretary, Economics Ministry, Germany (2005–11); Economic Adviser to Gerhard Schroder, Chancellor, Germany (2001–4); Deputy Head, Economics Department, Chancellor's Office, Germany (1992–2000): Berlin, 17 January 2023, 24 March 2024

Ploetz, Hans-Friedrich von Ambassador to Russia, Germany (1999–2002); Ambassador to the UK, Germany (1997–9); Secretary of State, Foreign Office, Germany (1994–7); Ambassador to NATO, West Germany, then Germany (1989–93): Berlin, 18 January 2023, 20 March 2023

Plötner, Jens Foreign and Security Policy Adviser to Olaf Scholz, Chancellor, Germany (2021–5); Director General for Political Affairs, Foreign Ministry, Germany (2019–21); German Ambassador to Netherlands (2014–19): Berlin, 4 April 2023

Powell, (Lord) Charles Private Secretary to Margaret Thatcher, Prime Minister, UK (1983–90); UK Ambassador to Spain (1991–4): London, 28 February 2023

Powell, Jonathan National Security Adviser, UK (2024–); Principal, Inter Mediate (2011–24); Chief of Staff to Tony Blair, Prime Minister, UK (1997–2007); Special Adviser, Foreign & Commonwealth Office, UK (1995–7): London, 12 September 2023

Praet, Peter Member of Board, European Central Bank (2011–19); Executive Director, National Bank of Belgium (2000–11); Chief of Staff, Minister of Finance, Belgium (1992–9): Brussels–London, 3 August 2023*, 27 October 2023*; Waterloo, 23 January 2024

Prodi, Romano President, European Commission (1999–2004); Prime Minister, Italy (1996–8, 2006–8): Bologna, 10 March 2023

Ramsden, (Sir) Dave Deputy Governor for Markets and Banking, Bank of England (2017–); Chief Economic Adviser, Treasury, UK (2008–17); Director General, Treasury, UK (2004–8): London, 12 June 2023

Redwood, (Sir) John Member of Parliament for Wokingham, UK (1987–2024); Secretary of State for Wales, UK (1993–5); Minister of State for Local Government, UK (1990–3): Wokingham, 14 April 2023, 22 June 2024

Rees-Mogg, (Sir) Jacob Member of Parliament for North East Somerset, UK (2010–24); Lord President of the Council, UK (2019–22); Chair, European Research Group (2018–19): London, 16 May 2023

Reuter, Edzard Chief Executive Officer, Daimler-Benz (1987–95); Chairman, Bertelsmann Foundation (1998–2001); Member of Board of Management, Daimler-Benz (1964–87): Stuttgart, 6 September 2023, *d. 27 October 2024*

Rice, Condoleezza Director, Hoover Institution, Stanford University (2020–); Secretary of State, US (2005–9); National Security Advisor, US (2001–5): Stanford–London, 23 May 2024*

Robbins, (Sir) Oliver 'Olly' Permanent Secretary, Foreign, Commonwealth and Development Office, UK (2025–); Managing Director, Goldman Sachs (2019–23); Prime Minister's Europe Adviser and Chief Negotiator for Exiting the EU, UK (2017–19); Permanent Secretary, Department for Exiting the EU, UK (2016–19): London, 12 June 2023

Rogers, (Sir) Ivan Permanent Representative to European Union, UK (2013–17); Prime Minister's Adviser for Europe and Global Issues, UK (2012–13); Director General, Treasury, UK (2006–11): London, 7 December 2022, 30 June 2023

Röller, Lars-Hendrik Founder and Chair, Berlin Global Dialogue (2022–); Chief Economic Adviser to Angela Merkel, Chancellor, Germany (2011–21); President, European School of Management and Technology (2006–11); Member, Council of Economic Experts, Germany (2005–11): London, 10 October 2022, 19 April 2023; Berlin, 25 January 2023, 23 May 2023

Rossi, Salvatore Chairman, Italian Insurance Supervisory Authority (2019–20); Senior Deputy Governor, Banca d'Italia (2013–19); Chief Economist, Banca d'Italia (2011–13): Rome, 8 March 2023, 12 March 2024

Rostagno, Massimo Director General, European Central Bank (2020–); Director, Monetary Policy, European Central Bank (2007–20); Director, Economic Outlook and Monetary Policy, Banca d'Italia (2001–7): Frankfurt, 25 July 2024

Saarenheimo, Tuomas President, Euro Working Group and Economic and Financial Committee of the EU (2020–); Permanent Secretary, Ministry of Finance, Finland (2013–20); Deputy Governor, Bank of Finland (2004–12): Brussels, 23 January 2024

Sawers, (Sir) John Chairman, Macro Advisory Partners (2015–); Chief, Secret Intelligence Service (MI6), UK (2009–4); British Ambassador, United Nations (2007–9): London, 18 June 2024

Schäuble, Wolfgang President, Bundestag (2017–21); Federal Minister of Finance, Germany (2009–17); Interior Minister, Germany (2005–9): Berlin, 18 January 2021, 16 January 2023, *d. 27 December 2023*

Schlesinger, Helmut President, Deutsche Bundesbank (1991–3); Board Member, Deutsche Bundesbank (1975–91): Frankfurt, 26 July 2024, 10 August 2024, *d. 24 December 2024*

Schnabl, Gunther Director, Flossbach von Storch Research Institute (2024–); Professor of Economics and International Economics Relations, Leipzig University (2006–): Berlin, 18 January 2023

Scholar, (Sir) Tom Chairman, Nomura Europe (2024–); Permanent Secretary, Treasury, UK (2016–22); Prime Minister's Adviser on European and Global Issues, UK (2013–16); Executive Director, UK, International Monetary Fund (2001–7): London, 11 January 2023, 30 October 2023

Schuknecht, Ludger Vice President and Corporate Secretary, Asian Infrastructure Investment Bank (2021–); Deputy Secretary-General, OECD (2018–21); Chief Economist, German Ministry of Finance (2011–20); Senior Economist, European Central Bank (1999–2011): Beijing–London, 14 March 2023

Selmayr, Martin Head of European Commission Representation to Vatican, Rome (2024–); Head of European Commission Representation in Austria (2020–4); Secretary-General, European Commission (2018–19); Chief of Staff to Jean-Claude Juncker, President, European Commission (2014–18): Vienna, 23 January 2012; Vienna–London, 23 November 2023

Sheets, Nathan Global Chief Economist, Citigroup (2021–); Chief Economist, PGIM Fixed Income (2017–21); Under Secretary of the Treasury for International Affairs, US (2014–17); Global Head of International Economics, Citigroup (2011–14): New York, 30 May 2023

Shirreff, (Sir) Richard Deputy Supreme Allied Commander Europe, NATO (2011–14); General Officer Commanding, Allied Rapid Reaction Corps (2007–10): London, 29 March 2023

Simpson, Anne Global Head of Sustainability, Franklin Templeton (2022–); Director, Board Governance and Sustainability, CalPERS (2009–21); Senior Faculty Fellow, Yale University (2020–): London, 25 February 2024

Singh, Daleep Chief Global Economist, PGIM Fixed Income (2025– and 2023–4); Deputy National Security Advisor for International Economics, US (2024–5 and 2021–2); Executive Vice President, New York Federal Reserve Bank (2017–21); Assistant Secretary of the Treasury for Financial Markets (2016–17): Washington–London, 5 September 2023

Smart, Christopher Managing Partner, Arbroath Group (2023–); Chief Global Strategist, Barings (2018–23); Special Assistant for International Economics, White House, US (2013–15); Deputy Assistant Secretary of the Treasury, US (2009–13): Boston–London, 2 August 2023

Smets, Frank Deputy Head, Monetary and Economic Department, Bank for International Settlements (2024–); Director General, Economics, European Central Bank (2017–24); Adviser to the President, European Central Bank (2013–17): Frankfurt, 26 July 2024

Sobel, Mark US Chair, Official Monetary and Financial Institutions Forum (2018–); Senior Advisor, Executive Director for US, International Monetary Fund (2015–18): Deputy Assistant Secretary for International Monetary and Financial Policy, Treasury, US (2000–14); Frankfurt, 10 May 2023

Stark, Jürgen Member, Board Member, European Central Bank (2006–12); Vice President, Deutsche Bundesbank (1998–2006); State Secretary, Federal Ministry of Finance, Germany (1995–8): Frankfurt, 25 April 2023, 10 May 2023, 15 December 2023

Stouranas, Yannis Governor, Bank of Greece (2014–); Minister of Finance, Greece (2012–14); Professor of Economics, University of Athens (1989–): Athens–London, 16 April 2024*

Stuart, (Baroness) Gisela First Civil Service Commissioner, UK (2022–); Chair, Wilton Park (2018–); Chair, Vote Leave, UK (2015–16); Member of Parliament for Edgbaston, UK (1997–2017): London, 2 September 2024

Stürmer, Michael Professor of History, University of Erlangen-Nuremberg (1989–); Chief Correspondent, *Die Welt* (2013–23); Director, Stiftung Wissenschaft und Politik (1988–98); Foreign Policy Adviser, Chancellor's Office, Germany (1980–6); Director, German Historical Institute, London (1976–89): Munich, 20 January 2023

Summers, Lawrence 'Larry' Charles W. Eliot University Professor, Harvard University (2001–); President, Harvard University (2001–6); Secretary of the Treasury, US (1999–2001); Scottsdale–London, 30 January 2024*, 21 April 2025*

Teltschik, Horst Board Member, BMW (1993–2000); Deputy Head, Chancellor's Office and Foreign Policy Adviser to Helmut Kohl, Chancellor, Germany (1982–90): Tegernsee, 20 January 2023, 5 September 2023

Tenreyro, Silvana Professor of Economics, London School of Economics and Political Science (2013–); External Member, Monetary Policy Committee, Bank of England (2017–23): London, 29 March 2023

Thimann, Christian Chief Executive Officer, Athora Germany (2017–23); Member of Executive Committee, AXA (2013–17); Director General, Financial Stability, European Central Bank (2008–13): Frankfurt–London, 23 July 2024*

Thygesen, Niels Chairman, European Fiscal Board (2016–24); Professor of Economics, University of Copenhagen (1971–); Member, Delors Committee on Economic and Monetary Union (1988–9): London, 15 June 2023, 4 March 2025

Toncar, Florian Parliamentary State Secretary (Deputy Finance Minister), Finance Ministry, Germany (2021–4): Berlin, 27 April 2023

Trichet, Jean-Claude President, European Central Bank (2003–11); Governor, Banque de France (1993–2003); Director, Treasury, France (1987–1993): Paris, 30 November 2021, 10 October 2023; Paris–London, 28 June 2024*, 12 March 2025*

Tucker, (Sir) Paul Research Fellow, Harvard Kennedy School (2013–); Deputy Governor, Bank of England (2009–13); Member of Monetary Policy Committee, Bank of England (2002–9): London, 8 February 2024

Tugendhat, (Lord) Christopher Chairman, Civil Aviation Authority (1986–91); Vice-President, European Commission (1981–6); Member of Parliament, City of London & Westminster South, UK (1970–7): London, 16 February 2023

Valla, Natacha Dean, School of Management and Innovation, Sciences Po, Paris (2020–); Deputy Director General for Monetary Policy, European Central Bank (2018–20); Head, Policy Strategy, European Investment Bank (2016–18): Paris, 4 October 2023

Vallée, Shahin Senior Research Fellow, German Foreign Policy Association (2019–); Senior Economist, Soros Fund Management (2015–18); Economic Adviser to Emmanuel Macron,

Economy Minister, France (2014–5); Economic Adviser to Herman Van Rompuy, President, European Council (2012–14): Paris–London, 1 May 2024*

Villeroy de Galhau, François Governor, Banque de France (2015–); Chairman, Bank for International Settlements (2019–22); Executive Director BNP Paribas (2003–15): Paris, 14 February 2023, 3 October 2023

Vimont, Pierre Executive Secretary General, European External Action Service (2010–15); Ambassador to US, France (2007–10): Paris, 3 October 2023

Visco, Ignazio Governor, Banca d'Italia (2011–23); Director General, Economics, Banca d'Italia (2007–11): Rome, 6 June 2022

Vujcic, Boris Governor, Croatian National Bank (2012–); Deputy Governor, Croatian National Bank (2000–12); Chairman, EU Economic and Financial Committee (2018–20): Zagreb–London, 24 June 2024

Weidmann, Jens Chairman, Supervisory Board, Commerzbank (2023–); President, Deutsche Bundesbank (2011–21); Chair, Bank for International Settlements (2015–21); Economic Adviser to Angela Merkel, Chancellor, Germany: Frankfurt, 16 June 2023, 12 December 2023

Wellink, Nout President, Nederlandsche Bank (2002–11); Chairman, Basel Committee on Banking Supervision (2009–11): The Hague, 14 July 2023, 10 April 2024, 13 April 2025

Weston, John Political Director & Deputy Under-Secretary (Europe), Foreign & Commonwealth Office, UK (1990–1): London, 8 June 2023, 11 September 2023

White, William 'Bill' Senior Fellow, C.D. Howe Institute (2019–); Chairman, Economic & Development Review Committee, OECD (2009–18); Head, Monetary & Economic Department, Bank for International Settlements (1995–2008); Deputy Governor, Bank of Canada (1999–2001): Toronto–London, 26 April 2023*

Wuttke, Joerg Partner, DGA Albright Stonebridge Group (2024–); Chief Representative, China, BASF (1996–2024); President, EU Chamber of Commerce in China (2007–10, 2014–17, 2019–23): Washington–London, 20 August 2024*

Zelikow, Philip Senior Fellow, Hoover Institution, Stanford University (2023–); Professor of History, University of Virginia (2014–23); Executive Director, 9/11 Commission (2003–4); Counselor, Department of State, US (2002–3): Stanford–London, 4 December 2023*

Zoellick, Robert 'Bob' President, World Bank Group (2007–12); Deputy Secretary of State, US (2005–6); Trade Representative, US (2001–5); Under Secretary of State for Economic & Agricultural Affairs, Counselor, US (1989–2): Washington–Berlin, 27 July 2023*; Washington–London, 2 April 2025*

* Telephone or video call. First place name indicates location of interview partner.
+ Conversation including other participants
E email exchange
d. date of death

SELECT BIBLIOGRAPHY

Acheson, Dean G., *Present at the Creation: My Years at the State Department* (New York: W.W. Norton, 1969)

Adonis, Andrew, *Ernest Bevin: Labour's Churchill* (London: Biteback, 2020)

——, *5 Days in May: The Coalition and Beyond* (London: Biteback, 2013)

Aeschimann, Éric, and Pascal Riché, *La Guerre de Sept Ans: Histoire secrète du franc fort 1989–1996* (Paris: Calman-Lévy, 1996)

Aglietta, Michel, *The Reform of Europe: A Political Guide to the Future* (London: Verso, 2018)

Ahamed, Liaquat, *The Lords of Finance: The Bankers Who Broke the World* (New York: Penguin Press, 2009)

Aldrich, Richard J., *The Hidden Hand: Britain, America and Cold War Secret Intelligence* (New York: Overlook Press, 2002)

Alexander Robin, *Die Getriebenen: Merkel und die Flüchtlingspolitik* (Munich: Siedler, 2017)

Aron, Raymond, *In Defense of Decadent Europe* (New York: University Press of America, 1979)

Ashcroft, Michael T., and Isabel Oakeshott, *Call Me Dave: The Unauthorised Biography of David Cameron* (London: Biteback, 2016)

Ashton, Catherine, *And Then What? Despatches from the Heart of 21st-Century Diplomacy* (London: Elliott & Thompson, 2023)

Arthuis, Jean, *Mondialisation: la France à contre-emploi* (Paris: Calman-Lévy, 2007)

Attali, Jacques, *C'était François Mitterrand* (Paris: Fayard, 2005)

——, *Verbatim I 1981–1986* (Paris: Fayard, 1993)

——, *Verbatim II 1986–1988* (Paris: Fayard, 1995)

——, *Verbatim III: Première partie, 1988–1989* (Paris: Fayard, 1996)

——, *Verbatim III: Deuxième partie, 1990–1991* (Paris: Fayard, 1996)

Baker, James A. III, with Thomas M. DeFrank, *The Politics of Diplomacy: Revolution, War and Peace, 1989–1992* (New York: G.P. Putnam's Sons, 1995)

Bakker, Age, Henk Boot, Olaf Skijen and Wim Vanthoor (eds), *Monetary Stability through International Cooperation: Essays in Honour of André Szász* (Dordrecht: Kluwer, 1994)

Baldwin, Richard, *Towards an Integrated Europe* (London: Centre for European Policy Research, 2004)

Balfour, Michael, *Germany: The Tides of Power* (London/New York: Routledge, 1992)

Baring, Arnulf, *Scheitert Deutschland?* (Stuttgart: Deutsche Verlags-Anstalt, 1997)

Barnier, Michel, *La grande illusion: Journal secret du Brexit, 2016-2020* (Paris: Gallimard, 2021)

Barucci, Piero, *L'Isola Italiana del Tesoro* (Milan: Rizzoli, 1995)

Barwell, Gavin, *Chief of Staff: Notes from Downing Street* (London: Atlantic, 2021)

Barzini, Luigi, *The Impossible Europeans* (London: Weidenfeld & Nicolson, 1983)

SELECT BIBLIOGRAPHY

Bayoumi, Tamim, *Unfinished Business: The Unexplored Causes of the Financial Crisis and the Lessons Yet to Be Learned* (New Haven/London: Yale University Press, 2017)

Belton, Catherine, *Putin's People: How the KGB Took Back Russia and Then Took on the West* (London: William Collins, 2020)

Bennett, Owen, *The Brexit Club: The Inside Story of the Leave Campaign's Victory* (London: Biteback, 2016)

Beschlosss, Michael R., and Strobe Talbott, *At the Highest Levels: The Inside Story of the End of the Cold War* (Boston, MA: Little, Brown, 1993)

Bini Smaghi, Lorenzo, *Il Paradosso dell'Euro* (Milan: Rizzoli, 2008)

Bishop, Graham, *The EU Fiscal Crisis: Forcing Eurozone Political Union in 2011?* (London: Searching Finance, 2011)

Bizouarne, Léon, *La Haute Banque: Son rôle dans la libération du territoire Français en 1871–1872 et 1873* (Paris: P. Dupont, 1892)

Blair, Tony, *A Journey: My Political Life* (London: Hutchinson 2010)

Blessing, Karl, *Im Kampf um gutes Geld* (Frankfurt: Fritz Knapp, 1966)

Bohlen, Charles E., *Witness to History 1929–1969* (New York: W.W. Norton, 1973)

Bollmann, Ralph, *Angela Merkel: Die Kanzlerin und ihre Zeit* (Munich: C.H. Beck, 2021)

Bordo, Michael D., and Anna J. Schwarz (eds), *A Retrospective on the Classical Gold Standard, 1821–1931* (Chicago, IL: University of Chicago Press, 1984)

Bower, Tom, *Gordon Brown* (London: HarperCollins, 2004)

Braithwaite, Rodric, *Across the Moscow River: The World Turned Upside Down* (New Haven/London: Yale University Press, 2002)

——, *Russia: Myths and Realities* (London: Profile, 2022)

Brandt, Peter, Hans-Joachim Gießmann and Götz Neuneck (eds), *'. . . aber eine Chance haben wir': Zum 100. Geburtstag von Egon Bahr* (Bonn: Dietz, 2022)

Brandt, Willy, *Erinnerungen* (Frankfurt: Propyläen, 1989)

Brawand, Leo, *Wohin steuert die deutsche Wirtschaft?* (Munich: Desch, 1971)

Brown, Brendan, *Euro Crash: The Implications of Monetary Failure in Europe* (London: Palgrave Macmillan, 2010)

——, *Euro on Trial: To Reform or Split Up?* (London: Palgrave Macmillan, 2004)

Brown, Gordon, *Beyond the Crash* (London: Simon & Schuster, 2010)

——, *My Life, Our Times* (London: The Bodley Head, 2018)

——, *Seven Ways to Change the World* (London: Simon & Schuster, 2021)

Brown, Gordon, Mohamed A. El-Erian and Michael Spence, *Permacrisis: A Plan to Fix a Fractured World* (London: Simon & Schuster, 2023)

Brunnermeier, Markus K., Harold James and Jean-Pierre Landau, *The Euro and the Battle of Ideas* (Princeton, NJ: Princeton University Press, 2016)

Bryant, Arthur, *Triumph in the West, 1943–1946* (London: William Collins, 1959)

Buchan, David, *Europe: The Strange Superpower* (London: Dartmouth Publishing, 1993)

Bullock, Alan (ed.), *The Twentieth Century* (London: Thames & Hudson, 1971)

Burns, William J., *The Back Channel: American Diplomacy in a Disordered World* (London: Hurst & Co., 2021)

Bush, George H.W., and Brent Scowcroft, *A World Transformed* (New York: Alfred A. Knopf, 1998)

Bush, George W., *Decision Points* (New York: Crown, 2010)

Callaghan, James, *Time and Chance* (London: William Collins, 1987)

Camdessus, Michel, *Le Soursaut: Vers une nouvelle croissance pour la France* (Paris: La documentation Française, 2004)

Cameron, David, *For the Record* (London: William Collins, 2019)

Campbell, Alastair, *The Blair Years* (London: Hutchinson, 2007)

——, *Diaries*, vol. 1: *Prelude to Power, 1994–1997* (London: Hutchinson, 2010)

——, *Diaries*, vol. 2: *Power and the People, 1997–1999* (London: Hutchinson, 2011)

——, *Diaries*, vol. 3: *Power and Responsibility, 1999–2001* (London: Hutchinson, 2011)

——, *Diaries*, vol. 4: *The Burden of Power: Countdown to Iraq* (London: Hutchinson, 2012)

——, *Diaries*, vol. 5: *Outside, Inside, 2003–2005* (London: Biteback, 2016)

——, *Diaries*, vol. 6: *From Blair to Brown, 2005–2007* (London: Biteback, 2017)

——, *Diaries*, vol. 7: *From Crash to Defeat, 2007–2010* (London: Biteback, 2018)

Chabot, Christian, *Understanding the Euro: The Clear and Concise Guide to the New Trans-European Currency* (New York: McGraw Hill, 1999)

Charlton, Michael, *The Price of Victory* (London: BBC Books, 1983)

Ciampi, Carlo Azeglio, *Dalla Crisi al Risanamento* (Rome: Treves Editore, 2005)

Clinton, Bill, *My Life* (New York: Alfred A. Knopf, 2004)

Cobham, David and George Zis (eds), *From EMS to EMU, 1979 to 1999 and Beyond* (London: Macmillan, 1999)

Cohen, Benjamin J., *The Future of Sterling as an International Currency* (London: Macmillan, 1971)

Colchester, Nicholas and David Buchan, *Europe Relaunched: Truths and Illusions on the Way to 1992* (London: Hutchinson, 1990)

Cole, Alistair, *François Mitterrand: A Study in Political Leadership* (Abingdon: Routledge, 1994)

Collignon, Stefan, *Europe's Monetary Future* (London: Pinter, 1994)

Connolly, Bernard, *The Rotten Heart of Europe* (London: Faber & Faber, 1995)

Coombs, Charles, *The Arena of International Finance* (New York: Wiley, 1976)

Cottrell, Philip, Even Lange and Ulf Olsson (eds), *Centres and Peripheries in Banking: The Historical Development of Financial Markets* (Abingdon: Routledge, 2007)

Cottrell, Philip, Gérassimos Notaras and Gabriel Tortella (eds), *From the Athenian Tetradrachm to the Euro: Studies in European Monetary Integration* (Abingdon: Routledge, 2007)

Crockett, Andrew, *International Money: Issues and Analysis* (London: Thomas Nelson, 1977)

Darling, Alistair, *Back from the Brink: 1,000 Days at Number 11* (London: Atlantic, 2011)

Davies, Norman, *Europe: A History* (Oxford: Oxford University Press, 1996)

Deane, Marjorie and Robert Pringle, *The Central Banks* (London: Hamish Hamilton, 1994)

Debré, Michel, *Mémoires: Gouverner autrement 1962–1970* (Paris: Albin Michel, 1993)

Deighton, Anne, *The Impossible Peace: Britain, the Division of Germany, and the Origins of the Cold War* (Oxford: Oxford University Press, 1990)

Deininger, Roman, and Uwe Ritzer, *Markus Söder: Der Schattenkanzler* (Munich: Droemer, 2022)

Delors, Jacques, *L'Europe Tragique et Magnifique: Les grands enjeux européens* (Paris: Éditions Saint-Simon, 2006)

——, *Mémoires* (Paris: Plon, 2004)

Desai, Meghnad, *Hubris: Why Economists Failed to Predict the Crisis and How to Avoid the Next One* (New Haven/London: Yale University Press, 2015)

——, *The Poverty of Political Economy* (Gurugram: HarperCollins India, 2022)

Deutsche Bundesbank (ed.), *Fünfzig Jahre Deutsche Mark: Notenbank und Währung in Deutschland seit 1948* (Munich: C.H. Beck, 1998), also published as *Fifty Years of the Deutsche Mark: Central Bank and the Currency in Germany since 1948* (Oxford: Oxford University Press, 1999)

——, *Hans Tietmeyer: Währungsstabilität für Europa* (Baden-Baden: Nomos Verlag, 1996)

——, *Währung und Wirtschaft in Europa, 1875–1975* (Frankfurt: Fritz Knapp, 1976)

Dollbaum, Jan Matti, Morvan Lallouet and Ben Noble, *Navalny: Putin's Nemesis, Russia's Future?* (London: Hurst & Co., 2021)

Dormel, Armand van, *Bretton Woods: Birth of a Monetary System* (London: Macmillan, 1978)

Driffill, John, and Missimo Beber (eds), *A Currency for Europe: The Currency as an Element of Division or of Union in Europe* (London: Lothian Foundation Press, 1991)

Duchêne, François, *Jean Monnet: The First Statesman of Interdependence* (New York: W.W. Norton, 1994)

Dumas, Charles, *Globalisation Fractures* (London: Profile, 2009)

Dyson, Kenneth, and Ivan Maes (eds), *Architects of the Euro: Intellectuals in the Making of European Monetary Union* (Oxford: Oxford University Press, 2016)

Dyson, Kenneth, and Kevin Featherstone, *The Road to Maastricht: Negotiating Economic and Monetary Union* (Oxford: Oxford University Press, 1999)

SELECT BIBLIOGRAPHY

Eichengreen, Barry, *The European Economy since 1945* (Princeton, NJ: Princeton University Press, 2007)

——, *Exorbitant Privilege: The Rise and Fall of the Dollar* (Oxford: Oxford University Press, 2011)

——, *Golden Fetters: The Gold Standard and the Great Depression, 1919–1939* (Oxford: Oxford University Press, 1992)

Eisenberg, Carolyn Woods, *Drawing the Line: The American Decision to Divide Germany, 1944–1949* (Cambridge: Cambridge University Press, 1996)

Eisenhower, Dwight D., *Mandate for Change: The White House Years, 1953–1956* (New York: Doubleday, 1963)

El-Erian, Mohamed A., *The Only Game in Town: Central Banks, Instability and Avoiding the Next Collapse* (New York: Random House, 2016)

Ellwood, David W., *Rebuilding Europe: Western Europe, America and Postwar Reconstruction* (Abingdon: Routledge, 1992)

Eltis, Walter, *Britain, Europe and EMU* (London: Macmillan, 2000)

Emminger, Otmar, *D-Mark, Dollar, Währungskrisen* (Stuttgart: Deutsche Verlags-Anstalt, 1986)

——, *Währungspolitik im Wandel der Zeit* (Frankfurt: Fritz Knapp, 1966)

Feis, Herbert, *Churchill, Roosevelt, Stalin* (Princeton, NJ: Princeton University Press, 1957)

Feldman, Gerald D., *The Great Disorder: Politics, Economics and Society in the German Inflation, 1914–1924* (Oxford: Oxford University Press, 1993)

Ferguson, Niall, *The War of the World: Twentieth-Century Conflict and the Descent of the West* (London: Allen Lane, 2006)

Foster, Peter, *What Went Wrong with Brexit: And What We Can Do About It* (Edinburgh: Canongate, 2023)

Fratzscher, Marcel, *Geld oder Leben: Wie unser irrationelles Verhältnis zum Geld die Gesellschaft spaltet* (Berlin: Berlin Verlag, 2020)

Fries, Herbert, *Churchill, Roosevelt, Stalin* (Princeton, NJ: Princeton University Press, 1957)

Fritsch, Rüdiger von, *Russlands Weg: Als Botschafter in Moskau* (Berlin: Aufbau, 2020)

——, *Zeitenwende: Putins Krieg und die Folgen* (Berlin: Aufbau, 2022)

Fursenko, Aleksandr, and Timothy Naftali, *Khrushchev's Cold War* (New York: W.W. Norton, 2005)

——, *'One Hell of a Gamble': Khrushchev, Castro, and Kennedy, 1958–1964* (New York: W.W. Norton, 1997)

Gaddis, John Lewis, *The Cold War* (London: Penguin, 2005)

——, *We Now Know: Rethinking Cold War History* (Oxford: Clarendon Press, 1997)

Galbraith, J.K., *Money: Whence It Came, Where It Went* (Boston, MA: Houghton Mifflin, 1975)

Garton Ash, Timothy, *Homelands: A Personal History of Europe* (London: Bodley Head, 2023)

——, *In Europe's Name: Germany and the Divided Continent* (London: Jonathan Cape, 1993)

Gates, Robert M., *Duty: Memoirs of a Secretary at War* (New York: Alfred A. Knopf, 2014)

Gaulle, Charles de, *Mémoires de l'Espoir, L'Effort 1962–1971* (Paris: Plon, 1971)

Gauron, André, *European Misunderstanding* (New York: Algora, 2000)

Gayer, Arthur D., *Monetary Policy and Economic Stabilisation: A Study of the Gold Standard* (London: A. & C. Black, 1935)

Geithner, Timothy F., *Stress Test: Reflections on Financial Crises* (New York: Crown, 2014)

Genscher, Hans-Dietrich, *Erinnerungen* (Berlin: Siedler, 1995)

George, Stephen, *An Awkward Partner: Britain in the European Community* (Oxford: Oxford University Press, 1990)

Gessen, Masha, *The Man Without a Face: The Unlikely Rise of Vladimir Putin* (London: Granta, 2012)

Giersch, Herbert, Karl-Heinz Paque and Holger Schmieding, *The Fading Miracle: Four Decades of Market Economy in Germany* (Cambridge: Cambridge University Press, 1992)

Giesbert, Franz-Olivier, *Jacques Chirac* (Paris: Éditions du Seuil, 1987)

——, *Le Président* (Paris: Éditions du Seuil, 1990)

Gilbert, Martin, *Churchill: A Life* (London: William Heinemann, 1991)

464

Gilbert, Milton, *Quest for World Monetary Order: The Gold-Dollar System and Its Aftermath* (New York: Wiley, 1980)

Gimbel, John, *The Origins of the Marshall Plan* (Stanford, CA: Stanford University Press, 1976)

Giordano, Francesco, *Storia del Sistema Banacario Italiano* (Rome: Donzelli, 2007)

Giscard D'Estaing, Valéry, *Macht und Leben: Erinnerungen* (Berlin: Ullstein, 1988), originally published as *Le Pouvoir et la Vie* (Paris: Compagnie 12, 1988)

Gorbachev, Mikhail, *Memoirs* (Berlin: Siedler, 1995)

——, *The New Russia* (Cambridge: Polity Press, 2016)

——, *Perestroika: New Thinking for Our Country and the World* (New York: Harper & Row)

Grant, Charles, *Delors: Inside the House That Jacques Built* (London: Nicholas Brealey, 1994)

Greenspan, Alan, *The Age of Turbulence: Adventures in a New World* (London, New York: Penguin, 2007)

Greider, William, *Secrets of the Temple: How the Federal Reserve Runs the Country* (New York: Simon & Schuster, 1987)

Gretschmann, Klaus (ed.), *Economic and Monetary Union: Implications for National Policymakers* (Maastricht: European Institute of Public Administration, 1993)

Groeben, Hans von der, and Ernst-Joachim Mestmäcker (eds), *Ziele und Methoden der europäischen Integration* (Frankfurt: Athenäum, 1972)

Gromyko, Andrej, *Erinnerungen* (Düsseldorf: Econ Verlag, 1989)

Gros, Daniel, and Niels Thygesen, *European Monetary Integration* (London: Longman, 1992)

Grubel, Herbert G., *The International Monetary System* (London: Penguin, 1969)

Guigou, Elisabeth, *Une Femme au Coeur de l'État* (Paris: Fayard, 2000)

Halle, Louis J., *The Cold War as History* (London: Chatto & Windus, 1967)

Halligan, Liam, and Gerard Lyons, *Clean Brexit: Why Leaving the EU Still Makes Sense* (London: Biteback, 2017)

Hankel, Wilhelm, Karl Albrecht Schachtschneider and Joachim Starbatty (eds), *Der Ökonom als Politiker: Europa, Geld und die soziale Frage: Festschrift für Wilhelm Nölling* (Stuttgart: Lucius & Lucius, 2003)

Harding, Rebecca, and William E. Paterson (eds), *The Future of the German Economy: An End to the Miracle?* (Manchester: Manchester University Press, 2000)

Healey, Denis, *The Time of My Life* (London: Michael Joseph, 1989)

Heath, Edward, *The Course of My Life* (London: Hodder & Stoughton, 1998)

Henderson, Nicholas, *Mandarin: The Diaries of an Ambassador* (London: Weidenfeld & Nicholson, 1994)

Henkel, Hans-Olaf, *Rettet unser Geld!* (Munich: Heyne Verlag, 2011)

Hennessy, Peter, *The Prime Minister: The Office and Its Holders since 1945* (London: Penguin, 2000)

Herzberg, Andert, *Der Sturz: Honecker im Kreuzverhör* (Berlin: Aufbau-Verlag, 1991)

Heusgen, Christoph, *Führung und Verantwortung: Angela Merkels Außenpolitik und Deutschlands künftige Rolle in der Welt* (Munich: Siedler, 2023)

Hill, Fiona, and Clifford G. Gaddy, *Mr Putin: Operative in the Kremlin* (Washington, DC: Brookings Institution Press, 2013)

Hitchcock, William I., *France Restored: Cold War Diplomacy and the Quest for Leadership in Europe, 1944–1954* (Chapel Hill, NC: University of North Carolina Press, 1998)

——, *The Struggle for Europe: The History of the Continent since 1945* (New York: Doubleday, 2003)

Hodson, Dermot, *Circle of Stars: A History of the EU and the People Who Made It* (New Haven/London: Yale University Press, 2023)

Hoffmeyer, Erik, *The International Monetary System* (Amsterdam: Elsevier, 1992)

Hogan, Michael J., *The Marshall Plan: America, Britain and the Reconstruction of Western Europe, 1947–1952* (Cambridge: Cambridge University Press, 1987)

Hogg, Sarah, and Jonathan Hill, *Too Close to Call: Power and Politics – John Major in No. 10* (London: Little, Brown, 1995)

Honecker, Erich *Aus meinem Leben* (Berlin: Dietz Verlag, 1980)

Horne, Alistair, *Harold Macmillan*, vol. 2, *1957–1986* (London/New York: Penguin, 1989)

Howe, Geoffrey, *Conflict of Loyalty* (London: Macmillan, 1994)

Hüfner, Martin, *Comeback für Deutschland* (Munich: Hanser Verlag, 2007)

——, *Europa: Die Macht von Morgen* (Munich: Hanser Verlag, 2006)

Hurd, Douglas, *Memoirs* (London: Little, Brown, 2003)

Ikenberry, G. John, *After Victory: Institutions, Strategic Restraint, and the Rebuilding of Order After Major Wars* (Princeton, NJ: Princeton University Press, 2001)

Ireland, Timothy P., *Creating the Entangling Alliance: The Origins of the North Atlantic Treaty Organization* (Westport, CT: Greenwood Press, 1981).

Issing, Otmar, *Der Euro: Geburt, Erfolg, Zukunft* (Munich: Franz Vahlen, 2008)

——, *Von der D-Mark zum Euro: Erinnerungen des Chefökonomen* (Munich: Franz Vahlen, 2024)

Jacobs, Lawrence R., and Desmond King, *Fed Power: How Finance Wins* (New York: Oxford University Press, 2016)

James, Harold, *Creation and Destruction of Value: The Globalization Cycle* (Cambridge, MA: Harvard University Press, 2009)

——, *The End of Globalization: Lessons from the Great Depression* (Cambridge, MA: Harvard University Press, 2001)

——, *International Monetary Cooperation since Bretton Woods* (Washington, DC: International Monetary Fund, 1999)

——, *Making the European Monetary Union* (Cambridge, MA: Belknap Press, 2012)

——, *Making a Modern Central Bank: The Bank of England 1979–2003* (Cambridge: Cambridge University Press, 2016)

——, *The Roman Predicament: How the Rules of International Order Create the Politics of Empire* (Princeton, NJ: Princeton University Press, 2006)

Jenkins, Roy, *The Chancellors* (London: Macmillan, 1998)

Joffe, Josef, *Der Gute Deutsche: Die Karriere einer moralischen Supermacht* (Munich: Bertelsmann, 2018)

Johnson, Boris, *Unleashed* (London, William Collins, 2024)

Johnson, Christopher, and Stefan Collignon (eds), *The Monetary Economics of Europe: Causes of the EMS Crisis* (London: Pinter, 1994)

Jörges, Hans-Ulrich (ed.), *Der Kampf um den Euro: Wie riskant ist die Währungsunion?* (Hamburg: Hoffmann & Campe, 1998)

Judt, Tony, *Postwar: A History of Europe since 1945* (London: Heinemann, 2005)

Kearns, Ian, *Collapse: Europe after the European Union* (London, Biteback, 2018)

Keegan, Victor, and Martin Kettle (eds), *The New Europe* (London: Fourth Estate, 1993)

Keegan, William, *The Prudence of Mr Gordon Brown* (Chichester: Wiley, 2003)

Keegan, William, David Marsh and Richard Roberts, *Six Days in September: Black Wednesday, Brexit and the Making of Europe* (London: OMFIF Press, 2017)

Kenen, Peter B., *Economic and Monetary Union in Europe: Moving beyond Maastricht* (Cambridge: Cambridge University Press, 1995)

Kennan, George F., *Memoirs: 1925–1950*, 2 vols, paperback edn (New York: Bantam, 1967–72).

Kennedy, Ellen, *The Bundesbank: Germany's Central Bank in the International Monetary System* (London: Pinter, 1991)

Kennedy, Paul M., *The Rise and Fall of the Great Powers: Economic Change and Military Conflict from 1500 to 2000* (New York: Random House, 1987)

Keohane, Robert O., *After Hegemony: Cooperation and Discord in the World Political Economy* (Princeton, NJ: Princeton University Press, 1984)

Keynes, John Maynard, *The Economic Consequences of the Peace* (London: Macmillan, 1919)

——, *Monetary Reform* (London: Macmillan, 1923)

——, *A Treatise on Money* (London: Macmillan, 1930)

Khlevniuk, Oleg V., *Stalin: New Biography of a Dictator* (New Haven/London: Yale University Press, 2015)

Kimball, Warren F., *The Juggler: Franklin Roosevelt as Wartime Statesman* (Princeton, NJ: Princeton University Press, 1991)

King, Mervyn, *The End of Alchemy: Money, Banking and the Future of the Global Economy* (London: Little, Brown, 2016)

Kissinger, Henry, *Diplomacy* (New York: Simon & Schuster, 1994)

——, *The White House Years* (Boston, MA: Little, Brown, 1979)

Koerfer, Daniel, *Kampf ums Kanzleramt: Erhard und Adenauer* (Stuttgart: Deutsche Verlags-Anstalt, 1988)

Kohl, Helmut, *Erinnerungen 1982–1990* (Munich: Droemer, 2005)

——, *Erinnerungen 1990–1994* (Munich: Droemer, 2007)

——, *Ich wollte Deutschlands Einheit* (Berlin: Propyläen, 1996)

Kolko, Joyce, and Gabriel Kolko, *The Limits of Power: The World and United States Foreign Policy, 1945-1954* (New York: Harper & Row, 1972)

Kozyrev, Andrei, *Firebird: The Elusive Fate of Russian Democracy* (Pittsburgh, PA: University of Pittsburgh Press, 2019)

Krause, Axel, *Inside the New Europe* (New York: HarperCollins, 1991)

Kwizinskij, Julij A. [Yuli Kvitsinsky], *Vor dem Sturm: Erinnerungen eines Diplomaten* (Berlin: Siedler, 1993)

Lamont, Norman, *In Office* (London: Little, Brown, 1999)

Laqueur, Walter, *Europe in Our Time: A History 1945–1992* (New York: Viking, 1992)

Larosière, Jacques de, *En finir avec le règne de l'illusion financière* (Paris: Odile Jacob, 2023)

——, *50 ans de Crises financières* (Paris: Odile Jacob, 2016)

——, *Le déclin français est-il réversible?* (Paris: Odile Jacob, 2024)

Lawson, Nigel, *The View from No. 11: Memoirs of a Tory Radical* (London: Bantam Press, 1992)

Leach, Rodney, *Europe: A Concise Encyclopaedia of the European Union* (London: Profile, 1998)

Ledwidge, Bernard, *De Gaulle* (London: Weidenfeld & Nicolson, 1982)

Leffler, Melvyn P., *A Preponderance of Power: National Security, the Truman Administration, and the Cold War* (Stanford, CA: Stanford University Press, 1992)

Leffler, Melvyn P., and David S. Painter (eds), *Origins of the Cold War: An International History* (Abingdon: Routledge, 1994)

Leonhardt, Rudolf Walter, *This Germany: The Story since the Third Reich* (New York: New York Graphic Society, 1964)

Llewellyn, John, and Peter Westaway, *Europe Will Work* (London/Tokyo: Nomura Global Economics, 2011)

Lloyd, John, *Rebirth of a Nation: An Anatomy of Russia* (London: Michael Joseph, 1998)

Lough, John, *Germany's Russia Problem: The Struggle for Balance in Europe* (Manchester: Manchester University Press, 2021)

Lucas, Edward, *The New Cold War: Putin's Threat to Russia and the West* (London: Bloomsbury, 2008)

Ludlow, Peter, *The Making of the European Monetary System* (London: Butterworth, 1982)

Lundestad, Geir, *'Empire' by Integration: The United States and European Integration, 1945–1997* (New York: Oxford University Press, 1998)

McFaul, Michael, *From Cold War to Hot Peace: An American Ambassador in Putin's Russia* (New York: Houghton Mifflin Harcourt, 2018)

McIntosh, Ronald, *Turbulent Times* (London: Biteback, 2014)

Macmillan, Harold, *Pointing the Way, 1959–1961* (London: Macmillan, 1972)

——, *Riding the Storm, 1956–1959* (London: Macmillan, 1971)

MacShane, Denis, *At the End of the Day, 1961–1963* (London: Macmillan, 1973)

——, *Brexit: How Britain Will Leave Europe* (London: I.B. Taurus, 2015)

——, *Brexiternity: The Uncertain Fate of Britain* (London: Bloomsbury, 2019)

Major, John, *The Autobiography* (London: HarperCollins, 1999)

Mak, Geert, *In Europe: Travels through the Twentieth Century* (London, Harvill Secker, 2007)

Mallaby, Christopher, *Living the Cold War: Memoirs of a British Diplomat* (Stroud: Amberley, 2017)

Mandelson, Peter, *The Third Man: Life at the Heart of New Labour* (London: HarperCollins, 2010)

Markwell, Donald, *John Maynard Keynes and International Relations: Economic Paths to War and Peace* (Oxford: Oxford University Press, 2006)

Marsh, David, *The Bundesbank: The Bank That Rules Europe* (London: Heinemann, 1992)

——, *The Euro: The Battle for the New Global Currency* (New Haven/London: Yale University Press, 2009)

——, *Europe's Deadlock: How the Euro Crisis Could Be Solved – And Why It Won't Happen* (New Haven/London: Yale University Press, 2013)

——, *The Germans: Rich, Bothered and Divided* (London: Hutchinson, 1989)

——, *Germany and Europe: The Crisis of Unity* (London: Heinemann, 1994)

Marshall, Matt, *The Bank: The Birth of Europe's Central Bank and the Rebirth of Europe's Power* (London: Random House, 1999)

Mastny, Vorjech, *The Cold War and Soviet Insecurity: The Stalin Years* (New York: Oxford University Press, 1996)

Merkel, Angela, *Freiheit: Erinnerungen 1954–2021* (Cologne: Kiepenheuer & Witsch, 2024), also published as *Freedom: Memoirs 1954–2021* (London: Macmillan, 2024)

——, *Mein Weg: Angela Merkel im Gespräch mit Hugo Müller-Vogg* (Hamburg: Hoffmann & Campe, 2004

Merkl, Peter H., *Germany: Yesterday and Tomorrow* (New York: Oxford University Press, 1965)

Merz, Friedrich, *Neue Zeit – Neue Verantwortung: Demokratie und Soziale Marktwirtschaft im 21. Jahrhundert* (Berlin: Econ Verlag, 2020)

Meyer, Christopher, *DC Confidential: The Controversial Memoirs of Britain's Ambassador to the US at the Time of 9/11 and the Iraq War* (London: Weidenfeld & Nicolson, 2005)

Mitterrand, François, *De l'Allemagne, de la France* (Paris: Odile Jacob, 1996)

——, *Mémoires interrompus* (Paris: Odile Jacob, 1996)

——, *Réflexions sur la Politique Extérieure de la France* (Paris: Fayard, 1986)

Mody, Ashoka, *EuroTragedy: A Drama in Nine Acts* (New York: Oxford University Press, 2018)

Monnet, Jean, *Mémoires* (Paris: Fayard, 1976)

Moore, Charles, *Margaret Thatcher*, vol. 2: *Everything She Wants* (London: Allan Lane, 2015)

——, *Margaret Thatcher*, vol. 3: *Herself, Alone* (London: Allen Lane, 2019)

Moravcsik, Andrew, *The Choice for Europe* (Ithaca, NY: Cornell University Press, 1998)

Morgan, Kenneth O., *Callaghan: A Life* (Oxford: Oxford University Press, 1997)

Naimark, Norman M., *The Russians in Germany: A History of the Soviet Zone of Occupation, 1945–1949* (Cambridge, MA: Belknap Press, 1995)

Naudin, François, *The European Central Bank: A Bank for the 21st Century* (London: Kogan Page, 2000)

Naughtie, James, *The Rivals: The Intimate Story of a Political Marriage* (London: Fourth Estate, 2001)

Nay, Catherine, *Le Noir et le Rouge* (Paris: Grasset, 1984)

Newhouse, John, *De Gaulle and the Anglo-Saxons* (London: André Deutsch, 1970)

Nölling, Wilhelm, *Unser Geld: Der Kampf um die Stabilität der Währungen in Europa* (Berlin: Ullstein, 1993)

Nölling, Wilhelm, Karl Albrecht Schachtschneider and Joachim Starbatty (eds), *Währungsunion und Wirtschaft: Festschrift für Wilhelm Hankel* (Stuttgart: Lucius & Lucius, 1999)

Norman, Peter, *Plumbers and Visionaries: Securities Settlement and Europe's Financial Market* (New York: Wiley, 2008)

Nye, Joseph S., *The Paradox of American Power: Why the World's Only Superpower Can't Go It Alone* (New York: Oxford University Press, 2002)

——, *Soft Power: The Means to Success in World Politics* (New York: Public Affairs, 2004)

Overy, Richard, *Russia's War: A History of the Soviet Effort, 1941–1945* (London: Allen Lane, 1998)

Owen, David, *Europe Restructured? The Eurozone Crisis and Its Aftermath* (London: Methuen, 2012)

——, *Hubris: The Road to Donald Trump – Power, Populism, Narcissism* (London: Methuen, 2018)

——, *Riddle, Mystery, and Enigma: Two Hundred Years of British–Russian Relations* (London: Haus, 2011)

Owen, David, and David Ludlow, *British Foreign Policy after Brexit* (London: Biteback, 2017)

Péan, Pierre, *Une Jeunesse Française* (Paris: Fayard, 1994)

Peston, Robert, *Brown's Britain* (London: Short Books, 2005)

Pickert, Philip (ed.), *Merkel: Eine kritische Bilanz* (Munich: FinanzBuch Verlag, 2017)

Pogue, Forrest C., *George C. Marshall: Statesman, 1945–1959* (New York: Viking, 1987)

Posen, Adam (ed.), *The Euro at Five: Ready for a Global Role?* (Washington, DC: Institute for International Economics, 2005)

Powell, Jonathan, *The New Machiavelli: How to Wield Power in the Modern World* (London: Bodley Head, 2010)

Putin, Vladimir, *First Person* (New York: Public Affairs, 2000)

Quinn, Josephine Crawley, *How the World Made the West: A 4,000-Year History* (London: Bloomsbury, 2024)

Rawnsley, Andrew, *Servants of the People: The Inside Story of New Labour* (London: Hamish Hamilton, 2000)

Reading, Brian, *The Fourth Reich* (London: Weidenfeld & Nicolson, 1995)

Redwood, John, *Just Say No! 100 Arguments against the Euro* (London: Politico's, 2001)

Rehn, Olli, *Walking the Highway: Rebalancing the European Economy in Crisis* (London: Palgrave Macmillan, 2020)

Reinhard, Carman M., and Kenneth S. Rogoff, *This Time Is Different* (Princeton, NJ: Princeton University Press, 2009)

Reuter, Edzard, *Schein und Wirklichkeit: Erinnerungen* (Berlin: Siedler, 1998)

Rice, Condoleezza, *No Higher Honor: A Memoir of My Years in Washington* (New York: Simon & Schuster, 2011)

Ridley, Nicholas, *My Style of Government: The Thatcher Years* (London: Hutchinson, 1991)

Roberts, Geoffrey K., *West German Politics* (London: Macmillan, 1972)

Roberts, Richard, and David Kynaston, *The Bank of England: Money, Power and Influence 1694–1884* (Oxford: Oxford University Press, 1994)

Rougemont, Denis de, *The Meaning of Europe* (London: Sidgwick & Jackson, 1965)

Ruge, Gerd, *Michail Gorbatschow: Biographie* (Frankfurt: S. Fischer Verlag, 1990)

Sandbrook, Dominic, *Never Had It So Good: A History of Britain from Suez to The Beatles* (London: Little, Brown, 2005)

Sarkozy, Nicolas, *Ensemble* (Paris: XO Éditions, 2007)

——, *Le Temps des Combats* (Paris: Fayard, 2023)

——, *Le Temps des Tempêtes* (Paris: L'Observatoire, 2020)

Sarotte, Mary Elise, *The Collapse: The Accidental Opening of the Berlin Wall* (New York: Basic Books, 2014)

——, *Not One Inch: America, Russia, and the Making of the Post-Cold War Stalemate* (New Haven/London: Yale University Press, 2021)

Schabert, Tilo, *Mitterrand et la Réunification Allemande: Une histoire secrète (1981–1995)* (Paris: Grasset, 2005)

Schabowski, *Günter, Der Absturz* (Berlin: Rowolt, 1991)

Scheller, Hanspeter K., *The European Central Bank: History, Role and Functions* (Frankfurt: European Central Bank, 2004)

Schiller, Karl, *Der schwierige Weg in die offene Gesellschaft: Kritische Anmerkungen zur deutschen Wiedervereinigung* (Berlin: Siedler, 1994)

Schmidt, Helmut, *Die Deutschen* und *ihre Nachbarn* (Berlin: Siedler, 1990)

——, *Menschen* und *Mächte* (Berlin: Siedler, 1987)

Scholl-Latour, Peter, *Russland im Zangengriff* (Berlin: Ullstein, 2006)

Scholz, Olaf, *Hoffnungsland: Eine neue deutsche Wirklichkeit* (Hamburg: Hoffmann & Campe, 2017)

Schönfelder, Bruno, *Der Fluch des Imperiums* (Berlin: Europolis, 2022)

Schönfelder, Wilhelm, and Elke Thiel (eds), *Ein Markt, Eine Währung: Die Verhandlungen zur Wirtschafts- und Währungsunion* (Baden-Baden: Nomos, 1994)

Schröder, Gerhard, *Entscheidungen: Mein Leben in der Politik* (Hamburg: Hoffmann & Campe, 2006)

——, *Klare Worte: Im Gespräch mit Georg Meck* (Freiburg: Herder, 2016)

Schweizer, Peter, *Reagan's War: The Epic Story of His Forty Year Struggle and Final Triumph over Communism* (New York: Doubleday, 2002)

Sebestyen, Victor, *Lenin: The Dictator* (London: Weidenfeld & Nicolson, 2017)

——, *Revolution 1989: The Fall of the Soviet Empire* (London: Weidenfeld & Nicolson, 2009)

Sédillot, René, Histoire Morale et Immorale de la Monnaie (Paris: Bordas, 1999)

Seldon, Anthony, with Chris Ballinger, Daniel Collings and Peter Snowdon, *Blair Unbound* (New York: Free Press, 2004)

Seldon, Anthony, and Peter Snowdon, *Cameron at 10: The Verdict* (London: William Collins, 2015)

Seldon, Anthony, and Raymond Newell, *Johnson at 10: The Inside Story* (London: Atlantic, 2023)

——, *May at 10: The Verdict* (London: Biteback, 2019)

Seldon, Anthony, with Jonathan Meakin, *Truss at 10: How Not to Be Prime Minister* (London: Atlantic, 2024)

Sheehy, Gail, *Gorbachev: The Making of a Man Who Shook the World* (London: Heinemann, 1991)

Shipman, Tim, *No Way Out: Brexit, from the Backstop to Boris* (London: William Collins, 2024)

Short, Philip, *Mitterrand: A Study in Ambiguity* (London: Bodley Head, 2013)

——, *Putin: His Life and Times* (London: Bodley Head, 2022)

Shultz, George P., *Turmoil and Triumph: My Years as Secretary of State* (New York: Scribner, 1993)

Silguy, Yves-Thibault de, *L'Économie, Fil d'Ariane de l'Europe* (Paris: Presses de Sciences, 2000)

Sinn, Hans-Werner, *Ist Deutschland noch zu retten?* (Munich: Econ Verlag, 2003)

Smyser, W.R., *The Economy of United Germany: Colossus at the Crossroads* (London: Hurst, 1992)

Snyckers, Alexander, *La Reichsbank et la Banque de France: Leur Politique* (Paris: Arthur Rousseau, 1908)

Snyder, Timothy, *Bloodlands: Europe between Hitler and Stalin* (London: Bodley Head, 2010)

Sobolewska, Maria, and Robert Ford, *Brexitland: Identity, Diversity and the Reshaping of British Politics* (Cambridge: Cambridge University Press, 2020)

Solomon, Stephen, *The Confidence Game: How Unelected Central Bankers Are Governing the Changed World Economy* (New York: Simon & Schuster, 1995)

Soros, George, *Financial Turmoil in Europe and the United States* (New York: Public Affairs, 2012)

——, *The New Paradigm for Financial Markets: The Credit Crash of 2008 and What It Means* (New York: Public Affairs, 2008)

——, *Open Society: Reforming Global Capitalism* (New York: Public Affairs, 1998)

Speier, Hans, *Divided Berlin: The Anatomy of Soviet Political Blackmail* (New York: Frederick A. Praeger, 1961)

Spierenburg, Dirk, and Raymond Poidevin, *The History of the High Authority of the European Coal and Steel Community: Supranationality in Operation* (London: Weidenfeld & Nicolson, 1994)

Steil, Benn, *The Marshall Plan: Dawn of the Cold War* (Oxford: Oxford University Press, 2018)

Stephens, Philip, *Politics and the Pound* (London: Macmillan, 1996)

Stern, Fritz, *Gold and Iron: Bismarck, Bleichröder and the Building of the German Empire* (London: Allen & Unwin, 1977)

Stoltenberg, Gerhard, *Wendepunkt: Stationen deutscher Geschichte 1947–1990* (Berlin: Siedler, 1997)

Strauss, Franz-Josef, *Die Erinnerungen* (Berlin: Siedler, 1989)

Stürmer, Michael, *The German Empire 1871–1919* (London: Weidenfeld & Nicolson, 2000)

——, *Russland: Das Land, das aus der Kälte kommt* (Hamburg: Murmann Verlag, 2008)

Stürmer, Michael, Gabriele Teichmann and Wilhelm Treue, *Wagen und Wägen* (Munich: Piper Verlag, 1989)

Szász, André, *The Road to European Monetary Union* (London: Palgrave Macmillan, 2000)

Talbott, Strobe, *The Russia Hand: A Memoir of Presidential Diplomacy* (New York: Random House, 2002)

Taubman, William, *Gorbachev: His Life and Times* (London: Simon & Schuster, 2017)

Taylor, A.J.P., *The Origins of the Second World War* (New York: Atheneum, 1962)

Taylor, Frederick, *The Berlin Wall: A World Divided 1961–1989* (London: Bloomsbury, 2006)

Teltschik, Horst, *Die 329 Tage zur deutschen Einigung: Das vollständige Tagebuch*, ed. Michael Gehler (Göttingen: Vandenhoeck & Ruprecht, 2024)

——, *329 Tage: Innenansichten der Einigung* (Berlin: Siedler, 1991)

——, *Russisches Roulette: Vom Kalten Krieg zum Kalten Frieden* (Munich: C.H. Beck, 2019)

Temperton, Paul (ed.), *The Euro* (New York: Wiley, 1997)

——, *The European Currency Crisis: What Chance Now for a Single European Currency?* (Cambridge/Chicago, IL: Probus, 1993)

Thatcher, Margaret, *The Downing Street Years* (London: HarperCollins, 1993)

Thumann, Michael, *Revanche: Wie Putin das bedrohlichste Regime der Welt geschaffen hat* (Munich: C.H. Beck, 2023)

Tietmeyer, Hans, *Herausforderung Euro* (Munich/Vienna: Hanser, 2005)

Tilford, Simon, *Will the Eurozone Crack?* (London: Centre for European Reform, 2006)

Toniolo, Gianni, with Piet Clement, *Central Bank Cooperation at the Bank for International Settlements 1930–1973* (Cambridge: Cambridge University Press, 2005)

Tooze, Adam *Crashed: How a Decade of Financial Crises Changed the World* (New York: Viking, 2018)

Treaster, Joseph B., *Paul Volcker: The Making of a Financial Legend* (New York: Wiley, 2004)

Truman, Harry S., *Memoirs*, vol. 1: *1945, Year of Decisions*, reprint edn (New York: Signet, 1965)

—— *Memoirs*, vol. 2: *Years of Trial and Hope, 1946–1952*, reprint edn (New York: Signet, 1965)

Tsoukalis, Loukas, *The New European Economy: The Politics and Economics of Integration* (Oxford: Oxford University Press, 1991)

Tucker, Paul, *Global Discord: Values and Power in a Fractured World Order* (Princeton, NJ: Princeton University Press, 2022)

——, *Unelected Power: The Quest for Legitimacy in Central Banking and the Regulatory State* (Princeton, NJ: Princeton University Press, 2018)

Tugendhat, Christopher, *The Worm in the Apple: A History of the Conservative Party and Europe from Churchill to Cameron* (London: Haus, 2022)

Vale de Almeida, João, *The Divorce of Nations: A Diplomat's View as the Global Order Collapses* (London: Flint, 2025)

Varoufakis, Yanis, *Adults in the Room: My Battle with Europe's Deep Establishment* (London: Bodley Head, 2017)

Védrine, Hubert, *Les Mondes de François Mitterrand* (Paris: Fayard, 1996)

Volcker, Paul, and Toyoo Gyohten, *Changing Fortunes: The World's Money and the Threat to American Leadership* (New York: Times Books, 1992)

Waigel, Theo, *Ehrlichkeit ist eine Währung: Erinnerungen* (Berlin: Ullstein, 2019)

——, (ed.), *Unser Zukunft heißt Europa: Der Weg zur Wirtschafts- und Währungsunion* (Düsseldorf: Econ Verlag, 1996)

Waigel, Theo, and Manfred Schell (eds), *Tage, die Deutschland und die Welt veränderten: Vom Mauerfall zum Kaukasus – Die deutsche Währungsunion* (Munich: Ferenczy, 1994)

Wall, Stephen, *A Stranger in Europe: Britain and the EU from Thatcher to Blair* (Oxford: Oxford University Press, 2008)

Wallace, Paul, *The Euro Experiment* (Cambridge: Cambridge University Press, 2016)

Walters, Vernon A., *Die Vereinigung war voraussehbar: Hinter den Kulissen eines entscheidenden Jahres* (Berlin: Siedler, 1994)

——, *In vertraulicher Mission* (Munich: Bechtle Verlag, 1990)

Wass, Douglas, *Decline to Fall: The Making of British Macro-Economic Policy and the 1976 IMF Crisis* (Oxford: Oxford University Press, 2008)

Weber, Manfred (ed.), *Europe auf dem Weg zur Währungsunion* (Darmstadt: Wissenschaftliche Buchgesellschaft, 1991)

Weidenfeld, Ursula, *Die Kanzlerin: Porträt einer Epoche* (Berlin: Rowolt, 2021)

Westoby, Adam, *Communism since World War II* (New York: St Martin's Press, 1981)

Williams, Charles, *The Last Great Frenchman: A Life of General de Gaulle* (London: Little, Brown, 1993)

Winkler, Allan M., *Home Front U.S.A.: America During World War II*, 2nd edn (Wheeling, IL, Harlan Davidson, 2000)

Yeltsin, Boris *Midnight Diaries* (London: Weidenfeld & Nicolson, 2021)

Young, Hugo, *One of Us* (London: Macmillan, 1989)

——, *This Blessed Plot* (London: Macmillan, 1998)

Young, Richard, *Europe Reset: New Directions for the EU* (London: I.B. Tauris, 2017)

Zeiler, Thomas W., *Free Trade, Free World: The Advent of GATT* (Chapel Hill, NC: University of North Carolina Press, 1999)

Zelikow, Philip, and Condoleezza Rice, *Germany Unified and Europe Transformed: A Study in Statecraft* (Cambridge, MA: Harvard University Press, 1995)

——, *To Build a Better World: Choices to End the Cold War and Create a Global Commonwealth* (New York: Twelve, 2019)

Zoellick, Robert B., *America in the World: A History of U.S. Diplomacy and Foreign Policy* (New York: Twelve, 2020)

Zubok, Vladislav, *Collapse: The Fall of the Soviet Union* (New Haven/London: Yale University Press, 2021)

Zubok, Vladislav, and Constantine Pleshakov, *Inside the Kremlin's Cold War: From Stalin to Khrushchev* (Cambridge, MA: Harvard University Press, 1996)

INDEX

Page references in **bold** show the Dramatis Personae.